Operation Barbarossa and Germany's Defeat in the East

Operation Barbarossa, the German invasion of the Soviet Union, began the largest and most costly campaign in military history. Its failure was a key turning point of the Second World War. The operation was planned as a blitzkrieg to win Germany its *Lebensraum* in the east, and the summer of 1941 is well known for the German army's unprecedented victories and advances. Yet the German blitzkrieg depended almost entirely upon the motorised panzer groups, particularly those of Army Group Centre. Using previously unpublished archival records, David Stahel presents a new history of Germany's summer campaign from the perspective of the two largest and most powerful panzer groups on the eastern front. Stahel's research provides a fundamental reassessment of Germany's war against the Soviet Union, highlighting the prodigious internal problems of the vital panzer forces and revealing that their demise in the earliest phase of the war undermined the whole German invasion.

DAVID STAHEL is an independent researcher based in Berlin.

T0382616

Cambridge Military Histories

Edited by

HEW STRACHAN, Chichele Professor of the History of War,
University of Oxford, and Fellow of All Souls College, Oxford

GEOFFREY WAWRO, Major General Olinto Mark Barsanti
Professor of Military History, and Director, Center for the Study of
Military History, University of North Texas

The aim of this new series is to publish outstanding works of research on warfare
throughout the ages and throughout the world. Books in the series will take a
broad approach to military history, examining war in all its military, strategic,
political and economic aspects. The series is intended to complement *Studies in
the Social and Cultural History of Modern Warfare* by focusing on the 'hard' military
history of armies, tactics, strategy and warfare. Books in the series will consist
mainly of single-author works – academically vigorous and groundbreaking –
which will be accessible to both academics and the interested general reader.

A full list of titles in the series can be found at:
www.cambridge.org/militaryhistories

Operation Barbarossa and Germany's Defeat in the East

David Stahel

CAMBRIDGE
UNIVERSITY PRESS

CAMBRIDGE
UNIVERSITY PRESS

University Printing House, Cambridge CB2 8BS, United Kingdom

One Liberty Plaza, 20th Floor, New York, NY 10006, USA

477 Williamstown Road, Port Melbourne, VIC 3207, Australia

314-321, 3rd Floor, Plot 3, Splendor Forum, Jasola District Centre, New Delhi-110025, India

79 Anson Road, #06-04/06, Singapore 079906

Cambridge University Press is part of the University of Cambridge.

It furthers the University's mission by disseminating knowledge in the pursuit of education, learning and research at the highest international levels of excellence.

www.cambridge.org
Information on this title: www.cambridge.org/9780521170154

First published 2009
Third Printing 2010
First paperback edition 2011

A catalogue record for this publication is available from the British Library

Library of Congress Cataloging in Publication data
Stahel, David, 1975–
Operation Barbarossa and Germany's defeat in the East / by David Stahel.
  p. cm. – (Cambridge military histories)
Includes bibliographical references and index.
ISBN 978-0-521-76847-4 (hardback)
1. World War, 1939-1945 – Campaigns – Eastern Front.   2. World War,
1939-1945 – Tank warfare.   3. Soviet Union – History – German occupation,
1941-1944.   I. Title.   II. Series.
D764.S795   2009
940.54′217–dc22   2009016993

ISBN 978-0-521-76847-4 Hardback
ISBN 978-0-521-17015-4 Paperback

Contents

Illustrations

TABLE

Maps

x   Maps

Acknowledgements

This book constitutes a revised version of my doctoral dissertation, which was submitted to the Philosophical Faculty I of the Humboldt-Universität zu Berlin with the title: *And the World Held its Breath. The July/August 1941 Crisis of Army Group Centre and the Failure of Operation Barbarossa.* The process of researching and writing this study was enormously rewarding, for which a good deal of thanks belongs to my supervisor Professor Rolf-Dieter Müller of the German Military Research Institute in Potsdam. His patience and selfless devotion to the project allowed me the benefit of his years of research and tremendous knowledge in the field. The end result is, I hope, a reflection of his faith in me and the project.

A number of others deserve special mention for their time, services and friendship. The distinguished American historian Colonel David M. Glantz provided useful commentary and promptly replied to all my questions during the research process. He also kindly agreed to allow the reproduction of his own privately produced maps for publication in this study. They are the most detailed and comprehensive maps available on the German/Soviet war, and an invaluable asset to my work. Historians Dr Alex J. Kay and Dr Jeff Rutherford both read drafts and provided much critical commentary and useful feedback. Their respective expertise in the area of Germany's eastern front also led to many enlightening discussions of the field.

During my first year of postgraduate studies at Australia's Monash University I wrote my first substantial research project on the eastern front under the skilled tutelage of Dr Eleanor Hancock. She went on to recommend future study at King's College Department of War Studies and throughout my time in England and Germany has remained a constant source of both helpful advice and encouragement.

My deepest gratitude also extends to two German families without whom my desire to undertake this research would not have been possible. Upon my arrival in Germany the Mogge family in Köln took in a simple friend of the family and made me feel like one of their own. The whole family tirelessly taught me German throughout my initial year in Germany and even supported me financially in that period. Furthermore, I would like to thank the Graichen family originally from Bonn, whose great kindness has provided an education in itself. They provided me with accommodation to do the bulk of my primary research at the military archive in Freiburg. More particularly, to my old friend Jakob Graichen, who provided technical assistance and cast a critical eye over my many translations, I owe a special debt of thanks. I should also like to add my thanks for the many years of friendship, good humour and countless travel adventures. Likewise, his lovely wife Mariana, who never failed in her interest for this project leading to much support and, at times, welcome distraction.

Anna Held did some excellent last-minute translations for which I was very grateful. Thanks also to Isabella Kessel for providing me with accommodation in Freiburg at short notice and to Stefan Sonneberger for numerous favours.

On a more personal note, I should like to thank my aunt Priscilla Pettengell for her thorough correction and commentary on the draft, as well as for all the years of loving dedication she has devoted to my education. To my father Warren and my brother Andy, my heartfelt thanks for all the blissful memories together in Cheltenham and everything else since.

Finally to Paddy Stahel who passed away in 1998. An extraordinary woman of strength, wit and compassion, who never failed to recognise the important things in life. I was privileged to call her my mother. This work is dedicated to her.

Glossary of terms

BA-MA	Bundesarchiv-Militärarchiv (German Military Archive)
Einsatzgruppen	'Action groups' of the SD and Security Police, used mainly for mass killings
Eisenbahntruppe	Railroad troops
FHQ	Führerhauptquartier (Führer Headquarters)
Gestapo	Geheime Staatspolizei (Secret State Police)
Grossdeutschland	'Greater Germany' Infantry Regiment
Grosstransportraum	'Large transport area'. Referring to the transport regiment responsible for bridging the gap between front-line divisions and railheads
Kleinkolonnenraum	'Small column area'. Referring to the transportation unit belonging to a division
KTB	Kriegstagebuch (War Diary)
Landser	German infantry man
Lebensraum	Living space
Luftwaffe	German Air Force
MGFA	Militärgeschichtliches Forschungsamt (Military History Research Institute)
NCO	Non-commissioned officer
NKVD	Narodnyi Komissariat Vnutrennych Del (People's Commissariat for Internal Affairs)
NSDAP	Nationalsozialistische Deutsche Arbeiterpartei (National Socialist German Workers Party)
OKH	Oberkommando des Heeres (High Command of the Army)
OKW	Oberkommando der Wehrmacht (High Command of the Armed Forces)
Panzerjäger	Anti-tank unit
POW	Prisoner of war
Pz. Div.	Panzer Division
RAF	Royal Air Force

Das Reich	'The Reich' 2nd SS Division
Reichsbahn	German railways
SD	*Sicherheitsdienst* (Security Service)
SS	*Schutzstaffel* (Protection Echelon)
Stavka	Soviet High Command
UK	United Kingdom
USA	United States of America
USSR	Union of Soviet Socialist Republics
Wehrmacht	German Armed Forces

Tables of military ranks and army structures

Table of equivalent ranks

German Army/Luftwaffe	Translation used in this study	Equivalent US Army ranks
Officer Ranks		
Generalfeldmarschall	Field Marshal	General of the Army
Generaloberst	Colonel-General	General
General	General	Lieutenant General
der Infanterie	of Infantry	
der Artillerie	of Artillery	
der Flakartillerie	of Flak Artillery	
der Flieger	of Aviation	
der Kavallerie	of Cavalry	
der Luftwaffe	of the Luftwaffe	
der Panzertruppe	of Panzer Troops	
der Pioniere	of Engineers	
Generalleutnaut	Lieutenant-General	Major General
Generalmajor	Major-General	Brigadier General
Oberst	Colonel	Colonel
Oberstleutnant	Lieutenant-Colonel	Lieutenant Colonel
Major	Major	Major
Hauptmann	Captain	Captain
Oberleutnant	1st Lieutenant	1st Lieutenant
Leutnant	Lieutenant	2nd Lieutenant
Enlisted Ranks		
Stabsfeldwebel	Master Sergeant	Master Sergeant
Oberfeldwebel	Technical Sergeant	Technical Sergeant
Feldwebel	Staff Sergeant	Staff Sergeant
Unterfeldwebel	Sergeant	Sergeant
Unteroffizier	Corporal	Corporal
Gefreiter	Private	Private 1st Class
Soldat	Private	Private 2nd Class

Source: Karl-Heinz Frieser, *The Blitzkrieg Legend. The 1940 Campaign in the West* (Annapolis, 2005) p. 355.

Structure and size of the German Army

Germany Army formation	English translation	Number of subordinate units	Average number of personnel[a]
Heeresgruppe	Army Group	Two or more armies	From 100,000 to over a million
Armee	Army	Two or more corps	From 60,000 to 250,000
Korps	Corps	Two or more divisions	From 40,000 to 70,000
Division	Division	Two or more brigades	From 12,000 to 18,000
Brigade	Brigade	Two or more regiments	From 5,000 to 7,000
Regiment	Regiment	Two or more battalions	From 2,000 to 6,000
Bataillon	Battalion	Two or more companies	From 500 to 1,000
Kompanie	Company	Two or more platoons	From 100 to 200
Zug	Platoon		From 30 to 40

Note: [a] Wide variations of these figures occurred especially after 1941
Source: Own records.

Introduction

On 3 February 1941 Hitler hosted an important military conference in preparation for Operation Barbarossa – Nazi Germany's upcoming invasion of the Soviet Union. Although Hitler was determined to crush the Soviet Union in a short summer campaign, this was destined to become a titanic clash between two ruthless empires, leading to the largest and most costly war in human history. Hitler was sufficiently aware of the profound scale of the conflict and the momentous consequences it would induce, even in the shortened form that he conceived for it that by the end of the conference he ominously pronounced: 'When Barbarossa begins the world will hold its breath.'[1] Nor was this just another bombastic outburst, typical of Hitler's unrestrained hubris. In a radio address on the day of the invasion (22 June 1941) the British Prime Minister, Winston Churchill, told his people:

So now this bloodthirsty guttersnipe must launch his mechanized armies upon new fields of slaughter, pillage and devastation . . . And even the carnage and ruin which his victory, should he gain it – though he's not gained it yet – will bring upon the Russian people, will itself be only a stepping stone to the attempt to plunge four or five hundred millions who live in China and the 350,000,000 who live in India into that bottomless pit of human degradation over which the diabolic emblem of the swastika flaunts itself. It is not too much to say here this pleasant summer evening that the lives and happiness of a thousand million additional human beings are now menaced with brutal Nazi violence. That is enough to make us hold our breath.[2]

If the spectre of an expanding Nazi empire caused the world a sudden collective gasp, Churchill's words of defiance signalled Britain's

---

[1] Hans-Adolf Jacobsen (ed), *Kriegstagebuch des Oberkommandos der Wehrmacht (Wehrmachtführungsstab)*, Band I/1: *1. August 1940–31. Dezember 1941* (Munich, 1982), p. 300 (3 February 1941). Hereafter cited as KTB OKW, Volume I.

[2] Max Domarus, *Hitler. Speeches and Proclamations 1932–1945. The Chronicle of a Dictatorship*, Volume IV: *The Years 1941 to 1945* (Wauconda, 2004), p. 2458; Winston S. Churchill, *Never Give In: The Best of Winston Churchill's Speeches* (New York, 2003), pp. 289–293. Also available online: www.jewishvirtuallibrary.org/jsource/ww2/churchill062241.html

determination to go on opposing Nazism and at the same time offered an open-ended alliance to the Soviet Union. It was an alliance born more of necessity than of pre-existing goodwill, for these were the darkest days of World War II. Nazi Germany had amassed the greatest invasion force in history. In the string of preceding campaigns the opposing nations of Europe had fallen in short order to German aggression, leaving the Soviet Union as the sole remaining continental power. With the planned conquest of Soviet territories, Hitler stood to gain immeasurable raw materials, freeing him forever from Britain's continental blockade and providing him with the strategic freedom to wage truly global warfare.

Yet the Soviet Union was a very different adversary from any of Germany's previous opponents and Hitler was well enough aware that Germany's internal constraints, most notably on the economic front, necessitated a short, victorious war. Thus Operation Barbarossa was designed to defeat the Soviet Union decisively in the summer of 1941.

The importance of Hitler's new war in the east was understood by all sides at the time as the definitive moment in the future fortunes of the expanding world war. Either Hitler would soon stand almost untouchable at the head of an enormous empire, or his greatest campaign would falter (something no government at the time believed to be likely) resulting in the dangerous Allied encirclement Hitler was aiming to eliminate forever. It is therefore not an overstatement to say that the German invasion of the Soviet Union represents an extraordinary turning point in world affairs, central not only in our understanding of World War II, but indeed as one of the most profound events in modern history.

Many histories have sought to understand the failure of Operation Barbarossa by tracing the movement of armies through to the great battle of Moscow in the winter of 1941/42. The central importance of this climactic battle in studies on Operation Barbarossa is effectively explained by its common acceptance as Germany's first major defeat in the war against the Soviet Union. Germany's sequence of unprecedented battle-field victories, ending in the ill-fated drive on Moscow, has sufficed to persuade many historians of its fundamental significance and fixated their attention on the winter battle as Operation Barbarossa's crucial point of demise. Long before the first snows of winter began to fall, however, and even before the first autumn rains brought most movement to a halt, in fact as early as the summer of 1941, it was evident that Barbarossa was a spent exercise, unavoidably doomed to failure.

Germany's failure in the early weeks of the campaign is perhaps not immediately apparent because it does not include the conventional historical benchmark of a great battlefield defeat. Indeed, according to most histories, the period is characterised by apparently extraordinary successes for the German armies. Encirclements at Belostok–Minsk,

Smolensk and Uman are often framed by emphatic references to the impending collapse of the Soviet Union. Accordingly, it is with a measure of scepticism that some readers may first judge the paradoxical claim that it was in fact Germany whose demise was being assured in the summer of 1941. A short explanation of Germany's defeat in this period might best be provided by a simple theoretical concept devised by the renowned German strategist and historian Carl von Clausewitz. Based in large part on his first-hand observations of the Napoleonic wars, Clausewitz's timeless study *Vom Kriege* (*On War*) established numerous maxims of war, which in many cases are still upheld today. Clausewitz's theory of the culminating point of the attack provides a useful intellectual framework through which to view Operation Barbarossa. Put simply, Clausewitz established that most attacks diminish in strength the longer they continue, whereupon a critical point is eventually reached at which the power of the attack is superseded by the strength of the defence. This he determined to be the culminating point or climax of the attack, which he then added was usually, but not always, followed by an extremely powerful enemy counter-blow.[3] This basic hypothesis formed an intriguing theoretical starting point for my own questioning of the literature concerning Operation Barbarossa and posed the problem of whether it was possible to pre-date the German military failure in 1941. As a result, Clausewitz's culminating point formed a conceptual beginning to what I believe subsequent research has confirmed – that German operations in the east had failed by the middle of August 1941.

Attempting any manageable re-examination of the Barbarossa campaign requires both a clear sense of purpose and a certain limitation of scope. Confronting the immense scale of Germany's invasion of the Soviet Union has been made somewhat easier by the relatively small number of motorised divisions which made up the German Army in 1941. These were concentrated into four 'panzer groups' upon which the success of the Barbarossa blitzkrieg was made dependent. This study focuses mainly on the two largest panzer groups (Panzer Groups 2 and 3) assigned to Army Group Centre in the middle of the German front. The study seeks to use these vital formations as a test case through which one can understand the overall success of German offensive operations in the earliest period of the war.

The bulk of the research was conducted in Germany at the German Military Archive (Bundesarchiv-Militärarchiv) in Freiburg im Breisgau, with additional resources provided by the Military History Research Institute (Militärgeschichtliches Forschungsamt) in Potsdam

---

[3] Michael Howard and Peter Paret (eds.), Carl von Clausewitz, *On War* (New York, 1993), p. 639.

and the Humboldt University in Berlin. The study is divided into two parts. In the first, there is a broad assessment of the conceptual planning for the campaign, as a basis for what would need to be achieved in the war itself. The second part, and the main body of the work, deals with the first two months of the war and follows the progress of the panzer groups towards their respective goals.

Research was concentrated on the four highest tiers of the army's field commands; Army Group Centre, the subordinate two panzer groups, the five corps making up the panzer groups and their constituent sixteen divisions. The wartime records for these various commands are not always complete with valuable elements sometimes unavailable. This either means the documents were destroyed in the war, have simply not been found and remain 'missing', or that they were captured and remain in Russian custody (where access for scholars has sometimes been limited or withheld). Nevertheless, the period covering Barbarossa is well served for detailed primary research on the motorised elements of Army Group Centre.

Once located the files reveal themselves to be something of a mixed bag. From the army group down to individual divisions all command structures were required to keep a daily war diary, but oddly there appears to have been little standardisation in content or style. Most of the war diaries were typed, but in some cases, as for example with XXIV Panzer Corps, the whole diary was recorded in a barely legible handwritten script. In many diaries entries were made continually throughout the day with the exact time of each entry recorded in the margin; in some cases, however, a single entry was recorded summarising the whole day. The content of the diaries also varied greatly. Some diarists limited themselves to recording strictly factual details (often only an updated positioning of the various units) without any other commentary. Others offered a more general coverage of the situation and even on occasion gave tactical details on the battles themselves. The diversity between the various war diaries suggests that there was no standard format for record keeping beyond what the diarist saw fit to include. A guideline was reported in the war diary of the 3rd Panzer Division, but more than likely it applied only to this division (perhaps because more than one man was charged with making entries or to ensure conformity with the express wishes of the commanding officer). At the top of specially printed pages for the war diary was the heading: 'Descriptions of the events (Important: Assessment of the situation (enemy and own) times of incoming and outgoing reports and orders)'.[4] Even so, and atypically of the normal rigidity of

---

[4] 'KTB 3rd Pz. Div. vom 16.8.40 bis 18.9.41' BA-MA RH 27–3/14.

German military bureaucracy, widespread discrepancies remain between the war diaries, making a large sampling essential to an accurate overview.

Beyond the war diaries themselves, there was also much to be gained from files containing numerous appendices, often only discussed in brief in the war diaries. Yielding further value were the files filled with incoming and outgoing daily orders (*Tagesmeldungen*).

Supplementing the archival research, there are a number of published primary materials that proved invaluable to this study. Among the most useful were the assembled collection of documents edited by Erhard Moritz in *Fall Barbarossa*, and Hugh Trevor-Roper's edited English translation of *Hitler's War Directives 1939–1945*. The OKW war diaries and the three volumes of Halder's own war dairy are standard works, but indispensable to any comprehensive study. The published version of Bock's diary is a trustworthy translation and another vital primary reference.

A selection of post-war memoirs have also been used, but it is important to add that a distinction was made between those sources produced at the time of the war (i.e. diaries, military reports/orders, speeches etc.) and those published after the war, usually by former German generals. These men generally sought to cast themselves in a more favourable light, either with full prescience of political and military events or as innocent functionaries subject to the baneful effects of Hitler's military interference. Accordingly, these post-war accounts are in many cases tainted, distorting their historical objectivity. Nevertheless, as problematic as they are, World War II memoirs cannot be entirely excluded as source material because the authors sometimes provide the only existing record of certain historical events. When used, they have been considered critically and backed, whenever possible, with collaborating evidence.[5]

Although this study is essentially a 'top-down' history focusing on events at the highest level, the 'bottom-up' perspective of individual soldiers has also been included. Using a wide selection of letters, war diaries and memoirs, the soldier's view is interspersed throughout the discussion of the military campaign.

As a matter of orientation for the reader it should be noted that some place names in the Soviet Union appear throughout the documents and

---

[5] See comments on these sources in Gerhard Weinberg, 'Some Thoughts on World War II', *The Journal of Military History*, 56(4) (October, 1992), 659–660; Gerhard Weinberg, *Germany, Hitler, and World War II – Essays in Modern German and World History* (New York, 1995), pp. 307–308; Wolfram Wette, *Die Wehrmacht. Feindbilder, Vernichtungskrieg, Legenden* (Frankfurt am Main, 2002), Teil V: 'Die Legende von der "sauberen" Wehrmacht', pp. 197–244; English translation: *The Wehrmacht. History, Myth, Reality* (Cambridge, 2006), Chapter 5, 'The Legend of the Wehrmacht's "Clean Hands"', pp. 195–250.

published literature with certain variations in spelling. To avoid confusion and assist readability these have been standardised in my text, even sometimes in direct quotations. As a matter of principle I have rejected the all too common inaccuracy of referring to 'the Russians' as if the Soviet Union consisted of a generic, singular national group. Exceptions have only been made when the point in discussion does refer to an individual national group. Direct quotations from German documents, which almost always refer to all members of the Soviet Union as 'the Russians', have not been changed.

It is sometimes suggested that histories written solely from the German perspective, or vice versa, are somehow one-sided and thereby unable to render as accurate a judgement as those studies which claim a duality of source material. This could be the case depending on the exact subject under examination but, on the whole, the mistrust of studies focusing exclusively on one aspect or participant is unwarranted. To argue otherwise shows no understanding of the fact that almost all good studies are built on the back of countless specialised works which illuminate specific aspects of the conflict from one side or the other. Furthermore, one must appreciate the enormity of the war in the east, which makes mastery of the mammoth stock of Soviet or German archival material, on any subject or period, an ambitious claim. It is certainly possible to combine the two successfully, but this should not be mistaken for the benchmark of good research. Specialised studies not only have a legitimate place in the discourse; they tell us a great deal that more general accounts cannot. Nor is it always necessary, or advantageous, to make comparisons between Soviet and Nazi views or methods, which often differed radically. In the English language the eastern front of World War II is already under-represented given its overall importance to the war, and asserting that researchers can only make a useful contribution if they possess a working knowledge of Russian and German is ridiculous. If the counter-claim is that it is only possible to understand the war by looking at it from the point of view of all participants then we will need to look far beyond just German and Russian sources. In many ways the eastern front is a smaller-scale world war in itself. A glance at a contemporary map of Europe, to identify where the many battles took place, reveals that more than a dozen countries hosted this war at various points between 1941 and 1945. Their people and their soldiers, who often worked and fought for one side or the other – or both – have their own stories to tell. Moreover, when one looks at the constituent countries which made up the Soviet Union one can count fifteen successor states whose people fought in the Red Army. Yet not all the conscripts plucked from Central Asia, the Trans Caucasus, the Baltic region or the Far East spoke Russian, nor did the countless ethnic minorities such as Tatars, Bashkirs, Chechens, Chukchis and many others who were drafted into army service. Germany's war was also shared by significant forces from Finland, Romania, Hungary, Italy, Slovakia and even a division from Spain. Additionally, thousands of volunteers from Norway, Denmark, France, Holland, Belgium, Croatia and Bosnia served in Hitler's Waffen SS. Although the war was dominated by forces using the Russian or German language, it was not exclusively so. Thus, charting the complexities of the war will require specialised studies on all participants and only through these can we gain a comprehensive overview of the war in the east.

Given the overall importance of Operation Barbarossa to the development of World War II it is surprising how limited the research has been. The planning phase of this enormous operation is a good example. Only a handful of specialised works exist and none is recent. The most comprehensive are those by Ernst Klink[6] and Barry Leach,[7] appearing in 1983 and 1973 respectively. Leach's work takes in more than simple military planning and therefore does not have the detail of Klink's study, but, building on the work of Andreas Hillgruber,[8] Leach clearly sets out the startling over-confidence of the Army High Command in 1940–41. Robert Cecil's 1975 study[9] backed this conclusion, but discussed the military planning in even less detail, which left Ernst Klink fertile ground to produce a definitive work and his endeavours remain until now unsurpassed. Klink was the first to identify the army's own independent planning for the invasion of the Soviet Union even before Hitler's order. He also explored in detail the emergent split between Hitler and the OKH over the strategic direction of the campaign, as well as detailing the concerns Hitler held in the region of the Pripet marshes. As groundbreaking as Klink's research was, Operation Barbarossa remains the largest military operation in history, and accordingly, more attention needs to be devoted to its origins.

Beyond simple military considerations, attempting any analysis of Germany's invasion of the Soviet Union inevitably brings one into contact with some of the most fervently contested debates of World War II.

[6] Ernst Klink, 'Die militärische Konzeption des Krieges gegen die Sowjetunion', in Militärgeschichtliches Forschungsamt (ed.), *Das Deutsche Reich und der Zweite Weltkrieg*, Band 4: *Der Angriff auf die Sowjetunion* (Stuttgart, 1983).
[7] Barry Leach, *German Strategy Against Russia 1939–1941* (Oxford, 1973).
[8] Andreas Hillgruber, *Hitlers Strategie. Politik und Kriegführung 1940–1941* (Bonn, 1965).
[9] Robert Cecil, *Hitler's Decision to Invade Russia 1941* (London, 1975).

Central among these is Hitler's rationale for turning against his Soviet 'ally' and the struggle between those who see the decision on purely pragmatic grounds and those who see it as the fruition of a long-espoused 'programme' for eastern expansion. This debate opens a wide-ranging discussion that is beyond the current scope of this study. However, the underlying assumptions and prejudices through which Hitler and his army commanders viewed their war against the Soviet Union up until the end of August 1941 are important for my purposes. For this reason, some discussion of the debate and its historical context is required.

With deserved moral authority and for the benefits of political necessity, the immediate post-war period encompassing the Nuremberg trials was largely devoid of serious debate surrounding the origins of the German–Soviet war. Instead, Germany's lone responsibility and guilt for having waged an aggressive war was judged both deliberate and absolute. The harmony did not last long, however, as Cold War rivalry, mixed with some honest quests for historical truth, prompted the US State Department to publish a volume of captured German documents[10] dealing with the Nazi–Soviet pre-war relationship, and indicating a degree of blame for Stalin's commitment to the secret protocols contained within the 1939 Molotov–Ribbentrop pact. The Soviets responded with their own publication entitled *The Falsifiers of History*[11] contesting the authenticity of the American evidence and asserting their own Marxist-Leninist interpretation which emphasised the role of monopoly capitalists in rearming Germany and later channelling German aggression eastward.

The first concerted scholarly study into the period immediately preceding the outbreak of war came from Swiss historian Walter Hofer and demonstrated an intentional, premeditated policy on the part of Germany for further expansion through war.[12] This was contested in the 1961 thesis by A. J. P Taylor, *The Origins of The Second World War*,[13] which caused considerable controversy and began years of debate over whether there was an established, planned programme for eastern expansion, as outlined in *Mein Kampf*, or whether, as Taylor argued, Hitler was a simple opportunist seizing his chances as they arose. Notwithstanding some of the more radical arguments forwarded by Taylor, his main

---

[10] Raymond James Sontag and James Stuart Beddie (eds.), *Nazi–Soviet Relations, 1939–1941. Documents from the Archives of the German Foreign Office* (Washington DC, 1948).
[11] Soviet Information Bureau, *The Falsifiers of History* (Moscow and London, 1948).
[12] Walter Hofer, *War Premeditated, 1939* (London, 1955).
[13] A. J. P Taylor, *The Origins of the Second World War* (London, 1961).

line of reasoning found its supporters,[14] as well as a significant body of detractors.[15] The debate extended to Germany where Taylor's 'revisionist' argument was largely rejected.

Shortly thereafter a landmark work by Andreas Hillgruber[16] appeared that contributed more than any other to the achievement of a factually based middle road between the competing extremes of communist and German apologist interpretations.[17] The latter, sponsored largely by former generals, suggested that Hitler alone dominated the decision-making process but that he was mentally too erratic to follow a detailed plan. Moreover, the generals asserted that Hitler's constant interference in military operations was solely responsible for most of the major military defeats. Many even subscribed to the preventive war theory which centred on an unproven assumption equating Soviet expansionism in eastern Europe with a determination to attack Germany.[18] Communist theories took the diametrically opposed view, blaming Hitler and his 'fascist cohorts' for unleashing a war of unsurpassed aggression, supported all

---

[14] Gerald Reitlinger, *The House Built on Sand. The Conflicts of German Policy in Russia 1939–45* (London, 1960), p. 10. E. M. Robertson stated that: 'Hitler seldom looked more than one move ahead; and the view that he had tried to put into operation a programme, carefully formulated in advance, is quite untenable.' E. M. Robertson, *Hitler's Pre-War Policy and Military Plans: 1933–1939* (London, 1963), p. 1. Even recent works have continued to reflect Taylor's thesis. Heinz Magenheimer considers the idea of Hitler harbouring preconceived plans as 'endeavours to explain a casual chain of incidents that extend over a long period and culminate in a multiple, complex combination of events, simply by pointing to statements made by one of the protagonists in the distant past'. Heinz Magenheimer, *Hitler's War. Germany's Key Strategic Decisions 1940–1945* (London, 1999), p. 42.

[15] Hugh Trevor-Roper, 'A. J. P Taylor, Hitler and the War' in *Outbreak of the Second World War: Design or Blunder?* (Boston, 1962), pp. 88–97. See also Hugh Trevor-Roper (ed.), *Hitler's War Directives 1939–1945* (London, 1964), pp. 13–14; Ian Kershaw, *Hitler 1936–1945. Nemesis* (London, 2001), p. 336; Alan Bullock, *Hitler. A Study in Tyranny* (London, 1962), p. 594; Lucy Dawidowicz, *The War Against the Jews 1933–45* (London, 1987), p. 157; William Shirer, *The Rise and Fall of the Third Reich* (New York, 1960), pp. 122–123, 1044.

[16] Hillgruber, *Hitlers Strategie*.

[17] See comments by Rolf-Dieter Müller in Rolf-Dieter Müller and Gerd R. Ueberschär, *Hitler's War in the East 1941–1945. A Critical Assessment* (Oxford, 1997), pp. 10–15.

[18] Erich von Manstein, *Lost Victories* (Novato, 1958), pp. 154, 169–171, 181–182; Franz Halder, *Hitler as Warlord* (London, 1950), pp. 17, 22–23; Albrecht Kesselring, *The Memoirs of Field-Marshal Kesselring* (London, 1953), pp. 86–87; Walter Görlitz (ed.), *The Memoirs of Field-Marshal Keitel. Chief of the German High Command, 1938–1945* (New York, 1966), pp. 124 and 243. In counterpoint to these assertions see the helpful essay by Manfred Messerschmidt, 'June 1941 Seen Through German Memoirs and Diaries' in Joseph Wieczynski (ed.), *Operation Barbarossa. The German Attack on the Soviet Union June 22, 1941* (Salt Lake City, 1993), pp. 214–227.

the while by western capitalist powers who accordingly were not seriously interested in containing Germany during the summer of 1939.[19] Similarly, the post-war contributions of the German generals were depicted to be those of a self-serving clique, aimed at absolving their caste of guilt and restoring militarism to western Germany.[20]

Hillgruber's study rejected both of these views in favour of a meticulous review of the available evidence which highlighted the dominance of an ideologically driven quest for 'living space' (*Lebensraum*) as the guiding principal of Nazi foreign policy. This set the tone for many instructive future studies, with the concept of an ideological interpretation interwoven with pragmatic considerations of the political and strategic kind,[21] as Hillgruber himself had emphasised.

The acceptance among many historians of ideology as a fundamental component of Hitler's strategic outlook did not exclude occasional challenges from new revisionists, nor alter the unrelenting attitude of Soviet and East German historians more interested in the ardent adherence to entrenched dogma than historical truth.[22] Debate also resurfaced with

[19] Lev Besymenski, *Sonderakte Barbarossa. Dokumentarbericht zur Vorgeschichte des deutschen Überfalls auf die Sowjetunion – aus sowjetischer Sicht* (Reinbek, 1973); Hans Höhn (ed.), *Auf antisowjetischem Kriegskurs. Studien zur militärischen Vorbereitung des deutschen Imperialismus auf die Aggression gegen die UdSSR (1933–1941)* (Berlin, 1970); A. A Gretschko (ed.), *Geschichte des Zweiten Weltkrieges 1939–1945*, Volume II: *Am Vorabend des Krieges* (East Berlin, 1975); P. A. Shilin, *Der Grosse Vaterländische Krieg der Sowjetunion*, Volume I (Berlin, 1975).

[20] Leach, *German Strategy Against Russia*, p. 2.

[21] Gerd R. Ueberschär, 'Hitlers Entschluß zum "Lebensraum" – Krieg im Osten. Programmatisches Ziel oder militärstrategisches Kalkül?' in Gerd Ueberschär and Wolfram Wette (eds.), *'Unternehmen Barbarossa'. Der deutsche Überfall auf die Sowjetunion 1941* (Paderborn, 1984), pp. 83–110; Klaus Hildebrand, 'Hitlers "Programm" und seine Realisierung 1939–1942' in Manfred Funke (ed.), *Hitler, Deutschland und die Mächte. Materialien zur Außenpolitik des Dritten Reiches* (Düsseldorf, 1976), pp. 63–93; Klaus Hildebrand, *Deutsche Außenpolitik, 1933–1945. Kalkül oder Dogma?* 4th edn (Stuttgart, 1980); Gerhard Schreiber, 'Deutsche Politik und Kriegführung 1939 bis 1945' in Karl Dietrich Bracher, Manfred Funke and Hans-Adolf Jacobsen (eds.), *In Deutschland 1933–1945. Neue Studien zur nationalsozialistischen Herrschaft* (Bonn, 1992), pp. 333–356; Eberhard Jächel, *Hitlers Weltanschauung. Entwurf einer Herrschaft* (Stuttgart, 1991), Chapter 2, 'Die Eroberung von Raum'. In English the most valuable studies are those by Norman Rich, *Hitler's War Aims. Ideology, the Nazi State, and the Course of Expansion* (New York, 1972); Cecil, *Hitler's Decision to Invade Russia 1941*; Leach, *German Strategy Against Russia*; Gerhard Weinberg, *A World At Arms. A Global History of World War II* (Cambridge, 1994).

[22] These views persisted in the Soviet Union up until its final years when Gorbachev's *glasnost* and *perestroika* decreed a new openness allowing fundamental change in the discourse of Soviet history. Central among these was the recognition of the secret protocols agreed to by Stalin in the Molotov–Ribbentrop pact. Curiously, the East German state opted not to partake in this new discussion choosing instead to hold doggedly to the long since discredited denial. Müller and Ueberschär, *Hitler's War in the East*, pp. 28, 31.

renewed vigour in the late 1980s over the preventive war theory with the old line of the German generals repackaged to include supposed 'new evidence' that amounted to no more than a reproduction of existing documents in an unconvincing attempt to provide a guise of academic merit.[23] The first-rate studies produced to rebut these pseudo-academic apologists' works not only revealed their yawning lack of credibility, but have contributed greatly to clarifying the pre-war motivations and political manoeuvring of Stalin and Hitler.[24]

While debates on the origins of Hitler's war against the Soviet Union form an important background to the first part of this study (dealing with the strategic conceptions and operational planning for the campaign), the central thesis, that the German military campaign failed in the summer of 1941, remains to be proven in the second part (looking at the progress of the war itself). Here the existing literature has far greater implications for the study and therefore a comprehensive orientation is required both to familiarise the reader with the field of study and to provide a clear historiographical context for the present work.

Seldom are works of military history popular bestsellers, but in 1998 that feat was achieved by Antony Beevor's *Stalingrad*, a comprehensive and authoritative account of that epic battle. For many readers, particularly in the English-speaking world, it was undoubtedly an introduction to the lesser-known conflict in eastern Europe during World War II. Beevor's study traced the fighting from the beginning of the war in June 1941 with the opening assertion: 'Seldom had an attacker enjoyed such advantages

---

[23] Victor Suvorov, *Icebreaker: Who Started the Second World War* (London, 1990); Ernst Topitsch, *Stalin's War: A Radical New Theory of the Origins of the Second World War* (New York, 1987); Joachim Hoffmann, 'The Soviet Union's Offensive Preparations in 1941' in Bernd Wegner (ed.), *From Peace to War. Germany, Soviet Russia and the World, 1939–1941* (Oxford, 1997), pp. 361–380; Constantine Pleshakov, *Stalin's Folly. The Tragic First Ten Days of WWII on the Eastern Front* (New York, 2005). In 2000 I had the opportunity to hear Victor Suvorov (this is only a pseudonym, his real name is Vladimir Rezun) speak at King's College Department of War Studies. He spoke at length on the general thesis of *Icebreaker* and included what he explained to be new research. Overall, however, I found the presentation (as with his book) thoroughly unconvincing and sorely lacking in documentary evidence for such outlandish claims.

[24] The most comprehensive overall survey is that by Gabriel Gorodetsky, *Grand Delusion. Stalin and the German Invasion of Russia* (New Haven, 1999). See also Gabriel Gorodetsky, 'Stalin and Hitler's Attack on the Soviet Union' in Bernd Wegner (ed.), *From Peace to War*, pp. 343–359; Gerd R. Ueberschär, 'Hitler's Decision to Attack the Soviet Union in Recent German Historiography' in Joseph Wieczynski (ed.), *Operation Barbarossa*. On a different tack from Gorodetsky, David M. Glantz argues the case through a pre-war analysis of the Red Army; see David M. Glantz, *Stumbling Colossus. The Red Army on the Eve of World War* (Lawrence, 1998). For a more complete listing of the large body of literature in this area see the selected titles in Müller and Ueberschär, *Hitler's War in the East*, pp. 390–397.

as the Wehrmacht in June 1941.'[25] Beevor's statement is certainly not exceptional. Histories lauding the victorious progress of the Wehrmacht in the first two years of the conflict form a characteristic representation of the war. With unprecedented victories and comparatively bloodless battles, the temptation to over-estimate German strength has always been great. In the case of Barbarossa this tendency has been further aided by the poor standing of the Red Army following Stalin's purges[26] and its chaotic reorganisation following its disastrous performance in the war against Finland (1939–40). Russel Stolfi has taken such logic so far as to suggest that historians have largely under-estimated the offensive capabilities of the German army and over-estimated those of the Red Army,[27] leading to his revisionist thesis that Operation Barbarossa represented a realistic war-winning alternative for Germany. Accordingly, Stolfi sees the invasion in glowing terms, allowing him to draw the ill-informed and dangerous conclusion: 'Hitler showed impressive decisiveness in ordering the attack against the Soviet Union, an indomitable will for which he has not received adequate recognition for the potential consequences.'[28] Not all histories which describe Germany's promising state of affairs in the prelude to Barbarossa hold to such radical and misguided views. Nevertheless, they lack a required understanding of Germany's core military and economic institutions that, in relation to the scale of the undertaking and Germany's wider geo-strategic position, offer little cause for optimism.

Histories covering the early stages of the campaign are often equally problematic. Striking statistics detailing the extraordinary number of Soviet prisoners of war, or the huge quantities of equipment seized and destroyed, tend to dominate many of these accounts, impressing upon the reader the magnitude of the German victory and suggesting the campaign was not only a realistic undertaking, but one that could only have failed by the narrowest of margins. This line of argument began, like so many falsehoods of World War II, in the memoirs of former German generals. As Field Marshal Erich von Manstein wrote after the war: '[T]hanks to the superiority of German staff-work and the performance of the combat troops, we achieved extraordinary successes that brought

---

[25] Antony Beevor, *Stalingrad* (London, 1998), p. 21.
[26] Between May 1937 and September 1938 an estimated 36,700 men were purged from the army and 3,000 from the navy (Gorodetsky, *Grand Delusion*, p. 115). These included three out of the Red Army's five marshals, fifteen out of sixteen army commanders, sixty from sixty-seven corps commanders, 70 per cent of all divisional commanders and a large number of the senior political commissars. Rodric Braithwaite, *Moscow 1941. A City and Its People at War* (New York, 2006), p. 46.
[27] R. H. S. Stolfi, *Hitler's Panzers East. World War II Reinterpreted* (Norman, 1993), p. 22.
[28] Ibid., p. 16.

the Soviet armed forces to the very brink of defeat.'[29] Such representations passed all too easily into established histories producing characteristically upbeat assessments of German operations in the early period of Barbarossa. Oxford historian R. A. C. Parker's 1989 study *Struggle for Survival* concluded:

> By any standard of military accomplishment, except that required by Barbarossa, the achievement of the German army in Russia was incomparable. This superb instrument, the most effective land force ever known, won the biggest victories in the history of war... The six months' campaign of 1941 can be summarized very simply: the immense German superiority was not quite great enough.[30]

In similar fashion the renowned British historian Richard Overy asserted in his 1995 book *Why the Allies Won*:

> The wide even grasslands of the Soviet Union showed German armoured forces at their most deadly in the summer of 1941. Against overwhelming odds – some 3,648 tanks against an estimated fifteen thousand Soviet tanks – the Panzer armies cut swathe after swathe through the Soviet defences, virtually destroyed the Soviet tank and air arm, and brought the Soviet Union almost to the point of collapse.[31]

While the shattering defeats suffered by the Red Army remain categorical, they were only achieved at a cost so great to the Wehrmacht as to quickly preclude any hope of final victory in 1941, and at no time succeeded in eliminating major Soviet resistance. Overy himself makes the valid observation that in truly explaining the outcome of wars, reliance on straightforward statistics or basic facts can be misleading[32] and it is on this point that many hitherto recorded histories of Operation Barbarossa may be found to be at fault. Indeed the German armies did make enormous territorial gains, destroy vast quantities of Soviet war material and capture enemy soldiers in the hundreds of thousands. A true appreciation of their success, however, can only be gauged from a relative accounting against the cost to German forces. The imposing figure cited by Overy of 15,000 Soviet tanks (of which the overwhelming majority were antiquated models, in varying states of disrepair and manned by barely trained crews) is of less significance to an industrial power capable of sustaining and ultimately replacing the loss, than it might represent to a nation less well resourced. By the same token, the much lower rate of loss suffered by

[29] Von Manstein, *Lost Victories*, pp. 177–178.
[30] R. A. C. Parker, *Struggle for Survival. The History of the Second World War* (Oxford, 1989), pp. 65–67.
[31] Richard Overy, *Why the Allies Won* (New York, 1996), p. 211.   [32] Ibid., pp. 3–4.

Germany proved calamitous to an army already heavily overtaxed and finding itself increasingly incapable of replacing losses or meeting its growing operational requirements.[33]

Robert Citino's various histories about the Prussian/German army have attracted a wide and deserved readership. Yet his 2007 book, on the Wehrmacht's demise in 1942, includes a chapter on 1941 that recounts the German army's initial progress in Operation Barbarossa in the most glowing terms. Citino writes:

[T]he opening of Operation Barbarossa saw the Wehrmacht pound the Red Army senseless, methodically encircling and destroying huge Soviet forces at Bialystok and Minsk. In this opening phase, the Germans fought the *Kesselschlacht* to perfection, taking hundreds of thousands of prisoners and overrunning a huge swath of territory as large as Britain. The operational plan for Barbarossa called for destroying as much of the Red Army as close to the border as possible before it could retreat into the endless depths of the country, and it could not have worked much better than it did.[34]

Citino later continues:

A month into the campaign, the Germans could look with satisfaction on their progress. The Red Army seemed to be coming apart at the seams . . . Things only got better through July. The third great *Kessel* at Smolensk yielded up another 348,000 Soviet prisoners by the end of the month . . . As always, the Wehrmacht maneuver scheme had been a thing of beauty, completely baffling Soviet attempts to counter it.[35]

Citino does go on to describe the difficulties of the 1941 campaign, but this arises in his narrative as something abrupt and sudden, as if the factors which undermined Barbarossa were not present, much less having a terribly corrosive impact, from the beginning of the war. Accordingly, it is only after the 'dizzying'[36] success of the initial weeks that Citino concludes: 'it was at this very moment – with Soviet Russia seemingly on the ropes and the Red Army having apparently dissolved – that Barbarossa began to fall apart'.[37] A comparable angle appears in Andrew Nagorski's 2007 history of the battle of Moscow. It is only in early October 1941, according to Nagorski, that German operations begin to lose what he presents as their lofty superiority: '[T]he German forces finally advancing on Moscow, while still victorious and formidable, weren't quite

[33] For a useful discussion of this process see chapters by Rolf-Dieter Müller in *Das Deutsche Reich und der Zweite Weltkrieg*, Band IV: *Der Angriff auf die Sowjetunion* (Stuttgart, 1983). See also Omer Bartov, *Hitler's Army. Soldiers, Nazis, and War in the Third Reich* (Oxford, 1992), Chapter 1, 'The Demodernization of the Front'.
[34] Robert M. Citino, *Death of the Wehrmacht. The German Campaigns of 1942* (Lawrence, 2007), pp. 34–35.
[35] Ibid., pp. 38–39.   [36] Ibid., p. 36.   [37] Ibid., p. 39.

the juggernaut that they had been during the early weeks of Operation Barbarossa.'[38]

With the early progress of the campaign still commonly recorded as a further laurel for the Wehrmacht, there should be little surprise that challenges to this portrayal, namely from East German and Soviet historians, were accorded little serious consideration. Albert Seaton, in his extensive history *The Russo-German War 1941–45*, dismissively concluded: 'On the Soviet side there has been an attempt to build up the Smolensk battle [July/August 1941] to the proportions of a victory.'[39] Following this lead, the long-since discredited historian David Irving[40] later claimed: 'Hitler had every reason to scent victory throughout July 1941.'[41] Although legitimate criticism may be made of the communist predisposition to explain Soviet successes as proof of the virtues encompassed in a Marxist-Leninist ideology, there remains surprising value in the strictly factual substance of their historical research. As early as 1961 Wolf Stern and Ernst Stenzel suggested that the West German preoccupation with the early success of Barbarossa gave it an artificial and undeserving prominence in the discourse.[42] In 1962 Hans Busse challenged what he saw as the West German attempt to aggrandise the Hitler–Halder command crisis of July/August 1941 into an explanation for the failure of the summer campaign. He argued that this belittled the role of the Red Army and placed the onus for failure on a German strategic decision rather than adequately acknowledging the counter-moves and strengths of the Soviet Union.[43] A few years later in 1965 Helmut Göpfert provided an insightful article assessing the early period of fighting on the eastern front in which he highlighted the sizeable inconsistency between Germany's operational goals and available forces. The resulting attempts to encircle large Soviet armies and operate in such depth, while exposed flanks were suffering constant, albeit ill co-ordinated, counter-attacks, was simply too taxing on German strength. The result, Göpfert argues, was an

---

[38] Andrew Nagorski, *The Greatest Battle. Stalin, Hitler, and the Desperate Struggle for Moscow That Changed the Course of World War II* (New York, 2007), p. 110. See also Andrew Nagorski, 'Stalin's Tipping Point' in *Newsweek* (US edition, 10 September, 2007), 44.

[39] Albert Seaton, *The Russo-German War 1941–45* (Novato, 1971), pp. 131–132.

[40] In spite of a once prominent standing in the field of military history, Irving is now notorious for his anti-Semitic views and his active role as a Holocaust denier.

[41] David Irving, *Hitler's War*, Volume I (New York, 1977), p. 308.

[42] Wolf Stern and Ernst Stenzel, 'Die Blitzkriegsstrategie des deutschen Militarismus und ihr Scheitern beim Überfall auf die Sowjetunion', *Jahrbuch für die Geschichte der UdSSR und der volksdemokratischen Länder Europas* 5 (1961), p. 32.

[43] Hans Busse, 'Das Scheitern des Operationsplanes "Barbarossa" im Sommer 1941 und die militaristische Legende von der "Führungskrise"', *Zeitschrift für Militärgeschichte* 1 (1962), 62–83.

unsustainable rate of loss in momentum rendering the operational plan doomed to failure, and this was clearly evident in the beginning phase of the campaign.[44]

The problem of gaining any form of acceptance for these works in the west was that their interpretation fitted all too well into the familiar communist mythology of a superior socialist society, pitting the heroic Soviet people against German fascist invaders and concluding that a Soviet victory was inevitable from the very beginning.[45] Not surprisingly, such an interpretation stimulated no special interest in the west and, with the end of communism in Europe, few have bothered to revisit such tainted works with any notion of uncovering historical truth. Yet judged on their intrinsic scholastic value alone, and without the heavy baggage of supporting a redundant ideology, the work of Soviet and East German historians provides an interesting starting point for a fresh discussion of the initial period of war on the eastern front.

A recently published study by Heinz Magenheimer highlights the need for a corrective approach. According to Magenheimer: 'It is . . . a gross distortion of the facts to claim that the energetic Soviet defence east of Smolensk had dealt the Germans a defeat and thereby prevented their immediate further advance on Moscow.'[46] However even Magenheimer had to concede: 'Even if resistance by the Red Army had diminished after the battle of Smolensk, the German troops would have required a break of about three weeks for replenishment and supply, *particularly in order to increase the offensive power of the weakened armoured formations.*'[47] In spite of dismissing the contention of communist historians, the question of how these armoured formations became so badly weakened, and the significance of this for the continuation of the campaign, does not appear to have influenced Magenheimer's earlier assessment of the fighting around Smolensk.

So far the only western historians to present major studies challenging conventional wisdom on the subject of Barbarossa's failure in the summer of 1941 are Bryan Fugate and Russel Stolfi. Both authors have attempted

---

[44] Helmut Göpfert, 'Zur Anfangsperiode des faschistischen Überfalls auf die Sowjetunion', *Zeitschrift für Militärgeschichte* 4 (2) (1965), 171–172. Not all of Göpfert's article can be viewed with such merit and he considerably over-estimates the state of Soviet preparations for war in 1941. The extraordinary losses which befell the Red Army in the early period of war he ascribes largely to Stalin's refusal to alert the army in sufficient time. Another article by Göpfert dealing with the failure of German operations in the east appeared later, see Helmut Göpfert, 'Das Scheitern des blitzkrieges der faschistischen Wehrmacht an der deutsch-sowjetischen Front' in Erhard Moritz (ed.), *Das Fiasko der antisowjetischen Aggression. Studien zur Kriegführung des deutschen Imperialismus gegen die UdSSR (1941–1945)* (East Berlin, 1978), pp. 45–73.

[45] Shilin, *Der Grosse Vaterländische Krieg*, Volume I, pp. 119–121.

[46] Magenheimer, *Hitler's War*, p. 85.   [47] Italics mine. Ibid., pp. 85–86.

far-reaching reinterpretations of the campaign, drawing thoroughly divergent conclusions that have remained deservedly marginalised. Fugate's 1984 study *Operation Barbarossa – Strategy and Tactics on the Eastern Front, 1941* elaborated the bold thesis that the Soviet High Command successfully carried out an ambitious plan, conceived of by Marshal Georgi Zhukov, to sacrifice its first strategic echelon in order to disrupt German concentrations and catch them unawares with a stronger second strategic echelon anchored on the Dvina–Dnepr River line. Thus, Bock's army group was being lured into a cleverly devised Soviet trap. Detractors of Fugate's theory rightly pointed to the absence of any solid archival evidence to back up this elaborate Soviet plan[48] and this probably inspired Fugate's second book, co-written with Russian historian Lev Dvoretsky, *Thunder on the Dnepr. Zhukov–Stalin and the Defeat of Hitler's Blitzkrieg,* which appeared in 1997. The second book expounded the same thesis, with supposedly new evidence in the form of a February 1941 war game that allegedly confirmed Zhukov's master plan for the coming war. Yet even Fugate and Dvoretsky acknowledge that the facts surrounding the February war game are less than certain[49] and they cannot hope to convince sceptical readers with scant footnotes and no bibliography.[50] The redeeming feature of Fugate's first study, particularly of value when one disregards his implausibly far-fetched theory of Soviet strategic planning, is his use of German archival sources in detailing the demise of German offensive strength over the summer of 1941. Here parallels with Göpfert's work acquire significance given Fugate's accurate assessment of the effects of heavy fighting on grinding down the German panzer and motorised divisions, particularly in the Yel'nya[51] salient.

The second study by Russel Stolfi, *Hitler's Panzer East – World War II Reinterpreted*[52] (1991) postulates the contrasting thesis that the German strategy for the conquest of the Soviet Union represented a perfectly realisable plan which was only confounded by Hitler's ruinous insistence on halting the drive on Moscow in August 1941. In addition to

[48] Jacob W. Kipp, 'Barbarossa and the Crisis of Successive Operations: The Smolensk Engagements, July 10–August 7, 1941' in Wieczynski (ed.), *Operation Barbarossa,* p. 117; Jacob W. Kipp, 'Barbarossa, Soviet Covering Forces and the Initial Period of War: Military History and Airland Battle', published online by the Foreign Military Studies Office (Fort Leavenworth, 1989) p. 1. http://fmso.leavenworth.army.mil/fmsopubs/issues/barbaros.htm

[49] Bryan Fugate and Lev Dvoretsky, *Thunder on the Dnepr. Zhukov–Stalin and the Defeat of Hitler's Blitzkrieg* (Novato, 1997), p. xiii.

[50] Earl F. Ziemke, 'Book Review – *Thunder on the Dnepr*', *The Journal of Military History,* 62(2) (April, 1998), 433.

[51] Yel'nya is sometimes spelled in the literature 'El'nia', 'Yelnia' or 'Yelnya'.

[52] See also R. H. S. Stolfi, 'Blitzkrieg Army, Siege Führer. A Reinterpretation of World War II in Europe' in Command Magazine (ed.), *Hitler's Army. The Evolution and Structure of German Forces, 1933–1945* (Boston, 2003), pp. 153–164.

glaring factual errors,[53] Stolfi's thesis is laden with contentious assertions and beset by dubious methodology, underlining the difficulty of
supporting a largely untenable case. Even if Moscow could have been
seized by the autumn of 1941, as Stolfi claims,[54] there is no evidence to
suggest that this would have precipitated the collapse of the Soviet war
effort as he assumes.[55] Furthermore, Stolfi's assessments of Soviet losses,
materiel strengths and intentions rely often on German wartime intelligence reports, which were naturally prone to prodigious inaccuracies.[56]
Elements of the study are so erroneous as to make it both unhelpful
in understanding the events of summer 1941 and, in many regards,
actively misleading especially to readers unfamiliar with the period. A
case in point is Stolfi's inexcusable omission of discussion relating to the
widespread German atrocities in the east by both the SS and the German
army, particularly given his repeated highlighting of war crimes committed by Soviet forces.[57] Indeed the only major point on which Stolfi's thesis
renders an accurate judgement is his final conclusion that the summer of
1941 represented a clear shift away from a Blitz-style campaign to one
already bogged down in an unwinnable war of attrition.

Although major studies are lacking, a number of West German historians have proved closer to the mark in describing the lessons of war in the
early period of conflict on the eastern front. Despite failing to acknowledge the much earlier contributions of their East German counterparts,
to which these works owed a degree of creative debt, during the 1980s

[53] Among the most outstanding is an alleged quotation from the commander of Panzer
Group 4, Colonel-General Erich Hoepner, written according to Stolfi 'after the war' for
which no footnote is given. In fact Hoepner was hanged in 1944 for his role in the July
plot to assassinate Hitler (Stolfi, *Hitler's Panzers East*, p. 53).

[54] For contrasting views see comments by Weinberg, *A World At Arms*, pp. 269–270;
David M. Glantz, *Colossus Reborn. The Red Army at War, 1941–1943* (Lawrence, 2005),
pp. 16–17; Domarus, *Hitler*, Volume IV, pp. 2461–2462.

[55] Casting doubt on Stolfi's contention, see Günther Blumentritt, 'Moscow' in William
Richardson and Seymour Freidin (eds.), *The Fatal Decisions* (London, 1956), p. 73;
Gerd Niepold, 'Plan Barbarossa' in David M. Glantz (ed.), *The Initial Period of War on
the Eastern Front 22 June–August 1941* (London, 1997), p. 77.

[56] To cite one example from early August 1941, Stolfi writes: 'Army Group Centre was so
successful that Soviet forces opposed to it, according to German intelligence estimates,
appeared to have been reduced to roughly half the strength of Army Group Centre.'
Stolfi, *Hitler's Panzers East*, p. 154. In fact, the enormous Soviet force generation undertaken in July and August 1941 was heavily concentrated in front of Bock's army group,
increasing overall Soviet numbers in spite of their great losses. See David M. Glantz
and Jonathan House, *When Titans Clashed. How the Red Army Stopped Hitler* (Lawrence,
1995), pp. 68–69 and 301.

[57] According to his distorted representation, 'without similar provocation, Red Army soldiers committed atrocities against German ground and air force personnel. The accounts
of murder, mutilation, and maiming come entirely from German sources': Stolfi, *Hitler's
Panzers East*, pp. 90–91.

West German historians presented the battle of Smolensk for the first
time as something other than a resounding German victory. Ernst Klink
provided one of the few German operational histories of the campaign
and succeeds well, in spite of relying too much on the diaries and files of
the OKH and OKW, which fail to reflect the full extent of the campaign's problems clearly made evident in the reports of the combat
units.[58] In another study, Andreas Hillgruber argued that the second
half of July 1941 was decisive for both the military developments on
Bock's front and the wider implications these were having on Japan's
strategic deliberations.[59] John E. Tashjean's short article complemented
Hillgruber's assessment by reviewing the battle of Smolensk through the
useful prism of Clausewitz's culminating point, which alludes to some
of the themes subsequently confirmed in this study.[60] In the same vein,
Anglo-American historians researching Soviet military operations have
provided an array of evidence suggesting that the battle of Smolensk
played a much more important role in blunting the German offensive
than previously thought.[61]

An attempt to understand the persistence of controversies surrounding the German–Soviet war requires a brief introduction to the difficulties confronting historians looking into the literature from and about
this period. First, because of the unprecedented scale and complexity
of the war in the east, the historian is confronted by a daunting array
of archival material. As a result, in spite of some fine studies published
over the years, many principal subjects of interest remain shrouded in
mystery.[62] The associated 'holes' in research have contributed to many

[58] Ernst Klink, 'Die Operationsführung' in Militärgeschichtliches Forschungsamt (ed.),
Das Deutsche Reich und der Zweite Weltkrieg, Band IV: *Der Angriff auf die Sowjetunion*
(Stuttgart, 1983).
[59] Andreas Hillgruber, 'Die Bedeutung der Schlacht von Smolensk in der zweiten Juli-
Hälfte 1941 für den Ausgang des Ostkrieges' in Inge Auerbach, Andreas Hillgruber and
Gottfried Schramm (eds.), *Felder und Vorfelder russischer Geschichte. Studien zu Ehren
von Peter Scheibert* (Freiburg, 1985), pp. 266–279. Reproduced in Andreas Hillgruber,
Die Zerstörung Europas. Beiträge zur Weltkriegsepoche 1914 bis 1945 (Frankfurt am Main,
1988), pp. 296–312. See also Andreas Hillgruber, *Der Zenit des Zweiten Weltkrieges Juli
1941* (Wiesbaden, 1977).
[60] John E. Tashjean, 'Smolensk 1941. Zum Kulminationspunkt in Theorie und Praxis'
in Militärgeschichtliches Forschungsamt (ed.), *Die operative Idee und ihre Grundlagen.
Ausgewählte Operationen des Zweiten Weltkrieges. Vorträge zur Militärgeschichte*, Volume X
(Herford, 1989) pp. 39–51.
[61] See studies by Kipp, 'Barbarossa and the Crisis of Successive Operations', pp. 113–150,
and Glantz, *The Battle for Smolensk: 7 July–10 September 1941* (privately published study
by David M. Glantz, 2001). See also the more general study by John Erickson, *The
Road to Stalingrad. Stalin's War with Germany*, Volume I (London, 1975).
[62] For an insight into research gaps see David M. Glantz, *Forgotten Battles of the German–
Soviet War (1941–1945)*, Volume I: *The Summer–Fall Campaign (22 June–4 December*

unproven conceptions about the war flourishing without basis in fact or scholarly methodology. These ideas, usually first recorded in popular post-war accounts, may fail the rigorous standards of serious examination, but have nevertheless made an indelible impact on the general understanding of events. The belief that 'General Mud' and 'General Winter' were the real culprits behind the 1941 failure of the Barbarossa campaign, is still commonly heard and even published today.[63] Furthermore, there is a persistent determination in some quarters to accept the post-war fabrication of a 'sanitised' German army, disbelieving the incontrovertible evidence relating to crimes by the Wehrmacht. Such notions have helped mould popular knowledge of the war in competition with 'accepted' understandings, and demonstrate the susceptibility of history to distortion.[64]

Nevertheless the challenge for historians is not simply one of a misinformed mass versus learned scholars. The field, like any other academic discipline, provides ample room for disagreements regarding many elements of the war.[65] The previously discussed controversies surrounding Hitler's decision to invade the Soviet Union (Barbarossa as a preventive war) as well as rival East/West interpretations have provided more than enough fodder for energising debate. Moreover, in the English-speaking world a further challenge has long existed because of the skewed representation of the German–Soviet war which is often subsumed within the Anglo-American war effort or largely eclipsed by it.[66] For the war on Germany's eastern front, which involved literally millions of combatants

---

1941) (privately published study by David M. Glantz, 1999) and Glantz, 'Forgotten Battles' in The Military Book Club (ed.), *Slaughterhouse. The Encyclopedia of the Eastern Front* (New York, 2002), pp. 471–496.

[63] Interestingly, in the wake of Napoleon's failed 1812 invasion of Russia, the French also took solace from the myth that they had been defeated by the Russian winter, rather than the Russians themselves or Napoleon's own mistakes. Adam Zamoyski, *1812. Napoleon's Fatal March on Moscow* (London, 2004), p. xvii.

[64] Ronald Smelser and Edward J. Davies II, *The Myth of the Eastern Front. The Nazi–Soviet War in American Popular Culture* (Cambridge, 2008).

[65] For one overview see Glantz, *Colossus Reborn*, pp. 14–17.

[66] According to David Glantz: 'The paucity of detailed information on the war available in the English language reinforces the natural American (and Western) penchant for viewing the Soviet–German War as a mere backdrop for more dramatic and significant battles in western theatres, such as El Alamein, Salerno, Anzio, Normandy, and the Ardennes Offensive.' Glantz, *The Soviet–German War 1941–1945: Myths and Realities: A Survey Essay* (privately published study by David M. Glantz) p. 2. See also Glantz, 'Introduction', in The Military Book Club (ed.), *Slaughterhouse*, p. 2. It is also worth remembering that the same historical distortion has taken place, to perhaps an even greater extent, in representing events in the war against Japan. Here events in the Pacific have dominated much of our understanding of this aspect of the conflict with the frightful war in mainland China accounting for only the most rudimentary historical research.

and countless battles along the Soviet steppe, including some on an extraordinary scale, typically struggle to register a mention even in the most detailed studies. By contrast much smaller battles in Northern Africa, France and Italy have been given far greater prominence and have become the subject of much research and debate. This pro-western orientation tends to take account of only the largest and best known battles on the eastern front and then frequently accords to them a prominence similar to those battles fought at the time by the western allies. Thus the Soviet offensives at Moscow and Stalingrad are commonly discussed with the same degree of detail as General Auchinleck's 'Crusader' offensive and General Montgomery's second battle of Alamein. The corresponding gulf in significance between these battles is too often overlooked, generating a disturbing misconception that continues to widen because of the further preoccupation with the Anglo-American bombing campaign and the battle of the Atlantic against German U-boats. Many western representations of World War II therefore offer a slanted perspective which belittles the contribution of the Soviet Union and consequently hinders our understanding of the eastern front in World War II.[67]

More recently, concern has also been raised about the methodology of the war's research and the dominance of German source material which, since the post-war era, has formed the backbone of many western accounts. Initially spawned by the flurry of memoirs by former German officers, who also produced many early studies for the US Army Historical Division, their groundwork was built on by the later release of German archival records, and the subsequent emergence of many proud, veteran inspired, wartime unit histories, often lacking a discerning historical objectivity. By contrast, the absence of free access to Soviet source material, and the brazen bias of official publications, largely removed a competing remedial. The result was a scripted appraisal of the Red Army laden with accounts of military ineptitude and assertions that the Red Army was saved from defeat by the huge size of the Soviet Union, the harsh climate, a pitiless disregard for human life and sheer weight of numbers. While these interpretations largely scorned Soviet combat performance, the burden of blame for German blunders and miscalculations was typically laid squarely at the feet of Adolf Hitler.[68] Although such stereotypical views have been debunked, their persistence in various quarters and to varying degrees has continued to exert influence, particularly

---

[67] The best single-volume guides to the war are Weinberg's *A World At Arms*, and from the German perspective Rolf-Dieter Müller's *Der letzte deutsche Krieg 1939–1945* (Stuttgart, 2005).

[68] David M. Glantz, 'The Red Army at War, 1941–1945: Sources and Interpretations', *The Journal of Military History* 62(3) (July, 1998), 596–598.

as a popular explanation for events in the opening stages of Operation Barbarossa. Consequently, secondary accounts have frequently adopted an uncritical approach presenting German successes as evidence of the lofty skill and professionalism of the Wehrmacht while, in contrast, the lamentable Red Army is seen to survive almost in spite of itself and owes its later success only to lessons learned from the Germans.

In addition to reassessing the famed German blitzkrieg on the eastern front in the summer of 1941, there is a need to review another event similarly fraught by oversight and worthy of investigation. Accurately referred to by Alan Clark as 'the first crisis' of the eastern front,[69] the struggle for operational control of the panzer groups between Hitler and the OKH has commonly been treated in the literature as little more than a through-way station on the road to disaster at Moscow. Yet it is because of this power struggle, against a backdrop of the failing strategic plan, lagging operational timetable and the rapidly eroding strength of the all-important panzer divisions, that the crisis acquires its heated intensity. Not only did Halder believe before the invasion that Moscow represented the surest war-winning solution, but as he grasped the seriousness of the complications arising from the campaign, Moscow assumed a critical status for him upon which all hope for victory hinged. Likewise, Hitler foresaw the attainment of economic objectives as the essential element in ensuring Germany's success. Yet the crisis in command has generally attracted only passing interest among historians, while the course of operations ending in the final demise of Barbarossa at Moscow has remained the principal focus of the literature.[70] A critical review of the German summer campaign tells us a great deal more about the significance of the crisis which, if anything, confirmed the defeat of Barbarossa rather than precipitated it. The campaign, which had by no means been won in the first stage of operations, now depended, with rapidly diminishing strength, upon a decisive blow in the second. The stakes for Germany could not have been higher, but even more alarming than the stark choice of options at hand was the realisation that German mobile forces, with their available strength, operating at such depth and against such large-scale ongoing resistance, could not possibly strike a war-winning blow in the remainder of 1941. Thus the vigour with which Hitler and his generals fought each other over the strategic direction of the campaign, paralleled to an extent by the vitality with which some historians have since debated the

---

[69] Alan Clark, *Barbarossa. The Russian-German Conflict 1941–1945* (London, 1996), Chapter 4, 'The First Crisis'.

[70] For some key points see Alan F. Wilt, 'Hitler's Late Summer Pause in 1941', *Military Affairs* 45(4) (1981), 190–191.

respective alternatives, seems neglectful of the real issue at stake – that by late August 1941 Germany's defeat of the Soviet Union was doomed to fail.

The eminent British military theorist and historian Sir Basil Liddell Hart observed in relation to Operation Barbarossa:

The issue in Russia depended less on strategy and tactics than on space, logistics, and mechanics. Although some of the operational decisions were of great importance they did not count so much as mechanical deficiency in conjunction with excess of space, and their effect has to be measured in relation to these basic factors.[71]

In the straightforward analysis of space, logistics and mechanics it becomes clear that a central failing of Barbarossa belongs to inherent structural flaws in the German army, which presented a fundamental problem to the prospects of the campaign beyond the not inconsiderable complications caused by the Red Army. When taken together these factors make it somewhat naive to frame Army Group Centre's strategic dilemma of July/August 1941 as the essential choice between victory and defeat, if only the correct option was chosen. In fact, the confrontation over strategy was brewing long before the invasion began and took little account of the deeper problems undercutting the German war effort, problems that were not recognised before the war, nor fully appreciated in its initial weeks. In short, the complex relationship between space, time and striking power reveals the extent to which Germany had overplayed its hand in the summer of 1941 and the consequent triviality of strategic manoeuvring after the fact.

An obvious conclusion that may be drawn from this particular appraisal of the initial period of the war is that, with the aggregate loss of momentum throughout the three German army groups and the resultant inability to end the war on the eastern front in a Blitz-style campaign, the culminating point of the attack had been reached and the war, as a result, had turned. Of course Germany was still capable of major offensives on certain sectors of the front and could achieve impressive successes at the operational level, but none of this could change the fundamental disparity between Soviet staying power and German offensive strength. As soon as Germany ceased to threaten a knockout blow and a longer, grinding war ensued, economic factors came into play which favoured the allied war effort even before the direct entry of the United States into the conflict. Indeed two days after the German invasion the US President, Franklin Roosevelt, pledged; 'we are going to give all the aid

---

[71] Basil Liddell Hart, *History of The Second World War* (London, 1970), p. 163.

we can to Russia', signalling his intention to extend the Lend-Lease aid programme, currently arming Britain, to the Soviet Union.[72]

Previous assessments of the German summer campaign in 1941 have assumed the implicit success of Hitler's armies, especially in Army Group Centre. Accordingly, the proposition of an early turning point in the war has centred solely on strategic options, pitting Kiev against Moscow and debating the best method of defeating the Red Army. Yet the two sides to this debate misrepresent the real determinant of what constituted the turning point in the early period of the war. Simply put, the issue is not a strategic question of when and along which axis of advance the drive to victory was to be achieved, for these questions assume that such an accomplishment was even possible in the late summer of 1941. In fact, the German motorised divisions were simply too exhausted to achieve anything more than operational successes on certain parts of the front (aided greatly in this endeavour by Stalin's baneful strategic direction) and certainly could not hope to end the war before the winter. Thus the turning point of the war took place in the summer of 1941, not as a result of any one decision or battle, but rather as the general consequence of many factors broadly represented by the harsh terrain, vast distances, fierce Soviet resistance and internal German weaknesses.

Previously, the debate over turning points in the war has focused on the great battles of the eastern front with opinions split between those advocating the battle of Moscow (winter 1941/42), Stalingrad (winter 1942/43) and Kursk (July 1943). Winston Churchill, in his comprehensive history of World War II, nominated the spring of 1943 as the eastern front's turning point,[73] while studies by Geoffrey Roberts[74] and Mark Healy[75] have argued for Stalingrad and Kursk respectively as the decisive encounters which determined the outcome of the war. More prominently, Richard Overy has taken a longer view which finds no answer in 1941 and instead asserts: 'Somewhere in the changing fortunes of war between 1942 and 1944 lies the heart of the answer to our question of why the allies won.'[76] If indeed this period does explain the allied road to victory

[72] Hubert P. van Tuyll, *Feeding the Bear. American Aid to the Soviet Union*, 1941–1945 (Westport, 1989), p. 4.
[73] Winston S. Churchill, *The Second World War. Abridged Edition* (London, 1959), p. 658.
[74] Geoffrey Roberts, *Victory at Stalingrad. The Battle that Changed History* (London, 2002), Chapter 8, 'Conclusion: The Battle That Changed History'. See also Max Hastings's comments in the Foreword to Willy Peter Reese, *A Stranger to Myself. The Inhumanity of War: Russia, 1941–1944* (New York, 2005), p. x.
[75] Mark Healy, *Kursk 1943: Tide Turns in the East* (Oxford, 2000), p. 7. See also Rupert Butler, *Hitler's Jackals* (Barnsley, 1998), Chapter 13, 'Kursk: The Turning Point'.
[76] Overy, *Why the Allies Won*, p. 17.

it may not necessarily address the timing of the Axis defeat. Yet Overy specifically singled out 1943, noting that in the aftermath of Stalingrad:

Then slowly the tide turned... The first major defeat of the war was inflicted. Over the next twelve months the Red Army drove German forces from much of western Russia, on a broad arc from Kursk to the Caucasus. These Soviet victories marked the turning-point of the whole war, as victory in 1919 had turned the tide of the civil war.[77]

In a more recent publication Overy has highlighted Kursk in July 1943 as the war's turning point.[78]

Klaus Reinhardt's thorough assessment of the battle for Moscow[79] provides a convincing case for the German army's demise in the east and certainly puts beyond doubt the ultimate failure of the Wehrmacht in 1941. Nevertheless, the focus is squarely on Moscow as the definitive turning point, in spite of acknowledging the overarching importance of a short war in the strategic conception of the campaign – the failure of which entailed numerous and fundamentally adverse military and economic consequences. Indeed one might say that irrespective of any other factors, the continued large-scale resistance of the Soviet Union in September 1941 points to the fact that Operation Barbarossa had already failed in its core function. Hence, it is instructive to look at the less familiar side to Germany's defeat in 1941 by focusing on its early failure which occurred, paradoxically, at the height of Germany's success in the east.

While most academic works require a certain historiographical orientation in order to familiarise readers with the field of study and underscore the value of the research to the discourse, an operational history of Barbarossa requires more. This is because it concerns an area of history that many in the German academic establishment reject. Even in the Anglo-American world there are those questioning the continuing relevance of

[77] Ibid., p. 64.
[78] '[The] many fundamental improvements in the way the Soviet forces fought were displayed fully in the battles that rescued Stalingrad between November 1942 and January 1943, when the German Sixth Army under General Friedrich Paulus was forced to capitulate. The turning-point came six months later, when the German armed forces launched Operation "Citadel" to seize a major salient around Kursk to try to unhinge the Soviet front and create the possibility for a renewed assault on Moscow.' Richard Overy, *The Dictators. Hitler's Germany and Stalin's Russia* (London, 2004), p. 529.
[79] Klaus Reinhardt, *Moscow – The Turning Point. The Failure of Hitler's Strategy in the Winter of 1941–42* (Oxford, 1992). See also Klaus Reinhardt, 'Moscow 1941. The Turning Point' in John Erickson and David Dilks (eds.), *Barbarossa. The Axis and the Allies* (Edinburgh, 1998), pp. 207–224.

military history.[80] Yet this takes on an entirely new dimension in Germany where the field has long since been absent from the universities. Aside from those historians teaching or otherwise involved within the *Bundeswehr* (Germany army) and Professor Bernhard Kroener at Potsdam University, there is no formal education in military history available in the country. What is even worse, many students and academics think this is to their benefit, and seem horrified at the suggestion of running courses discussing military campaigns and battles, instead of the more staple interactions with Homer and Luther. It strikes me as odd that such opinion can claim to be promoting the knowledge base of the student body, while at the same time arguing for a restriction of the university curriculum. Who can say what the loss is to German academic discourse when nobody bothers to study it and find out? The result has left the field poverty-stricken in Germany, a deficiency only somewhat mitigated by the outstanding works produced by the *Bundeswehr*'s MGFA (Military History Research Institute) in Potsdam. The underlying problem in Germany, as in the United States, is largely one of image. However, apologists for military history in Germany face such deep-seated antipathy that there is a burning need to counter the widespread misconceptions, and the damage resulting from them.

In Germany more than sixty-five years after the end of the war, histories such as mine are surprisingly rare because they have still not overcome the critical questioning of why such studies should even be attempted. No such taboo or equivalent phenomenon occurred in the Anglo-American world where the righteousness of the war and the ultimate military triumph led to a proliferation of literature which eagerly embraced military campaigns as a legitimate subject for academic pursuit and the popular press. In Germany, however, discussion throughout the long post-war period has often concluded that such questions of military history are of much lesser importance than the 'deeper' issues surrounding the rise of the Nazi party to power, the role of ideology, mechanisms of state control and the regime's litany of criminal activity. Questions of a military nature were, at best, seen as illuminating background to the progress of other more relevant issues and events or, at worst, a shameful and altogether irrelevant undertaking misconstrued as profiting from the lessons of war merely for the benefit of future conflicts. An entrenched pacifist sentiment born of the enduring national guilt Germany has felt since the end of the war accounts in large measure for such views. It also illustrates the deep sense of responsibility most Germans feel towards their past, as well as an overwhelming acceptance of their country's role as a highly

---

[80] John J. Miller, 'Sounding Taps. Why Military History is being Retired', *National Review Online* (October, 2006). http://nrd.nationalreview.com/article/?

aggressive power which committed acts of unrivalled brutality.[81] Until only recently these events forestalled any open expression of national pride among Germans, and only lately, as challenges have emerged, has debate begun about whether the country should re-embrace patriotism.[82]

In identifying the evils of their Nazi past, Germans have naturally taken aim at the rampant militarism that dominated the Third Reich and the regime's proud trumpeting of German/Prussian military history. Unquestionably the Nazis were skilful manipulators, especially when it came to propaganda, and the use of history as a powerful tool in this process was no different. The lavish indulgence in military history under the Nazis reflects only their self-deceiving interpretation of the past and cannot be taken as an accurate or representative view of what the field seeks to achieve. Indeed, given the central importance of the military ethos in Hitler's state and the unrelenting warfare the Nazis directed, discouraging the study of these events is more harmful to the legacy of their crimes. In coming to terms with its Nazi past, Germany's openness has allowed many encouraging lessons to be learned. In fact, I would contend that Germany serves as a fine model for other countries with proverbial skeletons in the closet. Banishing military history, however, is one of the wrong lessons, which has hindered rather than contributed positively to Germany's progress.

For an Australian historian familiar with the long persecution of our indigenous Aboriginals and the difficulties they endure to this day, Germany's unadorned candour in dealing openly with its painful past compares admirably. Yet Australia is not an exception. Many nations are unwilling to accept any measure of responsibility for their blackened pasts, particularly when it relates to nineteenth- and twentieth-century abuses that continue to impact on their societies.[83] Their reluctance reinforces the contrastingly open attitude Germany has adopted – although

---

[81] The actions and beliefs of German neo-Nazis notwithstanding, although in relation to some other extremist right-wing organisations in Europe they have retained comparatively little support in Germany. Only in the past few years have these groups gained a surge in popularity, particularly in the former eastern states.

[82] A convincing case highlighting the pitfalls of promoting national pride is made by Patrick Graichen, 'Deutsche Vergangenheitspolitik und deutscher "Nationalstolz"' in Stiftung für die Rechte zukünftiger Generationen (ed.), *Was bleibt von der Vergangenheit? Die junge Generation im Dialog über den Holocaust* (Berlin, 1999), pp. 222–229.

[83] Cases in point would be Japan's disputed role in its war of annihilation in Korea and China during World War II and Turkey's ardent denial of its genocide against Armenians during World War I. More general examples can be seen in the brutality and exploitation of colonial rule. These periods are still viewed by many in European countries – especially Britain – with unabashed pride as golden eras of nationhood. One can also add the generally appalling treatment of indigenous peoples around the world for whom histories of displacement, exploitation and even genocide have been followed in more recent years by neglect and discrimination.

there are those who would perhaps justifiably point to the unique nature of the Holocaust in fomenting this state of affairs.

Drawing attention to Germany's comparative historical openness is not intended as a mark of pride for Germans; it is nothing more than what is required. Nor is it a faultless process. Germany's internal debate over its history is not devoid of occasional challenges from radical quarters of the historical community. The West German *Historikerstreit* (historians' dispute) that erupted in the 1980s is a perfect example. Still, while Germany retains a comparatively clear conscience in its acceptance of the past, the unduly critical view of histories focused on military operations persists. When I began my research for this study I was initially surprised at how little work had been done in Germany on the strictly military side of Operation Barbarossa. The reason for this lack of material only became clear later in context of the prevailing taboo. The rejection of the field as a serious undertaking has undoubtedly stymied a good deal of work and left many gaps in our understanding of German militarism. The neglect was metaphorically exemplified when at least one map I ordered at the military archive had to be immediately returned for restoration because of damage sustained from years of accumulated mould.

It would surprise some in the English-speaking world to learn that, although German schoolchildren are taught much about Hitler's rise to power and the Holocaust, they learn next to nothing about the campaigns and battles their country fought in World War II. As a result the name 'Kursk' means more to many Germans as the namesake of a Russian submarine tragedy in which 118 sailors died in 2000 than as one of the most significant battles of World War II in which many thousands of German and Soviet lives were lost. Teaching children about wars is not a matter to be undertaken lightly and there can be no question of its sensitive nature, but neglecting our violent past should not be misconstrued as protecting children. Indeed, given the horrific impact of wars, particularly World War II, and the opportunity granted to learn valuable lessons from these periods, more education, not less, seems in order.

Whatever direction Germany's public education system takes is ultimately a matter for the Germans themselves and my comments express a preference, not a criticism. I reserve stronger judgement for higher levels of education in Germany. Of course there is no official restriction on the study of military history, nor is it difficult to gain access to the military archive in Freiburg, but this does not mean that the intellectual environment embraces, to say nothing of encouraging, the study of war. The tendency to reject military history as a serious undertaking is all the more disappointing because it discounts its inherent importance to related fields of study. The vital interaction between the radicalisation of Nazi policy in Europe and the day-to-day progress of the war would surely count as a noteworthy example.

Although there are some fine studies by German historians, a great deal of work, particularly on Germany's eastern front in World War II, remains to be done. Doubts by some German intellectuals, often backed, as I discovered in my time at the Humboldt University, by significant elements of the student body, about the underlying 'meaning' or suspected motives of such research, must be judged on a case by case basis and not be allowed to cloud the field as a whole. Certainly such fears are not completely unjustified. Any in-depth look at military histories in the English language reveals there is an all too common tendency for histories to adopt a brazen tone of glorification, becoming a medium for patriotic embellishment and national pride. Although such dubious contributions do not dominate the scholarly field, they are nonetheless present and, in some instances, have been well received by large audiences keen to embrace romantic depictions of their county's exploits in war. Still, misguided and potentially damaging rogue elements are a challenge to all fields of study which debate in an open forum. Indeed, it is the absence of informed opinion that allows radical theories to gain credibility.

Investigating Germany's military history is unlikely to spawn a rise of similarly ill-conceived, misguided publications. The well-established culpability of Germany for crimes perpetrated between 1933 and 1945 has left Germans much more inclined to assess their country's exploits in war critically and objectively. There is also a much more limited tolerance for forms of nationalistic expression because it is still inextricably linked to the rhetoric and actions of the Third Reich. Thus, advocating the proliferation of military history in Germany's contemporary historical discourse entails little risk, but promises a good deal of important research. To that end, I hope the following work can make a modest contribution.

Part I

Strategic plans and theoretical conceptions
for war against the Soviet Union

1   Fighting the bear

The evolution of early strategic planning

In August 1939 the signing of the Nazi–Soviet Non-Aggression Pact
(otherwise referred to as the Molotov–Ribbentrop Pact) set out the par-
tition of Poland following an agreed invasion, first by Hitler and later
Stalin. The pact heralded a new degree of co-operation between the two
nations, while the secret agreement on spheres of influence in eastern
Europe and Finland had the important ramification of ensuring security for Germany's eastern border. This freed Hitler's hand for the war
he found himself fighting against France and Britain and allowed for
the heavy concentration of his forces in the west. Hitler's subsequent
campaign in May and June of 1940 seized control of the Low Countries, knocked France out of the war and effectively secured control of
Germany's western flank.

It was only at this point that substantial forces were redirected towards
the Reich's eastern border, which was the result of both the changed
strategic situation in Europe and the events unfolding in the east beyond
Germany's frontier. Stalin was moving quickly to absorb his share of the
territory allocated to him under the Nazi–Soviet pact, and the remarkable
successes Germany achieved in the west added to his sense of urgency.
Finland had already been forced to yield territory in the Winter War
(1939–40) and by the middle of June the Baltic states were completely
occupied and eventually absorbed into the Soviet empire as member
republics. June also saw Soviet forces occupying the Romanian regions
of Bessarabia and Northern Bukovina, heightening German fears that
Soviet ambitions might extend as far as Romania's oil fields at Ploesti,
which were vital to Germany's war economy.[1]

With these concerns in mind, and indeed before the Soviet armies
had completed their occupations on the Baltic and in Romania, the first

---

[1] Geoffrey Roberts, *The Soviet Union and the Origins of the Second World War. Russo-German
Relations and the Road to War*, 1933–1941 (London, 1995), pp. 119–121.

operational plans were drawn up to provide contingencies in the unlikely event of a Soviet attack. This first plan envisaged an offensive type of defence, which placed emphasis on blunting the initial attack and then launching a counter-offensive at the earliest possible opportunity. As the Chief of the Army General Staff, Franz Halder, observed in his diary on 18 June: 'Everything we have should be used for offensive action.'[2]

On 26 June the transfer of the 18th Army was ordered from the west to shore up Germany's eastern defences, with the bulk of its 15 divisions in place by the end of July.[3] Following discussions between Halder, the 18th Army's commanding officer Colonel-General Georg von Küchler and his Chief of Staff Major-General Erich Marcks, a new directive was drawn up under the title, 'Deployment Instructions for Eighteenth Army'. This involved a fundamental departure from the earlier plan by adopting a wholly offensive posture based on the assumption that Soviet preparations could be identified and attacked before operations began against Germany. Even at this embryonic stage of Germany's concept for war in the east, the plan was not simply an offensive reaction to a war already in progress, but rather an action which represented the beginning of a war.[4] Thus we might well consider the 'Deployment Instruction for Eighteenth Army' as the first distinct plan for a German attack on the Soviet Union, even though this involved only limited immediate objectives and was not the result of any directive on Hitler's part.[5]

On 21 July the Commander-in-Chief of the Army, Walter von Brauchitsch, met Hitler to receive instructions regarding the future conduct of the war. The outcome of this meeting was reported back to Halder by Brauchitsch and the resulting account in Halder's diary offers many clues to Hitler's strategic deliberations, indicating consideration of an attack on the Soviet Union. Hitler believed that Britain was beaten, but that Churchill continued the war only in the hope that either the Soviet Union or the United States would soon come to his aid. The objective Halder noted was: 'To smash the Russian army'. Such an undertaking was estimated to require between 80 and 100 German divisions and they

---

[2] Franz Halder, *Kriegstagebuch: Tägliche Aufzeichnungen des Chefs des Generalstabes des Heeres 1939–1942*, Band I: *Vom Polenfeldzug bis zum Ende der Westoffensive (14.8.1939 – 30.6.1940)*, Hans-Adolf Jacobsen and Alfred Philippi (eds.) (Arbeitskreis für Wehrforschung, Stuttgart, 1962), p. 362 (18 June 1940). Hereafter cited as: Franz Halder, KTB I.

[3] Klink, 'Die militärische Konzeption', p. 206 and see note 61.

[4] Ibid., p. 210. See also Olaf Groehler, 'Goals and Reason: Hitler and the German Military' in Wieczynski (ed.), *Operation Barbarossa*, p. 56.

[5] Jürgen Förster, 'Hitler Turns East – German War Policy in 1940 and 1941' in Bernd Wegner (ed.), *From Peace to War. Germany, Soviet Russia and the World, 1939–1941* (Oxford, 1997), pp. 119–120. See also Müller, *Der letzte deutsche Krieg*, pp. 80–81.

could be expected to encounter only 50 to 75 'good' Soviet divisions.[6] The attack was thought possible as early as the autumn of 1940, but accordingly there was some concern about the ability of the Luftwaffe to support operations in the east as well as against Britain. German strength was to be concentrated in the north and south for advances along the Baltic Sea and into the Ukraine.[7] Halder also wrote of 'political aims' being the creation of a Ukrainian state, a separate Belorussia and a confederation of Baltic states.[8]

Hitler's strategic vision at this point was still rather erratic, jumping between options aimed at finding the elusive resolution to cement his victorious war.[9] The confusion was reflected in the emerging war plans of the OKW (Oberkommando der Wehrmacht – High Command of the Armed Forces) and OKH (Oberkommando des Heeres – Army High Command), where contrasting priorities required radically different armament programmes. The OKW called for U-boats and aircraft for the ongoing war against Britain, while the OKH would require tanks and men for the invasion of the Soviet Union. At this point Hitler did not yet see the invasion of the Soviet Union as the long prophesied showdown with Bolshevism and the achievement of 'living space' (*Lebensraum*), but rather as a chiefly strategic manoeuvre, designed to clarify to the British the hopelessness of their situation and result in a favourable peace for Germany.[10] Yet even in Hitler's proposed war on the Soviet Union, Halder's notes suggest that this was not a proposition for full-scale war, but rather something more limited, in line with the 'Deployment Instructions for Eighteenth Army' already prepared.[11] In either case, Hitler commented at the time of the French capitulation, in comparison to what had just been achieved, war against Russia would represent nothing more difficult than 'child's play' (*Sandkastenspiel*).[12]

Upon hearing Brauchitsch's report, Halder instigated a new round of strategic study briefing the Operations Department, the Department of Foreign Armies East and the Military Geography Department. The

[6] Franz Halder, *Kriegstagebuch: Tägliche Aufzeichnungen des Chefs des Generalstabes des Heeres 1939–1942*, Band II: *Von der geplanten Landung in England bis zum Beginn des Ostfeldzuges (1.7.1940 – 21.6.1941)*, Hans-Adolf Jacobsen (ed.) (Arbeitskreis für Wehrforschung, Stuttgart, 1963), pp. 32–33 (22 July 1940). Hereafter cited as: Franz Halder, KTB II.

[7] Ibid., p. 33 (22 July 1940). Leach, *German Strategy Against Russia*, p. 92; Klink, 'Die militärische Konzeption', pp. 213–214.

[8] Franz Halder, KTB II, p. 33 (22 July 1940).

[9] Domarus, *Hitler. Speeches and Proclamations* (Würzburg, 1997), p. 2067.

[10] Kershaw, *Hitler 1936–1945. Nemesis*, p. 305.

[11] Klink, 'Die militärische Konzeption', p. 214.

[12] Albert Speer, *Inside the Third Reich* (London, 1971), p. 188.

Figure 1.1 In the aftermath of the Polish campaign Hitler decorates many of the generals who would later spearhead the invasion of the Soviet Union. From left to right are generals Franz Halder, Heinz Guderian, Hermann Hoth, Adolf Strauss and Erich Hoepner.

first reports were presented a few days later and the discussions that followed centred on the deployment directive for the main German thrust. The head of the operations department, Colonel Hans von Greiffenberg, proposed a strong southern grouping in support of operations directly into the Ukraine, where intelligence indicated the large concentration of the Soviet 6th, 12th and 5th armies were located.[13] Halder, on the other hand, argued for a powerful northern deployment, capable of striking towards Moscow with a subsequent secondary operation into the Ukraine, compelling the Soviet forces there to fight with reversed fronts.[14] The notes of Lieutenant-General Gerhard Feyerabend, who served in the Army General Staff Operations Department, indicate that Halder believed the drive on Moscow would result in a decisive battle with the bulk of the Red Army, presumably involving a rapid redeployment

[13] See map for disposition and stationing areas of 22 July 1940, Klink, 'Die militärische Konzeption', p. 209.
[14] Ibid., p. 214.

from the south. Feyerabend noted that victory in such a campaign was regarded by Halder as the prerequisite for the political collapse of the Soviet Union.[15]

Despite the planning and preparations advanced until now by Halder, there had still been no formal decision announced by Hitler, nor had he issued specific orders that a plan for an aggressive war in the east be prepared. It was on 29 July that Hitler informed the head of the Wehrmacht Operations Department, Colonel-General Alfred Jodl, of his decision to invade the Soviet Union in May 1941. When told of this decision Jodl's deputy Major-General Walter Warlimont described 'a chorus of objection' followed by an hour of bitter debate.[16] The consternation Warlimont claimed to have witnessed centred on the dreaded prospect of a war on two fronts, long since the bane of German military planners. Jodl sought to counter with assurances that victory in the east would stimulate the Luftwaffe with 'a new pitch of efficiency' and allow it to be deployed once again in full strength against England in the autumn of 1941. He also asserted Hitler's belief in the inevitable confrontation with Bolshevism, claiming it was better that the war be fought now at the height of Germany's military dominance in Europe.[17]

Following the meeting with Hitler, Jodl ordered his staff to begin planning, under the operational name 'Build-up East' (*Aufbau-Ost*), facilitating the movement and concentration of forces into the poorly-developed regions of western Poland. Additionally, an operational study was ordered, to be authored by Lieutenant-Colonel Bernhard von Lossberg, in preparation for a campaign against the Soviet Union.[18] This study was later to prove the first document in the evidence of the prosecution at Nuremberg, charging German commanders with complicity in planning and waging a war of aggression.[19]

Two days after Jodl's meeting with Hitler, on 31 July, a major conference took place at the Berghof, Hitler's mountain retreat. Present along with Hitler were the Commander-in-Chief of the Navy, Grand Admiral Erich Raeder,[20] Chief of the High Command of the Wehrmacht, Field Marshal Wilhelm Keitel, Jodl, Halder, Brauchitsch and representing the Luftwaffe, Lieutenant-General Hans Jeschonnek.[21] The formalities began with a briefing by Raeder regarding the state of preparations

---

[15] Ibid., see note 70.
[16] Walter Warlimont, *Im Hauptquartier der deutschen Wehrmacht 1939 bis 1945*, Band I: *September 1939 – November 1942* (Koblenz, 1990), pp. 126–127.
[17] Ibid., pp. 126–127.   [18] Hillgruber, *Hitlers Strategie*, pp. 222–223.
[19] Warlimont, *Im Hauptquartier*, Band I, p. 127; also see note 19.
[20] Raeder however left the conference following his opening presentation.
[21] Klink, 'Die militärische Konzeption', p. 215; also see note 73.

for the invasion of England, the preference of the navy being for the postponement of any cross-channel attack until at least May of 1941. Hitler was made well aware of the risks involved owing to serious complications with the weather and German naval deficiencies. The Admiral even raised veiled objections to the army's invasion plan on such a broad front.[22] When Hitler finally spoke, it was clear that Raeder's address had only confirmed his own misgivings about the operation. Politically astute, Hitler was aware that Germany's prestige following the victory over France was at an all time high and could plainly see the risks involved in a cross-channel invasion in 1940. Thus he arrived at the question: if there was not to be an attempted landing until the spring of the following year, which even then would involve considerable risks, how best should Germany proceed in forcing Britain's recognition that the war was in fact lost? The root of such thinking stems from Hitler's belief that the British cause was a hopeless one and that refusal to accept terms was maintained only in the lingering hope that either the United States or the Soviet Union would eventually join the war against Germany. Hitler therefore resolved to eliminate the Soviet Union, which he believed would have the dual effect of directly removing one threat, and simultaneously removing the other by consequence of the tremendously increased power Japan would enjoy in the Far East and the Pacific. The result, Hitler prophesied, would leave Germany 'master of Europe and the Balkans'.[23]

Halder's diary spells out the new direction in Hitler's strategic thought and hints at some of the reckless assumptions, which astonishingly were allowed to persist throughout the numerous planning phases and operational studies.

With Russia smashed Britain's last hope would be shattered... Decision: *Russia's destruction must therefore be made part of this struggle. Spring 1941. The sooner Russia is crushed the better. Attack achieves its purpose only if Russian state can be shattered to its roots with one blow. Holding part of the country will not do*[24] ... If we start in May 1941, we would have five months to finish the job.

Object is destruction of Russian manpower.[25]

The campaign was to aim for nothing less than the total destruction of the Soviet state and the occupation of the industrial western regions of the country. To do this Hitler spoke of two operational thrusts, one through the south towards Kiev and the other striking north through the Baltic

[22] Irving, *Hitler's War*, p. 163.   [23] Franz Halder, KTB II, p. 49 (31 August 1940).
[24] This should be seen in terms of Hitler's earlier acceptance of the more limited objectives set out by Brauchitsch on 21 July 1940.
[25] Italics in the original. Franz Halder, KTB II, pp. 49–50 (31 August 1940).

states and then on towards Moscow. The two operational groups would
then link up for a subsequent drive on the oil fields near Baku. Following
the defeat of France and the reduction in the size of the army to 120
divisions, the demands of a major new campaign in the east prompted
Hitler to reverse his earlier decision by directing an increase in the size of
the army to a new total of 180 divisions. This denoted 120 divisions for
use in the east with the remainder on occupation duties in France (50),
Norway (7), Belgium and Holland (3).[26]

The conference on 31 July formalised the effort to prepare operational
studies for war against the Soviet Union and can thus be identified as a
watershed in Hitler's strategy for waging the war. Significantly, the recep-
tion of this momentous news by Hitler's most senior commanders was
without protest or dispute, and stands in sharp contrast to the impassioned disputes arising from the timing and operational plans for the
western campaign.[27] In particular, Halder noted only the day before that
maintenance of good relations with Russia would be preferable to the
alternative of confronting a two-front war.[28] This draws attention to the
twisted logic adopted by Hitler and accepted by his generals, that in
order to deny Britain her final hope of Soviet involvement in the war, an
invasion of that country was necessary. Ideological precepts were clearly
a guiding force in the army's conceptualisation of war with the Soviet
Union and this would become more and more evident as the planning
stages progressed. Some thought was given to the long-term challenge a
rearmed and modern Soviet army would pose to German hegemony in
Europe, but these concerns were by no means at the forefront of strategic planning or decision making in the summer of 1940.[29] Indeed, Soviet
prospects for offensive action in Europe posed concern only for Romania
and Finland, but certainly were not believed to include any aggressive
intentions towards the Reich.[30]

Two ways to skin a bear – the Marcks and Lossberg plans

The Chief of Staff of the 18th Army, Major-General Erich Marcks, had
already been working on contingency plans for war with the Soviet Union

---

[26] Ibid., p. 50. Curiously Halder does not include in his total forces for occupation duties
in Denmark, Poland or the Reich itself.
[27] Hillgruber, *Hitlers Strategie*, p. 211.
[28] Franz Halder, KTB II, p. 46 (30 August 1940).
[29] Andreas Hillgruber, 'The German Military Leaders' View of Russia Prior to the Attack
on the Soviet Union' in Wegner (ed.), *From Peace to War*, p. 179.
[30] Jürgen Förster, 'Hitlers Entscheidung für den Krieg gegen die Sowjetunion' in
Militärgeschichtliches Forschungsamt (ed.), *Das Deutsche Reich und der Zweite Weltkrieg*,
pp. 14–15.

since receiving orders from Halder in early July. On 29 July he arrived at the Army High Command headquarters in Fontainebleau to be briefed again by Halder on the increasing scope of the operations now being anticipated in the east.[31] A long-time acquaintance of Halder and a man of high standing within the General Staff,[32] Marcks was then charged with preparing an operational study that would become a principal cornerstone in the theoretical foundation of the final Barbarossa[33] plan.

Completed in the first week of August, Marcks's plan, entitled 'Operations Outline East' (*Operationsentwurf Ost*), envisaged two main thrusts, one to the north and one to the south of the Pripet marshes. The stronger of these two pincers was to be stationed in the north striking from East Prussia and Poland as Marcks, at Halder's urging,[34] determined Moscow to be the decisive key to 'eliminating the coherence of the Russian state' (*seine Eroberung zerreißt den Zusammenhang des russischen Reiches*).[35] To achieve this he directed the powerful northern army group to take the most direct approach to the Soviet capital, using one of the best road systems in the country, which proceeded via Minsk and Smolensk through the 'Orsha Corridor' between the Dvina and Dnepr Rivers. A secondary force would break off from the main group to strike north and seize Leningrad via Pskov.

In the second theatre of operations south of the Pripet marshes, the objective was to prevent a Soviet advance into Romania, vital for Germany's supply of oil, by advancing on Kiev and the middle Dnepr. From this point future operations would be worked out in close co-operation with the northern army group and could vary between an advance due east towards the industrial city of Kharkov or north-east towards a direct link up with formations in the north.

---

[31] Klink, 'Die militärische Konzeption', p. 219.

[32] Otto Jacobsen, *Erich Marcks: Soldat und Gelehrter* (Göttingen, 1971), p. 90.

[33] 'Barbarossa' was not yet a term in use; the code word used early on in Halder's diary is 'Otto'. Likewise, Lossberg had given his study the code-name 'Fritz'. The switch to 'Barbarossa' was adopted in Hitler's War Directive No. 21. The code-name 'Barbarossa' (originating from the Italian 'Red Beard') was selected in reference to the twelfth-century Holy Roman Emperor Frederick I. Barbarossa drowned while leading his Third Crusade in the east, but legend had it he survived and only awaited the call of his country to return. The name, chosen by Hitler, was thought to evoke the idea of Operation Barbarossa as a modern-day crusade. Barton Whaley, *Codeword Barbarossa* (Cambridge, 1973), p. 18; Warlimont, *Im Hauptquartier*, Band I, p. 154, footnote 11.

[34] Klink, 'Die militärische Konzeption', pp. 219–220.

[35] Friedhelm Klein and Ingo Lachnit, 'Der "Operationsentwurf Ost" des Generalmajors Marcks vom 5. August 1940', *Wehrforschung* 4 (1972), 116; Erhard Moritz (ed.), *Fall Barbarossa. Dokumente zur Vorbereitung der faschistischen Wehrmacht auf die Aggression gegen die Sowjetunion (1940/41)* (Berlin, 1970), p. 122, Document 31 'Aus dem Operationsentwurf des Generalmajors Marcks für die Aggression gegen die Sowjetunion, 5. August 1940'; Leach, *German Strategy Against Russia*, Appendix I, p. 250.

The elimination of the bulk of the Red Army in the western districts would enable a rapid advance into the distant hinterland thereby safeguarding Germany from the perceived danger of strategic bombing raids. The ultimate objective was to reach a line extending from Rostov in the South, to Gorki east of Moscow and up as far as Arckangel'sk on the White Sea. Such an advance, it was believed, would lead to the collapse of organised Soviet resistance and the denial of resources necessary for the further conduct of major operations. The Soviet Asiatic regions were not believed to be greatly developed and were consequently judged incapable of sustaining large-scale Soviet resistance.[36]

The campaign was to embody four distinct phases of operation through which Marcks hoped to achieve final victory. The first involved pushing back the vanguard of the Red Army to their older fortified lines of defence calculated to be roughly 400 kilometres from the German starting positions. This first stage was thought to require approximately three weeks and included the optimistic observation that if the German armoured units were able to penetrate the Soviet lines fast enough, an effective withdrawal of large-scale formations might be prevented and the outcome of the campaign decided in this first phase.

Failing that, a second phase would be necessary requiring the breakthrough and encirclement of the Soviet defensive positions extending to a distance of between 100 and 200 kilometres. Marcks stressed the importance of achieving a clean penetration of these lines or, he warned, there existed the danger of scattered Soviet units carrying on resistance and needing to be eliminated one at a time. For this stage of the operations Marcks anticipated that two to four weeks would be required.

The third phase was predicated on the success of the second. Its objective called for the simultaneous advance on, and capture of, Moscow, Leningrad and the eastern Ukraine, a distance of 400 kilometres further east. Yet the timing of the operation depended on the condition of the army's motor-vehicles and the extent to which German gauge railway tracks could be laid for re-supply.[37] There was also a question surrounding the condition of Red Army forces. If they were assessed to be still capable of offering resistance a further pause might be necessary in order to overhaul engines and carry out maintenance. The length of time allocated to this phase was between three and six weeks.

The fourth and final stage was the occupation of the Soviet Union up to the Don, middle Volga and upper Dvina. This was not thought to

---

[36] Klein and Lachnit, 'Der "Operationsentwurf Ost"', pp. 116–118; Moritz (ed.), *Fall Barbarossa*, pp. 121–125.

[37] The Soviet railway gauge was wider than the European standard and would have to be changed to accommodate German trains. The problems this posed to the German logistical apparatus will be dealt with in a later section.

involve any serious opposition and was even termed a 'railway advance', requiring between three and four weeks.[38]

Marcks believed the Soviet strategic response would suffer from a fundamental dilemma. On the one hand, they might wish to adopt a similar strategy to that used in 1812 and fall back into the depths of their country, but being unable in a modern war to abandon lines of supply and sources of production, Marcks concluded they would be forced to hold a defensive position in the western part of the country. The line Plozk–Beresina – the Pripet marshes – Zbrutsch–Pruth was thought most likely for this purpose by Marcks, but he also suggested a retreat as far as the Dnepr, with delaying actions being fought to slow the German advance and cover the Soviet withdrawal. In Marcks's opinion, the only exception to this defensive response was a possible Soviet offensive into Romania to cut off German oil supplies. He also held the Soviet air force and navy (he specifically made reference to the submarine arm) in high regard, expecting them to adopt an offensive posture, contributing to the blockade of Germany and launching strong air attacks on the Romanian oil fields.

The Red Army's strength was estimated to be 151 infantry divisions, 32 cavalry divisions and 38 motorised brigades. Of these Marcks believed 55 infantry divisions, 9 cavalry divisions and 10 motorised brigades were tied down on the borders of Finland, Turkey and Japan. The conclusion Marcks reached therefore was that only 96 infantry divisions, 23 cavalry divisions and 28 motorised brigades were available for operations against Germany. It is also significant that from Marcks's information no appreciable increase in the total number of Soviet units was thought possible before the spring of 1941.

German strength for the invasion of the Soviet Union, by the spring of 1941 was aimed at being 147 divisions (110 infantry and mountain divisions, 24 Panzer divisions, 12 motorised divisions and one cavalry division), a total which did not include occupation forces in Scandinavia or western Europe. In the conduct of operations the emphasis was on speed and surprise to penetrate Soviet lines and envelop their major formations before they could reach lines of prepared or natural defences. Marcks also planned to hold back a large part of his total force in a central reserve to compensate for the expanding funnel shape of the theatre into which the German armies were to advance. The allocation of forces is shown in Table 1.[39]

---

[38] Klink, 'Die militärische Konzeption', pp. 224–225.
[39] Klein and Lachnit, 'Der "Operationsentwurf Ost"', pp. 116–119; Moritz (ed.), *Fall Barbarossa*, pp. 122 and 126.

Table 1.1 *Division of forces in Marcks' plan.*

	Panzer Divisions	Motorised Divisions	Infantry Divisions	Cavalry Divisions
Army Group South	5	6	24	0
Army Group North	15	2	50	1
Army Group Reserve	4	4	36	0

Source: Erhard Moritz (ed.), *Fall Barbarossa*, p. 126.

The campaign to defeat the Soviet Union was estimated by Marcks to require between nine and 17 weeks, but interestingly he refused to rule out an indefinite state of war continuing in the distant east on a much smaller scale.[40]

In the weeks following Marcks's submission of his operational study he continued to reflect on the possible outcome of a war with the Soviet Union. Putting his thoughts to paper, he named his new study 'Evaluation of Situation Red' (*Beurteilung der Lage Rot*) which envisaged an outcome considerably different from that which he described in his initial analysis. His preliminary focus was on the larger geopolitical ramifications of a war with the Soviet Union, but he also addressed new considerations in his strategic analysis for a campaign in the east. To begin with he foresaw with certainty an enemy coalition between Britain and the Soviet Union, that would be joined shortly by the United States who, Marcks noted, were already involved economically. This would see the Axis placed in the grip of a powerful blockade, while having to defend on all sides. With this, the Allies would have achieved their precondition for offensive operations from both the east and in the west with an Anglo-American landing in Europe. The Soviets would just have to ensure their survival against the initial German blow to take advantage of the collective power and subsequent counter-attacks that would eventually be unleashed against Germany. These, Marcks thought, could arise towards the end of 1941, but were more likely in 1942. Such a scenario, therefore, placed great emphasis on defeating the Soviet Union quickly in order to eliminate a dangerous enemy and ensure Germany's economic survival. Marcks still held to his earlier belief that, once the most prosperous areas in the Soviet Union were occupied, Soviet resistance would crumble and 'Situation Red' would not materialise, but in order to occupy the European districts of the Soviet Union further study was needed to assess the

[40] Klink, 'Die militärische Konzeption', p. 225.

prospects of success. Marcks now concluded that the Soviet command would probably react systematically to the German invasion by constructing numerous defensive lines, rather than relying wholly on a stand along the Dnepr–Dvina line (as his earlier study assumed). Such a conclusion calls into question his whole timetable of advance as presented in the earlier draft.[41]

Marcks received responses to his 'Evaluation of Situation Red' from Lieutenant-General von Tippelskirch, Senior Quartermaster IV, and Lieutenant-Colonel Eberhard Kinzel, head of the Department of Foreign Armies East (*Abteilung Fremde Heere Ost*). Neither foresaw events with such potential foreboding as Marcks did, and consequently their respective answers concentrated less on dealing with the dire implications of 'Situation Red' than assuring Marcks how and why this would not come about. Significantly, there is no evidence to suggest Marcks's follow-up study ever reached Halder and, therefore, its veiled warnings had no impact on future planning.

While enlightening in its own right, Marcks's 'Evaluation of Situation Red' also reveals a great deal about the intellectual process employed in planning the eastern campaign from the earliest stages. The unquestioning assumptions of Marcks's 'Operations Outline East' that, as will be seen with subsequent army studies, made no assessment of the *ability* of the Wehrmacht to achieve victory in a single campaign, proved symptomatic of the responses he received to the 'Evaluation of Situation Red'. Such blind supposition of success – among the very body charged with establishing the operational parameters and feasibility of the campaign – is strong evidence of the 'closed circle' of discussion and debate that was fostered within the army General Staff. It also hints ominously at the vast and unseen implications of an invasion of the Soviet Union.[42]

Halder himself bears a significant degree of responsibility for such stifling of independent thought, having dissuaded Marcks from launching the main thrust of his attack into the Soviet Union from the south, emphasising instead the primary importance of Moscow for the victory in the east.[43] This further led to his discounting Marcks's forecast of an indefinite state of war continuing in the east, on a small scale, even after reaching the final line of advance.[44]

The General Staff's exuberant self-confidence towards an eastern campaign, no doubt boosted by the spectacular collapse of France only

[41] Ibid., pp. 226–227.
[42] Barry Leach, 'Halder' in Correlli Barnett (ed.), *Hitler's Generals* (London, 1989), p. 114.
[43] Bryan Fugate, *Operation Barbarossa. Strategy and Tactics on the Eastern Front, 1941* (Novato, 1984), p. 67.
[44] Klink, 'Die militärische Konzeption', p. 265.

weeks before, also reflected long-held prejudices of a racial and cultural kind, which memories of World War I appeared only to confirm.[45] Olaf Groehler has suggested that Prussian–German disdain for Russian military power can be traced back two hundred years to Frederick II of Prussia. The more recent set of beliefs were influenced by a so-called 'Tannenberg myth', which contrasted a natural German military superiority with barbaric Russian hordes capable of atrocities.[46] In addition, Germany's academic experts on the east (*Ostforscher*) were profoundly influenced by entrenched stereotypes, adding a guise of merit to the ingrained anti-Slavic and anti-Bolshevik beliefs.[47] The future commander of Panzer Group 3 in Army Group Centre's invasion of the Soviet Union, Colonel-General Hermann Hoth, described the 'bestial cruelty' of the Russians during their 1914 invasion of East Prussia, while his counterpart, Colonel-General Heinz Guderian, later to command Panzer Group 2, observed after World War I while in Mitau on the Baltic: 'the Bolsheviks . . . cavort like beasts'.[48]

As the inferior 'foe-image' supported central precepts of the National Socialist agenda and paralleled prevailing views already widespread within the armed forces, one begins to identify not only the willing acceptance of Nazi ideals, but the generals' own role in initiating and propagating them. As a case in point, Halder pre-empted even Hitler in strategic planning for a war in the east, which, much more than providing a defence of Germany's eastern border, called for a first strike attack against the Soviet Union. Christian Hartmann in his biographical study of Halder suggested that the Chief of the General Staff's views may have been shaped or at least influenced by his personal experience on Germany's eastern front in World War I. Halder only spent a few months in the east in 1917, but this was shortly before the final Russian political and military collapse.[49]

In spite of such self-inflicted deception, the audacious liberties taken in the early planning of the eastern campaign cannot simply be passed over as the by-products of blatant ignorance or diehard prejudices. The General Staff demonstrated a wanton lack of professionalism, ignoring

---

[45] A good discussion can be found in Jürgen Förster, 'Zum Russlandbild der Militärs 1941–1945' in Hans-Erich Volkmann (ed.), *Das Russlandbild im Dritten Reich* (Köln, 1994), pp. 141–163.

[46] Groehler, 'Goals and Reason', pp. 51–55.

[47] Michael Burleigh, *Germany Turns Eastwards. A Study of 'Ostforschung' in the Third Reich* (Cambridge, 1988); Michael Burleigh, *The Third Reich. A New History* (London, 2001), p. 490.

[48] Ben Shepherd, *War in the Wild East. The German Army and Soviet Partisans* (Cambridge, 2004), pp. 11 and 13.

[49] Christian Hartmann, *Halder Generalstabschef Hitlers 1938–1942* (Munich, 1991), pp. 230–231.

unfavourable intelligence and failing to consider in depth such critical questions as logistics, climate and the imposing spaces which extended not only the depth of operations but, owing to the expanding funnel of the Soviet land mass, the breadth of the front line.

Among the intelligence reports supplied to Marcks for his operational study there is believed to have been a draft copy of the Military Geography Department's soon-to-be-published study of the Soviet Union. This forwarded the standard arguments in favour of the occupation of the Ukraine, Moscow and Leningrad, but went on to suggest that the oil wells of the Caucasus were probably too distant to be included in the German sphere of control. Nevertheless, the report concluded, even if such far-flung regions could be directly administered, it would still not ensure a cessation of Soviet resistance owing to the substantial development of Asian Russia. This region was no longer a backwater of sparsely populated indigenous peoples living as nomads or in isolated settlements. On the contrary, the report presented an impressive picture of modern development. Beyond the Urals and Caspian Sea lived 40 million people with developed agricultural and industrial resources, and the western section had an increasing network of railroad communications. The report concluded that the principal enemies in any attack were space and climate with the vastness of territory being of the utmost importance.[50]

The German military attaché in Moscow, Lieutenant-General Ernst Köstring, the foremost German military expert on the Soviet Union, fluent in Russian and stationed in the Soviet capital since 1935,[51] was undoubtedly another source of authoritative information for Marcks. Although he did contribute to the intelligence-gathering process, his voice, unlike head of the intelligence-gathering 'Department of Foreign Armies East' Lieutenant-Colonel Kinzel,[52] was distinctly critical. He believed there was nothing to gain in a proposed war that could not be secured politically, so long as the German Wehrmacht remained strong and undefeated.[53] Militarily, Köstring observed in August 1938, the Red Army, even amidst the worst of Stalin's 'Great Purge', retained a formidable fighting capacity.

The Red Army, as a result of the liquidation of large numbers of senior officers, who applied themselves to their task very ably for ten years, advancing theoretical and practical training, has now lost a degree of its operational level ability . . . The

---

[50] Klink, 'Die militärische Konzeption', p. 220. See also Ludolf Herbst, *Das national-sozialistische Deutschland 1933–1945. Die Entfesselung der Gewalt Rassismus und Krieg* (Frankfurt am Main, 1996), pp. 348–349.

[51] With a previous period of service in Moscow lasting from 1931 to 1933.

[52] Hillgruber, 'The German Military Leaders' View of Russia', pp. 172, 177–178.

[53] Klink, 'Die militärische Konzeption', pp. 195–196.

best commanders are now gone, yet there is *no* indication or proof that the strike power of the *majority* has sunken so low as to no longer constitute a significant factor in the event of a war.[54]

In early September 1940 Halder recorded a conversation with Köstring, in which the veteran Soviet observer noted improvements within the Red Army, but added that it would still require a further four years before it reached its former level. Köstring also warned of the demands the terrain and conditions would cause the Wehrmacht to which Halder noted: '[M]ovement in the various parts of Russia will present significant difficulties for motorised units.'[55] The following month Köstring again emphasised caution in an intelligence report prepared for Foreign Armies East. Here he stressed the defensive qualities of the Red Army which reinforced the appearance of a formidable and serious opponent, although Köstring pointed out that it was still incapable of conducting large-scale mobile warfare. Köstring again highlighted the difficulties of movement in the east. He drew attention to the absence of roads and extremes in weather, which he concluded were the Soviet Union's greatest allies, along with time and space.[56] Yet not all of Köstring's urgings can be taken at face value, especially his post-war claim, accepted by some historians,[57] but unsupported by available records, professing his prescience of the Soviet industrial developments east of the Urals and emphasising therefore the irrelevance of Moscow as a strategic key to victory.[58]

Operating under orders from Jodl, Lieutenant-Colonel Bernhard von Lossberg began work on his 'Operational Study East' ('*Operationsstudie Ost*') on, or shortly after, 29 July and completed it, much later than Marcks, on 15 September. This meant of course, that Lossberg had the benefit of learning from Marcks's 'Operations Outline East' which, in addition to the fact that Lossberg was supplied with much the same material from the General Staff, accounts in large measure for their many similarities. Yet the delay between the completion of the two studies allowed Lossberg to incorporate into his planning the rapidly changing political situation unfolding in Eastern Europe, namely in Romania.[59]

---

[54] Italics in the original. Ernst Köstring, *Der militärische Mittler zwischen dem Deutschen Reich und der Sowjetunion 1921–1941*, ed. Hermann Teske (Frankfurt am Main, 1965), p. 202.

[55] Franz Halder, KTB II, p. 86 (4 September 1940).

[56] Seaton, *The Russo-German War 1941–45*, p. 45.

[57] George Blau, *The Campaign against Russia (1940–1942)* (Washington, 1955), p. 12.

[58] For associated critical literature see Hillgruber, *Hitlers Strategie*, p. 228, footnote 93; Hillgruber 'The German Military Leaders' View of Russia', pp. 177–180; Seaton, *The Russo-German War 1941–45*, pp. 45–46, also p. 46, footnote 5.

[59] Klink, 'Die militärische Konzeption', p. 230.

The imposed resolution to the escalating conflict with Hungary in the arbitration of Vienna (August 30) secured for Germany the ability to use Romania as a staging ground for the coming war against the Soviet Union, and thus created a strategic option not open to Marcks.[60] In essence, however, the Lossberg plan bore many similarities to the Marcks plan so, in order to avoid repetition, I shall focus on those factors which diverged appreciably from Marcks.

Lossberg opened his study with the following outline of objectives:

> The aim of a campaign against Soviet Russia is to destroy the mass of the Soviet Army in western Russia, to prevent the withdrawal of battle-worthy elements into the depths of Russia, and then, having cut western Russia off from the seas, to advance to a line which will place the most important part of Russia in our hands and on which it will be easy to form a shield against Asiatic Russia.[61]

Unlike Marcks, who anticipated a significant Soviet withdrawal to established defensive positions, Lossberg did not think that this was the most likely Soviet reaction in the event of a German invasion. He foresaw three possible scenarios. First, a pre-emptive Soviet attack that he discounted on military grounds, while acknowledging that a degree of risk existed to Finland and Romania. Second, and most likely in Lossberg's estimation, the Red Army would mount a vigorous defence of its western border to protect Soviet air force bases and because its status as a military power made a retreat, according to Lossberg, doubtful. Third, the Soviets would revert to their 1812 strategy of withdrawal in depth meeting the Germans only where necessary as rearguard actions. This, however, was also viewed as improbable owing to the valuable economic importance of the Ukraine which Lossberg judged could not be abandoned. The Red Army was therefore expected to hold the line in the west of the country on or near the border where, Lossberg concluded, in the event of an early commitment of strong Soviet forces, the Red Army would be defeated and an orderly withdrawal of the bulk of the army would become unmanageable.[62]

Lossberg's plan called for three simultaneous thrusts into the Soviet Union, each directed by its own army group and deployed, to the north (two groups), and to the south (one group) of the Pripet marshes. Of the two northerly army groups, one would attack through the Baltic states, across the Dvina towards Leningrad, while the second and most

---

[60] Weinberg, *A World at Arms*, pp. 184–185.
[61] Moritz (ed.), *Fall Barbarossa*, p. 126. Document 32, 'Operationsstudie des Gruppenleiters Heer in der Abteilung Landesverteidigung im OKW für die Aggression gegen die Sowjetunion (Lossberg-Studie), 15. September 1940'. Leach, *German Strategy against Russia*, Appendix II, p. 255.
[62] Moritz (ed.), *Fall Barbarossa*, pp. 127–129.

powerful army group, equipped with the bulk of the motorised and panzer divisions, would proceed due east towards Moscow with encirclement battles centred on Minsk and Smolensk. For the southern army group Lossberg envisaged two main areas of concentration, one striking from southern Poland and the other from Romania along the northern shore of the Black Sea. The goal was to enact a double envelopment of Soviet forces between the Pripet marshes and the Black Sea, eradicating resistance before attempting a crossing of the Dnepr. The army group would then have to assess the degree of continued Soviet resistance in ascertaining the scope of further operations which, Lossberg suggested, would be the occupation of the eastern Ukraine and a linking-up with elements of the northern army groups.[63]

Significantly, Lossberg perceived more clearly than Marcks the tremendous field of operations in which the campaign would have to be fought[64] and consequently planned his initial strategic movements with some consideration for the difficulties of logistics and supply in mind. Accordingly, the large central army group heading in the general direction of Moscow was to wheel north at some point (possibly east of the Dvina) and cut off the Soviet forces along the Baltic in a huge pocket. Apart from the military triumph this would represent, Lossberg foresaw the strategic importance of allowing forward supplies, through the Baltic ports, for the continued advance on to Moscow.[65]

Lossberg also appreciated to a greater extent the scale of the logistical problems confronting operations in the depths of the interior where possible re-supply through Baltic or Black Sea ports would have little influence.[66] For this he sought to alleviate the strain on standard resources by emphasising the use of captured broad gauge Soviet trains that he hoped could be acquired in the newly-won regions. Lossberg sought to underline this point by stating that without the use of Soviet railways to facilitate the latter stages of the advance, 'a transport system based only on roads will be insufficient'.[67]

In spite of Lossberg's enhanced consideration for the operation of large armies over such great distances, his improvised remedies appear woefully inadequate when, in conclusion, he resolved to select the final

---

[63] Ibid., pp. 130–131.

[64] Köstring's warning to Halder in early September regarding the difficulty of motorised movement over such long distances represents one possible explanation for Lossberg's heightened concern, yet in drawing any firm conclusions one must not underestimate the level of inter-service rivalry, nor the degree of separation which existed between the OKH and OHW.

[65] Moritz (ed.), *Fall Barbarossa*, pp. 130, 133.

[66] Although the capture of Black Sea ports could never have been a decisive option given the proportional strength of Soviet naval forces.

[67] Moritz (ed.), *Fall Barbarossa*, p. 129.

line of advance, Arckangel'sk – Gorki – Volga (to Stalingrad) – Don (to the Black Sea).[68] For the single campaigning season envisaged, such an effort represents optimism that has turned to folly.

Lossberg also identified internal dissent as a reliable source of support for the German effort to conquer the Soviet Union. He believed that the Ukrainian population's traumatic experience under Stalin's enforced drive for collectivisation would lead to German forces being greeted as liberators from communist oppression. Encouragement of a popular pro-German or, at the very least, anti-Soviet sentiment could be fanned by German espionage and extend as far as direct participation in the conflict, with Lossberg foreseeing a use for the population in the sabotage of crucial Soviet railway links. Looking even further ahead, Lossberg anticipated a Ukrainian 'government' could be formed, sub-servient to German wishes and aiding in the occupation of the immense territory.[69]

This brief insight into Lossberg's political aspirations for the war in the east represents the infancy of the planning stages in which he took part. In the final Barbarossa plan there would be no attempt to win over any of the Soviet people. Hitler was later to make clear the ominous racial and ideological dimensions of the war to be conducted against the Soviet Union and his disregard for the Slavic peoples who inhabited the region. Yet Lossberg's assumption that non-Russian peoples would largely support Germany's invasion, with the exception of the Baltic states and other newly acquired territories, was not backed at the time by substantive evidence and subsequently, in part as a result of Germany's brutal 'new order' of administration, proved not to be a widespread phenomenon in the initial period of the war. Much less than providing aid to the German advance, the likelihood of active hostility among the non-Russian peoples of the western Soviet Union would require an ever increasing deployment of strength to ensure German control. Such dire repercussions represented a significant reversal of a key assumption upon which Lossberg's plan was built, undercutting another basis of support and placing further demands on the already overstretched resources.

Just as Marcks had done, Lossberg's plan never questioned the *ability* of the Wehrmacht to achieve victory and concerned itself only with the best method of achieving that end. His outline of the campaign included no timetable for operations and is remarkably vague concerning the crit-ical advance of the main army groups. There appears a wanton lack of consideration for the difficulties Soviet counter-measures could repre-sent and an astounding under-estimation of the size and robustness of

---

[68] Ibid., p. 132.   [69] Ibid., pp. 131–132.

the Soviet economy. Lossberg believed that, even if one considered the Ural industrial area,[70] it was 'impossible that Russia can remain capable of resistance after losing her western territories and contact with the seas'.[71] In any case, attainment of the final line of advance would, in Lossberg's estimation, allow bombing of the Ural region.[72]

The delusory assumptions seen throughout Lossberg's study are symptomatic of the army's inflated self-assurance and unquestioning conviction of their own superiority. It is not without significance that Lossberg notes at the beginning of his study the considerable difficulty he encountered in obtaining accurate intelligence about the enemy.[73] Geoffrey Megargee has pointed out the tendency among senior figures in the Army High Command, including intelligence officers, to fill the void of information concerning the Soviet Union with cultural preconceptions of diehard stereotypes.[74] Central tenets of such preconceptions, identified by Andreas Hillgruber and Michael Burleigh, date back as far as the Crimean War and cast the Russian empire in the opposing roles of an aggressive colossus looking to expand westward and an internally fractured state unable to resist an external attack.[75] Such contradictory, double-sided notions fit well with National Socialist precepts allowing, on the one hand, convincing arguments for the pursuit of *Lebensraum* in the east, while also providing a 'foe image' which depicted the Soviet state as a threatening godless enemy of 'cultured' Europe, providing the justification for a pre-emptive war.

The early planning stages of Barbarossa reveal a muddled process where information was produced to match major decisions already taken, rather than information being gathered on which to base major decisions.[76] Here the exuberant over-estimation of the Wehrmacht's own 'blitzkrieg' represents an obvious source of blame. Most German generals were trained and educated in forms of military manoeuvre and organisation unsuited to the requirements of rapid mechanised warfare or close air support. Thus, while they showed little surprise at the swift defeat of Poland as a small secondary power, they were largely united in

---

[70] Which should have been made clear to him by the above-mentioned study from the Military Geography Department.

[71] Moritz (ed.), *Fall Barbarossa*, p. 132.   [72] Ibid., pp. 132–133.

[73] Ibid., p. 127. For a good study highlighting the many problems of intelligence gathering within Foreign Armies East see David Thomas, 'Foreign Armies East and German Military Intelligence in Russia 1941–45', *Journal of Contemporary History* 22 (1987), 274–279.

[74] George P. Megargee, *Inside Hitler's High Command* (Lawrence, 2000), p. 110.

[75] Hillgruber, 'The German Military Leaders' View of Russia', pp. 169–170; Burleigh, *The Third Reich*, p. 490.

[76] Megargee, *Inside Hitler's High Command*, p. 116.

their opposition to the western campaign and were therefore astounded at both the totality of the victory and the apparent ease with which it was carried through.[77] Consequently, their faith in blitzkrieg reigned supreme with little attention devoted to the necessary mechanics of this process in logistics and technical support, nor was there any real appreciation for the fundamental differences that existed between an eastern and a western theatre of war.[78] Such intellectual bankruptcy speaks strongly of the decline in excellence within the German General Staff and the ease with which events were allowed to overshadow judgement and reason.

The disassociation from reality not only affected the planning stages of the campaign but pervaded most levels of the Wehrmacht's organisation including its armaments programme. The large expansion in the number of infantry and motorised divisions forced such large production demands that they could not be met without everything being subordinated to the army.[79] The result was a prioritisation of equipment with the army favouring its much needed Mark III and Mark IV tanks in addition to the new 50mm anti-tank gun. Yet, even in this narrow selection, estimates for production capacity differed greatly from actual output, indicating that an immense effort needed to be made in order to lift production. In July 1940 a monthly goal of 380 tanks was envisaged, but by August this figure was revised down to 200. In September 1940 a mere 121 tanks were produced in the course of the month. This, however, did not stop new targets being set on 14 September which aimed for the extraordinary figures of 2,000 Mark III and 800 Mark IV panzers to be delivered by 1 April 1941, requiring a monthly output of 466 tanks starting immediately.[80] The absurdity of such projections is another plain confirmation of the regime's tendency towards delusional practices, forming a chief impediment to realising the extent of its limitations and responding accordingly.

The expansion of the army also had profound implications on the already serious shortage of motorised transportation within its ranks. Even before the army's expansion to 180 divisions was decided, Hitler wanted to double the number of panzer divisions to 20 as well as raise

---

[77] Karl-Heinz Frieser, *Blitzkrieg-Legende. Der Westfeldzug 1940* (Munich, 1996), pp. 110–116. English translation *The Blitzkrieg Legend. The 1940 Campaign in the West* (Annapolis, 2005), pp. 94–99.

[78] Leach, *German Strategy Against Russia*, pp. 88–89.

[79] Document 56 'Aktennotiz über eine Besprechung des Chefs des OKW über die forcierte Steigerung der Rüstungsproduktion zur Vorbereitung des Überfalls auf die Sowjetunion, 17. August 1940' in Moritz (ed.), *Fall Barbarossa*, p. 201.

[80] Rolf-Dieter Müller, 'Von der Wirtschaftsallianz zum kolonialen Ausbeutungskrieg' in Militärgeschichtliches Forschungsamt (ed.), *Das Deutsche Reich und der Zweite Weltkrieg*, pp. 171–173.

the number of motorised divisions to 10.[81] Production capacity simply
did not exist to achieve this fanciful goal in any realistic time frame
so the divisions were created by simply reducing the strengths of those
already in existence – a solution which immediately solved the problem
on paper, but offered no practical benefit to the army's strength.[82] In
managing this process Colonel-General Fritz Fromm, Chief of the Land-
Force Armaments and Commander-in-Chief of the Replacement Army,
informed Halder that the activation of new panzer divisions required so
many vehicles that those allotted to the infantry divisions would have
to be reduced further.[83] By the end of September 1940 Halder was
complaining in his diary that there was not enough motorised transport
to meet even the most urgent needs of the army and as a result, further
cuts would have to be made to the mobility of divisions in the 13th and
14th waves.[84]

Further considerations of even more fundamental importance to the
conduct of operations in the east arose in November 1940 when Halder
met with the Army Quartermaster-General, Major-General Eduard
Wagner. Concerned primarily with the issues of supply and logistics,
Wagner came to report his findings based on the premise of keeping some
two million men, 300,000 horses and 500,000 motor-vehicles supplied.[85]
Such an undertaking, he frankly assessed, would allow for an advance
of between 700 and 800 kilometres given projected fuel consumption.
In addition, foodstuffs and ammunition supply would suffice for only
the first 20 days.[86] Such a troubling appraisal should have evoked considerable concern with plans afoot to march far deeper into the Soviet
interior. At the very least a delay in operations of many weeks would
be required before the army groups could gather their strength to reach
Leningrad, Moscow and the eastern Ukraine. This was plainly not in
line with the rapid victories predicted by the operational studies, to
say nothing of reaching the distant Caucasus oil fields or the Volga.
Most probably Halder tempered such a foreboding forecast with the
optimistic anticipation of the Red Army's swift defeat, allowing for an

[81] Seaton, *The German Army 1933–45*, p. 145.
[82] Bernhard R. Kroener, 'Die Winter 1941/42. Die Verteilung des Mangels oder Schritte zu
      einer rationelleren Personalbewirtschaftung' in Militärgeschichtliches Forschungsamt
      (ed.), *Das Deutsche Reich und der Zweite Weltkrieg*, Band V/1: *Organisation und Mobil-
      isierung des deutschen Machtbereichs*. Erster Halbband: *Kriegsverwaltung, Wirtschaft und
      Personelle Ressourcen 1939–1941* (Stuttgart, 1988), pp. 871–872.
[83] Franz Halder, KTB II, p. 4 (1 August 1940).   [84] Ibid., pp. 117–118.
[85] The actual figures of German strength on 20 June 1941 proved much higher; three mil-
      lion men, 625,000 horses and 600,000 motor-vehicles. Klink, 'Die militärische Konzep-
      tion', p. 270.
[86] Franz Halder, KTB II, p. 176 (12 November 1940).

unopposed 'railway advance' further east. In any case it remains clear that the campaign was driven in its conception by grand strategic and macro-economic considerations[87] above more pertinent questions such as available strength, logistical possibilities and a sober respect for the ever present element in war which Clausewitz dubbed 'friction'.[88]

Crisis postponed – from war games to Directive No. 21

Although there is some debate among historians regarding the finality of Hitler's decision for an attack in the east between July and December 1940, it is enough to reassert the importance of his ideologically-driven programme for eastern expansion through which war and the conquest of *Lebensraum* remained inevitable components. Yet, throughout 1940 at least, Hitler chose to emphasise the more pragmatic rationale for his invasion plans.[89] Speaking at the beginning of December, Hitler told Field Marshal Fedor von Bock, the future commander of Army Group Centre in the invasion of the Soviet Union, that 'the eastern question is becoming acute'. He pointed to the supposed development of links between the Soviets and Americans that he said suggested a corresponding link existed with England. Awaiting such an outcome, Hitler insisted, was dangerous and thus he concluded, 'if the Russians were eliminated, England would have no hope left of defeating us on the continent'.[90]

In spite of Hitler's confused strategic manoeuvring, resulting from his lack of a clear direction as well as the unexpected developments in North Africa and Greece resulting from Mussolini's ill-fated invasions, there was remarkably little detraction from the overall planning for Operation Barbarossa. Even before his arrival, the state visit of Soviet foreign minister Vyacheslav Molotov was seen as irrelevant to the question of an approaching conflict. On the same day Molotov arrived in Berlin

[87] Müller, 'Von der Wirtschaftsallianz', pp. 116–117.
[88] Clausewitz defined 'friction' as 'Countless minor incidents – the kind you can never really foresee – combine to lower the general level of performance, so that one always falls far short of the intended goal.' Howard and Paret (eds.), Carl von Clausewitz, *On War*, p. 138.
[89] Kershaw, *Hitler 1936–1945*, p. 343.
[90] 'Tagebuchnotizen Osten – Vorbereitungszeit, 20.9.1940 bis 21.6.1941' BA-MA N-22/7. Fol. 2 (3 December 1940). Fedor von Bock, *Generalfeldmarschall Fedor von Bock. The War Diary 1939–1945*, Klaus Gerbet (ed.) (Atglen, 1996), p. 194 (3 December 1940). The editorial notes included in this otherwise first-rate English volume to its disadvantage, supporting the theory of Barbarossa as a preventive war. Hereafter references for Bock's diary will be cited first with the German archival reference and second with the published English translation: Fedor von Bock, KTB 'Vorbereitungszeit', Fol. 2. *War Diary*, p. 194 (3 December 1940).

(12 November), Hitler issued War Directive No. 18 which under the title 'Russia' stated:

Political discussions for the purpose of clarifying Russia's attitude in the immediate future have already begun. Regardless of the outcome of these conversations, all preparations for the East for which verbal orders have already been given will be continued.

Further directives will follow on this subject as soon as the basic operational plan of the Army has been submitted to me and approved.[91]

The Marcks and Lossberg plans formed the basis for the final draft of planning which was prepared under the supervision of Lieutenant-General Friedrich Paulus, the recently appointed Senior Quartermaster I. The two studies set out some of the basic underpinnings of the German plan. They reveal a great deal about the army's expectations for success and also hint at the many divergent operational objectives that, as we will see, become a major subject of contention between the army and Hitler.

The studies by Marcks and Lossberg shared a common acceptance that victory rested on the rapid penetration and encirclement of major Soviet forces positioned west of the Dnepr–Dvina Rivers. Further operations would be conducted in secondary phases, after periods of recuperation and based on indeterminate factors such as Red Army strength, position of neighbouring army groups and distance to major population centres. As the advance continued, resistance was calculated to weaken accordingly, reducing the strain on operating deep in the interior. Economic collapse was also seen as an unavoidable consequence of the Wehrmacht's occupation of Western Russia as the loss of essential raw materials, farming lands and industrial centres would cripple the Soviet Union. Finally, both plans settled on grossly unrealistic final lines of advance that, perhaps more than anything else, highlight the grandiose objectives set for the short campaigning season.

To test the effectiveness of the strategic thinking thus far formulated, General Paulus, under instruction from Halder, conducted detailed map exercises at the beginning of December, which brought together the departmental heads of the Army General Staff and utilised the 'Consolidated Files, Russia' provided by the Foreign Armies East intelligence branch.[92] In the exercise it was estimated that Germany could field 154

---

[91] Trevor-Roper (ed.), *Hitler's War Directives*, p. 86; Domarus, *Hitler*, Volume III, pp. 2121–2122, 2125.
[92] Walter Görlitz, *Paulus and Stalingrad* (London, 1963), pp. 99–100. This evidence is based on an account written by Paulus in August 1946. Although his account provides a unique insight into the undisclosed problems of the planning process, Paulus's contentions still need to be viewed critically.

divisions, including 18 panzer and 18 motorised infantry divisions as well as ten Romanian divisions. These would face 125 Soviet divisions with 50 tank and motorised brigades. Interestingly, after listing the relative army strengths and making no mention of German reinforcements, Paulus factored in a Soviet 'subsequent build-up' which he said would arise from Red Army units being transferred from other regions and newly raised formations. He calculated this would add another 30–40 divisions in the first three months of the war and within six months the figure would rise to 100 divisions.[93] In his appreciation of the unparalleled ability of the Soviet state to generate new forces, Paulus showed considerably more foresight than his contemporaries in the General Staff. Although still an under-estimation of real Soviet potential, it is significant that previous studies made no mention of, and therefore no allowance for, the critical element Soviet force generation could – and indeed did – play in the German failure in 1941.[94] Marcks and Lossberg concluded, as Paulus ultimately did, that the opening weeks would largely decide the campaign, although Paulus added, 'calculations of enemy strength . . . were of primary importance when it came to determining the objectives and the timetable of the German offensive'.[95]

Paulus recorded the results of his war game in two stages, the first being eight days after the start of operations and the second after twenty days. In the first period of analysis the most revealing observation concerns the movements of Army Group Centre which, Paulus stated, faced the problem of how to achieve its assigned task: '[B]old thrusts by columns of armoured formations will be made deep into enemy territory and the withdrawal of major enemy forces into the depths of Russia will be prevented.'[96] The two panzer groups designated to the army group soon found themselves overstretched, meeting strong opposition on both inner and outer flanks as they simultaneously tried to prevent the withdrawal of retreating armies while also meeting concentrated counter-attacks from forces not previously engaged. Third Panzer Army was attacked so heavily that it was compelled to stop and form a front, while also recalling its advanced units which were pushing further eastward. The conclusion reached by the Blue (German) commander was that the Red (Soviet) army aimed to counter-attack and destroy the leading Blue armies. The significance of this is clear. The forward elements of the Blue forces

[93] Ibid., p. 108.
[94] Glantz and House, *When Titans Clashed*, pp. 67–69. Paulus also stated that the lack of trained officers and equipment available to the freshly raised divisions would reduce their overall effectiveness. While this was certainly true, it does not effectively mitigate their enormous impact on the battlefield of 1941.
[95] Görlitz, *Paulus and Stalingrad*, p. 104.   [96] Ibid., p. 113.

represented the cutting edge of the operational knife upon which German 'blitzkrieg' theory depended. Blunt the knife and the opportunity for rapid penetration of the enemy front is lost, eliminating the mobility of the army and leaving the marching infantry with a predicament not unlike that faced by Napoleon's slow-moving *Grande Armée*.

In response, Paulus thought infantry corps should be attached to the panzer groups in order to assist in the initial attack and thereby free the motorised infantry to advance as quickly as possible. The infantry would then march in the wake of the column providing support where possible. Although such an initiative represented an improvement, and could aid the advance in the opening days of the campaign, it was nevertheless a temporary solution which failed to resolve the problem properly, as the inevitable gap quickly developed between man and machine.

The second period of assessment Paulus undertook focuses on events after twenty days of action which he described as 'severe fighting'. The line reached and the timetable of the advance, he stated, were proceeding in accordance with those planned. Yet Paulus's positive appraisal did not disguise the fact that major objectives of the campaign were still far from being fulfilled. In his assessment of the Soviet forces Paulus noted that as a result of its 'stubborn resistance'[97] the Red Army had suffered heavy casualties but had managed its withdrawal to the line Dnepr–Upper Dvina, establishing there a new continuous front.[98] This was a fundamental failing of the Blue forces. The outline for the campaign included among the army's tasks the instruction: 'Having made the initial break-through, to strive with every possible means to isolate and destroy in detail Russian formations before the enemy [is] able to form a new, corporate front.'[99] Other factors influencing the overall outlook included observation of road and railway traffic indicating the transfer of new forces from the Caucasus and the Far East that, in addition to large-scale army replacements and the formation of new units, was estimated to stiffen Soviet resistance considerably. Furthermore, the Blue Commanders doubted that the Soviets would remain on their current defensive line, electing instead to trade space for time and fight only delaying actions in a general withdrawal to Moscow.

On the German side, the condition of the Blue army necessitated a rest period of approximately three weeks for concentration and reorganisation of forces, reconditioning the panzer and motorised units and, most importantly, the establishment of frontal supply bases. For Paulus,

---

[97] Ibid., pp. 114–116.
[98] Although Paulus added that the line was weakly held in certain positions.
[99] Görlitz, *Paulus and Stalingrad*, p. 102.

the need to resume the advance as quickly as possible was clear, yet the tasks allotted to each of the three army groups, along with their current distribution of forces, soon gave rise to a new debate.

Army Group South's long front dispersed its armies over a wide area, hampering its efforts to produce a concentrated force capable of isolating Kiev. The group commander therefore asked for the temporary use of armoured units from Army Group Centre as well as the release of some reinforcements from the Army General Reserve. The same plea was made by the commander of Army Group North who needed to advance his right wing in order to provide essential flank support for the renewed drive of Army Group Centre. The commander of Army Group Centre recognised the importance of both operations but argued that the seizure of Moscow, as the principal objective, required the central panzer groups to be at their maximum possible strength and, as a result, Army Groups North and South would have to make do with their existing forces.[100] The discussion highlights a fundamental dilemma facing German commanders in the east – how to balance the ratio of force to space. As the advance continued, the front expanded substantially in depth and width resulting in an ever increasing dispersal of manpower that was exacerbated by casualties and logistical constraints. This ultimately forced a general weakening of the front which soon stalled the simultaneous advance of the army groups and forced choices to be made regarding priorities. In Paulus's war game the choice was clear; Moscow would be the objective towards which all army groups would work.

The lesson for Paulus seemed obvious; the Wehrmacht did not enjoy a substantial quantitative superiority and could not raise reinforcements on anything like the scale of the Soviet Union.[101] Given the geographic dimensions of the theatre, the size of the German deployment and the critical time factor, the effectiveness of the Wehrmacht's mobile units was of paramount importance in determining the outcome of German fortunes in the east.

[100] Ibid., pp. 116–118.
[101] Indeed German intelligence reports until 22 June 1941 repeatedly increased their estimates of Soviet strengths; see Glantz, *Stumbling Colossus*, Appendix C, p. 290; Leach, *German Strategy Against Russia*, Appendix IV, p. 270. The actual correlation between Soviet and German forces facing each other on the eve of war equalled a difference of 370,000 men in favour of the Germans. This must be set against the fact that the Red Army contained an overall total of 5.5 million men with many employed outside its western military districts and a mobilisation base of some 14 million men. By contrast the German invasion forces, numbering just over 3 million men, did not have recourse to substantial manpower reserves. Figures for the German army in the east on 20 June 1941 are taken from Klink, 'Die militärische Konzeption', p. 270. For the Soviet figures, see Glantz and House, *When Titans Clashed*, pp. 68 and 301.

Orders for the second phase of the campaign placed the highest priority on the capture of Moscow with operations to begin not later than forty days into the war. Leningrad in the north and the Donets Basin in the south were clearly designated as secondary objectives, with Army Groups North and South providing flank support for the main thrust.[102] Here the account provided by Paulus ends, but he does offer an insightful discussion of the overall exercise. This opens with the frank admission that the 'general conclusion' was that 'the German forces were barely sufficient for the purpose'.[103] This worrying assessment implies grave consequences given that Paulus's mandate limited the exercise purely to questions of military strategy[104] and that his war game offered no analysis of the logistical difficulties or the distinctively harsh conditions of climate and poor infrastructure prevalent in the east. Paulus then commented on the woefully inadequate size of the Army General Reserve which contained just 11 divisions for a front stretching 1,200 miles with poor means of lateral transportation. He declared that it was generally accepted that the whole reserve would have to be committed as early as the second phase and that, as a result, the armies would have to be self-sufficient, creating reserves from within their own front-line units.[105]

The line of final advance 'Volga to Archangel' was dismissed by Paulus as 'far beyond anything that the German forces available could hope to achieve'. He then added, 'but it is a typical example of the megalomaniac extravagance of National Socialist political thinking'.[106] If that is indeed the case, such a statement speaks for itself about the degree of National Socialist thinking within the armed forces, given that both Marcks and Lossberg, with the subsequent approval of higher command, suggested this line as their final objective.

It seems clear that the outcome of the war game demanded, at the very least, a reassessment of the plans for war against the Soviet Union. The mock battles had proved a far more sobering encounter for the Wehrmacht than was suggested by the conquering tone of the earlier operational studies. The many troubling questions and subjects of concern presented by the war game raise an essential question: in what new direction would Paulus take the planning of Barbarossa given the unpromising events he himself had witnessed? In order to answer this, one must consider the character of the man who throughout his career (and especially in his role as commander of the 6th Army at Stalingrad, 1942–43)

---

[102] Görlitz, *Paulus and Stalingrad*, pp. 118–120.   [103] Ibid., p. 106.
[104] Ibid., p. 100.   [105] Ibid., p. 106.
[106] Ibid. This statement should also be seen in context of the fact that Paulus was writing in 1946 while still in Soviet custody. He was no doubt also bitter about the great debacle he was led into at Stalingrad.

displayed a methodical devotion to duty and distinguished himself as an unquestioning supporter of Nazism, unaccustomed to conflict with his superiors or bold independent action.[107] General Erwin Jaenecke, a personal friend of Paulus and subordinate in the 6th Army, wrote: 'In spite of his intelligence, Colonel-General Paulus was far too pliable to cope with Hitler. I am convinced that this is the real and deeper cause of his failure.'[108] Given this assessment it is perhaps not surprising that Paulus took no action to persuade Halder or any others in the High Command of the results emerging from the war game. Indeed nothing at all was done to reflect what Paulus claims to have learned. Paulus had stated that the exercise's primary objective was to gather information and suggestions for the 'first strategic concentration [of troops] and [their] approach march'.[109] Seen in this light, Paulus may have deluded himself into thinking that such a far-ranging critique of the whole operation was uncalled for. Instead, Paulus preferred to trust in the general air of confidence fostered within the High Command rather than risk rocking the boat with pessimistic objections. This shameful inaction further demonstrates the depths to which senior officers within the General Staff had sunk, and the associated loss of professionalism. It also suggests that Paulus was a convert to the megalomaniac extravagances of National Socialist political thinking that he so readily attributed to others.

On 5 December 1940 Hitler met again with Halder and Brauchitsch, as well as the chiefs of the OKW, to hear the army's report on operational intentions. In typical fashion, before his generals could present their proposals Hitler used the high-level gathering as cause for another long-winded overview of the general military situation. This covered at length the many operational possibilities being considered in the Balkans and Mediterranean, but, as Halder noted, Hitler saw the definitive decision concerning German hegemony in Europe as arising from the struggle against Russia.[110] According to Hitler, in comparison to the German Wehrmacht, the Red Army was weaker in armaments, personnel and especially leadership. He predicted that, once hit, the Soviet state would suffer a collapse greater than France had earlier that year. Yet he also warned against simply pushing the Soviet forces back without breaking through the front and encircling the bulk of the Red Army. He cited the

---

[107] For a helpful overview, see Martin Middlebrook, 'Paulus' in Barnett (ed.), *Hitler's Generals*, pp. 361–372; Samuel Mitcham and Gene Mueller, *Hitler's Commanders. Officers of the Wehrmacht, the Luftwaffe, the Kriegsmarine, and the Waffen-SS* (Lanham, 2000), pp. 73–99.

[108] Samuel Mitcham, *Hitler's Field Marshals and Their Battles* (Chatham, 1988), p. 235.

[109] Görlitz, *Paulus and Stalingrad*, p. 105.

[110] Franz Halder, KTB II, p. 212 (5 December 1940).

Volga as the point where the campaign could conclude with air raids able to destroy the remaining armament industry in the distant east.[111]

When Halder was finally able to take the floor he kept his focus wholly concentrated on the planned operation against the Soviet Union, beginning his address with a summary of the geographical conditions to be encountered there. Halder reported that the most important armament centres lay in the Ukraine, Moscow and Leningrad with the Soviet Union's agricultural requirements also dependent upon the Ukraine. The Pripet marshes formed a natural barrier which divided the operational area into northern and southern zones, with the most favourable road and rail networks laying in the northern sector along the Warsaw–Moscow road. He described the transportation network in the southern zone as bad and emphasised the advantage of the northern sector for large-scale movement operations. Halder stated that the greater portion of the Soviet Army was deployed in the northern sector[112] in close formations set behind the former Soviet–Polish border with extensive field fortifications and supply routes. He postulated that the Dnepr–Dvina line represented the Soviets' easternmost point of defences given their need to protect vital industrial assets. Accordingly the army, with special emphasis on the panzer forces, would have to ensure that, once the initial breakthrough had been achieved, there was no re-establishment of resistance before the great rivers could be secured.[113]

Of critical importance in the evolution of the strategic planning was Halder's assertion that an especially powerful thrust should be made from the area around Warsaw to the Soviet capital, Moscow. This, he stated, would proceed through Minsk and Smolensk in tandem with advances by the northern and southern army groups on Leningrad and Kiev respectively. In outlining his objectives Halder allowed no room for ambiguity regarding the direction of Army Group Centre nor the primary importance he attached to Moscow. Like Hitler before him, he pointed to the Volga and to the area around Archangel as the overall area to be

---

[111] KTB OKW, Volume I, p. 205 (5 December 1940). Nicolaus von Below, *Als Hitlers Adjutant 1937–45* (Mainz, 1999), p. 253.

[112] This proved to be incorrect, highlighting a considerable failure of German intelligence. See John Erickson, *The Soviet High Command 1918–1941. A Military-Political History 1918–1941* (London, 1962), pp. 556–557; Glantz, *Stumbling Colossus*, pp. 92–95.

[113] KTB OKW, Volume I, p. 208 (5 December 1940). Hans-Adolf Jacobsen (ed.), *Kriegstagebuch des Oberkommandos der Wehrmacht (Wehrmachtführungsstab)*, Band I/2: *1. August 1940–31. Dezember 1941* (Munich, 1982), pp. 981–982, Document 41 (5 December 1940). Hereafter cited as: KTB OKW, Volume II. Moritz (ed.), *Fall Barbarossa*, p. 138, Document 34 'Aus der Niederschrift über die Vorträge des Oberbefehlshabers und des Generalstabschefs des Heeres zur Operationsplanung gegen die Sowjetunion und die Stellungnahme Hitlers, 5. Dezember 1940'; Helmuth Greiner, *Die Oberste Wehrmachtführung 1939–1943* (Wiesbaden, 1951), p. 327.

occupied in the campaign. The army, he suggested, would invade with 105 infantry and 32 panzer and motorised divisions.[114]

With the conclusion of Halder's address Hitler rose again to voice his general agreement with the proposals thus far presented by the army, but he also sought to redirect his audience's attention to the main points as he saw them. With careful attention to the language Hitler used it is not without significance that he began by pointing out that the most 'important objective' (*wichtigstes Ziel*) lay in not allowing the Red Army an orderly withdrawal. He went on to state that the blows dealt to the Red Army had to be of sufficient strength to prevent any prospect of recovery. This, he then explained, required the use of panzer forces to encircle the strongest enemy elements and destroy them. Army Group North was to seek encirclements in the Baltic states, Army Group South in combination with Romanian forces would do the same in the Ukraine, while Army Group Centre, far from then being assigned Moscow as its absolute priority, was to be prepared to send 'considerable forces' (*erhebliche Teile*) northward to assist in the drive on Leningrad. Hitler then declared that the question of whether Army Groups North and South, following the destruction of enemy forces opposing their fronts, should proceed to Moscow or into the region east of the capital could not yet be decided. Finally, Hitler acknowledged that the figure of 130–140 divisions for the whole operation was adequate.[115] Halder spoke one last time before the conclusion of the meeting, but rather than confronting Hitler over the apparent difference of opinion concerning the importance of Moscow, he commented only on the secondary issues of moving troops to their assembly areas and the number of divisions to remain garrisoning the occupied countries.[116]

Is it quite clear that the two men foresaw different objectives in the secondary stage of the campaign. For Halder the drive on Moscow was to be the decisive event of the war, whereas Hitler showed only marginal

---

[114] KTB OKW, Volume I, pp. 208–209 (5 December 1940); KTB OKW, Volume II, p. 982, Document 41 (5 December 1940); Moritz (ed.), *Fall Barbarossa*, p. 138; Greiner, *Die Oberste Wehrmachtführung*, pp. 327–328.

[115] KTB OKW, Volume I, p. 209 (5 December 1940); Moritz (ed.), *Fall Barbarossa*, pp. 138–139; Greiner, *Die Oberste Wehrmachtführung*, p. 328. Hitler's acceptance of force strengths supplied by the army for completion of the operation belies the post-war myth supported by many former generals, including Halder, that Hitler's gross underestimation of the Soviet Union was simply a result of his ideologically-inspired megalomania. Indeed through supplying such flawed factual information to their head of state the generals are implicated with at least as much guilt for the extent of the blunder. For further useful discussion see Leach, *German Strategy Against Russia*, pp. 119–120.

[116] KTB OKW, Volume I, p. 209 (5 December 1940); Moritz (ed.), *Fall Barbarossa*, p. 139; Greiner, *Die Oberste Wehrmachtführung*, p. 329.

interest and concerned himself more with the destruction of Soviet forces. It is typical of their relationship, and a reflection of the disjointed method of communication within the High Command itself, that Halder chose not to pursue his argument even though we know from subsequent events that he fiercely opposed any compromise on Moscow as the primary objective. Paulus confirmed that from the very beginning there existed 'a sharp divergence of opinion between Supreme Headquarters (Hitler) and the Army General Staff regarding both the manner in which the operations should be conducted and the intermediate objectives that should be set'.[117] Yet the blame in this case must lie more with Halder as Hitler undoubtedly assumed his preference predominated, while Halder either surreptitiously opted to try and force Hitler's hand at the opportune moment (i.e. during the campaign), or he simply felt that the initial blow would remove any serious threat from the Red Army, and the secondary phase of operations would be a straightforward drive eastward.[118] In any case the result postponed the conflict and ensured that this fundamental difference of opinion was to become a crisis in July/August 1941.

The degree of complacency demonstrated by a man of Halder's prominence and responsibility in such a fundamental aspect of the coming invasion highlights another facet of the conceited over-confidence shown by the Chief of the General Staff towards the most important military undertaking of the Third Reich. It also attests to his inflated perception of his own ability, confident that his plan held greater merit in spite of his poor, unimaginative and ultimately rejected proposal for the attack in the west (Plan Yellow).[119] Yet Halder was not alone in his supercilious estimations; Brauchitsch himself later described the coming campaign in the following terms: 'Massive frontier battles to be expected; duration up to four weeks. But in further development only minor resistance is then still to be reckoned with.'[120]

Halder's diary for 5 December 1940 took a confident tone towards the forthcoming campaign and stated simply that 'The Russian is inferior', but beyond such bias, indistinguishable from the standard National Socialist racial prejudice, he also commented on the state of Soviet equipment. He portrayed the Soviet air force as antiquated even in comparison with the older German models; their artillery batteries were noted to

[117] Görlitz, *Paulus and Stalingrad*, p. 106.
[118] The later argument is favoured by Christian Hartmann in his biography of Halder. Hartmann, *Halder Generalstabschef Hitlers 1938–1942*, p. 234.
[119] Len Deighton, *Blitzkrieg. From the Rise of Hitler to the Fall of Dunkirk* (London, 1980), pp. 243–254.
[120] Cecil, *Hitler's Decision to Invade Russia 1941*, p. 129; Leach, *German Strategy Against Russia*, p. 114; see also footnote 1.

include a few 'modern' designs but he dismissed the majority as 'rebuilt old material'. Most importantly Halder extolled the 'clear superiority' of the Mark III German panzer with its 5cm gun and estimated production of 1,500 units by the spring of 1941. Soviet tanks, Halder concluded, were largely distinctive for their poor armour.[121]

On 28 November 1940, OKH ordered the Chiefs of Staff of Army Groups A, B and C to carry out independent operational studies on the proposed invasion of the Soviet Union. Two of these by Generals Brennecke (Army Group C) and von Salmuth (Army Group B) were not dissimilar from the operational approach developed and tested by Paulus.[122] Yet the third study by the Chief of Staff for Army Group A, General Georg von Sodenstern, completed 7 December 1940, presented a novel approach which called for an envelopment by two army groups deployed to the north and south of the Pripet marshes. This would be aided by a smaller central army group advancing into the marshes and driving the assumed significant enemy forces into the developing German pincers. Upon completion of this first phase the united northern and southern army groups would then drive directly on Moscow with their flanks covered by subsidiary thrusts towards Pskov, Toropez, Kursk and Kharkov. Sodenstern's narrow front of advance (which neglected contact with either the Baltic or Black Seas) proceeded from a recognition of the vastness of the territory and the resulting dissipation of strength along the line. Having seized the vital industrial heart of the country it was then hoped that such a bargaining chip would help secure grounds for a favourable peace settlement.[123] Sodenstern's study seems radical in comparison with the other proposals presented and there is some unqualified evidence to suggest that he had doubts about the success of the campaign. This may account for the unorthodox operational approach he adopted, yet the degree of influence, if any at all, Sodenstern's study had on future planning within the OKH remains unclear.[124]

On 13 and 14 December Halder hosted a conference with the Chiefs of Staff of the Army Groups and Armies. Its purpose, as Halder put it, was to outline the military–political situation 'based on our version of a discussion with the Führer'.[125] The analysis encompassed the broader

[121] Franz Halder, KTB II, pp. 213–214 (5 December 1940).

[122] Wilhelm-Ernst Paulus, *Die Entwicklung der Planung des Russland Feldzuges 1940/41* (Bonn, 1957), pp. 179–180; Leach, *German Strategy Against Russia*, pp. 106–107.

[123] Alfred Philippi, 'Das Pripjetproblem: Eine Studie über die operative Bedeutung des Pripjetgebietes für den Feldzug des Jahres 1941' in *Wehrwissenschaftliche Rundschau*, Beiheft.2 (Darmstadt, 1956), pp. 13–15, 73–75. Also see Klink, 'Die militärische Konzeption', p. 233, footnote 117; Leach, *German Strategy Against Russia*, p. 107.

[124] Klink, 'Die militärische Konzeption', p. 233, footnote 117.

[125] Franz Halder, KTB II, p. 224 (13 December 1940).

European situation and was not restricted to the coming invasion of the Soviet Union, but Halder pointed out that the struggle for hegemony in Europe would be resolved only through 'war against Russia'.[126] The result for the army, he continued, was a single-front war[127] requiring between 130 and 140 divisions. The air force, however, would have to undertake a two-front war, while the navy cleared the Baltic. With no irony intended, Halder finished his summary: '*We do not seek conflict with Russia, but must* be prepared for this eventuality by spring 1941.'[128] Not surprisingly, Halder's selective account of his discussion with Hitler included no mention of the rift over Moscow nor, as will be seen, his determination to circumvent Hitler's authority on the matter.

Following the conference on 5 December 1940 and Hitler's broad satisfaction with the proposals presented by the army, preparations began in earnest on a new draft war directive to be compiled by the Operations Section of OKW. Walter Warlimont, Jodl's deputy in charge of OKW planning, later testified that the first drafts were completed with the firm approval of the Operations Section of the OKH, meaning that the concentration of effort was directed towards the unambiguous goal of Moscow.[129] As one may expect, Halder maintained a watchful eye on developments hoping to secure a written endorsement of his own plan in the form of one of Hitler's all-important war directives.

Lieutenant-Colonel von Lossberg composed the document and the first draft was presented to Jodl for his revision on 12 December 1940. Jodl expanded on the detail to include some matters of secondary importance, but in substance accepted the basic conclusions of the draft. The text was returned to Lossberg on 14 December for modification and resubmitted to Jodl on 16 December for final approval. On 17 December Jodl took the text to Hitler who, not surprisingly, ordered 'a considerable alteration'.[130] The new text, in line with Hitler's pronouncements of December 5, now read:

In the theatre of operations, which is divided by the Pripet Marshes into a Southern and a Northern sector, the main weight of the attack will be delivered in the *Northern* sector. Two Army Groups will be employed here.

---

[126] Ibid., p. 227.
[127] It is interesting that Hitler or Halder should characterise the army's role in the invasion as a one-front war given that Paulus's war game felt it necessary to assign no less than 56 German divisions to western defence, North Africa or occupation duties, while the success of the proposed Operation Marita (invasion of the Balkans) would no doubt tie down more units.
[128] Italics in the original. Franz Halder, KTB II, p. 228 (13 December 1940).
[129] Warlimont, *Im Hauptquartier*, Band I, p. 154.
[130] Ibid., p. 153. Klink, 'Die militärische Konzeption', pp. 238–239.

The more southerly of these two Army Groups (in the centre of the whole front) will have the task of advancing with powerful armoured and motorised formations from the area around and north of Warsaw, and routing the enemy forces in White Russia. This will make it possible for strong mobile forces to advance northwards and, in conjunction with the Northern Army Group operating out of East Prussia in the general direction of Leningrad, to destroy the enemy forces operating in the Baltic area. Only after the achievement of these essential first tasks has been made safe, which must include the occupation of Leningrad and Kronstadt, will the attack be continued with the intention of occupying Moscow, an important centre of communications and of the armaments industry.[131]

Importantly for Halder the main weight of the attack was still placed in the centre of the front and Army Group Centre was to start out along the road to Moscow, which remained consistent with his own plan. Yet in deference to the undisputed precedence enjoyed by Hitler's preference, Halder devised a cunning solution. In what probably seemed to Hitler a pedantic fuss over semantics of no real consequence, Halder arranged for some subtle word changes which he felt left the future course of operations open to some interpretation as well as denying Hitler the absolute endorsement such a document would otherwise have provided him. The fact that Halder resorted to such a deceitful technique shows he was fairly certain Hitler would oppose his recommendation. By the same token, this clash of equally unyielding wills leads one to question the wisdom of delaying such a dispute until the campaign was underway.

In the final text of Directive No. 21, issued 18 December 1940, Halder ensured Army Group Centre's redirection towards Moscow would take place once Hitler's northern objectives had been 'made safe' (*Sicherstellung*)[132] – a substantial amendment over what had formally been described as 'settled' (*Erledigung*).[133] The difference was the more subjective interpretation that one could apply towards the achievement of Hitler's goals. In an even more blatant example, Halder successfully arranged for the inclusion of a clause at the beginning of the section on 'Conduct of Operations' which declared Hitler in agreement

---

[131] Moritz (ed.), *Fall Barbarossa*, p. 142. Italics in the original. Document 36 'Hitlers Weisung Nr. 21 (Fall Barbarossa) für den Überfall auf die Sowjetunion, 18. Dezember 1940'. Trevor-Roper (ed.), *Hitler's War Directives 1939–1945*, pp. 95–96; Domarus, *Hitler*, Volume III, pp. 2157–2159. Domarus incorrectly attributes the date of the Directive to 16 December 1940.

[132] Ibid. all.

[133] KTB OKW, Volume I, p. 233 (17 December 1940); Klink, 'Die militärische Konzeption', p. 239. See also the first-rate English translation: Ernst Klink, 'The Military Concept of the War Against the Soviet Union' in Militärgeschichtliches Forschungsamt (ed.), *Germany and the Second World War*, Volume IV: *The Attack on the Soviet Union* (Oxford, 1998), p. 281. For referencing purposes the original German edition has been used except where otherwise stated.

with the army's plans. The passage opened: 'A. *Army* (Approving the intentions reported to me)'[134] (*In Genehmigung der mir vorgetragenen Absichten*).[135] Halder was evidently seeking to tie Hitler down to the Army's point of view, providing himself with pivotal counter-arguments against the resistance he expected in the future. Halder's scheming, unknown to Warlimont at the time, prompted the latter to conclude, 'the Army... suddenly faced with this major alteration in its plans, accepted the situation in silence.' As the situation developed, however, he noted: 'It later became known that their reasoning was that in time the course of the campaign would compel even Hitler to go back to the original Army concept.' Such a dangerous and naive assumption on the part of the army, Warlimont regarded as 'to a certain extent taking the easy way out'; furthermore 'it proved no more than self-deception'.[136] Thus, Directive 21 formalised the titanic clash between Nazi Germany and the Soviet Union and, unspoken and unknown to most, the same document drew the lines for a similar clash, clearly foreseen by Halder, which would plunge the German High Command into its own crisis.

The idea of shifting the main attack of Army Group Centre to the north did not originate with Hitler, but rather formed an integral part of Lossberg's Operational Study East. This has raised some questions about whether Hitler ever saw Lossberg's study or if in fact he came to this conclusion of his own accord.[137] Likewise, Jodl's role in advising Hitler remains a point of conjecture, as he was no doubt aware of Lossberg's study and could have presented the idea to Hitler and supported it again during their December 17 meeting.[138] A report by Lossberg of Hitler's discussion with Jodl on 17 December 1940 retraced many of the main points set out by his own Operational Study East, including the shift of armoured forces to the north to assist in the clearance of the Baltic states before the advance on Moscow was undertaken.[139]

Beyond the direct importance of Moscow in the coming campaign, Directive No. 21 also outlined the underpinnings for both the German

[134] Klink, 'The Military Concept', p. 282; Megargee, *Inside Hitler's High Command*, pp. 131–132.
[135] Klink, 'Die militärische Konzeption', p. 240.
[136] Warlimont, *Im Hauptquartier*, Band I, p. 154. There also exists an English translation: Walter Warlimont, *Inside Hitler's Headquarters, 1939–1945* (New York, 1964), p. 139.
[137] Although definitive evidence is lacking, divergent opinions are held; see Irving, *Hitler's War*, Volume I, p. 206; Klink, 'Die militärische Konzeption', p. 239.
[138] Klink, 'Die militärische Konzeption', p. 239 and footnote 137; Cecil, *Hitler's Decision to Invade Russia 1941*, p. 125. Warlimont writes that there is no evidence Jodl influenced Hitler's thinking, but this lack of evidence neither proves nor disproves the fact. Warlimont, *Im Hauptquartier*, Band I, p. 154.
[139] KTB OKW, Volume II, p. 996, Document 45 (21 December 1940).

plans for victory in the east and its associated assumptions about the Red
Army and the Soviet Union. Under the sub-heading 'General Intention',
the German aim was for 'daring' armoured thrusts to destroy the bulk of
the Red Army in the western regions of the country. The success of these
early operations would prevent the escape of battle-worthy elements and
allow the remaining enemy forces to be 'energetically pursued' to the
final line of advance along the Volga to Archangel.[140] Not surprisingly,
the absence of a rigorous critical review of the earlier operational studies
allowed many of their fundamental errors and misconceptions to flow
directly into Directive No. 21. Notably, the assumption that German
operations would continue after the initial encirclements, in the form of
a pursuit, suggests major operations would no longer be necessary. Even
in the question over Army Group Centre's deployment to the Baltic or
Moscow, the victory fever pervading the planning deemed it necessary to
add: 'a surprisingly rapid collapse of Russian resistance could justify the
simultaneous pursuit of both objectives.'[141]

Finland and Romania were identified as Germany's two main allies
offering direct involvement in the campaign at the extreme north and
south of the front. Finland would cover the flank of German detachments from Group XXI advancing out of Norway and pressure the Red
Army to the west with an advance to the shores of Lake Ladoga, while
Romania was enlisted to support the German southern flank tying down
Soviet forces and providing troops for rear area administration. Army
Group South, operating south of the Pripet marshes, was to eliminate all
resistance west of the Dnepr in a concentric two-pronged attack led by its
main force striking out of the Lublin area towards Kiev and supported by
a broad wheeling manoeuvre from German forces in Romania attacking
across the lower Pruth.[142]

With the conclusion of the main operations north and south of the
Pripet marshes, Directive No. 21, again characterising the attack within
the framework of a 'pursuit of the enemy', instructed the army groups
towards new objectives. Army Group South was to proceed towards
the mineral-rich Donets Basin, important to the Soviet war industry,
while in the north the main German forces, having secured the Baltic
and occupied Leningrad, would seek the immediate capture of Moscow.
In addition to the capital's crucial railway junction, the capture of the

---

[140] Trevor-Roper (ed.), *Hitler's War Directives 1939–1945*, p. 94; Moritz (ed.), *Fall Barbarossa*, p. 141.

[141] Trevor-Roper (ed.), *Hitler's War Directives 1939–1945*, p. 96; Moritz (ed.), *Fall Barbarossa*, p. 142.

[142] Trevor-Roper (ed.), *Hitler's War Directives 1939–1945*, pp. 95–96; Moritz (ed.), *Fall
Barbarossa*, pp. 141–143.

city was portrayed as representing 'a decisive political and economic success'.[143] Yet however much value one attributes to the term 'decisive' it cannot be denied that Moscow remained a secondary objective, only to be attempted following the battles in Belorussia, the Baltic and Leningrad. In that sense, Moscow's significance in Directive No. 21 was a far cry from Halder's conception of the Soviet capital as the vital and definite war-winning objective.[144]

The German air force was assigned the dual role of obtaining complete control over the theatre's airspace by eliminating the Soviet air force as well as offering ground support to the main operations of the army. Long-range air attacks against industrial targets located in the distant Urals region would not feature in the initial phase of the campaign, but would commence following the conclusion of mobile operations. The navy's focus was still to be directed primarily against British shipping, though in the Baltic Sea the navy was ordered first to secure the German coastline, with the prevention of Soviet ships escaping into the North Sea, and later, following the army's occupation of all Soviet naval bases, to seek the final destruction of the Soviet Baltic fleet. Final preparations for all services in accordance with Directive No. 21 were to be completed by 15 May 1941, indicating strongly the envisaged date for the opening of the campaign.[145]

---

[143] Trevor-Roper (ed.), *Hitler's War Directives 1939–1945*, pp. 96–97; Moritz (ed.), *Fall Barbarossa*, p. 143.

[144] Klink, 'Die militärische Konzeption', p. 240.

[145] Trevor-Roper (ed.), *Hitler's War Directives 1939–1945*, pp. 94, 97; Moritz (ed.), *Fall Barbarossa*, pp. 141, 143–144.

2   The gathering storm

The army deployment directive

On 23 December 1940 Halder held further discussions regarding the
effectiveness of Soviet tanks. Intelligence on the subject was acknowledged to be sparse, but their relative inferiority, in comparison with
German models, was identified in both armour and speed. The maximum thickness of Soviet armour was predicted to be 30mm, while
the 4.5cm Ehrhard armament could penetrate German armour up to
a range of only 800m. The Soviet panzer corps faced further disadvan-
tages with very poor communication equipment and optical sights which
were understood to be hazy and limited in range. In regard to the Wehrmacht, Halder noted that an additional 4,930 captured enemy tanks and
ammunition carriers were being incorporated into German units.

That same morning Fromm reported to Halder that stocks of steel and
non-ferrous metals were very low. As for food supplies Fromm remarked:
'We'll muddle our way through 1941.' The supply of rubber, vital to the
production of tyres, was also proving 'difficult' and Fromm believed that
new synthetics factories would be necessary. The next day General Paulus
highlighted the extent of the rubber shortage, informing Halder that ten
panzer divisions were operating at 10 per cent below strength purely as a
result of tyre wear. This, together with vehicles undergoing maintenance
or repair, resulted in a figure of 20 per cent of wheeled vehicles out of
commission.[1] This was a worryingly high figure considering the army
was not engaged in anything other than occupation and training duties.

The increasingly dire economic data also highlights the great depen-
dency Germany had on produce and raw material shipments supplied
by the Soviet Union, raising still more questions about the wisdom of
Barbarossa. Only seven of the thirty most important raw materials for the
armaments industry were available to Germany in adequate quantities.[2]

---

[1] Franz Halder, KTB II, pp. 240–242 (23 and 24 December 1940).
[2] Frieser, *Blitzkrieg-Legende*, p. 24. English translation: *The Blitzkrieg Legend*, p. 20.

As early as September 1939 Hitler made it clear that time was working against him and that a long war would not favour Germany either militarily or economically. Speaking to Halder, the dictator stated: "'Time" will, in general, work against us if we do not use it effectively. The economic means of the other side are stronger. The enemy can purchase and transport. Time does not work for us in the military sense either.'[3] A major study by Adam Tooze focusing on Nazi Germany's economy highlights the alarming shortages in oil, coal, food and industrial capacity for 1940–1941.[4] Given such dangerous prognoses, embarking on a major new war against the Soviet Union with Britain still undefeated is perhaps the best indication of the hubris encompassing not only Hitler and party officials, but also the OKW, OKH, air force and certain quarters of the navy. Accordingly, it is not surprising that the Department of Foreign Armies East reinforced many of the disdainful preconceptions regarding the Red Army in its 1 January 1941 report. The report concluded:

The strength of the Red Army is based upon its great mass, the number of its weapons and the simplicity, toughness and courage of its soldiers. The weakness lies in the lack of training, which does not satisfy modern standards, and in the lack of organization, which is obvious in all areas.[5]

Such notions were not without a basis in fact, but the tone entirely neglects the prospect of an enemy capable of offering sustained resistance, to say nothing of a level of co-ordination able to surprise or disrupt German intentions.

On 9 January 1941 Hitler gathered together many of his most senior commanders, as well as his foreign minister Joachim von Ribbentrop, to deliver a sweeping survey of the progress of the war and outline his most recent political and strategic forecast. When he finally came to addressing the issue of Barbarossa his justification returned to the theme of defeating Britain, seeing the two as being integrally tied. Britain, Hitler explained, was simply holding out, hoping to build a continental block against Germany together with the Soviet Union and the United States for which diplomatic preparations were already underway. The possibility of Soviet involvement, Hitler claimed, stiffened British resolve, but he predicted that the British would give in once their last potential continental ally was eliminated. The English had no interest in continuing

[3] Franz Halder, KTB I, p. 86 (27 September 1939).
[4] Adam Tooze, *The Wages of Destruction. The Making and Breaking of the Nazi Economy* (London, 2007), Chapters 12 and 13.
[5] Moritz (ed.), *Fall Barbarossa*, p. 80. Document 14, 'Aus der Einschätzung der politisch-moralischen Stabilität der Sowjetunion und der Kampfkraft der Roten Armee durch die Abteilung Fremde Heere Ost des Generalstabes des Heeres, 1. Januar 1941'.

a war that offered no chance of victory and could only jeopardise their whole Empire. On the other hand, if Britain was to raise 40–50 divisions and the Soviets and Americans were to join the war, Germany would face a very difficult situation. Up until that point, Hitler continued, he had always acted according to the principle of smashing his enemy's most important positions in order to advance a step. Following a war with the Soviet Union, Britain would either give in or Germany would face the ongoing struggle under more favourable circumstances. The elimination of the Soviet Union would also enable Japan to concentrate all of her power against the United States, impeding American intervention in the European war.[6]

Hitler described Stalin as 'the lord of Russia and a clever man'. He would not act openly against Germany but it would have to be assumed that, in situations already difficult for Germany, he would add to those difficulties. Stalin, Hitler presumed, clearly saw that a German victory would leave his nation in a very worrying position. The Soviet Union, Hitler therefore deemed, must be struck and it was better to undertake this now while the Soviet armed forces were leaderless, badly armed and before the development of the armaments industry, through foreign aid, had overcome many of its present difficulties. Hitler identified the time factor in the campaign as particularly important, while he described the Red Army as 'a headless clay colossus'. Yet Hitler also warned against complacency, insisting the Soviets were not to be under-estimated and that the German attack must proceed with great force. Under no circumstances should the front be simply pushed back, swift breakthroughs were necessary instead.

If Hitler was determined to avoid under-estimation among his subordinates he certainly exhibited his own failings in this regard. Pointing to the great distances in the Soviet Union he claimed that these were nothing the German Wehrmacht had not already mastered. He then turned his audience's attention to the post-victory rewards, speaking of the reduction of the army to the benefit of armament production and the use of the newly-won territories for the relocation of the most important industry, safe from aerial attack. With this, Hitler assured: 'Germany would be unassailable.' In conclusion Hitler stated that, once in possession of the 'immeasurable riches' the Soviet Union offered, Germany would be in a position to wage war against continents and stand impervious to attack. If such an operation were carried through, Hitler predicted, 'Europe would hold its breath' (*werde Europa den Atem anhalten*).[7]

---

[6] KTB OKW, Volume I, pp. 257–258 (9 January 1941).
[7] Ibid., p. 258 (9 January 1941).

Significantly, Hitler referred to the 'rapid severance of the Baltic region' (*die rasche Abschneidung des Ostseeraums*) as 'the most important task' (*die wichtigste Aufgabe*) and for that reason the army's right wing north of the Pripet marshes (Army Group Centre) was to be made especially strong. Furthermore, Hitler outlined his operational objectives listing in order of priority, 'the annihilation of the Russian army, seizure of the most important industrial regions and the destruction of the remaining industrial regions'.[8] This again clearly relegated Moscow to a position of secondary importance. Yet members of the army asked no awkward questions and raised no objections. The operational objectives, the rationale for a second front and premise for victory were all accepted without the slightest utterance of disapproval.[9] Indeed, echoing Hitler, Jodl is said to have exclaimed shortly afterwards, 'the Russian colossus will prove to be a pig's bladder, prick it and it will burst'.[10]

On 28 January 1941 Halder hosted a conference of senior administrators in the army and Luftwaffe to consider preparations for Operation Barbarossa. Production of trucks, vital to the motorisation of the army and its tenuous logistical apparatus, still remained in a low priority category despite facing a 30 per cent shortfall in the projected quota.[11] The conference opened with discussion of this shortfall, to which the expropriation of French army material and additional deliveries from Switzerland were deemed the most practical immediate solutions.[12] Supply of tyres was another increasingly grave problem, forming an industrial bottleneck affecting not only new stocks but Germany's entire fleet of wheeled vehicles. General Georg Thomas, Chief of the War Economy and Armaments Department, commented that they must have 13,000 tonnes of rubber a month although German industry could only process 7,300 tonnes. To make matters worse, current stocks would be expended by the end of February and replenishment was dependent on South American blockade runners and 12,000 tonnes of rubber ordered from Indochina. A further 25,000 tonnes had been bought from the French, but the Japanese were proving reluctant to release the shipment. Fuel stocks were also dwindling with the situation being described as 'serious' and projections indicating current supply would suffice for the deployment of forces in the east and just two months of active operations.[13] The grim economic data attains an even more menacing significance given

[8] Ibid., pp. 257–258 (9 January 1941).
[9] Von Below, *Als Hitlers Adjutant 1937–45*, p. 259.
[10] Warlimont, *Im Hauptquartier*, Band I, p. 156.
[11] Müller, 'Von der Wirtschaftsallianz', p. 178.
[12] Franz Halder, KTB II, p. 256 (28 January 1941).
[13] Ibid., pp. 256, 260–261. See also Thomas's report of 9 January 1941, KTB OKW, Volume II, pp. 997–998, Document 46 (9 January 1941).

that Halder, after hearing the foreboding assessment of his motorised transportation, made the astounding observation:

Speed. No stopping! No waiting for the railroads. Everything must be achieved with the motor. *Increased motorisation* (as opposed to 1940)... Since the railway (through destruction, watercourses, different gauge) cannot be counted on for maintaining the pace, the *continuous operation* of supply depends upon the motor.[14]

Only eight days earlier, on 20 January, following a similar meeting concerning preparations for Barbarossa which had ended without a conclusive result (and hence resulted in the current conference), Halder had drawn rather different conclusions regarding his re-supply problem.

Operational mission. Space – no pause; that alone guarantees victory. Continuous movement is a supply issue... Distances! Space relationships in the north... Complications through differing equipment types (troops, trucks, workshops). The railroads provide the only means to maintain the advance without additional transport.[15]

It is probably not too much to assume that Halder's shifting deliberations on the issue, which in each instance disregarded the alternative for its apparent inadequacy, reflect the intractable nature of the problem for which no practical solution existed. Halder could see from the distances and the shortness of the campaigning season that the advance would have to be rapid and in response to his own question: 'Why is an uninterrupted operation necessary?' Halder afforded the answer: 'We must destroy the Russian army without pause over the Dnepr–Duna line (500 kilometres into north Russia and other goals another 500 kilometres, in total 1,000 kilometres).'[16] Obviously Halder's reckoning between what 'must' and what *could* be achieved presented a differentiation he either could not identify or, in the light of his supreme confidence, chose not to consider. As a result, Halder as Chief of the German General Staff must bear considerable responsibility for this failing. Indisputable evidence of the deficiency was before him and, even if doubts did stir within him as some have suggested,[17] why did he not bring these to Hitler with all the weight of his person, rank and office?

At the conclusion of the conference on 28 January 1941 Halder set forth instructions that any further unresolved questions concerning the 'operational direction' (*Operationsführung*) in the east should be made clear for a final decision by Hitler.[18] In view of Halder's intransigence over yielding operational direction to Hitler in the case of Moscow, and the

---

[14] Italics in the original. Franz Halder, KTB II, p. 258 (28 January 1941).
[15] Ibid.   [16] Ibid.   [17] Leach, *German Strategy against Russia*, p. 140.
[18] Franz Halder, KTB II, p. 259 (28 January 1941).

lengths to which his subversion had already progressed, his willingness
for a deferral to Hitler suggests he feared no challenge to his designs.
Furthermore, the acceptance of Hitler in the role of ultimate decision-
maker testifies to the special privilege Halder afforded himself in his
scheming over Moscow.

Of particular note to 28 January 1941 are the oft quoted doubts Halder
expressed concerning Barbarossa. Following his meeting with the senior
army administrators Halder met with Brauchitsch to discuss the general
situation. Referring to Barbarossa, Halder wrote:

Purpose not clear. We do not hit the British that way. Our economic potential will
not be improved. The risk in the West should not be underestimated. It is even
possible that Italy may collapse after losing her colonies and we find ourselves
with a southern front through Spain, Italy and Greece. If we are then committed
against Russia our situation will become increasingly difficult.[19]

Such reservations may well have been influenced to a limited degree by
the discouraging reports of the previous meeting, yet there is no evidence
to support the theory that Halder or Brauchitsch saw the coming war in
the east as a significant military risk. The subject in question was simply whether the invasion of the Soviet Union was the most prudent step
towards defeating Britain, a consideration of such well-founded good
sense and reason that one wonders why this was not questioned more
openly by the army as indeed it was within the navy and from such committed Nazis as Joachim von Ribbentrop.[20] Characteristically, the army
leadership did nothing more than a little private grumbling, believing
as they did in the likelihood of their victory and reluctant to reprise
their roles as the cynical doubters who had openly opposed the successful 'Sichelschnitt-Plan' in the west.[21] There was also a wide-ranging
aversion to grand strategic matters within the army; a trend which had
begun in World War I and had recast itself in an even more virulent
form under the Nazis. Fearing relegation from its traditional position
of privilege within German society, the new Wehrmacht[22] of the Third

[19] Ibid., p. 261.
[20] Hillgruber, *Hitlers Strategie*, pp. 210–211; Leach, *German Strategy Against Russia*,
pp. 127–128; Cecil, *Hitler's Decision to Invade Russia 1941*, pp. 117–118. In January
1941 Ribbentrop's opposition to Barbarossa was expressed much more clearly and with
greater conviction. 'Would this war', Ribbentrop asked, 'bring us any closer to our goal
as regards England, even if it went entirely according to plan? Either we smash England,
in which case we don't need to become embroiled in the East, or we fail to force England
to capitulate, in which case a war in the East will be of no use to us.' Geoffrey Waddington, 'Rippentrop and the Soviet Union, 1937–1941' in John Erickson and David Dilks
(eds.), *Barbarossa. The Axis and the Allies* (Edinburgh, 1998), p. 27.
[21] Frieser, *Blitzkrieg-Legende*, pp. 110–114; *The Blitzkrieg Legend*, pp. 94–98.
[22] Replacing the old *Reichswehr* (German armed forces) of the Weimar Republic.

Reich became a functional elite largely blind to the costs or problems of Hitler's ideological strategy and opportunist methods.[23]

On 31 January 1941 Brauchitsch hosted a meeting attended by Halder and the army's top field commanders, Field Marshals Rundstedt, Leeb, Bock and Witzleben. Here it was made clear that the army's plan proceeded from the assumption that the Red Army could be engaged and defeated before the Dvina–Dnepr line. Field Marshal Bock, however, asked what would happen if the Red Army did not oblige OKH plans and instead fell back into the depths of the country. He received the curt reply from Halder, 'it might well happen otherwise'.[24] Disturbing as this must have been for Bock, who was returning from four months of sick leave and receiving his first detailed briefing on the Barbarossa campaign, Halder, after months of planning that he himself had overseen, was not about to be thrown off by having the whole theoretical conception called into question. As recently as November 1940, Halder had confided to his diary that the daunting scope of commitments around Europe suggested a limitation of operations in the east to the first operational objective (i.e. the Dvina–Dnepr line). He believed that 'starting from there, one could attempt an enveloping operation, but in the endless expanse of space this would have no prospect of success'.[25] Not surprisingly, the prospect of fighting on into the Soviet hinterland boded ill for Halder, but once again the Chief of the General Staff failed in the duty of his office, ordering no review or follow up, asking none of the difficult questions, trusting instead in the plans at hand and avoiding the glaring flaws so apparent to others.

Bock's concern, however, was not so easily assuaged and he took up the matter the following day (1 February 1941) during a meeting with Hitler. Bock expressed his certainty that the Soviet forces could be defeated if they stood their ground and fought, but questioned what could be done to force a settlement if they refused to give battle. To this Hitler replied that if the occupation of the Ukraine, Leningrad and Moscow did not bring about peace then the campaign would just have to carry on, using mobile forces, to Yekaterinburg, a staggering 2,000 kilometres further east from Moscow.[26] Bock recorded Hitler's response without comment but, as an experienced field commander, alarm bells should have sounded at the mere suggestion of such an audacious assertion. Yet early in the war Hitler still possessed the ability to allay many fears in the minds of

---

[23] Michael Geyer, 'German Strategy in the Age of Machine Warfare, 1914–1945' in Peter Paret (ed.), *Makers of Modern Strategy. From Machiavelli to the Nuclear Age* (Oxford, 1999), pp. 583–584.

[24] Fedor von Bock, KTB 'Vorbereitungszeit', Fol. 5, *War Diary*, p. 197 (31 January 1941).

[25] Franz Halder, KTB II, p. 198 (27 November 1940).

[26] Fedor von Bock, KTB 'Vorbereitungszeit', Fol. 5, *War Diary*, p. 198 (1 February 1941).

his generals with long, at times grandiose lectures, exuding unbounded confidence and showing off his meticulous acquaintance with military and political developments. Here Hitler's use of sweeping euphemisms, especially in military matters, often allowed little room for attention to detail; he was content with vague references to 'annihilation', 'collapse' and 'reduction to rubble'.[27] Bock would not be the first, or last, general to falter before Hitler.

Thus, the planning for Barbarossa proceeded without delay or revision and Hitler's unrestrained megalomania was left unchallenged by the principal army commanders. The dangers of this approach were only identified in retrospect by some in the High Command. Speaking in July 1945, Jodl told his American interrogators: 'He took part in the trench warfare . . . he had had no real experience with mobile warfare and all the difficulties that are caused in communications with the uncertain conditions of mobile warfare. He, therefore, tended to overlook the difficulties of executing some of the operations which he had planned.'[28] What Jodl neglected to mention was the gross failing of the German military in condoning and acting upon Hitler's wild gambles.

The first draft of the Army's Deployment Directive Barbarossa (*Aufmarschanweisung Barbarossa*) was issued on 22 January 1941 with a subsequent final version submitted to Halder and dated 31 January. It began by re-emphasising the need to eliminate the bulk of enemy forces in the western districts and prevent any withdrawal. The second section, entitled 'Enemy Situation', began with the important assumption that Soviet forces would accept battle west of the Dnepr and Dvina Rivers with at least strong parts of their forces, thereby fulfilling the German requirement for the subsequent destruction of the Red Army's main force.[29]

The substance of the document was based upon the guidelines set out in Directive No. 21 and accordingly followed Hitler's well-known preference regarding operational objectives. Under the title 'Intention', the Deployment Directive noted:

Army Group Centre – Field Marshal von Bock – will commit strong and fast-moving forces from the area around Warsaw and Suwalki to enact a breakthrough in the direction of Smolensk. This will permit the turning of strong, mobile elements northwards to assist *Army Group North – Field Marshal von Leeb –* attacking out

---

[27] Joachim Fest, *Hitler* (Orlando, 1974), p. 644.
[28] Richard Overy, *Interrogations. The Nazi Elite in Allied Hands, 1945* (London, 2001), p. 281.
[29] Franz Halder, KTB II, p. 464 (Appendix 2); Moritz (ed.), *Fall Barbarossa*, p. 151, Document 39, 'Aus der Aufmarschanweisung des Oberbefehlshabers des Heeres für die Aggression gegen die Sowjetunion (Aufmarschanweisung Barbarossa), 31. Januar 1941'.

of East Prussia to annihilate enemy forces in the Baltic and proceed in the general direction of Leningrad.[30]

Even so, the army, was keen to emphasise that in the event of a general collapse of Soviet forces 'the abandonment of the northward turn and an immediate thrust towards Moscow could be considered'.[31] The Deployment Directive was signed by Brauchitsch, although the Army High Command's own operational objectives remained, as ever, separate from those of Hitler. Their apparent acceptance was only another act of deception designed to concede only what they must. Evidence to this effect is provided by Paulus who, writing after the war, made clear:

In the Army Headquarters' plan the capture of Moscow was regarded as the principal objective. Its capture, however, was to be preceded by the capture of Leningrad, the fall of which would deprive the Baltic Fleet of its main base, the Russian war effort of the armament production of the city and, above all, the Russian Army of a strategic assembly area for a counter-offensive against the flank and rear of the German forces advancing on Moscow. For this last reason alone it was essential that Leningrad should be the first objective.[32]

What Paulus neglects to mention of course is that the army simply had no other choice but to accept the precedence of Leningrad over Moscow and that, left to their own devices, it seems highly unlikely the army would have subordinated Army Group Centre's mobile forces to its northern counterpart. On the contrary, if indeed there did exist a serious threat to the northern flank of Army Group Centre, the army would have re-designated Army Group North's priority to protecting the central front's flank, just as they had previously done in Paulus's December war game. Brauchitsch and Halder, however, knowing the limits to which their arguments and powers of persuasion could influence Hitler's reasoning, decided instead on a covert subversion of Hitler's plan. This cannot be seen in any way as an act of resistance to Hitler or his regime, rather a strictly military matter calculated to win Hitler's war in what was perceived by the army command to be a more efficient manner. The conspiracy of silence was a means to this end and was therefore in the service of the regime rather than in opposition to it. Almost certainly the plotters were restricted to the highest officers of the OKH and the extent to which any formal plan of action was developed, if indeed anything so exact was produced, is unknown. Most likely the plotting consisted simply of strongly voiced personal opinions followed by actions being taken,

[30] Italics in the original. Franz Halder, KTB II, pp. 464–465; Moritz (ed.), *Fall Barbarossa*, p. 152.
[31] Franz Halder, KTB II, p. 465; Moritz (ed.), *Fall Barbarossa*, p. 153.
[32] Görlitz, *Paulus and Stalingrad*, p. 127.

where possible, to meet the army's interests, but without raising Hitler's suspicions or incurring further interference. The overriding realisation of the difficulties in dealing with Hitler necessitated a patient resignation. The generals bided their time, seeking to force the issue only at the critical moment, convinced that events leading up to the secondary phase of operations would prove the intrinsic value of a direct assault on Moscow. Here again one identifies the overarching conviction of complete confidence in the coming campaign. The Soviet armies, in spite of their size, were believed to be so utterly inferior to the Wehrmacht and its relentless 'blitzkrieg' that the secondary phase of operations would have no more important goal than the immediate thrust on the Soviet capital. The certainty of a short, victorious war did not allow for dire predictions of German setbacks or troublesome Soviet counter-attacks. The question was only how best to win a war that none doubted would be won. As Colonel-General Heinz Guderian later observed: 'All the men of the OKW and the OKH with whom I spoke evinced an unshakable optimism and were quite impervious to criticism or objections.'[33] In a similar tone, Colonel-General Maximilian Freiherr von Weichs, who was to command the 2nd Army in Operation Barbarossa, wrote after the war: 'One began the war with an underestimation of the enemy that would be hard to surpass and an arrogance stemming from the surprisingly rapid victories of past campaigns.'[34]

On 3 February 1941 Halder met Hitler for further discussions concerning the preparations for Barbarossa. Halder was careful to base his report, at least in the realm of operations north of the Pripet marshes, on Directive No. 21 and presented an overall picture, not always in line with fact, of confident progression. He began with a detailed description of the enemy strengths, indicating available Soviet forces at 100 infantry divisions, 25 cavalry divisions and 30 motorised divisions;[35] these were to be seen against a German force of 104 infantry and 34 mobile divisions.[36] Halder acknowledged to Hitler a Soviet numerical advantage in tanks including those attached to infantry divisions, but dismissed their worth

---

[33] Heinz Guderian, *Panzer Leader* (New York, 1952), pp. 142–143. Guderian's account goes on to emphasise his own unclouded view in which his supposed prescience concerning Soviet strength led him to see the coming campaign as an 'infinitely difficult task' (p. 143). In fact, the only time Guderian's opinion was asked for in the planning of the campaign, he presented an optimistic view of German superiority over the Red Army. See Hillgruber, *Hitlers Strategie*, pp. 226–227.

[34] Weichs's letter cited by Johannes Hürter, *Hitlers Heerführer. Die deutschen Oberbefehlshaber im Krieg gegen die Sowjetunion 1941/42* (Munich, 2006), p. 282.

[35] KTB OKW, Volume I, p. 297 (3 February 1941).

[36] Franz Halder, KTB II, p. 266 (2 February 1941).

Figure 2.1 In the planning for Operation Barbarossa Halder (right) and Brauchitsch (left) privately disagreed with Hitler's objectives for Army Group Centre.

on account of German qualitative superiority.[37] The notes made in his diary on 2 February, in preparation for the meeting with Hitler, however, record the imposing figure of 10,000 Soviet tanks in comparison with 3,500 German panzers. Guderian's 1937 book on tank warfare also set the number of Soviet tanks at 10,000.[38] After the war, Guderian's memoir made the claim, impossible to substantiate, that Hitler remarked to him during a military conference in early August 1941: 'If I had known that the figures for Russian tank strength which you gave in your book were in fact the true ones, I would not – I believe – ever have started this war.'[39] As it was, Halder apparently did not quote the figure to Hitler. The low estimation of Soviet quality in tanks was tempered by the observation, 'Nevertheless surprises not impossible.'[40] Indeed, Soviet production of the KV-1 and T-34 would ensure surprises of the most profound kind awaited the Wehrmacht. Yet, for the time being, brash, self-assured impunity sustained the Army High Command in spite of

[37] KTB OKW, Volume I, p. 297 (3 February 1941).
[38] Heinz Guderian, *Achtung-Panzer! The Development of Tank Warfare* (London, 2002), p. 153.
[39] Guderian, *Panzer Leader*, p. 190.
[40] Franz Halder, KTB II, p. 267 (2 February 1941).

the acknowledged limitations in intelligence.[41] Hitler's army adjutant, Major Gerhard Engel, had earlier noted that Hitler and Halder shared a 'very optimistic' estimation of the Red Army, foreseeing 'obsolete equipment and above all few aircraft and old tanks'.[42] Soviet artillery, Halder informed Hitler, was outfitted to its units in the conventional manner, but suffered again from poor quality.[43] Halder's diary of the previous day, however, included the noteworthy addition, 'numerically strong'.[44]

Instructions for the three army groups generally aimed at breaking through the Soviet front and preventing an enemy withdrawal. Halder then specified the tasks of Army Groups North and Centre, detailing a joint action by the three panzer groups over the Dvina in a north-easterly direction. Yet, as he continued, Halder's commitment to the northern operation appeared less certain. While Army Group North's panzer group advanced towards Lake Peipus in Estonia, Halder stated the other two panzer groups from Army Group Centre would make Smolensk their first objective and follow on from there in co-operation with the northern group, 'further to the east'.[45] Undoubtedly, Halder was aware that reaching Smolensk would also ensure strong arguments in favour of Moscow simply on geographical terms. From this position the Soviet capital lay only a further 360 kilometres to the east, while Leningrad would necessitate a 90 degree turn northwards with an advance of 600 kilometres over terrain dotted with swamps and marshes.

Halder's handling of the operations for Army Group South help to illustrate further the degree of divergence in operational conception and the extent of departure he was prepared to risk from Hitler's strategy as set out in Directive 21. During the February 3 conference with Hitler, Halder made only passing reference to the task of Army Group South, deflecting attention from the subject on account of the fundamental alterations he had instigated in the issuing of the Army Deployment Directive. These included expanding the mandate of the 12th Army to include the taking of Odessa, if an opportunity arose for its surprise capture.[46] Moreover, flagrant liberties were taken concerning the staging of troops in Hungary to support an advance out of the Carpathian mountains for which Halder

[41] Ibid., p. 266.
[42] Hildegard von Kotze (ed.), *Heeresadjutant bei Hitler 1938–1943. Aufzeichnungen des Majors Engel* (Stuttgart, 1974), p. 93 (17 January 1941). Engel's book, although presented in the form of a diary, was in fact written after the war from his personal notes.
[43] KTB OKW, Volume I, p. 297 (3 February 1941).
[44] Franz Halder, KTB II, p. 267 (2 February 1941).
[45] KTB OKW, Volume I, pp. 297–298 (3 February 1941).
[46] Klink, 'Die militärische Konzeption', pp. 242–243. The 'Deployment Directive Barbarossa' as published in Halder's War Diary is incomplete and misleading (see Klink, p. 242, footnote 147). An accurate reference is found in Moritz (ed.), *Fall Barbarossa*, p. 154.

had been engaged in unauthorised negotiations.[47] This went expressly against Hitler's instructions of early December 1940 that excluded any participation by Hungary, which is why no mention of Hungary was included in Directive 21. Indifferent to such official obstructions, Halder proceeded with *his* planning. This went beyond commanding German troops into a theoretically neutral country to also include a provision for Hungarian formations to support the attack in the role of rear-area security forces.[48] In what must count as an outstanding example of insubordination well in excess of his position and authority, Halder undertook all this without the consent of his head of state. In an attempt to legitimise his actions Halder included a request to Hitler on 3 February for the active inclusion of Hungary in the planning for Operation Barbarossa. This request was flatly rejected and Halder was left to accept his first defeat in the battle with Hitler over the direction of the eastern campaign.[49] Significantly, Halder's rebuff over Hungary was a warning sign for his main gamble requiring Hitler's ultimate consent, namely Moscow.

Such underhand dealings speak strongly of the double standards upheld during Halder's tenure as Chief of the General Staff. While he was infuriated at Hitler's interference in the military sphere, he saw no contradiction in his own attempt to circumvent Hitler's authority. Moreover, Halder's subordinates were not permitted the independence of action that was encouraged within certain quarters of the army. Instead, strict obedience and a dedicated loyalty were valued above all else, a point which Lieutenant-Colonel Henning von Tresckow emphasised to Halder's secretary: 'We are trained to be machines and must adapt our opinions. Little value is placed on our development as individuals.'[50] Thus, it seems hypocrisy was also one of Halder's failings.

The issue of the army's supply was also a feature of Halder's presentation to Hitler during the 3 February conference, but again it remained unreflective of the grave reports Halder himself had received. None of the worrying economic details reported to him on 28 January were brought to Hitler's attention. The objective it seemed was to address how problems

[47] Klink, 'Die militärische Konzeption', pp. 237, 243.

[48] Jürgen Förster, 'Die Gewinnung von Verbündeten in Südosteuropa' in Militärgeschichtliches Forschungsamt (ed.), *Das Deutsche Reich und der Zweite Weltkrieg*, Band IV: *Der Angriff auf die Sowjetunion* (Stuttgart, 1983), pp. 355–356; Leach, *German Strategy Against Russia*, pp. 188–189.

[49] Förster, 'Die Gewinnung von Verbündeten', p. 356; Klink, 'Die militärische Konzeption', p. 242; KTB OKW, Volume I, p. 299 (3 February 1941). Ultimately the Hungarian leader Admiral Horthy, who was himself a committed anti-communist and feared Romania's increasing favour with Hitler, would of his own volition declare war on the Soviet Union and send an army to aid Army Group South.

[50] As cited by Leach, 'Halder', p. 116.

could be overcome, with contradictory evidence simply omitted. Halder emphasised to Hitler the great reliance on trucks owing to the fact that the Soviet railroads would first have to be reset to the German gauge.[51] Yet changing the gauge would not alter the fact, as Halder had noted in his diary, that the Soviet railway system was 'very dispersed, mostly single tracked and not maintained'.[52] Hitler was also informed of the need to open the Baltic ports as quickly as possible for re-supply and Halder recommended increased co-operation between the army and the Luftwaffe to avoid wastage of space in the transports heading east.[53] From such uncritical and clearly limited assessments of the supply situation, one can see the ease with which Hitler's obsessive ambitions would push the Wehrmacht far beyond the limits of its already fragile support system. Halder's unbounded confidence only fuelled Hitler's yearnings when he should have been restraining him with all the means at his disposal. The conference of 3 February ended its discussion of Barbarossa with Hitler's disquieting prediction: 'When Barbarossa begins the world will hold its breath.' (*Die Welt werde den Atem anhalten, wenn die Operation 'Barbarossa' durchgeführt werde.*)[54]

Perilous warning signs were already clearly visible to the army commanders and not just in the realm of motorised transportation but the whole war economy. Field Marshal von Bock was assured by Hitler on 1 February 1941, 'we are ready for anything. Materially we are well off and already have to think about the conversion of some factories . . . economically we are absolutely solid.'[55] Hitler's show of absolute confidence is in part due to his self-delusional character, but also sustained by his belief in the power of individual 'will'; he sought to convince those around him of his own infallibility as if this belief alone could alter fact. As eccentric as it was, it found no shortage of disciples in the Third Reich, including those within the armed forces. Brauchitsch's and Halder's unquestioning participation in Hitler's eastern schemes[56] not only condoned the flimsy basis upon which the schemes rested, but fired Hitler with their own conviction of superiority and faith in the operational plans. Halder in particular, who had been shown the critical weakness of his army and heard at first hand the excessive aspirations of Hitler, still managed an otherwise inexplicable reconciliation between the two.

---

[51] KTB OKW, Volume I, p. 299 (3 February 1941).
[52] Franz Halder, KTB II, p. 267 (2 February 1941).
[53] KTB OKW, Volume I, p. 299 (3 February 1941).
[54] Ibid., p. 300 (3 February 1941).
[55] Fedor von Bock, KTB 'Vorbereitungszeit', Fol. 5, *War Diary*, p. 198 (1 February 1941).
[56] Von Below, *Als Hitlers Adjutant 1937–45*, p. 262.

Halder's slide into the devout service of Hitler, like that of many of his fellow generals, was a subtle, but steady process. As recently as 1938 Halder had been a central figure in the anti-Hitler resistance, but abandoned such ideas in spite of Hitler's aggressive war-waging and the terrors he unleashed, with widespread assistance from the army, in Poland. Halder's desire for acceptance clouded his professional judgement and reduced the eminent position of Chief of the General Staff to outward obedience and inner deceit, aimed at achieving Hitler's growing ambitions without risking a confrontation over divergent strategies or the difficulties involved. Halder's own blindness to the corruption of his post and its forsaken ideals sees no greater reflection than his insistence in December 1940 that: 'So long as I am the keeper of the grail, I shall not retreat one hair's width from the spirit of the German General Staff.'[57] Yet for the army it was already much too late. Halder's betrayal of the time-honoured principles enshrined in the traditions of the German General Staff had allowed the foreboding problems and unanswered questions to remain unseen and unaddressed.

The dysfunctional order – delusion as operative discourse

Despite the bravado of Hitler's public ranting about German strengths and future conquests, this outward facade occasionally failed him, betraying misgivings and revealing indecision. Even upon the issuing of Directive 21 Hitler's army adjutant Major Engel observed: 'In my opinion the Führer himself does not yet know how things should be continued. Mistrust of his own military leadership, uncertainty over Russian strengths, disappointment at England's hard line all continue to occupy the Führer.'[58] Not surprisingly therefore, Hitler viewed with a degree of scepticism Halder's confident assessment of 3 February and, in an act which suggests Hitler to be more of a pragmatist than Halder, he ordered two further studies on 5 February in areas he saw to be potential threats.

The first concerned the imposing obstacle of the Pripet marshes and its defensive capabilities as well as the possibility of the Soviets establishing a centre of resistance there. Furthermore, Hitler instructed attention to be directed towards the possible use of Soviet forces, especially cavalry, against the flanks of the two bordering army groups. The second study was to be concerned with the different Soviet industrial areas, ascertaining how interdependent they were and assessing the possible

---

[57] Franz Halder, KTB II, p. 230 (13 December 1941).
[58] Von Kotze (ed.), *Heeresadjutant bei Hitler*, p. 92 (18 December 1940).

implications of the Soviets building a defensive zone at any point up to the Urals.[59] Obviously Hitler's thoughts were concerned with Soviet defensive counter-measures, something which hardly featured in the OKH plans and were certainly not a topic of great concern to the Army General Staff.

The army report into the Pripet marshes was compiled by Foreign Armies East and issued in its first draft on 12 February. While the study made reference to the difficulty of the terrain, it nevertheless arrived at the unsettling conclusion that, using the railways, Soviet armies could be transported in any direction. Furthermore the report judged: 'It seems therefore that a threat from the Pripet [marshes] to the flank and the rear of the armies advancing towards Moscow or Kiev is very much within the realm of possibilities.' When Hitler requested a copy of the study, however, this sentence was inexplicably deleted from the final version, in what was to be the latest example of an army censoring its own information to guard against a negative impression. Instead, the document suggested guerrilla actions and minor engagements (up to regimental strength) were the most likely form of combat to be expected, a far cry from a threat to the flanks of the two biggest army groups.[60] Hitler's mistrust of his military commanders was therefore not wholly without basis. Indeed, as if aware of the army's deceit, he ordered the mining of passages throughout the marshes and made an insightful observation to Halder that, 'supposedly armies could be moved in there'.[61]

The second study called for by Hitler proposed answers of an economic kind which General Thomas as head of the War Economy and Armaments Department was charged to answer. His study in fact predated Hitler's request, resulting instead from a meeting with OKW chief Field Marshal Keitel on 22 January 1941. Thomas on this occasion expressed some misgivings about the war-economic implications of the planned operation in the east and on this basis resolved to prepare a memorandum.[62] On 8 February, three days after Hitler's instruction that further studies be conducted, Thomas informed Keitel and Jodl of the fact that aircraft fuel would only last until the autumn, vehicle fuel for the first two months of operations and rubber supplies until the end of March. To this damning assessment Keitel flatly responded that 'the Führer would not allow himself to be influenced in his planning

---

[59] KTB OKW, Volume I, p. 306 (5 February 1941).
[60] Klink, 'Die militärische Konzeption', p. 244.
[61] Franz Halder, KTB II, p. 319 (17 February 1941).
[62] Müller, 'Von der Wirtschaftsallianz', p. 125.

by such economic difficulties'.[63] Thus it is considered doubtful Hitler was ever briefed on such details, providing yet another success for the internal army control over information and preservation of their confidently assured outcome.[64] Keitel's blunt dismissal, however, had an even more drastic ramification in that it sent a clear signal to Thomas of what was expected in the still pending memorandum for Hitler's examination. Accordingly the memorandum entitled 'The War-Economy Consequences of an Operation in the East' dated 13 February 1941 was not submitted to Hitler until 20 February. In this time Thomas was able to amend and re-draft his study, presenting a final version favourable to Hitler's wishes and in line with the established views of his commanding officers.[65]

Thomas thus delivered a report lavish in discussion of the long-term economic benefits to be derived from occupying the Soviet Union and entirely dismissive of contradictory evidence previously produced[66] as well as the dubious nature of his source material.[67] Furthermore, his study ignored questions relating to the military feasibility of achieving the distant economic goals even though they required the conquest of an enormous land mass. Specifically, Thomas emphasised the need for the rapid conquest of the Caucasus for oil and a connection to the Far East to ensure future rubber supplies. Grain was expected to flow from the Ukraine solving Germany's food shortage and 75 per cent of the Soviet armaments industry was to fall, it was hoped intact, under direct German control with the remainder posing little threat so long as the factories in the Urals were destroyed.[68] The folly of such optimistic predictions was apparent even to former diplomat and anti-Hitler conspirator Ulrich von Hassell, whose diary of 2 March 1941 observed with remarkable accuracy that the 'real results' of an invasion of the Soviet Union would be: '(1) the cutting off of imports from Russia, since the Ukraine will be useful only

[63] Georg Thomas, *Geschichte der deutschen Wehr- und Rüstungswirtschaft (1918–1943/45)*, ed. Wolfgang Birkenfeld (Boppard am Rhein, 1966), p. 18.

[64] Leach, *German Strategy Against Russia*, p. 144; Kershaw, *Hitler 1936–1945*, p. 345.

[65] I am indebted to Alex J. Kay for access to his doctoral work: ' "Neuordnung" and "Hungerpolitik": The Development and Compatibility of Political and Economic Planning within the Nazi Hierarchy for the Occupation of the Soviet Union, July 1940–July 1941', Chapter IV, 'Laying the Foundations for the Hungerpolitik'.

[66] This refers in particular to the Walther memorandum of October 1940 which foresaw no chance of an internal Soviet collapse and argued that the Ukraine, Belarus and the Baltic states would probably be more of a burden than a benefit to the economic situation of Germany. Robert Gibbons, 'Opposition gegen "Barbarossa" im Herbst 1940 – Eine Denkschrift aus der deutschen Botschaft in Moskau', *Vierteljahrshefte für Zeitgeschichte* 23 (1975), 337–340.

[67] Hillgruber, 'The German Military Leaders' View of Russia', p. 183.

[68] Thomas, *Geschichte der deutschen Wehr- und Rüstungswirtschaft*, pp. 515ff. See also Müller, 'Von der Wirtschaftsallianz', p. 127; Leach, *German Strategy Against Russia*, pp. 144–145.

after a long time; (2) a new and unprecedented strain on war material and energies; (3) complete encirclement, deliberately arranged.'[69]

Thomas's study is a characteristic example of what Ian Kershaw has referred to as 'working towards the Führer' in which service to the dictator and his ideals was pursued above and sometimes at the expense of other more practical or moral considerations.[70] In this case General Thomas provided more dangerous encouragement to Hitler's already overwrought ambition. More importantly still, his study solidified Hitler's conception of the campaign, substantiating as it did his preference towards economic objectives as a dual method of crippling the Soviet state and providing the resources he required to sustain his war. Indeed Hitler had ordered that a clear map accompany General Thomas's study and this became a constant source of reference for his operational decisions over the early months of the campaign.[71]

It is a further sign of the decline in excellence that the two studies, not ordered by the army command but by Hitler, that were to prove of such prophetic importance to the outcome of the campaign, could be so wantonly mismanaged and distorted in their conclusions, that they precluded the very real dangers each contained from being confronted. Far from being a 'haven' from the regime separate from the other more sinister Nazi agencies, Hitler's army was in fact a willing and integrated component,[72] determined to retain his favour and suffering in the process from an ever widening distortion of reality.

By 14 March 1941 preparations for the campaign were well advanced, but even at this stage, the over-extension of forces was becoming plainly apparent. Halder, together with his operations department chiefs, assessed the plans and objectives for each of the armies taking part in Barbarossa with the conclusion that more strength and greater concentration would be necessary. The extent of the problem was most evident in Army Group South where it was determined the 12th and 17th Armies would need to be strengthened by the active involvement of Romanian, Hungarian and Slovak units. In Army Group Centre Halder was concerned with the weakness of the 4th Army's southern flank, in spite of

[69] Ulrich von Hassell, *Vom andern Deutschland* (Freiburg, 1946), p. 183 (2 March 1941). For the English translation see Ulrich von Hassell, *The Von Hassell Diaries 1938–1944* (London, 1948), pp. 157–158 (2 March 1941).

[70] Examples are cited throughout his excellent two-volume biography, although only the second volume deals with the war years. See Kershaw, *Hitler 1936–1945*.

[71] Rolf-Dieter Müller, 'Das "Unternehmen Barbarossa" als wirtschaftlicher Raubkrieg' in Gerd R. Ueberschär and Wolfram Wette (eds.), *'Unternehmen Barbarossa'. Der deutsche Überfall auf die Sowjetunion 1941* (Paderborn, 1984), p. 188; Müller, 'Von der Wirtschaftsallianz zum kolonialen Ausbeutungskrieg', p. 126.

[72] Omer Bartov, 'Soldiers, Nazis, and War in the Third Reich', *Journal of Modern History*, 63 (1991), 53–54.

the fact that he perceived little threat emerging from the Pripet marshes. The 9th Army was expressing reluctance at giving up units to the 3rd Armoured Group. Likewise, Army Group North's 18th Army was having difficulty co-ordinating its activities with the 4th Armoured Group. The 16th Army was criticised for being spread too widely and would be dependent on reserves for increased striking power. Despite the clear pressure on German forces operating in the east Halder then matter-of-factly noted the observation of Major-General Wagner, that fuel reserves would last for just three more months. To this worrying observation Halder nevertheless added the note: 'Fuel preparations adequate.'[73] The importance of a short, victorious war could no longer be seen as a best-case scenario; it had become a vital necessity. The following day (15 March) Halder's concern at the army's strength for Barbarossa received a further setback when he learned that Brauchitsch was allocating additional forces to French coastal security at the expense of those deployed in the east. 'It is not the point', he recorded in frustration, 'to ensure 100% security everywhere, but rather to provide the necessary minimum security, allowing the fullest success for Operation Barbarossa.'[74]

Worse news was to come in Halder's meeting with Hitler on 17 March 1941. Halder had made extensive notes in preparation for the conference which included the addition of satellite forces to reinforce Army Group South. The enemy forces, he now noted, numbered a total of 155 divisions while Halder could muster just 134 divisions. German reserves totalled a mere 21 divisions and of these Halder noted nine were designated for Operation Marita (the planned invasion of the Balkans) leaving just 12 divisions, which Halder himself acknowledged as 'very few!'[75] The conference of 17 March opened with Hitler's insistence that Barbarossa must proceed from the very outset with great successes and no reverses. He then ruled out Halder's hope for allied armies in the south with the dismissive objection that there was no point building operations on unreliable forces. The Finnish forces, he believed, could only be counted on for local successes along the Baltic; the Romanians were seen as completely unreliable with no offensive strength; the Hungarians were mistrusted with no reason for joining the war and the Slovakians, he disdainfully remarked, 'are Slavs', perhaps of later use as occupation forces. German forces, Hitler stated, were the only ones which he could be sure to count on.[76]

---

[73] Franz Halder, KTB II, p. 312 (14 March 1941).
[74] Ibid., p. 313 (15 March 1941).   [75] Ibid., p. 316 (16 March 1941).
[76] Ibid., p. 319 (17 March 1941).

If Halder was disheartened by his stalled attempt to prop up Army Group South's strength with satellite forces, he was to suffer greater disappointment when Hitler declared his intention to reassign the 12th Army (soon to take part in the Balkan campaign). Hitler justified the move by casting doubt on Halder's plan, claiming it 'would be fundamentally wrong to attack everywhere' and insisting that the offensive across the Pruth and Dniester was doomed to fail. The result for Halder was an exacerbation of the problem he had hoped to solve. With the depletion of his forces, no additional allied armies, near non-existent reserves and a radical modification to his strategic plan, Halder should have been well disposed towards confrontation, but his conformist subservience to Hitler's bidding precluded that consequence. Instead, he accepted Hitler's reorganisation of the southern sector providing only for the defence of Romania and adding the remaining forces to the northern thrust of the army group.[77] Not without justification did Ulrich von Hassell write only the day before in his diary: 'Halder and Brauchitsch are nothing more than technical stooges [to Hitler].'[78]

Halder's concession to Hitler in the south was not so easily accepted by the commander of Army Group South, Field Marshal Gerd von Rundstedt, who, concerned for his southern flank and hoping to tie up Soviet forces near the border, made further pleas to Hitler for Hungarian involvement from the Carpathians and a reactivation of the offensive across the Pruth.[79] Such arguments failed to alter Hitler's decision, but reveal the anxiety of Rundstedt and the weakness of Halder in failing to deal directly with Hitler over such important concerns.

At another conference on 30 March Hitler again re-emphasised that Army Group Centre was to advance to the Dnepr and then, using the safety of the river, assemble its strength for the northward thrust. Moscow, Hitler added incidentally, without realising the strongly partisan opinion of Halder, was 'completely irrelevant!' (*völlig gleichgültig!*).[80] If Halder was not motivated to challenge Hitler over his changes to Army Group South, he was certainly not about to reveal his ardent insistence on Moscow as the central war-winning objective. Halder hoped this would be made clear by the early course of the campaign and only if Hitler persisted to oppose his plans would a more direct confrontation have to be contemplated.

---

[77] Ibid., pp. 319–320 (17 March 1941).
[78] Von Hassell, *Vom andern Deutschland*, p. 184 (16 March 1941); Ulrich von Hassell, *The Von Hassell Diaries 1938–1944*, p. 158 (16 March 1941).
[79] Franz Halder, KTB II, p. 338 (30 March 1941).   [80] Ibid., p. 319.

Halder's attempts to subvert Hitler's authority, most notably regarding Moscow, offer much room for misinterpretation of his character and may be regarded by some as evidence of his maverick, non-conformist status, perhaps even offering notions of an officer, formerly opposed to Hitler, and now seeking a war-winning solution for Germany to counter Hitler's confused strategy.[81] Yet such representations would be misleading. Throughout the war Halder's loyalty to the regime never wavered. Not even towards the bitter end in July 1944, when all hope of victory was long since gone and the last vestiges of honourable men within the army resolved to act, did Halder betray his Führer. If Halder was not prepared to abandon Hitler at Germany's lowest ebb, he was in no way inclined to do so before the war had turned and he had suffered the indignity of his dismissal in disgrace. Halder's motivations in circumventing Hitler's authority were governed solely by his desire to advance Germany's conquests through personal conviction of his superior military aptitude.[82] Yet his standing in Hitler's eyes was influenced by precisely the opposite impression. To Hitler, Halder was an acceptable Chief of Staff for his skills as a capable technocrat, but strikingly lacking in his grasp of modern strategic concepts, resulting primarily from his poor submissions prior to the French campaign.[83] Following the triumph in the west, Halder's failure to be recognised among the many newly-created Field Marshals is perhaps the most noteworthy indication of Hitler's disfavour. Halder thus suffered from a lack of prestige, especially on issues of strategic significance, which led to friction, seldom openly expressed, but present nevertheless. It also drove Halder in his quest for redemption and explains his timidity around Hitler, not wishing to set himself back with pessimistic assessments or objections, as he had done prior to the western campaign. The result was a Chief of Staff outwardly loyal and compliant, yet pursuing his own agenda, convinced of his ability and hoping to recapture Hitler's approval through it. The practical consequence in the day-to-day planning for Barbarossa, however, was a man observing unquestioning obedience, without the professional objectivity necessary to adequately evaluate the scope of the undertaking, or the personal courage to withstand Hitler's overbearing personality.

[81] Richard Brett-Smith treads this precarious line, suggesting: 'without Halder's meticulous planning Hitler would have been unable to frame the simplest military operation effectively . . . Halder was surely one of the best brains and ablest Staff officers of his time, but not even he could cope with the strain and uncertainty of working under a psychopath.' Richard Brett-Smith, *Hitler's Generals* (London, 1976), pp. 216, 218.

[82] Leach, 'Halder', pp. 111–112.

[83] Hitler even condemned Halder and Brauchitsch during the planning stages for 'thinking like military cadets': von Kotze (ed.), *Heeresadjutant bei Hitler 1938–1943*, p. 75 (19 February 1940).

Halder's nominal superior at OKH, Field Marshal von Brauchitsch, was a man of even weaker character, not only in his dealings with Hitler but in many respects with Halder too. His ascension to Commander-in-Chief of the Army in 1938 necessitated his willing compliance in Hitler's dictate 'to lead the Army closer towards the state and its philosophy'[84] and Brauchitsch's acquiescence set the tone for his tenure in command. On 18 December 1938 in a directive on army education Brauchitsch declared: 'The officer corps must not allow itself to be surpassed by anyone in the purity and genuineness of its National Socialist *Weltanschauung*' (world-view).[85] Along with Brauchitsch's appointment, a new command structure surrendered the army's previous hegemony over military affairs and installed one of the most spineless and contemptible of all Hitler's officers, Field Marshal Wilhelm Keitel, as chief of the combined armed services. Unlike Halder, Brauchitsch refused any decisive action in the planned coup during the crisis over Czechoslovakia and his passivity continued throughout the war. Worse still, Brauchitsch sanctioned the reprehensible acts of the Wehrmacht and SS in Poland and even sought to justify their atrocities to those courageous individuals who voiced objections.[86] Although portrayed by some to be an unwilling accomplice to the regime without the power to affect its political decisions,[87] an accomplice he nevertheless remains, with moral considerations after the fact counting for nothing. Brauchitsch was an integral and willing servant of the regime whose prosperity and future success were inextricably tied to his own. Yet his close association with Halder and the dominance exerted by the Chief of the General Staff over their relationship[88] caused Brauchitsch, in addition to his own misgivings, to voice doubts over the war in the west, incurring in consequence Hitler's great anger and resentment. The scathing verbal tirade this drew from Hitler and the ultimate success of the operation reduced Brauchitsch's confidence and standing even further.[89] He adopted a meek compliance to Hitler and relied even more on Halder for direction of the army and its

[84] Brian Bond, 'Brauchitsch' in Barnett (ed.), *Hitler's Generals*, p. 77. See also Megargee, *Inside Hitler's High Command*, p. 55.

[85] Jürgen Förster, 'New Wine in Old Skins? The Wehrmacht and the War of "Weltanschauungen", 1941' in Wilhelm Deist (ed.), *The German Military in the Age of Total War* (Warwickshire, 1985), p. 305.

[86] Bond, 'Brauchitsch', pp. 80–81. See also Mitcham, *Hitler's Field Marshals*, p. 63. Richard C. Lukas, *The Forgotten Holocaust. The Poles Under German Occupation 1939–1944* (New York, 1997), p. 3.

[87] Brett-Smith, *Hitler's Generals*, pp. 43–44.

[88] Basil Liddell Hart, *The Other Side of the Hill. Germany's Generals: Their Rise and Fall, With Their Own Account of Military Events, 1939–1945* (London, 1999), p. 87.

[89] Von Manstein, *Lost Victories*, p. 76; John Wheeler-Bennett, *The Nemesis of Power. The German Army in Politics 1918–1945* (New York, 1969), pp. 471–472.

military policy. Halder exploited this weakness, using it to garner support for his subversion of Hitler's Directive 21, and rapidly established himself as the true authority within the army.

Brauchitsch and Halder's scheming over Moscow did not include the field commanders of Army Group Centre and their instructions were accordingly vague and ambiguous. In his post-war memoir Guderian complained: 'I received at my headquarters only bare indications of the Supreme Command's intentions for the second phase of the operation after the first objective (in the case of my corps the area Roslavl–Elnya–Smolensk) had been reached.'[90] The commander of Panzer Group 3, Colonel-General Hermann Hoth, stated that he learned only after the war of the full text contained within War Directive 21 and the Barbarossa deployment directive. Until then Hoth claimed to have no knowledge of the plan to turn his forces northward and assist Army Group North. In this regard Brauchitsch and Halder's control of information was assisted by Hitler's January 1941 order limiting knowledge of the campaign to a commander's immediate zone of operations, which prohibited a more general conception of Hitler's intentions.[91] Utilising this advantage, Brauchitsch and Halder could pass on all orders through Army Group Centre giving their own subtle interpretation, always with emphasis on keeping the operation and its commanders directed towards Moscow. As Hoth wrote:

In fact within Panzer Group 3 itself, everyone was driven by the thought that they were on the way to Moscow. One must understand, if the Commander-in-Chief of the Army [Brauchitsch] would have been determined to fulfil Hitler's wishes, he would have informed the commander of the troops.[92]

Without question Brauchitsch and Halder avoided giving anything too exact in their instructions for the secondary phase of the operations, but they could not directly contradict Hitler by stating that the one and only goal was to seize Moscow. To accept that Hoth was really so utterly ignorant of the plan to turn his panzers northward may give Brauchitsch and Halder too much credit for concealment. Possibly Hoth had his own connections at OKH, or maybe there was something Bock or another of the Field Marshals learned and passed on; in any case, the first phase of the operational plans gave rise to some unwanted questioning by Hoth. The issue at stake was the direction of Hoth's initial thrust and where this would leave his forces for the secondary operation. As Bock observed in

---

[90] Guderian, *Panzer Leader*, p. 149.
[91] Hermann Hoth, *Panzer-Operationen. Die Panzergruppe 3 und der operative Gedanke der deutschen Führung Sommer 1941* (Heidelberg, 1956), p. 48.
[92] Ibid.

his diary on 18 March 1941: 'The initial deployment of Panzer Group 3 for the attack is difficult. Hoth is casting his eyes beyond the Dnepr and Dvina from the very outset and is paying scant attention to the possibility of attacking and defeating enemy forces which stand and fight somewhat farther forward.'[93] If Hoth was in fact oblivious to Hitler's intentions for his panzer group, his stance must be seen purely in terms of favouring a large encirclement for the first operational manoeuvre. If Hoth, however, was aware of Hitler's intentions, then making the rapid drive for the Dvina would provide the best springboard for a thrust northwards.

Naturally, Hoth was striving for the most economical employment of his forces and, irrespective of whether he was viewing Moscow or Leningrad as the secondary objective, both argued strongly for him to keep his weight on the left flank and not be drawn into the centre. Essentially he hoped for a direct thrust on the Dvina, seizing bridgeheads along the river west of Vitebsk and creating, in tandem with Panzer Group 2's drive to the Dnepr, a giant ring closed on the great rivers. From this position Hoth's further operations to either the north-east (Leningrad) or east (Moscow) would be best served. Yet the OKH insisted that the great mass of Soviet strength lay between the border zone and Minsk, allowing a decisive blow to be struck. There may also have been a latent fear on Brauchitsch and Halder's part that allowing Hoth's panzers such a favourable development for the northward swing towards Leningrad would endanger their own designs. Conceivably, they therefore sought to concentrate Hoth's armoured strength in the centre of the front before a continued advance eastward. The decision for a smaller encirclement centred on Minsk created the dilemma for Hoth, who clearly saw the incompatibitly of having to secure the Dvina rapidly, with a south-easterly diversion to Minsk. 'But', as Bock noted, 'the Army Command . . . in its directives is demanding that the panzer groups assist in the destruction of the enemy forces in the frontier zone [i.e. the region west of Minsk], I will have to reject Hoth's solution, even though there is much to be said in its favour.'

Foreseeing the bitterness the dispute could engender, Bock dispatched his operations officer, Lieutenant-Colonel Henning von Tresckow, to OKH to ensure the sincerity of their commitment to the Minsk operation, especially in the light of Hoth's justifiable concerns.[94] Brauchitsch and Halder did not welcome a discussion in detail of such sensitive operations and they refused to be drawn on the issue, placating Tresckow with vague, non-committal answers. Irritated at such vacillation, Bock

---

[93] Fedor von Bock, KTB 'Vorbereitungszeit', Fol. 9, *War Diary*, p. 203 (18 March 1941).
[94] Ibid. (18 March 1941).

took up the matter personally on 27 March during an OKH meeting with the army and panzer group commanders. Here Bock was under no illusions as to the fundamental issue at stake and was frustrated by the preoccupation with what he saw as 'minor details'. Indeed he was given the same treatment as Tresckow, with Halder attempting to skip over the issue,[95] forcing Bock to complain in his diary:

When I mentioned the matter of the linking up of both my panzer groups in the Minsk area and the difficulties of their subsequent advance from there, I received no clear statement on it, the same sort of answer Tresckow had received in Berlin recently. The question is important, for between Minsk and the 'gateway to Smolensk' – the land bridge between the Dniepr and the Dvina – lie the marshes from which the Beresina springs; massing armoured forces near Minsk would therefore be very detrimental to their further forward movement.[96]

We may safely surmise that Bock's attention was directed by Halder towards Smolensk as the next operational objective, adding to the Field Marshal's concern about the density of marshlands to be traversed. Unaware of the divergent plans of the OKH and Hitler pulling his armoured strength in different directions, Bock had cause to welcome an opportunity for discussion of the planned operations with Hitler a few days later on 30 March. The conference was also attended by Brauchitsch and Halder who were evidently prepared to play along with Hitler's intentions as they had done in all previous discussions, but neither had thought to forbid Bock from raising the matter openly with Hitler. When Hitler surveyed the operations in the Baltic and around Leningrad he made reference to the likelihood of Bock's armoured groups impacting events decisively. The difficulties this would entail with a diversion of forces first to Minsk and later Smolensk, as well as the entanglement of marshes and the ever-present vast distances, forced Bock to seize his moment. 'I once again spoke of the difficulties facing a subsequent advance by the tanks out of the area assigned to me at Minsk.' According to Bock, as he outlined the problem, Brauchitsch, somewhat embarrassed and desperate to play it down, interjected 'that "link-up at Minsk" was intended to mean the general area of Minsk'. This attempt to trivialise Bock's concern and

---

[95] This approach was also reflected in Halder's diary which contains no mention of the discussion and even makes the extraordinary statement next to his sub-heading 'AGp Centre' (Army Group Centre) 'No significantly new viewpoints'. Halder then goes on to record an issue of comparatively minor importance between 9th Army and Panzer Group 3. Given Bock's fury over the outcome it is hard to believe Halder was oblivious to his reaction. The avoidance of such an essential detail, however, is typical of Halder's diary on all questions concerning his covert plans for Moscow. Halder no doubt understood the explosive potential of keeping a written record of his deceit, especially since he must have assessed its future historical value in terms of Third Reich historians above all others.

[96] Fedor von Bock, KTB 'Vorbereitungszeit', Fol. 10, *War Diary*, p. 205 (27 March 1941).

belittle the issue in front of Hitler angered Bock all the more because specific orders to the contrary had been issued by the OKH – a fact Bock pointed out to Halder at the conclusion of the meeting when he remarked: 'You have issued written orders that the panzer groups are to advance "in close contact".' Like Brauchitsch, Halder sought again to make light of the fact, retorting with a laugh: 'Spiritual contact is what was meant!' The ambiguity of this response, coupled with the apparent failure of Halder and Brauchitsch to grasp the difficulties involved, especially with discussion of supporting operations as far north as Leningrad, disgusted Bock, whose final comment summed up his utter failure to resolve the matter: 'That clarified nothing!'[97] Importantly for Brauchitsch and Halder, Hitler seems to have been adequately convinced this was a minor internal matter of the army without perceiving any threat to his intended strike northwards. This could have a number of explanations; either Bock was cut off before he was able to outline the full extent of his concerns or Hitler, in a typically boundless over-estimation of German strength, simply did not share the Field Marshal's assessment.

The vague issue of closing the first armoured ring at Minsk remained unattended until Tresckow finally extracted a firm commitment from Brauchitsch in mid-May, which confirmed that Panzer Group 3 would advance over the Molodechno land bridge to link up with Panzer Group 2 in the area around Minsk. Further operations directed eastwards were to be preceded by an advance north around the Beresina marshes. Although Tresckow's report represented clear instructions and a welcome resolution to what Bock called the 'foggy order concerning the link-up of the two panzer groups',[98] it nevertheless did not satisfy Bock's or Hoth's initial concerns over closing the first armoured ring so soon. No open dialogue took place because in the closed circle of discussion that was not possible. For Brauchitsch and Halder, it was only important that OKH's orders be followed and that Hitler not be drawn into strategic questions concerning the direction of the campaign or, so far as possible, even be made aware of their existence.

Barbarossa – the zenith of war

Until spring 1941 the campaign in the east was presented and explained by Hitler largely in terms of the wider war against Britain and the related advantages for possible future conflict with the United States. Yet as the

---

[97] Ibid., Fol. 12, p. 208 (30 March 1941). Despite a lengthy entry for 30 March Halder's diary is again devoid of discussion of Bock's dissatisfaction, suggesting once more his desire for concealment.

[98] Ibid., Fol. 17, p. 214 (14–16 May 1941).

campaign approached, his interest shifted more and more from strategic and geopolitical considerations to his long-held racial and ideological beliefs. As early as his 1925 publication of *Mein Kampf* these ideas had been given clear expression:

We take up where we broke off six hundred years ago. We stop the endless German movement to the south and west, and turn our gaze toward the land in the east. At long last we break off the colonial and commercial policy of the pre-War period and shift to the soil policy of the future. If we speak of soil in Europe today, we can primarily have in mind only Russia and her vassal border states.[99]

Reiterating this point, his second book, written in 1928, asserted:

The size of a people is a variable factor. It will be a rising one in the case of a healthy people. Yes, the increase alone can secure the future of a people... The growth in population could only be compensated by growth – expansion – of the Lebensraum.[100] For Germany, a future alliance with Russia has no sense... On the contrary... that would have prevented us from seeking the goal of German foreign policy in the one and only place possible: space in the East.[101]

Upon his accession to power, Hitler declared to his generals on 3 February 1933 that the purpose of the new Wehrmacht was for 'conquering new Lebensraum in the East and ruthlessly Germanizing it'.[102] The advent of the Molotov–Ribbentrop Pact in August 1939 was the product of political convenience and represented no more than a short-term 'tactical maneuver'.[103] Finally, at the end of March 1941 Hitler gathered his generals to announce the beginning of what he called 'Colonial tasks!', requiring a '*Clash of two ideologies*' for which the Wehrmacht would have to partake in 'a war of extermination'.[104]

Hitler's words signalled a fundamental change in the nature of the war and the previous approach of the German army in conceptualising and engaging its enemy. Although atrocities had been perpetrated in Poland and in other occupied countries, the eastern front deserves careful attention in order to understand what kind of war Hitler was planning and the resulting implications for the war's turning point. For this purpose, a brief elaboration on terminology is in order.

---

[99] Italics in the original. Adolf Hitler, *Mein Kampf* (New York, 1999), p. 654.
[100] Although this book dates from 1928 it was not in fact published until after the war. Gerhard Weinberg (ed.), *Hitler's Second Book* (New York, 2003), p. 17. In English this book is sometimes referred to by the title of an earlier edition: '*Hitler's Secret Book*'.
[101] Ibid., p. 152.   [102] Ibid., p. xxii.
[103] Von Below, *Als Hitlers Adjutant 1937–45*, p. 184.
[104] Italics in the original. Franz Halder, *KTB II*, pp. 336–337 (30 March 1941). See also Hürter, *Hitlers Heerführer*, pp. 205–222.

Owing to its rapidly developing ideological nature, Operation Barbarossa represents a clear break from all previous German campaigns of World War II.[105] Even apart from the obvious military and strategic implications of open conflict between Germany and the Soviet Union, the campaign in the east represents a watershed in the basic character of the war itself. This differentiation is best understood through Erich Ludendorff's definition of 'total war' from his 1935 study *Der Totale Krieg*.[106] Defining this difference is not helped by the common usage of the term 'total war' in the vast annals of Anglo-American military literature, especially in regard to categorising the First and Second World Wars. The contention by Ludendorff is unique, however, for its radical, even extremist application of war and at the same time its close approximation to the methods adopted by National Socialist Germany. For Ludendorff, war should aim for 'the annihilation of the enemy Army and of the enemy nation',[107] the essential aspect being the lack of distinction between combatants and non-combatants, thus creating the precondition for unrestrained violence directed indiscriminately against a civilian populace. Ludendorff's definition of total war, Beatrice Heuser has concluded, encompassed two essential elements; the total application of the modern war machine combined with a genocidal policy.[108]

In pursuing the conquest of the Soviet Union, the German war aims began to envisage far more than a purely military victory, transforming the struggle into a war of annihilation or 'total war' directed against an enemy nation of perceived inferior racial stock with a competing and hostile ideology. The totality of the coming war was reflected in Hitler's instruction in early March 1941 that Barbarossa was to be 'more than a mere clash of arms; it is also a conflict between two ideologies. In view of the extent of the space involved, *the striking down of the enemy armed forces will not suffice to bring about an end to the war.*'[109] Clearly, Ludendorff's conception of war against the enemy nation was reaching its fruition.

---

[105] There is a strong case to be made for ideological similarities between Operation Barbarossa and the Polish campaign, but one should not under-estimate the drastic radicalisation of German policies between September 1939 and June 1941.

[106] Erich Ludendorff, *Der Totale Krieg* (Munich, 1935). The translation appears under the title *The Nation at War* (London, 1936).

[107] Ludendorff, *The Nation at War*, p. 168.

[108] Beatrice Heuser, *The Bomb. Nuclear Weapons in their Historical Strategic and Ethical Context* (Harlow, 2000), p. 109. In regard to applying this definition it could be argued that although the bulk of Germany's military might was employed against the Soviet Union from June 1941 it was only later that Germany's economy was likewise switched to a total war footing.

[109] Italics mine. KTB OKW, Volume I, p. 341 (3 March 1941).

The fanatical ideals contained within Hitler's 'total war' philosophy formed a radical departure from his past campaigns and necessitated a degree of brutality and harshness hitherto unseen in Europe since the genocidal campaigns of the Thirty Years' War (1618–1648). The concept of 'total war', however, was identified at the time by the more acceptable term of a 'New Order', which determined the methods and policies of occupation in the newly-won territories of the east. The ruthless ideological dictates of this work and the huge area to be administered demanded the willing complicity of the armed forces which would have to operate both directly and in close contact with the murderous excesses of the genocidal policy. Indeed, the cordial relationship between the Wehrmacht and the other agencies of the regime such as the SS and SD[110] belies the myth of ignorance or formal separation from the barbarous German rule, which many generals (and lower-ranking veterans) later claimed in their defence.

While a detailed assessment of the Wehrmacht's participation in the 'total war' to be fought in the east is beyond the scope of this study, it is important to establish its impact on the will of the Soviet people to resist. The methods of 'total war' threatened not only the existence of the Soviet state, but the survival of the Soviet people themselves, who responded with an indignant conviction of assured righteousness, maximised by the scale of German atrocities. In the advent of an unforeseen setback or major delay in the German campaign, the consequences of an unrestrained genocidal policy are plainly apparent. This highlights the German faith in their ultimate triumph and the belief that it could be achieved before an organised Soviet response would be possible. Given the tenuous state of German preparations for war, the planned ruthless exploitation and wanton cruelty towards the Soviet population attain greatly increased significance in determining the advent of a turning point once the assumed decisive military solution had failed to materialise.

Hitler's announcement at the end of March that a war of annihilation was to be conducted in the east was received by the 250 assembled army commanders with attitudes ranging from inactive ambivalence to fervent enthusiasm. Embracing a position more in line with the latter, Halder observed after Hitler's speech: 'commanders must make the sacrifice of overcoming their personal scruples'.[111] His diary records none of the shock or moral revulsion that he later claimed to have felt and there was no

---

[110] Helmut Krausnick and Hans-Heinrich Wilhelm, *Die Truppe des Weltanschauungskrieges: Die Einsatzgruppen der Sicherheitspolizei und des SD 1938–1942* (Stuttgart, 1981). See also Theo Schulte, *The German Army and the Nazi Policies in Occupied Russia* (Oxford, 1989), Chapter 9, 'German Army Relations with the SS/SD'; Raul Hilberg, *The Destruction of the European Jews* (Chicago, 1973), pp. 196–197.

[111] Franz Halder, KTB II, p. 337 (30 March 1941).

rush of complaints or criticism from his fellow officers.[112] However, even if one accepts Omer Bartov's well argued contention that the Wehrmacht was a deeply integrated and willing component of the National Socialist state,[113] this offers only part of the explanation of their complete failure to recognise the military implications of such a radicalised war. Without question, the severe measures of a 'total war' were bound to engender strong anti-German sentiment provoking popular resistance and legitimising Soviet propaganda attempts to provide a unifying cause for the struggle. Although difficult to assess accurately, a 'total war' would also preclude whatever opportunity existed for broad collaboration among the occupied populations. In addition, the exploitation of strong nationalist yearnings, particularly within the Ukraine and Baltic states, was largely squandered by the ardent imperative of racial supremacy and insistence on absolute German domination. Even considerations for the welfare of German prisoners of war, who could expect reprisals, failed to move the army commanders, who remained defiantly oblivious to the substantial military implications of a radicalised war on the scale being discussed. The only way to account for this staggering oversight or illogical acceptance by army commanders is the charged intensity of the inferior 'foe image' and associated self-assurance in the primacy of the Wehrmacht's training, technical capacity and even racial superiority. Indeed, as Gerhard Weinberg has argued, it was precisely their coloured ideological and racial world-view that provided Hitler and his generals with an added measure of confidence in casting their gaze to the east. Germany's most important and dangerous enemies were judged to have been in the west and the ease of their defeat only made the conquest of the Soviet Union appear all the more certain.[114] These factors left no doubt that a war would be won quickly without any regard for the prospect of a long and bitterly contested struggle.

In spite of the disadvantageous military implications, the army commanders did more than just accept Hitler's notion of the new 'total war'. Like many elements in the genocidal process undertaken within the Third Reich, its advancement was sustained not in spite of the army, but largely in accordance with its wishes and fervent desires.[115] This

---

[112] Warlimont, *Im Hauptquartier*, Band I, p. 177; Robert Cecil, *Hitler's Decision to Invade Russia 1941*, p. 157. Warlimont's contention that most officers present failed to follow Hitler's speech or could not grasp its true signifance is simply untenable.

[113] Bartov, 'Soldiers, Nazis, and War', p. 60.

[114] Gerhard Weinberg, '22 June 1941: The German View', *War in History* 3(2) (1996), 228–229.

[115] Helpful in understanding the evolution of the relationship between the Wehrmacht and the NSDAP is the insightful essay by Jürgen Förster, 'Motivation and Indoctrination in the Wehrmacht, 1933–45' in Paul Addison and Angus Calder (eds.), *A Time to Kill. The Soldier's Experience of War in the West 1939–1945* (London, 1997), pp. 263–273.

curiously detrimental effort on the part of the army, which was always in competition for resources, suggests the dominance of political allegiance above strictly practical considerations. In the same way high-ranking party officials operated with unquestioning obedience to Hitler first, before adequately addressing the confused and disjointed administrative structures that typified the Third Reich's organisations. The army was therefore the victim of its own ideological bias and political subservience, proving, to its detriment, only too willing to embrace the next chapter in the purest application of National Socialist doctrine as determined by Hitler.

Field Marshal von Brauchitsch, as the Commander-in-Chief of the Army, led this new call to arms, rousing his officers to carry out the upcoming campaign as 'a struggle between two different races, requiring... troops to act with all necessary harshness'.[116] His subordinate commanders followed suit with even more explicit and harshly worded orders. Colonel-General Erich Hoepner, commander of Panzer Group 4, proclaimed on 2 May 1941:

The objective of this battle must be the destruction of present day Russia and it must therefore be conducted with unprecedented severity. Every military action must be guided in planning and execution by an iron will to exterminate the enemy mercilessly and totally. In particular no adherents of the present Russian-Bolshevik system are to be spared.[117]

Hoepner's reference to eliminating Bolshevik elements, notably political commissars within the Red Army, was soon translated into army policy with the drafting of the Commissar Order formally issued on 6 June 1941.[118] This charged the army with responsibility for widespread executions to be administered immediately without recourse to any form of legal procedure. Equally severe was the Barbarossa Directive issued 13 May 1941[119] which decreed the execution of all civilians who 'attacked' German soldiers, with the formal interpretation of 'attacked' extended to

[116] Jürgen Förster, 'The German Army and the Ideological War against the Soviet Union' in Gerhard Hirschfeld (ed.), *The Politics of Genocide: Jews and Soviet Prisoners of War in Nazi Germany* (London, 1986), p. 17.
[117] Förster, 'New Wine in Old Skins?', p. 310; Jürgen Förster, 'Das Unternehmen "Barbarossa" als Eroberungs- und Vernichtungskrieg' in Militärgeschichtlichen Forschungsamt (ed.), *Das Deutsche Reich und der Zweite Weltkrieg*, p. 446.
[118] Moritz (ed.), *Fall Barbarossa*, p. 321, Document 100: 'Richtlinien des Chefs des OKW für die Verfolgung und Ermordung der Politischen Funktionäre der Sowjetunion (Kommissarbefehl), 6. Juni 1941'.
[119] Moritz (ed.), *Fall Barbarossa*, p. 316, Document 97: 'Erlaß Hitlers über Gewaltmaßnahmen gegen die sowjetische Bevölkerung und über die Einschränkung der Bestrafung von Wehrmachtangehörigen für Kriegsverbrechen in der Sowjetunion (Kriegsgerichtsbarkeitsbefehl), 13. Mai 1941'.

include such innocuous acts as the distribution of leaflets or the failure to follow German orders.[120] The Barbarossa Directive also exempted German soldiers from prosecution for all offences against the Soviet population deemed 'ideologically motivated'.[121]

As Christian Streit has ably demonstrated, despite the emphatic post-war denials of Halder and many of his fellow generals, the so-called 'criminal orders' were dutifully prepared by the army, with Halder play-ing a central part. Indeed it was through his insistence that a clause was introduced to the Barbarossa Directive which permitted officers to order the razing of villages and the outright execution of inhabitants if it was suspected that villages were supporting partisans.[122] At Army Group Centre, Bock made no attempt to protest against these orders and main-tained this stance even in August 1941 when the mass killing of innocent Jewish civilians was reported to him.[123] As Michael Geyer has accurately observed, it was through such policies that German strategy reached its zenith: 'where racist domination, and the reforging of German society into a master race were brought together, linking in a grand concen-tric movement all the previously disconnected and nascent dynamics of the state against a single target. The Russo-German war encompassed not just the battlefronts, but also the battle zones and the rear areas.'[124] Casting a deserved moral judgement on the leadership of the army, while retaining his perspective on the political liability, von Hassell recorded in his diary:

---

[120] Christian Streit, 'Partisans – Resistance – Prisoners of War' in Joseph Wieczynski (ed.), *Operation Barbarossa. The German Attack on the Soviet Union June 22, 1941* (Salt Lake City, 1993), p. 262.

[121] Christian Streit, 'The German Army and the Policies of Genocide' in Gerhard Hirschfeld (ed.), *The Policies of Genocide: Jews and Soviet Prisoners of War in Nazi Germany* (London, 1986), pp. 3–4; Jürgen Förster, 'The Dynamics of Volksgemein-schaft: The Effectiveness of the German Military Establishment in the Second World War' in Allan Millett and Williamson Murray (eds.), *Military Effectiveness*, Volume III: *The Second World War* (Winchester, 1988), pp. 196–197.

[122] Streit, 'Partisans', pp. 262–263; Christian Streit, *Keine Kameraden: Die Wehrmacht und die sowjetischen Kriegsgefangenen 1941–1945* (Stuttgart, 1978), pp. 37–46, 313. See also Gerd R. Ueberschär, *Generaloberst Franz Halder* (Zürich, 1991), pp. 63–64. Like most of the German generals, Halder's role in the war of annihilation only came into focus after his death. Prior to that he worked for fifteen years with the US Army Histor-ical Division and in 1961 was awarded the Meritorious Civilian Service Award, the highest American civilian award, for his services to the army. See Christian Hartmann, 'Franz Halder – Der verhinderte Generalstabschef' in Ronald Smelser and Enrico Syring (eds.), *Die Militärelite des Dritten Reiches. 27 biographische Skizzen* (Berlin, 1995), p. 218.

[123] Horst Mühleisen, 'Fedor von Bock – Soldat ohne Fortune' in Ronald Smelser and Enrico Syring (eds.), *Die Militärelite des Dritten Reiches. 27 biographische Skizzen* (Berlin, 1995), p. 72.

[124] Geyer, 'German Strategy', p. 574.

[I]t makes one's hair stand on end to learn about and receive proof of orders signed by Halder and distributed to the troops as to measures to be taken in Russia, and about the systematic transformation of military law concerning the conquered population into uncontrolled despotism – indeed a caricature of all law. This kind of thing turns the German into a 'Boche'; it develops a type of being which had existed only in enemy propaganda. Brauchitsch has sacrificed the honour of the German Army in submitting to these orders of Hitler.[125]

The close relationship between the German army's preparations in the lead up to Barbarossa and what Omer Bartov has dubbed 'the barbarisation of warfare'[126] cannot be called into question.[127] As a result, the conflict inadvertently incorporated a latent point of no return; failure to achieve a decisive military victory in the early phase of the war would ensure political solidification of the Soviet Union's war effort, allowing it to exploit fully the immense potential of its natural, industrial and manpower resources.[128]

Clearly, ideology was a driving force in the conceptualisation of the coming campaign, offering Hitler his long-desired showdown with Bolshevism and justifying the genocide about to be undertaken. Hitler, however, was also greatly influenced by what he saw as the direct practical benefits of Barbarossa. Hitler gave great weight to economic requirements, having always preferred conquest to meet his requirements over a more cautious or drawn-out strategy. His abiding economic advisors

---

[125] Von Hassell, *Vom andern Deutschland*, p. 200 (4 May 1941 – referring to a discussion on 8 April). See also von Hassell's comments, p. 209 (16 June 1941); von Hassell, *Diaries*, p. 173 (4 May 1941). See also von Hassell's comments, p. 189 (16 June 1941).

[126] Omer Bartov, *The Eastern Front, 1941–45, German Troops and the Barbarisation of Warfare* (London, 1985).

[127] See also Bodan Musial, '*Konterrevolutionäre Elemente sind zu erschiessen*'. *Die Brutalisierung des deutsch-sowjetischen Krieges im Sommer 1941* (Berlin, 2000). There is also no mitigating credibility to attempts by Ernst Nolte to ameliorate the deliberate German intent to pursue genocide with claims that these were simply a repetition of Soviet practices since the revolution and therefore not a new or profoundly significant development in the spiral of violence taking place in the east: Ernst Nolte, 'Zwischen Geschichtslegende und Revisionismus? Das Dritte Reich im Blickwinkel des Jahres 1980' in *Historikerstreit. Die Dokumentation der Kontroverse um die Einzigartigkeit der nationalsozialistischen Judenvernichtung*, 6th edn (Munich, 1987), pp. 13–15.

[128] Interestingly, Robert Thurston's research suggests that in spite of German brutality and the harsh rule of the Stalinist state, in particular the purges of the late 1930s, most Red Army men still fought out of a voluntary desire to serve the Soviet state. Robert Thurston, 'Cauldrons of Loyalty and Betrayal: Soviet Soldiers' Behavior, 1941 and 1945' in Robert Thurston and Bernd Bonwetsch (eds.), *The People's War. Responses to World War II in the Soviet Union* (Chicago, 2000), pp. 235–250. Additionally, a leading work by John Barber and Mark Harrison has noted that the Soviet population's widespread support for the war effort existed independently of the state terror apparatus. John Barber and Mark Harrison, *The Soviet Home Front 1941–1945: A Social and Economic History of the USSR in World War II* (London, 1991), pp. 12–13, 60, 68.

had fed this ambition with baseless optimism, not unlike that which had biased General Thomas's recent study. The state secretary in the ministry of food and agriculture, Herbert Backe, assured Hitler in January that 'the occupation of the Ukraine would liberate us from every economic worry'.[129] By the spring of 1941 such emphatic guarantees were assuming an acute importance given dwindling food stocks and the worrying forecast that, after July, Germany would be reliant, for better or worse, on the summer's harvest yield. Hitler was also heavily influenced by the collapse of the German home front in 1918, which resulted in large measure from the British naval blockade and the consequent food shortages.[130] Ever sensitive to public opinion, the experience of Germany's defeat in World War I was uppermost in Hitler's mind and he prioritised a high standard of living for the home front. Not only did these factors direct Hitler's attention to the economic solution that Barbarossa proposed to offer, but they also account, in large measure, for his fixation with grand strategic objectives of a war-economic kind, over the purely military and operational considerations which attracted Halder.[131]

Along with the grain shortage, Germany's limited access to basic raw materials essential to the war economy formed a growing component of the economic quandary consuming Germany by the spring of 1941, and driving Hitler's conception of the forthcoming campaign. Foremost among these was the supply of Romanian oil which proved insufficient to the demands of occupied Europe and the German war economy, prompting Hitler in May to slash domestic consumption and foreign exports to Axis allies. The rationing became so severe that Walther Funk, minister for economic affairs, complained to Jodl in June 1941 that the economy was receiving 'even less than 18 per cent of peacetime consumption' and that in consequence the economy had been 'threshed to the limit'.[132] The crippling shortages convinced Hitler to seek his remedy through direct control over the Caucasian oil fields, reinforcing further the role of economic considerations in Hitler's strategic deliberations, ultimately designed to alleviate industry bottlenecks and fulfil his long-desired goal of economic autarky.

[129] BA-MA, RW 19/164, 'OKW/Wehrwirtschafts- und Rüstungssamt', Fol. 126 (30 January 1941).
[130] Alex J. Kay, *Exploitation, Resettlement, Mass Murder: Political and Economic Planning for German Occupation Policy in the Soviet Union, 1940–1941* (Oxford, 2006), pp. 7–8; Cecil, *Hitler's Decision to Invade Russia 1941*, p. 137.
[131] Müller, 'Von der Wirtschaftsallianz', pp. 159–160; Christian Gerlach, *Kalkulierte Morde. Die deutsche Wirtschafts- und Vernichtungspolitik in Weißrussland 1941 bis 1944* (Hamburg, 2000), pp. 59–76.
[132] As cited by Joel Hayward, *Stopped at Stalingrad. The Luftwaffe and Hitler's Defeat in the East, 1942–1943* (Lawrence, 1998), p. 6.

Beyond the alluring economic benefits, Hitler was drawn to Barbarossa for its sweeping geo-strategic advantages, crucial to the continental empire he sought to build. Whatever dubious credence one may extend to Hitler's earlier justifications that Britain was only holding out in the hope of support from the Soviet Union, it cannot be denied that the elimination of such a large power would have dire consequences for the British war effort. Hitler's timing for Barbarossa was tied to the continuing war against Britain, not just for its obvious strategic value, but because it would realise his much-cherished expansionist goals before peace could intervene. Far from fearing the opening of a second front, Hitler's self-assurance meant he was more concerned about domestic rather than military considerations. 'A conflict is inevitable', Halder recorded him as saying in February 1941. 'Once England is finished, he would not be able to rouse the German people to a fight against Russia; consequently Russia would have to be disposed of first.'[133] Clearly Hitler foresaw absolute domination of the continent as integral not just to his immediate war plans against Britain, but to forging an empire capable of uninhibited potential.

Barbarossa therefore represented to Hitler the culmination of his lifelong struggle against alleged Jewish Bolshevik interests, achieving the destruction of what he perceived to be his natural enemies while ensuring the security and prosperity of the German people through *Lebensraum*. On at least equal par, the campaign incorporated more immediate strategic and economic objectives vital to the pressing needs of the day. The contrast this makes with Halder's divergent strategic concept, chiefly centred around Moscow, and the absence of an open dialogue between the two, which Halder purposefully avoided and Hitler was largely incapable of having, paves with certainty the road towards confrontation. Yet if there was one thing the two men did agree upon it was that Barbarossa would represent another stirring triumph of German arms. They foresaw the achievement of everything that was hoped for, without regard to the striking materiel and manpower shortages that would have to be overcome in order to meet the hefty demands of the operational plan.

[133] Franz Halder, KTB II, p. 283.

3 Barbarossa's sword – Hitler's armed forces in 1941

Carrying fear before them and expectation behind – Hitler's panzer arm

Materiel deficiencies within the army were in no way a sudden or surprising occurrence, having dogged it since the start of the war. They could hardly be attributed to battlefield losses which had been relatively light. Instead, the lack of coherent overall direction, systemic inefficiency, corrupt officialdom, rivalries between the armed services, stifling bureaucracy, and the poorly co-ordinated actions of economic planners, military commanders and industrialists led to the army's predicament. Added to this was the inherent shortage of manpower, raw materials and specialised machine tools. The result was plain; while the Soviet Union and Britain almost doubled their armament production in only the second year of the war, and the United States tripled theirs, Germany's armament production stagnated and achieved no further growth between 1940 and 1941.[1]

Beyond administrative complexities, Germany's armament industry also suffered from structural flaws owing to the specialised assembly process which, as a rule, turned out technically advanced, high-quality weapons in a daunting multiplicity of makes and designs, but for these reasons proved unsuited to the demands of mass production. Underscoring the extent of industrial dispersal and accordant organisational overlap is the bewildering array of armaments being constructed which at its height saw 425 different models of aircraft in production, and equipped the army with 150 different makes of trucks and motor-cycles.[2] Eventually the gross impracticality of this confused and inefficient system drew a harsh rebuke from Hitler, who insisted in May 1941 that 'more primitive, robust construction' must follow with the introduction of 'crude mass-production'.[3] Even if immediately enacted such measures would have

---

[1] Müller, 'Von der Wirtschaftsallianz', p. 183.
[2] Overy, *Why the Allies Won*, p. 201.   [3] Ibid., p. 203.

been too late to have any bearing on the assembling invasion force. However, they do reflect the lamentable state of the German war economy
and its inability to come of age before the crucial turning point of the war
was reached. Indeed, true reform of the armaments sector proved to be
another whimsical flirtation of Hitler's erratic mind and soon succumbed
to his over inflated self-assurance in the success of Barbarossa. Accordingly, War Directive 32 (issued 11 June 1941) opened with the conceited
claim: 'After the destruction of the Soviet Armed Forces Germany and
Italy will be military masters of the European continent.' It then went
on to formally direct the main industrial effort towards the air force and
navy.[4]

The shift away from army production was not a new occurrence, having
been a feature of the incoherent armaments policy pursued since the
defeat of France. After first reducing the size of the army in the wake
of the victory in the west, the later prospect of an eastern campaign
forced a reversal, increasing it to 180 divisions and doubling the number
of armoured divisions. Yet, in spite of the extensive expansion, the army
was relegated by the OKW to third place among the priorities of the three
services – a decision that went unchallenged by Hitler and the OKH.[5]
Again, rank over-confidence in the coming campaign was to blame, with
Jodl stating:

The next intended army operation can be easily carried through with the present
strength and munitions allotment . . . If we must soon carry out such a great
campaign then one can do it just the same with 12 panzer divisions as with 24
panzer brigades as more will not be available before spring anyway. In that case
one saves an enormous amount of auxiliary weapons and rearward services.[6]

Echoing this audacious assessment, the army's weapons department later
concluded that the reduced capacities and existing stockpiles would be
sufficient to cope with '*all* conceivable future requirements of the war'.[7]

The implications for Barbarossa were profound. Not only was the army
lightly armed, but rectifying the problem by switching resources back to
it would be a laborious process requiring many months before tangible
results could be seen on the battlefield. Yet the short campaigning season
and the time demands of the operational plan did not allow for this,
meaning the war would have to be won rapidly without recourse to,
or reliance on, new industrial production, which in any case was being
squeezed to a trickle.

---

[4] Trevor-Roper (ed.), *Hitler's War Directives 1939–1945*, p. 130.
[5] Müller, 'Von der Wirtschaftsallianz', p. 177.
[6] Thomas, *Geschichte der deutschen Wehr- und Rüstungswirtschaft (1918–1943/45)*, p. 437.
[7] As cited by Müller, 'Von der Wirtschaftsallianz', p. 179.

The one outstanding exception to the army's austerity measures was nevertheless a revealing one. In May 1941 production of armoured fighting vehicles was not only protected from being cut back, but plans were afoot to embark on a massive new initiative with all the hallmarks of illusory planning that typified the preparation for Barbarossa. The plan, known as 'armour programme 41', was based on achieving the projected target of June 1940, completely outfitting 20 panzer divisions and ten motorised divisions. At a minimum this would necessitate the construction of some 34,661 vehicles, requiring an unattainable fivefold expansion of the current manufacturing capacities and a completion date of December 1944. Beyond this the programme took no account of design modifications or new models and blindly included the continued construction of the Mark II light tank which was already considered obsolete.[8] Likewise, projections in August 1940 for properly fielding 180 divisions with all requisite men and materiel proved demanding enough to require a full three years to achieve.[9] Such impractical plans reflect the degree of delusion that pervaded the upper circles of the Wehrmacht, offering a further insight into the lack of reality underpinning the strategic thinking of Hitler and his senior commanders.

To make an informed analysis of the military campaign against the Soviet Union one must first gain a rudimentary grounding in the technical means by which it would be fought. The central component of the blitzkrieg strategic concept was without doubt the tank, a device commonly treated in much of the secondary literature as a generic, standardised instrument, without regard for the radical differentiation between designs and models which determined their use and effectiveness. Thus, the common citation of a total figure for the number of German tanks in the invasion of the Soviet Union tells us little without an appreciation of the different models involved.

The smallest and most feeble German tank to enter service against the Red Army was the Pz Kpfw I.[10] Produced in two main models since 1934, the design included a fully rotating turret mounted with two 7.92mm machine guns and an armour thickness of just 13mm, restricting its usefulness wholly to engagements with enemy infantry. It first saw action in the Spanish Civil War where, despite the primitive battlefield conditions, it was recognised to be lacking in armament and protection. The early campaigns of World War II only reinforced this point and by the time of Barbarossa it was plainly considered an obsolete model. Despite this

---

[8] Ibid., pp. 180–181.   [9] Förster, 'Hitler Turns East', p. 124.

[10] This is an abbreviation for 'Panzer-Kampfwagen I' (Armoured Fighting Vehicle I), commonly referred to as just 'Mark I'.

281[11] were included in the invasion force. Thereafter remaining stocks were relegated largely to training roles.[12]

A year after the Mark I came into service the Mark II appeared, a slightly heavier tank that saw many upgrades and variant adaptations. The improved D and E models known as 'fast fighting vehicles' (*Schnell-kampfwagen*) entered service in 1938. These were adapted with armour twice the thickness of earlier models (up to 30mm) and included a torsion bar suspension system with larger wheels which in addition to a new more powerful engine raised the top speed to 55 kph. The trade-off was that high speeds could only be achieved on sealed roads, while cross-country performance was hampered – an important factor for the barren landscape of the east.[13] The main armament was a 2cm L/55 gun with a secondary 7.92mm machine gun mounted next to it in the traversing turret. Panzer training regulations of 1939 classed the Mark II as being 'chiefly designed as an anti-tank weapon',[14] yet its record in France proved so poor as to be only effective in this role in the most exceptional circumstances.[15] By the beginning of 1941 the Mark II was remodelled in a new F series with only slightly thicker armour and no change to the main armament, rendering it, like the Mark I, outdated on the modern battlefield, particularly for combat with the Red Army. In spite of such deficiencies the army employed some 743 Mark II[16] tanks in Operation Barbarossa, which together with the Mark I makes up over 1,000 tanks. This meant that 28 per cent of the total tank force consisted of obsolete models.

As a result of the bloodless occupation of Czechoslovakia in 1939 the Wehrmacht was able to benefit from the considerable arsenal of high-grade Czech weapons and their well developed armaments industry. The tank arm of the Czech armed forces was of particular value owing to their advanced design, which outstripped both the Mark I and Mark II, at that time the mainstays of the German tank fleet. The heavier of the two Czech models was dubbed by the Germans Pz Kpfw 35 (t) and featured 35mm armour, a 3.7cm vz 34 anti-tank gun as main armament, plus two 7.92mm machine guns, one mounted in the turret and the other alongside the driver in the hull. The early service life of the Model 35 (t)

[11] See table on armoured fighting vehicles in Müller, 'Von der Wirtschaftsallianz', p. 185.
[12] George Forty, *German Tanks of World War II* (London, 1999), pp. 30–31.
[13] Ferdinand Maria von Senger und Etterlin, *German Tanks of World War II. The Complete Illustrated History of German Armoured Fighting Vehicles 1926–1945* (Harrisberg, 1969), pp. 24–25, 91–92.
[14] Forty, *German Tanks of World War II*, pp. 37–38.
[15] Von Senger und Etterlin, *German Tanks of World War II*, p. 25.
[16] See table on armoured fighting vehicles in Müller, 'Von der Wirtschaftsallianz', p. 185.

was beset by problems, most of which were overcome by the time the Germans took control, although some remained basic to the design. The armour was riveted, not welded like the German tanks. The rivets had the dangerous tendency to pop out under the impact of a heavy shells, sending the rivet shanks flying through the inside of the tank as secondary projectiles. By the launch of Barbarossa, the Model 35 (t) was in decline and, according to the account of one former officer from the 6th Panzer Division, was deemed 'no longer suitable for combat', a classification borne out by the fact that not one of the division's 105 Model 35 (t) tanks saw out the year 1941.[17] In total 157 Pz Kpfw 35 (t) tanks supported the German invasion.[18]

Following on from the early disappointment of the Pz Kpfw 35 (t), the Czech authorities commissioned a new design which evolved into what the Germans later called the Pz Kpfw 38 (t). Lighter than its predecessor, the first four designs had thinner armour (25mm) until November 1940 when the new series E and later F attempted to rectify this inadequacy with an extra 25mm plate added to the frontal surfaces and 15mm to the sides. The armament was similar to the Pz Kpfw 35 (t), supporting a 3.7cm KwK 37 (t) main gun and two 7.92mm machine guns. The Pz Kpfw 38 (t) was also adapted by the Germans to fit a four-man crew with the addition of a gun loader to the driver, radio operator and commander/gunner. Most outstanding of all, however, was the excellent performance and durability of the chassis, proving extremely reliable mechanically and offering itself as an appealing base for later variants in design including the *Panzerjäger* Marder III and Hetzer.[19] The Pz Kpfw 38 (t) represents the best of all the German light tanks at this time and some 651[20] were deployed for service in Operation Barbarossa, making up a large portion of Hoth's Panzer Group 3.[21] Yet, for all its assets and success in previous campaigns, the Pz Kpfw 38 (t) remained a light tank which, against the unparalleled strength of Soviet medium and heavy tanks as well as the numerous heavy calibre artillery of the Red Army, proved simply inadequate. Accordingly, the attrition rate of the Pz Kpfw

---

[17] Forty, *German Tanks of World War II*, pp. 48–51; Helmut Ritgen, '6th Panzer Division Operations' in David M. Glantz (ed.), *The Initial Period of War on the Eastern Front 22 June–August 1941* (London, 1997), p. 108; Peter Tsouras (ed.), *Panzers on the Eastern Front. General Erhard Raus and his Panzer Divisions in Russia 1941–1945* (London, 2002), p. 223.

[18] See table on armoured fighting vehicles in Müller, 'Von der Wirtschaftsallianz', p. 185.

[19] Forty, *German Tanks of World War II*, pp. 51–60.

[20] See table on armoured fighting vehicles in Müller, 'Von der Wirtschaftsallianz', p. 185.

[21] See the table: 'Die materielle Ausstattung des deutschen Ostheeres am 22. Juni 1941', ibid., pp. 186–187.

38 (t) in the east was exceedingly high with one source putting the figure at 796 tanks being lost in the first six months of the war[22] – a figure well in excess of the entire initial deployment. These losses also underline the basic weakness of the German tank force invading the Soviet Union, upon which so much of the operational plan rested. To break this down more clearly, if one adds the totals of all light tanks deployed for Barbarossa and takes that as a percentage of the overall total it equals 50 per cent, meaning that half of the German tanks gathered for the invasion of the Soviet Union were largely obsolete for that theatre.

Germany's panzer formations were initially conceived of with two main models in mind – one light and one medium. The lighter variant, the Mark II, was for reconnaissance and an anti-tank role – which even in 1934 was an optimistic assessment of its capabilities given the poor 2cm armament, although it was hoped that the heavier enemy tanks could be drawn into the fire of infantry-manned anti-tank guns. The medium model later became known as the Pz Kpfw IV (Mark IV) and was to be used in a close support role against fortified field positions. Yet it was not long before the inadequacies of the Mark II were recognised and the need for a purpose-built anti-tank model was realised. This model became known as the Pz Kpfw III (Mark III) with the first few being produced in 1936–37.[23] The Mark III had a troubled beginning with designers unable to perfect a suitable suspension and accordingly none of the first four series A–D, all produced in small quantities, were employed after Poland for action in France and the Low Countries. The E series saw the first run of large-scale production with almost a hundred being built. It adopted an entirely new suspension system, a better engine and upgraded frontal armour from a pitiful 15mm plate to 30mm, giving it a total weight of 19.5 tons. At the beginning of 1939 it was decided to replace the increasingly ineffectual 3.7cm main armament with a new 5cm L/42, yet the time taken to develop and adapt the new gun meant that three-quarters of the new F series (425 produced in total) were equipped with the old standard 3.7cm gun. The G series (600 produced) added the 30mm armour to its rear plating, while the H series (308 produced) benefited from a newly designed turret, transmission and running gear, as well as an extra 30mm armoured plate welded to its front. The last of the Mark III upgrades to be initiated before Barbarossa was the J series which commenced production in March 1941 and incorporated

[22] Forty, *German Tanks of World War II*, p. 58.
[23] Forty, *German Tanks of World War II*, pp. 18–19, 61; Kenneth Macksey, *Guderian. Panzer General* (London, 1975), pp. 65–66.

the new frontal armour in the basic design.[24] With so many upgraded variants it is difficult to talk of a standard Mark III. For that reason it is important to make a distinction between the models of tanks and also recognise the sometimes radical evolution of each series and the consequent differences that existed within a given model. In the case of the Mark III those equipped with a 5cm L/42 gun and additional armour represented a great improvement among the Barbarossa tank force. In total, 979 Mark III tanks[25] were to see action from the beginning of Barbarossa, with the later models bringing the first real backbone to the panzer divisions.

For the attack on the Soviet Union the Germans employed the first large-scale use of the so-called StuG III – *Sturmgeschütz* (assault gun). The main armament was mounted on the chassis of the Mark III and they were commissioned to provide close armour support for infantry and serve in an anti-tank role. The central difference between the StuG III and panzer was the absence of a revolving turret. In order to keep the silhouette low, the 7.5cm L/24 armament was built directly into the hull and the saving in weight from the turret was put towards extra armour, reaching a maximum thickness of 50mm. The total weight came to 20 tons and it was manned by a crew of four. Like the Mark III the design progressed through many series with the addition of a new engine and gearbox being the only major alterations before the StuG III took its place for the beginning of Barbarossa.[26] Mass production was only begun in 1940 with just six StuG III available for the French campaign. By June 1941, 250 were assigned to the invasion force,[27] forming a valuable addition to the German tank fleet.

The final German model to participate in the invasion of the Soviet Union was the Pz Kpfw IV (Mark IV) which first began production in 1936. All series produced before the Barbarossa campaign (A–F) were armed with a 7.5cm L/24 main gun. The Mark IV was originally designed to provide close infantry support,[28] with two machine guns fitted for local defence. Like all early tank models the A series (35 produced) was exceedingly weak in frontal armour, having a thickness of only 20mm. The latter B, C and D series improved on this somewhat with a maximum thickness of 30mm. Starting with the B series (42 produced) it was fitted with a more powerful engine and gearbox, increasing its weight

[24] Forty, *German Tanks of World War II*, pp. 61–62.
[25] See table on armoured fighting vehicles in Müller, 'Von der Wirtschaftsallianz', p. 185.
[26] Von Senger und Etterlin, *German Tanks of World War II*, p. 39.
[27] See table on armoured fighting vehicles in Müller, 'Von der Wirtschaftsallianz', p. 185.
[28] This changed when the main armament was upgraded in 1942, overtaking the role of the Mark III and becoming the main anti-tank tank.

to 17.7 tons. The C series (140 produced) saw few substantive changes aside from the removal of the hull machine gun, which was reinstated in the next series. Rear armour was increased from 15mm to 20mm in the D series (220 produced) but only a few were finished in time for the Polish campaign. The E series reflected the need for greater protection, with the armour strengthened to 50mm for the front glacis plate and additional plates secured to the front (30mm) and sides (20mm). The F series was the last version of the Mark IV to commence production before Barbarossa (April 1941) and included 50mm armour as standard to the turret, hull and superstructure, and 30mm for the sides.[29] As with the Mark III, the Mark IV underwent many improvements, meaning that earlier variants were markedly inferior to later ones, particularly in terms of armour. In total, 444 Mark IV tanks were deployed against the Red Army for the beginning of Operation Barbarossa.[30]

Without doubt, the Mark III, StuG III and Mark IV, which together numbered some 1,673 vehicles, represented the cream of the German tank force. Yet their true value is of course relative to their opponents. This therefore necessitates a brief comparison with Soviet models. Clearly the best in the Soviet arsenal were the medium T-34 and heavy KV-1[31] of which a combined total of 1,861 were available by the time of the German invasion.[32] The KV-1 was simply beyond anything the Germans had yet imagined and was a giant of its time. Weighing in at 43.5 tons, with 90mm armour and a 7.6cm F-34 main gun plus three 7.62mm machine guns, the KV-1 could penetrate 69mm armour at a range of 500 metres and was effective against the thickest German armour up to a range of almost 2,000 metres.[33] In similar fashion, the T-34 proved greatly superior to its German contemporaries, with 45mm armour, twice the cross-country speed of the German medium tanks and a main armament identical to the KV-1.[34] The qualitative advantage of these Soviet tanks was enormous. In practical terms it meant that none of the German tanks regardless of armament could penetrate the armour on the T-34 at ranges above

---

[29] Forty, *German Tanks of World War II*, pp. 79–80.

[30] See table on armoured fighting vehicles in Müller, 'Von der Wirtschaftsallianz', p. 185.

[31] 'KV' stands for Kliment Voroshilov, the Soviet Commissar of War (renamed Commissar of Defence in 1934) from 1925 to 1940.

[32] Glantz, *Stumbling Colossus*, p. 117; Glantz and House, *When Titans Clashed*, p. 36. John Erickson cites a lower figure 1,475 (508 Kv-1s and 967 T-34s); Erickson, *The Soviet High Command 1918–1941*, p. 567.

[33] Earlier designs in the KV-1 series supported slightly weaker guns, but even the weakest variant of these (the 76.2mm F-32) was capable of penetrating 52mm armour at a range of 1,000 metres.

[34] The earlier model T-34 possessed a smaller gun (the 76.2mm L-11) which could still penetrate 56mm armour at a range of 1,000 metres.

500 metres. Indeed, only the later models of the Mark III equipped with 5cm L/42 main guns could effectively penetrate the armour of the T-34 at less than 500 metres. The KV-1 was simply impervious to all tank-mounted German firepower as well as the standard 3.7cm anti-tank guns issued to infantry divisions.

By contrast, even the older model Soviet light tanks such as the T-26 and the BT-5 and 7 series employed 4.5cm main guns capable of penetrating 52mm armour (more than the thickest German armour) at a range of 100 metres. These light Soviet tanks had been produced in vast quantities during the 1930s (an estimated 12,000 T-26s and 3,000 of the BT series), which taken together with all other models gives the imposing figure of some 23,767 Soviet tanks in existence by the eve of war.[35] Although equipped with powerful main armaments, these tanks were lightly armoured and certainly unequal to the rigours of the coming war, which their losses in the opening phase undoubtedly reflect. Furthermore, the Soviet tanks were at a considerable technical disadvantage because of their lack of radios and rudimentary communication equipment which hindered co-ordination on the battlefield.

The remarkable number of Soviet tanks and the fact that this figure included hundreds of T-34s and KV-1s has given cause for some historians to explain the apparent early success of Operation Barbarossa through a tremendous German superiority in mobile operations. Such representations, in addition to the well worn memoir literature of former generals, have contributed to the rise of a semi-mythical status surrounding the German panzer divisions and their execution of the so-called 'blitzkrieg'. In fact, the preparation of the German motorised and panzer divisions was far from perfect, with Halder noting in his diary five weeks prior to the campaign: 'we will be lucky if we're finished with their equipping; the training of the last equipped divisions will in any case be incomplete'.[36] Ultimately, shortcomings in training affected no fewer than six of the 13 motorised infantry divisions and two of the panzer divisions (20th and 18th, both committed to Army Group Centre).[37] This is not to question that the German armoured units had a qualitative advantage in the organisation and level of training and experience of their tank crews. Such advantages, however, do not fully explain the extent of German success in the summer of 1941, which was in no small part due to astonishing Soviet ineptitude as opposed to simple German brilliance.

[35] David M. Glantz, 'Introduction: Prelude to Barbarossa. The Red Army in 1941' in Glantz (ed.), *The Initial Period of War*, p. 33; Glantz, *Colossus Reborn*, p. 247.
[36] Franz Halder, KTB II, pp. 411–412 (14 May 1941).
[37] 'Oberkommando des Heeres/Generalstab des Heeres', BA-MA RH 2/v. 247, Fol. 151.

Since 1940 the Red Army had pursued a radical restructuring and modernisation programme which began with the creation of nine new mechanised corps and followed in early 1941 with a further twenty.[38] Fulfilling the manpower and materiel requirements of such an ambitious reform was truly a mighty undertaking with the result that many of the mechanised corps were woefully disorganised, ill-equipped and under-manned by the summer of 1941. In the western military district opposing Army Group Centre, mechanised corps averaged shortages of 75 per cent in personnel and 53 per cent in equipment, greatly impairing their ability to function effectively.[39] Compounding the shortages, many tank drivers had as little as one-and-a-half to two hours' driving experience, and com-mand staff lacked specific training in the direction of motorised units.[40] Furthermore, there was an appalling degree of negligence in the mainte-nance and servicing of older model Soviet tanks. A report from 15 June 1941 stated that among the great mass of T-26s and BT models, 29 per cent were in need of capital repair and 44 per cent of lesser maintenance, making a total of 73 per cent being in need of some kind of work.[41] During the winter of 1940–41 an analysis was conducted to assess the professional knowledge of the commanding officers serving in the bor-der military districts and its conclusion was damning. The southernmost Odessa Military District was marked 'Average' while all the others were marked 'Poor'.[42]

Clearly the German panzer divisions were to encounter a foe scarcely prepared for war, which in spite of its numerical and technological supe-riority could not help but be at a severe disadvantage. The hapless state of the Red Army in the summer of 1941 was most definitely exploited by the German attack, but not caused by it. The great number of Soviet tanks subsequently captured or destroyed must be seen in this context. Yet the disparity of arms also points to a further consideration in the early progress of the war. If Germany could not achieve the outright success it aimed for and crush the Red Army in its weakened state, the reality was that future battlefields would only see an ever greater proportion of newer model Soviet tanks and a heightened degree of competence among those Soviet officers and men who survived earlier encounters.

The German tank force at the start of the western campaign in May 1940 numbered some 2,445 vehicles of all models.[43] In the last six

---

[38] Each corps was destined to field 36,080 men, 1,031 tanks (half of these being either KV-1s or T-34s), 358 guns, 268 armoured cars, 5,165 vehicles and 352 tractors.

[39] Glantz, *Stumbling Colossus*, pp. 116–118.

[40] Erickson, *The Soviet High Command 1918–1941*, p. 567.

[41] Glantz, *Stumbling Colossus*, pp. 117–118.   [42] Braithwaite, *Moscow 1941*, p. 50.

[43] Figures cited in Rolf-Dieter Müller's table on armoured fighting vehicles includes armoured staff cars, which I have subtracted from my total (Müller, 'Von der

months of 1940 tank production averaged 182 units a month (all types) with this rising slightly to 212 in the first six months of 1941.[44] By 22 June 1941 the combined figure for all tanks in the four panzer groups of Operation Barbarossa reached 3,505 (see Figure 3.1).[45] Of the 21 panzer divisions in existence by the summer of 1941, two were engaged in northern Africa, another two were in the process of being reorganised and refitted for future operations, leaving 17 panzer divisions available for service on the eastern front.[46] Yet, just as caution should be exercised in a differentiation between tank models, so too must attention be paid to the divisions in which they were organised. Radical differences in the number of tanks assigned to each division resulted in considerable disparities of strength which directly impacted the overall performance of the panzer groups. By far the weakest, Panzer Group 1, assigned to Army Group South, had an average of 154 panzers in its four panzer divisions. In contrast, Panzer Group 3 of Army Group Centre averaged 253 tanks per division with the most numerous being the 7th Panzer Division, fielding 299 tanks. Panzer Group 2, the second arm of Army Group Centre, was considerably smaller, averaging 191 tanks per division, but this was offset in overall strength by the addition of a fifth panzer division. Panzer Group 4, attached to Army Group North, averaged 210 tanks per panzer division, although this panzer group contained only three panzer divisions, giving it roughly the same strength as Panzer Group 1. Thus, from a standpoint of overall tank numbers, Panzer Groups 2 and 3 had approximately one-third more tanks than Panzer Groups 1 and 4 which, in addition to the fact that both were deployed in the central Army Group, reinforces the paramount importance of this sector.[47]

Taken together, the relative strengths of Panzer Groups 2 and 3 reflect a considerable disparity in the composition of forces making up each group. While Panzer Group 2 was mainly stocked with tanks and trucks of German origin, Panzer Group 3 was a far less homogenous force, reflecting the spoils of past conquests. It comprised a core of Czech Pz Kpfw 38 (t) tanks and its motorised infantry was largely dependent upon

Wirtschaftsallianz', p. 185). Karl-Heinz Frieser's figure does not include the six StuG IIIs which I have added (Frieser, *Blitzkrieg-Legende*, p. 44).

[44] Matthew Cooper, *The German Army 1933–1945. Its Political and Military Failure* (New York, 1984), p. 276.

[45] Figures cited in Rolf-Dieter Müller's table on armoured fighting vehicles include armoured staff cars, which I have subtracted from my total (Müller, 'Von der Wirtschaftsallianz', p. 185).

[46] Klink, 'Die militärische Konzeption', p. 270.

[47] Statistical calculations have been made from figures given in Burkhart Müller-Hillebrand, *Das Heer 1933–1945*, Band III: *Der Zweifrontenkrieg. Das Heer vom Beginn des Feldzuges gegen die Sowjetunion bis zum Kriegsende* (Frankfurt am Main, 1969), p. 205.

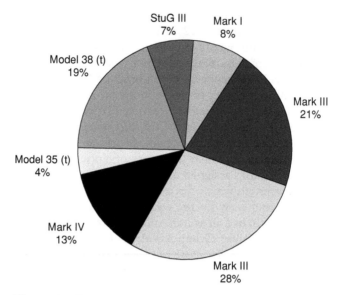

Figure 3.1 Panzer models available for Operation Barbarossa on 22 June 1941. Rolf-Dieter Müller, 'Von der Wirtschaftsallianz zum kolonialen Ausbeutungskrieg', p. 185.

requisitioned French vehicles.[48] All forms of wheeled transport suffered greatly on the deplorable Soviet roads, but the less robust French trucks proved even more susceptible on summer roads choked with dust and potholes, and soon converted to an impassable morass with every downpour. The commander of Panzer Group 3, Colonel-General Hoth, would later complain: 'It seems the allocation of trucks was totally unsuitable for an eastern campaign.'[49] The addition of so many foreign vehicles also exacerbated the problem of standardisation within the army and made the process of conducting repairs and finding spare parts much more complicated. The result was a higher rate of attrition and a slower rate of return to service, affecting the overall performance of the panzer group and emphasising yet again the importance of a speedy victory before mobility was decisively compromised.

On 19 June 1941, only three days before Barbarossa was due to begin, the OKW issued a directive to Brauchitsch relating Hitler's intentions for the future use and deployment of panzer divisions. With undisguised conceit Hitler's instruction read:

[48] Müller, 'Von der Wirtschaftsallianz', pp. 186–187.
[49] Hoth, *Panzer-Operationen*, p. 44.

1. Eastern Front: The eastern front should as much as possible live from its own materiel reserve. In case of heavy losses panzer divisions should be consolidated together. Newly-established panzer divisions in Germany shall be staffed by personnel vacated due to the consolidations.
2. From these newly-formed units 2 panzer divisions are for France, 1 panzer division for Norway.[50]

The document goes on to direct that tank losses in Africa must be replaced as soon as possible, leaving nothing in reserve for those on the eastern front. From this it is clear that Hitler's lofty confidence was as delusional as it was self-destructive, reinforcing yet again the absolute dependence on the forces at hand for the fullest achievement of the operational plan. The panzer divisions now carried not only the profound expectations of their leaders, but the fate of Germany's greatest military campaign.

Standing before the precipice – the infantry and Luftwaffe on the eve of Barbarossa

In spite of the central importance of the motorised and panzer divisions, an analysis focusing on the make-up and employment of the infantry divisions is not without merit for gaining a wider appreciation of both the weaknesses of the German army and the complex function of managing armour and infantry in combined operations. Just as one must guard against a generalised accounting for tanks and panzer divisions, avoiding the inaccurate representation of a generic standard, it is likewise important to differentiate between the large sum of German infantry divisions. According to an army document assessing the combat value of divisions, dated 20 June 1941, a full 73 divisions were deemed to be at a level below the highest classification which determined a division to be capable of 'any offensive action'. These 73 were described as follows: '[S]omewhat lesser offensive strength', 8 divisions in total; 'reduced offensive strength and mobility', 19 divisions; 'little offensive strength and mobility', 22 divisions; and lastly 24 divisions equipped and trained only for rear-area security operations. Among those in the highest classification were 95 infantry divisions, four mountain divisions and one cavalry division, the great bulk of which were deployed in the east ready for the start of operations against the Soviet Union.[51] Yet the reality of so many second- and

[50] 'Beurteilung des Kampfwertes der Divisionen nach dem Stand vom 20. Juni 1941', BA-MA RH 2/v. 247, Fol. 154.
[51] Ibid., Fols. 151–153.

third-class divisions discouraged the prospect of a rotational reserve existing between units on the eastern front and those stationed in quieter sectors. In any case, when German losses eventually demanded this course of action it proved difficult to implement quickly owing to the substantial distances and the Soviet Union's poor transportation network. Thus, while Barbarossa proceeded with the finest elements of the German army, it was largely self-reliant in dealing with the Red Army, and had to meet all operational requirements without recourse to an appreciable reserve of quality or quantity.

Compounding such limitations, the training of the German infantry proved insufficient to cope with the many challenges of the new theatre, as well as the stubborn and unorthodox tactical approach of Soviet soldiers.[52] One post-war study of small unit actions on the eastern front concluded that several months of acclimatisation were often necessary before units could adapt and stem the high tide of casualties. The learning curve was large enough that occasionally full-strength combat units, without previous experience on the eastern front, were incapable of achieving the same tasks as those units greatly depleted by previous engagements.[53]

Even more problematic were the constraints of equipment which greatly hampered the performance of the infantry and directly exposed them to the structural failings of the German army. Given the plainly inadequate state of motorisation and the clear priority enjoyed by the motorised and panzer divisions, the great mass of German infantry was largely self-reliant for its means of transportation. In practice this led to an advance at the pace of a march, with some 625,000 horses[54] employed to draw guns and supplies. Thus the tempo of the German advance progressed at two entirely different speeds, preventing the close mutual reliance of the two most basic arms of the army. The dire complications this caused to the German strategic and operational position will be fully explored in Part II but, in short, it meant that two separate armies were invading the Soviet Union. One army was highly mobile and armoured, but relatively small in size and without depth in manpower or endurance for battles of long, grinding duration. The other army was large, slow and cumbersome, bearing the great bulk of the three million men invading

---

[52] Kroener, 'Die Winter 1941/42', p. 879.

[53] Department of the U.S. Army (ed.), *Small Unit Actions During the German Campaign in Russia* (Washington, 1953), pp. 1–2. One former German soldier of the eastern front wrote of November 1941: 'Missions were carried out with a few men that would have seemed nearly incredible in earlier months and that would have occasioned an unbelieving smile from every teacher of tactics at the war college.' Helmut Günther, *Hot Motors, Cold Feet. A Memoir of Service with the Motorcycle Battalion of SS-Division 'Reich' 1940–1941* (Winnipeg, 2004), p. 207.

[54] Klink, 'Die militärische Konzeption', p. 270.

the Soviet Union, and proving not greatly more manoeuvrable than the Kaiser's army of 1914, or even that of Napoleon in 1812.[55] Particularly in reviewing the period from June to August 1941, this distinction between the infantry armies and panzer groups must be kept in mind. Indeed, one easily gains a deceptive impression from countless maps produced in the secondary literature, as they almost always limit themselves to showing the furthermost point of advance and thereby disguise a critical structural deficiency within the army, as well as giving a misleading impression of rapid, early success.[56]

The firepower of the standard infantry division in both offensive and defensive action rested largely with its artillery complement. This placed a premium on its ability to be used in as much concentration as possible and be kept well supplied with shells. The width of the front and depth of operations did not afford such beneficial conditions and its overall employment was complicated by the comparatively small number of German guns, and an alarming shortfall in the production of ammunition. Soviet field armies operated some 32,900 guns and mortars of all calibres over 50mm, while the whole Red Army together possessed the startling figure of 76,500 guns and mortars over 50mm.[57] By comparison, the Germans could muster only 7,146 artillery pieces along their whole front.[58] As with their tank forces the Soviets were let down by poor organisation, training and support services, which initially compensated in some measure for the German numerical inferiority.[59] German ammunition shortfalls were most starkly observed in production of armour-piercing shells for the infantry anti-tank guns, whose output was only 50 per cent of projected targets. Batteries of other calibres were likewise affected, although there were exceptions where production exceeded projections.[60]

---

[55] Overy, *Why the Allies Won*, p. 215; Richard L. DiNardo, *Mechanized Juggernaut or Military Anachronism: Horses and the German Army in World War II* (London, 1991), pp. 39–40; Mary Habeck, *Storm of Steel. The Development of Armor Doctrine in Germany and the Soviet Union, 1919–1939* (London, 2003), p. 292.

[56] The best source available for maps of the period are the many dozens which accompany David Glantz's edited work *The Initial Period of War on the Eastern Front 22 June–August 1941*. His privately published *Atlas and Operational Summary The Border Battles 22 June– 1 July 1941* and *Atlas of the Battle of Smolensk 7 July–10 September 1941* are indispensable.

[57] Glantz and House, *When Titans Clashed*, p. 306. Evan Mawdsley suggests that the Red Army only had a total of 33,200 artillery pieces in June 1941, but even this lower figure still gives the Soviets an almost fivefold advantage over the Germans. Evan Mawdsley, *Thunder in the East. The Nazi–Soviet War 1941–1945* (London, 2005), p. 26.

[58] 4,760 light artillery pieces, 104 army AA guns (88mm), 2,252 heavy artillery pieces and 30 super-heavy high/low angle guns (Klink, 'Die militärische Konzeption', p. 270).

[59] Glantz, *Stumbling Colossus*, pp. 163–164.

[60] See table: 'Das Rüstungsprogramm B. Die Fertigung von Waffen Gerät und Munition für das Heer vom 1.9.1940 bis 31.3.1941' in Müller, 'Von der Wirtschaftsallianz', p. 184.

From the very beginning of Barbarossa, the infantry also suffered from obsolescence in certain key areas. The standard 3.7cm anti-tank gun was to prove largely useless against the new medium and heavy Soviet tanks, acquiring the unflattering nickname 'door knocker' in certain divisions.[61] To rectify the problem, captured French 4.7cm anti-tank guns were pressed back into service and the army distributed its new 5cm anti-tank guns to units in ones and twos to offer a small, generalised boost. Nevertheless these proved only makeshift solutions and many companies had to be supplemented by field guns from divisional artillery.[62]

Just as the necessity of a short war affected Germany's strategic, operational and economic plans, it also had a fundamental bearing on the personnel situation, through the need to keep infantry and panzer divisions at full strength. As studies by Bernhard Kroener have well demonstrated, the importance of manpower shortages in 1939/1941 were bound up with what he called the 'Blitzkrieg plan', which juggled Germany's scant manpower resources between its army and factories both to meet economic objectives and win successive short campaigns. This, however, ran the double-edged risk that high losses in the eastern campaign would, in each case, require replacement of both a trained soldier and a skilled worker, while the longer the campaign dragged on the longer industry would suffer manpower shortages.[63] By the summer of 1941 some 85 per cent of German men aged between 20 and 30 were already in the Wehrmacht and those remaining were judged to be too important to the war economy to be drafted for military service.[64] The commander of the Replacement Army, Colonel-General Fritz Fromm, outlined the limitations to Halder in a discussion on 20 May 1941. With surprising candour Halder noted that 275,000 casualties were expected in the initial border battles, with a further 200,000 expected in September. Going into Barbarossa the Replacement Army was left with just 385,000 men, after deducting a share for the Luftwaffe (90,000 men). Thus, by Halder's own figures the Replacement Army would not suffice for the demands of the campaign through to the end of September and nothing at all would remain if the

[61] Tsouras (ed.), *Panzers on the Eastern Front*, p. 223.
[62] Chris Perello, 'German Infantry on the Eastern Front in 1941' in Command Magazine (ed.), *Hitler's Army. The Evolution and Structure of German Forces, 1933–1945* (Boston, 2003), p. 20.
[63] Bernhard R. Kroener, 'Squaring the Circle. Blitzkrieg Strategy and the Manpower Shortage, 1939–1942' in Wilhelm Deist (ed.), *The German Military in the Age of Total War* (Warwickshire, 1985), pp. 294–295; Bernhard R. Kroener, 'The "Frozen *Blitzkrieg*". German Strategic Planning against the Soviet Union and the Causes of its Failure' in Bernd Wegner (ed.), *From Peace to War. Germany, Soviet Russia and the World, 1939–1941* (Oxford, 1997), pp. 142–143. Also see Förster, 'Hitler Turns East', pp. 124–125.
[64] Tooze, *Wages of Destruction*, p. 437.

war dragged on longer. The seriousness of being without trained reserves in the middle of a major campaign forced Halder to consider an early call up of the 1922 generation, but ultimately he decided the risk 'could be borne'.[65] Yet again, the inability of Germany to sustain anything but a short, decisive campaign was strikingly clear.

Between the invasion of France in 1940 and Operation Barbarossa in 1941, the army raised an additional 52 divisions, but the increase did not translate into increased striking power as no fewer than 49 divisions were required for occupation details or in Northern Africa. By contrast, in May 1940 only 14 divisions were required for this purpose, leaving a far greater share of German manpower in the attacking armies or the factories.[66]

In the post-war era the size of the Red Army and the allegedly inexhaustible human resources of the Soviet Union were often cited as central reasons behind Germany's defeat. The image frequently portrayed presents a picture based more on the defensive battles taking place from 1943 until the end of the war, in which the hard-pressed German infantry fought tenaciously against an enemy with a vast numerical superiority. This representation, however, cannot be applied to the earliest stages of the campaign when Germany was the dominant military force, but its pervasiveness has helped build the perception of the army as an expert military organisation which operated a masterful 'blitzkrieg'. In truth, the size of the Red Army in 1941 overstated its value and effectiveness, which in any case numbered less than the invading Germans in the western military districts.[67] The success of the German infantry armies and panzer groups was greatly aided by the lamentable state of the Red Army – a point too often overlooked or under-emphasised in much of the existing literature focusing on the German experience in Operation Barbarossa. The immense quantity of equipment seized, the enormous areas overrun, and the Red Army's losses, soon to number in the millions (killed, wounded and captured) appeared to present the virtue of the German armies and their operational art as self-evident. Yet more recent scholarship by Roger Reese, Mark von Hagen and David Glantz, on the organisation and internal functioning of the Red Army, has supported the view that the military disasters of 1941 were at least as much a result of Soviet ineptitude as German military prowess.[68] Such insights

---

[65] Franz Halder, KTB II, p. 422 (20 May 1941).

[66] Kroener, 'Die Winter 1941/42', p. 872.

[67] Glantz and House, *When Titans Clashed*, p. 301.

[68] Roger R. Reese, *Stalin's Reluctant Soldiers. A Social History of the Red Army 1925–1941* (Lawrence, 1996), Chapter 7, 'The Predictable Disaster and the End of the Red Army: 22 June to December 1941'; Mark von Hagen, 'Soviet Soldiers and Officers on the

go a long way towards reconciling the initial successes enjoyed by the Wehrmacht, with its own considerable shortcomings and deficiencies.

The success of the German blitzkrieg depended firstly on the role of its armoured formations, with aircraft and the formula of close air support forming an important second. Like all major powers of the 1930s, the rejuvenated German air force placed strong emphasis on strategic bombing, but what distinguished the new Luftwaffe was its close integration with army operations.[69] Given Germany's geographic position, confronting potential enemies in both east and west, there was less opportunity for the Luftwaffe's planners to pursue a doctrine that ignored the predominance of the army in overall German strategy. There were also practical factors to consider. The development of an effective long-range, strategic bomber had floundered because of design and production errors, and the high demands it placed on limited resources. As a result, shorter-range aircraft, better suited to tactical rather than strategic uses, were produced, although the notion of the Luftwaffe as an overtly tactical air force was only one element in its intended service.[70]

The principal aircraft employed by the Luftwaffe to support Operation Barbarossa can be broadly categorised into three types; fighters, dive-bombers and bombers.[71] The fighters were important for winning aerial superiority, protecting bombers and strafing ground targets. For this the Luftwaffe was well served by the fast and manoeuvrable Me Bf-109 (series E and F), a single-engine fighter that could perform well against the new Soviet models, including the Iak-1, LaGG-2 and MiG-3.[72] The twin-engine fighter known as the Me Bf-110 or 'destroyer' (*Zerstörer*) was less numerous and not as proficient, but able to operate at much longer ranges.[73] The standard German dive-bomber, which operated with such devastating effect in the first two years of the war, was the

Eve of the German Invasion: Towards a Description of Social Psychology and Political Attitudes' in Robert Thurston and Bernd Bonwetsch (eds.), *The People's War. Responses to World War II in the Soviet Union* (Chicago, 2000), pp. 187–210; Glantz, *Stumbling Colossus*, Chapter 3, 'The Soviet Soldier'.

[69] Richard R. Muller, 'Close Air Support. The German, British and American Experiences, 1918–1941' in Williamson Murray and Allan R. Millett (eds.), *Military Innovation in the Interwar Period* (Cambridge, 1998), p. 160.

[70] Williamson Murray, 'Strategic Bombing. The British, American and German Experiences' in Williamson Murray and Allan R. Millett (eds.), *Military Innovation in the Interwar Period* (Cambridge, 1998), pp. 131–132; Muller, 'Close Air Support', p. 160.

[71] There were also a sizeable number of long- and short-range reconnaissance aircraft in service which I have excluded owing to their non-tactical role.

[72] Seaton, *The Russo-German War 1941–45*, p. 87.

[73] Peter Young (ed.), *The World Almanac of World War II. The Complete and Comprehensive Documentary of World War II* (London, 1981), pp. 469–470.

Ju-87, commonly known as the 'Stuka'.[74] Against the RAF in the Battle of Britain the Stuka had suffered heavily, lacking speed and armament but, given adequate protection, or in the absence of serious opposition, the Stuka could provide remarkable accuracy, while its screeching air brakes had an often terrifying psychological effect on ground forces.[75] A number of different bomber designs saw service in Operation Barbarossa, performing a variety of roles and proving more effective than their largely obsolete Soviet equivalents. The principal aircraft were all twin-engine, medium bombers with limited range and payload. These included the hardy and versatile Ju-88 A, the Do-17 Z, Do-217 E and the He-111 H and He-111 P.[76]

In contrast to the army, from the opening of the campaign against France in May 1940 through to the invasion of the Soviet Union the following year, the Luftwaffe was required to perform in almost constant combat, fighting a long and costly campaign over Britain. Figures for the period between May and September 1940, covering both the defeat of France and the Battle of Britain, illustrate the toll these operations took on the Luftwaffe. Taken as a percentage of the early May total, losses for single-engine fighters amounted to 57 per cent, twin-engine fighters 94 per cent, bombers 64 per cent and dive-bombers 50 per cent.[77] Such an erosion of strength was clearly unsustainable in the long term and boded ill for the further commitment of the Luftwaffe in the campaign over England as well as the expansion of aerial operations into new theatres. The chief of the operations department of the Luftwaffe, Major-General Hoffman von Waldau, reported to Halder in October 1940 that operations against Britain would have to be scaled back over winter to stem losses, while force levels could not be replenished until early 1941 at best. The prospect of the Luftwaffe fighting a two-front war, to include the Soviet Union, was dismissed outright by Waldau who regarded the prospect as 'impossible'.[78] Such a shrewd assessment did not, however, meet with the required orders of the German political and military leadership. Hitler's War Directive 21 of December 1940 gives a clear indication of the lurch towards over-extension that Barbarossa represented for the Luftwaffe. The new tasks were outlined as follows:

[74] An abbreviation of *Stukageschwader* – dive-bomber groups.
[75] Young (ed.), *The World Almanac of World War II*, pp. 484–485.
[76] Ibid., pp. 495–497; Horst Boog, 'Die Luftwaffe' in Militärgeschichtliches Forschungsamt (ed.), *Das Deutsche Reich und der Zweite Weltkrieg*; see table: Taktisch-technische Daten der hauptsächlichsten im Sommer 1941 im Osten eingesetzten Flugzeugmuster der deutschen Luftwaffe, p. 314.
[77] Williamson Murray, *The Luftwaffe 1933–45. Strategy for Defeat* (Washington, 1996). See Table X: Aircraft Losses – May–September 1940, p. 54.
[78] Franz Halder, KTB II, p. 129 (7 October 1940).

The air force will have to make available for this Eastern campaign supporting forces of such strength that the Army will be able to bring land operations to a speedy conclusion and that eastern Germany will be as little damaged as possible by enemy air attack. This build-up of a focal point in the east will be limited only by the need to protect from air attack the whole combat and arsenal area which we control, and to ensure that attacks on England, and especially upon her imports, are not allowed to lapse.[79]

Given the Luftwaffe's high losses and related difficulties in attempting to subdue England from the air in 1940, it seems absurd to believe that those efforts could be matched in 1941, while at the same time embarking on a war with the scale and scope of Barbarossa. To make matters worse, in late 1940 X Air Corps was being transferred to the Mediterranean which, as Horst Boog has observed, was leading the Luftwaffe towards a three-front war by the summer of 1941.[80]

Between autumn 1940 and the spring of 1941 the bombing of Britain and attacks on British shipping resulted in a reduced, but still steady attrition of German aircraft. January 1941 recorded the minimum monthly loss with 4.8 per cent of the German bomber force lost and 2.1 per cent of the fighter force. As the year wore on, each month recorded a new increase in the Luftwaffe's losses.[81] The spring 1941 Balkan campaign and the subsequent aerial invasion of Crete placed significant demands on the Luftwaffe's resources, while in the final months preceding Barbarossa, the Luftwaffe was ordered to intensify the air war against Britain to camouflage German intentions in the east and feign that a German invasion of Britain was finally at hand.[82] Not surprisingly, aircraft losses rose correspondingly and by May 1941 bombers were suffering 12 per cent and fighters 6.8 per cent losses a month.[83] In practical terms, from the beginning of August 1940 to June 1941 the Luftwaffe had lost 3,700 aircraft (all types) as well as almost 3,700 members of flying crews killed, 3,000 missing and 1,500 wounded.[84] As Williamson Murray aptly points out, the demand on the Luftwaffe's resources even before Barbarossa began, and the great strain that would be subsequently added by the war in the east, left many fundamental questions concerning the Luftwaffe's

---

[79] Trevor-Roper (ed.), *Hitler's War Directives 1939–1945*, pp. 93–94.
[80] Boog, 'Die Luftwaffe', p. 278. See also Richard Muller, *The German Air War in Russia* (Baltimore, 1992), p. 38.
[81] Murray, *The Luftwaffe 1933–45*. See figures presented in Table V: German Fighter Losses 1940, p. 42; Table IV: German Bomber Losses 1940, p. 43; Table XVI: German Fighter Losses 1941, p. 92; Table XV: German Bomber Losses 1941, p. 91.
[82] Boog, 'Die Luftwaffe', pp. 279–280.
[83] Murray, *The Luftwaffe 1933–45*. See figures presented in Table XVI: German Fighter Losses 1941, p. 92 and Table XV: German Bomber Losses 1941, p. 91.
[84] Boog, 'Die Luftwaffe', p. 281.

capabilities unanswered.[85] Adding further concern, the great bulk of the Luftwaffe's aircraft were due, or even overdue, for replacement by a new generation of models. The battles against the RAF made this painfully clear, although the technical gap was much less evident on the eastern front in 1941. The problem was that many of the Luftwaffe's new models proved hopelessly inadequate, wasting precious time and millions of Reichsmarks, and giving the Allies an overall qualitative as well as numerical superiority against German aircraft.[86]

Difficulties in gathering intelligence about the Soviet air force allowed many gaps in German assessments to be filled by the rampant Nationalist Socialist thinking that pervaded the Luftwaffe.[87] At the onset of the campaign the Luftwaffe estimates of the Soviet Air Force in the European theatre were set at 5,800 aircraft with only 1,300 bombers and 1,500 fighters classed as fully operable.[88] Even these conservative expectations figures still left the Soviet Air Force at a significant numerical superiority, but the reality was that more than 7,000 Soviet aircraft (all types) were stationed in its western military districts[89] with thousands more in the interior.[90] Assessments of the poor Soviet command and control structures, training, experience and tactics proved largely accurate, helping to offset the Soviet numerical advantage. As with the Red Army, the Soviet Air Force was undergoing a major reorganisation at the time of the German attack which, together with the achievement of tactical surprise and the marked German superiority in aircraft quality and crew training, allowed such devastating losses in the earliest period of the war.[91] The most striking German under-estimation centred on their assessment of the Soviet aircraft industry,[92] which even before the war was far larger than the Luftwaffe's industrial base[93] and would continue to outperform the Germans even through the great disruption of 1941.[94] Conversely, the Luftwaffe's commanders tended to over-estimate their own effectiveness. The adverse ratio of aircraft to space prevented the Luftwaffe from making their advantages felt over the vastness of the operational area,

---

[85] Murray, *The Luftwaffe 1933–45*, p. 77.
[86] For a good overview of the problems within the German aircraft industry see Tooze, *Wages of Destruction*, pp. 446–452; Overy, *Why the Allies Won*, pp. 218–220.
[87] Boog, 'Die Luftwaffe', p. 287.
[88] Ibid., p. 298; Schwabedissen, *Russian Air Force*, p. 49.
[89] Glantz, *Stumbling Colossus*, p. 204.
[90] David M. Glantz, *Barbarossa. Hitler's Invasion of Russia 1941* (Stroud, 2001), p. 27.
[91] Glantz, *Stumbling Colossus*, pp. 186–191; Boog, 'Die Luftwaffe', pp. 297–298.
[92] Schwabedissen, *Russian Air Force*, p. 51.
[93] Muller, *The German Air War in Russia*, p. 41; Glantz, *Stumbling Colossus*, p. 184.
[94] Boog, 'Die Luftwaffe', p. 299.

meaning that aerial support could only be offered selectively and Soviet aircraft could operate on parts of the front with a degree of impunity.

In sustaining its operations against the Soviet Union, the Luftwaffe was forced to confront many practical problems also shared by the army. Material problems were recognised in the area of supply with a short-fall of some 15,000–20,000 tons in transport capacity.[95] Furthermore, it became apparent prior to the campaign that many vehicles were in such poor mechanical condition that a great effort had to be made to recondition as many as possible before the beginning of operations. Even so, the Luftwaffe suffered the widespread problem that its motor vehicles were simply unsuited to the rigours of the eastern theatre. Personnel was another hindrance to the Luftwaffe's performance with previous losses of air crews being easy to replace numerically, but lacking the vital experience of combat and formation flying.[96]

Aerial support for the eastern front was organised into four so-called 'Air Fleets' (*Luftflotte*), one for each of the three army groups plus a much smaller force to operate from northern Norway and Finland. Army Group Centre was supported by Air Fleet 2, under the able command of Field Marshal Albrecht Kesselring. This was the largest German air fleet and by far the best outfitted for close support operations with the army, underlining the overall importance of Army Group Centre's progress. Air Fleet 2 commanded all 425 dive-bombers and 98 'destroyers' deployed in the east, with Fourth and First Air Fleets, supporting Army Groups South and North respectively, receiving none.[97] The previous success of the Wehrmacht's land campaigns had highlighted the great advantage Germany possessed in combined-arms operations and Kesselring under-lined the importance of this co-operation by instructing his generals that the wishes of the army were to be considered as his own orders.[98]

Air Fleet 2 was made up of two Air Corps: VIII and II; the first was assigned to support 9th Army and more particularly Armoured Group 3. Air Corps II was to co-operate with 4th Army, yet concentrate especially on supporting Armoured Group 2.[99] Air Corps VIII was the larger of the two corps and was heavily engaged in the capture of Crete which, due to the battle concluding in early June, meant that there was little time to accomplish its transfer and make adequate preparations for Barbarossa.

---

[95] Ibid., p. 305.

[96] Hermann Plocher, *The German Air Force Versus Russia, 1941* (New York, 1965), p. 24.

[97] Boog, 'Die Luftwaffe'. See table: Ist-Stärke und Einsatzbereitschaft der fliegenden Verbände (einschl. Ergänzungsgruppen) der Luftwaffe im Osten am Vortage 'Bar-barossa' (21.6.1941), p. 313. The small Fifth Air Fleet deployed in the extreme north of the front did however command 40 dive-bombers and four destroyers.

[98] Kesselring, *Memoirs*, p. 89.   [99] Boog, 'Die Luftwaffe', p. 309.

Accordingly, on 21 June Air Corps VIII was still short of some 600 motor-vehicles, 40 per cent of its aircraft and vital communications equipment – a crucial deficiency on the eve of war.[100] The commander of Air Corps VIII, Colonel-General Wolfram von Richthofen, noted on 21 June: '[w]e are greatly concerned that our units are as yet unready'.[101]

Keeping hundreds of aircraft at peak operational efficiency presented an ongoing technical challenge which disguised the critical difference between aircraft numbers and those actually combat ready. For example, of the 425 dive-bombers cited above, only 323 were in fact combat ready and of the 98 'destroyers' only 60 were fit for service. Air Fleet 2 also numbered some 384 fighters with just 284 listed as combat ready, while the bomber force totalled 299 aircraft, but only 222 were serviceable. Overall, the Air Fleet numbered some 1,367 aircraft (all types), yet of this figure just 994 were able to conduct combat operations. The same was true for the Luftwaffe along the whole of the eastern front with an average 25 per cent fallout rate among aircraft totals – thus the 2,995 combined aircraft strength meant in real terms 2,255 combat ready.[102]

By the summer of 1941 it was clear that the Luftwaffe was only going to be able to meet all its obligations if the war in the east could be won quickly and without substantial losses. Either for practical reasons, such as the availability of oil, or for strategic considerations concerning Britain, a long campaign was simply untenable. The Luftwaffe was already engaged in a multi-front war which was tying down some 1,566 aircraft in western Europe, the Mediterranean, North Africa and Germany.[103] This major dispersion of strength to theatres of secondary importance prevented concentration on the most important front and the one with the smallest window for success.

The impossible equation – the logistics and supply of Barbarossa

Although my discussion of the major armed components making up Germany's invasion force reveals many of the institutional flaws within each service, the Achilles heel upon which all rested was logistics.

[100] Ibid., p. 307.
[101] Muller, *The German Air War in Russia*, p. 40. On this note, aviation historian Richard Muller added: 'While not every Luftwaffe unit had undergone such extensive recent use, the fact remains that the German air force commenced its largest operation of the war with a force structure and serviceability at dangerously low levels.'
[102] Boog, 'Die Luftwaffe'; see table, p. 313. See also Plocher, *German Air Force Versus Russia*, p. 35.
[103] Boog, 'Die Luftwaffe', p. 316.

The extent to which many Germans saw Hitler as a revolutionary leader was not only reflected by the disdainful vigour with which he denounced the Weimar Republic and international conventions. The Third Reich was to be an archetypal expression of modernisation, encompassing both a nationalist, spiritual renewal and technical progression. An essential element of this was the embracing of the motor vehicle and its promotion under the Nazis to supersede the railways. Accordingly, by the autumn of 1939 neglect had led to a critical deterioration of the railways with fewer locomotives and rolling stock than had existed in 1914.[104] Yet motorisation had by no means filled the void in Germany's transportation sector, which hindered economic progression and impeded the rate of conversion from rail to road based infrastructure. At its root were unalterable economic considerations that persistently failed to impress upon the Nazi leadership the futility of their goal. As many as 1,600 trucks were required to equal the capacity of a double-tracked railway line, while the consumption rates of fuel, personnel, spare parts and maintenance decisively favoured the railways for distances over 200 miles. Furthermore, Germany could not domestically produce the rubber and oil needed for motorisation, whereas coal and steel for the railways were readily available.[105]

For the Wehrmacht, motorisation offered the promise of a return to movement on the battlefield and a solution to the impasse of World War I. Many officers, however, held to their traditional reliance on the railways and warned against a one-sided approach. In spite of these concerns, Klaus Schüler makes clear that such reservations, particularly within Halder's General Staff, were regarded as matters of secondary importance and were not allowed to impinge on the primacy of operational command.[106] It is evident that, by pursuing motorisation and neglecting the railways, Germany created a situation where neither infrastructure was able to meet the demands of war.

By the advent of the war in 1939 the results of a partial motorisation of the armed forces produced, as we have seen, two separate armed forces each governed by an operational doctrine that proved mutually exclusive. In the invasion of Poland Germany fielded only 16 armoured,

---

[104] Klaus Schüler, 'The Eastern Campaign as a Transportation and Supply Problem' in Bernd Wegner (ed.), *From Peace to War. Germany, Soviet Russia and the World, 1939–1941* (Oxford, 1997), p. 206, footnote 2. See also Klaus Schüler, *Logistik im Russlandfeldzug. Die Rolle der Eisenbahn bei Planung, Vorbereitung und Durchführung des deutschen Angriffs auf die Sowjetunion bis zur Krise vor Moskau im Winter 1941/42* (Frankfurt am Main, 1987).

[105] Martin van Creveld, *Supplying War. Logistics from Wallenstein to Patton* (Cambridge, 1984), pp. 143–144.

[106] Klaus Schüler, 'The Eastern Campaign', p. 207.

motorised and 'light' formations which were fully motorised and, therefore, to a certain degree independent of the railways. For the rest of
the army, movement and supply were divided between the 'small column area' (*Kleinkolonnenraum*), in which the division operated, and the
'large transport area' (*Grosstransportraum*), responsible for bridging the
gap between the divisions and railheads. In the case of the *Kleinkolonnenraum*, the authorised establishment for each infantry division was 942
vehicles (excluding motorcycles) and 1,200 horse-drawn wagons. In the
case of the *Grosstransportraum*, only three transport regiments existed for
the whole army and these together numbered a pitiful 9,000 men and
operated 6,600 vehicles, of which 20 per cent were routinely undergoing
maintenance at any given time. In total, a maximum capacity of 19,500
tons could be delivered to the front, offering only the most limited re-
supply and dependent for this on relatively short distances.[107] To meet
even these most modest demands, the army's logistical apparatus had
been anxiously absorbing civilian trucks and vehicles into its ranks. While
this had the short-term effect of increasing capacity, it also exacerbated
the standardisation problem already prevalent within the army.

In 1938 there were 100 different types of trucks, 53 types of cars and
150 varying motorcycle designs in service. The resulting chaos led to the
'Schell Programme' which sought uniform standardisation but, given
Germany's limited resources, could not hope to make any real headway
before the Polish campaign was underway. The jumble of vehicles in
service was complicated further by the addition of those commandeered
from the civilian sector. These were not the robust six-wheeled, four-
wheel-drive, Krupp models, but instead the ordinary two-wheel-drive
variants, unsuited to the rigours of war on dust-choked, unsealed Polish
roads. As a result some units suffered vehicle losses of up to 50 per
cent, which factory replacements, consisting largely of two-wheel-drive
models, simply could not make good.[108]

Confronting this problem in February 1940 Halder noted that the
army possessed 120,000 trucks, which did not allow any to be held in
reserve. There was already a shortfall of 2,668 trucks (more than 2 per
cent[109] of the overall total) which, added together with those trucks out of
service due to maintenance or repair, created a deficit of more than 4 per
cent of the total.[110] Thus, the army was already some 5,000 trucks under
strength. Even more worrying was the monthly loss of roughly 2,400

---

[107] Van Creveld, *Supplying War*, p. 144.   [108] Deighton, *Blitzkrieg*, pp. 204–205.
[109] Halder records this figure as being 'less than 2%', which is mathematically incorrect.
[110] The fact that the overall figure for trucks undergoing maintenance and repair is so
     much lower than that for those in the *Grosstransportraum* (20 per cent) may reflect the
     added strain placed on this arm of the service.

trucks (2 per cent) from accidents or simple mechanical wear, with a replacement figure per month of just 1,000 vehicles. The end result, as Halder recorded, was 'a deterioration in the operational ability'.[111]

What is most striking about the dire shortage being experienced by the army was that it was worsening at a rate of 1 per cent of the total every month, even without the mechanical fallout rates of a sustained campaign or the battlefield losses this would entail. When one takes into account the great distances and poor infrastructure of the Soviet Union, the issue of logistics, with all its foreboding implications, stands at the forefront of problems to be encountered.

Obvious possible remedies included increasing production, but owing to the limited availability of rubber a projected maximum of only 4,000 vehicles a month (for the whole armed forces, allowing 2,500–2,600 for the army) could be produced. Requisitioning 16,000 trucks from the civilian economy was considered, although this would prove only a short-term solution and leave the army facing the same dilemma in seven months. Thus, as extraordinary as it may seem, Halder therefore undertook an 'extensive de-motorisation' (*großzügige Entmotorisierung*) programme in which the seven-month respite granted by the civilian truck allocation could be used to achieve a balance in the loss/replacement ratio. Halder reasoned that with a reduction in the total number of vehicles, one could expect a decrease in the fallout rate, allowing production to close the gap on the shortfall. Consequently, orders were to be issued immediately to implement the necessary preparations for the procurement of more horses, harnesses and carriages.[112]

Clearly, such a plan would further polarise the spilt between motorised divisions and the rest of the army. The worst, however, was yet to come as continued tank production, and Hitler's later decision to arbitrarily double the number of panzer divisions, resulted in many more trucks being required to provide for their movement and supply. The infantry divisions were thus forced to shed an even greater share of motorised vehicles, finding themselves ever more dependent on horses and wagons.[113] In the spring of 1941 the drain was somewhat offset by the expropriation of French war materiel, furnishing the Wehrmacht with 13,000 trucks[114] and 341 trains.[115] In addition, the army gained between 3,000

---

[111] Franz Halder, KTB I, pp. 180–181 (4 February 1940).   [112] Ibid., p. 181.

[113] Franz Halder, KTB II, p. 4 (1 July 1940).

[114] General Guderian later wrote that these French vehicles were 'in no way capable of meeting the demands of warfare in eastern Europe' (Guderian, *Panzer Leader*, p. 143). See also comments by General Hoth (Hoth, *Panzer-Operationen*, pp. 44–45).

[115] Franz Halder, KTB II, p. 321 (18 March 1941).

and 4,000 trucks from French North Africa[116] and was able to purchase more from Switzerland.[117] The trade-off for alleviating the immediate strain on resources was a further exacerbation of the standardisation problem, which had grown so out of proportion that by the launch of Barbarossa some 2,000 different types of vehicle were in service and Army Group Centre alone had to stock and distribute over a million types of spare parts.[118] The administrative complexity inevitably led to time-consuming delays in returning vehicles to service. It also complicated the smooth function of panzer divisions. The 18th Panzer Division, for example, fielded no fewer than 96 different types of personnel carriers, 111 types of trucks and 37 types of motorcycles.[119] The evidence suggests that Hitler's eastern army resembled a pieced-together, mismatched construction – not the imposing, purpose-built, uniformly-equipped war machine often portrayed in the immediate post-war literature.[120]

A further complication of primary importance to a motorised supply system was the availability of fuel. Only nine days before the beginning of the campaign Thomas visited Halder and outlined for him, in the bleakest of terms, the grossly inadequate state of Germany's oil reserves. 'Fuel supplies', Thomas explained, 'will be exhausted in the autumn, aviation fuel will be down to one-half, regular fuel to only a quarter. Diesel and heating oil would be at only half the required levels.'[121] The Wehrmacht operations department had been observing the dwindling oil stocks since the beginning of the planning for Operation Barbarossa and had exerted some of its influence to push for economic objectives. These were focused on the Soviet oil-producing region of the Caucasus and necessitated that part of Army Group South's strength march towards the Donets region and then on to Krasnodar and Maykop-Grozny. In accordance with these objectives the War Economic Staff issued a request to the 17th Army dated 12 June in which it asked that the oil region of Drogobycz in Galicia be occupied as soon as possible. Halder, however, refused to pass on the request[122] and noted in his diary on the following day: 'Political Questions – I refuse to allow economic considerations to influence the operational direction.'[123] Not only does this highlight the urgency of Germany's fuel shortage, at least according to the War Economic Staff,

[116] Many of these, however, were destined to remain in Africa to support Rommel's Africa corps. Franz Halder, KTB II, p. 390 (2 May 1941).
[117] Van Creveld, *Supplying War*, p. 151.   [118] Overy, *Why the Allies Won*, p. 217.
[119] Rudolf Steiger, *Armour Tactics in World War II. Panzer Army Campaigns of 1939–41 in German War Diaries* (Oxford, 1991), p. 127.
[120] Müller, 'Von der Wirtschaftsallianz', pp. 188–189.
[121] Franz Halder, KTB II, p. 454 (13 June 1940).
[122] Klink, 'Die militärische Konzeption', p. 272.
[123] Franz Halder, KTB II, p. 454 (13 June 1940).

but it also illustrates Halder's refusal to allow any encroachment on his operational concept, especially for objectives he saw as extraneous to the task of defeating the Soviet Union. Importantly for the coming war, a good deal of Hitler's operational conception in the secondary stage of the campaign was fixed on economic objectives.

In a reversal of logical procedure characteristic of Halder's General Staff, the feasibility of the operation was assumed from the outset and planning for its logistical support only begun on that basis. It is not surprising, therefore, that on the same day (1 August 1940) that Major-General Marcks was reporting to Halder his planned conduct of the operation, the Quartermaster-General was instructed to begin his own planning.[124] This was entrusted to Major-General Wagner, who would be faced with the seemingly intractable task of giving the campaign an equitable chance of realising its grand objectives, which, if at all possible, necessitated a short campaign that could largely be won between the German border and the Dvina–Dnepr line. The German army's supply system was simply incapable of adequately sustaining anything further than a penetration of about 500 kilometres into the Soviet Union.[125]

After the defeat of France in 1940 Germany's army was initially to be expanded from 120 to 180 divisions, but by the eve of Barbarossa it had ballooned to some 209 divisions.[126] As a result, availability of motor transport for the divisions had both shrunk as a percentage of the pre-war total, and been heavily concentrated into the new panzer and motorised divisions. In the same period, an equivalent expansion of the logistical apparatus had proved utterly impossible owing to materiel shortages, namely of trucks. Supplying an army of such size necessitated the extensive use of railways; this, however, faced the cardinal problem that the Soviet railway gauge was wider than the rest of Europe. The lines would first have to be reset to accommodate German trains, but this could not be undertaken at anything approaching the speed necessary to sustain the operational timetable. The solution therefore hinged on supporting the panzer and motorised divisions as far to the east as possible with wheeled transport. Determining whether this was possible or not depended entirely on estimates of fuel consumption and ammunition expenditure which, owing to the many unknown variables, were ultimately decided upon by the maximum transport capacity of the vehicles,

---

[124] Ibid., p. 51 (1 August 1940).

[125] Dr Ihno Krumpelt and a small staff were commissioned by Wagner at the beginning of October 1940 to commence planning for an eastern campaign. See Ihno Krumpelt, *Das Material und die Kriegführung* (Frankfurt am Main, 1968) p. 149.

[126] 'Beurteilung des Kampfwertes der Divisionen nach dem Stand vom 20. Juni 1941', BA-MA RH 2/v. 247, Fols 151–153.

and not any informed projection of conditions.[127] As such, the panzer spearheads would be dependent on a logistical system already pushed to full capacity, without any available reserves.

To propel the panzer groups forward as far as possible even the tanks were heavily loaded with supplies. The Mark II, III and IV tanks were fitted with two-wheeled trailers each carrying two 200-litre petrol tanks, while some were further loaded with 20-litre petrol cans strapped to their turrets. Moreover, twice the standard complement of ammunition was squeezed inside each tank, making them as self-sufficient as possible during the earliest phase of the campaign.[128] Despite such improvisations, supplying operations to ranges hundreds of kilometres beyond the German border clearly required a more sustained approach. A reorganisation of the army's rear services, which included stripping the infantry divisions of all but the most essential motorisation and replacing the loss with 15,000 Polish '*Panje*' horse-drawn wagons, eventually raised the capacity of the *Grosstransportraum* behind the three army groups to 15,880 tons in the south, 25,020 tons in the centre and 12,750 tons in the north.[129] This was then chiefly concentrated in support of the panzer groups, which gave Army Group Centre the only chance of securing the Dvina–Dnepr line before a major halt became necessary. In practice, however, estimates indicate that the trucks could only provide the motorised divisions with about 70 tons of supplies per day when they required on average 300 tons.[130] Specifically, the supply operation employed a new method of distribution known to the troops as 'hand baggage' (*Handkoffer*). This determined that supply columns advanced with the panzer units replenishing them as they went and dumping the remainder of their loads at a forward point about 100 kilometres from the border. While these columns then returned for new loads, others would continue with the advance to establish a second supply dump 300 kilometres from the border. The panzer divisions would use their own *Kleinkolonnenraum* to supply themselves from the dump sites.[131] Obviously the efficiency of

[127] Leach, *German Strategy Against Russia 1939–1941*, p. 138.

[128] Von Senger und Etterlin, *German Tanks of World War II*, p. 45.

[129] Franz Halder, KTB II, pp. 382 and 384 (26 and 28 April 1941); van Creveld, *Supplying War*, p. 151; Wilhelm Deist, 'Die militärische Planung des "Unternehmens Barbarossa"' in Roland G. Foerster (ed.), *'Unternehmen Barbarossa'* (Munich, 1993), p. 115.

[130] Rolf-Dieter Müller, 'Das Scheitern der wirtschaftlichen "Blitzkriegstrategie"' in Militärgeschichtliches Forschungsamt (ed.), *Das Deutsche Reich und der Zweite Weltkrieg*, p. 961.

[131] Elisabeth Wagner (ed.), *Der Generalquartiermeister. Briefe und Tagebuchaufzeichnungen des Generalquartiermeisters des Heeres General der Artillerie Eduard Wagner* (Munich, 1963), p. 285; Leach, *German Strategy Against Russia 1939–1941*, pp. 138–139;

the system deteriorated with distance, while complications owing to poor roads, vehicle breakdowns and enemy action only weakened the already tenuous basis upon which it all rested.[132]

Included in the administrative regulations for the Soviet territories was a directive entitled: 'Guidelines for booty, confiscation and exacting of services', which translated into the open exploitation of the occupied areas for the army's benefit. Yet, in recognition of the enormous burden carried by the motorised transport columns, Wagner issued his own 'Order for the securing of booty during operations'. This was intended for army and corps commands and aimed at keeping the operations moving by utilising captured stocks of vital resources and materials such as foodstuffs, motor-vehicles, fuel, horses, wagons and ammunition.[133] The great need to supplement the existing supply system was not limited to the employment of captured Red Army equipment, but extended to the plunder of the local populace. Accordingly, the German army undertook a ruthless programme of expropriation which, in addition to further exposing the shortcomings of its own logistical apparatus, also had the profound effect of rapidly alienating the Soviet population. Before the invasion the 18th Panzer Division ordered its troops to undertake 'full exploitation of the land', which later resulted in instances where whole villages were looted with anyone who resisted being shot.[134] One SS report denounced such practices of the army, complaining:

The positive attitude towards the Germans[135] is being jeopardised by the indiscriminate requisitions by the troops, which become generally known, further by individual instances of rape, and by the way the Army treats the civilian population, which feel handled as an enemy people.[136]

This is not only a moral indictment on the conduct of the army, underlining its direct liability in hardening the resolve of the Soviet cause, but, at its root, it highlights the great inadequacy of the motorised-based logistical system for the size of the army driving into the Soviet Union.

According to the operational plans the achievement of the Dvina–Dnepr line would see the bulk of the Red Army cut off and facing destruction, leaving only weak reserves further east. Yet it was also recognised that, irrespective of the enemy situation, this point would represent the

---

van Creveld, *Supplying War*, p. 153; Müller, 'Das Scheitern der wirtschaftlichen "Blitzkriegstrategie"', pp. 961–962.

[132] Krumpelt, *Das Material und die Kriegführung*, pp. 150–151 and 154–155.

[133] Klink, 'Die militärische Konzeption', pp. 257–258.

[134] Bartov, *The Eastern Front, 1941–45*, pp. 130 and 135.

[135] In some regions such as eastern Poland, the Ukraine and the Baltic states the Germans were initially seen as liberators from communist domination.

[136] Alexander Dallin, *German Rule in Russia 1941–1945. A Study of Occupation Policies* (London, 1957), p. 215.

furthest possible extension of the motorised logistical system. Beyond this the railroads would assume a decisive importance, re-establishing stockpiles for the next thrust and providing for the great mass of infantry now drawing up behind the panzer and motorised divisions.

If the initial vehicle-based advance appeared tenuous at best, the conceptual foundation for the railway-based supply system should be characterised as sheer wishful thinking. Overwrought by buoyant optimism, the calculations made during the spring 1941 planning stage assumed the absolute minimum requirement for the repair and operation of the railways in the occupied areas. To make matters worse, planning assumed the widespread capture of broad-gauge Soviet trains and only insignificant damage to the Soviet rail network. The general disappointment of this absurd expectation forced heavy reliance on the immediate eastward extension of the standard-gauge rail lines, while the deficit in locomotives and rolling stock had to be borne by the already over-strained *Reichsbahn* (German railways).[137] From a cursory study of the battlefield movements, the impending crisis was not at first evident, as the panzers raced ahead still supported by their motorised columns and the infantry were sustained by their own wagon trains. The railroad troops (*Eisenbahntruppe*), however, were faced with critical shortages of both manpower and materials, making rapid progress impossible. Dependent on the army groups for their allocation of fuel, they suffered from a low priority ranking, made worse by the fact that only one-sixth of the formations were fully motorised and two-thirds had to make do without any vehicles at all. In total only 1,000 vehicles were allocated to the *Eisenbahntruppe* (mostly inferior French and British models) across the whole eastern front.[138]

Administrative difficulties also encroached on the operation of the logistical system. Wagner's position as the Army Quartermaster-General gave him authority over the stockpiles of supplies, the depots at which these were stored and the haulage vehicles, but not the railways, which were under the control of Lieutenant-General Rudolf Gercke, the Chief of Wehrmacht Transport. Gercke was thus working under the timetables and constraints of the OKW while Wagner served the OKH, and the interests of the two command organisations did not always coincide. Thus, while Wagner was responsible for the organisation and distribution of supplies at each end of the railways, he held little power over what quantities could be shipped or when these would arrive.[139]

---

[137] Schüler, 'The Eastern Campaign', pp. 209–210.

[138] Van Creveld, *Supplying War*, p. 153.

[139] Müller, 'Das Scheitern der wirtschaftlichen "Blitzkriegstrategie"', p. 962. It was only in the summer of 1942 that the army groups in the east were at last given command over their supply apparatus. Krumpelt, *Das Material und die Kriegführung*, p. 153.

On a technical level, the adaptation of German trains to the eastern theatre was much more complex than the conversion of rails to the standard gauge. In theory, converting the rails was a relatively straightforward procedure of removing the spikes, moving the rails and hammering the spikes down again. In practice, however, the Soviets were to prove particularly effective in damaging or destroying the rail beds and twisting rails, forcing the Germans to bring up new materials and engage in a much more time-consuming construction process. To make matters worse, most Soviet locomotives were much bigger machines, capable of carrying a greater load of water and fuel, which allowed them to travel about twice the distance of their German counterparts. This left an absence of service stations for the German trains, which had to be built from nothing and often required locomotive sheds, repair shops, slag pits, turntables, sidings and water towers. In contrast to the relative ease of rail conversion, these would require skilled personnel, scarce heavy construction equipment and considerable materials, not to mention much precious time. Such unforeseen complications altered the premise upon which all timetables were fixed and placed in doubt the relief of the hard-pressed panzer divisions.

In his 1937 book *Achtung-Panzer* the German tank commander, Heinz Guderian, wrote:

The extensive mechanization of the army has raised two important issues: how will the army as a whole be supplied with fuel, spares and replacement vehicles? And how will we be able to move our large mechanized formations, and especially the ones that are road-bound? A positive answer to these two requirements is a precondition for the deployment of large tank formations, not least for their use in the operational dimension.[140]

In answer to his own pertinent questions, Guderian cited three areas of concentration – fuel, sustained replenishment of military vehicles with spare parts and access to a network of highways and roads. While each of these three conditions presented their share of problems during the French campaign, the ultimate success of the operation has suggested to some that none of these posed insurmountable difficulties.[141] In casting an eye forward to the eastern campaign, maintaining faith in the army's logistical apparatus should have taken into account both the expansion

[140] Guderian, *Achtung-Panzer!*, p. 207.
[141] Much less than a major inhibiting factor, R. H. S Stolfi's argument even suggests that the German supply system could have supported operations as far as Moscow in the summer of 1941 (Stolfi, *Hitler's Panzers East*, Chapter 11, 'German Logistics: Could the Germans Support an Advance into the Moscow-Gorki Space in the Summer of 1941?').

of the German army and the fundamental geographic differences to be encountered. Whereas shortages of fuel proved substantial in France, their effect was mitigated firstly by the much shorter distances (the longest stretches of the advance were undertaken only after effective Allied resistance had been broken), secondly by the seizure of Allied fuel dumps, and thirdly by the fact that German tanks were fitted with petrol engines, which allowed them to refuel at roadside petrol stations.[142] By contrast, not only was the Soviet Union a much larger theatre of operations, but Soviet fuel contained a lower octane content rendering captured stocks useless until they could be treated in specially-constructed installations.[143]

Guderian's second condition, the need to ensure the replenishment of military vehicles and spare parts, has already been identified as failing to meet even the most basic requirements of the army. This was evident even from the Polish campaign and the problem became so acute in the invasion of France that ten days into the campaign Wagner, then Chief of Staff at the Quartermaster-General's office, requested and received permission to 'gather all available motorised transport in Germany' to provide for the needs of the army.[144] By comparison with the conditions in the west, the eastern campaign presented logistical challenges so profound that the prospect of a greater crisis of over-extension was not only likely, it was preordained.

The third point raised by Guderian was the need for access to roads or highways to facilitate supply. Given the extremely limited degree of German motorisation in 1937, such an assertion neglects the vital role railways would have to play in any foreseeable war, but it also makes the implicit assumption that supplying mobile divisions is only possible in developed areas.[145] The barren and open plains to the east, crossed only by minor farming tracks and occasional dirt roads, often ruined by the heavy traffic of horse and cart, were not what Guderian had in mind. Indeed, of the 850,000 miles of road in the Soviet Union, only 40,000 miles were hard surfaced, all-weather roads.[146]

---

[142] Deighton, *Blitzkrieg*, p. 179.
[143] Franz Halder, KTB II, p. 422 (20 May 1941); van Creveld, *Supplying War*, p. 150.
[144] Wagner (ed.), *Der Generalquartiermeister*, p. 256.
[145] Guderian suggested that Italian achievements in building roads during their Abyssinian campaign presented a model for adapting his operations to desolate landscapes. Thus, he called for the establishment of special road-construction units, equipped with modern machines and tools. Yet he does not address how these special units could possibly keep pace with the rapid forward movement of operations, especially over long distances. Guderian, *Achtung-Panzer!*, p. 209.
[146] Earl F. Ziemke and Magna E. Bauer, *Moscow to Stalingrad: Decision in the East* (New York, 1988), p. 14.

There can be no doubt that the German operations in the east were underpinned by irresponsible staff work and shameless over-confidence. In 1940–1941 Germany stood at the height of its overwhelming military success and, flushed with the accolades of past victories, Hitler's generals eagerly accepted each new task. The challenges presented by Operation Barbarossa seemed less threatening than those faced by the ultimately victorious campaign in the west. The collective shame of those generals, who had dared doubt the invasion of France and the Low Countries, soon extinguished future scepticism and confused the line between reasoned objection and pessimistic cynicism. Accordingly, the flaws so plainly apparent in the conception of the coming campaign were allowed to pass, at times with both a measure of official acknowledgement and indifference.[147] Reminiscent of Hitler's constant extolment of the primacy of 'will', irrespective of difficulties, the generals remained steadfastly undeterred by problematic or negative reports and concentrated simply on implementing the orders at hand. Beginning such a major campaign with such a deplorable base in logistics and supply was an obvious symptom of the larger problem.

---

[147] Richard Lakowski, 'Between Professionalism and Nazism. The Wehrmacht on the Eve of its Invasion of the USSR' in Bernd Wegner (ed.), *From Peace to War. Germany, Soviet Russia and the World, 1939–1941* (Oxford, 1997), pp. 162–164.

4   The advent of war

'Welcome to hell on earth'

Hitler's War Directive 21 stated that preparations for the campaign against the Soviet Union were to be concluded by 15 May 1941.[1] While planning for the eastern campaign went ahead, the wider war was developing in its own direction, rapidly engulfing the nations of south-eastern Europe, until events finally came to a head in the spring of 1941, compelling Hitler to intervene. The Balkan campaign is sometimes narrowly portrayed as Hitler's response to the successful Yugoslav coup against the regent Prince Paul, who was deposed after finally acceding to the Tripartite Pact, following months of German pressure. In truth, however, Hitler's rationale for the new campaign ultimately aimed at restoring the Axis position in the south and ensuring Germany's flank for the invasion of the Soviet Union.

Since October 1940 Mussolini had been embroiled in a disastrous attempt to invade Greece, which soon saw his beleaguered army thrown back into Albania and forced to defend itself against further Greek counter-attacks.[2] The following months saw increasingly bold British action in the eastern Mediterranean and North Africa, leading to heavy Italian losses and the eventual Greek consent to the landing of four British divisions. The Greek hesitation in accepting direct British assistance was closely tied to their well-founded concerns about provoking Hitler,[3] who feared the British were seeking to recreate a 'Salonika front' like the one that had proved such a thorn in Germany's side in 1916–1918. Of even greater concern to Hitler was the prospect that British bombers might be committed to new RAF airfields and used to strike the vital oil fields

---

[1] Trevor-Roper (ed.), *Hitler's War Directives 1939–1945*, p. 94.
[2] For a detailed discussion of this little-known war see Gerhard Schreiber, 'Mussolinis Überfall auf Griechenland oder der Anfang vom Ende der italienischen Großmachtstellung' in Militärgeschichtliches Forschungsamt (ed.), *Das Deutsche Reich und der Zweite Weltkrieg*, Band III: *Der Mittelmeerraum und Südosteuropa. Von der 'non belligeranza' Italiens bis zum Kriegseintritt der Vereinigten Staaten* (Stuttgart, 1984), pp. 368–414.
[3] Franz Halder, KTB II, p. 212 (5 December 1940).

in Romania. In addition, Hitler was undoubtedly aware of the economic implications control over south-eastern Europe held for Germany. Half of Germany's cereal and livestock came from the region, 45 per cent of its bauxite (aluminium ore), 90 per cent of its tin, 40 per cent of its lead and 10 per cent of its copper.[4] Finally, a major operation to occupy Yugoslavia and Greece would provide a somewhat more convincing explanation for the growing German military build-up in the east, helping to allay any Soviet fears of an impending attack.

Planning for what later became known as Operation Marita began in early November 1940,[5] although Hitler made it clear to Mussolini and the Italian foreign minister, Galeazzo Ciano, that German intervention could not be expected before the following spring.[6] In spite of the continuing turmoil in the south, the army's deployment and timing for Barbarossa remained almost unaltered until the Yugoslav coup. The heavy commitment of first-rate German combat formations to Operation Barbarossa required the immediate dispatch of nine divisions and two corps headquarters to new assembly areas in the south,[7] inducing a delay in the launch of the eastern campaign, which Halder estimated at being around four weeks.[8] Some have questioned the wisdom of this postponement,[9] but a delay was almost certainly inevitable given that the late spring thaw had swelled and in some cases flooded the major waterways, impeding mobile operations over the sodden ground.[10]

Even though the time lost was unavoidable owing to the unseasonable weather, the Balkan campaign still exacted a military price. From the divisions committed to action in Yugoslavia, two-thirds were simply replaced in the line by OKH reserves and all combat divisions were en route back to the eastern border by the end of May. The forces committed to Greece, however, were a different matter. Combat losses were slight yet, as would soon be the case in Operation Barbarossa, the long distances and inhospitable terrain took a much greater toll on the German panzers and motorised transports.[11] As a result, these divisions had to make the long journey back to Germany to receive thorough overhauls and partial

---

[4] John Keegan, *The Second World War* (New York, 1989), p. 146.

[5] KTB OKW, Volume I, p. 150 (4 November 1940).

[6] Domarus, *Hitler*, Volume III, p. 2139; Detlef Vogel, 'Die deutsche Balkanpolitik im Herbst 1940 und Frühjahr 1941' in Militärgeschichtliches Forschungsamt (ed.), *Das Deutsche Reich und der Zweite Weltkrieg*, Band III, p. 422.

[7] Leach, *German Strategy Against Russia 1939–1941*, p. 165.

[8] Franz Halder, KTB II, p. 332 (28 March 1941).

[9] Von Below, *Als Hitlers Adjutant 1937–45*, pp. 271–272.

[10] Guderian, *Panzer Leader*, p. 145;. Günther Blumentritt, *Von Rundstedt. The Soldier and the Man* (London, 1952), p. 101; Hillgruber, *Hitlers Strategie*, pp. 506–507; Detlef Vogel 'Der deutsche Überfall auf Jugoslawien und Griechenland' in Militärgeschichtliches Forschungsamt (ed.), *Das Deutsche Reich und der Zweite Weltkrieg*, Band III, p. 483.

[11] Leach, *German Strategy Against Russia 1939–1941*, p. 166.

re-equipping. It proved a time-consuming process and meant that the 2nd and 5th Panzer Divisions, as well as the 60th Motorised Infantry Division, only arrived on the eastern front well after the initial attack.[12] The two panzer divisions were then held in the OKH reserve and did not see action until October 1941. The delay in returning motorised units to service proved an important setback given the brief window of opportunity for the success of Barbarossa. Compounding this was the loss of the entire 12th Army, which was needed to provide occupation forces and coastal defence in south-eastern Europe. This complicated the already difficult task of Army Group South, which made the slowest progress of the three army groups in the opening weeks of Operation Barbarossa.[13] In the longer term, partly because of the brutally repressive measures enacted against the Serb and later Greek populations, the Balkans rapidly became the centre of an intense guerrilla war, harming Germany's economic exploitation and demanding increasingly large security forces.[14] Finally, one must consider the resultant military cost of seizing Crete in May 1941, where some 220 transport aircraft were lost and 4,000 German soldiers killed, devastating the elite 7th Parachute Division and ending Hitler's enthusiasm for further airborne operations.[15]

The Balkan campaign placed yet another drain on Germany's eroding military resources and contributed in no small measure to the mounting over-extension of the Wehrmacht. Alone these burdens could be borne, at least in the short term. The added risk posed by invading the Soviet Union presented an entirely different proposition and one which entailed very real dangers for the Reich. Operation Barbarossa was always going to be a great gamble and in many regards the odds were stacked against Germany. Still, Hitler chose this course and, resolutely backed by his generals, there was no dispute about the wisdom of war, or the prospect of victory. If Hitler bears the guilt of being an obsessive megalomaniac, driven by a fanatical and irrepressible will, the generals too must be accorded their share of blame for blindly following and even encouraging him.[16]

On the last day of April 1941 Hitler settled on 22 June as the new date for the start of Operation Barbarossa.[17] Despite the months of planning

[12] Franz Halder, KTB II, p. 387 (30 April 1941); Blumentritt, 'Moscow', p. 36.
[13] Cecil, Hitler's Decision to Invade Russia 1941, p. 134.
[14] Vogel, 'Der deutsche Überfall', p. 483; Seaton, The German Army 1933–45, p. 171. For a detailed study see Mark Mazower, Inside Hitler's Greece. The Experience of Occupation, 1941–1944 (London, 1993).
[15] Keegan, The Second World War, pp. 171–172.
[16] Kershaw, Hitler 1936–1945, pp. 368–369.
[17] Franz Halder, KTB II, p. 387 (30 April 1941); Cecil, Hitler's Decision to Invade Russia 1941, p. 134; Hillgruber, Hitlers Strategie, pp. 507–508; Kershaw, Hitler 1936–1945, p. 368.

and the fact that the postponement of the operation was a relatively recent occurrence, the generals were still undecided on basic questions concerning the deployment of panzers and infantry in the initial attack. This had been debated since Paulus's December 1940 war game, where the old issue of the panzer groups operating as independent entities was again a subject of contention.[18] A further war game conducted in February 1941 under Guderian's direction raised the issue once more. In this instance Hoth, commander of Panzer Group 3, was worried that the presence of infantry divisions would congest the roads and slow the advance of his own forces. Neither Bock nor Guderian agreed, although Hoth was somewhat placated by assurances that these forward infantry divisions would be subordinated to him, allowing him to ensure that their movement did not impede his panzers. Explaining the decision, Bock, as Army Group Centre's commander, was clearly concerned at the speed with which a gap could open up between his infantry divisions and those of the motorised and panzer divisions. 'If I gave into Hoth's demand', Bock wrote, 'the leading infantry might not cross the border until four or five days after the tanks in Panzer Group 3's attack area, meaning the entire northern sector of the 9th Army.'[19] For Hoth's part, he insisted upon the promised control of the infantry divisions, pursuing the matter all the way to Halder to ensure his authority.[20]

By the middle of May, the suggestion that Guderian's Panzer Group 2 should likewise accommodate infantry divisions in its forward area provoked an apparent change of heart in the general. According to Bock, Guderian now spoke out harshly against the proposals, claiming they would split up his panzer units in the first attack. Bock also now expressed reservations. The additional infantry was to be provided by the strategic reserve, causing Bock to complain: '[A]rtillery and combat engineers of the reserve are already being committed in the first attack; if they are now joined by the infantry, there will be practically nothing left of the reserves.'[21] The impatient desire to move the infantry closer to the border was Brauchitsch's initiative and not only the panzer units were affected; he also wanted the reserves packed more tightly together on the army group's right wing. Bock feared this would produce mass confusion and obstruct movement throughout the entire army group. Summing up his view, Bock wrote:

---

[18] Görlitz, *Paulus and Stalingrad*, p. 100.
[19] Fedor von Bock, KTB 'Vorbereitungszeit', Fol. 8, *War Diary*, p. 201 (27 February 1941).
[20] Franz Halder, KTB II, p. 325 and 330 (21 and 27 March 1941).
[21] Fedor von Bock, KTB 'Vorbereitungszeit', Fol. 16 (14–16 May 1941). See also Fol. 21 (4 June 1941), *War Diary*, p. 213 (14–16 May 1941), and p. 218 (4 June 1941).

The same dictate as the year before at Wesel, where they forced me to move them [the reserves] closer! That led to dangerous traffic jams, which were overcome only with great difficulty. It will be exactly the same here, for days will pass before Panzer Group 2 departs and before the XII Corps is across the Bug, in which the reserves can close ranks calmly.[22]

In the end, Guderian was appeased in much the same manner as Hoth, which may well have formed the impetus for his change of heart. At his own request, Guderian was temporarily given command of XII Corps to assault the defences at Brest Litovsk.[23] The resolution was only agreed as late as 12 June 1941, which may explain why Brauchitsch, in spite of his aversion to the plan, grudgingly accepted it. Bock was also disturbed, writing: 'I too can see no advantage to this solution . . . And up front is a huge mass of infantry, which can easily lead to large and unnecessary losses.' Bock then added: 'Behind it all is the failure of those in charge to clearly and in good time order what they wanted; that would have elim- inated all discussions and compromises.'[24] Bock's insightful comment forms a rare instance of general criticism which, although unknown to Bock at the time, deserves to be seen in the wider context of Halder's and Brauchitsch's deception over Moscow.

As the date of attack drew nearer, the final intelligence reports from the deputy military attaché in Moscow, Colonel Hans Krebs, and the chief of Foreign Armies East, Colonel Kinzel, reaffirmed the general tone of confidence within the German High Command. Towards the end of April, Kinzel noted that estimates of the Red Army had grown to a peacetime strength of 170 divisions, but that many divisions were short of equipment, especially artillery. Officers were also said to be in short supply with regiments being commanded by young majors and divisions by colonels.[25] Krebs gave his report to Halder upon returning from Moscow on 5 May. The Soviets, he said, would do anything to avoid war and yield on every issue short of making territorial concessions. The officers' corps was decidedly bad and, compared with 1933, the over- all picture was strikingly negative. Indeed, despite Soviet rearmament, Krebs maintained it would take the Red Army twenty years to reach their former position.[26] The reports only confirmed the impression, shared throughout the upper circles of the Wehrmacht, that the Soviet Union was still a backward land with a large but clumsy army, lacking modern equipment, training and above all leadership. In early May, as the

[22] Ibid., Fol. 16, p. 213 (14–16 May 1941).   [23] Macksey, *Guderian*, p. 131.
[24] Fedor von Bock, KTB 'Vorbereitungszeit', Fol. 23, *War Diary*, p. 220 (12 June 1941).
[25] Franz Halder, KTB II, p. 382 (26 April 1941).
[26] Ibid., pp. 396–397 (5 May 1941).

commander of Army Group South, Field Marshal Gerd von Rundstedt, bid goodbye to his counterpart at Army Group North, Field Marshal Wilhelm Ritter von Leeb, he made the laconic remark: 'Well then, see you in Siberia.'[27] In a further dose of sober realism, Ulrich von Hassell commented a week before the campaign on 15 June 1941: 'The prospects of a swift victory against Russia are still judged by the soldiers as stirringly bright.'[28]

While the accuracy of German intelligence amounted to little more than an accumulation of fanciful misinformation, a glaring failure of Halder's General Staff was its blatant unwillingness to consider the other side to the Soviet empire. The remarkable increases in industrialisation, the vast manpower reserves, the adaptability of a centralised economy to wartime mobilisation and the absolute authority of the state administration headed by Stalin, all merited closer attention. The prospect of the Soviet Union as an emerging great power with modern military concepts and technical sophistication was not an entirely new idea, nor one unknown to the German military. Describing the Soviet state in 1937 Guderian wrote:

Russia possesses the strongest army in the world, numerically and in terms of the modernity of its weapons and equipment. The Russians have the world's largest air force as well, and they are striving to bring their navy up to the same level. The transport system is still inadequate, but they are working hard in that direction also. Russia has ample raw materials, and a mighty armaments industry has been set up in the depths of that vast empire. The time has passed when the Russians had no instinct for technology; we will have to reckon on the Russians being able to master and build their own machines, and with the fact that such a transformation in the Russians' fundamental mentality confronts us with the Eastern Question in a form more serious than ever before in history.[29]

Clearly, if the Soviet people were committed to fighting a serious war, it would be nothing less than that – a serious war, whatever the Germans might have planned.

Juxtaposing Guderian's insightful comprehension of Soviet potential with his subsequent participation in the hopelessly ill-conceived war plans[30] provides a good example of the contradiction which characterised the whole General Staff. Even assuming a positive impression of Soviet

---

[27] Burleigh, *The Third Reich*, p. 491; Hillgruber, 'The German Military Leaders' View of Russia', p. 181.

[28] Von Hassell, *Vom andern Deutschland*, p. 209 (15 June 1941); von Hassell, *Diaries*, p. 180 (15 June 1941).

[29] Guderian, *Achtung-Panzer!*, pp. 153–154.

[30] Hillgruber, *Hitlers Strategie*, pp. 226–227; Engel, *Heeresadjutant bei Hitler 1938–1943*, p. 86 (10 August 1940).

capabilities at the height of Tukhachevsky's influence,[31] which was by no means shared among all German generals of the period, the Red Army's fall from grace in the intervening years was probably only surpassed in its magnitude by the Wehrmacht's swift ascendance to domination of Europe.[32] By 1940–41 questioning the strategic wisdom of Hitler's all-knowing vision for Germany was tantamount to 'defeatism' within the General Staff and career-minded officers, emboldened by past triumphs and looking forward to a victorious conclusion to the war, were not about to risk professional estrangement.[33] Thus, while purporting to offer a sound and objective review of all intelligence for the purpose of devising reasoned military responses, the General Staff had in fact become so corrupted in its core function as to fulfil Hitler's every whimsical desire unswervingly. The extent of these desires went as far as issuing War Directive No. 32, signed by Warlimont, projecting future military operations into the Middle East from Transcaucasia and Turkey, even before the invasion of the Soviet Union had begun.[34] The chief of the Operations Department in the Army General Staff, Colonel Adolf Heusinger, wrote after the war: '[E]stimations of the military, economic and internal political power of the Soviet Union were completely false.'[35]

The last major military conference before the start of operations was held on 14 June at the Reich Chancellery in Berlin. The participants included a large number of the highest ranking officers from the army groups, armies and air fleets, as well as the usual representatives from the OKH including Halder and Brauchitsch. After a brief welcoming speech from Hitler, the formalities began with each army commander reporting his intentions for the first days of action, followed by an assessment of how operations should proceed. Through all of this Hitler listened attentively and hardly spoke. The picture portrayed of the Red Army was again one of great mass, but little qualitative substance.[36]

---

[31] Mikhail Nikolayevich Tukhachevsky was a Marshal of the Soviet Union who staunchly advocated the mechanisation of the Red Army and sought to employ these technological advancements in a new method of warfare which he described as 'Deep Battle'. Tukhachevsky authored the Red Army's 1936 field manual which included many of the principal formulas of modern military operations and cemented his places as one of the great military minds of the twentieth century. In spite of his brilliance Tukhachevsky never enjoyed good relations with Stalin and was one of the most prominent victims of the military purge, being arrested and shot in 1937.

[32] Manfred Zeidler, 'Das Bild der Wehrmacht von Russland und der Roten Armee zwischen 1933 und 1939' in Hans-Erich Volkmann (ed.), *Das Russlandbild im Dritten Reich* (Cologne, 1994), pp. 116–123.

[33] Warlimont, *Im Hauptquartier*, Band I, pp. 64–65.

[34] Trevor-Roper (ed.), *Hitler's War Directives 1939–1945*, pp. 131–134.

[35] As cited in Georg Meyer, *Adolf Heusinger. Dienst eines deutschen Soldaten 1915 bis 1964* (Berlin, 2001), p. 150.

[36] Von Below, *Als Hitlers Adjutant 1937–45*, p. 277.

When Hitler finally spoke after lunch, he revisited the long eulogised theme that defeating the Soviet Union would compel Britain to give in.[37] The campaign itself, he anticipated, would be a hard fought affair in which the Soviets would put up tough resistance, but the worst of the fighting would be over after six weeks. Hitler also underlined the ideological nature of the coming war, insisting that every soldier must know what he was fighting for – not the acquisition of land, but rather the destruction of Bolshevism.[38]

According to Hitler's Luftwaffe adjutant, Nicolaus von Below, who observed the proceedings, in the afternoon Hitler held further talks with the commanders of Army Group South, in which he emphasised the immense size of the theatre in which they would be operating. Hitler then drew attention to the mass of Soviet troops stationed before Army Group Centre and stated that, once these had been defeated, Army Group South would be reinforced from Army Group Centre. Hitler's address was watched by both Halder and Brauchitsch, who must have viewed with some alarm the idea that Hitler was now proposing to send forces to the south as well as north towards Leningrad. Still, as Below noted, neither raised a word of protest.[39] In Halder's case, his silence on these occasions did not go entirely unnoticed and Below stated that shortly before the invasion he feared that the curious absence of discussion, to say nothing of debate, disguised a much deeper divergence between Hitler and his Army Chief of Staff. The friction which had characterised relations between Hitler and the OKH in the early months of the war had all but ceased, at least openly, yet nothing in Halder's behaviour indicated he had really changed his belief regarding where command and control of the army rested. The change on Halder's part was a tactical one, calculated not to engage Hitler directly, but to win Hitler's confidence and then use his position to supply Hitler with all the evidence that might lead him into supporting his own operational choices. Only after the failure of that more subtle approach would something more direct have to be contemplated. For the time being, however, Halder swallowed his pride and made no comment. As Below observed: 'Hitler's concept of the war in the east was completely different from that of the army.' Below then overstated the opposition within the army to Hitler's Commissar Order, before continuing:

At the same time I realized that there could be other orders that might be system-atically sabotaged. The reason for this was that I had observed on various occa-sions an oppositional stance by Halder to Hitler's judgements and instructions,

---

[37] Franz Halder, KTB II, p. 455 (14 June 1941); Fedor von Bock, KTB 'Vorbereitungszeit', Fols. 23–24, *War Diary*, pp. 220–222 (14 June 1941).
[38] Von Below, *Als Hitlers Adjutant 1937–45*, p. 277.   [39] Ibid., p. 278.

without the general voicing his differing views. I had the impression that Halder was forever eating something he didn't like, but swallowed anyway.

Thus we embarked upon a truly massive offensive with a disjointed leadership and with leaders pulling in different directions. I saw this as a great danger for the success of the operation.[40]

Whether Below really foresaw events with such clarity in June 1941, or whether his account was somewhat coloured by the benefit of hindsight, he clearly spelled out the dangers lurking ahead for the German war effort. With its grand operational objectives and the tremendous demands these would place on the ill-equipped Wehrmacht, the success of Operation Barbarossa was at best going to be a tenuous proposition. The fact that almost the entire German military leadership were so unsuspecting of the hazards awaiting them in the east is the first major fault of Halder's General Staff. The second concerns Halder's role in deliberately seeking to blur Army Group Centre's second operational objective in order to assert his own preference over that of Hitler. His subsequent complaints of Hitler's interference in the military sphere carry less weight when one considers that Hitler's intentions were clear from the beginning, and Halder's muted response was no doubt interpreted by Hitler as an endorsement. It was therefore Halder who was seeking to modify what Hitler saw as the accepted strategic arrangement. The merits of either preference are not in discussion here; rather it is the cardinal fault of Halder to have allowed such a fundamental disagreement to persist, even into the campaign.

While Hitler and Halder were certainly at odds over the strategic direction of the war in the east, it would not be correct to infer that there was any general opposition to Hitler or his aggressive war plans among the overwhelming majority of German generals. If one was to believe the fog of distortions generated by the numerous memoirs of senior members of the Wehrmacht, the general representation of the army's wartime role would be very misleading.[41] Less discerning studies, especially many of those produced up until the end of the 1970s, have consequently given too much weight to this point of view and disproportionately emphasised the activities of the relatively small opposition groups that existed within the German armed forces. The work of Admiral Canaris's military intelligence group and the later efforts of Major-General Henning von Tresckow and Colonel Claus Schenk Graf von Stauffenberg, culminating in the July 1944 attempt to assassinate Hitler, distracted attention from the wider, more representative view of the army, as an agency very much within the Nazi fold. It was only with the collaboration of the army that Hitler's European empire was possible, but even

---

[40] Ibid., pp. 279–280.   [41] Streit, 'Partisans', pp. 262–263.

worse, the systematic brutality of the regime and its organised extermination policies required both the backing and in many cases the direct involvement of the armed forces. All of this was forthcoming and it was only after the war was irretrievably lost that the most serious acts of resistance, by a minority of officers, were attempted.

Given the close relationship between the army, Hitler and Nazi policies it is hardly surprising that Hitler's great undertaking to invade the Soviet Union, whether viewed for its ideological, geo-strategic or military rationale, was able to gain the common acceptance of the men charged with carrying it out. From a military point of view, the likelihood of a German victory was also shared in Britain, with the Joint Intelligence Committee estimating that the Germans would require just six weeks to occupy the Ukraine and reach Moscow.[42] A similarly pessimistic assessment was reached by the US Secretary of War, Henry Stimson, and his Chief of Staff, General George Marshall, who predicted that the German armies would require a minimum of one month, and a possible maximum of three months, to defeat the Soviet Union.[43] The Italians, as Germany's envious junior ally, were so convinced of another sweeping triumph that Mussolini told his foreign minister: 'I hope for only one thing, that in this war in the east the Germans will lose a lot of feathers.'[44] In Japan the head of the army's military intelligence, General Okamoto Kiyomoto, predicted a campaign would last only a few weeks, not longer.[45] Within the Nazi leadership itself there was a buoyant optimism. Joseph Goebbels, the German propaganda minister and one of Hitler's most fanatical supporters, wrote on 16 June 1941: 'The Führer estimates that the operation will take four months, I reckon on fewer. Bolshevism will collapse like a house of cards.'[46] The *Reichsmarschall* Hermann Göring, Hitler's chosen successor and Commander-in-Chief of the Luftwaffe, had made a similar

---

[42] H. F. Hinsley, 'British Intelligence and Barbarossa' in John Erickson and David Dilks (eds.), *Barbarossa. The Axis and the Allies* (Edinburgh, 1998), p. 72; Cecil, *Hitler's Decision to Invade Russia 1941*, p. 121. See also Churchill, *The Second World War*, p. 461.

[43] Hillgruber, *Hitlers Strategie*, pp. 444 (footnote 93) and 558; Hillgruber, *Der Zenit des Zweiten Weltkrieges*, pp. 26–27; Gerd R. Ueberschär, 'Das Scheitern des Unternehmens "Barbarossa". Der deutsch-sowjetische Krieg vom Überfall bis zur Wende vor Moskau im Winter 1941/42' in Gerd Ueberschär and Wolfram Wette (eds.), *'Unternehmen Barbarossa'. Der deutsche Überfall auf die Sowjetunion 1941* (Paderborn, 1984), pp. 150–151.

[44] Malcolm Muggeridge (ed.), *Ciano's Diary 1939–1943* (Kingswood, 1947), p. 365 (1 July 1941). See also comments on p. 354 (6 June 1941).

[45] Although Kiyomoto's view represented the prevailing view within the army, the Japanese Navy, favouring a southward strike into the Pacific, were by no means as convinced. John Chapman, 'The Imperial Japanese Navy and the North-South Dilemma' in John Erickson and David Dilks (eds.), *Barbarossa. The Axis and the Allies* (Edinburgh, 1998), p. 176.

[46] Elke Fröhlich (ed.), *Die Tagebücher von Joseph Goebbels*, Teil I: Aufzeichnungen 1923–1941, Band 9, Dezember 1940–Juli 1941 (Munich, 1998), p. 377 (16 June 1941).

assessment, declaring, 'with the entry of German troops into Russia, the entire Bolshevist State will collapse'.[47] The SS chief, Heinrich Himmler, was equally dismissive of Soviet strength and claimed it represented no threat.[48]

In the days before the launch of Barbarossa, Hitler showed signs of nervous anxiety and apprehension.[49] As Goebbels's diary had indicated, for all of Hitler's protestations proclaiming the great success of Barbarossa, he was now the most guarded in his optimism. In a letter to Mussolini announcing his decision to attack the Soviet Union, Hitler referred to 'months of anxious deliberation', ending in what he described as 'the hardest decision of my life'.[50] Reflecting back in October 1941, Hitler revealed the true fear these days had held for him: 'On the 22nd June, a door opened before us, and we didn't know what was behind it . . . The heavy uncertainty took me by the throat.'[51]

The German invasion of the Soviet Union was to begin the largest and most brutal war in history. Given the enormous numbers of men and material involved, the war in the Soviet Union was without question the most decisive battleground of World War II. Even by conservative estimates the fighting in this theatre claimed between 27 and 28 million Soviet lives,[52] which dwarf the 700,000 combined war dead of the United Kingdom and the United States.[53] To put it another way, the total Soviet war dead alone equalled more than three times the total war dead of *all* the nations involved in the carnage of World War I.[54] Four-fifths of all the fighting in World War II took place on Germany's eastern front and never less than two-thirds of the German army was engaged in the war against the Soviet Union, even after D-Day.[55] The conflict would last almost four years, being fought on an enormous front extending 2,768 kilometres from the Barents Sea in the north to the Black Sea in

---

[47] Thomas, *Geschichte der deutschen Wehr- und Rüstungswirtschaft*, p. 18.
[48] Eleanor Hancock, *The National Socialist Leadership and Total War 1941–45* (New York, 1991), p. 27.
[49] Fest, *Hitler*, p. 647.   [50] Domarus, *Hitler*, Volume IV, p. 2455.
[51] Hugh Trevor-Roper (ed.), *Hitler's Table Talk, 1941–1944. His Private Conversations* (London, 2000), p. 71 (17–18 October 1941).
[52] Barber and Harrison, *The Soviet Home Front 1941–1945*, pp. 40–41. See also John Erickson, 'Soviet War Losses. Calculations and Controversies' in John Erickson and David Dilks (eds.), *Barbarossa. The Axis and the Allies* (Edinburgh, 1998), pp. 255–277.
[53] Weinberg, *A World At Arms*, p. 894.
[54] The total war dead of both the Allied and Central Powers was in excess of 8 million men. Brian Bond, *The Pursuit of Victory. From Napoleon to Saddam Hussein* (Oxford, 1998), p. 124. Barber and Harrison looked at Soviet losses another way: 'for every dead Briton or American (including both soldiers and citizens), some seven Japanese, twenty Germans and eighty-five Soviet citizens had died' (Barber and Harrison, *The Soviet Home Front 1941–1945*, p. ix).
[55] Braithwaite, *Moscow 1941*, p. 310.

the south.[56] To Hitler's mind the war could only result in another great triumph bringing unrivalled power or absolute defeat and ruin; there could be no compromise peace.[57] In its sheer scale and ferocity, the eastern front bears no comparison with any of Germany's other theatres of warfare between 1939 and 1945. For this reason, nowhere else is the explanation for Germany's defeat more profoundly rooted.

As a German soldier would later write of his entry onto the eastern front: 'Mother Russia opened her arms wide in embrace. Welcome to the war . . . Welcome to hell on earth.'[58] Operation Barbarossa had begun.

---

[56] This figure is a linear measurement of the front; the actual length was about half as much again. See Glantz, *The Soviet-German War 1941–1945*, p. 5. For a partial reproduction of this essay see Glantz, 'Introduction', p. 5.

[57] In January 1943 with the German disaster at Stalingrad entering its final stages, Hitler was clear about the cost of losing the war. It was not to be seen as one of victory and defeat, but rather one of 'survivors and annihilated'. Overy, *Why the Allies Won*, p. 321.

[58] Taken from the World War II memoir of eastern front veteran Rick Holz. Rick Holz, *Too Young to be a Hero* (Sydney, 2000), p. 132.

Part II

The military campaign and the July/August
crisis of 1941

5 Awakening the bear

Indecisive border battles and the surfacing of strategic dissent

The war on Germany's eastern frontier began at 3.15 a.m. on 22 June 1941 with powerful artillery bombardments at the points of main concentration along the front. The barrage was soon followed by the advance of panzer and motorised divisions with the Luftwaffe poised to strike Soviet airfields at first light. The largest military operation in history was underway.

Aiding the German advance, Soviet deployments in their first strategic echelon opposite Army Group Centre were set well forward, with only the most rudimentary of prepared defences[1] and, owing to Stalin's intransigence, received no warning of the impending invasion until it was literally underway. Compounding the problem, the strategic deployment of the Soviet 3rd, 10th and 4th Armies, which according to pre-war Soviet plans were to absorb an initial German blow, were heavily concentrated in the west of the Belostok salient largely between the joint armoured thrusts of 2nd and 3rd Panzer Groups, thus greatly facilitating their encirclement.[2] Not surprisingly therefore, in the early hours of 3rd Panzer Group's surge eastward, forward units reported 'only very weak or no enemy contact'.[3] Luftwaffe reconnaissance counted just one enemy artillery battery in its

---

[1] The new forward 'Molotov Line' was still at an early stage of construction in the recently occupied eastern part of Poland, but some of the materials were furnished from the old 'Stalin Line', which had been partly dismantled. The result was that neither line was adequately fortified (Mawdsley, *Thunder in the East*, p. 23). When the Germans attacked there were gaps of anywhere between 10 and 80 kilometres in the defences of the new Molotov Line and only 1,000 out of the 2,500 completed concrete emplacements were equipped with artillery; the rest had no more than machine guns. Alan Bullock, *Hitler and Stalin. Parallel Lives* (London, 1993), pp. 765–766.

[2] David M. Glantz, 'The Border Battles on the Bialystok–Minsk Axis: 22–28 June 1941' in David M. Glantz (ed.), *The Initial Period of War on the Eastern Front 22 June–August 1941* (London, 1997), p. 187.

[3] 'Panzerarmeeoberkommandos Tagesmeldungen 21.6 – 31.8.41', BA-MA RH 21–3/43, Fol. 11 (22 June 1941).

153

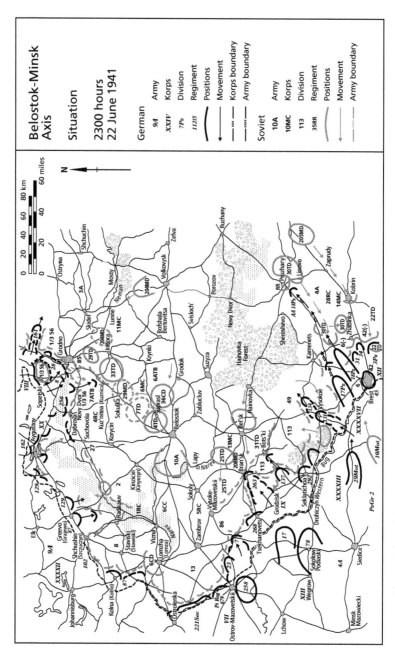

Belostok–Minsk Axis

Situation

2300 hours 22 June 1941

German

9A	Army
XXIV	Korps
7Pz	Division
1215	Regiment
	Positions
	Movement
	Korps boundary
	Army boundary

Soviet

10A	Army
10MC	Korps
113	Division
35RR	Regiment
	Positions
	Movement
	Army boundary

Map 1 Dispositions of Army Group Centre 22 June 1941: David M. Glantz, *Atlas and Operational Summary The Border Battles 22 June–1 July 1941*

path.[4] Before the end of the day Hoth's panzer group was on the Neman River with captured bridges at Olita and Merkine. The penetration of the Soviet front, Halder suggested, had already won the panzer group freedom of operational manoeuvre.[5] Yet, in spite of its success, the panzer group's war diary includes the observation:

Where the enemy appears he fights tenaciously and courageously to the death. Defectors and those seeking to surrender were not reported from any positions. The struggle, as a result, will be harder than those in Poland and the Western campaign.[6]

In similar fashion the commander of the XXXXIII Army Corps[7] in Kluge's 4th Army, General of Infantry Gotthard Heinrici, wrote home to his family on 24 June that the Soviet solder fought 'very hard'. Heinrici then concluded: 'He is a much better soldier than the Frenchman. Extremely tough, devious and deceitful.'[8]

The 2nd Panzer Group, operating 190 kilometres to the south of Hoth, had a more difficult advance (see Map 1). While some bridges across the Bug River (which then formed the German/Soviet border) were seized in the initial German assault, Field Marshal Bock observed that at Brest, which sat on the road to Moscow, the first bridge over the river was only secured at noon. Complicating matters, General of Panzer Troops Joachim Lemelsen, the commander of the XXXXVII Panzer Corps (17th and 18th Panzer Divisions, 29th Motorised Division and 167th Infantry Division[9]) reported that he was having difficulties crossing the captured bridges because the approach roads were literally sinking into the swamplands under the heavy weight of traffic.[10] Even once across the Bug, German forces still had to contend with the Brest fortified district which

---

[4] Ibid.

[5] Franz Halder, *Kriegstagebuch: Tägliche Aufzeichnungen des Chefs des Generalstabes des Heeres 1939–1942*, Band III: *Der Russlandfeldzug bis zum Marsch auf Stalingrad (22.6.1941 – 24.9.1942)*, ed. Hans-Adolf Jacobsen and Alfred Philippi (Arbeitskreis für Wehrforschung, Stuttgart, 1964), p. 5 (22 June 1941). Hereafter cited as: Franz Halder, KTB III.

[6] '3rd Pz. Gr. KTB 25.5.41 – 31.8.41' BA-MA Microfilm 59054, Fol. 36 (22 June 1941). Further expressions to this effect by German officers are recorded in Anatoli G. Chor'kov, 'The Red Army During the Initial Phase of the Great Patriotic War' in Bernd Wegner (ed.), *From Peace to War. Germany, Soviet Russia and the World, 1939–1941* (Oxford, 1997), pp. 425–426.

[7] The XXXXIII Army Corps was made up of three infantry divisions, 131st, 134th and 252nd.

[8] Johannes Hürter, *Ein deutscher General an der Ostfront. Die Briefe und Tagebücher des Gotthard Heinrici 1941/42* (Erfurt, 2001), p. 63 (24 June 1941).

[9] The 167th Infantry Division was only subordinated to the XXXXVII Panzer Corps for the initial phase of operations.

[10] Fedor von Bock, KTB 'Osten I', Fol. 1, *War Diary*, p. 224 (22 June 1941).

was to prove a thorn in the army's side long after the armoured spearhead had passed it by. Difficulties continued to mount when a central route of the panzer group's right wing, made up of the XXIV Panzer Corps (3rd and 4th Panzer Divisions, 10th Motorised Division, 1st Cavalry Division and 255th Infantry Division[11]) under General of Panzer Troops Freiherr Geyr von Schweppenberg, was found to consist of 'catastrophic road conditions' that were deemed 'impossible' to traverse.[12] As a result 3rd and 4th Panzer Divisions had to share the same road, which was deemed 'hardly traversable' for wheeled vehicles.[13] The delays and subsequent loss of the bridge over the Muchaviec River meant that in the course of the day the distance advanced was only 18 kilometres when it should have been 80 kilometres.[14]

On the Soviet side the invasion induced nothing short of utter chaos which was most strikingly evident in the Western Military District opposite Army Group Centre.[15] Here the Soviet command structure was rendered largely redundant almost from the very beginning owing to a near total loss of communication at most levels of the chain of command. The complete disarray prevented coherent knowledge of the current situation from being gathered and consequently the development and execution of a co-ordinated Soviet response. Racked by internal confusion and the growing external pressure, the Western Military District's hasty slide towards disintegration was worsened by the Soviet High Command's erroneous adherence to pre-war plans, which called for immediate counter-attacks.[16] Unable to properly prepare or direct these attempts, they inevitably resulted in piecemeal attacks of little effect, but carried out at great cost to Soviet forces.[17]

On the second day of the offensive Halder proclaimed operations at Army Group Centre to be proceeding 'according to plan' and talked of soon achieving 'full operational freedom' behind the shattered Soviet front.[18] On the same day, in response to Paulus's assessment that the campaign would be of short duration, Brauchitsch is said to have responded:

---

[11] The 255th Infantry Division was only subordinated to the XXIV Panzer Corps for the initial phase of operations.

[12] 'KTB 3rd Pz. Div. vom 16.8.40 bis 18.9.41' BA-MA RH 27–3/14, p. 39 (22 June 1941). See also Franz Halder, KTB III, p. 5 (22 June 1941).

[13] 'Kriegstagebuch 4.Panzer-Division Führungsabtl. 26.5.41 – 31.3.42' BA-MA RH 27–4/27, p. 7 (22 June 1941).

[14] Horst Zobel, '3rd Panzer Division Operations' in David M. Glantz (ed.), *The Initial Period of War on the Eastern Front 22 June–August 1941* (London, 1997), p. 241.

[15] Sergei M. Shtemenko, *The Soviet General Staff at War 1941–1945* (Moscow, 1975), pp. 33–34.

[16] Earl F. Ziemke, *The Red Army 1918–1941: From Vanguard of World Revolution to US Ally* (London, 2004), pp. 275–276.

[17] Glantz, 'Border Battles', p. 200.   [18] Franz Halder, KTB III, pp. 7–8 (23 June 1941).

Figure 5.1 The advancing German columns stirred up great clouds of dust, which soon infiltrated motors and caused severe irritation to horses and men.

'Yes, Paulus, you may be right, we shall probably need six to eight weeks for finishing Russia.'[19] In contrast to his superiors Field Marshal Bock's impression was a far more guarded one. His diary noted the stubborn resistance of the Soviet defenders prompted by political commissars who

[19] Niepold, 'Plan Barbarossa', p. 70.

were spurring their men to 'maximum resistance'. He also recorded with a note of unease that the state of the roads was 'indescribable'.[20] More worrying still, Bock was again starting to question the wisdom behind the operational plan, foreseeing the closure of a pocket at Minsk as unlikely to achieve a decisive success. In Bock's view a direct drive by Hoth's panzer group in the direction of Vitebsk-Polotsk would save time and prevent an organised Soviet force being assembled on the eastern banks of the great rivers. As Bock noted:

I fear the enemy will already have withdrawn strong elements from there [Minsk]. By turning the panzer group towards Minsk time will be lost, which the enemy can use to establish a new defence behind the Dvina and Dnepr.[21]

After failing to convince Halder of his concerns, Bock attempted to persuade Brauchitsch only to receive a similar rejection. It was only the second day of the campaign and far from winning operational freedom behind the Soviet line, as Halder believed, Bock was already convinced that the deepest possible penetration was required to cut off the great mass of the Red Army and forestall the building of a new defensive line. Bock's anxiety would have been further heightened by a report from 4th Army communicated to OKH which, according to Halder, characterised the overall picture: 'The enemy in the Belostok salient is not fighting for his life, rather to gain time.'[22]

In the meantime, XXXXVII Panzer Corps was already reporting fuel shortages among its furthermost elements, while the roads leading to and from the Bug crossings had deteriorated so much that it was difficult moving the great volume of traffic – a considerable complication when a large portion of the wheeled transport, containing vital fuel supply, was still queued up on the western bank of the river.[23] On the other flank, Hoth's wheeled columns had penetrated deeper, but were experiencing even greater problems maintaining contact with the armoured spearheads. On 24 June the panzer group's war diary complained that road conditions restricted movement to a single-file column, reducing speeds to the slowest moving vehicle and stretching out even further when the heavily loaded tracks became bogged. Furthermore, the diary observed: 'All routes marked as roads turned out to be unsealed, unmaintained sand tracks. The difficulties are placing great demands on

[20] Fedor von Bock, KTB 'Osten I', Fol. 1, *War Diary*, p. 225 (23 June 1941).
[21] Ibid., Fol. 2, p. 225 (23 June 1941).
[22] Franz Halder, KTB III, p. 8 (23 June 1941).
[23] 'KTB Nr.1 Panzergruppe 2 vom 22.6.1941 bis 21.7.41' BA-MA RH 21–2/927, Fol. 31 (23 June 1941).

the divisions.'[24] The situation was not helped by the panzer group's high proportion of French vehicles which were already revealing their fragility. The 20th Panzer Division reported that their vulnerability to overland conditions was already 'very noticeable'. 'The trucks can only manage a few metres alone before needing to be dug out and then pulled and pushed.'[25] Furthermore, their fuel consumption was 'many times more than normal', inhibiting the supplies that could be brought forward.[26] Even Halder noted that lubricant and fuel utilisation was 'very high'.[27] The mass of infantry divisions were also finding movement exceedingly difficult owing to the severe traffic congestion. Doctor Hermann Türk noted in his diary on 24 June: 'The march goes dreadfully slowly. Always only a few metres forwards . . . Overtaking is impossible . . . We should be another 150 kilometres further ahead . . . Time is vital, but what can we do given the fully clogged roads?'[28]

Although large-scale Soviet counter-attacks were essentially ineffectual, and suffered in most cases appalling losses, at the very least they forced the panzer or infantry corps to halt their advance in order to meet and repel the desperate onslaughts. As Bock noted for 24 June:

The Russians are defending themselves desperately; heavy counterattacks near Grodno against the VIII and XX Army Corps; Panzer Group Guderian is also being held up near Slonim by enemy counterattacks.[29]

Whatever delays and casualties these early Soviet counter-attacks caused German forces, because they involved such horrendous Soviet losses their significance in much of the literature has largely been to prove the one-sided nature of the conflict, favouring the notion of an unremitting German blitzkrieg. Yet what this focus tends to obscure is that, from the earliest stages of the war, German losses were far from inconsiderable. Typically, German casualties were not the result of major battles in conventional engagements with the Red Army. Rather it was the very dissolution of organised Soviet fighting formations, caused by the utter breakdown in command and control, which led to countless smaller actions that were of no prominence in their own right, but collectively extracted a significant toll on the invading forces. On only the third day of the conflict Halder noted that casualties were 'bearable' but then added: 'Remarkably

[24] '3rd Pz. Gr. KTB 25.5.41 – 31.8.41' BA-MA Microfilm 59054, Fol. 52 (24 June 1941).
[25] 'KTB 20th Pz. Div. vom 25.5.41 bis 15.8.41' BA-MA RH 27–20/2, Fol. 14 (24 June 1941).
[26] Ibid.   [27] Franz Halder, KTB III, p. 9 (24 June 1941).
[28] Walter Kempowski (ed.), Das Echolot Barbarossa '41. Ein kollektives Tagebuch (Munich, 2004), p. 79 (24 June 1941).
[29] Fedor von Bock, KTB 'Osten I', Fol. 3, War Diary, p. 226 (24 June 1941).

high losses among officers'.[30] Soviet tactics in this period were crude, but effective. Characteristic engagements were initiated by small groups of Soviet soldiers, often in selected positions, against unsuspecting German forces. This provided a far more even playing-field against the German superiority in heavy weapons, mobility and airpower. The dense Belorussian forests and high summer cornfields provided excellent cover for these forces, allowing them to prepare ambushes close to the roads on which the Germans depended. With ever longer German columns stretching out across the countryside, an inevitable gap opened between the panzer spearheads and the trudging infantry, leaving the vital, but poorly armed supply columns exposed to attack, even from small bands of men without heavy weapons. In essence it gave rise to an immediate and effective form of guerrilla resistance, with the advantage that it was carried out by soldiers with military-issue equipment instead of by peasants. Already on 24 June, the 3rd Panzer Group reported that the forests were full of fugitive Soviet soldiers who were 'attacking from the flank and rear' causing unrest and 'slowing the advance'. The request was therefore made that reserves from Colonel-General Adolf Strauss's 9th Army be dispatched to 'clean out the woods'.[31] The enormous area in question made this an impossible task, especially for the exceedingly limited German reserves. Indeed at no point in the war did German security forces succeed in eliminating partisan resistance in Belorussia – on the contrary, these forces grew in number and effectiveness. The same pattern of attacks also dogged 2nd Panzer Group's rear area from the very beginning of the war. A former officer in the 3rd Panzer Division reported:

During the first two days of combat, unarmoured troops and rear echelons suffered considerable losses inflicted by hostile enemy troops cut off from their main bodies. They hid beside the march routes, opened fire by surprise, and could only be defeated in intense hand-to-hand combat. German troops had not previously experienced this type of war.[32]

General Heinrici wrote on only the second day of the war: 'All over the large forests, in countless homesteads, sit lost soldiers who often enough shoot at us from behind. The Russian fights war in devious ways.'[33]

---

[30] Franz Halder, KTB III, p. 9 (24 June 1941).
[31] '3rd Pz. Gr. KTB 25.5.41 – 31.8.41' BA-MA Microfilm 59054, Fol. 52 (24 June 1941). For an informative individual insight into the extent of the guerrilla warfare from the beginning of the war, see Heinrich Haape in association with Dennis Henshaw, *Moscow Tram Stop. A Doctor's Experiences with the German Spearhead in Russia* (London, 1957), Chapter I, 'Operation "Barbarossa"'.
[32] Zobel, '3rd Panzer Division Operations', p. 242.
[33] Hürter, *Ein deutscher General an der Ostfront*, p. 62 (23 June 1941).

Having failed to win over Halder or Brauchitsch to his idea of a deep encirclement on the Dvina and Dnepr Rivers, Bock tried again on the following day (24 June), but to no avail.[34] In part, as a result of Bock's strenuous urgings and perhaps with a view to the divisive disputes which arose in May 1940 over the speed of the advance through Belgium, Halder and Brauchitsch were already conceiving a radical new reorganisation of Army Group Centre's command structure. Halder was determined that the OKH would maintain a tight grip on the motorised and panzer divisions, setting the pace and direction of operations without having its hand forced by independently minded field commanders operating on their own initiative. Halder had in mind that the two panzer groups should no longer be directly answerable to Bock, whom he suspected of being too sympathetic to a headlong rush eastwards favoured by Hoth and Guderian. Instead Halder favoured uniting the two panzer groups under the more conservative direction of Field Marshal Günther von Kluge, currently employed in command of the 4th Army. The new combined panzer group would be known as 'Fourth Panzer Army', with the 4th Army now under the command of Colonel-General Maximilian Freiherr von Weichs and re-designated 2nd Army. The 2nd Army, in collusion with the 9th Army, would then have the task of completing the encirclement of the Belostok salient, relieving the panzer and motorised divisions for further operations.[35]

Bock's fervent opposition to sealing off the Belostok–Minsk pocket was keenly matched by Hoth, who likewise considered the operation an unconscionable delay and wanted to exploit the initial penetration immediately and push on into the easterly Vitebsk–Orsha region to secure the land-bridge between the Dvina and Dnepr Rivers. Aware of Bock's stalled efforts to influence matters at OKH, Hoth dispatched Lieutenant-Colonel Hünersdorff, the OKH liaison officer attached to 3rd Panzer Group, to present the panzer commander's case personally. It must have dawned on Halder that the very same issue had already arisen in March 1941, long before the campaign was underway, and resolved at that time to the satisfaction of the OKH, with the first operational movement closing in the region of Minsk. In his memoirs, Hoth makes reference to a pre-war understanding with Bock favouring a direct push on the Vitebsk–Orsha region as the priority of 3rd Panzer Group.[36] Furthermore, a report from 3rd Panzer Group noted that in spite of OKH's preference for closing the first ring at Minsk, the army group command decided

[34] Fedor von Bock, KTB 'Osten I', Fol. 3, *War Diary*, p. 226 (24 June 1941).
[35] Franz Halder, KTB III, p. 12 (24 June 1941).
[36] Hoth, *Panzer-Operationen*, pp. 62–63; Bryan Fugate, *Operation Barbarossa*, p. 106.

before the war to leave the final decision open.[37] Clearly, Hoth and Bock sought to pursue their own preference, effectively seeking to bypass the instructions of Halder and Brauchitsch. The irony is that this was the very same tactic Halder and Brauchitsch had adopted in relation to Hitler's unyielding opposition to Moscow and suggests the OKH leadership were not the only ones engaged in silent duplicity.

On the morning of 25 June, the subject of the Belostok–Minsk pocket took on a new urgency at Bock's headquarters when Colonel Rudolf Schmundt, the Führer's chief military adjutant, arrived and informed Bock that Hitler was worried the proposed encirclement at Minsk was too large and that he feared German forces would prove insufficient to destroy the trapped Soviet units or force them to surrender. Either Bock immediately recognised the futility of pursuing operations further to the east if Hitler was now threatening to close a ring at Novogrudok, or Bock's sense of soldierly duty and unquestioning loyalty prevented him from adopting the quarrelsome tone with Hitler that he so frequently took with his fellow officers.[38] In any case, he telephoned 3rd Panzer Group and ordered that priority be shifted from securing the Dvina to proceeding now with all speed for Minsk. Hitler's decision on the matter had been deferred until the afternoon and Bock wanted to gain as much ground as possible towards Minsk in the hope of ensuring the lesser of two evils was now adopted. He also contacted 9th and 4th Armies with instructions for the encirclement and an emphasis on haste. Bock's change of heart towards Minsk did little to improve his standing with Halder as the debate now shifted to where exactly the 9th and 4th Armies would meet, with Halder again seeking a tighter concentration than that favoured by Bock.[39] The renewed wrangling incensed Bock, who was already of the opinion that too much had been forsaken, and his diary reflects the ire of indignation: 'I am furious, for here we are unnecessarily throwing away a major success!'[40]

While Bock focused his frustrations on his superiors at OKH, their stance was in fact more moderate than the increasingly conservative attitude emanating from Hitler's 'Wolf's Lair' (*Wolfschanze*) headquarters in East Prussia. By the evening of 25 June Halder's headquarters received orders expressing the concern that Army Group Centre and

---

[37] 'Panzerarmeeoberkommandos Anlagen zum Kriegstagesbuch "Berichte, Besprechungen, Beurteilungen der Lage" Bd.III 25.5.41 – 22.7.41' BA-MA RH 21-3/46, Fols. 80–81 (29 June 1941).

[38] For a summation of the relationship between Hitler and Bock see Alfred W. Turney, *Disaster At Moscow: Von Bock's Campaigns 1941–1942* (Albuquerque, 1970), p. 10.

[39] Fedor von Bock, KTB 'Osten I', Fol. 3, *War Diary*, pp. 226–227 (25 June 1941).

[40] Ibid., Fol. 4, p. 227 (25 June 1941).

South were operating in too much depth – a charge Halder dismissively rejected as: 'The old song!' This referred to Hitler's faltering nerve in sustaining operations towards the English Channel the year before. Halder then obstinately declared: 'Our intentions will as a result of this not be changed.'[41]

On the same evening Halder sent orders to Army Group Centre informing Bock of his intended reorganisation of the command structure.[42] This would not in fact take effect until 3 July but, when Bock discovered what was intended, he again found himself at odds with his superiors at OKH and protested against the decision. He even implied his own refusal to comply with the orders, writing in his diary for 26 June: 'The "pocket" can best be taken care of by the two armies that created it and that is how I am going to do it.'[43] Evidently Bock shared Halder's rigid stubbornness and contempt for higher authority, which were paralleled in the wilful ego of each man and embittered the process of strategic direction, particularly given their respective agendas privately being pursued. Adding a further complication was the erratic flow of instructions from Hitler's headquarters which were received as unwelcome interference in the exclusive preserve of army affairs. Not surprisingly, the outcome was an undeclared wrestle for control in which each man assumed foremost authority for the direction of Army Group Centre. It was now that the lamentable planning process with its confused strategic conception was making itself evident, engendering much ill-feeling and frustration, even though the campaign was only days old and the army was clearly dominating the battlefield.

When Brauchitsch paid a visit to Army Group Centre's headquarters on the morning of 26 June to offer his congratulations on the developing pocket, Bock was still so annoyed at its premature closure that he tersely slighted Brauchitsch's praise, retorting: 'I doubt there's anything left inside now!'[44] This, however, was only sarcasm on Bock's part and the new task of sealing the eastern perimeter of the pocket, containing hundreds of thousands of Soviet troops, many attempting to fight their way out, presented a formidable problem. Reluctantly, Bock agreed to re-assign the 29th Motorised Division from 2nd Panzer Group to 4th Army to help plug the gap[45] but, even so, the pocket's eastern border remained extremely porous.

The speed of the German advance and the depth at which the army was now operating left the main force of the Soviet Western Front

---

[41] Franz Halder, KTB III, p. 15 (25 June 1941).   [42] Ibid.
[43] Fedor von Bock, KTB 'Osten I', Fol. 5, *War Diary*, p. 228 (26 June 1941).
[44] Ibid., Fol. 4, p. 228 (26 June 1941).   [45] Ibid. (26 June 1941).

out-flanked, but as yet undefeated behind the panzer spearheads. The result was an astonishingly large and varied area of combat which, unlike conventional wars, was by no means limited to the frontal zone of the attacker's advance. With every mile of progression eastwards, German strength had to be dissipated vertically, to cover the expanding funnel of Soviet geography, and horizontally to isolate and close the main pocket as well as eliminate bypassed strongpoints and protect supply routes and installations. In the vanguard, massed panzers made swift thrusts often sweeping aside weak and unsuspecting opposition, while in other quarters set-piece battles took place between main elements of each side. Small arms fire-fights and hit and run tactics were an increasingly common feature along the length of the German penetration, and there remained the bloody task of overcoming fanatical Soviet resistance from troops held up in entrenched fortifications. From 2nd Panzer Group's point of entry into the Soviet Union at Brest, the entire 45th Infantry Division, with the aid of the enormous rail-borne artillery piece known as 'Karl', was still heavily engaged in reducing the Soviet stronghold and weeding out resistance.[46] On 26 June Bock commented: 'All parts of the citadel at Brest have still not fallen . . . Unfortunately casualties there are high. The enemy is also holding out in other, smaller groups of fortifications far behind the front.'[47] One such smaller group encountered by 9th Army's 28th Division presents a closer picture of the toll these battles were taking. The report, coming from a former company commander, noted that in this instance the Soviet position consisted of a line of bunkers and half-finished fortifications protected by a system of trenches. One regiment of the division was assigned to assault the Soviet defences which resulted in a tenacious three-day battle. The company commander's battalion alone suffered 150 casualties.[48] In another infantry division from 4th Army, Lieutenant Georg Kreuter noted on 25 June: 'We cannot move forward, everywhere there are small battles. Above all at night . . . Very close to me four officers have fallen. They will soon be buried together with other comrades in the town [Ozgmowicz]. Under no circumstances can this continue!!'[49]

[46] Fugate, *Operation Barbarossa*, p. 111; Franz Halder, KTB III, p. 14 (25 June 1941). An insight into the fanatical resistance of the Soviet garrison at Brest is provided in Albert Axell, *Russia's Heroes, 1941–45: An Epic Account of Struggle and Survival on the Eastern Front* (London, 2001), Chapter 2, 'The Hero Fortress'. See also the first-hand accounts provided in Robert Kershaw, *War Without Garlands. Operation Barbarossa 1941/42* (New York, 2000), pp. 47–51, 59–60, 65–67, 78–79.
[47] Fedor von Bock, KTB 'Osten I', Fol. 5, *War Diary*, p. 229 (26 June 1941).
[48] Alfred Durrwanger, '28th Infantry Division Operations' in David M. Glantz (ed.), *The Initial Period of War on the Eastern Front 22 June–August 1941* (London, 1997), p. 235.
[49] Kempowski (ed.), *Das Echolot Barbarossa '41*, p. 100 (25 June 1941).

After the many disparaging pre-war assessments of the Red Army, the initial days of the campaign left a contrasting impression. The Soviet Union's predicted strategic debacle was tempered somewhat by the impressive display of fervour among the vast majority of its rank and file. It was also in these opening days that the Germans were confronted with the startling reality of the latest Soviet armour and its clear superiority to their own. With a measure of aloof detachment Halder simply recorded the imposing dimensions of the KV-1,[50] noting that the only defensive possibilities for the standard German infantry division were to use the new 5cm anti-tank guns and aim shots under the turret. As Halder must have known, the new 5cm anti-tank guns were in short supply and greatly outnumbered by the obsolete 3.7cm standard anti-tank guns. In any case, the prospect of the 5cm anti-tank gun hitting a moving target with such precision was exceedingly doubtful. The more powerful 8.8cm anti-aircraft gun, which could be lowered to fire at a flat trajectory, was also a defensive option, but Halder was not even sure if this mighty weapon could penetrate the thick side armour of a KV-1.[51]

Although the utter disarray consuming the Soviet Western Front's position doomed most counter-moves to failure, the impact of the Red Army's new tanks was evident even in the most one-sided contest. Attempting to cut off the German penetration and seal the perilous breach in the Soviet front, Lieutenant-General Dmitri Pavlov, the commander of the Western Front, launched frantic counter-attacks on 24 and 25 June against Army Group Centre's left wing using his 11th and 6th Mechanised Corps. The 11th Mechanised Corps was comparatively weak with only 60 T-34s and KV-1s supported by 200 of the outdated T-26s and BT series. By contrast, of the 960 tanks fielded by the 6th Mechanised Corps, approximately half were of the newer medium and heavy T-34 and KV-1 design. Plagued by communication problems and a lack of precise intelligence, the Soviet offensive was hopelessly ill co-ordinated and, as a result, missed its intended target of Hoth's 3rd Panzer Group, ploughing into the XX and VIII Army Corps of the following 9th Army instead. Even before contact was made, the counter-attack, directed by Pavlov's adroit operations officer Lieutenant-General Ivan Boldin, was greatly hindered by the unceasing aerial attack of Colonel-General Wolfram von Richthofen's VIII Air Corps. Boldin's scattered forces suffered terribly just trying to reach the designated assembly areas in the Lunna–Indura–Sokolka area

---

[50] Understandably it seems that some of these early figures were inaccurate.
[51] Franz Halder, KTB III, p. 14 (25 June 1941). In fact the answer depends on the type of ammunition fired, the distance to target and the angle of impact, but under favourable conditions it was possible, except on the frontal turret armour.

south of Grodno. His long, armoured convoys proved easy prey for the redoubtable Ju-87 Stuka dive-bombers, in some instances equipped with phosphorus bombs. Complicating matters further, the complement of T-34s and KV-1s were a recent addition to the two Mechanised Corps, arriving in April and May 1941. Many of the KV-1s still had no ammunition, while drivers for the new models were only assigned in late May and early June, ensuring that training was rudimentary at best.[52] As a result, Boldin's counter-stroke ended up being a mere shadow of what was intended. Even so, the appearance of massed Soviet tanks led by the previously unknown T-34s and KV-1s stirred panic among the German *Panzerjäger* anti-tank units as they watched round after round bounce off the Soviets' impenetrable armour. Frantic calls were sent out for more armour-piercing shells and again Richthofen's squadrons provided invaluable close-air support.[53] The almost total absence of aerial cover cost the Soviets dearly and the offensive soon developed into another calamitous Soviet defeat with heavy losses, but two factors of significance emerged. One was the delay the battle caused to the forward progress of 9th Army's right wing and the resultant widening of the gap between 3rd Panzer Group and its infantry support. Even more importantly, the battle revealed the vulnerability of German units to attacks by the latest model Soviet tanks which, with Soviet tank factories now working at an exhausting pace, boded ill for the Germans if the war was to drag on longer than its prescribed duration.

A report about a junior Soviet officer, Lieutenant Pavel Gudz, commanding five KV-1s and two T-34s on the first day of the war on the southern part of the front, was recorded as follows:

The Germans started bombing the column . . . A shell from a German anti-tank gun bounced off the tank's heavy armour . . . Gudz, who was the tank's gunner as well as its commander, fired a single shot in return and the gun was destroyed. He and his platoon went on to knock out five German tanks, three armoured personnel carriers and several cars . . . After lunch the Germans attacked again. Gudz knocked out three more tanks. His driver Galkin rammed another German tank, dislodging its caterpillar track and forcing it into a ditch. The fields were covered with burned-out tanks and dead Germans.[54]

Ammunition and fuel soon ran short as German aircraft systematically attacked the Soviet rear, forcing Gudz's division to retreat. Ultimately, Gudz and his tanks got as far as Kiev where he and his men were forced to burn the tanks to prevent their capture.[55]

[52] Glantz, 'Border Battles', pp. 189, 202, 207.
[53] Fugate, *Operation Barbarossa*, pp. 106–107.
[54] Braithwaite, *Moscow 1941*, pp. 77–78. For another example see pp. 275–276.
[55] Ibid., p. 78.

Further evidence of the looming danger was provided by an attack of
Soviet KV-1s against leading elements of the German 6th Panzer Division on 24 June in the area of Army Group North. It is significant to note
that aerial cover for Army Group North, provided by Colonel-General
Alfred Keller's Air Fleet 1, contained none of the dive-bombers afforded
to Army Group Centre.[56] Accordingly, ground forces were left to fend
for themselves, but without prior knowledge or forewarning of the preponderant Soviet advantage in tank design, this was not understood to
constitute a risk. The Soviet attack was directed against the newly formed
German bridgehead across the Dubyssa River, north-east of Rossienie.
The following account comes from Colonel Erhard Raus of the neighbouring battle group:

It was not so much the numerical superiority of the enemy which made the
situation precarious for our command and troops, but the totally unexpected
appearance of colossal tanks for which German tanks and anti-tank weapons
appeared to be no match... Even the concentrated fire of the artillery and all
other heavy weapons of the *Kampfgruppe* [Battle Group] was not able to keep
off the steel pachyderms. Though enveloped in fire and smoke, they immediately
started attacking and crushed everything in their paths. Untroubled by the shower
of heavy howitzer shells and earth falling down upon them, they attacked road
block 121 in spite of the flanking fire of the anti-tank guns from the wooded areas,
rolled over the anti-tank guns dug in there and broke into the artillery area.
    About one hundred friendly tanks, one-third of them were Panzer IVs, now
assembled for a counterattack. Some of them faced the enemy in front, but the
bulk made an assault from the flanks. From three sides, their shells hammered
against the steel giants, but the effort to destroy them was in vain. On the other
hand, very soon we had casualties ourselves.[57]

It has been suggested with due merit that this clash, as one of the first
major tank battles of the eastern campaign, heralded a new era in the
role of the German tank. Previously tanks had primarily been employed
against infantry and their supporting arms. Now, however, the KV-1's
menacing appearance proved a watershed by introducing an instrument
beyond the reach of almost anything on the existing battlefield and transforming future German tank design into larger, heavier models with

[56] Boog, 'Die Luftwaffe', see table: Ist-Stärke und Einsatzbereitschaft der fliegenden
    Verbände (einschl. Ergänzungsgruppen) der Luftwaffe im Osten am Vortage 'Bar-
    barossa' (21.6.1941), p. 313.
[57] Tsouras (ed.), *Panzers on the Eastern Front*, pp. 36–37. For more details of this battle, see
    Ritgen, '6th Panzer Division Operations', pp. 113–116. A further example of the vexing
    predicament the KV-1 caused German commanders is provided by the appearance of a
    solitary tank in the rear area of Battle Group Raus (6th Panzer Division). The lone tank
    sat astride an important supply road defying all attempts at destruction for two days. See
    Tsouras (ed.), *Panzers on the Eastern Front*, pp. 38–45. Also published in Department
    of the U.S. Army (ed.), *Small Unit Actions During the German Campaign in Russia*,
    pp. 76–84.

Figure 5.2 During the German advance the dust and the dreadful state of Soviet roads accounted for far more German tank losses than battles with the Red Army.

much greater firepower, primarily aimed at meeting this new threat.[58] Tangible results, however, would not be seen on the battlefield until 1943 – far too late to influence Germany's fate in World War II.

If the KV-1 represented something of a wonder weapon in 1941, it was an achievement paralleled in innovation and complemented in battlefield performance by the medium T-34 tank. This remarkable machine was heavier and better armoured than the German Mark IV, yet also considerably faster. The main armament surpassed anything on the German models, its wide tracks offered better traction in mud and snow, while the design incorporated angled armour helping to make it impervious to all but the heaviest German anti-tank guns.[59] The sum effectiveness of these innovative enhancements in tank design was largely obscured by the tumultuous events following the start of Barbarossa, but again local encounters revealed the extent of the Soviet advantage. In one such illustration on the first day of the war, forward elements of the 7th Panzer Division, made up primarily of Czech Pz Kpfw 38s backed by Mark IVs, were ambushed by a single Soviet T-34. According to one observer, after hitting one German panzer: '[T]he Russian tank rushed

[58] Ritgen, '6th Panzer Division Operations', p. 116.
[59] Ziemke and Bauer, *Moscow to Stalingrad*, p. 11.

back to its unit by passing [*sic*] approximately 30 German tanks which were dispersed throughout a large area. Several tanks, including mine, tried to destroy the enemy tank using our 37mm gun. These attempts, however, had no effect on the T-34 which we were observing for the first time.'[60] Another German soldier, Franz Frisch, who served in an artillery regiment recalled: 'Our men were terrified of the T-34.'[61] Colonel-General Ewald von Kleist, commander of Panzer Group 1 in Army Group South, dubbed the T-34, 'the finest tank in the world'.[62]

Fortunately for the Germans the new Soviet tanks were still few in number and suffering from deficiencies in fuel and ammunition, poorly trained crews and flawed tactical employment on the part of inexperienced Soviet officers. Nevertheless, the warning signs were plainly apparent that the Red Army had to be defeated in its stricken and diminished state, or the remarkable potential of Soviet industry would deliver the truly ominous prospect of a reconstituted Red Army.[63]

On the whole, the initial success of Operation Barbarossa was a qualified one at best. From the narrowest perspective, the desired breakthroughs had been achieved and the panzer corps, slowly followed by their infantry support, were rolling eastwards towards their first major objective. Yet the great German blow, both military and psychological, had produced no indication that the Soviet state was paralysed by fear or on the brink of internal collapse. On the contrary, even in the most hopeless of circumstances, Soviet forces were resisting stubbornly, often to the bitter end. The defiant attitude was paralleled by the great majority of the civilian population who, upon hearing the news, spontaneously rallied to the call of the nation.[64] Military losses for the Germans, while sustainable in the short term, were nevertheless unexpectedly high and there was a disturbing realisation that the war would demand a lot more sacrifice before it was over. The vast distances also warranted renewed concern given the dreadful state of Soviet roads and the corresponding unsuitability of the wheeled transports. Finally, and perhaps most worrying, was the inability of the German leadership to find common ground in their strategic outlook – in fact the internal strife had only just begun. Consequently the campaign resembled a perilously wayward and

---

[60] Horst Ohrloff, 'XXXIX Motorized Corps Operations' in David M. Glantz (ed.), *The Initial Period of War*, pp. 173–174.

[61] Franz A. P. Frisch in association with Wilbur D. Jones, Jr., *Condemned to Live. A Panzer Artilleryman's Five-Front War* (Shippensburg, 2000), p. 84.

[62] Liddell Hart, *The Other Side of the Hill*, p. 330.

[63] In 1942 Soviet industry would produce some 12,600 T-34s and 1,800 KV-1s. (Mawdsley, *Thunder in the East*, p. 27).

[64] Barber and Harrison, *The Soviet Home Front 1941–1945*, p. 60.

insecure enterprise, where troubles loomed large on the horizon and the main actors jostled for position to lead there.

The Belostok–Minsk pocket – anatomy of a hollow victory

While Army Group Centre's advance held the key to German operations in the east, its success was nevertheless tied to the simultaneous progress of the northern and southern army groups, which, beyond their own objectives, also had responsibility for ensuring flank support for Army Group Centre. Rundstedt's Army Group South was faced with by far the most difficult task, confronting the Soviet South-Western Front commanded by Colonel-General Michail Kirponos. As the Ukraine was incorrectly believed by the Soviets to constitute the primary focus of a German invasion, South-Western Front was well endowed with mechanised formations and constituted the strongest of all the Soviet military districts.[65] Accordingly Rundstedt, with only one panzer group at his disposal, had an especially difficult advance and was forced to fend off heavy Soviet counter-attacks. On 26 June Halder stated in his diary 'Army Group South is advancing slowly, unfortunately with considerable losses.'[66] The Operations Officer at OKH responsible for Army Group South further noted: 'Russians are standing their ground excellently; down here there is exceptionally systematic command.'[67] The enduring delay caused to Army Group South later had a direct bearing on the dissipation of strength forced upon Army Group Centre, when it was compelled to cover its exposed southern flank. It also later encouraged Hitler's deliberations by inflaming his desire to resolve matters decisively in the Ukraine.

Army Group North made better progress in its initial days and by 26 June General Erich von Manstein's LVI Panzer Corps had established a bridgehead at Dvinsk on the Dvina. Yet here Manstein became the victim of his own success, having to pause his operations for six days to await the arrival of Colonel-General Ernst Busch's 16th Army which was threatened on the right flank as a result of 9th Army's turn south to begin its encirclement east of Belostok. Manstein was also far ahead of Fourth Panzer Group's second panzer corps, General Georg-Hans Reinhardt's XXXXI Panzer Corps, delayed in large part by the above-mentioned Soviet counter-attacks at Rossienie.[68] Lacking support, Manstein's halt was a prudent measure but, as Halder's diary indicates, it afforded the

[65] Glantz and House, *When Titans Clashed*, p. 53.
[66] Franz Halder, KTB III, p. 16 (26 June 1941).
[67] Karl Wilhelm Thilo, 'A Perspective from the Army High Command (OKH)' in David M. Glantz (ed.), *The Initial Period of War*, p. 298 (26 June 1941).
[68] Von Manstein, *Lost Victories*, pp. 183–186; Klink, 'Die Operationsführung', p. 463.

Figure 5.3 The motorised divisions had right of way on the roads, which soon led to the opening of a great gap between the small number of panzer divisions and the mass of supporting infantry.

Soviets the chance to fall back over the Dvina River. Halder also observed that in the Army Group's rear area: 'Strong wedged-in enemy elements are causing the infantry a lot of trouble even far behind the front.'[69]

The activity in the northern and southern army groups illustrates the interdependence of each sector on the progress of the war as a whole. Yet, even in this initial period of the war, the inability of the armies to maintain contact between neighbouring units simultaneously, pacify the rear areas, and provide infantry support to the panzer spearheads, speaks strongly of the army's over-extension which was already becoming apparent.

By 26 June, with Pavlov's Western Front collapsing around him and the combined German panzer groups surging deep into his rear, the front headquarters finally issued orders for a general withdrawal. With the prospect of encirclement all but assured, what remained of the mechanised corps after the furious counter-attacks of the preceding days was now used to force a passage to the east.[70] For its part, Hoth's Panzer Group seized Vilnius on 24 June[71] and then General Rudolf Schmidt's

[69] Franz Halder, KTB III, p. 17 (26 June 1941).
[70] Glantz, 'Border Battles', pp. 216–217.
[71] KTB OKW, Volume II, p. 418 (24 June 1941).

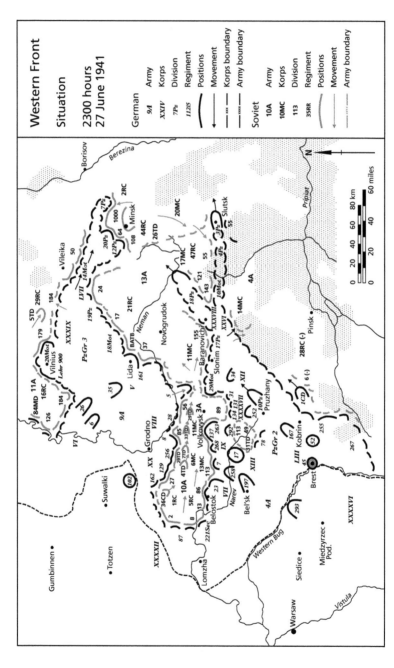

Western Front

Situation

2300 hours
27 June 1941

German

9A	Army
XXIV	Korps
7Pz	Division
112S	Regiment
➤	Positions
→	Movement
—xxx—	Korps boundary
—xxxx—	Army boundary

Soviet

10A	Army
10MC	Korps
113	Division
35RR	Regiment
	Positions
	Movement
	Army boundary

Map 2 Dispositions of Army Group Centre 27 June 1941: David M. Glantz, *Atlas and Operational Summary The Border Battles 22 June–1 July 1941*

XXXIX Panzer Corps (7th and 20th Panzer Divisions, 14th and 20th Motorised Divisions) supported by General of Panzer Troops Adolf Kuntzen's LVII Panzer Corps (12th and 19th Panzer Divisions and 18th Motorised Division) thrust down to the south-east towards the fortified region north of Minsk. Although this movement closed the northern pincer of the pocket, it was not without its cost. Here again the Soviet troops proved themselves unrelenting adversaries and, due to a lack of infantry support, the panzers were compelled to assault fixed defensive positions. On 27 June the diary of the 20th Panzer Division noted: 'The enemy is offering tenacious resistance from modern concrete positions. Our losses are noticeable.'[72] On the following day Hoth's panzer group advised Bock's headquarters: 'The battle north of Minsk on 28.6 against exceptionally well defended bunkers is considerably more difficult than anything so far . . . Against such tough defences and constant enemy reinforcements, the 20th Panzer Division could only slowly win ground in the area around Minsk.'[73] Operating on the left flank of the 20th Panzer Division, the 7th Panzer Division had occupied Smolewiecze 20 kilometres north of Minsk by 27 June (see Map 2), but the headlong advance over terrible roads had exacted a great toll.[74] By the evening of 28 June overall losses in the 7th Panzer Division constituted a hefty 50 per cent of all the Mark II and III tanks, while the Mark IV tanks suffered 75 per cent losses. As a result, barely a week into the campaign, the division had to request panzer reinforcements from the nearby 20th Panzer Division in order to carry out its next assigned objective.[75]

While overall material losses for the German army at this point remained low, the central importance of the tank and its alarming rate of attrition made its losses particularly critical. With production capacity in Germany still relatively meagre, and Hitler's determination to hold back all new tanks for future operations, the basis of Germany's battlefield mobility and striking power was threatened out of all proportion to the numerical strength of its other arms. The Red Army's resilience was also making an indelible impression, giving rise to some restive trepidation.

---

[72] 'KTB 20th Pz. Div. vom 25.5.41 bis 15.8.41' BA-MA RH 27–20/2, Fol. 20 (26 June 1941).

[73] 'Panzerarmeeoberkommandos Tagesmeldungen 21.6 – 31.8.41' BA-MA RH 21–3/43, Fols. 46–47 (28 June 1941).

[74] Ohrloff, 'XXXIX Motorized Corps Operations', pp. 168 and 180.

[75] 'Kriegstagebuch Nr.3 der 7.Panzer-Division Führungsabteilung 1.6.1941 – 9.5.1942' BA-MA RH 27–7/46, Fol. 21 (28 June 1941). Although not specifically stated in the war diary for the 7th Panzer Division, the number of tanks destroyed or 'total losses' were probably only a very small percentage of these figures. Most tanks were simply broken-down and therefore salvageable. As the example illustrates, however, the rate of attrition exacted by the poor Soviet infrastructure was extremely high.

Following the war from his office in Berlin, Goebbels noted in his diary: 'The first big pocket is beginning to close . . . But they are fighting well and have learned a great deal even since Sunday.'[76] At the front, a liaison officer from Panzer Group 3 visiting the 20th Panzer Division reported: 'Of the enemy there exists the impression that his infantry is many times numerically superior and very good to the bitter end. Colonel von Bismark used the expression "fantastic".'[77]

To the south in Guderian's Panzer Group 2, spirited Soviet resistance had significantly delayed the progress of Lemelsen's XXXXVII Panzer Corps on the road to Minsk and accordingly Guderian was lagging well behind Hoth's progress in closing the pocket. Western Front's withdrawal east also started creating problems for the panzer group's long left flank, and the commitment of Lemelsen's only motorised division (the 29th) to von Kluge's 4th Army to help contain the pocket and safeguard the panzer group's rear area was hardly sufficient. Even so, Guderian resented having any of his forces removed from his command and was especially perturbed to lose them to von Kluge for whom he held a keen personal and professional dislike. The antipathy between the two stretched back to past clashes, first in the Polish campaign and later with greater gusto in the Western campaign. Kluge regarded the junior ranking Guderian as a habitual risk-taker and an unwarranted hazard to the army, while Guderian viewed Kluge's caution as outdated and stifling to the new, rapid war of movement he sought to enact.[78] When Guderian received word of 29th Motorised Division's transfer he immediately dispatched one of his officers, Captain Euler, to 4th Army to argue for its immediate reinstatement. Failing this, the request was made that the division remain only so long as absolutely necessary and that it be relieved by elements of the OKH reserve. Euler also carried the request that 4th Army's XII Army Corps be diverted to secure the panzer group's main supply route or else 'the secure provisioning of the Panzer Group would stand in question'. A third request appealed for an official order forbidding elements of 4th Army from using the main thoroughfares necessary for the movement of Guderian's reserve panzer corps (General of Panzer Troops Freiherr von Vietinghoff's XXXXVI Panzer Corps).[79]

---

[76] Fröhlich (ed.), *Die Tagebücher von Joseph Goebbels*, Teil I: Aufzeichnungen 1923–1941, Band 9, Dezember 1940–Juli 1941, p. 405 (27 June 1941).

[77] 'Panzerarmeeoberkommandos Anlagen zum Kriegstagesbuch "Berichte, Besprechungen, Beurteilungen der Lage" Bd.III 25.5.41 – 22.7.41' BA-MA RH 21–3/46, Fol. 69 (29 June 1941).

[78] Kenneth Macksey, 'Guderian' in Barnett (ed.), *Hitler's Generals* p. 450.

[79] 'KTB Nr.1 Panzergruppe 2 vom 22.6.1941 bis 21.7.41' BA-MA RH 21–2/927, Fols. 63–64 (27 June 1941).

By all accounts the response from Kluge's headquarters was hardly promising. The next OKH reserves were still 90 kilometres to the rear, meaning the 29th Motorised Division's nearest relief was 4th Army's XII Army Corps, but even this was still a long way off. The sheer distance between Panzer Group 2 and 4th Army meant there was little Kluge could do about securing Guderian's supply lines, vast stretches of which still lay ahead of him, but he nevertheless promised what he could. On the final point, Kluge seemed to resent the inference that the best roads belonged to the panzer group and complained that the worse roads would slow the infantry's pace even further.[80]

With the campaign only in its sixth day, the tensions created by the two speeds of the army, one motorised and the other on horse and foot, were coming into sharp focus. In a private letter home to his wife on 27 June Guderian hinted at his frustration: 'In addition there is some annoyance, one incident of some importance. But nothing of that in this letter.'[81] Days later in a second letter home he conceded that the source of his irritation lay with his immediate superiors and singled out Kluge for having 'distinguished himself to good effect as a brake on progress'.[82] Bock too was starting to become impatient with Kluge's progress, complaining that: 'Indications of "standing still" are becoming apparent; 4th Army conceals this saying that it wants to build a "battle front".'[83] Bock's concern for the south-east side of the pocket, where the 29th Motorised Division alone held the line, forced him to the conclusion that, with 4th Army still too far off, the commitment of Guderian's reserve panzer corps (Vietinghoff's XXXXVI) would be necessary. Bock was very reluctant to give the order as he wished to preserve Guderian's armoured strength for the thrust east and leave the reduction of the pocket to the infantry, but he reasoned that having encircled Western Front, 'I must not allow the enemy out.'[84] The 10th Panzer Division was therefore subordinated to Kluge on the morning of 28 June in order to effect the closure of a gap at Zelwianka quickly. Kluge's vacillation, however, again became evident. In response to Bock's urging, Kluge declared: 'I haven't been able to make up my mind to do so yet.' When he finally did decide to attack, it was already too late and the operation had to be postponed until the following day.[85]

To the north, on 28 June Hoth's panzers entered Minsk, but Halder noted that the struggle to prevent Soviet forces from fighting their way

---

[80] Ibid., Fol. 65 (27 June 1941).
[81] Guderian's letter as cited by Macksey, *Guderian*, p. 136.   [82] Ibid.
[83] Fedor von Bock, KTB 'Osten I', Fol. 5, *War Diary*, p. 229 (27 June 1941).
[84] Ibid., Fol. 7, p. 230 (27 June 1941).   [85] Ibid., Fol. 7, p. 231 (28 June 1941).

out of the pocket north of Novogrudok was straining the northern ring to breaking point.[86] Meanwhile, when Guderian received word that the 10th Panzer Division was being diverted to Kluge he immediately contacted the army group headquarters to complain that this made his whole operation towards Minsk 'impossible'.[87] Furthermore, upon learning that plans were afoot to bring the two panzer groups directly under Kluge's new command, Guderian promptly dispatched an officer to Halder at OKH to insist that such an action would force him to ask for relief from his command.[88] Headstrong and impetuous, Guderian was known for his temper and it was not beyond him to threaten brash action to get what he wanted. In the event his incorrigible ego and driving ambition led him to suffer under Kluge rather than sit out the war on the sidelines. Similarly, his reaction to the loss of 10th Panzer Division and the alleged impossibility of reaching Minsk were characteristic overstatement, calculated for effect.

In addition to the transfer of the 10th Panzer Division, on 28 June Bock also subordinated Guderian's 1st Cavalry Division[89] to Kluge. This was operating on the extreme southern flank of the Army Group and according to Bock was out of reach of the panzer group.[90] The orders did not however reach Panzer Group 2 until the morning of 29 June, whereupon Guderian again protested[91] and, to Bock's surprise, the cavalry division was now reported to be 100 kilometres north of its position on the previous day. Accordingly, the Field Marshal relented to Guderian's insistence that the division be returned to his command.[92] Emboldened by his success, Guderian tried again later that morning to regain command of the 29th Motorised Division. This led to a series of strongly worded communiqués between the respective headquarters of Bock, Kluge and Guderian, with Panzer Group 2 insisting that 'the release must without fail take place today'.[93] Ultimately Guderian's demand was denied by Bock, who also recommended that the line from Slonim to Minsk be reinforced by 1st Cavalry Division and the SS *Das Reich* Division.[94]

[86] Franz Halder, KTB III, p. 21 (28 June 1941).
[87] 'KTB Nr.1 Panzergruppe 2 vom 22.6.1941 bis 21.7.41' BA-MA RH 21–2/927, Fols. 73–74 (28 June 1941).
[88] Franz Halder, KTB III, p. 22 (28 June 1941).
[89] This was the only division of its kind remaining in the German army.
[90] Fedor von Bock, KTB 'Osten I', Fol. 7, *War Diary*, p. 231 (28 June 1941).
[91] 'KTB Nr.1 Panzergruppe 2 vom 22.6.1941 bis 21.7.41' BA-MA RH 21–2/927, Fols. 78–79 (29 June 1941).
[92] Fedor von Bock, KTB 'Osten I', Fol. 8, *War Diary*, p. 232 (29 June 1941).
[93] Underlining in the original; 'KTB Nr.1 Panzergruppe 2 vom 22.6.1941 bis 21.7.41' BA-MA RH 21–2/927, Fol. 80 (29 June 1941).
[94] Beyond the role of the Waffen SS in Hitler's ideological war of annihilation, the organisation also fielded a limited number of elite military formations in Operation Barbarossa,

Guderian, on the other hand, was impatient to press on eastward with all the force he could muster and was contemptuous of the strength of Soviet forces attempting to escape the pocket. With a flight to Hoth's headquarters planned for the following day, Guderian was eager to see for himself the 'supposed strong enemy-occupied forested area ... from where 4th Amy and Army Group Centre expect breakout attempts towards the south-east'.[95]

The wrangling for control of divisions represented much more than matters of prestige or the personal animosity of the commanding officers; these quarrels were the tangible result of the more important division over strategy and how the war was to be waged. Kluge was fixed on sealing the pocket as tightly as possible and thereby netting the greatest bag of prisoners. He was not in principle opposed to Guderian's desire to continue the advance eastwards, but the hasty continuance of the advance did not concern him to anywhere near the extent it did Guderian, and he was certainly not interested in winning more ground at the expense of undermining the accomplishment at Minsk. Guderian, by contrast, saw little point in expending precious time and strength on forces he regarded as beaten and of only modest threat to his rear area. In his opinion, rather than fretting about rounding up every last prisoner, it was better to maintain the momentum of the advance, keeping the enemy off balance, and seize the next objective. The two views proved irreconcilable and indicative of the fundamental strategic divide splitting the German command. For resolution both men looked to higher authority to win support, which found Bock and Halder thirsting for both alternatives and ultimately supporting neither fully. The compromise between the competing extremes soured Kluge's triumph and left Guderian's continued drive conspicuously under-resourced. Yet it would be improper to suggest an obvious choice existed or that a golden opportunity was somehow missed. The fact remained that German forces were simply attempting too much. Guderian was right to seek a rapid solution through the deepest possible penetration, but he under-estimated the threat to his rear between Slonim and Minsk, as well as the strength of opposition further to the east, for which he would desperately need Kluge's infantry. The same dilemma confronted Hoth but, for the panzer generals, bold action in the face of danger was the hallmark of previously victorious campaigns and neither

which steadily expanded in number as the war continued. For a good overview of the military role of the Waffen SS see Bernd Wegner, '"My Honour is Loyalty." The SS as a Military Factor in Hitler's Germany' in Wilhelm Deist (ed.), *The German Military in the Age of Total War* (Warwickshire, 1985) pp. 220–239.

[95] 'KTB Nr.1 Panzergruppe 2 vom 22.6.1941 bis 21.7.41' BA-MA RH 21–2/927, Fol. 80 (29 June 1941).

man was about to shy away from the perils of forward operations, or give in to the wary reservations of army commanders. Even after the war Guderian maintained that the single greatest hindrance to his advance resulted from the unremitting doubts of Field Marshal von Kluge, who, he commented; 'was inclined to stop the advance of the panzers at every difficulty arising in the rear'.[96]

In spite of his ardent determination that Army Group Centre's first priority be the closure of the ring at Minsk, Halder still favoured sending elements of both panzer groups on towards the Dvina and Dnepr to secure bridgeheads for the next stage of the advance. Indeed, on 29 June Halder revealed in his diary for the first time his objective for the advance of Army Group Centre, namely the attack on Moscow. Upon expressing his hope for the seizure of Rogachev and Mogilev on the Dnepr, Halder added that this would 'open the road to Smolensk and from there the course to Moscow'.[97] Meanwhile, at Hitler's headquarters a very different picture was emerging. Hitler too was casting an eye to the continuation of the campaign following the elimination of the pocket, and the question was posed whether the main thrust of operations should be directed towards Moscow or Leningrad. Brauchitsch is known to have been in attendance at the Wolf's Lair on this day (29 June) and, although the record does not specify, he may well have recommended the Moscow option to Hitler. Even if not, he most certainly would have supported it. Hitler, however, was more attracted to cutting the Soviets off from the Baltic Sea, thereby denying them access to the North Sea, securing Germany's ore transports from Scandinavia and allowing the concentration of Finland's strength for their attack in the east. As for an eventual thrust on Moscow, Hitler contended that the drive on Leningrad would secure the left flank of the later operation and that for the time being the Soviet capital should simply be subjected to bombing. The following day (30 June) Hitler expanded on such sentiments, adding that the addition of panzer forces from Army Group Centre would allow the rapid seizure of Leningrad's industrial area and only then should the attack on Moscow be launched.[98]

In more immediate concerns Brauchitsch reported that Hitler was once again expressing a nervous anxiety about the depth of Schweppenburg's XXIV Panzer Corps, which on that day (29 June) had reached Bobruisk and was building a bridgehead on the eastern bank of the Beresina River.

[96] Liddell Hart, *The Other Side of the Hill*, p. 272.
[97] Franz Halder, KTB III, p. 25 (29 June 1941).
[98] KTB OKW, Volume II, pp. 1019–1020, Documents 64 (29 June 1941) and 65 (30 June 1941).

Brauchitsch placated Hitler with assurances that this was nothing more than flank protection for the main operation at Minsk, but Halder (who was not present, but later received a report from Brauchitsch) recognised that Guderian would be content with nothing less than the quickest possible crossing of the Dnepr. Personally, Halder supported Guderian in this endeavour as, with the encirclement at Minsk almost complete, the Chief of the General Staff now wanted to press on eastwards and capitalise on what he saw as the destruction of the Soviet front. Yet Hitler remained worried that the XXIV Panzer Corps had over-extended itself and forbade the army command from issuing any further orders for the further eastward advance of the panzer corps, meaning that Halder's hands were officially tied. Halder regarded this as a grave mistake, but was not about to concede direction of the campaign so readily to Hitler. In his diary Halder defiantly stated: 'Let us hope that the middle levels of command will do the right thing on their own and without express orders, which we cannot issue because of the Führer's orders to Brauchitsch.'[99] Thus, while a strict interpretation of his orders prohibited the issuing of a command to advance, they did not explicitly require him to forbid the action if it was undertaken independently by the generals themselves – which he assumed it would be. Using this frail logic Halder convinced himself that he could still have his way without disobeying orders.

While Germany's leading generals fought amongst themselves and against Hitler's headquarters for direction of the eastern campaign, the infighting was if anything even more intense among Germany's political institutions headed by some of the most unscrupulous personalities within the Third Reich, most notably Hermann Göring and Heinrich Himmler. With the toppling of the Soviet state predicted from all quarters, each man vied for the largest slice of the lucrative Soviet prize, seeking to build on their respective empires which made up the internal authorities of the Nazi state. Observing the unruly scene, Goebbels (who was himself involved in a dispute with the OKW and the designated minister for the new eastern territories, Alfred Rosenberg, over the dissemination of propaganda in the east), complained in his diary: 'Always the same thing: spheres of authority'. He then perceptively added: 'If we go down, then it will be as a result of these disputes.'[100]

On 29 June contact was finally established between Hoth and Guderian at Minsk, ostensibly closing the outer ring, although in practice the

[99] Franz Halder, KTB III, p. 25 (29 June 1941). See also Guderian, *Panzer Leader*, p. 167.
[100] Fröhlich (ed.), *Die Tagebücher von Joseph Goebbels*, Teil I: Aufzeichnungen 1923–1941, Band 9, Dezember 1940–Juli 1941, p. 411 (29 June 1941).

south-east side was far from hermetically sealed. At Army Group Centre, Bock was also now anxious to proceed on to the great rivers, but despaired at the lost opportunities higher command had cost him by insisting on the Belostok–Minsk pocket. Venting his frustration, Bock wrote:

That is the curse of the evil deed! If we turn near Minsk, there will inevitably be a stop there until the entire Belostok–Minsk pocket has largely been cleared. I wanted to take possession of the Dnepr or at least the Beresina bridges quickly, so as not to have to fight for them later – which unfortunately will now be the case![101]

As it turned out, the challenge for Bock was not just quickly clearing the pocket, but ensuring all the gaps were plugged in the outer ring. Despite Guderian's reckless insistence that the presence of the 29th Motorised Division was no longer necessary, events on the ground proved quite the opposite to be true. On the evening of 24 June as the 18th Panzer Division swept eastwards forming the southern arm of the encirclement, Lemelsen's XXXXVII Panzer Corps was inundated with radio messages from the division reading: '"Alarm", "Help", "enemy panzer breakthrough"'.[102] As the division continued to battle through the gauntlet of escaping Soviet units instances of panic occurred among the supply columns of the rear, resulting from the fear of enemy tanks along their long exposed flank. One report noted: 'Whole battalions have turned around on their tracks and fled back to the rear.'[103] As the 18th Panzer Division continued eastwards, however, it was left to the following 29th Motorised Division and the smaller 5th Machine-gun Battalion to hold the long southern arc of the ring, which, by the morning of 27 June, extended to an impractical 60 kilometres.[104] The length of front allowed no depth to the defences and, facing constant attacks which included Soviet armour, a mounting crisis developed within the division. Individual units of the 29th Motorised Division were frequently cut off from neighbouring units and then surrounded and forced to fight costly close-quarters battles in dense forests and swamps.[105] By the night of 29 June

[101] Fedor von Bock, KTB 'Osten I', Fol. 9, *War Diary*, pp. 232–233 (29 June 1941).
[102] 'Kriegstagebuch Nr.2 XXXXVII.Pz.Korps. Ia 25.5.1941 – 22.9.1941' BA-MA RH 24–47/2. This war diary has no folio stamped page numbers so references must be located using the date (24 June 1941).
[103] Bartov, *Hitler's Army*, p. 102.
[104] 'Kriegstagebuch Nr.2 XXXXVII.Pz.Korps. Ia 25.5.1941 – 22.9.1941' BA-MA RH 24–47/2 (27 June 1941).
[105] 'Kriegstagebuch der 29.I.D. (mot) vom: 25.5.1941 bis 29.7.1941' BA-MA RH 26–29/6. This war diary has no folio stamped page numbers so references must be located using the date (27, 28, 29 June 1941).

massed Soviet breakout attempts proved beyond the division's strength and the units of Infantry Regiment 71 and Panzer Regiment 7 had to withdraw and allow Soviet forces to surge past them to the east. Nor was this an isolated case. A great number of Soviet troops simply marched through the German lines.[106]

Guderian, however, was blinded to such problems and his post-war memoir similarly glossed over the incomplete nature of the encirclement, seeking only to crown his achievements up to Minsk as an outstanding success. Recalling the final days of June Guderian wrote: 'The Russian forces, which had been in the Belostok area and had been attempting in vain to break through our encircling pincers, were now completely surrounded . . . The foundations had been laid for the first great victory of the campaign.'[107] The confident tone of these later reflections disguised a more genuine picture of the fighting which Guderian set down in a letter to his wife on 27 June. After describing the first days as 'strenuous' he wrote of the loss of several officers who had been close to him and the sadness this caused him. When he came to the subject of the Red Army he noted with a trace of grim resignation: 'The enemy resists bravely and bitterly. The fighting, therefore, is very hard. One just has to put up with it.'[108] By nature Guderian was by no means a pessimist and indeed in past campaigns he had been accused of viewing events from quite the opposite extreme. His letter simply related the character of the new war in the east, which possessed an element of fervent hostility and ardent fanaticism, unlike anything he had hitherto witnessed.

By the end of June a similarly grudging acknowledgement of the Red Army's unexpectedly zealous resistance was taking root throughout some of the upper circles of the Wehrmacht and Nazi party, reflecting the dramatic contrast between the reality of the war and the elevated pitch of confidence that had consumed the German leadership prior to the launch of operations. In many cases this realisation was only just beginning to dawn and, although it would be too much to suggest that any yet doubted Germany's ultimate triumph, the shock of encountering genuine resistance was palpable. On 29 June Goebbels noted in his diary: 'The Russians are fighting bravely. Their command is functioning better than during the first few days.'[109] On the following day he remarked:

---

[106] Joachim Lemelsen, *29.Division* (Bad Nauheim, 1960), p. 114; Edgar Röhricht, *Probleme der Kesselschlacht. Dargestellt an Einkreisungs-Operationen im zweiten Weltkrieg* (Karlsruhe, 1958), pp. 30–31.

[107] Guderian, *Panzer Leader*, p. 158.

[108] Guderian's letter as cited by Macksey, *Guderian*, p. 136.

[109] Fröhlich (ed.), *Die Tagebücher von Joseph Goebbels*, Teil I: Aufzeichnungen 1923–1941, Band 9, Dezember 1940–Juli 1941, p. 410 (29 June 1941).

'In foreign countries our military situation is, if anything, being judged rather too optimistically, even by our enemies. They think our Wehrmacht capable of the most amazing achievements.'[110] By 1 July, despite maintaining a general satisfaction with developments, Goebbels betrayed a telling sense of disquiet: '[T]he Russians are putting up more of a fight than one would have expected. Our losses in men and equipment are not completely insignificant.'[111]

Echoing such sentiments, Bock described the enduring problem of defeating the sizeable Soviet armies, which the swift breakthroughs to Minsk had by no means fully achieved. Unlike previous campaigns, where surrounded enemy units acknowledged their defeat and willingly gave themselves up, Red Army units did not,[112] and the implications for Barbarossa were profound. Reviewing the course of events in his rear area on 28 June Bock observed:

Our losses are not inconsiderable. Thousands of Russians soldiers are sitting in the forests, far behind the front, some in civilian clothes... catching them all is impossible given the tremendous size of the area. 100km behind the front, at Siemiatycze, the 293rd Division is still fighting for a row of strongly-fortified bunkers, which have to be taken one at a time. In spite of the heaviest fire and the employment of every means the crews refuse to give up. Each fellow has to be killed one at a time.[113]

A report from 4th Army to the Army Group command noted the commencement of a planned 'cleaning action' on 29 June against what it expected to be 'exceptionally tough and stalwart' resistance in the forested areas of the pocket. The report also noted that the enemy was repeatedly attempting to escape through a series of uncoordinated attacks.[114] Already on 26 June Ernst-Günter Merten, a soldier in 4th Army, noted the difficulty of fighting in the densely wooded terrain.

These bloody Russian forests! One loses the overview of who is a friend and who is an enemy. So we are shooting at ourselves... The II company was encircled and came back with 55 men. 'Worse than at Verdun!' said Lieutenant-Colonel von Löhneysen.[115]

---

[110] Ibid., p. 413 (30 June 1941).   [111] Ibid., p. 415 (1 July 1941).

[112] 'Tagesmeldungen der Heeresgruppe Mitte vom 22.6.41 bis 15.7.41' BA-MA RH 19 II/128, Fol. 87 (29 June 1941). In this same report it was later noted that the motivation for Red Army resistance was the common belief among Soviet troops that they would be either immediately shot or mistreated. A similar statement is found in the same file on 24 June (Fol. 29).

[113] Fedor von Bock, KTB 'Osten I', Fol. 8, *War Diary*, p. 231 (28 June 1941).

[114] 'Tagesmeldungen der Heeresgruppe Mitte vom 22.6.41 bis 15.7.41' BA-MA RH 19 II/128, Fol. 76 (29 June 1941).

[115] Walter Kempowski (ed.), *Das Echolot Barbarossa '41*, p. 113 (26 June 1941).

This drag on German forward operations caused by intense Soviet rearward action was not unique to the large concentrations in the Belostok–Minsk pocket. The diary of the 3rd Panzer Division, which was surging eastward at the vanguard of Schweppenburg's XXIV Panzer Corps well to the south of the main pocket, noted the danger of sending prisoners of war towards the rear and instead indicated that prisoners were to be held in forward collection zones and only dispatched to the rear under special guard.[116] The turmoil in the division's rear area was simply too great. A former officer in the division explained how soldiers from headquarters and those ferrying supplies were often forced to fight like infantry, while it even became necessary to station tanks at 50–100 metre intervals in the most endangered areas to ensure the safety of unarmed vehicles.[117] Such measures sapped the strength of the forward drive, while the insecurity added a major complication to the already hard-pressed supply columns. The diary of the quartermaster of the 3rd Panzer Division noted on 28 June that supplies were 'very critical', but that their efforts to alleviate the shortage were hampered by 'very strong aerial and artillery activity',[118] indicating that bypassed Soviet units still employed heavy weapons and that the Soviet air force was still effective, at least in certain sectors, in spite of its immense losses in the opening days of the war. The diary also mentioned the destruction of many bridges in the rear area which forced the diversion of the supply columns onto 'very bad overland roads'. As a result, the diary noted, the fluid advance of the division was being impeded.[119]

Renegade Soviet units refusing to give up the fight in spite of finding themselves behind enemy lines and, in many cases, cut off from higher command were not the only menace confronting the army group's rear area. A report from 4th Army on 29 June described road conditions for the greater part of the dual carriageways as being 'exceptionally bad'.[120] In practical terms this naturally slowed the tempo of the advance but, more worryingly, it was also having a shattering effect on the army's horses. Given the almost total reliance of the 4th and 9th Armies on horses for the movement of equipment and supplies, their well-being and good health represented a pivotal concern for maintaining the gruelling

---

[116] 'KTB 3rd Pz. Div. vom 16.8.40 bis 18.9.41' BA-MA RH 27–3/14, p. 48 (26 June 1941).

[117] Zobel, '3rd Panzer Division Operations', p. 244.

[118] 'KTB 3rd Pz. Div. I.b 19.5.41 – 6.2.42' BA-MA RH 27–3/218 (28 June 1941). This war diary has no folio stamped page numbers so references must be located using the date. See also comments in Zobel, '3rd Panzer Division Operations', p. 246.

[119] 'KTB 3rd Pz. Div. I.b 19.5.41 – 6.2.42' BA-MA RH 27–3/218 (28 June 1941).

[120] 'Tagesmeldungen der Heeresgruppe Mitte vom 22.6.41 bis 15.7.41' BA-MA RH 19 II/128, Fol. 92 (30 June 1941).

pace of advance. Although the carnage of winter for the horses of Army Group Centre has long been recognised, the extremes of summer and its grim toll on the army's horse population have attracted less attention. Operation Barbarossa incorporated 625,000 horses.[121] Of these, 4th Army commanded 130,000 and the smaller 9th Army 87,000.[122] With the time-consuming delay of switching the Soviet Union's rail gauges to the European standard, the war began with the horse bearing the great burden of the German army's push eastward. The operational time constraints, and ever pressing demands of the panzer commanders for greater infantry support led to a punishing routine of exhausting marches, that, under the sweltering conditions, rapidly fatigued the horses and drained their strength. General Heinrici, commanding the XXXXIII Army Corps, wrote in a letter to his wife on 8 July: 'Now we are a long way back [from the motorised divisions,] marching 30–35 kilometres every day, the horses hardly make it along the sand [roads], but we must go on.'[123] Likewise, in only the second week of the campaign, Heinrich Haape, a doctor in the 9th Army's 6th Infantry Division, described how captured horses were already being used to replace those that had begun the campaign. 'My ambulance horses had been replaced; old Westwall [Haape's former personal mount] had dropped dead in the harness and the other had reached total exhaustion.'[124] In the circumstances, long and frequent halts had to be made to water and rest the horses,[125] but this cost precious time and could not always be guaranteed depending on the immediate demands of the individual unit. Accordingly, 4th Army informed the army group command on 29 June that the horse-drawn vehicles and, in particular, the heavy artillery were reporting 'heavy losses in horses'.[126] It was precisely these larger draft horses that proved most susceptible to the intense climate and rigorous demands of the campaign, but the problem remained a general one. The German army's horses were principally made up of stout breeds raised in the temperate climates of central Europe and unaccustomed to the searing conditions and dreadful roads of the east. The long hours of work soon took their toll and the heavy losses created new dilemmas for the army. On the one hand, the infantry divisions typically started the war with a quickly exhausted reserve of only about 150 horses. Since

---

[121] Klink, 'Die militärische Konzeption', p. 270.
[122] DiNardo, *Mechanized Juggernaut*, p. 40.
[123] Hürter, *Ein deutscher General*, p. 66 (8 July 1941).
[124] Haape with Henshaw, *Moscow Tram Stop*, p. 60.
[125] DiNardo, *Mechanized Juggernaut*, pp. 41–43.
[126] 'Tagesmeldungen der Heeresgruppe Mitte vom 22.6.41 bis 15.7.41' BA-MA RH 19 II/128, Fol. 92 (30 June 1941).

transporting new steeds to their units usually meant marching them long distances to the constantly advancing front, the horses often arrived in correspondingly worn-out condition. Further complications concerned the availability of fodder. The army considered oats to be the best feed for its horses, but such crops were not widely sown in the Soviet Union. The substitute of green fodder, while widely available in the Soviet Union, took time to harvest in the amounts required and proved problematic to obtain on the constant march.[127] Theodor Mogge, a non-commissioned artillery officer in the 4th Army, recorded that the tempo of the campaign was 'a great strain' on the horses and 'above all those pulling the artillery'. The availability of fodder was also highlighted by Mogge. As the army advanced further east, he noted that provisions for the horses could not keep pace and, as supplies of oats soon ran out, the horses were reduced to eating the straw from peasant houses. This, however, was no replacement for their usual diet, especially in the circumstances.[128] On 30 June Bock noted in his diary, 'the horses are tired out – with these roads they should receive much more oats'.[129] The statement echoed Halder's blunt assessment of 29 June: 'Horses very fatigued'.[130] Beyond the harsh physical demands placed on the horses, the extension of the combat zone throughout the rear area presented the additional problem of losing horses in direct engagements with Soviet troops, or in some instances to Soviet aircraft which proved devastating to the long, strung-out columns.[131]

In his memoirs Hoth proclaimed the closure of the Belostok–Minsk pocket as a 'battle of annihilation with few precedents in the history of warfare'.[132] It is an assessment similar to that presented in Guderian's memoir and repeated in countless military histories as a glowing example of the triumphant German blitzkrieg waged in the summer of 1941. While there can be no doubt that the encirclement of Pavlov's Western Front represented a calamity for the Red Army, it was by no means the one-sided victory commonly portrayed. The southern flank of the pocket haemorrhaged like an open wound for the Germans, with Kluge unable to close it, and Guderian unwilling even to recognise the problem. In addition, merely creating the vast pocket taxed German strength considerably, a factor that needs to be assessed in the fullness of the German operational plan, and not solely on the tally of encircled Soviet soldiers.

---

[127] DiNardo, *Mechanized Juggernaut*, pp. 43–45.

[128] Theodor Mogge's unpublished personal account of his experiences on the eastern front were recorded in 1978 and kindly provided to me by his son Klaus Mogge.

[129] Fedor von Bock, KTB 'Osten I', Fol. 10, *War Diary*, p. 233 (30 June 1941).

[130] Franz Halder, KTB III, p. 25 (29 June 1941).

[131] DiNardo, *Mechanized Juggernaut*, p. 44.   [132] Hoth, *Panzer-Operationen*, p. 69.

The battle was not an end in itself, but rather the first stage of the long march east, for which it was essential that the panzer forces retained their fluid mobility and at least partial infantry support. The strain of maintaining the equilibrium of arms was eased in this first period of the war by the close starting positions of the infantry and panzers. Yet now, as the panzer divisions raced away for their next big objective, leaving the mass of infantry, already far behind and with the stubborn remnants of the surrounded Soviet armies to deal with, Army Group Centre would split in two and face the dire consequences of this foreboding development.

Complicating matters still further, the barely restrained antagonism between the principal commanders reflected their stark differences in operational thinking. This was destined to worsen with the increasing depth of operations and the correspondent thinning of German resources. Threatening to eclipse even this embittered divergence was the pending, although still dormant, strategic pariah of Moscow.

Straining the limits – Bock's race to the rivers

With the northern ring of the pocket comparatively secure, Hoth was setting his sights on securing the Dvina River as far down as the Orsha corridor and closing the next big ring at Smolensk. Yet there was concern within his panzer group that its southern counterpart, Panzer Group 2, had not fulfilled its assignment of firmly preventing Soviet breakouts to the south-east.[133] The ramifications of this failing were serious. At Hoth's headquarters it was believed that the mass of Soviet troops opposite their northern ring, that previously had largely failed to break through, were now proceeding south to take advantage of the opening.[134] While in the short term this offered improved security for Hoth's continued advance, it ensured even greater problems for Guderian; these would doubtless slow the latter's advance and ultimately affect Hoth through the delay caused to the right hook of the next operational movement centred on Smolensk. Yet such distant concerns were secondary to Hoth's immediate goal of resuming the advance as rapidly as possible with the bulk of his forces. To do this, he faced the same battle with higher command that Guderian had been waging. Hoth's sense of urgency was heightened by aerial intelligence that, as early as 26 June, had indicated the massing of Soviet forces in the Orsha region.[135] Officially, however, the further advance of

---

[133] '3rd Pz. Gr. KTB 25.5.41 – 31.8.41' BA-MA Microfilm 59054, Fol. 71 (29 June 1941).
[134] Ibid., Fol. 72 (29 June 1941).   [135] Hoth, *Panzer-Operationen*, p. 65.

the panzer groups was still prohibited and only 'reconnaissance forces' were to be sent east over the Beresina and towards the Dnepr.[136]

On 30 June Guderian flew to Hoth's headquarters for discussion of the next stage of their advance. Both commanders were becoming increasingly infuriated at the perceived procrastination of higher command and it is not outside the realm of possibility that their joint disobedience to the restrictive orders was discussed and even planned. Although it is important to point out that nothing so exact exists among the primary material, subsequent events strongly indicate a degree of co-ordinated action in blatant defiance of orders. It was also well within the character of each man to 'interpret' their orders in terms of the wider strategic goals of the campaign and therefore implement actions as they saw fit, conveniently excusing themselves from any meticulous definition of insubordination.[137] This introduces the question of whether a commander's operational freedom, practised under the concept of *Auftragstaktik*[138] (mission tactics), was sometimes abused, especially by the panzer commanders.

Given the need to reorganise forces for the renewed attack, Halder was not prepared to release the panzer divisions until 5 July.[139] Subsequent pressure finally brought this forward to 3 July, although even this represented more of a delay than the panzer commanders would have liked. Agreeing on an exact starting date was in many respects aimed purely at placating higher command, as in practice there were already much

---

[136] Fedor von Bock, KTB 'Osten I', Fol. 11, *War Diary*, p. 234 (1 July 1941).

[137] Knowing very well his actions directly contravened Kluge's intentions Guderian evokes just such a defence in his memoir: 'My views concerning the next stage of operations were as follows: to detach the minimum amount of the Panzer Group for the destruction of the Russians in the Belostok pocket, while leaving the major part of this operation to the following infantry armies: thus our rapidly mobile, motorised forces would be able to push forward and seize the first operational objective of the campaign, the area Smolensk-Yel'nya-Roslavl . . . I was thus in agreement with the original orders that had been issued' (Guderian, *Panzer Leader*, p. 159).

[138] Developed in the nineteenth century under the tutelage of Helmuth von Moltke the Elder (Chief of the General Staff 1857 to 1888), *Auftragstaktik* was 'a command method stressing decentralized initiative within an overall strategic framework' (definition by Gunther E. Rothenberg). The concept sought to reduce 'friction' in the command process by making lower-level commanders responsible for set objectives and empowering them to make independent decisions, while freeing the higher command of tactical details. Strictly speaking it is not a tactic, nor, as seen in the above discussion, is it limited to the tactical level of command, rather *Auftragstaktik* is best understood as a leadership method. A key element of this process is forward control, which accounts in large measure for the German army's high rate of officer casualties. The success of the concept rested on the receiver of the orders correctly understanding the *intent* of the issuer, which in Barbarossa provided Guderian and Hoth with a potential loophole in conducting their own operations.

[139] Franz Halder, KTB III, p. 26 (29 June 1941).

more than just reconnaissance forces striking out to the east. From their meeting, both Hoth and Guderian reaffirmed their determination that it was 'high time' for forthright action towards the Dvina and Dnepr Rivers to prevent Soviet forces consolidating their defensive positions.[140]

In addition to the obstructions of higher command, they faced sizeable obstacles in implementing the next stage of the advance because of the hard fought battle at Minsk. On 29 June a tour of inspection by General of Panzer Troops Wilhelm Ritter von Thoma reported that while an extensive halt in operations was not necessary, the 3rd Panzer Group would nevertheless have only 70 per cent of its panzer forces fit for service by 2 July.[141] Although a sizeable number of the 30 per cent shortfall were only broken down and therefore salvageable in the long term, the significance of such a dire rate of attrition in tank numbers was made all the more striking by the fact that it was only the eighth day of the war.

A further omen of foreboding consequence, reminiscent of Hitler's obtuse belief that ardent conviction alone could alter fact, appeared in the form of Guderian's baseless confidence in the security of his southern side to the ring. Contrary to intelligence reports and events on the ground, Guderian's belief that no serious threat existed to his rear area was further reinforced by his flight to Hoth's headquarters, which swept over the Puszcza Nalibocka forested area and convinced Guderian that, in contrast to the army group and 4th Army, 'there were no considerable enemy forces in the forest and that there was, therefore, no danger from this quarter'.[142] Although excluded from his memoirs, events would prove otherwise, questioning the merit of Guderian's airborne assessment and the dependence he placed upon it. This was especially true given his own observation that the Red Army's 'battle technique, particularly his camouflage, was excellent'.[143]

At the same time as Guderian and Hoth had been planning the next phase of their operations, Brauchitsch hosted a meeting at his home attended by Hitler, Halder and Heusinger. Halder began proceedings with a summary of operations and then Hitler spoke of the importance he attached to securing the Gulf of Finland and eliminating the threat to ore shipments posed by the Soviet fleet. In contrast to Hitler's intentions over the preceding months, Halder's record of the meeting claimed that

---

[140] Hoth, *Panzer-Operationen*, p. 66.

[141] '3rd Pz. Gr. KTB 25.5.41 – 31.8.41' BA-MA Microfilm 59054, Fol. 71 (29 June 1941).

[142] Guderian, *Panzer Leader*, p. 160; 'KTB Nr.1 Panzergruppe 2 vom 22.6.1941 bis 21.7.41' BA-MA RH 21-2/927, Fols. 90–91 (30 June 1941).

[143] Guderian, *Panzer Leader*, p. 161.

Hitler was 'not sure' whether additional panzer forces for the rapid seizure of Leningrad would have to be made available by Bock.[144] Conceivably, under pressure from Halder and Brauchitsch, who may only have had to laud the successes of Leeb's progress, Hitler was compelled to waver on the issue of diverting strength from Army Group Centre. The encouraging reports left Hitler in a buoyant mood, giving Heusinger the impression that one was 'completely free to speak with him', even to the point of telling him things 'that maybe he wouldn't normally accept'.[145]

In addition to his discussion of operations in the north, Hitler also expanded on the importance of the Ukraine for its food supply and industry, underlining the importance of economic goals in Hitler's strategic conception. Yet significantly the one available record of the meeting (from Halder's diary) includes no indication that Hitler was yet considering an alternative diversion of Bock's panzers to the south. In Hitler's estimation, comparatively little significance was attached to the march on Moscow, which he forecast could only be undertaken by infantry units, at the earliest in August, once Smolensk had been secured. Only when the northern theatre of operations had been satisfactorily dealt with would Hitler release armoured forces to assist the infantry in the drive on Moscow.[146] Whatever the case, the future employment of Army Group Centre was still undecided following the 30 June meeting and would not be conclusively settled until Smolensk was in German hands.

On the surface, the result of the meeting seemed to offer Halder and Brauchitsch a promising format to end Hitler's opposition to their plans for a continued drive on Moscow with the full force of Army Group Centre. The key would be ensuring Army Group North carried out the drive on Leningrad under its own strength, allaying Hitler's fears of cutting the Soviets off from the Baltic and freeing Bock's panzer forces for a direct thrust on Moscow. Yet Halder and Brauchitsch must also have recognised that there were few certainties in dealing with Hitler, who could be as impetuous as he was stubborn, especially with the ever changing fortunes of war. Above all, an amicable solution was hoped for, but the army commanders were determined to drive for Moscow. In their view this was the linchpin of victory against the Soviet Union and accordingly a matter of uncompromising importance. If Hitler overruled the army on a matter of such decisive significance, it would constitute a direct challenge to the authority of Halder and Brauchitsch – an issue which had long since become a persistent and tiresome source of irritation for

---

[144] Franz Halder, KTB III, p. 29 (30 June 1941).
[145] As cited in Meyer, *Heusinger*, pp. 152–153.
[146] Franz Halder, KTB III, p. 29 (30 June 1941).

both men. For the moment, however, the external facade of harmonious relations was maintained, with the army commanders hoping anxiously to win Hitler over.

Reviewing preparations for the continuation of the advance scheduled for 3 July, Halder noted the disparity between the 9th Army and Panzer Group 3 in the north and the 4th Army and Panzer Group 2 in the south, with the latter two noticeably less prepared. The liquidation of the pocket was dominating all 4th Army's resources, while Panzer Group 2, Halder complained, 'against all orders and with a measure of defiance has failed to mop up the territory traversed by it and now has its hands full with local enemy breakthroughs'.[147] Personnel losses were another stark indication of the difficulties confronting Guderian in the south, particularly as a result of his exposed left flank. On 2 July Hoth's panzer group reported officer casualties at 125 men and all other ranks at 1,644 men;[148] by contrast Guderian's group, in a casualties report from two days earlier on 30 June, recorded officer losses to be already twice those of Hoth (246 men) and all other ranks at well over double Hoth's losses (4,143 men).[149] Guderian, however, remained resolutely undeterred and focused himself entirely on the next big push east. Yet the issue of firmly closing the eastern pocket was again a matter of central importance at Hitler's headquarters on 2 July and Brauchitsch was summoned to see what could be done.[150] By the time Brauchitsch had concluded his report, which was based in some measure on an earlier discussion with Bock that confirmed the pocket was far from hermetically sealed, Hitler's nervous anxiety had reached such heights that he was considering a postponement to the renewed advance of the panzer forces. When Bock was later informed of this possibility, he reacted with exasperation, claiming that the operation had already been delayed too long.[151] Halder too was now eager to avoid any delay and, after receiving a clarification of the situation from Bock and garnering the support of Brauchitsch and Jodl, the Army

---

[147] Ibid., p. 31 (1 July 1941).
[148] 'Panzerarmeeoberkommandos Tagesmeldungen 21.6 – 31.8.41' BA-MA RH 21–3/43, Fol. 67 (2 July 1941). Exact figures reported: Officers fallen 48, wounded 75, missing 2, totalling 125. Non-commissioned officers and lower ranks: fallen 387, wounded 1,111, missing 146, totalling 1,644. Research by Bernhard Kroener revealed that during the first year of the war in the east, out of every 1,000 casualties 229 (on average) were killed in action (Kroener, 'Die Winter 1941/42', p. 879).
[149] 'Verlustmeldungen 5.7.1941 – 25.3.1942' BA-MA RH 21–2/757, Fol. 1 (Casualty lists until 30 June 1941, report dated 5 July 1941). Exact figures reported: Officers fallen 89, wounded 151, missing 6, totalling 246. Non-commissioned officers and lower ranks: fallen 1,058, wounded 2,796, missing 289, totalling 4,143.
[150] Franz Halder, KTB III, pp. 34–35 (2 July 1941).
[151] Fedor von Bock, KTB 'Osten I', Fol. 12, *War Diary*, p. 235 (2 July 1941).

Chief of Staff visited the Wolf's Lair personally to allay Hitler's fears and assure him that the renewed offensive could proceed as planned.[152]

Among the tangible measures Halder took to seal the perimeter of the pocket and restore Hitler's confidence was a particular order to Guderian that units of his panzer group were forbidden 'from being pulled out of the encircling ring without orders'.[153] The order came about as it had become evident Guderian was siphoning-off forces from the ring to strengthen his main attack, a circumstance that produced the first open clash between Kluge and Guderian and plainly illustrated the difficulties commanders were having balancing operational demands with available forces.

As recently as 1 July, Guderian had again been specifically ordered by the army group command not to endanger the encirclement of enemy forces west of Minsk by drafting more forces into the upcoming offensive.[154] Attributing such hesitation to another bout of Hitler's over-anxious trepidation, Guderian wrote to his wife on 1 July: 'Everybody is scared of the Führer and nobody dares say anything. Regrettably, this is what causes a useless waste of blood.'[155] Unyielding as always and contrary to his instructions, Guderian ordered the 17th Panzer Division away from the encircling ring towards Borisov, only to have his order quickly countermanded by Kluge (see Map 3).[156] On the following day (2 July) Guderian visited the 17th Panzer Division holding the long, eastern segment of the pocket front and, although no record exists of what was said,[157] the 17th Panzer Division subsequently departed for Borisov. When Guderian returned to his headquarters he dispatched a communiqué to Kluge at 4th Army claiming that a mishap had occurred in the transmission of orders to the 17th Panzer Division and that the division had not received the order to remain on the encirclement front and had instead set off for Borisov. According to Guderian, it was too late to do anything about it. On the same day a similar 'mishap' had occurred on Hoth's front, causing Kluge to seethe with fury that, on the eve of his ascension to the new command of 4th Panzer Army, which controlled Hoth's and Guderian's panzer groups, he was being confronted by

[152] Franz Halder, KTB III, pp. 35–36 (2 July 1941).   [153] Ibid., p. 35 (2 July 1941).
[154] 'KTB Nr.1 Panzergruppe 2 vom 22.6.1941 bis 21.7.41' BA-MA RH 21-2/927, Fol. 96 (1 July 1941).
[155] Guderian's letter as cited by Macksey, *Guderian*, p. 136. See also Hürter, *Hitlers Heerführer*, p. 285, footnote 22.
[156] Guderian, *Panzer Leader*, p. 161.
[157] In his memoirs Guderian merely states that he visited the division and learned that enemy breakout attempts had been successfully repelled. General Weber, the divisional commander, left no record as he was later mortally wounded.

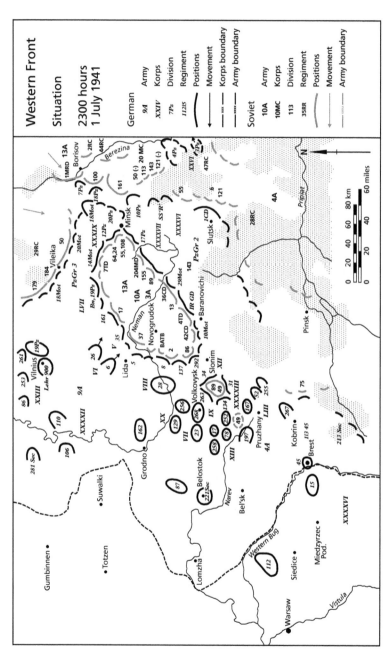

Map 3 Dispositions of Army Group Centre 1 July 1941[1]: David M. Glantz, *Atlas and Operational Summary The Border Battles 22 June–1 July 1941*

Western Front

Situation

2300 hours
1 July 1941

German

9A	Army
XXIV	Korps
7Pz	Division
1125	Regiment
	Positions
→	Movement
xxx	Korps boundary
	Army boundary

Soviet

10A	Army
10MC	Korps
113	Division
35RR	Regiment
	Positions
→	Movement
	Army boundary

a generals' conspiracy.[158] He demanded that Guderian present himself
the following morning at 8 a.m. with the intention of having both panzer
generals brought before a court-martial for insubordination. When Guderian appeared he was strongly taken to task for what he subsequently
referred to as 'the accident', but in the end Guderian was able to convince Kluge that it was indeed only a misunderstanding and that it would
be best to let the matter rest.[159]

The escalation in tension between Kluge and his panzer generals highlights the widening disparity in opposing strategic conceptions, brought
to the fore so quickly by the headstrong refusal of Guderian to compromise his own plans or defer to higher authority even in the face of direct
orders. Yet, the overall strategic problem confronting the army group was
not a simple one, and certainly presented more of a danger than either
of the two panzer generals was aware of or prepared to admit. An un-
titled memorandum sent to Army Group Centre on 3 July outlined the
problem categorically, which confirms that the imposing nature of the
predicament, as well as its seriousness, was not unknown to the army.
The memorandum stated:

The problem, appearing from now on in its full magnitude which must be the
constant worry of all responsible departments of the army group commands, . . . is
the daily widening of the distance between the panzer groups and the [infantry]
armies.
  While until now this distance had relatively little effect, the early renewal of
the advance by the panzer groups, with an objective over 500 km away, will have
the result that 100–200 km long stretches behind the panzer groups are more
or less empty of German troops. That these extensive areas are traversed by the
panzer troops almost entirely on the road, means that everywhere there are still
strong enemy elements roaming and a constant danger exists to the supply and
communications of the panzer groups.[160]

It was precisely this paradoxical method of waging war, whereby the
front was extended without actually winning the traversed ground, which
caught the attention of Wilhelm Prüller, a non-commissioned officer in
a motorised infantry regiment. His diary entry for 3 July summed up, in
straightforward terms, the wider dilemma:

---

[158] Guderian's defiance of higher authority was already evident from a number of previous
    instances in the 1940 Western campaign when he openly defied the orders of his
    superior von Kleist (Frieser, *Blitzkrieg-Legende*, pp. 187–190. English translation: *The
    Blitzkrieg Legend*, pp. 154–156).
[159] Guderian, *Panzer Leader*, p. 162.
[160] Underlining in the original. 'Tagesmeldungen der Heeresgruppe Mitte vom 22.6.41
    bis 15.7.41' BA-MA RH 19 II/128, Fol. 138 (3 July 1941).

The whole war takes place, more or less, on the road. Without securing the land lying to the right and left of the road, we move along and reach the appointed goals. How many Russians must be cruising around the country still! How many enemy tanks are off the road, hidden in protected positions, waiting for the right opportunity to rush up behind the troops and raise hell. Funny the way this war is being waged.[161]

Another soldier, Udo von Alvensleben, noted: 'We are advancing without a firm front. The huge area, which the panzers have long since passed through, remains enemy occupied and must be laboriously cleared.'[162] It was this rearward danger that Kuntzen's LVII Panzer Corps was becoming increasingly concerned with, not just because of its limited ability to deal with the problem, but because of the threat an exposed rear posed to its supply. On 3 July the corps reported to Hoth's Panzer Group 3: 'In the rear area there are unknown numbers of Russians lurking in the woods, who cannot be captured by the corps with its present manpower, but who pose a serious threat to supply convoys.'[163] Indeed the German army was attempting something unique in modern military history – advancing a major element of their supply apparatus *ahead* of the bulk of the army into what was essentially still hostile territory. Inevitably, losses would be heavy.[164]

Clearly, with the next stage of the advance beginning, the warning signs were evident that the panzer and motorised forces, already hard pressed by the preceding days, were about to face a much greater challenge in their race to the Dnepr. The supply columns of the panzer spearheads would be principally threatened; these were in any case struggling to keep pace with demands, especially over the dreadful network of roads.[165] A report from Panzer Group 3 on 3 July informed Kluge's 4th Panzer Army that the roads and byways used in the advance were becoming even worse the further they travelled east with the result that numerous losses were being suffered in trucks.[166] On the previous day (2 July) the Quartermaster-General's war diary for Panzer Group 2 noted that panzer losses were beginning to mount due to the shortage in replacement parts of all kinds.

[161] H. C. Robbins Landon and Sebastian Leitner (eds.), *Diary of a German Soldier* (London, 1963), p. 73 (3 July 1941).
[162] Kempowski (ed.), *Das Echolot Barbarossa '41*, p. 111 (26 June 1941).
[163] As quoted in Steiger, *Armour Tactics*, p. 119.
[164] Müller, 'Das Scheitern der wirtschaftlichen "Blitzkriegstrategie"', p. 963.
[165] There is evidence that Guderian was particularly unaware of the logistical dangers his forces faced, but the under-estimation was a general flaw seen throughout the army (Krumpelt, *Das Material und die Kriegführung*, p. 165).
[166] 'Panzerarmeeoberkommandos Tagesmeldungen 21.6 – 31.8.41' BA-MA RH 21-3/43, Fol. 73 (3 July 1941). See also '3rd Pz. Gr. KTB 25.5.41 – 31.8.41' BA-MA Microfilm 59054, Fol. 86 (3 July 1941).

Furthermore, as a result of the constant advance and the absence of rear-area security troops, the securing of captured foodstuffs and oil was noted to be 'impossible' and the subsequent loss of these resources by the plundering of the local population was deemed 'unavoidable'.[167] In the town of Pukhovichi half of the military supplies were pillaged in a single day by the local population. As a German report noted, this amounted to 'an average per family of 200 kilos of sugar, 200 kilos of fats, almost 350 kilos of grits, and a quantity of fish, individual rations and vegetable oils... The population had not seen such opulence for a long time.'[168]

To supplement their inadequate supply and sustain their momentum, the panzer groups themselves undertook widespread looting and pillaging among the civil population. The methodical exploitation of the population had already been incorporated into the pre-war planning for the campaign, with a distinction supposedly to be made between 'organised' requisitioning under the orders of an officer and 'wild' plundering by the men. In practice, however, the latter was a frequent occurrence, resulting from the many shortages experienced by the army and the common perception, backed by the ideologically driven official declarations, that the Slavic peoples of the Soviet Union were simply 'sub-humans' (*Untermenschen*). The pillaging of the Soviet population began from the very beginning of the German invasion. One German general mockingly wrote: 'Everywhere our people search for draft horses and take them from the farmers. In the villages scenes of great commotion and despair. In this way the population is being "liberated".'[169] A report from the XXXXVII Panzer Corps in early July pointed out that 'the wild requisitions of cattle and poultry... from the impoverished inhabitants cause extraordinary bitterness among the villagers'.[170] Similarly, a later report by the 255th Infantry Division noted that the practice of routine looting 'embitters the population and practically drives it into the arms of the partisans'.[171] Ernst Kern, who arrived on the eastern front in the late summer of 1941, reported: 'Some of our veterans returned back from the village loaded with milk, eggs and fruit; they had "organized" (scrounged) these provisions.'[172] The personal diary of a pastor in the

[167] 'Kriegstagebuch der O.Qu.-Abt. Pz. A.O.K.2 von 21.6.41 bis 31.3.42' BA-MA RH 21-2/819, Fol. 324 (2 July 1941).
[168] As cited in Catherine Merridale, *Ivan's War. Life and Death in the Red Army, 1933–1945* (New York, 2006), p. 107.
[169] Hürter, *Ein deutscher General an der Ostfront*, p. 63 (23 June 1941).
[170] Bartov, *The Eastern Front, 1941–45*, pp. 130 and 134.
[171] Gerhard Weinberg, 'The Yelnya–Dorogobuzh Area of Smolensk Oblast' in John A. Armstrong (ed.), *Soviet Partisans in World War II* (Madison, 1964), p. 408.
[172] Ernst Kern, *War Diary 1941–45. A Report* (New York, 1993), p. 5.

German army recorded what he saw in peasant homes after German soldiers had passed through them.

> Now everything in these dwellings is lying topsy-turvy. All cupboards, drawers and chests have been pried open, their contents scattered all over the floor. The locks are knocked out of the doors, which is no doubt not the handiwork of the Russians. I know as a fact that many musical instruments were smashed by our soldiers just out of sheer mischief... the 'blond beast' creates the best impression at a distance of ten yards.[173]

Such ruthless actions and the callous disregard for the civilian population were bound to vilify the German army, underlining again the necessity of a rapid end to large-scale military operations in order to forestall, or at least weaken, the beginnings of a vigorous partisan war spreading throughout the occupied territories.[174]

Reading between the lines of the army's daily reports and communiqués, it appears that the confident expectation of a great triumph at Minsk is overshadowed by the undercurrent of intractable difficulties steadily mounting in a campaign far from won. At the OKH and OKW, however, the great confidence of the pre-war period seemed entirely vindicated and the impending victory over the Soviet Western Front reinforced a rash optimism oblivious to any looming obstacles. To Halder, it appeared that the main bulk of the Red Army facing Bock and Leeb had been destroyed before the Dnepr–Dvina line, as called for by the operational plan. According to his own calculations, backed by figures from the intelligence department Foreign Armies East, Halder concluded that just 15–20 Soviet infantry divisions and about six armoured divisions remained north of the Pripet marshes.[175] With Soviet resistance apparently crumbling, Halder brashly wrote on 3 July:

> On the whole one can already now say that the objective to destroy the mass of the Russian army in front of the Dvina and Dnepr [Rivers] has been accomplished. I do not doubt... that eastwards of the Dvina and Dnepr we would only have to contend with partial enemy forces, not strong enough to hinder realisation of the German operational plan. Thus it is probably not too much to say, when I claim

---

[173] *True To Type. A Selection From Letters and Diaries of German Soldiers and Civilians Collected on the Soviet–German Front* (London), p. 13 (24 August 1941). This book makes no reference to its editor or date of publication.

[174] An outstanding new study by Jeffrey Rutherford provides a rare insight into three Infantry Divisions from Army Group North. In addition to his main thesis, Rutherford's work shows that the practice of plundering was a common feature of the Wehrmacht's attempt to supply itself throughout the summer advance. See Jeffrey Rutherford, 'Soldiers into Nazis? The German Infantry's War in Northwest Russia, 1941–1944' (unpublished PhD dissertation from the University of Texas at Austin, 2007), pp. 125–128, 134, 138–140.

[175] Franz Halder, KTB III, p. 36 (2 July 1941).

Figure 5.4 Attempting to close the widening gap with the motorised divisions, the German infantry were ordered to undertake excruciating forced marches for the first month of the campaign.

that the campaign against Russia was won within fourteen days. Naturally it is not yet over. The wide open spaces and the stubborn resistance, conducted with all means, will still claim our efforts for many more weeks to come.

Once we are across the Dvina and Dnepr, it will have less to do with the destruction of enemy forces than with taking from the enemy his centres of production and thereby preventing him from raising a new army from his enormous industrial potential and inexhaustible reserves of manpower.[176]

Halder's buoyant outlook was also shared at the Wolf's Lair, where Below later reported: 'The month of July found most in an optimistic frame of mind at FHQ [Führer Headquarters]. Hitler saw himself confirmed in his judgement. Neither Brauchitsch and Halder, nor Keitel and Jodl had a word to say to the contrary.'[177] Although Joseph Goebbels evinced an equally unshaken confidence in the final outcome of the campaign, he at least sounded a more realistic tone in reviewing the demands of the fighting and difficulties that were being encountered. On 2 July he observed: 'In total the fighting is very hard and bitter . . . The Red regime has mobilised the people. Plus there is the proverbial stubbornness of the

[176] Ibid., pp. 38–39 (3 July 1941).
[177] Von Below, *Als Hitlers Adjutant 1937–45*, p. 285.

Russians. Our soldiers have their hands full.'[178] If Goebbels was closer
to the mark than many of those in the High Command he was still a long
way off from understanding the men at the front and the looming danger
of fighting on into the endless east. Siegfried Knappe, a lieutenant in
the 9th Army's 87th Infantry Division, recounted the following exchange
with Major-General von Studnitz on the march to Minsk.

'How do you think the campaign has gone so far?' he asked. 'Great,' I said
enthusiastically. 'Everything seems to be going according to plan.' He did not
respond for a moment, his thoughts seeming to be far away. 'I was in Russia
during the last war,' he said finally. 'I have experienced the Russian winter. It
is savage, like nothing we have ever experienced. It will come, and it will come
soon. We are just in this little part of Russia. We have a vast empty country ahead
of us, and if we do not take Moscow before the weather turns bitter cold, I worry
about what will happen.'
    He was clearly not optimistic. I was amazed, . . . but I knew he was intelligent,
experienced, and capable, and I began to tone down my own optimism after
that.[179]

From the Soviet point of view the next stage of operations had many
advantages over the initial border battles. First, the disaster which befell
Pavlov's forces was in considerable part a result of their appalling strategic
deployment deep into the Belostok salient, half encircled by the Germans
before the invasion got underway. Second, there could no longer be any
question of strategic surprise which played an equally important role
in deciding Pavlov's fate, especially with communications so badly dis-
rupted. The encirclement of Pavlov's armies west of Minsk was not, however, the end of the Soviet Western Front as the German generals were
inclined to believe. Soviet pre-war planning called for a first strategic echelon, deployed between 20 and 100 kilometres from the border, intended
to counter-attack and stop the enemy advance in order to facilitate a general Soviet offensive carried out by a second strategic echelon located well
back from the frontier between 100 and 400 kilometres away.[180] With
the first strategic echelon doomed to defeat, Pavlov was ordered back to
Moscow and shortly thereafter tried and shot on Stalin's orders.[181] His
replacement was the strong-willed Marshal Semen Timoshenko, who,
upon his arrival at Western Front headquarters, promptly undertook the

[178] Fröhlich (ed.), *Die Tagebücher von Joseph Goebbels*, Teil I: Aufzeichnungen 1923–1941,
    Band 9, Dezember 1940–Juli 1941, p. 418 (2 July 1941).
[179] Siegfried Knappe with Ted Brusaw, *Soldat. Reflections of a German Soldier, 1936–1949*
    (New York, 1992), pp. 212–213.
[180] Kipp, 'Soviet Covering Forces', pp. 7–8.
[181] For a good discussion of Pavlov's role in the collapse of Western Front during the first
    days of the war see Mawdsley, *Thunder in the East*, pp. 61–65.

vital task of defending the Dnepr River line, using all means provided by the second strategic echelon as well as the mobilisation of the civilian population for constructing defensive works.[182]

Beyond the immediate measures implemented at Timoshenko's Western Front, the Soviet Union as a whole, in contrast to Germany, was fully mobilising for a long and gruelling war. On 22 June 1941 the Supreme Soviet drafted most of its reservists born between 1905 and 1918 into the ranks of the Red Army, while an emergency labour decree conscripted all able-bodied men aged between 18 and 45 and women between 18 and 40, who were not already working, to build defences. On 24 June martial law was declared throughout the western part of the Soviet Union and on 26 June mandatory overtime of up to three hours a day was placed at the discretion of factory managers, while all leave and holidays were suspended.[183] For the western regions already overrun by the Germans, Stalin's first public address on 3 July called on the occupied Soviet people to: '[F]oment partisan warfare everywhere, to blow up bridges and roads, damage telephone and telegraph lines, and to set fire to forests, stores and transport. Conditions in the occupied regions must be made unbearable for the enemy and all of his accomplices.'[184]

On 3 July when Guderian and Hoth's panzer groups officially continued their thrust for the Dnepr and Dvina, Germany clearly held the strategic initiative. It was not enough, however, just to dictate the course of the ongoing battles; the advantage had to be turned into a final victory capable of ending the war. To achieve this Halder had no recourse to substantial reserves of manpower or equipment and the intangible factor of time was equally irreplaceable. With the Soviet Union rapidly mobilising every aspect of its enormous military potential, Army Group Centre had to deliver on the hopes of its leaders and crush the remaining Soviet resistance in the second phase of its operations.

As the renewed offensive got underway on 3 July, orders for Hoth's panzer groups directed Schmidt's XXXIX Panzer Corps towards Vitebsk and Kuntzen's LVII Panzer Corps[185] to Disna on the Dvina.[186] To the south Guderian's advance was already in motion and on this day (3 July) Schweppenburg's XXIV Panzer Corps penetrated as far the Dnepr at

---

[182] Viktor Anfilov, 'Timoshenko' in Harold Shukman (ed.), *Stalin's Generals* (London, 1993), p. 253.

[183] Barber and Harrison, *The Soviet Home Front 1941–1945*, pp. 60–61; Richard Overy, *Russia's War* (London, 1997), p. 80.

[184] Leonid Grenkevich, *The Soviet Partisan Movement 1941–1944* (London, 1999), p. 75.

[185] Minus the 12th Panzer Division which was not yet released from the main pocket.

[186] Hoth, *Panzer-Operationen*, Anlage 3: 'Gruppenbefehl Nr. 10 für den 4. und 5. Juli 1941', p. 155.

Rogachev. The other two panzer corps advanced on a broad front to the north with Vietinghoff's XXXXVI Panzer Corps heading towards the Dnepr at Mogilev and Lemelsen's XXXXVII Panzer Corps[187] to Orsha. As they set out eastward once again, the panzer and motorised divisions found themselves delayed more by the elements and the miserable Soviet infrastructure than the Red Army. Wilhelm Prüller noted in his diary: 'It's raining again. The rain is especially bad for us, an armoured division, because we can barely get through the bottomless mud of Russia.'[188] In a report to the 4th Panzer Army, Panzer Group 3 stated that, on account of the awful roads, speeds were seldom above 10 kilometres per hour.[189] The bad weather and road conditions occasioned Timoshenko a short window of opportunity, in which space could be traded for time, to build defences and summon reinforcements. The Red Air Force also attacked German bridges across the Beresina River with some success and, according to one Soviet pilot, destroyed nine bridges and delayed the advance of some German motorised units for up to three days.[190] West of the Dvina and Beresina Rivers Panzer Group 3 also reported countless individual enemy strongpoints,[191] which would have to be dealt with later by the following infantry. Just as in the advance to Minsk, the panzer groups newly-won rear area would have to remain a treacherous war zone, which was especially problematic given that the vast Belorussian countryside was still far from pacified. As Bock noted on 3 July: 'There is still shooting everywhere in the rear.'[192]

The lack of control in the rear areas contests the over-simplified representation in much of the secondary literature, that shows the extent of the German advance in the summer of 1941 by depicting the deepest points of the German penetration along the length of the eastern front with simple north–south lines on the map. In addition to disguising the war still to be won behind the main front, the use of such lines to portray the early weeks of Barbarossa also gives the false impression that the German advance was an uninterrupted north–south sweep through the Soviet Union, undertaken on a broad unbroken front. In fact, great swathes of land were entirely bypassed as the German armies advanced largely between or around the great forests and swamps of the western

---

[187] Minus the 17th Panzer Division which was not yet released from the main pocket.

[188] Landon and Leitner (eds.), *Diary of a German Soldier*, p. 74 (3 July 1941).

[189] 'Panzerarmeeoberkommandos Tagesmeldungen 21.6 – 31.8.41' BA-MA RH 21-3/43, Fol. 73 (3 July 1941).

[190] Vasily B. Emelianenko, *Red Star Against the Swastika. The Story of a Soviet Pilot over the Eastern Front* (London, 2005), p. 59.

[191] 'Panzerarmeeoberkommandos Tagesmeldungen 21.6 – 31.8.41' BA-MA RH 21-3/43, Fol. 73 (3 July 1941).

[192] Fedor von Bock, KTB 'Osten I', Fol. 13, *War Diary*, p. 237 (3 July 1941).

Soviet Union, leaving much work to be done in the rear area and slowing the advance considerably as the distances grew greater.

While the euphoria of an expected victory pervaded the halls of the OKH and OKW,[193] the precise road to that victory was still unclear and it was this question that occupied discussion at the Wolf's Lair on 3 July. The future advance of Army Group Centre's two armoured groups beyond Smolensk was identified as the key decision for the defeat of the Soviet Union and centred on three possibilities. An advance to the north-east towards Leningrad, a further push eastwards on Moscow or for the first time there was discussion of a drive south-east to the Sea of Azov. Hitler's role in this discussion is not specifically stated by the document, but the new consideration for a drive to the south-east was almost certainly his idea and was made dependent on the success of Kleist's 1st Panzer Group seizing Zhitomir: 'If that is not the case, a push on Moscow by weaker forces and an advance to the southeast by Kluge's Panzer Army would be the best method of annihilation.' It was also added, however, that the great distance from Smolensk to the Sea of Azov (1,150 kilometres) made an advance by Kluge's forces 'questionable'.[194]

On the following day (4 July) Hitler reaffirmed his confidence in victory, informing his staff: 'I constantly try to put myself in the position of the enemy. He has practically already lost this war.' Hitler then again raised the question of what should be done once the so-called Stalin-Line (on the Dvina and Dnepr rivers) had been broken through. 'Turn to the north or to the south? This might be the most difficult decision of this war.'[195] Significantly, Hitler made no mention of a further advance to the east and there is no indication that Halder or Brauchitsch received word of the new developments in Hitler's evolving strategic conception. To their minds Hitler's fixation was with Leningrad and this was to be kept in check by the strong advance of Army Group North, which they hoped would dispel the dictator's desire to divert Bock's forces away from Moscow as the principal objective. Until now, however, there had been no indication that Hitler would consider a diversion to the south.

On 3 July the Belostok pocket, the smaller of the two main encirclements in Belorussia, was finally eliminated by elements of Strauss's 9th Army and Weichs's 2nd Army. The following day these forces were again marching east to support the panzer groups but, as Halder noted: '[T]he distance has grown so great, particularly behind Guderian, that

---

[193] Henrik Eberle and Matthias Uhl (eds.), *The Hitler Book. The Secret Dossier Prepared for Stalin from the Interrogations of Hitler's Personal Aides* (New York, 2005), p. 74.
[194] KTB OKW, Volume II, p. 1020, Document 66 (3 July 1941).
[195] Ibid., Document 67 (4 July 1941). Peter de Mendelssohn, *Die Nürnberger Dokumente. Studien zur deutschen Kriegspolitik 1937–45* (Hamburg, 1947), pp. 366–367.

special measures will have to be taken to bridge the gap.'[196] General Heinrici noted on 8 July that the motorised divisions were 200 kilometres ahead of his infantry divisions.[197] For the infantrymen this meant forced marches of punishing duration with little time for sleep or rest. The strain this caused the men was described by Heinrici on 11 July:

Yesterday one regiment marched 54, another 47 km. To do that once is possible. To do that having already had numerous marches of 30–40 km with more to come, that is something else, it makes it tremendous. To do it no one gets to sleep at night, rather it starts at 2 or 3 [a.m.] and lasts until the evening, sometimes 10 [p.m.].[198]

The individual accounts of the soldiers forced to endure this torment are even more explicit. On 30 June infantryman Bernhard Ritter wrote that substantive rest periods were no longer to be had which, after 'strenuous battles' he declared were 'urgently necessary'.[199] On the same day another soldier, Harald Henry, wrote home that in one day he had undergone a march of 44 kilometres, fighting a battle in the middle of it in which he was ordered to carry a 14-kilogram ammunition box cross country for almost three hours. 'I was completely worn out', he wrote, 'exhausted to the last reserve.'[200] Four days later, Henry wrote home again of the terrible strain he was under after another march of 45 kilometres.

We're wet through all over, sweat is running down our faces in wide streams – not just sweat, but sometimes tears too, tears of helpless rage, desperation and pain, squeezed out of us by this inhuman effort. No-one can tell me that someone who isn't an infantry man can possibly imagine what we're going through here.[201]

Alexander Cohrs wrote in his diary on 1 July that the demands of the march that day had led to the loss of three men in his company, one of whom died. Cohrs explained that the men were lost, 'Not as a consequence of battle, but from exhaustion resulting from the exertions.' Cohrs

---

[196] Franz Halder, KTB III, p. 40 (4 July 1941).

[197] Hürter, *Ein deutscher General an der Ostfront*, p. 66 (8 July 1941). On 11 July in another letter to his wife, Heinrici wrote of his belief that after the eastern campaign the infantry would have to be disbanded, owing to the inability of his slow-moving formations to support the motorised units. As Heinrici concluded: 'The difference between motor and manpower is too great' (Hürter, *Ein deutscher General an der Ostfront*, p. 68 (11 July 1941)).

[198] Ibid., p. 67 (11 July 1941). See also Knappe with Brusaw, *Soldat*, p. 208.

[199] Walter Bähr and Hans Bähr (eds.), *Kriegsbriefe gefallener Studenten, 1939–1945* (Tübingen and Stuttgart, 1952) p. 48 (30 June 1941).

[200] Ibid., p. 70 (30 June 1941).

[201] Ibid., p. 71 (4 July 1941). Hans Joachim Schröder, 'German Soldiers' Experiences During the Initial Phase of the Russian Campaign' in Bernd Wegner (ed.), *From Peace to War. Germany, Soviet Russia and the World, 1939–1941* (Oxford, 1997), pp. 313–314.

then related the physical and mental rigours of the march, concluding:
'Towards the end, when one is fighting painfully against collapse, one
occasionally hears words of suicide.'[202] Helmut Pabst complained that,
'[t]his marching is more strenuous than action'.[203] Another infantryman,
marching with Army Group North, talked of falling into what he called
'a quasi-sleepwalk'. Watching the steady rhythm of marching boots in
front of him he entered into a state of semi-consciousness, 'waking only
briefly whenever I stumbled into the body ahead of me'.[204] The adjutant
to the divisional commander of the 7th Panzer Division recalled after
the war that in the initial weeks of Barbarossa the 'inhuman hardships'
of the infantry 'made us feel sorry for them'.[205] Heinrich Haape vividly
described the conditions of the march.

With dry, cracked lips, red eyes and dust covered faces, the men marched eastwards with only one wish – to lie down for a few hours' rest. But the march continued relentlessly over roads and tracks, through woods and open fields . . . Each
man's war at this stage was circumscribed by the next few steps he would take,
the hardness of the road, the soreness of his feet, the dryness of his tongue and
the weight of his equipment. Beckoning him on was the thought of the next halt.
Just to stop, to have no need to put one foot in front of the other for a few hours,
was the dream of every man.[206]

While marching constituted its own torments, Haape also alluded to a
worse fate for the infantrymen – the so-called 'push commandos'. Two
or three sections of each company were selected for this purpose and
were detailed to accompany their heaviest wagons. As Haape explained:

As soon as a wagon slowed down, the men would spring forward, grab the spokes
and throw their weight forward to keep the wheels moving . . . The men stripped
off their tunics and shirts. Sweat ran down their backs, the red dust settled on
them and caked hard. One squad would be relieved from its push commando
duties by another, and would find blessed relief in marching.[207]

Even as the infantry divisions struggled desperately forward, they could
hardly be expected to close the gap on the motorised units that were
also pressing forward with all speed. Still, while the panzer commanders gave little thought to the slow and cumbersome infantry, the 9th

[202] Kempowski (ed.), *Das Echolot Barbarossa '41*, pp. 176–177 (1 July 1941).
[203] Helmut Pabst, *The Outermost Frontier. A German Soldier in the Russian Campaign*
(London, 1957), p. 14.
[204] William Lubbeck with David Hurt, *At Leningrad's Gates. The Story of a Soldier with
Army Group North* (Philadelphia, 2006), p. 85.
[205] Hans von Luck, *Panzer Commander. The Memoirs of Colonel Hans von Luck* (New York,
1989), p. 55.
[206] Haape with Henshaw, *Moscow Tram Stop*, pp. 51–53.   [207] Ibid., p. 57.

and 2nd Armies were in fact the backbone of the army group and would be urgently needed in a sustained contest with the Red Army. As Alexander Stahlberg, an officer in the 12th Panzer Division, later observed: 'Ultimately, even in 1941, the marching troops dictated our speed.'[208]

On the evening of 3 July Kluge spoke with his two new subordinates in the 4th Panzer Army, Hoth and Guderian, about the continuation of operations. Guderian, as might be expected, used the opportunity to press again for the release of all elements of his panzer group still engaged in reducing the remaining pocket west of Minsk. His request was backed by Hoth who added that the enemy had been observed retreating eastwards. Ultimately Kluge agreed to a limited release of panzers from the 17th Panzer Division but, probably with a view to the earlier 'mix-up', made it clear that the rest of the division could only be relieved of its duties with his express permission.[209]

As the two panzer groups set their sights on forging crossings over the Dvina and Dnepr rivers, they both reported on 4 July innovative new tactics on behalf of the Red Army. Instead of launching reckless, headlong counter-attacks, or obstinately attempting to hold every metre of ground, Soviet forces west of the Dnepr and south of the Dvina were primarily fighting rearguard actions while withdrawing to their fortified river crossings. In addition to hindering the German advance, the Soviet delaying actions won precious time to build up defences and assemble forces at the rivers, which, as the war diary of Panzer Group 2 noted, were gaining strength 'from day to day'.[210] At Panzer Group 3 a similar development was reported to 4th Panzer Army: 'The enemy fights delaying actions while evading us on route to the Dvina, there in strong battle groups he prepares to defend the Dvina crossings.'[211] Although Timoshenko's Western Front was still threatened by a grave crisis, a learning curve in strategic direction was already establishing itself, even if the cost had been great. The main problem for Timoshenko was rebuilding his shattered front along the river line and to this end Stalin transferred four of the five armies from the Reserve Front (19th, 20th, 21st, 22nd) to his command. These forces, like much of the Red Army, exhibited numerous command

[208] Alexander Stahlberg, *Bounden Duty. The Memoirs of a German Officer 1932–45* (London, 1990), p. 161.
[209] 'KTB Nr.1 Panzergruppe 2 vom 22.6.1941 bis 21.7.41' BA-MA RH 21-2/927, Fols. 119–120 (3 July 1941).
[210] Ibid., Fol. 127 (4 July 1941).
[211] 'Panzerarmeeoberkommandos Tagesmeldungen 21.6 – 31.8.41' BA-MA RH 21-3/43, Fol. 78 (4 July 1941).

Figure 5.5 A field conference on 8 July 1941 between Bock (left), Hoth (centre) and Richthofen (with back to camera). As Army Group Centre's advance east continued the field commanders, who received their instructions directly from the OKH, had no idea that Hitler intended to divert their attack away from Moscow.

and control failings and suffered shortages in a number of critical areas, but the German command was almost totally unaware of their existence and soon to be surprised at their strength.[212]

On 4 July, in spite of its hardships, Hoth's panzer group secured a small bridgehead across the Dvina near Disna and Guderian another in the vicinity of Rogachev. Recognising the danger, these bridgeheads were the subject of intense Soviet counter-attacks, which, in concert with stubborn resistance along the length of Panzer Group 3's front, brought its advance to a complete standstill by 5 July.[213] Guderian's attack was faring little better and he reported to Brauchitsch and Kluge at a conference in Minsk on 5 July that: 'As a result of personnel and material losses the momentum of the attacks by 3rd and 18th Panzer Divisions has been lost.'[214] These

---

[212] Glantz and House, *When Titans Clashed*, p. 58.
[213] Hoth, *Panzer-Operationen*, p. 80.
[214] 'KTB Nr.1 Panzergruppe 2 vom 22.6.1941 bis 21.7.41' BA-MA RH 21–2/927, Fol. 133 (5 July 1941).

206 Operation Barbarossa and Germany's Defeat in the East

two divisions were spearheading his advance and Guderian maintained that, to restore the offensive, reinforcements had to be brought forward either from the encirclement front near Minsk or by the infantry relieving his forces from security and guard duties in the rear area.[215] Hoth's attack was facing the same difficulties, not only because of the tenacious resistance he was meeting, but from the cumulative loss of panzers he had suffered since the beginning of the campaign. On 4 July, after merely 13 days of action, Hoth reported that the overall number of combat-ready tanks in his panzer group had fallen to the alarming figure of just 50 per cent, while the uninterrupted march tempo and bad roads were claiming constant losses in trucks.[216] In addition, the findings of General Thoma's recent inspection tour of Panzer Group 3 noted that the German Mark I tank,[217] far from assisting the German advance, was proving such a burden to the panzer troops that he recommended they all be pulled out of the line and returned to Germany.[218] At Army Group Centre, Bock too was taking stock of the toll the advance was taking on his forces. His diary for 5 July reads: 'Casualties have in places been serious. Equipment, too, has suffered considerably from the uninterrupted fighting and the hair-raising roads. Among the infantry divisions it is the heavy horses which are suffering the worst.'[219] Expanding on this problem, a former officer of the 6th Infantry Division recalled in his memoir:

It had taken only twelve days of the campaign to show how completely unsuited was our transport to this type of country. The wagons were far too heavy for moving on these incredibly bad roads and tracks. Our beautiful well-bred horses were altogether too food-conscious and were not acclimatised... our German horses needed long rest periods, heavy meals – and food for them was rarely obtainable in quantity... They had been ideal for France, but were a hindrance for this campaign.[220]

While touring the IX and XII Army Corps, Bock added that the march conditions for the men were 'made especially strenuous by the dust and heat and the frightful roads'.[221] Just as Napoleon's *Grande Armée* of 450,000 men withered on its march to Moscow even without sustained contact with the enemy, so too was Army Group Centre to lament the tyranny of distance and suffer its own rapid demise.

---

[215] Ibid. (5 July 1941).   [216] Franz Halder, KTB III, p. 40 (4 July 1941).

[217] Of which 281 were incorporated into Operation Barbarossa. See table on armoured fighting vehicles in Müller, 'Von der Wirtschaftsallianz', p. 185.

[218] Franz Halder, KTB III, p. 42 (4 July 1941).

[219] Fedor von Bock, KTB 'Osten I', Fol. 15, *War Diary*, p. 238 (5 July 1941).

[220] Haape with Henshaw, *Moscow Tram Stop*, p. 60.

[221] Fedor von Bock, KTB 'Osten I', Fol. 15, *War Diary*, p. 238 (5 July 1941).

Figure 5.6 Even in the summer months sudden downpours could turn the roads into a morass, slowing the advance.

Surveying the inordinate effort expended by Army Group Centre to traverse such great distances hastily with all the articles of war necessary for supplying and equipping well over a million men,[222] one is struck by the enormous dissipation of strength resulting from advancing across such a vast and inhospitable landscape. With many hundreds of kilometres still remaining in the advance, and an enemy by no means as badly beaten as the German command anticipated, winning the campaign was not only a race against time, but also a race against the German army's own exhaustion. For good reason the German operational plans had mandated the destruction of the bulk of the Red Army between the border and the great rivers. The consequences of this failure were compounded by the fact that the German command, from Hitler to his

---

[222] At the beginning of the war Bock's Army Group Centre numbered some 1,180,000 men (including reserves). These were allocated as follows: 9th Army 248,000 men; 4th Army 310,000 men; Panzer Group 2 248,000 men; Panzer Group 3 145,000. The rest of the army group's manpower was divided between reserve divisions, security divisions and the Luftwaffe. Brian Taylor, *Barbarossa To Berlin. A Chronology of the Campaigns on the Eastern Front 1941 to 1945*, Volume I: *The Long Drive East 22 June 1941 to 18 November 1942* (Staplehurst, 2003), pp. 17–19.

generals, scarcely recognised the rapid over-extension of their forces as well as the growing threat posed by the second echelon of the Red Army. The numerous expressions of optimism in this stage in the campaign reveal the seriously ill-informed judgement of the German High Command and should not be uncritically accepted by historians as proof of the Wehrmacht's success in the early period of Barbarossa.

6   The perilous advance to the east

Forging across the Dvina and Dnepr – the threshold to demise

As Army Group Centre heaved its way forward in the centre of Germany's long eastern front, there was a steadily emerging concern for its southern flank. Throughout June, Rundstedt's Army Group South had struggled to advance against vigorous Soviet counter-strokes and, by early July, its rapid forward movement was further hindered by the primitive Soviet infrastructure and intermittent downpours which turned the roads to seas of mud. The Operations Officer at OKH responsible for Army Group South, Major Karl Thilo, noted in his diary on 7 July that, 'the tanks "suffocate" in the mud of the Ukrainian *chermozem* [black earth]'.[1] The following day he recorded the situation estimate by Army Group South's High Command: 'Enemy well commanded . . . At first, defensive operations close to the border, then withdrawal to the Stalin Line with heavy counterattacks against our armoured wedge . . . Operational breakthrough by Panzer Group 1 *still not* achieved'. Thilo also noted that the army group was still sizeably outnumbered with 61 major Soviet units versus 46 German and allied formations.[2] Contemplating the further advance of Army Group Centre on 5 July, Brauchitsch raised the difficulty of screening Bock's right flank pointing out the emerging problem that Army Group South's 6th Army and 1st Panzer Group, 'are still quite far back'.[3]

On Army Group Centre's northern flank, Leeb's Army Group North was making better progress but, as the renowned General Manstein, commander of the LVI Panzer Corps, would later observe: 'the enemy, though pushed back to the east, was still not destroyed – as was very

---

[1] Karl Wilhelm Thilo, 'A Perspective from the Army High Command (OKH)', p. 301 (7 July 1941).
[2] Italics in the original. Ibid., pp. 301–302 (8 July 1941).
[3] 'KTB Nr.1 Panzergruppe 2 vom 22.6.1941 bis 21.7.41' BA-MA RH 21–2/927, Fol. 133 (5 July 1941).

soon to become apparent'.[4] After the capture of the Latvian capital Riga, Leeb was compelled to continue his drive to the east to support Bock's left flank, but also had to support a major offensive northwards up into Estonia in order to cover his own left flank. Accordingly, the army group's width of front was rapidly expanding which, as the smallest of the three German army groups, would soon heavily tax its offensive momentum. The commander of Army Group North's Panzer Group 4, Colonel-General Erich Hoepner, wrote to his wife on 16 July of his dissatisfaction with the halted drive on Leningrad: 'The deciding cause remains our weakness... The number of divisions is as inadequate as their equipment.... The men are tired, the losses increase, the fallout rate of vehicles rises.'[5]

At Army Group Centre the tussle over the allocation of forces between Kluge and Guderian was again embittering relations within 4th Panzer Army. Guderian desperately wanted to continue his offensive onto the eastern bank of the Dnepr, but on 5 July a surprise attack by the 3rd and 4th Panzer Divisions failed to break through the 'strong enemy resistance'.[6] Guderian preferred to blame Kluge's intransigence about releasing forces from the rapidly shrinking encirclement near Minsk, and Bock noted the 'visible dissatisfaction in Panzer Group 2 with being under the command of [Kluge's] Headquarters, 4th Army'.[7] As was characteristic of his intractable nature, and in spite of the acrimonious confrontation with Kluge on 3 July where the panzer general had been threatened with dismissal, Guderian issued repeated orders to his forces to break off from the encirclement front and drive east. The result, Guderian observed in his memoir, was that 'Kluge was simultaneously issuing contradictory orders by which all units were to remain in position about the encircled Russians and the advance eastwards was not to be resumed until further instructions were received.'[8] The idiocy of this state of affairs reflected the irreconcilable strategic divergence between Kluge and Guderian, which, beyond the negligent liability of both commanders for failing to ensure unified direction, also reflected the lack of clear strategic direction from above. The ongoing dispute exposed the unworkable command structure of 4th Panzer Army, for which Guderian (and to a lesser extend Hoth) showed little respect, and left Kluge virtually

---

[4] Von Manstein, *Lost Victories*, p. 193.
[5] Hoepner's letter cited by Hürter, *Hitlers Heerführer*, pp. 287–288, footnote 37.
[6] 'KTB Nr.1 Panzergruppe 2 vom 22.6.1941 bis 21.7.41' BA-MA RH 21-2/927, Fol. 134 (5 July 1941).
[7] Fedor von Bock, KTB 'Osten I', Fol. 15, *War Diary*, p. 239 (5 July 1941).
[8] Guderian, *Panzer Leader*, p. 167.

powerless to assert his authority. Apart from rescinding Guderian's orders, Kluge probably knew, as did Guderian, that he did not really have the authority to replace the panzer group commander, even though he was his nominal superior. Beyond the harmful message such an action would send, Guderian simply enjoyed too much support from above, not least from Hitler himself.

On the evening of 5 July Halder met with Brauchitsch, who was returning from a visit to Bock's army group and told of the difficulties being experienced in the large, occupied area. In addition to the widespread insecurity, the population was taking to the roads in large numbers and the enormous number of Soviet POWs was creating serious problems.[9] On the following day Bock wrote that one of his staff officers had encountered many thousands of Soviet POWs marching on the road south of Minsk unarmed, but also completely unsupervised. Under such lax conditions it was hardly surprising that the dense forests of Belorussia were teeming with hostile enemy troops, a good number of whom had conceivably already been captured at some point. Reluctantly, Bock concluded: 'We have no choice but to leave divisions behind to clear and watch over the rear areas.' In practical terms this meant that, apart from the three security divisions already designated for this purpose, a further two active service divisions were to be withheld for these duties.[10] Yet difficulties for German occupation forces behind the front were not just limited to rounding up stray Soviet soldiers and fighting off clandestine attacks. Two weeks after the invasion, the 45th Infantry Division was still heavily engaged at Brest clearing the border fortress of its resilient defenders. Indeed, the Soviet garrison continued to hold out under the most extreme conditions until the last pocket of resistance was finally extinguished on 24 July – more than a month after the launch of Barbarossa.[11] Scrawled on the walls of the bunkers around Brest are solemn declarations by many of the fortress's defenders; these might be taken as a collective epithet dedicated to its faithful garrison. Inscriptions read: 'Things are difficult, but we are not losing courage.' 'We die confidently July 1941.' 'We die, but we defended ourselves. 20.7.41.'[12] 'I am dying but I do not surrender. Farewell Motherland.'[13] The fervent

---

[9] Franz Halder, KTB III, p. 45 (5 July 1941).
[10] Fedor von Bock, KTB 'Osten I', Fol. 17, *War Diary*, p. 240 (6 July 1941).
[11] Alexander Werth, *Russia at War 1941–1945* (New York, 1964), p. 157.
[12] Kershaw, *War Without Garlands*, p. 79.
[13] Harrison E. Salisbury, *The Unknown War* (London, 1978), p. 26. For further examples see Paul Carell, *Hitler's War on Russia. The Story of the German Defeat in the East* (London, 1964), p. 44.

resistance at Brest is only the best known example of many valiant last stands which tied down German troops and inflicted a hefty toll in casualties.[14]

On 6 July Halder received the army's overall casualty figures spanning the period 22 June to 3 July. Illustrative of the intense fighting, in these first 11 days of the war the army's total casualties numbered 54,000 men, to which Halder added an additional 54,000 German soldiers who were listed as 'sick'.[15] Losses to the field armies stemmed from three sources. First, those resulting from enemy action (killed and wounded); second, men missing in action including men taken prisoner and, third, those listed as sick. The problem is that most German casualty reports list statistics only for the first two categories and the number of sick is simply ignored. Depending on local conditions and the time of the year, the number of sick men could exceed the numbers of casualties caused by the enemy by a sizeable margin. Reports from the summer of 1941 very seldom made references to the number of sick men, disguising a hidden loss, repeatedly overlooked in assessments of combat strength.[16] By early July Barbarossa had already cost more soldiers than the total number of killed and missing men sustained throughout the six weeks of the 1940 western campaign (49,000).[17] Furthermore, in comparison to the Polish and western campaigns, Halder noted a rising percentage of casualties among officers. Up to this point officer casualties constituted 6.6 per cent of the total killed, 3.8 per cent of the wounded and 1.7 per cent of the missing.[18] With personnel losses already spiralling and the war only in its earliest phase, the importance of ending the war rapidly was again conspicuously underlined.

In many ways the first ten days of July 1941 constituted a race to the Dvina and Dnepr Rivers, as both Bock and Timoshenko struggled to bring up enough strength to meet the opposing force. The rapid collapse of the Soviet Western Front in June, and the ensuing chaos among his scattered and makeshift forces, put Timoshenko on the back foot in this race, but the German blitzkreig was also rapidly losing its momentum.

[14] See examples provided in Chor'kov, 'The Red Army', pp. 424–425.

[15] Franz Halder, KTB III, p. 47 (6 July 1941). The commander of Army Group Centre's Army Corps IX, General of Infantry Hermann Geyer, stated in his memoir that after 17 days of action, the so-called 'Polish illness' had claimed 500–600 men among his 3 divisions. More than likely the 'Polish illness' was a reflection of the poor sanitary conditions and inadequate diets of the men; Hermann Geyer, Das IX. Armeekorps im Ostfeldzug 1941 (Neckargemünd, 1969), p. 77.

[16] Kroener, 'Die Winter 1941/42', p. 884.

[17] Frieser, Blitzkrieg-Legende, p. 400 (Karl-Heinz Frieser, The Blitzkrieg Legend, p. 318).

[18] Franz Halder, KTB III, p. 47 (6 July 1941).

The Soviet roads were the main impediment, accounting for far more destruction among the panzer and motorised divisions than the Red Army. Supporting the German advance into the Soviet Union were large numbers of civilian vehicles (trucks as well as motor-cars) pressed into service to offset the lack of motorisation within the army. Yet these did not have the ground clearance for such conditions and frequently bottomed out on the rutted and uneven roads, causing irreparable damage to the transmission and oil sumps. Civilian vehicles also had much weaker suspension that was prone to snap, quickly leaving a trail of wreckage behind the German advance.[19] Yet even the military vehicles suffered. Assigned to a panzer division, Alexander Cohrs gave a striking description of the perilous roads his unit traversed on 5 July. After referring to 'very bad roads, full of holes', his diary continued:

Some [vehicles] tipped over. Luckily none in our company. After 18 kilometres of marching on foot I sat on an armoured vehicle. It tipped so much that it balanced on two wheels, while the other two temporarily stood in the air; still it did not tip over. Along the way was a moor where the vehicles had to make a big detour . . . one by one vehicles got stuck or even turned over, resulting in breaks and a slow tempo.[20]

On 6 July General Heinrici, commanding three infantry divisions, wrote to his wife:

The compression of the troops [onto narrow avenues of advance] makes forward progress slower than we would like, to this must be added the unbelievable roads which increase the difficulties. Lord God this is a primitive country north of the Pripet marshes, forest, everywhere forest, between them kilometre wide swamps, where one can sink in up to the knee.[21]

Alongside the inhospitable terrain, vast distances and dreadful roads, as of early July, bad weather created a new obstacle for the advancing German armies. As a result of rainfall, a report from Kluge's 4th Panzer Army on 6 July noted that the roads over the vast Beresina swamplands, extending from the west of Minsk to the Dnepr, were 'exceptionally bad' and 'often bottomless'. The report continued that the motorised units were being 'greatly slowed' and that as many engineers and as much building strength be urgently brought forward.[22] As Hans von Luck of the 7th Panzer Division described:

---

[19] Müller, 'Das Scheitern der wirtschaftlichen "Blitzkriegstrategie"', p. 964.
[20] Kempowski (ed.), *Das Echolot Barbarossa '41*, p. 238 (5 July 1941).
[21] Hürter, *Ein deutscher General an der Ostfront*, p. 65 (6 July 1941).
[22] 'A.O.K.4 Ia Anlage zum K.T.B. Nr.8 Tagesmeldungen der Korps von 21.6.41 – 9.7.41' BA-MA RH 20–4/162, Fol. 74 (6 July 1941).

After brief downpours of rain, they [the roads] turned into muddy tracks which were only passable in some places after engineers or off-loaded grenadiers had felled trees to make a wooden runway with the trunks. It was not so much our opponents that held up our advance as the catastrophic roads.[23]

Field Marshal Kesselring, the commander of Army Group Centre's Air Fleet 2, observed that the intermittent rain made the primitive roads much worse, and revealed 'the real face of the Russian theatre'. Summing up the difficulty of movement in the east, Kesselring concluded: 'even the fully tracked vehicles, including tanks, and most of all the supply services, had to rely on the arterial roads [which] helped to warn the troops of difficulties ahead'.[24] On 7 July Bock added: 'It has been raining on 4th Panzer Army for two days. This has made conditions on the roads frightful and placed an unusually heavy strain on men and material.'[25] At one point the sunken roads caused the 7th Panzer Division to struggle for two days to advance 90 kilometres.[26]

While the summer downpours caused many roads to simply disappear into the swamps, in other areas the thick mud quickly reverted to the army's other great encumbrance – dust. On 6 July Wilhelm Prüller wrote in his diary:

The advance goes very slowly. Numerous obstacles keep slowing down our charge. You can't really call what we're on a road. It's better than this in the tiniest hamlet in Germany. And we're marching on a main road! The shoulders of the road are all muddy from the previous rain – you sink up to your knees – but in the middle of the road there's dust already... each vehicle [is] surrounded by an impenetrable cloud of dust.[27]

The same remarkable spectacle was observed by 4th Panzer Army's Chief of Staff, Major-General Günther Blumentritt, who wrote after the war: 'A vivid picture which remains of those [first] weeks is the great clouds of yellow dust... The heat was tremendous, though interspersed with sudden showers which quickly turned the roads to mud before the sun reappeared and as quickly baked them into crumbling clay once again.'[28] The commander of the XXXXIII Army Corps wrote on only the second day of the war: 'Every step, every vehicle sends up an impenetrable cloud [of dust]. The march routes are marked by a yellow brown cloud, which

[23] Von Luck, *Panzer Commander*, p. 54. See also Department of the U.S. Army (ed.), *Military Improvisations During the Russian Campaign* (Washington, 1951), pp. 53–55.
[24] Kesselring, *Memoirs*, p. 92.
[25] Fedor von Bock, KTB 'Osten I', Fol. 18, *War Diary*, p. 242 (7 July 1941).
[26] Hermann Rothe and H. Ohrloff, '7th Panzer Division Operations' in David M. Glantz (ed.), *The Initial Period of War*, p. 380.
[27] Landon and Leitner (eds.), *Diary of a German Soldier*, p. 76 (6 July 1941).
[28] Blumentritt, 'Moscow', pp. 47–48.

hangs for a long time like mist before the sky.'[29] For man, machine and beast the dust proved a torment for the German advance. It was ironic that the very roads upon which the rapid German blitzkrieg depended were also a primary factor in slowing their drive to the east. For the infantry, one soldier wrote of the summer advance:

Our feet sank into the sand and dirt, puffing dust into the air so that it rose and clung to us. The horses coughing in the dust produced a pungent odour. The loose sand was nearly as tiring for the horses as the deep mud would have been. The men marched in silence, coated with dust, with dry throats and lips.[30]

In the early days of the campaign the fine dust of the Soviet Union proved more deadly to the German panzer and motorised divisions than the Red Army's counter-attacks. The dust soon overwhelmed the inadequate air filters and then infiltrated the engines, initially greatly increasing oil consumption, and ultimately immobilising the engines altogether. Yet, for all the danger the dust posed to the German mechanised forces, it remained as unavoidable as it was pervasive. Claus Hansmann wrote that his motorised column drove 'as if in a sandstorm', and he observed how 'the wheels churned up fountains of sand that blackened out the sun...The dust burnt in our nose and throat.'[31] Not surprisingly, the fallout rate among vehicles of every kind soon began to rise alarmingly.

In Guderian's panzer group, figures for the number of combat-ready tanks in his divisions vary rather widely, although all denote a striking rate of attrition which was eroding force strengths to critical levels. Even the most optimistic assessment recorded on 7 July in the war diary of the panzer group classed the tanks in the 18th and 3rd Panzer Divisions as being at just 35 per cent combat readiness. The 4th and 17th Panzer Divisions were said to be at 60 per cent combat readiness, while the 10th Panzer Division was strongest at 80 per cent.[32] Yet, as an example of the difference in figures, the quartermaster's war diary for the panzer group claimed on the same day that the 18th Panzer Division was at only 25 per cent strength and the 17th Panzer Division at 50 per cent.[33] Two days earlier (5 July) the war diary of the XXXXVII Panzer Corps, to which both divisions belonged, claimed the 18th Panzer Division was

[29] Hürter, *Ein deutscher General an der Ostfront*, p. 63 (24 June 1941). See also Pabst, *Outermost Frontier*, pp. 13–14.
[30] Knappe with Brusaw, *Soldat*, p. 213.
[31] Claus Hansmann, *Vorüber – Nicht Vorbei. Russische Impressionen 1941 – 1943* (Frankfurt, 1989), p. 119.
[32] 'KTB Nr.1 Panzergruppe 2 vom 22.6.1941 bis 21.7.41' BA-MA RH 21–2/927, Fol. 149 (7 July 1941).
[33] 'Kriegstagebuch der O.Qu.-Abt. Pz. A.O.K.2 von 21.6.41 bis 31.3.42' BA-MA RH 21–2/819, Fol. 312 (7 July 1941).

at 30 per cent strength and the 17th Panzer Division at 33 per cent of its starting total.[34] Obviously there was some confusion regarding the precise figures, possibly stemming from definitions of what constituted 'combat ready', but what remains clear is the toll the first two weeks of operations took on the German panzers. Without question the bad roads and dust accounted for most of the high fallout, though reports show that the use of captured Soviet low octane fuel stocks proved highly destructive to German engines and accounted for a further noteworthy share of losses.[35]

Although a sizeable percentage of Army Group Centre's panzer fleet was out of commission by the time they reached the great rivers, the majority of these were not irreparably damaged and therefore not 'total losses'. The process of undertaking repairs, however, was complicated by the inadequate supply of spare parts and the insufficient resources of field maintenance companies. Facilities for major overhauls in the field were practically non-existent because they had not been necessary for past blitzkrieg campaigns in Poland, France and the Balkans. In each of these cases a victorious end to hostilities was rapidly achieved, allowing for the trouble-free return of tanks to German factories for major overhauls and rebuilding. In the Soviet Union such measures were impractical, not only because the Red Army remained unbeaten in the field, but because the railways still lagged far behind the advanced panzer groups.[36] The panzer troops were discovering what would soon become the scourge of the whole German army in the east – that their support basis was thoroughly inadequate, and that maintaining effective force levels required desperate ingenuity and improvisation.

In addition to the high fallout of tanks for technical reasons, combat losses or 'total losses' represented, according to Guderian's panzer group on 7 July, 10 per cent of his whole panzer fleet.[37] While this is a low figure in comparison with the number of Soviet tanks already destroyed, seen in the light of the small German domestic production and the excessive operational demands placed by Barbarossa on the panzer groups, even low combat losses pushed the remote chance of a blitzkrieg victory further from realisation. In the summer of 1941, the tank represented a

---

[34] 'Kriegstagebuch Nr.2 XXXXVII.Pz.Korps. Ia 25.5.1941 – 22.9.1941' BA-MA RH 24–47/2 (5 July 1941).

[35] On 6 July Schweppenburg's XXIV Panzer Corps reported the loss of 30 Panzer Mark IIIs and four Panzer Mark IVs as a result of using captured fuel supplies; 'Kriegstagebuch der O.Qu.-Abt. Pz. A.O.K.2 von 21.6.41 bis 31.3.42' BA-MA RH 21–2/819, Fol. 318 (6 July 1941).

[36] Macksey, *Guderian*, pp. 138–139.

[37] 'KTB Nr.1 Panzergruppe 2 vom 22.6.1941 bis 21.7.41' BA-MA RH 21–2/927, Fol. 149 (7 July 1941).

finite resource to the army's striking power, which was steadily eroded
in the early weeks of the campaign. This erosion crippled the central
instrument required for achieving the strategic plan. Accordingly, even
minor Soviet victories over the German panzer arm, like the destruction of 22 German tanks in an ambush north of Zhlobin on 6 July,[38]
assume disproportionate significance for depleting Germany's powerful,
but very limited, mechanised weapons. Referring to the previous ambush
one German officer noted on 7 July: 'Our panzers have heavy losses. One
company has just one tank which is still serviceable.'[39]

It was not only the loss of tanks in the panzer divisions that was
impairing their performance. On 6 July the 18th Panzer Division was
deemed 'no longer fully combat ready' because of numerous losses in
men and material during the two-week uninterrupted march.[40] Three
days later the divisional war diary observed: 'The troops make an exas-
perated impression. They are missing rest and the high officer losses
are noticeable. Combat strength greatly constricted. Weapons in need
of overhauling.'[41] Perhaps the most insightful comment came from the
divisional commander, Major-General Walther Nehring, who even at this
early stage cautioned: 'This situation and its consequences will become
unbearable in the future, if we do not want to be destroyed by winning.'[42]
Another observer commenting on the men in the 12th Panzer Division
stated: 'Not one of them dared to express a doubt or his own opinion
about the war in which they were all involved, even though day after day
the corpses of their fellow soldiers – bullet-riddled and torn by shrapnel –
became more numerous.'[43]

As Bock's forces were still moving up to the great rivers, the Soviet High
Command (Stavka) insisted Timoshenko launch an offensive with his
20th Army towards Lepel (see Map 4). Spearheading the advance were to
be the newly arrived 5th and 7th Mechanised Corps fielding about 1,420
tanks between them, but lacking vital infantry support, anti-aircraft guns
and air cover.[44] The counter-stroke was launched on 6 July and initially
gained some success with the 7th Panzer Division being pushed out of

[38] Department of the U.S. Army (ed.), *Small Unit Actions*, pp. 91–92; see also: Horst
Zobel, '3rd Panzer Division's Advance to Mogilev' in David M. Glantz (ed.), *The Initial
Period of War*, p. 393; Steiger, *Armour Tactics*, p. 79.
[39] Kempowski (ed.), *Das Echolot Barbarossa '41*, p. 273 (7 July 1941).
[40] 'Kriegstagebuch Nr.2 XXXXVII.Pz.Korps. Ia 25.5.1941 – 22.9.1941' BA-MA RH
24–47/2 (6 July 1941).
[41] '18. Panzer Division, Abt. Ia. Kriegstagebuch Teil I vom: 22.6 – 20.8.41' BA-MA RH
27–18/20, Fol. 31 (9 July 1941).
[42] Bartov, *Hitler's Army*, p. 20.
[43] Solomon Perel, *Europa Europa* (New York, 1997), pp. 35–36.
[44] Glantz, *Battle for Smolensk*, pp. 14–15; Erickson, *Road to Stalingrad*, pp. 161–162.

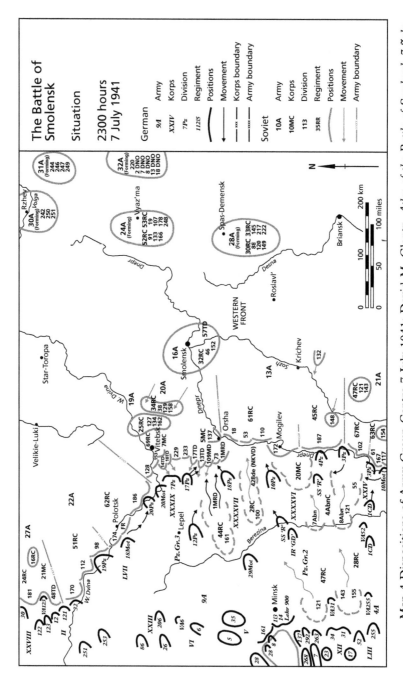

The Battle of
Smolensk

Situation

2300 hours
7 July 1941

German

9A	Army
XXIV	Korps
7Pz	Division
112S	Regiment
	Positions
	Movement
xxx	Korps boundary
xxxx	Army boundary

Soviet

10A	Army
10MC	Korps
113	Division
35RR	Regiment
	Positions
	Movement
	Army boundary

N

200 km

100 miles

0   50   100

Map 4 Dispositions of Army Group Centre 7 July 1941: David M. Glantz, *Atlas of the Battle of Smolensk 7 July–
10 September 1941*

Senno,[45] but the cumulative effects of poor concentration, inadequate support and the 7th Panzer Division's skilled anti-tank defence, quickly halted the drive. Successive Soviet counter-attacks failed to break the German lines and effectively decimated the two mechanised corps.[46] On 8 July the Germans re-took Senno with 'few panzer losses, but heavy losses in the dead and wounded'.[47]

The Lepel counter-attack was clearly a wasteful failure for the Red Army, but its significance should also be seen in the extent to which the battle impacted on the German command, who simply didn't realise Timoshenko possessed the strength for anything so audacious.[48] Before the attack on 6 July Bock acknowledged that his forces were too widely scattered and that 'now "a fist has to be made" somewhere'.[49] Yet, on the following day, in the wake of widespread Soviet attacks west of the Dnepr, Bock's plan to redeploy Vietinghoff's XXXXVI Corps northwards, to create a powerful 'fist' in the centre of the front together with Lemelsen's XXXXVII and Schmidt's XXXIX Panzer Corps, was judged by Bock to be 'no longer feasible'.[50] As a result, the Field Marshal resolved to continue the attack on a broad front, which, in spite of his intentions to regroup his forces once the western bank of the Dnepr was fully secured, never materialised. The dangerous consequence of continuing east on a broad front would become evident in the long drive beyond the Dnepr.

While Timoshenko expended his available strength in attempting to force the Germans back in the centre of his front, his forces along the Dvina were left dangerously thin. Holding the long front against Hoth's panzer group was Western Front's 22nd Army which had been unable to eliminate Kuntzen's small bridgehead at Disna and was now about to face a concerted attack by Schmidt's XXXIX Panzer Corps at Ulla. Unlike Guderian's broad advance, Hoth now stripped Kuntzen's LVII Panzer Corps of the 12th Panzer Division and the 18th Motorised Division (leaving him only the 19th Panzer Division at Disna) and directed them to follow Schmidt's attack, in order to exploit the breakthrough.[51] On 7 July the 20th Panzer Division supported by the 20th Motorised Division

[45] 'Panzerarmeeoberkommandos Tagesmeldungen 21.6 – 31.8.41' BA-MA RH 21–3/43, Fol. 93 (6 July 1941).
[46] Glantz, *Battle for Smolensk*, p. 15; Erickson, *Road to Stalingrad*, pp. 161–162.
[47] 'Tagesmeldungen der Heeresgruppe Mitte vom 22.6.41 bis 15.7.41' BA-MA RH 19 II/128, Fol. 196 (9 July 1941).
[48] 'Panzerarmeeoberkommandos Anlagen zum Kriegstagebuch "Berichte, Besprechungen, Beurteilungen der Lage" Bd.III 25.5.41 – 22.7.41' BA-MA RH 21–3/46, Fol. 90 (7 July 1941).
[49] Fedor von Bock, KTB 'Osten I', Fol. 15, *War Diary*, p. 239 (6 July 1941).
[50] Ibid., Fol. 18, p. 241 (7 July 1941).   [51] Hoth, *Panzer-Operationen*, p. 83.

successfully forced a crossing at Ulla and then proceeded east to Vitebsk, which was taken on 9 July.

Hoth's success effectively broke Timoshenko's left flank and rendered the Soviet defensive position anchored on the Dvina hopeless. With Soviet forces outmanoeuvred and the operational freedom to exploit the breakthrough, Hoth seemed set for another deep penetration of Soviet lines. Yet the immediate operational opportunities and the seriousness of Western Front's strategic position disguised the fatigue of Hoth's armoured group, which was rapidly exhausting itself and struggling to remain mobile. On 8 July the panzer group's war diary stated that its battles over the past few days had resulted in 'substantial losses in men and material, including panzers'. Consequently it noted: 'The resulting losses in officers, panzers and vehicles had to be taken into account, although the mobile divisions would desperately miss them in a further push towards Moscow.'[52] The gravity of the problem was clearly detailed in a report compiled by the panzer group and sent to 4th Panzer Army and Bock's army group command on 8 July. The document began by pointing out that the daily radio transmissions could not adequately convey to higher command many of the underlying problems slowing down operations and causing difficulties. The report therefore listed eight points of fundamental concern to the panzer group, for which it concluded: 'The danger therefore exists that in the future, mobile units will be expected to perform duties which they cannot fulfil.'[53]

Point one discussed the unsuitability of civilian vehicles, captured French buses and motorcycles (which made up the great majority of 3rd Panzer Group's wheeled transport) for service in the east. They were not robust enough for the roads and conditions, resulting in high fallout rates and constant traffic-jams. The section ended: 'The fluid advance suffers.'

Point two referred to the extensive problems brought about by the poor roads which were so sandy and marshy that 'a march tempo of maximum 10 km per hour is attainable. Every time estimate is questionable.' The report cited an example where on one stretch 17 hours were needed to drive 110 kilometres. Further delays were caused by having to almost always strengthen bridges over the streams and tributaries that dotted the landscape. It was also stated that overtaking and two-way traffic were 'often only possible with great difficulty'.

---

[52] '3rd Pz. Gr. KTB 25.5.41 – 31.8.41' BA-MA Microfilm 59054, Fol. 108 (8 July 1941).

[53] 'Panzerarmeeoberkommandos Anlagen zum Kriegstagesbuch "Berichte, Besprechungen, Beurteilungen der Lage" Bd.III 25.5.41 – 22.7.41' BA-MA RH 21-3/46, Fols. 100–101 (8 July 1941).

The third point emphasised the problem of conducting operations on a solitary road with troops stretched out in a long column. This limited the breadth of the advance and the capability of getting specialised units, such as engineers or anti-aircraft guns, to the front quickly.

The fourth point stated: 'The troops, in particular the drivers, are very tired after 14 days of advance.' The report continued that the bad roads had cost the army its planned rest period and, as a result, a sufficient respite could not be granted.

Point five highlighted the difference in quality between the motorised and panzer divisions with experience in past campaigns, and those newly formed in the spring of 1941. The new divisions were said to have less experience in the movement of large columns and also less 'driving skill'. The example of the new 18th Motorised Division was cited that, the report stated, was being expected to perform duties even the experienced units would have great difficulty conducting.

The sixth point noted the panzer group's relatively high losses among officers, particularly among the more experienced and eager officers. A more hesitant approach to the conduct of operations was therefore sometimes evident.

The seventh point referred to the menacing activity of the Soviet air force, which was causing sporadic halts to the advance through the revival of aerial attacks.

The eighth and final point concerned the nature of opposition the 3rd Panzer Group was meeting from Soviet soldiers. The report stated:

The Russian fights tough and fiercely, attacks continually, is very skilled in defence and on the Dvina is apparently well commanded. Resistance in the countryside constantly resurges. Often the Russian waits, well camouflaged and only when the distance is short does he then open fire.[54]

The report concluded that, while these issues did not halt the advance of the panzer group, they did slow all movement.

While Hoth's panzer group was breaching Soviet defences on the Dvina, to the south Guderian's forces were still closing up on the Dnepr, slowed by sabotaged bridges, sporadic enemy encounters and the usual terrain difficulties. In addition, Guderian conceded that 'the panzer divisions after 16 days of uninterrupted fighting are somewhat exhausted'.[55] Nevertheless, the panzer general was pushing his men as hard as ever, determined to force a crossing of the Dnepr, which he complained on

---

[54] Ibid. (8 July 1941). See also '3rd Pz. Gr. KTB 25.5.41 – 31.8.41' BA-MA Microfilm 59054, Fols. 113–115 (9 July 1941).
[55] 'KTB Nr.1 Panzergruppe 2 vom 22.6.1941 bis 21.7.41' BA-MA RH 21–2/927, Fol. 167 (8 July 1941).

8 July could have been achieved 'about 3 days earlier' against weaker resistance if Kluge had not withheld elements of his panzer group near Minsk.[56] The vexing frustration existing between the two commanders was not alleviated by the elimination of the Minsk pocket and the release of all Guderian's remaining forces. As the panzer and motorised divisions assembled along the western bank of the Dnepr on 9 July, Guderian ordered arrangements for immediate crossings along the length of his front. Kluge's opinion was neither asked for nor desired, and when he appeared at Guderian's headquarters the resulting clash was, according to Guderian, 'exceptionally heated'.[57] Kluge insisted that any attempt to cross the Dnepr must be supported by infantry and that Guderian must therefore await the arrival of Weichs's 2nd Army. Guderian, however, would have none of this. According to his own testimony he believed that crossing the Dnepr would decide the campaign in 1941 and, after failing to convince Kluge of the need for an immediate attack, he simply stated that offensive preparations had gone too far to be cancelled. In the face of Guderian's inexorable obstinacy, Kluge was again reminded that his authority over him was largely token and thus, presented with a *fait accompli*, he grudgingly accepted Guderian's plan with the solemn warning: 'Your operations always hang by a thread!'[58]

Kluge was not the only one to have reservations about 2nd Panzer Group's crossing of the Dnepr. Nor was this just an example of a panzer-minded general in opposition to an infantry commander. Within Panzer Group 2 strong differences were beginning to emerge that stemmed from the constant demands being placed on the increasingly worn-out troops and equipment. Geyer von Schweppenburg, the commander of the XXIV Panzer Corps, asked Guderian to delay the attempt to cross the Dnepr until at least some of the infantry divisions could reach the river and support the attack, but Guderian dismissed the idea. Meanwhile, the commander of the 3rd Panzer Division, Lieutenant-General Walther Model, had earlier had to disappoint his subordinates who were pleading for a 24-hour rest to regroup and refit. Model, who was later to rise to the rank of Field Marshal and develop a fearsome reputation as a ruthless commander, explained his decision in grave terms: 'Every minute that we lose will cost us great losses later that we will not be able to afford...We must push forward now, otherwise we risk everything.'[59] On 9 July Bock ordered 4th Panzer Army to direct Guderian's rearward units towards the north to pass through the crossing made by Hoth.[60]

[56] Ibid. (8 July 1941).
[57] Guderian, *Panzer Leader*, pp. 168–169.   [58] Ibid., p. 169.
[59] Steven H. Newton, *Hitler's Commander. Field Marshal Walther Model – Hitler's Favorite General* (Cambridge MA, 2006), pp. 126 and 129.
[60] Fedor von Bock, KTB 'Osten I', Fol. 21, *War Diary*, pp. 244–245 (9 July 1941).

Guderian, however, remained a law unto himself and Bock's attempts to direct the course of operations within the panzer group were no more successful in disrupting Guderian's own plan than Kluge's had been. Ultimately, Guderian's boldness would largely pay off with assaults across the river successfully conducted on 10 July to the north and south of Mogilev (see Map 5). Yet the accomplishment was a qualified one. A direct assault by elements of 3rd Panzer Division on Mogilev proved a costly failure[61] and the 17th Panzer Division's attack near Orsha was repulsed.[62] Beyond these immediate setbacks, Guderian's success in pushing through on the weaker sectors of the front still left behind powerful enemy strongpoints that would cause havoc in the rear areas and further delay the infantry who would eventually have to deal with them. Outstanding among these was the fanatical resistance offered at Mogilev, drawing parallels with the Soviet garrison at Brest and ultimately earning the Soviet Union's exalted distinction of 'Hero City'. Such fortresses of the rear further exacerbated the drain on resources, as the increasingly exposed southern flank of the army group was now to be greatly extended. If there was an especially dark cloud on the German horizon, it was caused by the German command's wilful over-extension.

On 8 July, as Hoth was exploiting his breakthrough on the Dvina and Guderian's three corps were still advancing on the Dnepr, Army Group Centre announced the end of the fighting near Minsk. The remaining pocket around Novogrudok had been eliminated by the infantry of Strauss's 9th Army and Weichs's 2nd Army. However, even the official declaration to the troops hailing the success admitted that, of the 32 Soviet rifle divisions encircled, one-third had escaped albeit with a 'reduction in their fighting strength'.[63] The fact that these forces were now moving east as disparate mobile bubbles into the vulnerable rear area of the panzer groups, or holding up in the forests of Belorussia, appears to have been inconsequential to claiming a great success.[64] Heusinger was representative of the OKH at the time in viewing the battle as a decisive blow in deciding the campaign.[65] Yet as Major-General Blumentritt, the 4th Panzer Army's Chief of Staff, wrote after the war:

There were not enough German troops available completely to seal off a huge encirclement such as that of Belostok–Slonim. Our motorised forces fought on or near to the roads: in the great trackless spaces between them the Russians were left largely unmolested. This was why the Russians were not infrequently

[61] Zobel, '3rd Panzer Division's Advance to Mogilev', pp. 395–396.
[62] Guderian, *Panzer Leader*, p. 171.
[63] Fedor von Bock, KTB 'Osten I', Fol. 20, *War Diary*, p. 243 (8 July 1941).
[64] Edgar Röhricht, *Probleme der Kesselschlacht*, Beispiel III, Der Ansatz der Heeresgruppe Mitte bei Beginn des Rußlandfeldzugs im Juni 1941.
[65] Meyer, *Heusinger*, pp. 153–154.

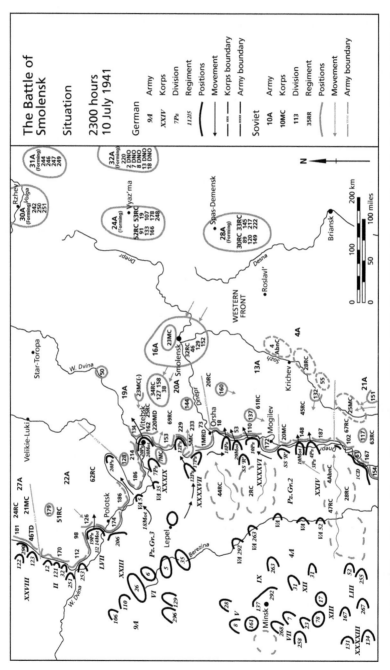

Map 5 Dispositions of Army Group Centre 10 July 1941: David M. Glantz, *Atlas of the Battle of Smolensk 7 July–10 September 1941*

Figure 6.1 Attempting to avoid the time-consuming delay of strengthening minor bridges tank commanders often risked crossings.

to break out of our encirclements, whole columns moving by night through the forests that stretched away eastwards. They always attempted to break out to the east, so that the eastern side of each encirclement had to be held by our strongest troops, usually panzer troops. Nevertheless, our encirclements were seldom entirely successful.[66]

In Army Group Centre's official proclamation of 8 July the total number of prisoners captured was put at 287,704 men, with 2,585 tanks destroyed or captured and 1,449 guns taken.[67] Time and again historians have quoted these figures to underscore the tremendous success of the German blitzkrieg in the summer of 1941, and while on the surface they do represent an impressive booty, it does not follow that the Soviet Union was on the brink of collapse – indeed far from it.

While German offensive strength was increasingly waning, the Soviet Union was enacting the most remarkable mobilisation programme in military history. For much of the 1920s and 1930s the Red Army had developed an extensive system of cadre forces, which consisted of small numbers of active duty soldiers in peacetime, but could be rapidly expanded by reservists in wartime. To support this system the 1938 Universal Military Service Law extended the age of those obligated to serve in the army reserves to 50, and created many new military schools to accommodate the influx. By the eve of the German invasion, the Red Army possessed a mobilisation base of 14 million men. By the end of June, 5.3 million reservists had been called up, with further mobilisations following in succession.[68] The cadre system allowed for an unheard-of rate of force generation, which completely outwitted German intelligence estimates, and disguised the real strength of the Soviet state. In July 1941 no less than 13 new field armies appeared and in August another 14 came into service. These new reserve armies were not as well equipped or as well trained as the professional armies they replaced, but as the German mobile forces weakened, more and more of the front settled down to positional warfare, allowing the new armies time to improve both. Thus, without attempting to trivialise the scale of the Western Front's military disaster in Belorussia, the fact remains that the Soviet Union's force generation scheme was able to replace its losses quickly and then dramatically expand the size of the Red Army.[69] On 22 June 1941 the Red Army numbered 5,373,000 men; by 31 August, in spite of its losses, it had grown to 6,889,000 and by 31 December 1941 the

[66] Blumentritt, 'Moscow', p. 48.
[67] Fedor von Bock, KTB 'Osten I', Fol. 20, *War Diary*, p. 243 (8 July 1941).
[68] Glantz and House, *When Titans Clashed*, pp. 67–68.
[69] Geyer, 'German Strategy', p. 591.

army had reached an estimated eight million men.[70] After the war Blumentritt also acknowledged the fundamental problem of latent Soviet military strength. Recalling the German offensive plans to cut off and destroy the Red Army before the Dnepr and Dvina Rivers, Blumentritt posed the rhetorical question: 'But what if armies, millions strong, had not yet even been mobilized and only parts of the Red Army were in western Russia?'[71]

The Soviet loss of tanks was more deeply felt as they were harder to replace and this added further strain to Soviet attempts to stop the German advance, although here too it has proved tempting for historians to overstate the extent of the German success. The Soviet Union's tank park at the start of the war numbered an incredible 23,767 tanks, but this reflected Soviet tank production since the 1920s and therefore included many that were obsolete on the modern battlefield. Some 15,000 tanks were of the older T-26 and BT series and estimates suggest that the great majority of these were in need of some form of repair.[72] Added to this, the untrained crews, the severe lack of ammunition, fuel and spare parts, as well as the absence of supporting arms such as air cover, make it small wonder that Soviet tanks littered the battlefields, if they even made it that far.[73] Accordingly, the apparently astounding German successes, often suggested by the sheer numbers of Soviet tanks destroyed, are better understood as a Soviet disaster waiting to happen. Put simply, inept Soviet planning and direction played a major role in handing the Germans their first major victory with the vast quantities of old and outdated equipment inflating the notion of an exceptional triumph. In reality, even in the absence of certain Soviet blunders, not much could probably have been expected from the great bulk of the Soviet mechanised arm. What was, however, of fundamental importance to the future of the war, was the production of new tanks and in this regard the Soviet leadership acted with astute resolve.

In the face of the unrelenting German advance, the enormous evacuation of Soviet industry to the east in 1941 was indispensable in ensuring the economic durability of the Soviet Union. Accomplished with extraordinary speed and under the most adverse circumstances, which included aerial attacks from the Luftwaffe, hundreds of factories were

---

[70] Glantz, *Barbarossa*, p. 68. See also Mawdsley, *Thunder in the East*, pp. 112–113.

[71] Blumentritt, *Von Rundstedt*, pp. 102–103.

[72] Glantz, 'Introduction', p. 33; Merridale, *Ivan's War*, p. 103; Glantz, *Colossus Reborn*, p. 247.

[73] David Glantz stated that: 'at least half of those mechanized corps [in the border battles] never made it into combat. They either broke down or never moved in the first place' (Glantz, 'Introduction', p. 39).

simply uprooted, transported into the interior and rapidly reassembled. The scale and complexity of such an undertaking is difficult to imagine, especially in the light of the national crisis overtaking the country, yet here post-war Soviet literature's propensity for grandiose superlatives such as 'heroic' and 'historic' seem justified.[74] Between July and November, 1,523 industrial enterprises were moved to the Volga region, Siberia or Central Asia, amounting in total to some 1.5 million railway wagon-loads.[75] Even more remarkable, the production of vital war materials actually increased in the second half of 1941, with official production quotes in some cases, such as tanks, being exceeded.[76] Indeed the Soviet Union produced more tanks in 1941 than Germany[77] and 66 per cent of these were of the newer T-34 and KV-1 variety.[78] Soviet industry also turned out more aircraft and a great many more artillery pieces than Germany, helping to meet the most immediate needs of the army.[79]

In assessing the outcome of Germany's first great battle of encirclement on the eastern front, it is plainly apparent that the German military leadership over-estimated the effect their victory would have on the Soviet Union's capacity to maintain a coherent front. Conversely, the Germans failed to recognise and adequately reconcile the opposing demands of ensuring a tight perimeter around the eastern edge of the pocket, with the need to exploit their success through a rapid continuation of the advance. The root cause of the problem, evident even in the earliest stage of the war, concerned the lack of sufficient mobile forces to accomplish the tasks at hand. Consequently, when losses began to mount and the campaign proceeded towards new and more ambitious objectives over great distances, the spectre of over-extension loomed large.

'The Russian is a colossus and strong' (Adolf Hitler)

In the early days of July, while the army command was concerned with the day-to-day issues of the campaign, Hitler was looking further ahead. His lack of enthusiasm for a continuation of the operation beyond the great rivers towards Moscow was well known to Halder and Brauchitsch, but the continued success of the campaign seemed to them the best guarantee

---

[74] For a helpful overview of the process see G. A. Kumanev, 'The Soviet Economy and the 1941 Evacuation' in Joseph Wieczynski (ed.), *Operation Barbarossa. The German Attack on the Soviet Union June 22, 1941* (Salt Lake City, 1993), pp. 163–193.

[75] Werth, *Russia at War 1941–1945*, p. 216.

[76] M. R. D. Foot, 'USSR' in I. C. B. Dear and M. R. D. Foot (eds.), *The Oxford Companion to the Second World War* (Oxford, 1995), Table 7: Production of New Weapons, p. 1231; ibid., p. 220.

[77] Overy, *Russia's War*, Table I: Soviet and German Wartime Production 1941–45, p. 155.

[78] Foot, 'USSR', Table 7: Production of New Weapons, p. 1231.

[79] Overy, *Russia's War*, Table I: Soviet and German Wartime Production 1941–45, p. 155.

of ensuring a continued forward advance on all fronts. Yet, as early as 3 and 4 July, Hitler had expressed an interest in halting Kluge's panzer groups and using them to support the advance on the flanks.[80] On 5 July Jodl telephoned Brauchitsch to request that the Army Commander-in-Chief meet with Hitler to offer his opinion on the northern and southern alternatives. Jodl also posed a number of questions relating first to the necessity and second to the feasibility of each operation. Perhaps sensing difficulties between the OKW and OKH over the issue, Jodl stressed to Brauchitsch the urgency of the army's involvement in the matter. The document in the OKW war diary concluded: 'Given that the Führer's thoughts, and those of others, are heading towards an early turning of the panzer groups towards the northeast or south, General Jodl considers it necessary that the Commander-in-Chief of the Army promptly meets with the Führer for a discussion.'[81]

The meeting took place at Hitler's headquarters on 8 July with Halder accompanying Brauchitsch and both men making presentations before Hitler and his staff. Brauchitsch first summarised the latest tactical reports and then Halder outlined the army's assessment of the enemy situation and the progress of operations in the three army groups. The tone of Halder's presentation was typically upbeat, designed to instil confidence in the army's running of the war and ensure its continued hegemony in the field of strategic direction. Yet Halder also firmly believed that the German armies were now in an unassailable position to win the war. In evidence of this, Halder gave details of Kinzel's latest intelligence report which noted that, of the 164 identified Soviet rifle divisions, 89 had been totally or largely eliminated. From the remaining 75 divisions, 46 were still opposing the German front, 18 were tied down on other fronts (14 in Finland and four in the Caucasus) and the last 11 divisions were probably still in the interior in reserve.[82] Other elements of Kinzel's report noted: 'The enemy is no longer able to organise a continuous front, not even behind strong terrain features . . . [Army Group] Centre, which was stronger from the beginning, now has a crushing superiority and can maintain it even if the enemy, as is expected, should bring up new units to that front.'[83] In addition to encouraging an atmosphere of great confidence in the progress of the war, the buoyant optimism of Halder's report[84] dismissed the urgency of making a definitive operational decision concerning Bock's panzer groups.[85] The jubilant mood also

---

[80] KTB OKW, Volume II, p. 1020, Documents 66 and 67 (3 and 4 July 1941).
[81] Ibid., pp. 1020–1021, Document 68 (5 July 1941).
[82] Ibid., p. 1021, Document 70 (8 July 1941); Franz Halder, KTB III, p. 52 (8 July 1941).
[83] Franz Halder, KTB III, p. 52 (8 July 1941); Hoth, *Panzer-Operationen*, pp. 90–91.
[84] Hoth, *Panzer-Operationen*, p. 91.
[85] KTB OKW, Volume II, p. 1021, Document 69 (8 July 1941).

seems to have inspired in Hitler and Halder a brief measure of concilia-
tion, allowing a glimmer of compromise previously inconceivable on the
question of Moscow.

Hitler spoke of his 'ideal solution' to the continuation of the campaign in which Army Group North was to accomplish with its own
forces the tasks already assigned to it in the Baltic states and Leningrad.
Army Group Centre was charged with finishing off the last of the organised resistance along the over-extended Soviet front north of the Pripet
marshes. This, Hitler stated, 'would thereby open the road to Moscow'.[86]
Upon reaching their assigned positions east of Smolensk, Hoth could
halt and then either render assistance to Leeb (if necessary) or continue
eastwards with a view to investing Moscow. Guderian could be used to
strike in a southern or south-eastern direction in co-operation with Army
Group South.

With the war proceeding so well, Halder too was suddenly much less
concerned about Hitler's desire to turn Guderian's forces south. On
the one hand, Halder was aware of Bock's increasingly exposed southern flank, but more importantly, he was sufficiently confident about the
campaign's success that he foresaw no means by which the Red Army
could obstruct his march on Moscow even without Guderian's forces.
Indeed, Halder was already setting his sights well beyond the Soviet capital, writing in his diary that after the battle of Smolensk 'we shall block
the railways across the Volga, occupy the country as far as that river and
then, by means of armoured expeditions and aerial operations, destroy
the remaining Russian industrial centres'.[87] Obviously the misguided
confidence evinced in the planning stages of the campaign continued
unabated despite the dangerous warning signs plainly emerging as the
reality of the campaign unfolded.

The degree of Halder's self-deception was evident even as he spoke of
the great triumph in the east. In the course of his meeting with Hitler,
Halder emphasised the urgency of tank replacements for the eastern
front, to which Hitler made clear his desire to retain all new production
in Germany for future missions 'that will again extend over thousands of
kilometres'. The result, Hitler stated, was that the tank losses suffered so
far in the east 'would necessitate an amalgamation of the panzer divisions'
with the surplus personnel being returned to Germany to outfit the new
tanks. It was only at the end of the meeting when Halder pleaded 'the
urgent requirements of the front' that Hitler conceded to the release of
70 Mark IIIs, 15 Mark IVs and the Czech tanks for use on the eastern
front.[88]

---

[86] Franz Halder, KTB III, p. 53 (8 July 1941).   [87] Ibid., p. 53 (8 July 1941).
[88] Ibid., pp. 53–54 (8 July 1941).

Halder's selective reading of the military situation in the east did not prevent others from drawing far more accurate conclusions about the progress of the war. The Italian foreign minister, Galeazzo Ciano, noted in his diary on 9 July: 'The German advance in Russia proceeds at a somewhat slower pace. Resistance is serious; I saw a set of documents sent by Goebbels in which this is clearly evident.'[89] On the following day he continued: 'From the Russian front news is quite serious; the Russians are fighting well, and, for the first time in the course of the war, the Germans admit withdrawing at two points.'[90] Although the Italians tended to look at Germany's successes with a degree of resentful spite, Ciano's remarks were not merely the result of Italian scorn or pessimism. The Japanese naval attaché in Rome, Captain Mitsunobu Tōyō, expressed deep scepticism about the prospects for German military operations in the east, comparing it with Japan's mired war in China. Even if Moscow and the whole western industrial area of the Soviet Union could be conquered, Tōyō argued that this would 'not deliver the fatal blow'. The Soviets, he said, had developed the area beyond the Urals meaning the Germans would face 'in the vast and barely accessible hinterland an enemy which will resort to the means of guerrilla warfare which tie down vast numbers of one's own troops without being able to bring about a decisive military victory.'[91] German diplomatic circles were also monitoring the situation in the east with growing unease. On 11 July Ciano recorded: 'A meeting with Domberg. He is calm but not joyful. Losses in Russia are heavy, and the war may bring us big surprises. His wife is more sprightly than he, and she does not conceal her judgment of the situation. "This is a war," she said, "that we cannot get away with."'[92] In his first diary entry since the outbreak of war former diplomat Ulrich von Hassell wrote on 13 July that in spite of the suddenness of the German attack, 'the struggle is much harder than had been expected' and had resulted in 'heavy losses among German officers'.[93] Hassell also perceptively alluded to the dangers of Hitler's occupation policies, placing the Soviet Union under Nazi Gauleiters and rejecting the co-operation of anti-Stalinist Russians. The result he foresaw: 'Stalin may yet succeed in forming a patriotic Russian front against the German enemy.'[94]

Having penetrated Timoshenko's defences along the Dvina and Dnepr, Guderian and Hoth pressed the attack forward across the breadth of their

---

[89] Muggeridge (ed.), *Ciano's Diary*, p. 368 (9 July 1941).
[90] Ibid. (10 July 1941).   [91] Chapman, 'The Imperial Japanese Navy', p. 176.
[92] Muggeridge (ed.), *Ciano's Diary*, p. 369 (11 July 1941).
[93] Von Hassell, *Vom andern Deutschland*, p. 211 (13 July 1941); von Hassell, *Diaries*, p. 182 (13 July 1941).
[94] Von Hassell, *Vom andern Deutschland*, p. 211 (13 July 1941); von Hassell, *Diaries*, p. 183 (13 July 1941).

front, causing Bock to worry that the army group was not achieving a decisive concentration. The Field Marshal, therefore, directed an inquiry to 4th Panzer Army stating that the front was 250 kilometres wide and asking if it was possible to align their forces to give them greater strength and focus. The answer came back that this was impossible on account of road conditions, meaning that the panzer corps would have to remain dispersed and essentially isolated from one another by the sheer size of the operational theatre.[95] The menacing difficulty of conducting deep operations into the immensity of the Soviet Union, a country which encompassed a staggering 22.4 million square kilometres,[96] was one of the most striking oversights of the operational planning for a war in the east. To a large extent Bock's success hinged on eliminating major Soviet resistance west of the great rivers and the prospect of lunging further into the country, while still facing a formidable foe, entailed grave consequences. For good reason Goebbels commented at the start of the war: 'I am refraining from publishing big maps of Russia. The huge areas involved can only frighten our people.'[97] Yet the sheer size of the Soviet Union could not help but impact on the soldiers who, according to one, entered into a 'realm of eternal horizons, where the land is like the sea'.[98] Such sentiments pervade the personal accounts of the soldiers, reflecting a sense of isolation, detachment, helplessness, melancholy and even despair. Liddell Hart cited the remarks of an unnamed German general:

The spaces seemed endless, the horizons nebulous. We were depressed by the monotony of the landscape, and the immensity of the stretches of forest, marsh and plain. Good roads were so few, and bad tracks so numerous, while rain quickly turned the sand or loam into a morass.[99]

On 8 July Harry Mielert lamented the 'endless space in which we feel after all eerily insecure'.[100] Another soldier, Bernhard Ritter, wrote of the internal conflict this caused:

We must protect ourselves against it, must overcome it, to reach our goal, which this country with all its features attempts to prevent. It is the embodiment of the 'without a goal', the infinite, the never to be able to achieve one's objective. In

[95] Fedor von Bock, KTB 'Osten I', Fol. 23, *War Diary*, p. 246 (11 July 1941).
[96] Krumpelt, *Das Material und die Kriegführung*, p. 141.
[97] Fröhlich (ed.), *Die Tagebücher von Joseph Goebbels*, Teil I: Aufzeichnungen 1923–1941 Band 9, Dezember 1940-Juli 1941, p. 402 (25 June 1941).
[98] As quoted in Stephen G. Fritz, *Frontsoldaten. The German Soldier in World War II* (Lexington, 1995), p. 124.
[99] Liddell Hart, *History of the Second World War*, p. 169.
[100] As quoted in Fritz, *Frontsoldaten*, p. 124.

this country I am always in a conflict between the necessity of overcoming it and feeling its essence.[101]

Willy Peter Reese wrote of the 'boundless, the ungraspable, the overwhelming quality of this soil', which, he concluded, 'we eyed doubtfully, and were afraid of, and could not bear as if the daemon and the spirit of Russia preserved the land from such unsolicited, unqualified visitors'.[102] Perhaps the most vivid observation was offered by Siegfried Knappe, who alluded to the despair of endless distances and the implications for waging a war in such a country:

Everything seemed to blur into uniform grey because of the vastness and sameness of everything. We traversed treeless plateaus that extended as far as the eye could see, just one vast open field overgrown with tall grass. We encountered grain fields of unimaginable vastness that sometimes concealed Russian infantry. Fields of sunflowers stretched for kilometer after weary kilometer. In other places we encountered immense forests that were like jungles in the density of their tangled underbrush. We struggled through marshes in Byelorussia that were as large as two German provinces...

Nothing could have prepared us for the mental depression brought on by this realization of the utter physical vastness of Russia. Tiny little doubts began to creep into our minds. Was it even possible that such vast emptiness could be conquered by foot soldiers?[103]

Beyond the draining psychological ramifications of fighting on into the vast Soviet hinterland, the difficulties of the infantry in having to manoeuvre on foot greatly reduced their flexibility in dealing with Soviet counterattacks, as well as their ability to provide timely assistance at trouble spots. This placed all the more importance on the motorised and panzer divisions maintaining their mobility but, in Hoth's estimation, this was already coming to an end. Assessing the situation on 11 July Hoth foresaw hard fighting over the coming days, including counter-attacks from Soviet panzer divisions, to which he rendered the judgement: 'Hereby the mobility of our motorised divisions will succumb.' In Hoth's opinion the only chance of maintaining his panzer group's offensive was to finally break through Soviet defences.[104]

The extent of the problem was just as pressing in Panzer Group 2. Guderian recalled that there were 'the dense clouds of dust put up by our advancing columns [that had] endured now for weeks on end [and]

101 Bähr and Bähr (eds.), *Kriegsbriefe gefallener Studenten*, pp. 49–50 (14 August 1941).
102 Reese, *A Stranger to Myself*, p. 67.
103 Knappe with Brusaw, *Soldat*, pp. 214 and 222.
104 'Panzerarmeeoberkommandos Anlagen zum Kriegstagesbuch "Berichte, Besprechungen, Beurteilungen der Lage" Bd.III 25.5.41 – 22.7.41' BA-MA RH 21-3/46, Fol. 115 (11 July 1941).

was equally hard on men, weapons, and engines. In particular the cylinders of the tanks became so clogged that their efficiency was considerably affected.'[105] In these conditions fuel consumption dramatically increased with supplies usually sufficient for 100 kilometres only reaching 70 kilometres on Soviet roads. The need for extra fuel further burdened the increasingly overstretched supply system with the daily requirement rising from an original estimate of 9,000 tons to 12,000 tons by only 11 July. Not only were the roads ruining the engines, but the long distances and heavy loads were taking their toll on the tyres of the trucks which were unable to withstand the abrasion of the sandy tracks. For a long time rubber had been in seriously short supply and there were few replacement tyres to be found, but as of 10 July the OKH informed the armies that no more tyres were to be supplied.[106]

If the harsh Soviet terrain had exacted a severe toll on the German motorised and panzer divisions in their advance to the great rivers, Blumentritt later recalled that even worse was to come as they continued further east. Referring to the drive beyond the Dnepr and Dvina, Blumentritt told Liddell Hart after the war:

It was appallingly difficult country for tank movement – great virgin forests, widespread swamps, terrible roads, and bridges not strong enough to bear the weight of tanks. The resistance also became stiffer, and the Russians began to cover their front with minefields. It was easier for them to block the way because there were so few roads.[107]

If the hinterland of the Soviet Union was troublesome for the tracked vehicles, the wheeled transport, according to Blumentritt, had an even harder time. Unlike the panzers, the heavily laden supply columns possessed no overland capabilities and were therefore bound to the abysmal road network irrespective of sand, dust or mud.[108] As Wilhelm Prüller noted in his diary on 11 July: 'When I see even at this time of the year how our vehicles, after it's rained a little, can barely make the grade, I just can't imagine how it will be in autumn when the rainy period really sets in. We're fighting in a solid mass of dirt.'[109] Blumentritt also alluded to the problem of summer downpours and the effect these had on the pace of the advance: 'An hour or two of rain reduced the panzer forces to stagnation. It was an extraordinary sight, with groups of them strung out over a hundred mile stretch, all stuck – until the sun came out and the ground dried.'[110]

[105] Guderian, *Panzer Leader*, p. 171.
[106] Müller, 'Das Scheitern der wirtschaftlichen "Blitzkriegstrategie"', pp. 963–964.
[107] Liddell Hart, *The Other Side of the Hill*, p. 271.   [108] Ibid.
[109] Landon and Leitner (eds.), *Diary of a German Soldier*, p. 81 (11 July 1941).
[110] Liddell Hart, *The Other Side of the Hill*, p. 271.

The size and strength of bridges was another critical weakness of Soviet infrastructure which had a detrimental effect on the swift movement of Bock's panzers. According to one post-war study written by German officers, the eastern theatre was marked by an 'almost complete absence of solidly constructed bridges'. The simple wooden bridges that did exist (often no more than fords across small streams or brooks) often needed reinforcing by engineers before the tanks could cross and in many cases these simple constructions were destroyed by fire during the Soviet retreat.[111]

Complications also arose from the poor quality of German maps which were on a scale of 1:100,000 and were described by one former officer as 'too old and almost of no use'.[112] Another officer told of brown printed maps dating as far back as 1870 with just the Smolensk–Moscow highway highlighted in violet ink.[113] Not surprisingly, units collided on roads, became lost and missed their objectives by large distances, leading to much unnecessary fuel consumption, lost time and wear and tear on the vehicles. Captured Soviet maps could not immediately be issued to the subordinate units because few could read the Russian Cyrillic alphabet and so these had to be overprinted with German names that did not always help readability. A further complication arose from the fact that, within a very small area, there could be three villages all bearing the same or a similar name.[114] Alexander Stahlberg, an officer in the 12th Panzer Division, described the Soviet maps they were issued with as 'fit only for use as lavatory paper'. He thought it 'irresponsible' to issue such maps to a panzer division and noted that the roads were 'sloppily penned' and 'not at all accurately plotted'.[115] Beyond problems of accuracy, William Lubbeck added that there were too few to go around.[116] Even General Staff officers, like Blumentritt, complained that the maps he dealt with 'in no way corresponded to reality'. On these maps the main roads were marked in red and appeared to be numerous, encouraging a deceptive confidence in what was to come. The reality, however, was often nothing more than sandy tracks, for which Blumentritt criticised the intelligence service for being 'badly at fault'.[117]

[111] Department of the U.S. Army (ed.), *German Armored Traffic Control*, p. 4.
[112] Durrwanger, '28th Infantry Division Operations', p. 438.
[113] General Lingenthal, 'Discussion' in David M. Glantz (ed.), *The Initial Period of War*, p. 444.
[114] General Lemm, 'Discussion' in David M. Glantz (ed.), *The Initial Period of War*, p. 444.
[115] Stahlberg, *Bounden Duty*, p. 172.
[116] Lubbeck with Hurt, *At Leningrad's Gates*, p. 88.
[117] Liddell Hart, *The Other Side of the Hill*, p. 271. See also Hermann Geyer, *Das IX. Armeekorps*, p. 100.

For all of Halder's optimism in assessing Army Group Centre's prospects for success, the fact remained that Timoshenko was still managing to co-ordinate a ramshackle front opposing Bock's advance, as well as mustering new forces for renewed counter-offensives. Nevertheless, Halder placed little worth in the continuing Soviet opposition which he portrayed as 'broken divisions' being fed by 'totally disorganised masses of men' without officers or NCOs. 'Under these conditions', Halder concluded, 'it is clear that the front, which also has no reserves left, cannot hold out much longer.'[118] Curiously, in contrast to the Red Army's infantry divisions, Halder saw the Soviet motorised units as a far more enduring problem owing to their ability, as he saw it, to almost always escape encirclement. He even envisaged the possibility that the Soviets might carry on the war with two or three large armoured groups assisted by smaller subsidiary groups. On the same day (11 July) Colonel Ochsner reported back to Halder after a visit to Hoth's and Guderian's panzer groups and stated that the panzer troops had suffered heavy losses in men and material and that all the men were tired. Ochsner also commented that the Red Army was well led and 'fought fanatically and determinedly'.[119]

The relative harmony between Hitler and the OKH expressed in their meeting of 8 July was already becoming strained by 12 July. Now that the great rivers had been crossed, Hitler was becoming impatient for the triumph over the Red Army which he had been led to believe was soon at hand. Yet it was not only the motorised forces of Army Group Centre that were suffering from the arduous affects of campaigning in the east. By 12 July Leeb's smaller Army Group North was also feeling the paralysing effects of distance, dispersal, and substantial losses. After a visit to Hoepner's 4th Panzer Group, Leeb wrote in his diary of 'heavy losses' and concluded: 'If further attacks are to be conducted at this pace we will soon reach a state of exhaustion.'[120] The slowing pace of operations in Army Group North was leading Hitler to renew his advocacy for a northward turn by elements of Hoth's panzer group, namely the 19th Panzer Division. Halder was reluctant to make any such diversion of forces, although his intelligence confirmed the increasing strength of Soviet forces on Bock's northern and southern flank.[121] Thus, while in his response to Hitler he conceded that operations might well have to be conducted to the north and south of Army Group Centre, he

[118] Franz Halder, KTB III, p. 64 (11 July 1941).   [119] Ibid., pp. 64–65 (11 July 1941).
[120] Georg Meyer (ed.), *Generalfeldmarschall Wilhelm Ritter von Leeb. Tagebuchaufzeichnungen und Lagebeurteilungen aus zwei Weltkriegen* (Stuttgart, 1976), p. 292 (12 July 1941). Hereafter cited as: Wilhelm Ritter von Leeb, KTB.
[121] Franz Halder, KTB III, p. 68 (12 July 1941).

stressed 'that the prerequisite for either move is that Hoth and Guderian break through towards the east and thereby achieve operational freedom'. Clearly, Halder favoured securing his road to Moscow before diverting his strength to the flanks and Heusinger was already working on a compromise plan aimed at seizing Velikie Luki, which Halder hoped would cut off Soviet forces in front of Leeb's right flank, while still allowing for the intended drive on Smolensk. A similar solution was adopted to clear Guderian's southern flank with joint operations envisaged towards Yel'nya in the north and Roslavl in the south.[122]

Although Halder's new plan was calculated to alleviate Hitler's concerns and deal with the threat to the army group's flanks, the great distances involved and the dispersed objectives proved the plan was unmistakably a product of Halder's misplaced confidence in the demise of the Red Army. From Velikie Luki in the north to Roslavl in the south, the army group would be stretching its front to some 300 kilometres in width, while simultaneously supporting a major offensive in the middle of its front at Smolensk. The dilemma for the German command was, from this point on, to become an increasingly acute one, although Halder's diehard faith in the success of the campaign prevented a timely realisation of the army's dire predicament. As Army Group Centre's advance to the east continued ahead of its two neighbouring army groups, its flanks became dangerously extended. Even if Strauss's and Weichs's infantry had been far enough forward, their respective 9th and 2nd Armies did not possess sufficient strength to cover the long flanks as well as support the panzer groups in the vanguard. Thus, Halder sought an offensive solution to clear the flanks and align the front, but in doing so he demonstrated his serious over-estimation of German offensive strength and a corresponding under-estimation of Soviet opposition. The result would push the motorised and panzer divisions beyond their offensive capacity, costing valuable strength and irreplaceable time.

By 13 July the problem on the flanks was becoming precarious. The continued progress at the centre of the front, where Hoth's and Guderian's forces were strongest, could not be matched by Kuntzen's LVII Panzer Corps (19th Panzer Division) in the north, which was too weak to make any headway (see Map 6).[123] In the south the problem was even more pronounced. The Pripet marshes formed a substantial natural barrier with Army Group South and, facing stiff resistance, Rundstedt's forces had no chance of keeping pace with Bock's advance and thereby covering his flank. Accordingly, it was here on 13 July that Timoshenko's offensive for the first time gained a worthy measure of success against the

---

[122] Ibid., p. 69 (12 July 1941).   [123] Ibid., p. 72 (13 July 1941).

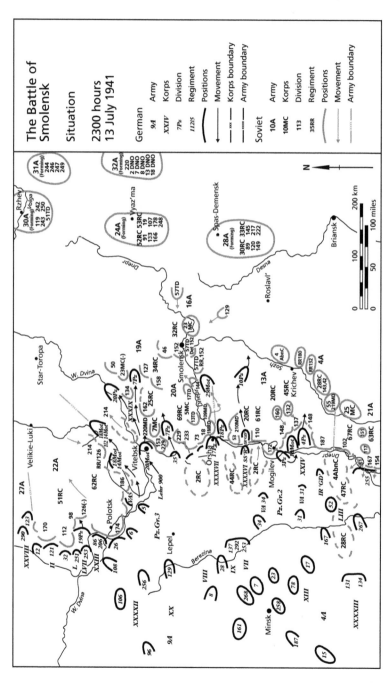

Map 6 Dispositions of Army Group Centre 13 July 1941: David M. Glantz, *Atlas of the Battle of Smolensk 7 July–10 September 1941*

dispersed and weakened German forces. The Soviet 21st Army proved the most successful, assaulting across the Dnepr River in the south and forcing the Germans out of Rogachev and Zhlobin. At the same time another corps of 21st Army thrust deep into the German rear towards Bobruisk with the 232nd Rifle Division advancing 80 kilometres and seizing bridges across the Beresina and Ptich Rivers. The drive was soon checked by Weichs's 2nd Army, which was forced to commit its reserves to help restore the situation. Rogachev and Zhlobin were also re-taken within a week, but the collective effort stalled Weichs's progress east and ultimately delayed his relief of Guderian's panzer forces.[124]

Timoshenko's offensive was also causing trouble further north where Schweppenburg's XXIV Panzer Corps was attempting to expand its bridgehead south of Mogilev. Of Schweppenburg's two panzer divisions, the 3rd Panzer Division was so exhausted, according to its Chief of Staff, that he requested support from the corps reserve.[125] This left the 4th Panzer Division to bear the brunt of attempts by the Soviet 13th and 4th Armies to lift the German siege at Mogilev. The result was much confused fighting with field units often unsure who was encircling whom. The Soviets also fought with a profound show of strength in artillery and anti-tank guns, exacting a great toll on the 4th Panzer Division's panzer regiment.[126] According to the divisional war diary, already on 13 July the regiment had only 'about 24 vehicles available'.[127] One former officer of the 4th Panzer Division recalled after the war:

If enemy resistance up to that time had been stiff in places but not so well organized, in the area south of Mogilev, we now had to defend against well-led counterattacks in divisional strength. Between 10 and 14 July several times we were forced to change over to a defence with open flanks and in all directions.[128]

In fact the divisions of the Soviet 13th and 4th Armies, both scarred veterans of the previous battles further west, were well below their nominal divisional strength. Guderian also assumed greater numbers after the war when he wrote of Timoshenko's offensive and attributed no fewer

[124] Glantz, *Battle for Smolensk*, p. 22.
[125] 'KTB 3rd Pz. Div. vom 16.8.40 bis 18.9.41' BA-MA RH 27–3/14, pp. 90–91 (12 July 1941).
[126] In the summer of 1941 a typical German panzer division was made up of a panzer regiment divided into three battalions. In addition, there was also a brigade of infantry, a battalion of anti-tank guns, a battalion of armoured reconnaissance, a regiment of artillery, a signals battalion and an engineers' battalion.
[127] 'Kriegstagebuch 4.Panzer-Division Führungsabtl. 26.5.41 – 31.3.42' BA-MA RH 27–4/27, p. 43 (13 July 1941).
[128] R. Koch-Erpach, '4th Panzer Division's Crossing of the Dnepr River and the Advance to Roslavl' in David M. Glantz (ed.), *The Initial Period of War*, p. 403.

than 20 divisions to the attack on his southern flank.[129] Actually the Soviet divisions in both armies numbered fewer than 3,000 men each and, although they did not achieve their objective of relieving Mogilev, their success is best understood by the impression they made on the Germans.[130] It was not the numerical strength of the Soviet armies that caused the 4th Panzer Division such difficulties, but more the division's own reduced manoeuvrability over the swampy terrain, physical fatigue, material losses and the fact that it was operating alone over an extensive battlefield without adequate flank protection. In other words, even a Soviet offensive launched with badly depleted forces was now encountering a German enemy on a far more even playing field, where the deadly German formula of concentrated strength and firepower, together with high battlefield mobility, was much less evident. Clearly a watershed was being reached, the character of the war was changing, and it was not just evident in 4th Panzer Division, but across the breadth of Army Group Centre and, indeed, the whole eastern front. The fighting was transforming the German war machine from a fine instrument into a blunt weapon, whereby the opposing armies were increasingly locked together in confused and ever more bloody encounters. The declining German ability to dictate the terms of battle added to the 'fog of war' prevailing on the battlefield and, according to one account, left command and control of operations at times in turmoil.

The Russians did not confine themselves to opposing the frontal advance of our Panzer Divisions. They further attempted to find every suitable occasion to operate against the flanks of the wedges driven in by our motorised elements, which, of necessity, had become extended and relatively weak... Situations were sometimes so confused that we, on our side, wondered if we were outflanking the enemy or whether he had outflanked us.[131]

In spite of Halder's continual optimism in the progress of the campaign, the slowing pace of the advance was becoming steadily more evident, causing Hitler to voice his concerns to his chief military adjutant Colonel Schmundt. 'The Führer', Schmundt told Hoth on 13 July, 'is somewhat worried that the panzer groups in the current battle may expend themselves before the coming wide-ranging operations.' According to Schmundt, Hitler also remarked: 'The Russian is a colossus and strong',[132] causing the dictator to reassert his intention to turn

---

[129] Guderian, *Panzer Leader*, p. 173.   [130] Glantz, *Battle for Smolensk*, pp. 21–22.
[131] As quoted in Clark, *Barbarossa*, p. 80.
[132] 'Panzerarmeeoberkommandos Anlagen zum Kriegstagesbuch "Berichte, Besprechungen, Beurteilungen der Lage" Bd.III 25.5.41 – 22.7.41' BA-MA RH 21–3/46, Fol. 151 (13 July 1941).

Guderian's panzer group south into the Ukraine to seize the harvest. Hoth's panzer group would be expected to conserve its strength by awaiting the arrival of the infantry and later continuing the drive on Moscow.[133] As a result of Hitler's heightened fears, Halder and Brauchitsch again appeared at Hitler's headquarters on 13 July with a summary of the campaign that once again exuded a sanguine confidence. Halder stated that the enemy front was in places 'thin' and held by forces of 'questionable strength'. He then reviewed the various sectors along the eastern front, expressing no hint of concern and even concluding that the attack on Guderian's southern flank was not worthy of any significant consideration, save that Guderian must protect his own flank. Halder also matter-of-factly observed that the main offensive along the Orscha–Vitebsk axis towards Smolensk 'was planned as a pincer movement, but for the most part is taking place as a frontal assault'.[134]

It is hard to know to what degree Halder's buoyant assessment reflected his own deluded understanding of events, and what was calculated to impress Hitler with the goal of maintaining the dictator's trust in the strategic direction of the OKH. From discussions of the previous day (12 July), Halder was aware of Hitler's renewed apprehension, particularly for the north. It is hardly surprising, therefore, that he now presented to Hitler Heusinger's hastily devised plan aimed at alleviating those fears and resolving any looming threat to the flanks. In the presentation of this plan, Halder deliberately ignored the fact that the main drive would still be centred on Smolensk and not on the flanks. In fact, Halder now gave Hitler the impression that his intention was to halt the drive on Moscow in favour of operations to the north-east and south-east of Smolensk, although his diary entry from the previous day makes clear that these new operations were to be conducted alongside continued thrusts around Smolensk. In all likelihood Halder's portrayal was nothing more than a ruse, telling Hitler what he wanted to hear, for in practice no new orders to this effect were forwarded to the panzer groups and the advance, with the bulk of the two panzer groups, continued unabated towards Smolensk. In all probability Halder did not foresee this fraudulent dishonesty as any great risk, for he doubtless also believed that the German armies were on the verge of breaking through the remaining elements of the Red Army and thereby prompting the collapse of the Soviet front.[135]

At the conclusion of Halder's presentation Hitler expressed his approval of the submitted plans and then went on to reiterate the importance of crushing the remaining Soviet military strength over a further

---

[133] Ibid. (13 July 1941).   [134] Franz Halder, KTB III, p. 72 (13 July 1941).
[135] Ibid., p. 73 (13 July 1941).

advance to the east. To this end, Hitler made special reference to elements of Hoth's armoured group assisting Leeb in the north, but the details were left to the army. This underscored Halder's perceptive understanding of Hitler's anxieties, and his cunning ability to manipulate reports to appease them, while maintaining the bulk of forces at the centre of Bock's front.

On the subject of Moscow, Hitler stated that the Soviet capital was to be subjected to a 'terror air raid' which, interestingly, he justified in part 'to disprove enemy propaganda which speaks of exhaustion of the German offensive capabilities'.[136] Yet, even Hitler's own characterisation of the Soviet state, according to Schmundt, as a strong colossus, suggests such enemy protestations were hardly fictional works of propaganda without any basis in fact. Certainly Bock was more aware of the diminishing strength of his motorised forces and when Halder's instruction reached him on 13 July, stating that operations would need to be extended towards the north and south, in addition to the ongoing eastward push at the centre of the front, Bock reacted with indignation. The army group commander immediately drove to 4th Panzer Army's headquarters to discuss the matter with Kluge and pressed his view that: 'If the armoured groups now fly apart to the south, east and north, it means forgoing the exploitation of our success.'[137] Bock was quickly becoming aware that as the drain on the army group's motorised forces grew, the orders of the higher command demonstrated little corresponding awareness of this fact. Consequently, overly ambitious orders were being issued without the sober remedial of sound judgement.

In Bock's discussion with Kluge the two Field Marshals were in complete agreement and so the army group commander instructed his Chief of Staff, Major-General Hans von Greiffenberg, to relay his dissatisfaction to Halder and press the need for a concentrated thrust eastwards with all the remaining resources under his command. Leaving nothing to chance, Bock also followed this up with a similarly-worded telegram to the OKH. That evening Bock elaborated in his diary on the problem:

I consider diverting elements of Panzer Group Hoth to the north while elements continue to march east to be futile. Because of the tremendous wear and tear on their equipment, the panzer groups are only still an effective striking force if employed in unison. I consider employing individual panzer corps to operate alone pointless, their fighting strength has become too low.[138]

Halder's reply exemplified his desire to placate Bock's concerns while maintaining his insistence on turning elements of Hoth's panzer group

[136] Ibid. (13 July 1941).
[137] Fedor von Bock, KTB 'Osten I', Fol. 23, *War Diary*, p. 247 (13 July 1941).
[138] Ibid., Fol. 24, p. 247 (13 July 1941).

north to aid Leeb. The swing north was described as taking place 'in the course of its forward movement', which, as Bock complained, was so loosely worded as to allow one to interpret it as he might wish.[139] Yet it was not as though Halder was ignorant of the declining state of the panzer forces. In addition to the concerns expressed by Bock, on 13 July Halder received a briefing from General Walter Buhle in which he was told that the panzer divisions were on average down to 50 per cent strength and the personnel losses had now exhausted the field replacement battalions.[140]

With the next stage of the German offensive becoming an increasingly open question, the field commanders too began debating the competing options, which, as Blumentritt stated, resulted in 'sharp exchanges of opinion'.[141] Bock did not mince words about the importance of an unhindered drive on Moscow with all the strength that could be mustered. Kluge on the other hand, in spite of having agreed with Bock's views on 13 July, was already advocating a new position by the following morning. According to the 3rd Panzer Group's war diary, when Kluge appeared on the morning of 14 July he declared that, of the three options at hand (southern, eastern and north-eastern), 'the southern would be the best, as there one could capture the strongest enemy forces, whereas Moscow would be a more political objective'.[142] Kluge's Chief of Staff confirmed after the war that in the dispute, Kluge 'was inclined to prefer Hitler's strategic concept'.[143] Blumentritt also noted Kluge's keen interest in Napoleon's campaign of 1812, reading General Armand de Caulaincourt's account 'with the greatest attention'.[144] This may have cautioned him, in the same fatalistic way it did Hitler, about treading the same path towards Moscow. Kluge's propensity for vacillation and at times agreeable subservience, especially in the presence of higher authority, soon earned him the nickname 'Clever Hans' (*Der kluge Hans*) and was to become decidedly more evident in later campaigns and the plot to assassinate Hitler.[145] Weichs likewise advocated the drive south and maintained this position even after the war when the generals found it convenient to blame the loss of the war on Hitler's diversion from Moscow.[146] Guderian has been said to have unreservedly favoured the push towards

[139] Ibid., Fol. 24, p. 248 (13 July 1941).
[140] Franz Halder, KTB III, p. 74 (13 July 1941).   [141] Blumentritt, 'Moscow', p. 51.
[142] 'Panzerarmeeoberkommandos Anlagen zum Kriegstagesbuch "Berichte, Besprechungen, Beurteilungen der Lage" Bd.III 25.5.41 – 22.7.41' BA-MA RH 21–3/46, Fol. 150 (14 July 1941).
[143] Blumentritt, 'Moscow', p. 51. See also Blumentritt's comments to Liddell Hart in Liddell Hart, *The Other Side of the Hill*, p. 275.
[144] Blumentritt, 'Moscow', pp. 34–35.
[145] Richard Lamb, 'Kluge' in Correlli Barnett (ed.), *Hitler's Generals* (London, 1989), pp. 404–408; Mitcham, *Hitler's Field Marshals*, p. 299.
[146] Hürter, *Hitlers Heerführer*, pp. 294–295, footnotes 78 and 79.

Moscow,[147] but there is evidence for some doubt. During a visit to Panzer Group 2 by Bock and Kesselring on 14 July, Guderian was away at the front and his place was taken by his Chief of Staff who, in the course of discussions, stated: 'The commander of the panzer group [Guderian] believes that the turn to the south and the link-up with panzer group Kleist should not be started after reaching the area around Smolensk, rather it should be carried out later from the Oka sector.'[148] Guderian later expressed a more emphatic commitment towards the seizure of Moscow, but his degree of devotion remains unknown, especially given his sudden about-face before Hitler in late August. Hoth, like Bock, was fixated by Moscow and saw little merit in rival alternatives for his panzer group. On 13 July, while acknowledging the difficulties of the campaign, he nevertheless advised that 'the last vehicle be set in the direction of Moscow'.[149]

By the middle of July 1941 Hitler's desire to rule the great expanses of the east finally seemed within his grasp. Certainly Halder's military briefings had done nothing to dissuade Hitler from this viewpoint – quite the contrary in fact. Halder's buoyant reporting on the military situation, with its brazen tone of optimism, upheld the most fanciful pillars of Hitler's *Weltanschauung*. At every stage the triumph of German arms was lauded over that of the inferior Soviet armies, providing a strident confirmation of Hitler's perverted racial conceptions and fuelling his unbridled thirst for conquest in an ever widening departure from reality. At the same time veiled qualms, voiced from various quarters, were either left unattended or dismissively rejected. It was in this atmosphere of unmitigated delusion that Hitler's revised War Directive 32a was issued on 14 July 1941, calling for a future reduction in the size of the army with resources being redirected towards the air force. Although retaining the ambitious tank building programme, the directive nevertheless stated: 'The extension of arms and equipment and the production of new weapons, munitions, and equipment will be related, with immediate effect, to the smaller forces which are contemplated for the future.'[150] As an instructive indication of the recurring importance of economic factors

---

[147] Macksey, 'Guderian', pp. 452–453; Macksey, *Guderian*, p. 142; Kenneth Macksey, 'Generaloberst Heinz Guderian' in Gerd R. Ueberschär (ed.), *Hitlers militärische Elite* (Darmstadt, 1998), p. 83.

[148] The 'Oka sector' pertains to the Oka River which runs north until it reaches Kaluga about 150 kilometres southwest of Moscow. 'KTB Nr.1 Panzergruppe 2 vom 22.6.1941 bis 21.7.41' BA-MA RH 21-2/927, Fol. 222 (14 July 1941).

[149] 'Panzerarmeeoberkommandos Anlagen zum Kriegstagesbuch "Berichte, Besprechungen, Beurteilung der Lage" Bd.III 25.5.41 – 22.7.41' BA-MA RH 21-3/46, Fol. 153 (13 July 1941); Hoth, *Panzer-Operationen*, p. 93.

[150] Trevor-Roper (ed.), *Hitler's War Directives 1939–1945*, p. 137.

Figure 6.2 As the Soviet armies near the border dissolved, countless armed groups hid in the extensive forests of Belorussia ambushing German supply columns.

in Hitler's strategic deliberations, the directive specifically pointed out: 'It is particularly important to ensure supplies of *raw materials and mineral oil*.'[151] Conspicuously for the intensifying strategic debate, it was only in the south of the Soviet Union, namely the mineral-rich Donets Basin in the eastern Ukraine and the oil-producing Caucasus, that Hitler could secure such commodities.

Caught in the hinterlands

As the swift advance east began to falter, observations made by Hoth on 13 July in his panzer group's war diary make clear the intractable predicament undercutting the German army's apparent success. Assessing the advance to distant objectives, Hoth bluntly observed: 'The expenditure of strength is greater than the success.' Yet with Soviet armies reeling in barely restrained chaos, there could be no question of a respite and so the motorised forces pressed on, mindful of their own dwindling strength, but unable to do anything about it. In substance, the Germans were damned if they stopped and damned if they did not, although Hoth was not yet drawing such an arrantly bleak conclusion. Instead the panzer

[151] Italics in the original; ibid, p. 138.

general acknowledged the 'heavy losses' of the campaign, but added that these were not in excess of those experienced in the previous western campaign. On the other hand, the physical strains, he stated, 'are very much greater', and he highlighted the oppressive conditions created by the heat and dust. For the first time, Hoth also called into question the morale of his men, citing a multitude of factors beginning with the 'barren expanses of the land and the doggedness of the enemy'. Furthermore, Hoth remarked on the state of the roads and bridges, as well as the fact that throughout the enormous operational area: 'Everywhere the enemy is taking up arms.' In conclusion the panzer general summed up the emerging frustration of his men, among whom there was 'constantly the feeling, should the motorised troops have to do everything alone?'[152]

Certainly Hoth illustrated a perceptive understanding of the burdens of his men, for which he was commonly known among them by the affectionate nickname 'Daddy Hoth' (*Papa Hoth*). Yet Hoth's commentary on the motivation of enemy soldiers was equally enlightening and, if accurate, constituted a decidedly adverse development for the Germans. 'The Russian soldier', Hoth judged, 'fights not out of fear, rather idea. He does not want to return to the tsarist time.'[153] Given the ruthlessly despotic rule the Germans were bringing to the east, and their genocidal practices, the worst fears of the Soviet people were soon confirmed, which greatly helped solidify their support for Stalin's cause.[154] In the occupied territories, suddenly freed from Stalin's own brand of repressive rule, active opposition to the Germans was not always an immediate instinct. The extraordinarily brutal German occupation, however, which included the pitiless exploitation of the population (often begun by the first waves of German troops), the murderous practices of the SS *Einsatzgruppen*

---

[152] 'Panzerarmeeoberkommandos Anlagen zum Kriegstagesbuch "Berichte, Besprechungen, Beurteilungen der Lage" Bd.III 25.5.41 – 22.7.41' BA-MA RH 21-3/46, Fol. 153 (13 July 1941). See also Hoth, *Panzer-Operationen*, pp. 92–93.

[153] 'Panzerarmeeoberkommandos Anlagen zum Kriegstagesbuch "Berichte, Besprechungen, Beurteilungen der Lage" Bd.III 25.5.41 – 22.7.41' BA-MA RH 21-3/46, Fol. 153 (13 July 1941).

[154] One Red Army Captain told a British correspondent in Autumn 1941: 'This is a very grim war. And you cannot imagine the hatred the Germans have stirred up amoung our people. We are easy-going, good-natured people, you know; but I assure you, they have turned our people into spiteful *mujiks*. *Zlyie mujiki* – that's what we've got in the Red Army now, men thirsting for revenge' (Werth, *Russia at War 1941–1945*, p. 194). Another Red Army soldier wrote to his wife in early 1942: 'However much they write in the newspapers about their atrocities the reality is much worse. I've been in some of the places where the beasts have been. I've seen the burned-out towns and villages, the corpses of women and children, the unhappy, plundered residents, but also I've seen the tears of joy when these people encountered us. . . . The spirit of these places has affected me and it has grown in all our soldiers' (as cited in Merridale, *Ivan's War*, p. 127; see also p. 133).

(action groups), the army's own criminal orders and the harsh rule of the rear-area security divisions, soon banished any hopes of a better life under German rule. As a result, the great majority of the occupied Soviet Union (outside of the Baltic states and parts of the Ukraine) were either ambivalent to the German cause or actively hostile to it. There was no attempt by the Germans to win over the people because in a short, decisive war their participation would not be necessary; what was needed could simply be taken and thereafter the population would be reduced to servitude.

On 14 July Halder took heart from Guderian's 'surprising progress' and Hoth's 'very good forward movement',[155] yet, as in the initial operations, the advance continued at the expense of bypassing formidable Soviet formations, which were again to plague the rear area of the panzer groups. While this had caused its share of problems during the formation of the Belostok–Minsk pocket, the much greater distances and increased vehicle losses made the newly developing encirclement centred on Smolensk an immensely more difficult undertaking. Operating in the vast depths of the Soviet Union, the neglect of logistical considerations was rapidly presenting the army with a new set of serious complications. As Clausewitz warned, from his intimate knowledge of Napoleon's disastrous campaign in 1812, the importance of maintaining supply lines was fundamental to an attacking army. 'These arteries', as Clausewitz termed supply lines, 'then, must not be permanently cut, nor must they be too long or difficult to use. A long road always means a certain waste of strength, which tends to cripple the condition of the army.'[156]

In the initial stage of the advance the panzer groups were principally dependent on the truck-based *Grosstransportraum* bringing supplies to the front from border depots. As the front advanced and the distances grew, only a corresponding advancement of the railways could maintain an adequate forward flow of provisions capable of meeting the needs of the army. Yet this depended on a number of factors not least of which was security in the rear areas. Expecting a short and conclusive end to the border battles, General Wagner, the army Quartermaster-General, told Halder on 1 July of his 'serious worry' for the pacification of the rear areas. 'The particularities of our military approach', Wagner told Halder, 'have resulted in an extensive insecurity in the rear area by insurgent enemy elements. The security divisions alone are not enough for the great spaces. We must also employ several divisions from the front line

---

[155] Franz Halder, KTB III, p. 76 (14 July 1941).
[156] Howard and Paret (eds.), Carl von Clausewitz, *On War*, p. 412.

troops.'[157] By 7 July, 9th Army was complaining it was receiving only one-third of its allotted daily entitlement in rail supply and the following day even this meagre allocation was cut off in favour of giving maximum support to Panzer Group 3. This now meant that 9th Army had to supply itself using its largely horse-drawn *Grosstransportraum* over terrible roads to a distance of 400 kilometres.[158] Not surprisingly, Bock remarked to Halder a few days later about the 'overexerted' state of the army group's horses.[159]

Even with the concentrated effort of directing the railroads to supply the motorised divisions, the fact remained that demand still greatly outstripped what the feeble rail network could supply. The assumption had been made during Barbarossa's planning stage that large quantities of Soviet rolling stock and locomotives would be captured in the initial phase of the campaign, providing support for the drive into the Soviet Union, while the railroad troops (*Eisenbahntruppe*) extended the German gauge. Yet, once the initial shock and confusion of the invasion had passed, the Soviets were quick to institute an extensive evacuation of their trains with the subsequent demolition of those remaining behind. This was so effective that, by the end of August 1941, the Germans had captured only around 1,000 Soviet locomotives of which just half were still operational.[160] This critical setback had two major repercussions for the German campaign. First, the army became almost immediately reliant on extending the narrow-gauge lines as quickly as possible in order to assume the enormous burden of sustaining operations to the east. Planning for this conversion did not anticipate the effects the Soviet 'scorched earth' policy[161] would have on the railroads and installations, nor the extent of destruction caused by the Luftwaffe and front-line units in earlier combat operations. The conversion was therefore slower than expected and achieved only by the most rudimentary standards of quality control.[162] The second complication of the German failure to capture large numbers of Soviet trains was that the deficit had to be made up by the already overextended *Reichsbahn* (German railways). By the autumn of 1941 some 2,500 German locomotives and 200,000 railcars had to be employed in the east, creating additional stresses for the German economy.[163]

Given the inadequate quantity of captured Soviet equipment and the difficulties of conversion, it was hardly surprising that by 10 July Wagner

---

[157] Franz Halder, KTB III, p. 32 (1 July 1941).
[158] Van Creveld, *Supplying War*, p. 168.
[159] Franz Halder, KTB III, p. 62 (10 July 1941).
[160] Schüler, 'The Eastern Campaign', p. 210.   [161] Glantz, *Barbarossa*, pp. 73–74.
[162] Schüler, 'The Eastern Campaign', pp. 210–211.
[163] Reinhardt, *Moscow – The Turning Point*, p. 147.

was expressing his concern at the limited railroad capacity towards Minsk, to which Halder added the note, 'in the last few days very poor capacity'. Wagner added that the average losses in the *Grosstransportraum*, which were running at 25 per cent, were compounding the problem.[164] With the depth of operations from the supply depots constantly increasing and the overstretched *Grosstransportraum* simultaneously contracting, it was no surprise that units throughout Army Group Centre were rapidly outrunning their supply apparatus. It was therefore something of an understatement when Halder described the logistics of the army group on 11 July as merely 'strained', especially since he expressed his belief that the strain would be overcome in two days.[165] Characteristically, the Chief of the General Staff gave no impression that he grasped the true gravity of the crisis, or the dire implications this held for his incessantly optimistic conception of the campaign. Halder, it seems, was largely basing his opinion on the highly subjective information provided to him by Wagner, but the scale of disparity between reality and delusion was far too great to exonerate Halder – and indeed a large part of the General Staff – of a significant degree of blame.

Among the litany of oversights and falsehoods that underscored the German conception of Operation Barbarossa, the OKH's fixation with Moscow is perhaps most conspicuous for the fact that it was simply an unattainable goal within the prevailing time frame. The paramount importance of logistics rendered the various strategic arguments advanced by the generals, however favourable they might have been, entirely superfluous. Equally so, the questionable preoccupation of some historians with hypothetical 'what if' scenarios[166] likewise tends to ignore or understate logistical considerations, which alone made the seizure of Moscow, within the confines of the operational timetable, a preordained impossibility.[167] Like so much of the stubborn confidence pervading the German high command, however, negative conclusions were rapidly supplanted by adherence to Hitler's maxim: 'To the German soldier nothing is impossible!'[168] Thus, in spite of all the encroaching difficulties Wagner nevertheless assured Halder on 12 July that the panzer groups could reach Moscow, although he left open the question

---

[164] Franz Halder, KTB III, p. 63 (10 July 1941); Krumpelt, *Das Material*, p. 167.
[165] Halder, KTB III, p. 66 (11 July 1941).
[166] Stolfi, *Hitler's Panzers East*, Chapter 12, 'Constructing an Alternate Historical Past: Taking Moscow and Defeating the Soviet Union. August–October 1941'.
[167] Schüler, 'The Eastern Campaign', pp. 211–213; Weinberg, *A World At Arms*, pp. 269–270. Geoffrey P. Megargee, *War of Annihilation. Combat and Genocide on the Eastern Front 1941* (Lanham, 2006), pp. 80–81.
[168] Cecil, *Hitler's Decision to Invade Russia 1941*, p. 134. See also Fest, *Hitler*, p. 647.

of whether the infantry armies could reach even as far as Smolensk.[169] Two days later on 14 July, as the motorised forces were again striking out to the east, Wagner's assessment underwent a abrupt change, which reflected for the first time the cold reality of the German predicament. The Quartermaster-General conceded to Halder: 'The situation is still difficult. The railway capacity is not yet sufficient. Pz. Gr. [2 and 3 of Kluge's] 4th Army will reach to the east of Smolensk. The 2nd Army, given its provisioning, will not get far beyond the Dnepr with the mass of its troops. The 9th Army not far beyond the area of Vitebsk [on the Dvina].'[170] As the newly appointed commander of the 17th Panzer Division, General of Panzer Troops Wilhelm Ritter von Thoma,[171] stated after the war: 'In modern warfare the tactics are not the main thing. The decisive factor is the organisation of one's resources – to maintain the momentum.'[172]

Wagner's sudden acknowledgement of Army Group Centre's logistical limitations did not mean that solutions were any easier to come by as all available resources were already being utilised to sustain the fragile supply system. Nor did it mean that there was any perceptible change in the practices of the OKH; they were simply responding to the steadily rising cries for help from the field units. In essence, one might say they only became aware of how deep the hole was when they fell to the bottom of it. Guderian's Panzer Group 2, for example, complained on 15 July that the supply situation was becoming more and more difficult as a result of the distances, bad roads and insecure rear areas. Such factors, the panzer group's war diary concluded, 'are what make an eastern campaign such a special case. All considerations and tactical actions are dependent to a great degree on this. Operations that do not take this into account are condemned to failure.'[173] On the following day (16 July) the panzer group's Quartermaster-General was more specific in his criticism. 'Fuel is especially lacking. The supplies arrive only sparsely, above all the railway situation is by no means enough.'[174] Combined with the abysmal planning for the provisioning of the army, the poor road conditions exacerbated the problem by instituting more demands on the supply services while at the same time weakening their ability to carry out such requests.

[169] Franz Halder, KTB III, p. 71 (12 July 1941).

[170] Ibid., p. 78 (14 July 1941). See also p. 87 (16 July 1941).

[171] The previous commander, General Ritter von Weber, was mortally wounded on 18 July 1941.

[172] Liddell Hart, *The Other Side of the Hill*, p. 247. See also the informed discussion in Krumpelt, *Das Material und die Kriegführung*, Chapters 14 and 16.

[173] 'KTB Nr.1 Panzergruppe 2 vom 22.6.1941 bis 21.7.41' BA-MA RH 21–2/927, Fols. 234–235 (15 July 1941).

[174] 'Kriegstagebuch der O.Qu.-Abt. Pz. A.O.K.2 von 21.6.41 bis 31.3.42' BA-MA RH 21–2/819, Fol. 296 (16 July 1941).

An entry from the war diary of the 3rd Panzer Division's Quartermaster-General made clear that stocks of tyres, on which the truck-based supply system depended, were 'extremely limited' and in fact consisted of only one sixth of the total requirement.[175]

In Hoth's Panzer Group 3 the same difficulties were also hampering its ability to sustain operations further east. On 15 July the 20th Panzer Division was at the forefront of the German charge into the Soviet Union, but its war diary talked of 'the greatest worry' being the consumption of fuel which had 'drastically surged'.[176] Part of the problem for Hoth was that the terrain north of Vitebsk was less favourable to mechanised warfare with the landscape dominated by swamps, lakes and woods, and punctuated by rolling hills which extended down to Smolensk.[177] On 14 July General Schmidt, even after having travelled along countless Soviet roads, described 20th Panzer Division's route as simply 'unbelievable'.[178] Further north the 19th Panzer Division, after having been restricted to the Disna bridgehead from 4 July to 12 July, was at last making headway on the army group's northern flank.[179] Yet Bock's concern that his forces had become too weak to attempt such a far-reaching operation was soon confirmed by the nearly impassable terrain, to say nothing of enemy resistance. On 14 July the war diary of the LVII Panzer Corps recorded that the 19th Panzer Division's forward march 'suffered greatly throughout the day because of the indescribable road condition... In places the vehicles must be pulled or pushed separately through the deepest sand, which results in hold ups of hours on end.'[180] The problem was that every mile of difficult terrain for the front-line units was a further mile the seriously over-extended supply columns would also have to traverse between the distant railheads and the forward depots. Added to this was the ever threatening security situation in the expanding rear areas, which the exposed and badly armed supply columns were poorly disposed to counter.

By the middle of July the security situation in the army group's rear area was dire. As the large Soviet forces concentrated along the great rivers were bypassed by Bock's swift moving motorised divisions, the Soviets found themselves cut off to the east but in many places unchallenged,

[175] 'KTB 3rd Pz. Div. I.b 19.5.41 – 6.2.42' BA-MA RH 27–3/218 (14 July 1941).
[176] 'KTB 20th Pz. Div. vom 25.5.41 bis 15.8.41' BA-MA RH 27–20/2, Fol. 47 (15 July 1941).
[177] Kipp, 'Barbarossa and the Crisis', p. 126.
[178] '3rd Pz. Gr. KTB 25.5.41 – 31.8.41' BA-MA Microfilm 59054, Fol. 129 (14 July 1941).
[179] Hoth, *Panzer-Operationen*, p. 93.
[180] 'Gen.Kdo.LVII.Pz.Korps Kriegstagesbuch Nr.1 vom 15.2. – 31.10.41' BA-MA RH 24–57/2, pp. 173–175 (14 July 1941). See also 'Kriegstagesbuch 19.Panzer-Division Abt.Ib für die Zeit vom 1.6.1941 – 31.12.1942' BA-MA RH 27–19/23, Fol. 14 (15 July 1941).

leaving them in the veritable eye of the German storm. One front had largely passed them by but the following infantry had not yet arrived. Thus, the panzer group's supply columns still had to run the gauntlet of this treacherous area over terrible roads and makeshift river crossings because the Soviets still defended the major centres where the infrastructure was at least somewhat better. Even where the Germans had forced their crossings and continued on to the east, there was scarcely any such thing as a secured area and it was soon realised that this would not change until the mass of Soviet forces had been rooted out of their fortified river front positions. In the meantime, however, the flow of supplies was threatened with strangulation and this led to some disagreement at the lower levels on the virtue of continuing the advance. The Quartermaster-General's diary for the 3rd Panzer Division reported:

The supply situation does not permit a further advance to the east. The Quartermaster-General's section reported this to the general [Lieutenant-General Walther Model] and his staff, nevertheless the general ordered a further thrust eastward... The supply route of the division is extremely bad and insecure, enemy elements in the forests on both sides of the highway.[181]

This worrisome situation was common to both panzer groups and also troubling to Bock, who was equally mindful that the OKH and Hitler were keen to embark on new operations on the flanks, which Bock recognised was beyond his army group's strength. On 15 July he telephoned Brauchitsch and told him: 'I have the impression that there is a fundamental difference in the assessment of the situation between the Army High Command and the army group.' He then went on to detail the strength of Soviet forces attacking his southern flank from Gomel, the presence of Soviet strongholds in his rear at Mogilev and Orsha on the Dnepr and Polotsk on the Dvina, and another group he reported was operating north of Gorodok. In addition, the large area in the triangle between Smolensk–Orsha–Vitebsk contained, according to Bock, between 12 and 20 enemy divisions. Thus Bock cautioned that while the crossing of the Dnepr was a favourable development: 'One must be careful not to take the overall situation there too lightly based on local impressions. A victory has not yet been won!'[182]

Brauchitsch's response was one of indifference. He insisted that the planned battle of Smolensk be brought to a conclusion, while at the same time 'guarding the southeast flank' and conducting the northern operation to assist Leeb's forces, 'in accordance with the directive issued by me'. As if deaf to Bock's pleas for a curtailment of the operation, at the

[181] 'KTB 3rd Pz. Div. I.b 19.5.41 – 6.2.42' BA-MA RH 27–3/218 (17 July 1941).
[182] Fedor von Bock, KTB 'Osten I', Fol. 27, *War Diary*, pp. 249–250 (15 July 1941).

end of the meeting Brauchitsch made the astonishing observation that 'by and large, the views of the army group and of the Army High Command coincided!' Perhaps Brauchitsch thought that Bock had momentarily lost his nerve and was overstating the danger, yet, immediately after issuing his instructions which merely restated the standing orders agreed upon by Hitler and Halder, Brauchitsch unexpectedly expressed to Bock his own grim outlook regarding further operations beyond Smolensk. With surprising frankness, Brauchitsch told Bock:

A continued drive to the east by the panzers after the capture of the area around Smolensk is out of the question... We must be clear that after taking the area around Smolensk a continued advance by the entire body of infantry is no longer possible for reasons of supply. We will have to make do with a sort of 'expeditionary corps', which together with tanks will have to fulfil far-reaching missions.[183]

Clearly there was a paradox in the army's understanding of the war. Army Group Centre was reaching the limit of its advance, mobility within the motorised divisions was sharply declining, panzer losses were rapidly mounting and the Red Army, far from being beaten, was in fact fielding numerous new armies further east. The end of the blitzkrieg was already in sight and the so-called 'expeditionary corps' were a fanciful substitute, grossly inadequate for carrying through the planned operations to distant objectives. Yet none of the military professionals, not even Bock who seemed to possess the clearest head, could see how menacing the signs really were. Certainly none were yet talking of failing to win the war or worse – being bogged down in a slogging positional war over the winter. Interestingly, Admiral Wilhelm Canaris, the chief of the military intelligence and counter-intelligence department of the OKW, visited Bock on the evening of 17 July, for which Bock's only comment was: 'he fears the worst' ('er sieht schwarz in schwarz').[184] Five days earlier on 12 July Weichs wrote home to his wife that the operational situation was cause for 'some worry, because the Russian was fighting far better than we anticipated'. He then went on to express the hope that the Red Army would not escape behind Moscow or the winter period would not be 'entirely simple'.[185] Further afield, the Italian dictator Mussolini was likewise airing grave reservations about the war. As Ciano recorded on 16 July:

The Duce [Mussolini] is not convinced as to the course of events in Russia. The tone of his conversation today was distinctly pessimistic, particularly as the

---

[183] Ibid., Fols. 27–28, p. 251 (15 July 1941).
[184] Ibid., Fol. 32 (17 July 1941). The English edition of Bock's diary incorrectly dates the visit by Canaris as taking place on 15 July. Fedor von Bock, *The War Diary 1939–1945*, p. 252 (15 July 1941).
[185] Hürter, *Hitlers Heerführer*, p. 286.

Anglo-Russia alliance makes Stalin the head of a nationalist Russia. He is afraid
that Germany is facing a task that is too much for her, and will not reach a
complete solution of the whole problem before winter, which always reveals a lot
of unknown factors.[186]

In attempting to compile an accurate appraisal of the war on the eastern
front in the summer of 1941, no aspect is more elusive or shrouded in
ambiguity than the war being fought behind the front by cut-off Red
Army units or newly established partisan brigades.[187] A central problem
in drawing any general conclusions from this aspect of the conflict is the
variety of factors which influenced the insurgents' success and varied
from region to region according to population, geography or presence of
occupation forces. The clandestine nature of the fighting and presence
of irregular forces also left far fewer records with which to reconstruct
the events taking place. For a number of years western scholars have
been keen to downplay the often wildly exaggerated mythology spawned
by Soviet histories which encouraged the impression of a spontaneous
national revolt against the German invasion.[188] Accordingly, western
studies have been at pains to point out the inauspicious beginnings of the
partisan movement and have emphasised their diminutive contribution
in the early period of the war.[189] It is by no means the intention of this
study to seek a reinterpretation of this conclusion, but in addition to
the already formidable difficulties confronting the German blitzkreig in
the east, the importance of rear-area engagements in slowing or wearing
down the all-important motorised and panzer divisions should not be
under-estimated. Most commonly, the contribution of partisan forces
did not result from conventional attacks on front-line forces, but rather
from attacks on the vulnerable supply columns following in the rear. The
Quartermaster-General for Panzer Group 2 reported on 16 July that the
supply difficulties resulted from 'frequent obstruction of the roads by
insurgent enemy elements'.[190]

---

[186] Muggeridge (ed.), *Ciano's Diary*, p. 370 (16 July 1941).

[187] For the most recent overview of the Soviet partisan movement in World War II see
Kenneth Slepyan, *Stalin's Guerrillas. Soviet Partisans in World War II* (Lawrence, 2006).

[188] Joachim Hoffmann, 'Die Kriegführung aus der Sicht der Sowjetunion' in
Militärgeschichtliches Forschungsamt (ed.), *Das Deutsche Reich und der Zweite Weltkrieg*,
Band IV, p. 752.

[189] Alexander Hill, *The War Behind the Eastern Front. The Soviet Partisan Movement in
North-West Russia 1941–1944* (New York, 2005); Matthew Cooper, *The Phantom War.
The German Struggle Against Soviet Partisans 1941–1944* (London, 1979), Chapter 2,
'The Failure of the Partisan Movement – 1941'. See also the useful discussion in
Grenkevich, *The Soviet Partisan Movement*, pp. 157–162.

[190] 'KTB Nr.1 Panzergruppe 2 vom 22.6.1941 bis 21.7.41' BA-MA RH 21-2/927,
Fol. 241 (16 July 1941).

A cause for some confusion in our understanding of the early partisan movement is one of definition. Strictly speaking it is impossible to talk of the partisan movement as a unified entity. Political objectives varied so much that, while some groups pursued nationalist aspirations against both German and Soviet regimes, others cared little for any higher authority and distinguished themselves only as opportunist gangs striking whatever target promised the most lucrative booty. Even among those groups committed to fighting the German occupation, there were radical differences in the vigour with which this resistance was conducted as well as in ability to carry out planned actions. The better organised and more centrally controlled partisan forces, in the form we commonly understand them from 1942/43, hardly existed in the early months of the war. The tide of fierce resistance in the rear areas was instead largely carried out by the countless thousands of Soviet soldiers cut off behind the German advance and determined to continue resisting.[191] Whether one chooses to acknowledge these forces as 'partisans' or not (those that were not killed, captured or able to fight their way back to Soviet lines often formed the nucleus of partisan detachments) they played a pivotal role in striking at one of the German army's weakest links in the vacuum of security that existed behind the German motorised divisions.[192] On 16 July Halder noted: 'In the area passed through by Hoth and Guderian countless battle-worthy enemy groups are forcing our motorised divisions to form fronts in all directions. Even west of the Dnepr enemy groups are resurging.'[193] Another German officer alluded to the problem of dealing with POWs in a forward unit and the subsequent danger this posed to the rear area.

During our advance we took a lot of prisoners. We sent them back, but had not too much control over whether they arrived at the collecting points. (You could not detach a full APC [armoured personnel carrier] with six men to guard three or four prisoners.)
   This certainly contributed very much to the amazingly quick establishment of the partisan units.[194]

Even as the infantry of the 9th and 2nd Armies retraced the path of the motorised divisions there was no time to flush out the vast swamps and forests systematically looking for rogue enemy elements that were, in any

---

[191] Rudolf-Christoph Frhr. von Gersdorff, *Soldat im Untergang* (Frankfurt am Main, 1977), p. 103.
[192] Edgar M. Howell, *The Soviet Partisan Movement 1941–1944* (Washington, 1956), p. 42.
[193] Franz Halder, KTB III, p. 83 (16 July 1941).
[194] Koch-Erpach, 'Crossing of the Dnepr River', p. 404.

case, not yet fully recognised for the threat they posed. Yet to the German soldiers operating in the densely wooded regions the perils were soon well known. On 25 June Ernst-Günter Merten wrote: 'Yesterday afternoon we learned a new art of warfare: tree sniper fire. Unfortunately there were a few killed in the battalion . . . As the march continued everyone was a little nervous.'[195] Three days later Doctor Hermann Türk noted in his diary: 'Last night some more of our soldiers were shot by snipers.'[196] By early July Army Group Centre's rear area was becoming enormous, making control over the vast forests impossible. One soldier's letter, written at the beginning of July, suggested that the forests were more deadly than the battlefields:

> Any snipers who fall into our hands are of course shot; their bodies lie everywhere. Sadly, though, many of our own comrades have been lost to their dirty methods. We're losing more men to the bandits than in the fighting itself.
>
> Hardly any sleep to be had. We're all awake and alert almost every night. You have to be in case they attack suddenly. If the sentry drops his guard just once then it could be all over for us all. Travelling alone is out of the question.[197]

With the passing of the combat formations, Army Group Centre's vast rear area was then to be governed by a handful of poorly equipped security divisions assisted by a collection of SS and police.[198] What these forces lacked in manpower and mobility to control the vast area, they sought to make up for by the unrestrained spread of terror throughout the occupied territories. Mass shootings and draconian rule were the order of the day – a formula which General Lothar Rendulic bluntly illustrated with the maxim, 'success comes only through terror'.[199] On 16 July Hitler also expressed his endorsement for such methods. 'The Russians', he declared, 'have now ordered partisan warfare behind our front. This also has its advantages: it gives us the opportunity to . . . exterminate . . . all who oppose us.'[200] Conducting his war of annihilation under the veiled cover of a military operation against insurgents, Hitler soon enlisted the support of the OKW when Keitel issued orders calling for the most ruthless measures to counter resistance in the rear areas.[201] The directive

---

[195] Kempowski (ed.), *Das Echolot Barbarossa '41*, p. 98 (25 June 1941).
[196] Ibid., p. 141 (28 June 1941).
[197] As quoted in Shepherd, *War in the Wild East*, pp. 77–78.
[198] For a complete listing of these forces see Antonio Munoz and Oleg V. Romanko, *Hitler's White Russians: Collaboration, Extermination and Anti-Partisan Warfare in Byelorussia 1941–1944. A Study of White Russian Collaboration and German Occupation Policies* (New York, 2003), p. 122–126.
[199] Shepherd, *War in the Wild East*, p. 45.
[200] As quoted in Ziemke and Bauer, *Moscow to Stalingrad*, p. 207.
[201] Jürgen Förster, 'Die Sicherung des "Lebensraumes" Sowjetunion' in Militärgeschichtliches Forschungsamt (ed.), *Das Deutsche Reich und der Zweite Weltkrieg*, Band IV, pp. 1036–1037.

appeared on 23 July and stipulated that resistance should be quelled 'not by legal punishment of the guilty, but by striking such terror into the population that it loses all will to resist'.[202] Although the fierce resistance in the rear was initially sustained by the isolated mass of Red Army units trapped behind enemy lines, the lurid German terror sought to forestall any further popular resistance among the peasant population.

For all the burgeoning problems of logistics and security in the rear areas, the panzer and motorised divisions drove vigorously on, oblivious to the fading hope of eradicating organised Soviet resistance. On the surface the armoured forces still seemed capable of impressive action, with deep advances by all the armoured corps in the week following the penetration of the Dvina and Dnepr rivers (see Map 7), resulting most notably in the 29th Motorised Division fighting its way into Smolensk on 16 July.[203] Yet the rigours of the advance meant the two panzer groups were fast running themselves into the ground. On 16 July Lemelsen, the commander of the XXXXVII Panzer Corps, advised higher command that the 18th Panzer Division could no longer be looked on as fully combat ready. His report stated that after 25 days of uninterrupted heavy fighting the division had suffered heavy losses in officers and men as well as weapons and trucks. 'The heavy exhaustion of the troops', the corps diary recorded, 'had at times led to a completely apathetic attitude. Also the remaining serviceable material is so run-down, that further heavy fallout must be expected.'[204] Nor was the example of the 18th Panzer Division atypical. From an initial strength of 169 tanks, the 4th Panzer Division could field only 40 tanks by the evening of 17 July.[205] Likewise, the 10th Panzer Division reported on 16 July that the fallout rate among its tanks had 'alarmingly increased'[206] with just 30 per cent of its original strength still serviceable.[207] The 7th Panzer Division began the war with close to 300 tanks, but by 21 July 120 of these were in repair and another 77 total losses, leaving only about one-third of its original

[202] Trevor-Roper (ed.), *Hitler's War Directives 1939–1945*, p. 144.
[203] The city of Smolensk had a wartime population of just 170,000 inhabitants and early on fell under complete German control. The city's name, however, is given to the wide-ranging battles between Timoshenko's Western Front and Bock's Army Group Centre in July and August.
[204] 'Kriegstagebuch Nr.2 XXXXVII.Pz.Korps. Ia 25.5.1941 – 22.9.1941' BA-MA RH 24–47/2 (16 July 1941).
[205] 'Kriegstagebuch 4.Panzer-Division Führungsabtl. 26.5.41 – 31.3.42' BA-MA RH 27–4/10, p. 58 (17 July 1941).
[206] 'Kriegstagebuch der 10.Panzer Division Nr.5 vom: 22.5. bis: 7.10.41' BA-MA RH 27–10/26a. This war diary has no folio stamped page numbers so references must be located using the date (16 July 1941).
[207] 'KTB Nr.1 Panzergruppe 2 vom 22.6.1941 bis 21.7.41' BA-MA RH 21–2/927, Fol. 243 (16 July 1941).

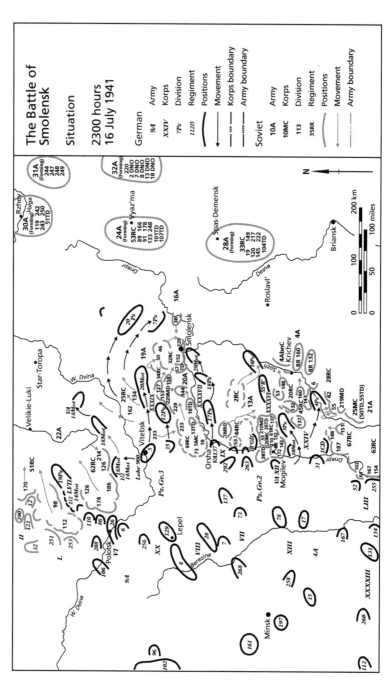

Map 7 Dispositions of Army Group Centre 16 July 1941: David M. Glantz, *Atlas of the Battle of Smolensk 7 July–10 September 1941*

strength available for action.[208] Beyond motorised vehicles the army's other main source of transportation, the horse, was suffering too. In the sole cavalry division in the German army (1st Cavalry Division) a total of 2,292 horses had been lost in the period up to 12 July with just 1,027 captured horses to offset the deficit.[209]

Although of less immediate importance to the prosecution of the war, personnel losses throughout the German army were also rising sharply, illustrating the intensity of the fighting. In just the first three and a half weeks (from 22 June to 16 July) German casualties had reached 102,588 men,[210] a rate of loss sustainable given the available reserves, but only if the war remained short and hostilities were largely concluded by the end of the summer.[211]

One of the central conditions for victory in Germany's war against the Soviet Union was the necessity of retaining mobility – both to outmanoeuvre and defeat the large Soviet armies and to ensure the occupation of enough industrial and economic centres to forestall continued large-scale resistance from the east. In short, the German army depended upon maintaining the swift pace of operations which typified its earlier successes. The fatal over-extension of its logistical system and the exhaustion of its panzer and motorised divisions before Smolensk may appear to be an unspectacular measure of defeat by the historical comparatives of Waterloo or Tannenberg, but a fundamental and ultimately ruinous defeat it remains. Germany did not fail in Operation Barbarossa by a crushing defeat in a major battle, nor can the performance of the Red Army take the credit; they failed by losing the ability to win the war. Yet it is for this same reason that the German defeat was not a knockout blow, but rather one which doomed Germany to fighting a war far different from the one the generals had planned and consequently were not prepared for. Caught in the vast Soviet hinterlands, the front promptly started to settle down into gritty positional warfare more reminiscent of World War I, while the war of manoeuvre became more and more limited to specific sectors of the front.

---

[208] Rothe and Ohrloff, '7th Panzer Division Operations', p. 389. The source gives individual figures for each model of tank in the division, but the addition of these figures is inconsistent with the totals given. The corrected totals have been quoted here.

[209] '1.Kav.Div. Ia: KTB Anl. Von 1.4.1941 – 23.7.1941' BA-MA RH 29–1/5. This war diary has no folio stamped page numbers so references must be located using the date (15 July 1941).

[210] Franz Halder, KTB III, p. 95 (19 July 1941).

[211] Interestingly, figures indicate that some 30 per cent more wounded soldiers died of their wounds on the eastern front than in the recent western campaign. In the winter of 1941–1942 the percentage rose to 49 per cent. The vast distance and the often overwhelmed medical resources probably accounted for this. Kroener, 'Die Winter 1941/42', p. 879.

7 The battle of Smolensk

The end of blitzkrieg

The declining strength of the motorised divisions was not the only factor compromising their ability to function effectively. The discordant strategic deployment of each corps – fanning out towards divergent objectives over wide areas – denied them the benefits of concentration and forced them to operate in a degree of isolation. The most far-flung and wayward operation was that of Kuntzen's LVII Panzer Corps, which, on Halder's orders (and against Bock's better judgement), was sent to enact a joint encirclement with Leeb's Army Group North. After a difficult drive over sunken roads, the spearhead of the corps (19th Panzer Division) took Nevel on 15 July.[1] From here the division could have swung north and encircled the Soviet 51st Rifle Corps (as intended by Halder) or south to envelope the 62nd Rifle Corps,[2] yet both of these options were disregarded by Hoth who instead ordered a continued forward drive to the northeast to seize Velikie Luki.[3] There can be no question of Velikie Luki's strategic importance, yet Bock's concern that individual panzer corps had become too weak to operate alone[4] was especially relevant to Kuntzen's corps given that it only consisted of two divisions (19th Panzer Division and 14th Motorised Division). With strong enemy forces on each flank from the retreating Soviet 22nd Army and the newly constituted Soviet 29th Army forming to the east of Velikie Luki, Hoth's thrust shifted from bold forward operations to senseless folly. The war diary of the LVII Panzer Corps makes clear that just reaching its objective required the fullest commitment of all its resources with no available reserves,[5] and although the 19th Panzer Division captured Velikie Luki on 19 July

---

[1] Hoth, *Panzer-Operationen*, p. 96.
[2] Jacob Kipp, 'Overview Phase 1: to 20 July 1941' in David M. Glantz (ed.), *The Initial Period of War*, p. 375.
[3] '3rd Pz. Gr. KTB 25.5.41 – 31.8.41' BA-MA Microfilm 59054, Fol. 139 (17 July 1941).
[4] Fedor von Bock, KTB 'Osten I', Fol. 24, *War Diary*, p. 247 (13 July 1941).
[5] 'Gen.Kdo.LVII.Pz.Korps Kriegstagesbuch Nr.1 vom 15.2. – 31.10.41' BA-MA RH 24–57/2, p. 197 (18 July 1941).

the success was short lived. Holding the rear flanks of the corridor was the hapless 14th Motorised Division which, by the afternoon of 19 July, was expecting massed Soviet attacks on multiple fronts. The division's materiel was noted to be 'completely worn out' and widely dispersed meaning that 'a massed Russian attack can hardly be held.'[6] In the early hours of 20 July the vigorous Soviet attack broke through the German line in multiple places, forcing an indignant Kluge to order the 19th Panzer Division back to the aid of the 14th Motorised Division.[7] Bock too was unswerving in his criticism. Having opposed the operation from the beginning, he now chastised Kuntzen in his diary (it seems Bock was unaware that the operation was ordered by Hoth's Panzer Group 3) for acting against his wishes and unnecessarily weakening his position by striking out for Velikie Luki.[8]

Hoth's vanity drove him to defend this operation in his memoir, even to the point of suggesting that Velikie Luki could have been held.[9] Yet Hoth's decision to attempt such an ill-fated move demonstrates how far removed even experienced field commanders were becoming from a pragmatic appraisal of what their forces could achieve. It was an archetypal example of what Clausewitz had warned against in the waning stages of an offensive. 'The diminishing force of the attack', Clausewitz wrote, 'is one of the strategist's main concerns. His awareness of it will determine the accuracy of his estimate in each case of the options open to him.'[10] Understanding the relative strength of the enemy force is equally critical to making an accurate assessment of the available options. The Germans were to discover in the second half of July that Soviet forces were nowhere near as exhausted as they had imagined. Far from shattering the Soviet front in the main operation towards Smolensk, the Soviet forces reeling under the German onslaught were now being aided by new Soviet armies moving up from the east.

Hoth's debacle at Velikie Luki was only a taste of things to come and the lesson of over-extending the weakened motorised divisions was by no means yet learned. The stubborn tendency to under-estimate Soviet forces persisted despite the growing evidence, as Bock discovered in a meeting with General of Infantry Hermann Geyer, commander of the IX Army Corps. Bock recorded in his diary: 'Geyer thinks all the reports

---

[6] 'Kriegstagesbuch Ia. 14.Inf.Div. (mot) vom 25.5.41 – 1.10.41' BA-MA RH 26–14/10, Fol. 66 (19 July 1941).
[7] 'Kriegstagesbuch Ia. 14.Inf.Div. (mot) vom 25.5.41 – 1.10.41' BA-MA RH 26–14/10, Fols. 69–70 and 74 (20 July 1941); Hoth, *Panzer-Operationen*, p. 99.
[8] Fedor von Bock, KTB 'Osten I', Fol. 36, *War Diary*, pp. 255–256 (20 July 1941).
[9] Hoth, *Panzer-Operationen*, p. 99.
[10] Howard and Paret (eds.), Carl von Clausewitz, *On War*, p. 638.

on the enemy are exaggerated and doesn't believe that there are serious enemy forces near Mogilev or in the pocket around Smolensk.'[11] In fact Mogilev was garrisoned by a large portion of the 13th Army, commanded by the 61st Rifle Corps commander, Major-General F. A. Bakunin, who was to ensure the defence of the city on all sides, mobilising workers' militia and transforming the city into what one historian described as the 'Belorussian Madrid'.[12] The developing encirclement at Smolensk was much larger and included the Soviet 19th, 20th and 16th Armies. These formed a large bulge in the German front that tied down a good deal of Bock's motorised forces for the rest of the month. Dealing with the pocket would prove taxing enough, but the real danger was as yet unknown – the new Soviet reserve armies that were massing between the Soviet front and Moscow. Far from being aware of what was to come, the latest intelligence report from Kinzel reflected an incessant confidence in the progress of the war, which even Halder dubbed in parts 'very optimistic'. Beyond Bock's immediate front were estimated to be just eight or nine Soviet infantry divisions and two or three panzer divisions.[13] Accordingly, Halder's faith in the coming victory remained unshaken and his intelligence supported the view that, once the Soviet front was ruptured at Smolensk, the absence of substantive Soviet reserves would ensure ample operational freedom to accomplish the march on Moscow.[14]

While spreading forces too thinly on Army Group Centre's northern flank had resulted in Kuntzen's panzer corps getting thrown back, the situation on the southern flank threatened far more serious consequences. The headlong drive at the centre of Bock's front was expanding his already elongated southern flank, and it was not long after forging across the Dnepr that Schweppenburg's XXIV Panzer Corps (Guderian's southernmost corps) was fully engaged in holding off Soviet attacks and keeping the army group's precarious flank intact. On 16 July Schweppenburg even feared that the strength of Soviet thrusts, striking south from the encirclement at Mogilev and north from Novy Bykhov, might sever his rearward communications. Accordingly, he requested that the XII Army Corps, of Weichs's following 2nd Army, be sent immediately to his aid.[15]

---

[11] Fedor von Bock, KTB 'Osten I', Fol. 33, *War Diary*, p. 253 (18 July 1941).

[12] A reference to Madrid's defiant role in the Spanish civil war, which was kept under siege from November 1936 to its fall in March 1939 (Kipp, 'Barbarossa and the Crisis,' p. 134).

[13] Franz Halder, KTB III, p. 88 (17 July 1941).

[14] In spite of the remarkably poor performance of Foreign Armies East under Kinzel, Halder did not have him replaced until 1 April 1942. The new head was Lieutenant-Colonel Reinhard Gehler (Thomas, 'Foreign Armies East', pp. 262–263).

[15] 'KTB Nr.1 Panzergruppe 2 vom 22.6.1941 bis 21.7.41' BA-MA RH 21–2/927, Fol. 241 (16 July 1941).

While Schweppenburg did his best to hold the line against the attacking formations of Timoshenko's 21st,13th and 4th Armies, the front was far from hermetically sealed and gaps were constantly opening and closing. The attempts to resume the advance eastward only stretched these lines further and therefore had to be broken off before any real progress was made. The solution sought by Weichs was to use the bulk of 2nd Army's strength to attack southwards, which, together with Schweppenburg's panzer corps, could seize the Soviet concentration point at Gomel and clear the troublesome enemy forces on the southern flank. Bock, however, was unconvinced and remained adamant that 2nd Army stay on a north-easterly course towards the main objective – the pocket forming at Smolensk. Just as Bock had disputed Halder's plan for an offensive operation on the northern flank, Bock again sought to pool his resources and not be distracted by secondary operations which pulled his forces further from the centre.

In spite of Bock's clear instructions, Weichs demonstrated a wilfulness befitting Guderian and sought to compromise Bock's demand. On 18 July Weichs informed Bock of the growing enemy strength in the south and declared that he would probably have to commit XIII Army Corps to shore up the line. Bock was very reluctant to agree and insisted that such a move was only to be considered 'in the most extreme emergency'. Later that day Bock discovered that Weichs was considering committing two army corps to attack in the south. He immediately telephoned 2nd Army and spoke with Weichs's Chief of Staff who confirmed the report, saying: 'Nothing has happened with piecemeal attacks and the situation there can't be cleared up by fighting a defensive battle. Therefore the Commander-in-Chief [Weichs] wants to commit XII and XIII Corps to attack to the south.'[16] Bock was incensed. He tersely forbade the operation and restated that Weichs's primary mission was to advance to the north-east leaving only the minimum possible forces to guard the flank. He then issued written instructions to 2nd Army so as avoid any further misunderstandings. Yet the matter did not end there and the following day (19 July) Bock had the impression from the morning report that 2nd Army 'was not acting as I wished'. Bock therefore dispatched Greiffenburg, his Chief of Staff, to Weichs's headquarters to set things straight and assert his view.[17]

Although Bock was essentially right in seeking to concentrate his forces at the main battle and relieve the hard-pressed motorised forces in the centre of the front, his ardent disregard for Weichs's concern in

[16] Fedor von Bock, KTB 'Osten I', Fol. 33, *War Diary*, p. 253 (18 July 1941).
[17] Ibid., Fol. 34, p. 254 (19 July 1941).

the south was foolhardy. Here Bock must be faulted for slipping into the all too common tendency among German generals of the period – under-estimating the strength of Soviet forces. On 19 July Bock derisively referred to the enemy forces attacking in the south as 'scraped-together elements' and judged Weichs's concerns 'exaggerated'.[18] Thus, while Weichs might rightfully be accused of failing to grasp the bigger picture by seeking an offensive towards Gomel, Bock certainly failed to appreciate the swelling threat intensifying on his southern wing. Not even on 20 July, when heavy attacks pounded Schweppenburg's 10th Motorised Division from all sides, forcing 4th Panzer Division to race to the rescue, did Bock recognise the scale of the problem (see Map 8).[19] It was only on 21 July, when the whole southern flank was threatening to buckle under the pressure, that Bock relented, admitting in his diary: 'The situation facing XXIV Panzer Corps on the southern wing was so threatening that I had to order the 2nd Army to restore it.' Weichs estimated this required the full commitment of two army corps (XIII and IV). The setback also made an indelible impression on Bock who remarked: 'A quite remarkable success for such a badly-battered opponent!'[20]

Despite the importance of the action on the flanks, it was at the centre of Bock's front that the main German forces were concentrated and where the battle of Smolensk would have to be won. To this end Hoth employed Schmidt's reinforced XXXIX Panzer Corps to advance in a long arching manoeuvre around the main Soviet force north of Smolensk. The advance proceeded swiftly and by 15 July the spearheading 7th Panzer Division captured the main Moscow–Smolensk railroad and highway junction at Yartsevo. It was a potentially definitive achievement but for the fact that the southern arc of the encirclement was missing. Guderian's panzer group was still a significant way off – a source of some irritation in Hoth's panzer group. On the evening of 15 July the war diary noted: 'Unfortunately the link-up with Panzer Group 2 is lacking, just as at Minsk.'[21]

Of Guderian's panzer group, composed of three panzer corps, the southernmost, Schweppenburg's XXIV Panzer Corps, was tied up holding the southern flank. On Guderian's northern wing, Lemelsen's XXXXVII Panzer Corps was entirely committed to holding the southern side of the encirclement and accordingly could spare no units to link up with Hoth east of Smolensk. This left Vietinghoff's XXXXVI Panzer Corps which operated in the middle of Guderian's group and could have been used to swing north-east to seal the gap. Instead, Guderian was

[18] Ibid. (19 July 1941).   [19] Ibid., Fol. 35, p. 255 (20 July 1941).
[20] Ibid., Fol. 38, p. 258 (21 July 1941).
[21] '3rd Pz. Gr. KTB 25.5.41 – 31.8.41' BA-MA Microfilm 59054, Fol. 132 (15 July 1941).

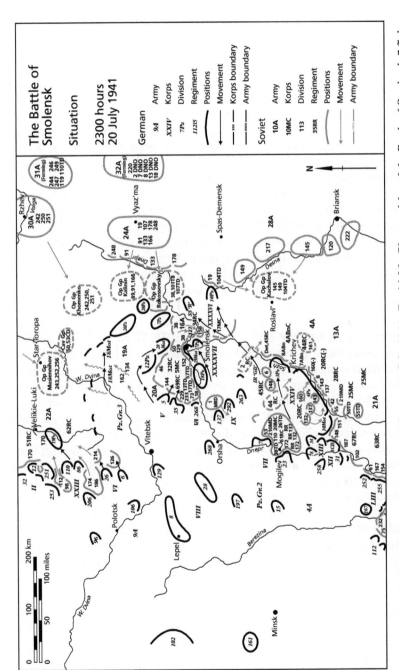

The Battle of Smolensk

Situation

2300 hours 20 July 1941

German

9A	Army
XXIV	Korps
7Pz	Division
112S	Regiment
(solid loop)	Positions
→	Movement
xxx	Korps boundary
—	Army boundary

Soviet

10A	Army
10MC	Korps
113	Division
35RR	Regiment
(loop)	Positions
→	Movement
xxxx	Army boundary

N

Map 8 Dispositions of Army Group Centre 20 July 1941: David M. Glantz, *Atlas of the Battle of Smolensk 7 July–10 September 1941*

already thinking about the next stage of the offensive and therefore drove this corps further east to seize the high ground at Yel'nya. This fateful decision illustrated yet again the ineptitude of the German generals in grasping the dangers of over-extension.

Understanding this harmful, and ultimately self-defeating predisposition is inconceivable without realising the power of the superiority myth which pervaded the German army at the time. In spite of the mounting obstacles, confidence in victory was still palpable. Problems or doubts, in so far as they were acknowledged or reported, were often treated as localised occurrences, or matters of short-term duration. In the end, however bad things may have appeared, solace was taken from the fact that things must have been much worse for the Soviets and consequently the war would have to be over soon. On 15 July the collapse of Timoshenko's front at Smolensk was predicted by Panzer Group 3 to be only days away.[22] It was a confidence shared by many of the rank and file. Karl Fuchs, a tank gunner in the 7th Panzer Division, wrote home on 15 July: 'We are now positioned outside the city of Smolensk and have penetrated the highly acclaimed Stalin lines. I would imagine that within eight to ten days this campaign will be over.'[23] Ernst Guicking, a soldier from the 52nd Infantry Division, wrote to his wife on 14 July: 'If you could see the frantic advance here you would surely be completely speechless. Something like this has never been recorded in the history of the world. The main thing is that the campaign will soon be over, of that we are all convinced.'[24] Walter Tilemann, an orphan from a German family living in the Soviet Union, noted after being adopted by a German unit early in the campaign: 'The word "Blitzkrieg" did not seem to be only an empty phrase. Many believed in it and that the war would soon be won.' Yet he also added: 'It was more hope than belief and the dull feeling that it must not turn out differently.'[25] A general of the Waffen SS, Max Simon, later attested to the valour of the Soviet infantry and their powers of resistance in this early phase of the war. He then cited Germany's failure to comprehend this as a key failing of their war in the east. 'Very soon we had to admit that we were up against a very different adversary from the one we had expected and I believe that this underestimation was one of the reasons for the unfortunate course [sic] which the campaign in Russia

[22] Ibid., Fol. 131 (15 July 1941).
[23] Horst Fuchs Richardson (ed.), *Sieg Heil! War Letters of Tank Gunner Karl Fuchs 1937– 1941* (Hamden, 1987), p. 118 (15 July 1941).
[24] Jürgen Kleindienst (ed.), *Sei tausendmal gegrüßt. Briefwechsel Irene und Ernst Guicking 1937–1945* (Berlin, 2001), p. 86 (14 July 1941).
[25] Walter Tilemann, *Ich, das Soldatenkind* (Munich, 2005), p. 136.

Figure 7.1 In the early days and weeks of the fighting German war cemeteries, neatly ordered and well prepared, were established, but as losses soared simple birch crosses were erected.

took.'[26] Other events such as the capture of Stalin's son on 18 July (he was a battery commander in the 14th Tank Division) seemed to suggest that the disintegration of the Red Army was closer than ever.[27] Indeed, the accolades of success were already flowing. Throughout July 1941 the Knight's Cross[28] was awarded to Lemelsen, Schweppenburg and Model (commander of the 3rd Panzer Division), while Schmidt, Hoth,

[26] James Lucas, *War of the Eastern Front 1941–1945. The German Soldier in Russia* (London, 1980), p. 53.

[27] Senior Lieutenant Yakov Dzhugashvili (Stalin's son) was captured near Smolensk by elements of the 12th Panzer Division. A German report stated that he maintained the outcome of the war was still unclear and refused to give up the hope of a Soviet victory. 'Kriegstagebuch Nr.1 der 12.Pz.Div. vom 25.5.41 – 30.9.41' BA-MA RH 27–12/2, Fols. 53–54 (18 July 1941). See also Perel, *Europa Europa*, pp. 33–34; Nagorski, *The Greatest Battle*, p. 71; Axell, *Russia's Heroes, 1941–45*, Chapter 5, 'Stalin's Son'.

[28] Hitler reinstated the Iron Cross on 1 September 1939 and it was awarded in four grades: Iron Cross 2nd Class, Iron Cross 1st Class, Knight's Cross and the Grand Cross (Herman Göring was the only man to received the Grand Cross). The Knight's Cross was awarded in four grades; with Oakleaves, with Oakleaves and Swords, with Oakleaves and Swords and Diamonds and with Golden Oakleaves and Swords and Diamonds. This last award was issued to only one man, Hans-Ulrich Rudel, who was a Luftwaffe war hero and flying ace. See Norman Davies, *No Simple Victory. World War II in Europe, 1939–1945* (London, 2007), pp. 264 and 267.

Guderian and Richthofen (the commander of the VIII Air Corps) were all awarded the prodigious Oak Leaves to the Knight's Cross.[29]

Thus it was with a resplendent confidence that Guderian, like so many of his fellow officers, viewed the progress of the war and, accordingly, he saw little danger in the bold move to seize Yel'nya before ensuring the closure of the main pocket around Smolensk. Yet, just as in the Belostok–Minsk pocket, Soviet forces were able to escape the encirclement and rejoin Soviet lines through the open corridor to the east. On 17 July Panzer Group 3 observed with frustration: 'In the hole left by Panzer Group 2, eastwards of Smolensk, countless enemy groups are succeeding in escaping to the southeast.'[30]

Not surprisingly, pressure was soon mounting on Guderian to close the pocket, but he was not prepared to do this at the expense of giving up his drive on Yel'nya. On 18 July Bock emphasised to Kluge the importance of closing the ring near Yartsevo[31] and on the following day he requested that 4th Panzer Army ask Guderian 'whether or not he is in a position to carry out the order of three days ago to link up with Panzer Group 3'. Bock's further questioning even implied a degree of dissatisfaction with Kluge's handling of the matter, given that he was Guderian's nominal superior and in Bock's view should have dealt with the matter earlier. This provoked an outburst from Kluge and resulted in a brief argument.[32]

In fact Guderian had been attempting to close the gap by mustering forces for a drive on Dorogobuzh, south-east of Yartsevo. On 18 July he visited the stricken 18th Panzer Division and, in spite of acknowledging its wretched state, ordered it towards Dorogobuzh.[33] The division had lost more than three quarters of its initial panzer strength and almost half of its anti-tank guns. In one regiment which had started the campaign with 2,359 men, losses by 19 July had reached 1,000. The terrible road conditions also had a devastating affect on the division's mobility with 1,300 trucks classed as total losses and a further 1,000 trucks in repair.[34] Beyond the division's internal difficulties, Guderian's decision to move it from the southern flank of the Smolensk pocket, before the arrival

---

[29] '3rd Pz. Gr. KTB 25.5.41 – 31.8.41' BA-MA Microfilm 59054, Fol. 139 (17 July 1941); Guderian, *Panzer Leader*, p. 178. See also Hürter, *Hitlers Heerführer*, p. 280.

[30] 'Panzerarmeeoberkommandos Tagesmeldungen 21.6 – 31.8.41' BA-MA RH 21-3/43, Fol. 166 (17 July 1941); '3rd Pz. Gr. KTB 25.5.41 – 31.8.41' BA-MA Microfilm 59054, Fol. 139 (17 July 1941).

[31] Fedor von Bock, KTB 'Osten I', Fol. 33, *War Diary*, p. 253 (18 July 1941).

[32] Ibid., Fols. 34–35, pp. 254–255 (19 July 1941).

[33] '18. Panzer Division, Abt. Ia. Kriegstagebuch Teil I vom: 22.6 – 20.8.41' BA-MA RH 27–18/20, Fol. 40 (18 July 1941).

[34] 'Kriegstagebuch Nr.2 XXXXVII.Pz.Korps. Ia 25.5.1941 – 22.9.1941' BA-MA RH 24–47/2 (19 July 1941).

of the replacement infantry, imperilled the panzer group's rear area. In essence, he was attempting to close one hole by opening another, but Guderian was firmly of the opinion that his panzer forces should not stand on static lines when they could be used in the attack. Consequently, just as at the Belostok–Minsk pocket, Guderian fell foul of Kluge, who immediately countermanded the order to remove the division. Such was the antipathy between the two men that Kluge didn't even bother to inform Guderian.[35]

If Guderian was aware of the strain his forces were under, his orders did not reflect it. In addition to trying to pull the 18th Panzer Division off the encirclement front, he also sought to send a part of the 10th Panzer Division, still fighting its way to Yel'nya, towards Dorogobuzh. Yet, the division was so hard pressed in the battle for Yel'nya that the divisional commander, Lieutenant-General Ferdinand Schaal, informed Vietinghoff's XXXXVI Panzer Corps that only one of the two objectives could be undertaken. Vietinghoff's response denied the request to break off either attack, adding that the panzer corps itself was under strict orders to carry through both operations.[36] As it quickly became clear that the 10th Panzer Division would be stretched thin even with one objective, Guderian eventually relented and on 20 July named Yel'nya the 'main objective . . . Dorogobuzh is extraneous'.[37] After the war Hoth looked on this decision with embittered resignation, writing in his memoir: 'To Panzer Group 2 the taking of the heights at Yel'nya, for the later continuance of the advance eastward, appeared more important than the completion of the [Smolensk] encirclement.'[38] Indeed, Guderian's flagrant disregard for prudence beggars belief given that his forces were clearly exhausted, unsupported by infantry, at the end of tenuous supply lines and facing increasing Soviet resistance from the east. Kluge was so concerned that he even broached the topic of a general withdrawal of Guderian's line to the Sozh River south of Smolensk.[39] By 20 July Bock's patience was also at an end. 'At the moment', Bock wrote in his diary, 'there is only one pocket on the army group's front! And it has a hole!'[40] It was five days previously that Hoth's 7th Panzer Division had reached

---

[35] Guderian, *Panzer Leader*, p. 179. Guderian's memoir makes the claim that the 18th Panzer Division was being moved to relieve the Infantry Regiment *Grossdeutschland*, not to attack towards Dorogobuzh, but this contradicts wartime records.

[36] 'Kriegstagebuch der 10.Panzer Division Nr.5 vom: 22.5. bis: 7.10.41' BA-MA RH 27–10/26a (19 July 1941).

[37] 'KTB Nr.1 Panzergruppe 2 vom 22.6.1941 bis 21.7.41' BA-MA RH 21–2/927, Fol. 287 (20 July 1941).

[38] Hoth, *Panzer-Operationen*, p. 97.

[39] 'KTB Nr.1 Panzergruppe 2 vom 22.6.1941 bis 21.7.41' BA-MA RH 21–2/927, Fol. 282 (20 July 1941).

[40] Fedor von Bock, KTB 'Osten I', Fol. 36, *War Diary*, p. 256 (20 July 1941).

Yartsevo and since then innumerable Soviet units had fled the German trap. Bock did not mince words in characterising Kluge's command as useless for not having taken a stronger line with Guderian and ensuring the closure of the pocket. As a result, Bock bypassed 4th Panzer Army altogether and sent a General Staff officer to Panzer Group 2, but as soon as he had captured Yel'nya, talk at the panzer group was centred on exploiting the success with further gains to the east. It was immediately made very clear that this was not what mattered and that the sealing off of the Smolensk pocket was the panzer group's top priority. Greiffenberg, Bock's Chief of Staff, also spoke with Guderian to further underline the army group's instructions.[41]

While Guderian and Kluge were procrastinating over closing the ring from the south, Hoth had been asked to do so from the north by thrusting the 7th Panzer Division further south. Although Hoth was willing, his plans were quickly overtaken by intense pressure from Soviet attacks emanating from the east, preventing any chance of resuming the southward drive.[42] As one former commander in the 7th Panzer Division noted: 'The battles at Yartsevo lasted longer than we would have liked. The blitzkrieg seemed to be over . . . Resistance grew stiffer and stiffer.'[43]

The 7th Panzer Division's inability to break away from the front and regain freedom of movement was symptomatic of the paralysis gripping the whole of 4th Panzer Army. The enormous theatre of operations had forced a wide dispersal of Hoth and Guderian's limited resources and the marching infantry were still too far off to relieve them. This had not been foreseen as a problem because the panzer and motorised forces were supposed to have shattered all remaining Soviet resistance in the second phase of operations east of the great rivers. Yet, to the increasing dismay of the German command, there were still numerous Soviet formations holding together a ramshackle front beyond the main Soviet encirclement at Smolensk. What was worse, these forces showed themselves to be far from inert and exerted constant pressure on the German front from all directions. As Bock observed on 20 July: '[R]epeated attacks on the elements of Panzer Group 2 . . . from the east, southeast and south. Panzer Group 3, too, has not only been attacked from inside the pocket, or from Smolensk and west, but from the east and northeast as well.'[44] Bock was finding out the hard way how utterly erroneous German intelligence

[41] Ibid., Fol. 35, p. 255 (20 July 1941).
[42] 'KTB Nr.1 Panzergruppe 2 vom 22.6.1941 bis 21.7.41' BA-MA RH 21-2/927, Fol. 287 (20 July 1941); Fedor von Bock, KTB 'Osten I', Fols. 36–37, *War Diary*, p. 255 (20 July 1941).
[43] Von Luck, *Panzer Commander*, p. 59.
[44] Fedor von Bock, KTB 'Osten I', Fol. 36, *War Diary*, p. 256 (20 July 1941).

reports had been – and the worst was yet to come.[45] That Bock had an inkling of this is also reflected in his diary.

The assumption that is voiced here and there, that the enemy is not acting according to a plan, does not coincide with the facts. Given the energy that he has shown in the last few days, I think it doubtful that the enemy will allow the fighting here to cease when it suits us, even following the destruction of the forces almost encircled around Smolensk. If full freedom of action is to be won, then the forces which the enemy has brought up to the army group's front in recent days must also be destroyed.[46]

Even the more perceptive Bock did not yet fully appreciate just how much fight Timoshenko's Western Front still had in it, and his stated intention to destroy this force by renewed offensive action only reflected a lack of understanding for the feeble state of his own forces. Army Group Centre's ailing condition, compounded by increasing shortages and severe over-extension, was indeed serious and, as the advance reached its limit, the initiative temporarily passed to the *Stavka* who were able to take advantage of the strung-out German armies to plunge them into their first military crisis of the war.

While the beleaguered Soviet 20th, 19th and 16th Armies fought for their lives inside the large pocket around Smolensk, the *Stavka*, under Stalin's direction, decided the time had come for a major counter-offensive to relieve the nearly encircled formations and re-take Smolensk. Timoshenko's command was reinforced with the entire first echelon of the new Front of Reserve Armies (29th, 30th, 24th and 28th Armies) that had been raised throughout June and July.[47] On 20 July Stalin informed Timoshenko of the offensive, stating: 'Until now you have counted on help in the form of two or three divisions at a time, but nothing really has come of this. Therefore it is time to give up this practice and to begin to create a fist of 7–8 divisions with cavalry on the flanks.'[48] With the backbone at last to deliver powerful attacks, a plan was devised by Marshal Georgi Zhukov, the Chief of the General Staff, to launch simultaneous concentric blows against Army Group Centre from each of the four new armies.[49] Unbeknown to the German generals, they had reached the high point of the summer blitzkrieg to the east.

---

[45] At a meeting five days later (on 25 July), Kinzel reported to Halder and Heusinger that he still had no clear picture of the strength or size of Soviet reserves, but nevertheless concluded his presentation: 'Large enemy operations I consider to be hardly possible.' Adolf Heusinger, *Befehl im Widerstreit. Schicksalsstunden der deutschen Armee 1923–1945* (Tübingen, 1957), p. 130.

[46] Fedor von Bock, KTB 'Osten I', Fol. 37, *War Diary*, p. 257 (20 July 1941).

[47] Glantz, *Battle for Smolensk*, p. 30.

[48] Kipp, 'Barbarossa and the Crisis', p. 140.   [49] Glantz, *Battle for Smolensk*, p. 31.

Figure 7.2 After weeks of hard marching, Army Group Centre's infantry arrived exhausted at the over-extended front of the panzer groups.

The rapidly expanding crisis on the army group's flanks and centre was debated by the generals as isolated questions of where to deploy the available forces, but this was really only a symptom of the underlying problem. At its root, Army Group Centre, like the whole eastern front, was already suffering from a debilitating lack of military resources, which forced the juggling of units between crisis points and gave rise to increasingly bitter disputes among commanders. There were simply not enough resources to meet the mushrooming demands of the war, and this was bringing the whole advance to a sudden and dangerous halt before the completion of the second major encirclement. With units strung out over many miles, and aggressive Soviet counter-attacks growing in frequency and strength, the culmination of exhaustion, resource depletion and supply difficulties spelled the end of the German blitzkrieg. The next phase of the war was marked by an increasingly static German defence with the pooling of resources for limited offensives. The initiative was only briefly lost and the German advances would later continue, but ending the war according to the timetable set out in the Barbarossa plan was doomed – the question was now whether the war could be won at all.

Crisis rising – the German command at war

As the armies of Army Group Centre were still tightening the noose around the great pocket, Hitler, at his East Prussian headquarters, was again considering the next stage of operations once the battle of Smolensk had concluded. On 17 July Hitler returned to his preferred option of swinging Hoth's panzer group north to cover Leeb's drive on Leningrad, and at the same time diverting Guderian's panzer group south, along with strong support from Weichs's infantry, to form a new pocket with Rundstedt's Army Group South.[50] Hitler expressed no interest in attacking Moscow and, perhaps sensing that this might result in a dispute with the OKH, without bothering to consult them, he quickly proceeded to enshrine his strategic vision in a new war directive. However, it is perhaps more likely that Hitler was completely unaware of Halder's careful scheming and simply expected the OKH to support his new directive. Dated 19 July, War Directive 33 formalised the divergent north/south thrusts by Bock's panzer forces with the drive on Moscow relegated to the remaining infantry on Bock's front – perhaps a frail concession to the OKH.

To Hitler's mind the conclusion of the battle at Smolensk would see the road to the east torn open leaving little opposition in front of Army Group Centre and allowing the use of its armour to roll up the flanks of the Soviet armies still resisting in the north and south. Essentially the tone of the directive pointed to a war already won on the central front.[51] 'The second series of battles in the East has ended', it proclaimed, with

---

[50] KTB OKW, Volume II, p. 1029, Document 76 (17 July 1941); Mendelssohn, *Die Nürnberger Dokumente*, p. 369.

[51] Indeed, on 16 July Hitler had already hosted a meeting of top officials to make selections for the posts of Reich and General Commissar (senior civil administrators) in the occupied Soviet territories. See Kay, *Exploitation*, pp. 180–185.

'mopping up' operations in Army Group Centre required to eliminate the remaining resistance. Thereafter the next phase of the campaign would have to 'prevent any further sizable enemy forces from withdrawing into the depths of Russia, and to wipe them out'.[52] Even for a man so prone to delusional fantasies of aggrandisement, presenting the eastern front's military situation in such terms betrayed a remarkable departure from reality, reflecting both Hitler's exorbitant self-assurance and the excessive bias in information flowing through the high command. Timoshenko's Western Front was still far from beaten and the Soviet high command was certainly not considering a headlong retreat eastwards. An example from the Italian diplomatic community plainly reveals just how differently the war's development was being viewed in circles uncorrupted by the German superiority myth. On 18 July Ciano wrote in his diary:

Hitler went to war believing that the struggle against Bolshevism might lead the Anglo-Saxon countries to end the conflict. Von Ribbentrop did not agree; in fact, he was convinced that Churchill is ready to make an alliance even with the devil himself if he can only destroy Nazism. And this time he was right. Now the struggle is hard and bloody, and the German people, who are tired, wonder why. Frau Mollier used harsh terms. She said Hitler is a blockhead. In fact, the war is harder than the Germans had foreseen. The advance continues, but it is slow, and harassed by the very vigorous Soviet counterattacks. Colonel Amé and General Squero, who made a report on the military situation today, believe that the Russians will succeed in maintaining a front even during the winter. If this is true, Germany has started a haemorrhage that will have incalculable consequences.[53]

Just as Hitler was unswervingly fixated by victory, Halder too remained defiantly optimistic in spite of a notable downturn in the confident mood at OKH. On 20 July Halder noted in his diary:

The gruelling battles involving some groups of our motorised forces, in which the infantry arriving from the west can only slowly become involved, together with the time taken on bad roads which restrict movement and the exhaustion of the troops who have been marching and fighting without rest, have dampened the spirits at high command. Nowhere is this better seen than in the thorough despair into which Brauchitsch had been plunged. However there is really no call for this.[54]

---

[52] Trevor-Roper (ed.), *Hitler's War Directives 1939–1945*, pp. 139–141.
[53] Muggeridge (ed.), *Ciano's Diary*, p. 371 (18 July 1941).
[54] Franz Halder, KTB III, p. 98 (20 July 1941). In his post-war writings Halder conveniently disassociated himself from such rash judgements and even suggested that he had warned Hitler against attempting too much. 'Hitler's keen ears had heard the warning of his military advisors . . . The boundaries of military possibilities he did not acknowledge.' Franz Halder, *Hitler als Feldherr* (Munich, 1949), p. 39.

While Halder appeared unperturbed by the military situation, the revelations contained within Hitler's new war directive were certainly of much greater concern to him. It is unclear exactly what Halder did in response to War Directive 33, as there is no mention of it in his diary on the date it was issued (19 July). Some form of discussion with Hitler, however, is not beyond the realm of possibility, given that only two days later on 21 July, during Hitler's visit to Leeb's Army Group North, the issue of Hoth's panzers striking north was suddenly far less certain. As Leeb wrote in his diary: 'The Führer spoke of the *possibility* that Panzer Group 3 would turn to the north.'[55] Furthermore, the OKW war diary for the same day (21 July) presented the northern operations as something to be decided upon 'at the latest in 5 days' and then concluded:

In this regard it could then happen, that Panzer Group 2 turns to the south, so that for the thrust on Moscow only infantry armies of Army Group Centre remain.

This eventuality does not worry the Führer because Moscow is for him only a geographical term.[56]

Clearly something had taken place to weaken Hitler's recent commitment to Directive 33 and this may well have prompted his decision to visit Army Group North and gain a first-hand account of its progress. With perhaps a similar motive Halder had flown to Army Group South the day before (20 July), to see what could be done to improve the slow progress being made and conceivably work on deflecting Hitler from diverting Guderian south.

In any case, Halder's diary for 21 July talked of continuing the advance on Moscow with just Hoth's panzer group, a circumstance he was probably only willing to consider because his upbeat assessment of the war deemed it sufficient for the task. Outlining the future operation to Brauchitsch and Heusinger, Halder stated that Moscow would be 'liquidated' by a combined attack of Weichs and Strauss, with Hoth driving in the centre or on the left flank.[57] Although Halder does not record Brauchitsch's response to this revised plan, Brauchitsch's increasingly diminished enthusiasm for the prospects of a German success probably led him to a much starker criticism of the new directive and the implications it held for his much hoped for assault on Moscow. Accordingly, on the following day Brauchitsch visited Hitler, most likely with a view to airing his grievances about the new war directive, but in the process he

[55] Italics mine. Wilhelm Ritter von Leeb, KTB, p. 303 (21 July 1941).
[56] KTB OKW, Volume II, p. 1030, Document 77 (21 July 1941); Mendelssohn, *Die Nürnberger Dokumente*, p. 373.
[57] Franz Halder, KTB III, p. 100 (21 July 1941).

was subjected to one of Hitler's ranting diatribes proclaiming his great dissatisfaction with Leeb's command.[58] Unexpectedly, as a result of this meeting, Hitler felt it necessary to issue a supplement to his previous war directive entitled War Directive 33a. The supplement began with the preface: 'After a report by Commander-in-Chief Army [Brauchitsch], the Führer on 22 July issued the following orders to amplify and extend Directive 33.'[59] As details of the meeting are vague, one can only suppose what exactly might have taken place to warrant this action, but given the stern tone of the supplement, which essentially only reinforced the strategic intentions outlined in Directive 33, it is reasonable to assume that Hitler was reacting somewhat angrily to complaints raised by Brauchitsch, and to what he saw as the ineptitude of Leeb.

If a despondent Brauchitsch had elaborated on the difficulties of Halder's scheme to attack Moscow with only Hoth's panzer group, Hitler may well have felt a sudden sense of betrayal, for he had certainly not agreed to any such operation and, for the first time in the unfolding dispute over Moscow, Hitler may have sensed he had been manipulated by Halder. Although only a theory, it remains a plausible explanation, together with Leeb's faltering advance, to answer the otherwise speculative question of why the OKW issued a second war directive which only reiterated what had been previously stated and added minor details. Furthermore, it explains the renewed purpose of mind and tart disregard for his generals that Hitler now displayed in committing Hoth's panzer group to the north. As for Halder, Hitler had never shared a great fondness for the Chief of the General Staff whom he regarded, at best, as competent in his role as a military bureaucrat and, at worst, as an insubordinate officer and a decidedly inept strategist. Yet Hitler, who often expressed an ingrained suspicion of his generals, now became even more distrustful, relying more and more on his own judgement against the mounting chorus of objections that would arise from his military commanders.

When Brauchitsch received the new Directive 33a he was no doubt deeply disappointed. His concern over the weakness of Army Group Centre's drive on Moscow was given no further consideration, while Halder's intention to use Hoth's panzer group to attack Moscow was now specifically ruled out as the group was being reassigned to Army Group North for the investment of Leningrad, and later to be used in 'thrusting forward to the Volga'. With Guderian's forces still being sent south, there were to be no panzers sent to Moscow, only the infantry. Yet Hitler was adamant that these were enough and the text of the new directive was

[58] Ibid., p. 102 (22 July 1941).
[59] Trevor-Roper (ed.), *Hitler's War Directives 1939–1945*, p. 143.

emphatic. 'After mopping-up operations around Smolensk and on the southern flank, Army Group Centre, whose infantry formations drawn from both its armies are strong enough for the purpose, will defeat such enemy forces as remain between Smolensk and Moscow, by an advance on the left flank if possible. It will then capture Moscow.'[60]

The new directive was signed by Keitel, although it reflected Hitler's reasoning, and it was therefore to Keitel that Brauchitsch directed a second appeal on 23 July. Brauchitsch complained that, given the situation at the front, the operational intentions of the new directive, especially those for Army Group Centre, were 'not possible'. He therefore unsuccessfully requested that Keitel postpone 33a until the current battles had produced a clearer outcome. Brauchitsch should probably have known better than to place much hope in Keitel, who was well known (and soon reviled) as Hitler's dependable mouthpiece and habitual yes-man. Brauchitsch then sought another audience with Hitler in which the Commander-in-Chief of the Army again tried to explain the difficulties of the army. Hitler, however, refused to be drawn on such matters and instead replied with a lecture on the advantages of smaller encirclements.[61]

Like Brauchitsch, Halder too appeared at the Wolf's Lair on 23 July and for the first time gave a presentation openly recommending Moscow as the best choice for attack. Halder reported that the infantry divisions were at only 80 per cent of their full strength with some having to be left behind because losses of horses were so high. In addition, the diversion of some infantry divisions to support Guderian's southern operation, and the loss of Hoth's panzer group to the north, rendered the remaining strength on Bock's front 'insufficient' for an offensive towards Moscow. He then pleaded for Hoth's panzer group, stating that while it was 'urgently needed by Army Group Centre', the thrust north would 'probably find no worthwhile objective'.[62] Moscow, on the other hand, Halder endeavoured to show, was of great importance. It was now protected by the greatest concentration of Soviet forces, it possessed the best infrastructure, was a major industrial area and the centre of military power.[63] That Halder was purposefully trying to sway Hitler by indulging his delusional fantasies of grandeur is most evident from his conclusion. Here Halder deceptively pronounced that German troops would be at

[60] Ibid.
[61] KTB OKW, Volume II, p. 1031, Document 79 and pp. 1034–1035, Document 80 (23 July 1941); Mendelssohn, Die Nürnberger Dokumente, pp. 378–379.
[62] Halder later described Hitler's decision to strike towards Leningrad as entirely motivated by 'political fanaticism' without any military grounding (Halder, Hitler als Feldherr, p. 40).
[63] Franz Halder, KTB III, pp. 104–106 (23 July 1941).

Leningrad, Moscow and the line Orel–Crimea in about a month, with the Volga reached by the start of October and Baku by the start of November. Later that day, when Hitler restated these same goals, Halder took a disdainfully cynical tone and mocked him in his diary. 'Apparently he believes that the motorised units alone can make it to the Volga and into the Caucasus as we head into the wet autumn.'[64] By promising Hitler everything he could want, Halder hoped he would change his mind, but unlike the early days of the conflict when it appeared an outright victory had been won, Hitler was no longer so easily seduced by Halder's assurances, especially when they ran contrary to his own ideas. Indeed when Hitler spoke at the conclusion of Halder's presentation, the break with the OKH was clearer than ever.

In spite of everything that Halder and Brauchitsch had had to say, Hitler was resolute and remained firmly behind the position of his new war directive. Bock, Hitler made clear, would be sent to attack Moscow with just infantry divisions, while the armour was to be diverted to the flanks. Halder noted that the Soviet capital held 'no interest at all' for Hitler, but Leningrad became the subject of a verbose monologue, which took in the mistakes made by Leeb and why Hoth must be directed north. Ultimately, Hitler declared, the objective of the operation was the elimination of the enemy, to which an affronted and sceptical Halder added: 'One can only hope that he is right. As for the rest: Shame about the time lost for such a presentation.'[65]

On 23 July the plans of Halder and Brauchitsch seemingly lay in ruin. Ideally Hitler was to have been subtly coerced, abiding in the wisdom of his generals and trusting that each new success was proof of the OKH's war-winning strategy. Yet, the evident failure to maintain a joint offensive with all three army groups forced choices about which axis of advance promised the best avenue for success. Suddenly the direct confrontation that Halder and Brauchitsch had hoped to avoid was thrust upon them. To their minds, Hitler was forgoing the great success in the centre and pushing everything towards the flanks before Bock had been able to achieve full operational freedom. Hitler's fixation with Leningrad, as a secondary target, endangered the whole campaign by failing to strike the decisive blow at Moscow where real Soviet power resided. Thus, on 23 July there could be no more pretence or outward posturing: to forestall Hitler's fatal step the OKH would have to declare themselves and openly show their hand, pleading the case for a continued offensive towards

[64] Ibid., pp. 107–108 (23 July 1941).
[65] Ibid. (23 July 1941). See also KTB OKW, Volume II, pp. 1030–1031, Document 78 (23 July 1941).

Moscow and hoping it was enough to convince Hitler. Their failure on 23 July was not the end of the dispute, but only the opening salvo in the now openly declared conflict which was to become a crisis of command that paralleled the rising crisis on the battlefield. As Halder wrote after the war, the OKH's open opposition to Hitler's plan was abhorred by the Führer and '[t]he effect was explosive'.[66]

As the *Stavka* began moving up the new reserve armies to strengthen Timoshenko's fragile front, Army Group Centre's front was in scarcely better condition. Without infantry support and at the end of long supply lines, the state of the fatigued motorised divisions became more and more desperate. In Panzer Group 2 the fact that large segments of the infantry were being diverted to the southern flank engendered 'very bitter' resentment among the troops, who felt they were being abandoned after shouldering the heaviest fighting for 30 straight days.[67] The mental strain on the men was not just the result of physical exhaustion; there were also the psychological effects of growing gaps in the ranks, declining tank support and the increasing worry about shortages of munitions desperately needed to parry the relentless Soviet counter-attacks. This often resulted in the drastic measure of allowing only sighted firing, which under the harrowing onslaught of repeated enemy attacks only frayed nerves more rapidly. Casualties in the two panzer groups were also starting to make themselves felt. After less than one month on the eastern front Guderian's group alone had suffered 830 casualties among its officers,[68] while Hoth's group reported 562 officers lost.[69] The figures were so high that Halder noted how some units had already lost half of their officers.[70] Other ranks were also heavily affected with Guderian's group citing 15,228 men killed, wounded and missing,[71] while Hoth's group gave the lower figure of 10,509.[72]

---

[66] Franz Halder, *Hitler als Feldherr*, p. 42.

[67] 'KTB Nr.1 Panzergruppe 2 vom 22.6.1941 bis 21.7.41' BA-MA RH 21–2/927, Fol. 294 (21 July 1941).

[68] 'Verlustmeldungen 5.7.1941 – 25.3.1942' BA-MA RH 21–2/757, Fol. 4 (casualty lists until 19 June 1941, report dated 23 July 1941). In fact the real figure is a little higher as the information for the report was collected from all the divisions, with one submitting its data on 16 July, one on 17 July and two on 18 July.

[69] 'Panzerarmeeoberkommandos Anlagen zum Kriegstagesbuch "Berichte, Besprechungen, Beurteilungen der Lage" Bd.III 25.5.41 – 22.7.41' BA-MA RH 21–3/46, Fol. 180 (21 July 1941).

[70] Franz Halder, KTB III, p. 103 (23 July 1941).

[71] 'Verlustmeldungen 5.7.1941 – 25.3.1942' BA-MA RH 21–2/757, Fol. 4 (casualty lists until 19 June 1941, report dated 23 July 1941).

[72] 'Panzerarmeeoberkommandos Anlagen zum Kriegstagesbuch "Berichte, Besprechungen, Beurteilungen der Lage" Bd.III 25.5.41 – 22.7.41' BA-MA RH 21–3/46, Fol. 180 (21 July 1941).

Operating in the depths of the Soviet hinterland, the size of the operational theatre also assumed daunting proportions which exacerbated the internal weaknesses of the combat units. Appealing for more infantry support, the war diary for Guderian's panzer group included this excerpt from its request to 4th Panzer Army on 22 July:

> The fighting of the panzer group reaches to a depth of several hundred kilometres and along an exceptional width... The security of the deep flanks, not just the outer flanks of the panzer group, but also the inner flanks of the widely dispersed and engaged panzer corps, is very difficult and absorbs much strength, which results in the loss of the spearhead. Motorised troops cannot be used for this security activity if the panzer corps is to be used as a powerful attacking force. For the security of the flanks, the supply routes and the airfields requires the commitment of the infantry.[73]

The consequence of the German strategic position was not just the distant horizontal dispersal of forces along the line, but also the vertical problem of keeping adequate supplies moving east to support them. This had been a considerable problem even with the frail rail network prioritising the panzer groups and the bulk of the motorisation servicing their *Grosstransportraum*. Yet every day the hundreds of thousands of men in the 9th and 2nd Armies were marching further east, straining the woeful logistical network ever more. On 21 July the LIII Army Corps was stuck in bloody positional warfare in front of the Dnepr at Rogatschew and reported: 'The munition consignment for the division is for a war of rapid movement. The necessary quantities for positional warfare (heavy shelling) are not available.'[74] At the forefront of the German penetration eastward, the quartermaster-general's war diary of Guderian's panzer group pronounced the munitions situation on 22 July 'critical', especially in Schweppenburg's XXIV Panzer Corps.[75] Two days later the supply of Vietinghoff's XXXXVI Panzer Corps was also being singled out as 'critical', while Lemelsen's XXXXVII Panzer Corps was judged 'tight'.[76] What this meant to the fighting units is most apparent from Vietinghoff's arduous struggle at Yel'nya. Guderian noted how ammunition for the 10th Panzer Division had to be fetched by road from supply depots a staggering 440 kilometres to the rear.[77] The divisional war diary

[73] 'KTB Nr.1 Panzergruppe 2 Bd.II vom 22.7.1941 bis 20.8.41' BA-MA RH 21–2/928, Fol. 6 (22 July 1941).

[74] Walther Lammers (ed.), *'Fahrtberichte' aus der Zeit des deutsch-sowjetischen Krieges 1941. Protokolle des Begleitoffiziers des Kommandierenden Generals LIII. Armeekorps* (Boppard am Rhein, 1988), p. 205 (21 July 1941).

[75] 'Kriegstagebuch der O.Qu.-Abt. Pz. A.O.K.2 von 21.6.41 bis 31.3.42' BA-MA RH 21–2/819, Fol. 289 (22 July 1941).

[76] Ibid., Fol. 285 (24 July 1941).   [77] Guderian, *Panzer Leader*, p. 181.

noted on 21 July that 'in spite of all efforts by the corps in the coming days there will be no oil for the panzers. The munitions situation is also strained... in particular artillery shells must be used sparingly.' By the evening the division reported to the corps that the 7th Panzer Regiment (the tank arm of the division) would only be operational again when oil and a number of new motors were delivered. Until then the report stated: 'In view of the constant Russian counterattacks a few panzers have been made provisionally operational.'[78] The fact that one month into Operation Barbarossa a panzer division was struggling to make even a handful of its tanks operational, and even then with only extremely limited fuel and ammunition, says much about the state of equipment and the supply system. Nor was this the exception. On 22 July the 18th Panzer Division was reinforced by 30 new Panzer Mark IIIs and IVs, which still only brought the division up to 20 per cent of its full operational strength[79] and, as the heavy fighting continued, by 24 July the divisional strength had again shrunk to just 12 operational tanks.[80] Figures are not always readily obtainable for all the panzer divisions, but from those available the overall picture is a consistently bleak one. Among the strongest in Guderian's panzer group were the 17th and 4th Panzer Divisions which on 22 July were operating at 40 and 35 per cent strength respectively.[81] In Hoth's panzer group the situation on 21 July was marginally better, but still only amounted to an average strength of around 42 per cent for each of his four panzer divisions. In addition, the number of destroyed or totally lost panzers (i.e. those tanks which could not be repaired and returned to active service) had risen to 27 per cent (see Figure 7.3).[82] These figures from Panzer Group 3's war diary and Panzer Group 2's divisional and corps diaries seem to refute Halder's oft cited figure from 23 July in which he reported a 50 per cent average strength among the panzer divisions, although he himself added the note, 'here and there apparently less'.[83]

---

[78] 'Kriegstagebuch der 10.Panzer Division Nr.5 vom: 22.5. bis: 7.10.41' BA-MA RH 27–10/26a (21 July 1941).

[79] 'Kriegstagebuch Nr.2 XXXXVII.Pz.Korps. Ia 25.5.1941 – 22.9.1941' BA-MA RH 24–47/2 (22 July 1941).

[80] Bartov, *Hitler's Army*, p. 20.

[81] 'Kriegstagebuch Nr.2 XXXXVII.Pz.Korps. Ia 25.5.1941 – 22.9.1941' BA-MA RH 24–47/2 (22 July 1941); 'Kriegstagebuch 4.Panzer-Division Führungsabtl. 26.5.41 – 31.3.42' BA-MA RH 27–4/10, pp. 67–68 (22 July 1941). The 4th Panzer Division had in fact raised the number of its operational tanks by repairing and returning to service about 20 panzers since 17 July.

[82] 'Panzerarmeeoberkommandos Anlagen zum Kriegstagebuch "Berichte, Besprechungen, Beurteilungen der Lage" Bd.IV 22.7.41 – 31.8.41' BA-MA RH 21–3/47, Fol. 112 (23 July 1941).

[83] Franz Halder, KTB III, p. 104 (23 July 1941).

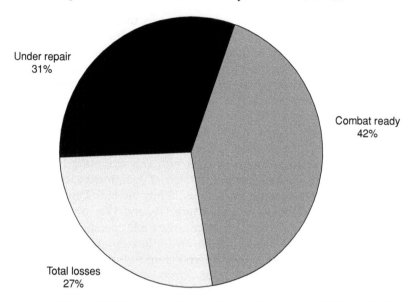

Under repair
31%

Combat ready
42%

Total losses
27%

Figure 7.3 Combat readiness of Panzer Group 3 on 21 July 1941. 'Panz-erarmeeoberkommandos Anlagen zum Kriegstagesbuch "Berichte, Besprechungen, Beurteilungen der Lage" Bd.IV 22.7.41 – 31.8.41' BA-MA RH 21-3/47. Fol. 112 (23 July 1941).

Lacking adequate resources, elements of the panzer groups were resort-ing to extraordinary measures to meet the demands of their extended fronts. On 21 July 4th Panzer Division, having cut off ten to twelve thousand Soviet soldiers in a forest near Cherikov, took around 2,000 prisoners in the fighting and then, lacking adequate air, artillery and panzer support, opted to allow the rest to return to Soviet lines rather than endure what was expected to be heavy material and personnel losses in continuing to oppose their breakout.[84] It was a reflection of the tacti-cal choices confronting commanders all along the line, as the changing relationship between individual strength and external pressure forced pragmatic responses to engagements. No longer did the panzer divisions reign supreme on the battlefield with superior firepower and mobility. Clashes were increasingly being fought on far more equal terms, with the Red Army even able to dominate in some sectors. The inability of Army Group Centre to cut down the constant pressure from the east led to a form of strategic deadlock with forces pinned down all along the front

[84] 'Kriegstagebuch 4.Panzer-Division Führungsabtl. 26.5.41 – 31.3.42' BA-MA RH 27-4/10, pp. 67–68 (21 July 1941).

and incapable of supporting each other or being assembled in enough mass to close the troublesome opening in the pocket around Smolensk. As Bock observed on 21 July: 'Pilots report that strong enemy forces are marching out of the pocket to the east.'[85]

The continued presence of this hole and the inability of the panzer groups to close it forms the best example of the failing military solution to the developing strategic crisis engulfing Army Group Centre. Unaccustomed to setbacks on the battlefield, and seemingly incapable of seeing the many integral failings that accompanied the whole concept of Operation Barbarossa, the frustrated generals of Army Group Centre sought answers by pointing the finger at each other. Hoth clearly believed that responsibility for closing the gap lay with Guderian and bemoaned his decision to strike instead towards Yel'nya.[86] Guderian, on the other hand, blamed Kluge for interfering in his panzer group and overriding his orders.[87] Kluge in turn directed the same accusation against Bock – a charge that Bock strenuously rejected in a meeting with Brauchitsch on 21 July. Bock then responded with a personal attack on Kluge's character.

I have scrupulously avoided any intermixing in Kluge's area of command, because of my awareness of his ego . . . I outlined in broad strokes Kluge's strange behaviour . . . I told Brauchitsch that it was very hard not to wound his vanity.[88]

The pettiness of such infighting must have seemed tiresome to Brauchitsch who was worried about the overall situation and had not come to arbitrate the personal disputes of the men he trusted to conduct the operation. Yet being egotistical is not an uncommon trait among men who rise to command armies, with all the pitfalls this brings out when the fortunes of war sour.

As the ferocity of the fighting continued with unabated violence, appeals from units within the panzer groups to be pulled out of the line for a period of rest and refitting were gaining in frequency. Panzer Group 3 noted the widespread feeling among the armoured troops that they were fighting the war almost alone, without the mass of the infantry, giving rise to the wish for a few days of quiet.[89] Such calls were echoed in Panzer Group 2, but as Lemelsen's XXXXVII Panzer Corps observed, gaining any kind of breathing space was 'extremely problematic' and could only be achieved when the infantry arrived in force to replace them on

---

[85] Fedor von Bock, KTB 'Osten I', Fol. 38, *War Diary*, p. 258 (21 July 1941).
[86] Hoth, *Panzer-Operationen*, p. 97.   [87] Guderian, *Panzer Leader*, p. 179.
[88] Fedor von Bock, KTB 'Osten I', Fols. 38–39, *War Diary*, pp. 258–259 (21 July 1941).
[89] '3rd Pz. Gr. KTB 25.5.41 – 31.8.41' BA-MA Microfilm 59054, Fol. 153 (22 July 1941).

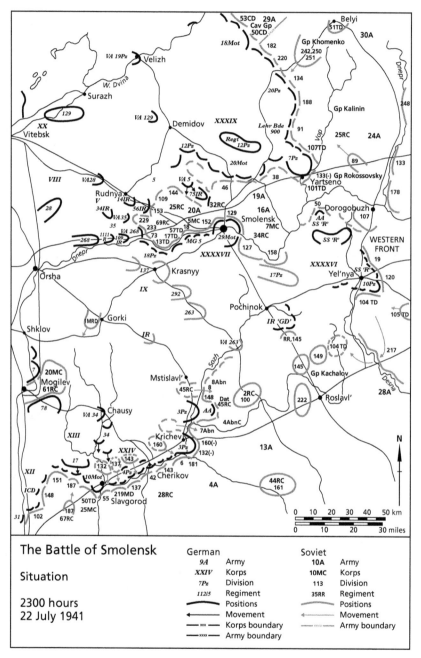

Map 9 Dispositions of Army Group Centre 22 July 1941: David M. Glantz, *Atlas of the Battle of Smolensk 7 July–10 September 1941*

the front (see Map 9).[90] In the meantime, despite all their deficiencies, the panzer and motorised divisions remained bound to the front,
enduring the daily grind of relentless battle and hardening the strategic
stalemate gripping the whole army group. It is not surprising, therefore,
that without the ability to concentrate and deal decisively with the enemy,
the motorised and panzer units of Army Group Centre found themselves
embroiled in an ever more costly struggle, eroding their strength in an
inescapable war of attrition.

On 23 July the major Soviet counter-strike planned by Zhukov began,
but from the beginning it was complicated by problems of poor co-
ordination and delays in the deployment of formations. As a result, the
offensive developed in a staggered fashion and was further complicated
by shortages of tanks, aircraft and logistical support,[91] which quickly
ruled out any prospect of a Soviet-style blitzkrieg. Instead, the offensive
developed as a kind of crude blunt instrument hammering away at the
German front, gaining little ground, but inflicting fearsome casualties
on both sides. Although the Soviet offensive, which ebbed and flowed
until early August, did not come close to achieving its stated objective
of pushing Army Group Centre back and relieving the Soviet position
around Smolensk, the cumulative effect of its bludgeoning attacks on
Bock's panzer groups means that the Soviet offensive cannot be depicted
as a comprehensive failure. The furious close quarters engagements and
violent artillery bombardments exacted a cost which, in the long run,
proved especially detrimental to the high-quality German formations.

Beyond material and personnel losses, the Soviet offensive also frustrated renewed German attempts to close the pocket around Smolensk.
By 23 July Bock's increasing exasperation at the inability of his two
panzer groups to make any headway over such a relatively short distance
was becoming more and more conspicuous. Both Hoth and Guderian
were in the process of scraping together the necessary force to be used
for the operation,[92] but as Timoshenko's offensive developed, every available unit was needed to hold the line and repulse the attacks. A thrust
by Hoth was the most favourable option to both Hitler and Bock, but
the panzer group's war diary makes it clear that nothing in Schmidt's
XXXIX Panzer Corps, on the northern flank of the pocket, could be
spared before infantry support arrived. The 7th Panzer Division, the

---

[90] 'Kriegstagebuch Nr.2 XXXXVII.Pz.Korps. Ia 25.5.1941 – 22.9.1941' BA-MA RH
    24–47/2 (23 July 1941).
[91] Glantz, *Battle for Smolensk*, pp. 33–41; Kipp, 'Barbarossa and the Crisis', pp. 142–143.
[92] '3rd Pz. Gr. KTB 25.5.41 – 31.8.41' BA-MA Microfilm 59054, Fol. 156 (23 July 1941);
    'KTB Nr.1 Panzergruppe 2 Bd.II vom 22.7.1941 bis 20.8.41' BA-MA RH 21–2/928,
    Fol. 14 (23 July 1941).

unit best placed strategically for an attack south, was caught in 'intense defensive battles to the east and the west' and could not risk thinning its lines further by thrusting south.[93] The neighbouring 12th Panzer Division was likewise extremely hard pressed with the divisional diary noting that there was 'not one man in reserve' and that as a result '[we] must trust in the troops.'[94] The 18th and 20th Motorised Infantry divisions as well as the 20th Panzer Division were all similarly engaged and in any case, the more distant elements lacked the necessary fuel supplies to make the journey.[95]

Attempting to close the pocket from the south, Guderian sought to make a thrust north from the Yel'nya salient using the 2nd SS Division known as *Das Reich*, but as Guderian discovered from a visit to the front on 23 July this was a hopeless venture and would require the additional commitment of the Infantry Regiment *Grossdeutschland*. Over the following days, however, Guderian later recalled: 'the Russian attacks went on with undiminished violence . . . all attempts to advance towards Dorogobuzh were a complete failure'.[96] Yet this passage from Guderian's memoir only tells part of the story. Much less than thrusting forward in attack, *Das Reich* was under enormous pressure just holding its position and suffering debilitating losses in the process (see Map 10). At midday on 24 July the war diary of Panzer Group 2 described the situation as 'extremely tense', which then became 'critical' by the afternoon and eventually became a retreat.[97] As one survivor, Heid Ruehl, later recalled from the fierce battles in the northwest of the salient on 24 July:

The gunners, working like fury, finally beat off the first Russian tank attacks, but these were then renewed in greater strength and then our motorcycle battalion came under heavy pressure. We were smothered in a drum fire such as we had never before experienced . . . Because of the severe losses which it had sustained [the] motor-cycle battalion had to be taken out of the line and was replaced by an East Prussian engineer battalion. With the help of that formation we stemmed the Russian advance, albeit only temporarily, for soon ammunition for the guns began to run out and we were only allowed to fire against certain, specified targets.[98]

[93] '3rd Pz. Gr. KTB 25.5.41 – 31.8.41' BA-MA Microfilm 59054, Fols. 159–160 (24 July 1941).
[94] 'Kriegstagebuch Nr.1 der 12.Pz.Div. vom 25.5.41 – 30.9.41' BA-MA RH 27–12/2, Fol. 67 (24 July 1941).
[95] '3rd Pz. Gr. KTB 25.5.41 – 31.8.41' BA-MA Microfilm 59054, Fol. 160 (24 July 1941).
[96] Guderian, *Panzer Leader*, p. 181.
[97] 'KTB Nr.1 Panzergruppe 2 Bd.II vom 22.7.1941 bis 20.8.41' BA-MA RH 21–2/928, Fols. 22, 24–25 (24 July 1941).
[98] As cited in James Lucas, *Das Reich. The Military Role of the 2nd SS Division* (London, 1991), p. 61.

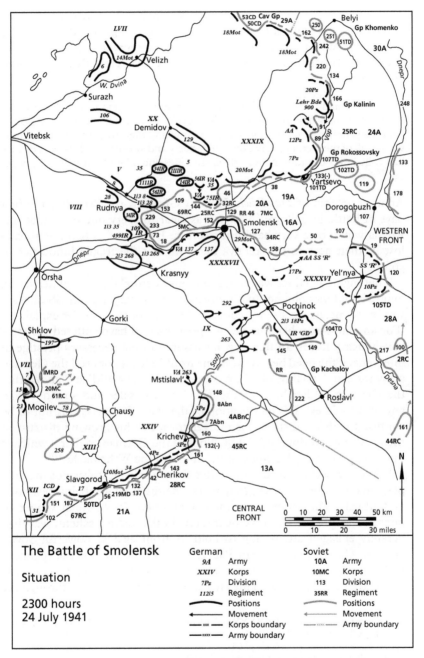

Map 10 Dispositions of Army Group Centre 24 July 1941: David M.
Glantz, *Atlas of the Battle of Smolensk 7 July–10 September 1941*

The severe shortages were common to Vietinghoff's entire corps and the possibility of solving these was, for the time being, noted to be 'very unlikely'.[99] When the relentless Soviet pressure forced *Das Reich* to pull back from its positions on the left flank of Yel'nya, Heid Ruehl's account continued:

> The battery had been ordered to pull back from its position near Ushakova. We were not the only ones on the road. Motorcycles loaded with wounded and other comrades, either alone or in groups, were making their way out of the burning village, all of them completely exhausted, dusty and sweaty. The Russian advance had rolled over our thin infantry defensive lines and a lot of our lads did not get out.[100]

Another veteran of *Das Reich*, Helmut Günther, recalled after the first days of battle in Yel'nya: 'Now it was clear to every one of us that this Russia would be a very hard nut to crack. If some of us had not already lost it, then here in the Yel'nya bend we lost the fragile innocence of youth.'[101]

That night, as Hitler was engaged in his habitual pastime of delivering long-winded monologues to his inner circle, the plight of the SS division was by no means a cause for concern. On the contrary, Hitler explained: 'For an elite force, like our SS, it's great luck to have suffered comparatively heavy losses. In this way, it's assured of the necessary prestige to intervene, if the need be, on the home front.' He also praised the German army for being 'technically the most perfect in the world' and added that the German soldier 'in a moment of crisis, is safer and sounder than any other soldier'. His glorification of the army, however, was not to be confused with his distaste for the generals, nor his growing distrust of them. 'I've never doubted the qualities of the German soldier – which is more than I can say for some of the chiefs of the Wehrmacht.'[102]

While the battles raged around the Yel'nya salient, it was not the only place in Guderian's panzer group where the situation was being described as 'critical'. The infantry regiment *Grossdeutschland*, which Guderian intended to use for offensive operations in the Yel'nya salient, was desperately engaged attempting to hold its front against powerful Soviet attacks. The supporting 18th Panzer Division noted that the regiment had 'not the slightest reserve available' and that '[t]he situation is repeatedly extremely critical' with the enemy having already broken through the

[99] 'Kriegstagebuch Nr.2 des XXXXVI.Pz.Korps Teil II. 8.7.41 – 23.8.41' BA-MA RH 24–46/8, Fol. 99 (24 July 1941).
[100] As cited in Lucas, *Das Reich*, p. 63.
[101] Günther, *Hot Motors, Cold Feet*, pp. 101–102.
[102] Trevor-Roper (ed.), *Hitler's Table Talk*, p. 13 (night of 24–25 July).

lines twice in regimental strength.[103] The 18th Panzer Division therefore strenuously opposed the orders for the removal of part of *Grossdeutschland* for the offensive towards Dorogobuzh. Yet this went ahead in spite of intelligence indicating additional enemy strength, including 40–50 tanks, were moving up behind the Soviet front and it was anticipated that 'it is not possible to prevent the enemy breakthrough under the current conditions'.[104]

While the centre of Bock's front strained under the immense pressure, the first major elements of Strauss's 9th Army and Weichs's 2nd Army were at last arriving on the western segments of the Smolensk pocket, but the desperate call to bring up more infantry was again endangering the hard-pressed southern flank. On 20 July Heinrici, commanding the XXXXIII Army Corps, wrote home of the many problems his infantry divisions faced.

The Russian is very strong and fights desperately, driven by his commissars. Worst of all are the forest battles. Everywhere the Russian suddenly appears and shoots, attacking columns, single transports, dispatches, and so on. The war here is without doubt very bad and to this must be added the tremendous road difficulties, the enormous spaces, the unending forests, the difficulties with the language and so on. All past campaigns seem like child's play in comparison with the present war. Our losses are heavy . . .[105]

Describing the heavy fighting on the army group's southern flank one junior doctor, Gerhard Meyer, wrote home in a letter on 23 July:

After weeks of very tiring marching my division reached the Dnepr, at that place the Russians in a great counterattack crossed the river to the west. This first encounter against the superior enemy, unable to be softened up with artillery, cost us much blood. In four places there was an enduring and very costly back and forth, whereby the two or threefold Russian superiority, above all in artillery, was very noticeable. The active strength of the division has sunken to less than half, with 80 per cent of the officers lost.[106]

On 24 July Weichs gave Bock 'a very pessimistic description of the situation' in which the loss of Bobruisk was suggested as the possible outcome of moving more infantry east. Bock, however, was adamant and accepted full responsibility.[107] By 26 July the LIII Army Corps defending Bobruisk

[103] '18. Panzer Division, Abt. Ia. Kriegstagebuch Teil I vom: 22.6 – 20.8.41' BA-MA RH 27–18/20, Fol. 46 (23 July 1941).
[104] Ibid., Fol. 48 (24 July 1941).
[105] Hürter, *Ein deutscher General an der Ostfront*, p. 69 (20 July 1941).
[106] Bähr and Bähr (eds.), *Kriegsbriefe gefallener Studenten*, p. 209 (23 July 1941).
[107] Fedor von Bock, KTB 'Osten I', Fol. 41, *War Diary*, p. 261 (24 July 1941). See also Franz Halder, KTB III, pp. 109–110 (24 July 1941).

reported that the individual companies of the 255th Infantry Division had to defend an average front of 1,200 metres.[108]

In addition to the delays caused to Weichs's infantry on the southern flank, the continuing Soviet resistance at Mogilev, in spite of the gravest deprivations, was holding up a further three infantry divisions, plus the artillery of a fourth, on the Dnepr. As Bock observed with a degree of irritation: 'The Russians are unbelievably stubborn!'[109] The siege continued until 27 July when supplies of food and ammunition were finally exhausted and the weary defenders, numbering 35,000 men,[110] passed into captivity. Yet they had fought valiantly, making the Germans pay dearly for the capture of the city in both expenditure of strength and loss of time. Such fanaticism on the part of the Soviet soldiers prompted the first private doubts about the course the war might take. Writing to his wife, Heinrici despaired that the Soviet will to resist was unbroken, and then added; 'Presently, one has the impression that even if Moscow was taken, the war would go on from the depths of this unending country.'[111]

'I am on the brink of despair' (Franz Halder)

The issuing of Directive 33a on 23 July had already sent a shock wave through the OKH command and as the orders were passed down to the field commands the effect was no less dramatic. Bock, whose army group was most directly affected, was incensed and even suggested the abolition of his command, presumably a veiled threat of resignation. In his diary for 24 July Bock gave voice to the ire of his discontent:

I sent a report to Brauchitsch opposing the new operation and suggested that they remove the army group headquarters if they stick to the announced plan of action. Perhaps they will correctly construe from this suggestion that I am 'piqued.' That is rubbish! But if the army group is carved up into three parts there will be no need for the headquarters.[112]

Bock's profound resentment of the new operational orders stemmed from two sources. On the one hand, he fundamentally disagreed with shifting the point of main concentration away from Moscow. In December 1940 during his convalescence from a serious stomach ailment, Bock read a series of articles in the *Neue Züricher Zeitung* entitled 'How France Lost

[108] Lammers (ed.), *'Fahrtberichte'*, p. 205 (26 July 1941).
[109] Fedor von Bock, KTB 'Osten I', Fol. 41, *War Diary*, p. 261 (24 July 1941).
[110] Ibid., Fol. 45, p. 265 (27 July 1941). David Glantz citing Soviet sources offers the much lower figure of 12,000 men (Glantz, *Battle for Smolensk*, p. 41).
[111] Hürter, *Ein deutscher General an der Ostfront*, p. 70 (22 July 1941).
[112] Fedor von Bock, KTB 'Osten I', Fol. 41, *War Diary*, p. 261 (24 July 1941).

the War'; here he noted: 'I found Maurois' [the journalist] view of the fall of Paris especially interesting.' Bock then copied into his diary the following passage from the article: 'After the loss of Paris France became a body without a head. The war was lost!'[113] Conceivably, Bock attached a similar importance to the capture of Moscow and now saw that hope squandered. A second motivating factor for Bock was the prestige blow; he had already suffered the frustration of being switched to the secondary role in the French campaign and now with all his panzer forces going to Leeb and Rundstedt, he was facing an even greater relegation.[114]

On 25 July Keitel arrived at Bock's headquarters ostensibly to discuss the hole in the Smolensk pocket, but in substance Keitel's presentation was entirely concerned with Hitler's most recent obsession – smaller tactical encirclements. Reports that sizeable Soviet forces had escaped the German pocket, with the panzer groups incapable of closing the pincers, had no doubt convinced Hitler that large-scale encirclements were invariably flawed and should be replaced by smaller movements where the enemy could be completely eliminated.[115] Given the increasingly limited offensive capacity of the panzer groups, such a theory had merit but, as Bock immediately observed, it appeared inconsistent with the wider objectives of the campaign. There were still numerous Soviet armies to be destroyed and many distant objectives to be reached, requiring in Bock's view broad strategic movements, which were impossible to reconcile with smaller tactical operations.[116] Thus in addition to Hitler altering the strategic direction of Bock's armies, the Field Marshal was now being instructed on the operational parameters for conducting new offensives.

Keitel then related Hitler's concern for the southern flank of Army Group Centre and proposed that Guderian turn south to encircle enemy forces 'in individual small packages'[117] around Gomel and Mosyr. Such a suggestion was met with bewilderment on Bock's part.

I told him that this conflicted with the directive given to me yesterday by the Army High Command. According to it, the forces of my right wing, together with Panzer Group Guderian, are supposed to be sent against objectives far to the southeast, while Keitel's proposal calls for these elements to be turned southwest.[118]

---

[113] Fedor von Bock, KTB 'Vorbereitungszeit', Fol. 3, *War Diary*, p. 195 (14 December 1940).
[114] Leach, *German Strategy Against Russia*, p. 116.
[115] KTB OKW, Volume II, pp. 1035–1036. Document 81 (25 July 1941).
[116] Fedor von Bock, KTB 'Osten I', Fol. 42, *War Diary*, p. 262 (25 July 1941).
[117] KTB OKW, Volume II, p. 1036, Document 81 (25 July 1941).
[118] Fedor von Bock, KTB 'Osten I', Fol. 42, *War Diary*, p. 262 (25 July 1941).

When news of the operation reached Guderian he too was confounded by the apparent contradiction between his new orders and the goals of the campaign.

I expected to be told to push on towards Moscow or at least Briansk; to my surprise I learned that Hitler had ordered that my 2nd Panzer Group was to go for Gomel in collaboration with Second Army. This meant that my Panzer Group would be swung round and would be advancing in a south-westerly direction, that is to say towards Germany; but Hitler was anxious to encircle the eight to ten Russian divisions in the Gomel area. We were informed that Hitler was convinced that large-scale envelopments were not justified: the theory on which they were based was a false one put out by the General Staff Corps...All officers who took part in this conference were of the opinion that this was incorrect: that these manoeuvres on our part simply gave the Russians time to set up new formations and to use their inexhaustible man-power for the creation of fresh defensive lines in the rear area: even more important, we were sure that this strategy would not result in the urgently necessary, rapid conclusion of the campaign.[119]

Understandably, Hitler's latest ideas produced much antipathy and confusion within the army command, not least because they seemed to contradict his own broad strategic movements outlined in Directives 33 and 33a. Emerging even at this early period of the war was Hitler's alarming propensity for a schizophrenic military policy, which could change according to his mood or the latest military reports to reach his headquarters. Ever more divorced from reality, Hitler sought to counter the escalating dimensions of the war through his increased personal involvement, convinced that victory should not be trusted to the imperfect judgement of his generals. Insisting upon tactical encounters, but proposing the war be won with grand strategic goals divided between Leningrad, Moscow and the Volga, was only the beginning of Hitler's chaotic foray into military affairs, further widening the gulf with the OKH. As Heusinger privately wrote on 25 July: 'Ceaseless disquiet and perpetual interference from the highest position, that is totally unnecessary. Aggravation is the result.'[120]

In further reaction to Hitler's interference, an OKH meeting on 25 July that brought together the chiefs of staff of the three army groups operating in the east was warned by Brauchitsch that it was 'not possible' for the OKH to 'protect against intervention from above'.[121] Yet, in his private notes before the meeting Halder determined that the '[s]tray shots from the stratosphere' had to be met with 'patience, but also timely refutation'.[122] In essence, the meeting was an attempt by Halder to achieve a consensus on basic principles of strategy and thus remove

---

[119] Guderian, *Panzer Leader*, pp. 182–183.   [120] As cited in Meyer, *Heusinger*, p. 154.
[121] Franz Halder, KTB III, p. 117 (25 July 1941).   [122] Ibid., p. 111 (25 July 1941).

the danger that the army groups would make contrary or competing demands to Hitler.[123] This was particularly important as Halder correctly recognised that '[t]he front is more trusted than us!' By this he meant the generals at the front, as opposed to himself and the other the 'desk generals' at OKH. This realisation instilled in Halder the idea that some reports to Hitler should be made through courier generals from the front[124] – a prospect which emphasised the importance of a unified pro-Moscow position.

In a discussion with Brauchitsch on 26 July, it seems Halder heard for the first time of Hitler's recent scheme for smaller tactical encirclements like the one being planned around Gomel and Mosyr. Like Bock, Halder not only now feared for the strategic direction of the campaign, but also the operational method for engaging the Red Army. The inherent contradictions of Hitler's strategy were also plainly evident to him and he complained in his diary that:

If striking at small local enemy concentrations becomes our sole objective, the campaign will resolve itself into a series of minor successes which will advance our front only slowly by steps. Pursuing such a policy would eliminate tactical risks and enable us to close the gaps between the army groups, the result would be that we use up our strength expanding the front in width at the expense of depth – and end up in positional warfare![125]

Halder then discussed the matter with Bock who was vehemently opposed to sending panzers back towards Gomel from the east, and spoke of Hitler's plan sabotaging the operational conceptions of the campaign.[126] Bock still clung to the fading hope that his entire army group would be employed for a concentrated drive east to destroy Timoshenko's remaining armies. Bock believed that: 'Securing the attack's southern flank would, for the most part, be a matter for Army Group South. From all that I heard, however, I doubt that the Supreme Command will be talked into it.'[127] Halder, on the other hand, remained defiant and went to see Hitler that evening in a meeting that he later described as 'long-winded', but at times erupting into 'heated argument'. 'The Führer's analysis', Halder recorded, 'indicates a complete break with the strategy of large operational conceptions.'[128] According to Hitler, the Red Army could not be beaten with such operational manoeuvres because they simply did not know when they were defeated. Soviet armies needed to be destroyed

[123] Klink, 'Die Operationsführung', p. 492.
[124] Franz Halder, KTB III, p. 111 (25 July 1941).   [125] Ibid., p. 121 (26 July 1941).
[126] Ibid. (26 July 1941).
[127] Fedor von Bock, KTB 'Osten I', Fol. 44, War Diary, p. 263 (26 July 1941).
[128] Franz Halder, KTB III, pp. 122–123 (26 July 1941).

Figure 7.4 Upon reaching the line east of Smolensk Army Group Centre had to repel desperate counter-attacks against its thinly held front.

piecemeal in actions of a more tactical character. To a point Halder was prepared to acknowledge that the large operational encirclements were less than perfect, but he could not reconcile Hitler's preference for smaller encirclements with the attainment of Barbarossa's goal to reach the Volga.

The Russians have plenty of manpower and I don't believe that we could pursue the new policy to the point where the enemy cracks and the way is again clear for large scale operations. In my view, these ideas mark the beginning of a decline in our previously dynamic operations and a readiness to throw away the opportunities offered to us by the impetus of our infantry and armour.[129]

Halder's sceptical questioning of Hitler's latest contribution to the war in the east did nothing to mend the rift between the two men, and consequently Halder's attempts to re-engage Hitler on the importance of Moscow were abruptly dismissed without Hitler offering any rationale for his position.[130] As a result, Halder's mounting exasperation at Hitler's overbearing interference in the military campaign caused him to blame every hindrance on Hitler's baneful influence, but in truth, even without the internal troubles of the German command, Operation Barbarossa was already in serious trouble.

[129] Ibid., p. 123 (26 July 1941).   [130] Ibid. (26 July 1941).

The paralysis caused by spreading its resources too thinly gripped Army Group Centre and was also being felt in the neighbouring two army groups, which led to calls for greater concentration of resources against a unified objective. During a visit by Paulus to Army Group North on 26 July the armoured commanders of Panzer Group 4 (Hoepner, Manstein and Reinhardt) all agreed that the terrain between Lake Ilmen and Lake Peipus on the approach to Leningrad was in no way suited to armoured warfare.[131] Due to this assessment and the undiminished enemy resistance, Leeb judged the further advance of Manstein's LVI Panzer Corps to be 'very unfavourable'. By contrast General Reinhardt's XXXXI Panzer Corps was better placed, but was momentarily halted with heavy losses.[132] Confronting such difficulties, Manstein did not mince words in his report to Paulus:

I put him in the picture about the battles we had fought to date and pointed out how run-down our panzer corps had become in country which was most unsuitable for the use of armoured troops...The losses of our corps' three mobile divisions already amounted to 6,000 men, and both the troops and the equipment were being subjected to excessive strain... I told Paulus that in my opinion the best thing to do would be to withdraw the entire Panzer Group from an area where a rapid advance was almost out of the question and to use it against Moscow.[133]

Yet unlike his decisive role in shaping German strategy in 1940, Manstein had no access to Hitler and would be at the serious disadvantage of arguing against Hitler's favoured conceptions, as opposed to confirming them as he had done the year before.

If there was one man who was to prove an indispensable ally to Halder in arguing the case for Moscow it was Jodl. Exactly how much influence he exerted is difficult to gauge, but Jodl's stance is probably as significant for the arguments he advanced as the office he represented. The well-known rivalry between the OKW and the OKH undoubtedly added weight to their common cause when, for once, they found themselves on the same side, rather than vying for Hitler's favour. The exception to this was Keitel, but as the eastern front was the sole theatre outside the mandate of the OKW he possessed no direct responsibility and, accordingly, involved himself little in the dispute except to refer the complaints of the generals back to Hitler. Keitel's own position was, predictably, never in any real doubt given his notorious devotion to Hitler, but for that same

---

[131] Ibid., p. 124 (26 July 1941).
[132] Wilhelm Ritter von Leeb, KTB, p. 309 (26 July 1941).
[133] Von Manstein, *Lost Victories*, pp. 197–198. See also Hürter, *Hitlers Heerführer*, p. 288, footnote 38.

reason his opinion was scarcely sought.[134] In Warlimont's account, Jodl was the key figure inside Hitler's headquarters backing the cause of the OKH, so that the opposition to Hitler was now a unified chorus of central figures in the OKW, the entire OKH and practically all the relevant field commanders.

Either in the scheduled discussions or alone with Hitler, Warlimont claimed that Jodl 'found a soft spot and took the next opportunity to speak out in favour of the attack on Moscow'.[135] This took place on 27 July when Jodl confronted Hitler with arguments centred, not on the importance of capturing the Soviet capital, as Halder had emphasised, but on his conviction that it was only here that the remaining strength of the Red Army could be found and defeated. This approach wisely took up Hitler's own reasoning that the enemy had to be destroyed where it was found.[136] Typically, Hitler countered with his now familiar arguments emphasising the economic importance of the Ukraine and Caucasus,[137] but Jodl's vocal intervention in the debate proved a vital ingredient. 'On the following day', Warlimont wrote, 'probably under weight of new unfavourable situation reports coming in from [Army Groups] Centre and North, he [Hitler] suddenly appeared ready to give up his large-scale operations in the south.'[138] The true extent of Jodl's role in swaying Hitler remains in question, but he certainly contributed an influential voice to the opposition against Hitler's plan. The effect on the German dictator was not always obvious from his unfailingly steely facade in the daily situation reports, and his unequivocal language with the generals, but in fact the burden of indecision about what to do next was gnawing at him.

On 28 July during a short walk with his army adjutant, Major Gerhard Engel, and his chief military adjutant, Colonel Rudolf Schmundt, Hitler gave a rare insight into his private thoughts. According to Engel, Hitler confided that he was not sleeping at night because he was 'not yet clear about some things'. Expanding on this further, the Führer revealed that he was torn between political and economic objectives in the Soviet Union. Political objectives necessitated the capture of Leningrad and Moscow, while economically he needed to secure his *Lebensraum* in the

---

[134] The disdainful tone Keitel used to describe the opposition to Hitler's preference makes clear where his sympathies lay even after the war (Gorlitz (ed.), *Memoirs of Field-Marshal Keitel*, pp. 150–151).

[135] Warlimont, *Im Hauptquartier*, Band I, p. 199.

[136] KTB OKW, Volume II, p. 1019, Document 62 (27 June 1941).

[137] KTB OKW, Volume II, pp. 1036–1037, Document 82 (27 July 1941); Mendelssohn, *Die Nürnberger Dokumente*, p. 386.

[138] Warlimont, *Im Hauptquartier*, Band I, p. 199.

south, 'where honey and milk flow'.[139] The next day (29 July) on a visit to Panzer Group 2, Schmundt too revealed to Guderian Hitler's indecisiveness over how to proceed with the war. Leningrad, Moscow and the Ukraine were the three objectives under consideration, but according to Schmundt no final decision had yet been reached. In his memoir Guderian professed to have urged Moscow to Schmundt, 'with all the force of which I was capable'.[140]

Not only was Hitler grappling with the strategic direction of the campaign, but also its projected timing. Shortly after the launch of Barbarossa, Hitler told the former German ambassador in Moscow, Friedrich Werner Graf von der Schulenburg, that he expected to be in Moscow by 15 August and to have won the whole campaign by 1 October.[141] Both estimates were now clearly unattainable and the issue of time was becoming an increasingly urgent problem in the impasse over how to win the eastern campaign. The breaking point in Hitler's tough outward resolve to follow his own strategic vision came on 28 July when he abruptly announced to his staff that owing to the developing situation over the last few days, 'above all the appearance of strong new enemy formations before the front and the flanks of Army Group Centre', it had become necessary to reassess the launch of large-scale operations as outlined in Directive 33a.[142] In essence, the rapidly changing character of the war in the east, which had slowed the German blitzkrieg to a halt, had forced Hitler to waver on the feasibility of ordering further wide ranging operations against an opponent who was clearly far from beaten. Instead, Hitler now insisted that the 'most urgent task' of Bock's army group was to clear the southern flank around Gomel – an operation reflecting his commitment to the doctrine of smaller encirclements.[143]

While Directive 33a was no longer the guiding principle of German strategy, Hitler remained very much undecided about the new strategic direction of the campaign and, for this reason, he probably did not wish to inform the army commanders of their potential opportunity. Thus, in spite of Brauchitsch being present for at least part of the meeting on 28 July, it seems Hitler only informed the Army Commander-in-Chief of the urgent need to resolve the situation at Gomel on Bock's southern

---

[139] Von Kotze (ed.), *Heeresadjutant bei Hitler 1938–1943*, p. 107 (28 July 1941).
[140] Guderian, *Panzer Leader*, p. 185.
[141] Ernst von Weizsäcker, *Erinnerungen. Mein Leben*, ed. Richard von Weizsäcker (Munich, 1950), pp. 315–316.
[142] KTB OKW, Volume II, p. 1040, Document 86 (28 July 1941); Mendelssohn, *Die Nürnberger Dokumente*, p. 387.
[143] KTB OKW, Volume II, p. 1040, Document 86 (28 July 1941); Mendelssohn, *Die Nürnberger Dokumente*, p. 387.

flank. Evidence that Brauchitsch did not yet know of Hitler's shifting deliberations on Directive 33a comes from his encounter with Halder that evening, upon returning to the OKH. From Halder's diary there is not a word of relief at the apparent modification of Directive 33a. Instead, Brauchitsch only seems to have related the substance of Hitler's order for the Gomel operation which infuriated Halder, who wrote in disgust about the 'absurdity of the operations now ordered. They are leading to a dispersal of our forces which will bring the deciding operation towards Moscow to a standstill.'[144] Halder then confided in a letter to his wife his true feelings about Hitler's ruinous meddling:

He is playing warlord again and proposing such absurd ideas, that he is putting in question everything our splendid operations have won so far. The Russian won't simply go away, like the French, when he has been operationally beaten. He has to be killed one at a time in a country that is half forest and marsh. This takes time and his nerves [Hitler's] won't stand it. Every few days I have to go there. Hours of empty talk with the result that there is only one man who knows how to wage wars. I am on the brink of despair, because I can predict exactly where this nonsense will end. If I didn't have my faith in God and my self assurance, I'd be like Brauchitsch, who is at the end of his tether and hides behind his rank so as not to betray his inner helplessness.[145]

Barely five weeks into a war that was supposed to be the decisive blitzkrieg campaign to secure hegemony in Europe against an inferior opponent, the demands of the conflict were overwhelming the army, and the German command was expending as much energy fighting within itself as addressing the problems of the front. On 29 July Heusinger noted that together with Halder he had 'to fight against much resistance, particularly against the ideas of the Führer'.[146] It all boded very ill for the outcome of the war, but like so many fundamental aspects of Barbarossa, the German command had to learn its lessons the hard way, often at the expense of time and strategic confusion.

On the battlefield at Army Group Centre a different lesson was being learned, which underscored the dangers of over-extension and resource depletion. Here, however, the price was paid in blood and the loss of irreplaceable equipment. Bock himself was still grappling with the dawning realisation of what it meant to wage war against the Soviet colossus and his diary for 26 July reflects his burgeoning astonishment.

---

[144] Franz Halder, KTB III, p. 129 (28 July 1941).
[145] Halder's letter as cited by Heidemarie Gräfin Schall-Riaucour, *Aufstand und Gehorsam. Offizierstum und Generalstab im Umbruch. Leben und Wirken von Generaloberst Franz Halder Generalstabchef 1938–1942* (Wiesbaden, 1972), p. 167 (28/29 July 1941).
[146] As cited in Meyer, *Heusinger*, p. 154.

It turns out that the Russians have completed a new, concentrated build-up around my projecting front. In many places they have tried to go over to the attack. Astonishing for an opponent who is so badly beaten; they must have unbelievable masses of material, for even now the field units still complain about the powerful effect of the enemy artillery. The Russians are also becoming more aggressive in the air.[147]

Bock was not overstating the matter. As many sectors of Germany's extensive eastern front were settling into the first stages of positional warfare, the Soviets revealed their preponderant advantage in artillery with an unremitting rain of fire that was quickly to become the bane of the German infantryman up and down the line. Making its first appearance in July 1941 was the experimental Soviet BM-13 *Katyusha* multiple rocket launcher (later dubbed by the German soldiers 'Stalin's organs'). This new weapon delivered a ten-second barrage of 132mm rockets. The effect was devastating and the weapon was soon moved into mass production.[148] One soldier who had fought in Poland, France and later Italy described his first experience of the Katyusha battery as 'the most terrible and shocking thing I have ever encountered'.[149] Observing the first usage of the new weapon at Rudnya near Smolensk, Marshal Andrei Yeremenko recalled:

On the afternoon of 15 July the earth shook with the unusual explosion of jet mines. Like red-tailed comets, the mines were hurled into the air . . . The effect of the simultaneous explosions of dozens of these mines was terrific. The Germans fled in panic, and even our own troops, . . . who for reasons of security had not been warned that this new weapon would be used, rushed back from the front line.[150]

Yet the real Soviet advantage lay not in specialised weaponry, but in the proportionate number of guns they could assemble and supply with ammunition. This is not to say there were not considerable imperfections in the Soviet employment and handling of artillery early in the war, but the Germans by comparison were frequently outgunned, and even then had great trouble bringing up sufficient stockpiles of shells.

Under the conditions of static warfare now beginning along the vast eastern front, the pre-eminence of the infantryman was on the rise, no

---

[147] Fedor von Bock, KTB 'Osten I', Fol. 43, *War Diary*, p. 263 (26 July 1941).
[148] Kipp, 'Overview Phase 1', p. 371. See also Glantz, *Colossus Reborn*, p. 307.
[149] Frisch with Jones, Jr., *Condemned to Live*, p. 82.
[150] As cited in Merridale, *Ivan's War*, pp. 110–111; Werth, *Russia at War 1941–1945*, p. 172. See also Chris Bellamy, *Absolute War. Soviet Russia in the Second World War* (New York, 2007), pp. 242–243.

longer in just securing the territory won by the panzers, but now holding the long front together. In this role the German infantry proved themselves well trained, but their equipment was deficient, especially in comparison to their Soviet opponents. One officer from the 4th Panzer Division remarked after the war: 'The equipment, which had proved efficient in the previous campaigns, was not robust enough for battle under the conditions prevailing in Russia. Russian equipment seemed to be more robust and less sensitive. Therefore, whoever got hold of a Russian tommy-gun kept it.'[151] An Italian officer who inspected a Russian machine gun for the first time remarked: 'I loved the simplicity, easy handling and firepower of this gun.'[152] Likewise, Colonel-General Ewald von Kleist, who later rose to the rank of Field Marshal and remained on the eastern front until March 1944, stated after the war: '[The Soviet] equipment was very good even in 1941, especially the tanks. Their artillery was excellent, and also most of the infantry weapons – their rifles were more modern than ours, and had a more rapid rate of fire.'[153] Colonel-General Erhard Raus, another former German commander with extensive experience on the eastern front, wrote for a post-war US military study:

The best weapon of the Russian infantryman was the machine pistol. It was easily handled, equal to Russian winter conditions, and one which the Germans also regarded highly . . . The mortar also proved highly valuable as the ideal weapon for terrain conditions where artillery support was impossible. At the beginning of the Eastern Campaign, Russian infantry far surpassed the German in mortar equipment and its use. The same was true for the Russian anti-tank gun, which at the beginning of the campaign considerably surpassed the anti-tank gun of the German infantry divisions in efficiency, and therefore was readily put to use whenever captured.[154]

Another element of the Red Army which is incorrectly regarded as antiquated for the time, is their extensive early use of horse cavalry. Fundamental to its success was the ability to maintain constant movement in difficult terrain (marshes and forest) where cover was plentiful and the German motorised forces could not operate. These advantages allowed for surprise raids on weak German positions, or long forays into the German rear to cut supply lines and destroy vital infrastructure.[155]

---

[151] Koch-Erpach, 'Crossing of the Dnepr River', p. 404.
[152] Giorgio Geddes, Nichivó. Life, Love and Death on the Russian Front (London, 2001), p. 18.
[153] Liddell Hart, The Other Side of the Hill, p. 330.
[154] Although originally written in the early 1950s Raus's work was later republished; Erhard Rauss, 'Russian Combat Methods in World War II' in Peter G. Tsouras (ed.), Fighting in Hell. The German Ordeal on the Eastern Front (New York, 1998), pp. 35–36.
[155] Ibid., pp. 40–41. See also Haape with Henshaw, Moscow Tram Stop, pp. 96–97.

Although not a replacement for mechanised operations, the cavalry was useful when employed on a limited scale against the exposed flanks of the over-extended German armies.[156]

The air battle on the eastern front was a more one-sided affair, but not to the degree that many histories have suggested hitherto.[157] In the opening days of Barbarossa the Luftwaffe inflicted carnage upon the Soviet air force, with staggering aircraft losses reaching into the thousands.[158] One authority put the figure at 4,614 Soviet aircraft destroyed by the end of June, 3,176 of these being eliminated on the ground and 1,438 in the air. By comparison, German losses amounted to just 330 planes.[159] Such figures underline a clear German superiority in the air, but for a variety of reasons this did not translate into anything more than a very short period of air supremacy on the eastern front.

In accordance with the precepts of a successful blitzkrieg, the Luftwaffe's first priority in the east was to win control of the immediate Soviet airspace, and then to concentrate resources on tactical support for the advancing army. Within just two days, the Luftwaffe had achieved total domination of the skies and had wreaked havoc on Soviet airfields in the western districts,[160] allowing the tactical switch towards assisting army operations. Yet there were still thousands of Soviet aircraft stationed well back from the western border districts, as well as many more in the Soviet interior. These had survived the initial devastation and could gradually be moved west to new airfields. In this brief period the Luftwaffe's dominance over the front was absolute, but not without pointed concerns. The chief of the operations department of the Luftwaffe, Major-General Hoffman von Waldau, commented to Halder on 1st July: 'The air force has greatly underestimated the numerical strength of the enemy. It is quite evident that the Russians initially had far more than 8,000 planes.'[161] Two days later Waldau wrote in his diary:

[156] The Red Army employed traditional cavalry throughout the war and even in September 1943 when the Soviet offensives began in earnest there were still eight Soviet cavalry corps, supported by light tanks (Mawdsley, *Thunder in the East*, p. 217).
[157] Many standard works on Barbarossa and World War II recount the initial successes of the German Luftwaffe on the eastern front, but tend not to follow up on the development of the air war in which, as early as late July 1941, the Luftwaffe's increasingly limited resources could only dominate narrow sectors of the front.
[158] This resulted in another round of arrests among the top echelon of the Soviet Air Force with many being severely beaten and imprisoned by the NKVD (Braithwaite, *Moscow 1941*, p. 134).
[159] Boog, 'Die Luftwaffe', pp. 653–654.
[160] Kesselring, *Memoirs*, p. 90; Plocher, *German Air Force Versus Russia, 1941*, p. 85.
[161] Franz Halder, KTB III, p. 32 (1 July 1941).

The military means of the SU [Soviet Union] are considerably stronger than studies before the start of the war... indicated... The material quality is better than expected... As a result we scored great successes with relatively low losses, but a large number of Soviet aircraft remain to be destroyed.[162]

Not only was the Soviet air force still far from eradicated, but the Luftwaffe was now forced to divide itself between servicing the hefty demands of the army and combating a resurgent Soviet aerial presence.[163] As the size of the operational theatre rapidly expanded, the already limited resources of the German air force soon became seriously over-extended. Air bases had to be relocated eastwards to new, sparsely equipped airfields where the feeble supply situation proved as detrimental to the Luftwaffe as it was to the army.[164] Moreover, these new airfields were particularly vulnerable to attacks by the roving enemy bands infesting the rear area.[165] Although by no means as successful as the Luftwaffe, the Soviet air force also had a share of successes raiding German airfields in July 1941. As one Soviet pilot recalled:

Approaching Bobruisk the Shturmoviks were flying very low... The leader turned and launched the attack. Missiles hit the rows of bombers and exploded, tracer bullets shredded the wings with black crosses. Just above the ground Shturmoviks dropped their hundred-kilo bombs. Junkers and Messerschmitts ready for operational flights blazed up. Our aircraft came in time and did not allow the enemy planes to take off!... The regiment flew to attack Bobruisk airfield three times and caused much damage to the enemy. It destroyed and damaged dozens of bombers and Messerschmitts.[166]

German aircraft losses were starting to take a heavy toll on operations. Although light by comparison with Soviet losses, by 12 July a total of 550 German planes had been destroyed with another 336 damaged, representing about 40 per cent of all the combat ready aircraft available on 22 June.[167] By contrast the enormous Soviet losses must be seen in light of three important factors. First, like the pre-war Soviet tank force, the Soviet air force was a ramshackle collection of aircraft, with some models

[162] Boog, 'Die Luftwaffe', p. 656.
[163] Plocher, German Air Force Versus Russia, 1941, p. 44.
[164] Murray, The Luftwaffe 1933–45, pp. 83–84.   [165] Kesselring, Memoirs, p. 99.
[166] Emelianenko, Red Star Against the Swastika, pp. 65 and 67. For more such accounts of successful Soviet actions in the summer of 1941 see Artem Drabkin (ed.), The Red Air Force At War. Barbarossa & the Retreat to Moscow. Recollections of Fighter Pilots on the Eastern Front (Barnsley, 2007), pp. 7 and 25–27.
[167] Boog, 'Die Luftwaffe', p. 654. On the following day (13 July) Halder cited figures which indicated 33 per cent of the Stuka dive-bombers and 39 per cent of the Messerschmitt fighters had been lost. Franz Halder, KTB III, p. 75 (13 July 1941).

dating back as far as the 1920s, meaning the overwhelming majority of the large losses were long since obsolete aircraft.[168] Up to 80 per cent of the 15,599 pre-war Soviet aircraft fleet were old designs and could not have posed a serious threat to the modern designs of the German Luftwaffe.[169] Second, since a sizeable majority of Soviet planes were destroyed on the ground in the initial German attacks, the loss of skilled pilots was correspondingly much lower.[170] Third, the Soviet industrial base for aircraft production significantly exceeded the output of German industry, and would continue to maintain its dominance even through the chaos and disruption of 1941.[171] Between July and December the Soviet Union produced some 5,173 modern fighters, easily surpassing the Luftwaffe's 1,619 fighters.[172] One must also remember that the Luftwaffe's lower production levels had to be divided between the demands of the eastern front and the ongoing war against the British RAF,[173] which was also far exceeding the Luftwaffe in fighter production.[174]

While the Luftwaffe certainly proved superior in the earliest period of Barbarossa, it was incapable of eliminating the Soviet air force and, by the end of July, could not even guarantee aerial superiority above the German front. On 26 July Leeb wrote in his diary: 'From day to day the enemy air force are winning more the upper hand and increasingly interfering in the ground operations.'[175] Similarly, Kleist stated after the war: 'such air superiority as we enjoyed during the opening months was local rather than general. We owed it to the superior skill of our airmen, not to a superiority in numbers.'[176] Army Group Centre was afforded the support of the strongest of the Luftwaffe air fleets (Air Fleet 2) commanded by the redoubtable Field Marshal Albrecht Kesselring, but even Kesselring was unable to ensure comprehensive cover to guard against costly Soviet airborne attacks. The war diary of the 14th Motorised Infantry Division complained on 25 July that while on a march it suffered from regular 'attacks by bombers which cost time and resulted in particular in

---

[168] Von Hardesty, *Red Phoenix. The Rise of Soviet Air Power 1941–1945* (Washington DC, 1982), p. 59.

[169] Glantz, *Stumbling Colossus*, p. 187.   [170] Von Hardesty, *Red Phoenix*, p. 59.

[171] Muller, *The German Air War in Russia*, p. 41; Glantz, *Stumbling Colossus*, p. 184; Boog, 'Die Luftwaffe', p. 299.

[172] Richard Overy, *The Air War 1939–1945* (London, 1980), p. 49.

[173] For more on the difficulties this was causing see von Below, *Als Hitlers Adjutant 1937–45*, pp. 293–294.

[174] 4,408 fighters were produced for the RAF in last six months of 1941 (Overy, *The Air War 1939–1945*, p. 49).

[175] Wilhelm Ritter von Leeb, KTB, p. 309 (26 July 1941). See also Franz Halder, KTB III, p. 124 (26 July 1941).

[176] Liddell Hart, *The Other Side of the Hill*, p. 266.

Figure 7.5 Operation Barbarossa exacted a huge toll on the German army with more men killed in July 1941 than in any other month of the war until December 1942. Countless roadside graves marked Army Group Centre's advance.

personnel and material losses'.[177] Two days later on 27 July Lemelsen's XXXXVII Panzer Corps reported: 'Strong enemy air superiority, many low-level strafes and bomber attacks, many casualties'.[178]

In addition to the great demands being made on the Luftwaffe's dwindling resources, three weeks into the campaign Hitler insisted upon 'terror air raids' to be launched against Moscow.[179] Extraneous to its duel tasks of suppressing Soviet air activity, and providing tactical support to the army, the demands of a strategic bombing campaign were well beyond the capacity of the Luftwaffe. Kesselring spoke of a 'harmful dissipation',[180] while Bock wanted the Luftwaffe concentrated 'without any limitation to smash the enemy's reserves'.[181] Yet, as Warlimont explains, the raids had nothing to do with the operational objectives of the campaign, Hitler ordered them in reprisal for Soviet raids against

[177] 'Kriegstagesbuch Ia. 14.Inf.Div. (mot) vom 25.5.41 – 1.10.41' BA-MA RH 26–14/10, Fol. 83. See also Fols. 87–88 (25 July 1941).
[178] As quoted in Steiger, *Armour Tactics*, p. 168.
[179] KTB OKW, Volume II, pp. 1021–1022, Document 69 (8 July 1941) and Document 71 (14 July 1941); Franz Halder, KTB III, p. 73 (13 July 1941).
[180] Kesselring, *Memoirs*, p. 89.
[181] Fedor von Bock, KTB 'Osten I', Fol. 37, *War Diary*, p. 257 (20 July 1941).

Bucharest and Helsinki.[182] In the end they proved both costly and wasteful. In the first raid on 22 July almost two hundred bombers flew in four waves towards Moscow, dropping 104 tons of high explosive and 46,000 incendiary bombs. In total, 22 planes were shot down at a cost to the Soviets of 130 people killed and 37 buildings destroyed.[183] Moscow was exceedingly well defended[184] and too far from the German airfields, meaning that bombs had to be substituted for extra fuel, with the result that the damage done could not justify aircraft losses. As Kesselring stated: 'The raids on Moscow caused me great anxiety. Crews shot down had to be written off, the effectiveness of the Russian anti-aircraft guns and searchlights impressing even our airmen who had flown over England. Also as time went on Russian defence fighters appeared in increasing numbers.'[185]

In the final analysis Luftwaffe operations over the eastern front in the summer of 1941 suffered from the same debilitating deficiencies as the army. Although the initial performance was impressive, the Luftwaffe's strength was clearly insufficient to sustain the momentum into the vast spaces of the Soviet Union. Indeed, by the end of July 1941 the Luftwaffe was reduced to a mere 1,045 serviceable aircraft across the whole eastern front.[186] As losses mounted and the demands of the war sharply increased, it took very little time for the Luftwaffe to become over-extended, giving the badly mauled Soviet air force time to revive. In practice, the Luftwaffe became a kind of flying fire brigade, rushed to trouble spots along the front or used to support the spearhead of new offensives, but an aerial superiority of the kind enjoyed in the earliest days of the conflict was never again achieved.

[182] Warlimont, *Im Hauptquartier*, Band I, pp. 198–199, footnote 74.
[183] Braithwaite, *Moscow 1941*, pp. 174 and 176.
[184] The approaches to Moscow were defended by almost 800 medium anti-aircraft guns, over 600 large searchlights and nearly 600 fighters. Inside the city itself more anti-aircraft guns were positioned on the top of buildings, along with smaller searchlights and over 100 barrage balloons intended to make the Germans fly high and confuse their aim (ibid., pp. 169 and 186).
[185] Kesselring, *Memoirs*, p. 94. See also Muller, *The German Air War in Russia*, pp. 51–54.
[186] Overy, *The Air War 1939–1945*.

8   The attrition of Army Group Centre

The killing fields at Yel'nya

The arduous exertion of the long thrust into the Soviet Union, followed by the savage ongoing battles around Smolensk, Yel'nya and along the flanks of the army group, necessitated a period of rest and refitting for Guderian's and Hoth's armoured groups. On 23 July this was optimistically assessed to require only ten days in order for the panzer divisions to return to about 60–70 per cent of their former strength. Yet to reach this lofty goal it was acknowledged that 'panzer replacements from Germany will arrive too late' for the renewed offensive operations. Halder's information indicated that the goal could not be achieved by merely repairing mechanical faults and battle damage to the existing pool of tanks in the panzer divisions. It was therefore suggested that one panzer division in each panzer group (Halder's notes recommended 17th and 20th Panzer Divisions) be broken up and used to reinforce the other divisions. Thus, in order to avoid 'very quickly sinking to an unbearably small panzer strength' in the armoured divisions, the rehabilitation process would have to include disbanding divisions, as well as undertaking a great many repairs to the existing quantity of tanks. Here the time factor also constituted a serious problem, not only in carrying out the repairs, but first receiving all the required spare parts, especially tank engines, via the dismal logistical system.[1]

By 25 July the supply capacity of the hopelessly overstretched logistical network behind Army Group Centre was threatening some sectors of the precariously held front with collapse. Ihno Krumpelt, a general staff officer who at the time was serving in an infantry division, later wrote in a study of the Barbarossa campaign that the combination of the supply situation and the defensive battles in the summer constituted in his opinion; 'the culminating point of the offensive operations'.[2] Nowhere was this

---

[1] Franz Halder, KTB III, pp. 115–116 (25 July 1941).
[2] Krumpelt, *Das Material*, p. 167.

better seen that at Yel'nya, where the XXXXVI Panzer Corps was fighting off immense Soviet pressure with fewer and fewer resources. Most particularly, artillery shells were sorely lacking,[3] while the Soviet guns were capable of delivering a bombardment, according to one participant, 'to be compared with the heaviest days of the western front in the [First] World War'.[4] In the zone of one company, 156 artillery shells landed in just five minutes, while the Soviet air force dominated the skies above. According to one account: 'Unhindered, [Soviet] bombers and fighters attacked the infantry the whole day.'[5] When the next Soviet assault came it was led by Soviet T-34 tanks which the SS *Das Reich* division encountered here for the first time. It was during this attack that the SS men discovered to their horror the uselessness of their 3.7cm and 5cm anti-tank guns. The T-34s could only be destroyed once inside the German lines by setting them ablaze with Molotov cocktails or, in one instance, climbing onto the tank from behind and emptying a can of petrol onto the hulk which was then ignited.[6] Helmut Günther, a motorcycle dispatch rider assigned to *Das Reich*, noted how the Soviets displayed no shortage of ammunition and even opened fire with heavy artillery during his lone dash to deliver orders. Given that Günther was constantly ferrying dispatches around the Yel'nya bend he saw a great deal more of the carnage and destruction than the average soldier. Early on in the battle he recalled: '[M]y journey continued through Yel'nya, which had changed greatly in recent days. Only ruins indicated that buildings once stood and people had lived here. I continued past the German military cemetery, where long rows of graves gave notice what the Yel'nya bend signified.' Days later Günther brought back a dispatch from divisional command which one of the officers read aloud. 'All that I remember of it is that the enemy we were facing greatly outnumbered us. Several Russian divisions and mechanised regiments were listed with their unit designations. It was doubtful whether our division could long stand these debilitating enemy attacks. I saw extremely black prospects for the continued advance.'[7] It was desperate and costly fighting, but, for the sake of renewing the thrust towards Moscow, the heights of Yel'nya were ordered to be held at all costs.

[3] 'KTB Nr.1 Panzergruppe 2 Bd.II vom 22.7.1941 bis 20.8.41' BA-MA RH 21-2/928, Fol. 34 (25 July 1941).
[4] Werner Haupt, *Die Schlachten der Heeresgruppe Mitte. Aus der Sicht der Divisionen* (Friedberg, 1983), p. 66.
[5] Ibid.
[6] This report comes from a reporter attached to a propaganda company who wrote of an attack by '30 ton heavy T-28' tanks, but owing to their lighter weight and much thinner armour, that could be pierced by German anti-tank guns, I have assumed that the tanks being referred to were in fact the 30 ton T-34s (ibid.).
[7] Günther, *Hot Motors, Cold Feet*, pp. 105–106.

308   Operation Barbarossa and Germany's Defeat in the East

The bulging salient at Yel'nya was not the only sector of Bock's front straining at the seams. To the south on 25 July the 18th Panzer Division defended against heavy Soviet attacks from the direction of Roslavl, and made the worrying observation '[e]verywhere new enemy columns with artillery'.[8] On the following day the divisional diary recorded; 'constant heaviest artillery fire, of a kind the troops have seldom experienced'. The diary then went on to question the morale of the men,[9] which a report by a battalion doctor diagnosed as collective battle fatigue:

A state of absolute exhaustion is noticeable... among all men of the battalion. The reason is... far too great mental and nervous strain. The troops were under a powerful barrage of heavy artillery... That the men were promised a few days of rest... but instead found themselves in an even worse situation... had a particularly grave effect. The men are indifferent and apathetic, are partly suffering from crying fits, and are not to be cheered up by this or that phrase. Food is being taken only in disproportionately small quantities.[10]

Casualties were also extremely high with one battalion reduced in size to almost company strength.[11]

To the north in Hoth's panzer group, the pressure was equally fierce with Halder noting on 26 July: '[i]ncreased enemy aircraft activity and also panzer deployment, especially against Hoth's left shoulder'.[12] Kuntzen's LVII Panzer Corps reported the difficulty its four divisions had defending a 200-kilometre-long front covered by large marshes and forests. 'This does not make the defence any easier', the war diary noted, as the terrain could not be traversed by motorised forces, but enemy infantry and cavalry 'can break through in many places'.[13] The defensive battles were further hindered by the fact that Kuntzen's divisions were far from full strength. The 20th Panzer Division reported on 27 July that its motorcycle component was 'very weakened', while the other motorised forces had suffered 'numerous losses, also in panzers'.[14] Helmuth Dittri, a soldier in the division, wrote in his diary for 26 July: 'On taking stock of our regiment we are driven to the sad conclusion that there is very little left of it... There isn't enough to make a decent detachment. Our losses

---

[8] '18. Panzer Division, Abt. Ia. Kriegstagebuch Teil I vom: 22.6 – 20.8.41' BA-MA RH 27–18/20, Fols. 50–51 (25 July 1941).
[9] Underlining in the original. Ibid., Fol. 52 (26 July 1941).
[10] Bartov, *Hitler's Army*, p. 21.
[11] '18. Panzer Division, Abt. Ia. Kriegstagebuch Teil I vom: 22.6 – 20.8.41' BA-MA RH 27–18/20, Fol. 54 (27 July 1941).
[12] Franz Halder, KTB III, p. 124 (26 July 1941).
[13] 'Gen.Kdo.LVII.Pz.Korps Kriegstagebuch Nr.1 vom 15.2. – 31.10.41' BA-MA RH 24–57/2, p. 249 (27 July 1941).
[14] 'KTB 20th Pz. Div. vom 25.5.41 bis 15.8.41' BA-MA RH 27–20/2, Fol. 62 (27 July 1941).

have been heavy, not only in men, but also in material.' On the following day (27 July) Dittri described the ordeal of life at the front:

From early dawn the enemy [artillery] rake our lines with his accurate, well-directed fire... The Russians have been shooting for 48 hours now, the only lull having been 3 hours during the night. ...

[S]everal [German] bombers wheeled above our heads and as long as they were about the Russians warily abstained from firing. But as soon as they disappeared... we landed in a cross-fire so terrific that we did not know if we were dead or alive. A few more tanks went the way of all flesh – or metal, rather, to be exact. They're bringing in an endless line of wounded. The motor-cyclists fared very badly. Their casualties were tremendous.[15]

The desperate situation along Bock's extensive front heightened calls for more infantry to be brought forward to release the motorised and panzer units for rest and refitting. However, the infantry divisions were themselves not without losses, and the strain of forced marches lasting over a month had greatly tired them before they even made contact with the main Soviet formations on the eastern front. Adding to the gloomy outlook, Halder noted on 26 July the presence of new Soviet armies moving up to support the Soviet offensives against Army Group Centre.[16] In addition, he noted that at Yel'nya the enemy attacks were to continue 'supported by new divisions and new panzers from the east'.[17]

By 26 July Panzer Group 2 judged the situation at Yel'nya to be 'exceedingly critical'[18] and the war diary of the 10th Panzer Division reported: 'Heaviest attacks on all fronts with bombers, fighters and tanks'. Vietinghoff, the corps commander, insisted a mobile reserve was urgently needed behind the front of the SS *Das Reich* division, but he refused to countenance a withdrawal of men believing it to be only a temporary crisis (see Map 11).[19] Throughout the day, however, reports coming back from the SS division to Vietinghoff's command spoke of copious losses in men and material.[20] By the afternoon the tone had become increasingly critical with the situation in Regiment *Der Führer* described

---

[15] *True To Type*, p. 16 (27 July 1941). The book in which this diary is printed claimed that Dittri was serving in the 21st Panzer Division (not the 20th Panzer division) but this is not possible given that the 21st Panzer Division was not even in existence in July 1941 (it was created later in 1941 and then deployed in North Africa). The confusion probably stems from the fact that Dittri was serving in the 21st Panzer Regiment, which was part of 20th Panzer Division.

[16] Franz Halder, KTB III, p. 124 (26 July 1941).   [17] Ibid., p. 121 (26 July 1941).

[18] 'KTB Nr.1 Panzergruppe 2 Bd.II vom 22.7.1941 bis 20.8.41' BA-MA RH 21–2/928, Fol. 48 (26 July 1941).

[19] 'Kriegstagebuch der 10.Panzer Division Nr.5 vom: 22.5. bis: 7.10.41' BA-MA RH 27–10/26a (26 July 1941).

[20] 'Kriegstagesbuch Nr.2 des XXXXVI.Pz.Korps Teil II. 8.7.41 – 23.8.41' BA-MA RH 24–46/8, Fol. 111 (26 July 1941).

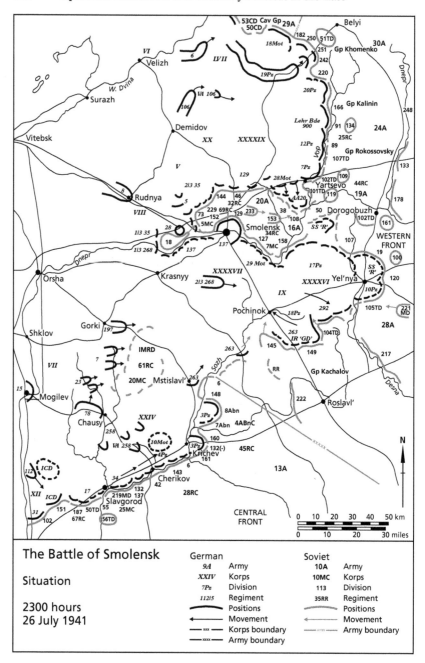

The Battle of Smolensk

Situation

2300 hours
26 July 1941

German			Soviet		
9A	Army		10A	Army	
XXIV	Korps		10MC	Korps	
7Pz	Division		113	Division	
112I5	Regiment		35RR	Regiment	
⟶	Positions		⟶	Positions	
←	Movement		←	Movement	
── xxx ──	Korps boundary		── xxx ──	Army boundary	
── xxxx ──	Army boundary				

Map 11 Dispositions of Army Group Centre 26 July 1941: David M.
Glantz, *Atlas of the Battle of Smolensk 7 July–10 September 1941*

as 'unbearable'. This was then followed by a plea to the higher command that something had to be done immediately: 'Action must be taken now. There exists the danger that otherwise the division will be completely pummelled.'[21] The deteriorating situation was well known at Guderian's headquarters and the panzer group's war diary tellingly illustrates the horrific cost of defending the Yel'nya salient. On the late afternoon of 26 July the panzer group's diarist recorded:

At the fighting around Yel'nya the situation is especially critical. The corps has been attacked all day from strongly superior forces with panzers and artillery. The enemy achieved a breakthrough at Lipnja which has not yet been dealt with . . . Constant heavy artillery fire is inflicting heavy casualties on the troops. In addition there is the impact of enemy bombers. As a result of the artillery fire, the evacuation of the many wounded has so far not been possible . . . The corps has absolutely no reserves available. Artillery munitions have been so depleted that no shells remain for bombarding the enemy artillery. For the last few days the panzer brigade of the 10th Panzer Division has been immobilized because oil and fuel supplies are lacking. The corps can maybe manage to hold on to its position, but only at the price of severe bloodletting.[22]

For reasons of both prestige and the much hoped for continuation of the advance on Moscow, none of the senior commanders advocated the evacuation of the Yel'nya salient and so the frightful attrition of Vietinghoff's XXXXVI Panzer Corps continued.

On 27 July the Smolensk pocket was finally closed by Hoth in a final drive from the north.[23] This still left sizeable forces inside the pocket which would attempt to break out to the safety of Soviet lines,[24] as well as the ongoing pressure from the east resulting from Timoshenko's stolid offensives to relieve the pocket. Wary of the weakness of his forces and with a view to the difficulty of sealing off large encirclements, Bock was unsure whether his units could withstand the expected counter-pressure.[25] Unlike in the Belostok–Minsk pocket, the Soviet forces fleeing the destruction of the pocket had only a relatively narrow corridor of German lines to penetrate, and although this was a treacherous undertaking, smaller groups continued to escape.

---

[21] Ibid., Fol. 115 (26 July 1941).

[22] 'KTB Nr.1 Panzergruppe 2 Bd.II vom 22.7.1941 bis 20.8.41' BA-MA RH 21–2/928, Fols. 49–50 (26 July 1941).

[23] Fedor von Bock, KTB 'Osten I', Fol. 44, *War Diary*, p. 264 (27 July 1941); '3rd Pz. Gr. KTB 25.5.41 – 31.8.41' BA-MA Microfilm 59054, Fols. 168–169 (27 July 1941). Guderian's memoir puts the date at 26 July (Guderian, *Panzer Leader*, p. 182).

[24] For a Soviet soldier's account of attempting to escape encirclement see Nikolai I. Obryn'ba, *Red Partisan. The Memoir of a Soviet Resistance Fighter on the Eastern Front* (Washington DC, 2007) Chapter 5.

[25] Fedor von Bock, KTB 'Osten I', Fol. 44, *War Diary*, p. 264 (27 July 1941).

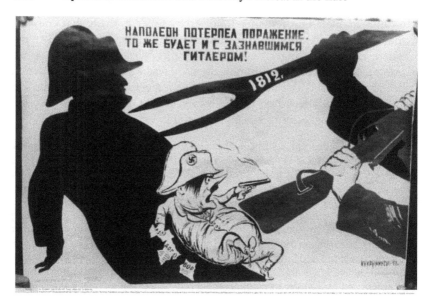

Figure 8.1 A 1941 Soviet propaganda poster which reads: 'Napoleon suffered defeat and so will Hitler!'

On 28 July Bock hosted a meeting of all the senior commanders of the army group (Kluge, Weichs, Strauss, Hoth and Guderian) to discuss the latest directive and set new operational objectives. None were happy about the switch to smaller tactical encirclements, and the generals were right to question the ramifications of this decision for achieving the audacious strategic goals required by the Barbarossa plan.[26] Yet, realistically the army group was presently incapable of anything more ambitious than small-scale local operations. Bock himself commented: 'Whatever can be found in the rear army area is being scraped together for the coming missions, for the army group is much too thin, especially south of the Dnepr, to undertake anything serious.'[27] Guderian was fiercely opposed to the operation ordered by Hitler towards Gomel and bluntly informed Bock that deployment of his forces into this area would be 'impossible'. Instead the panzer commander wanted to amass strength for an operation towards Roslavl which, along with the Yel'nya salient, he regarded as the most threatened sectors of his front. Typically, Guderian did not attribute the critical situation his forces faced in these sectors to overextension, but rather blamed Kluge for retaining his forces on the Dnepr

[26] Guderian, *Panzer Leader*, p. 183.
[27] Fedor von Bock, KTB 'Osten I', Fol. 45, *War Diary*, pp. 264–265 (27 July 1941).

and west of Smolensk. Consequently, according to Guderian, 'crises and losses had occurred ... which could have been avoided.' The dispute further embittered the relationship between the two men and led to an almost unbearable atmosphere, which Guderian guardedly described in his memoir as 'strained to an undesirable degree'.[28] Thus, in order to relieve his threatened front, Guderian was determined to use the prospect of a renewed offensive to end the critical situation near Roslavl caused by the Soviet 28th Army (otherwise referred to as the Kachalov Group, see Map 12). This move was supported by Bock and, seemingly in defiance of Hitler's order, planning proceeded for an offensive towards Roslavl, not Gomel. As Guderian recalled in his memoir: 'Regardless of what decisions Hitler might now take, the immediate need of Panzer Group 2 was to dispose of the most dangerous enemy threat to its right flank.'[29] Moreover, much to Guderian's delight, his panzer group was removed from Kluge's command and renamed 'Army Group Guderian'[30] with the allotment of the VII Army Corps for the attack on Roslavl and the IX Army Corps for the relief of the Yel'nya bulge.[31] Likewise Hoth's panzer group was re-subordinated to Strauss's 9th Army,[32] dissolving Kluge's 4th Panzer Army (although Kluge's Fourth Army, made up of infantry divisions only, was later reinstated between 2nd and 9th Armies).[33]

While the Roslavl operation offered a tactical solution to an immediate problem confronting Guderian's front, its consequence was to extend Army Group Centre's threadbare forces even further to the south, while still not alleviating the threat to the southern flank emanating from around Gomel. The flank was simply too long, and Army Group South was still too far off and too heavily opposed to offer any aid in the foreseeable future. Thus, the army group was drawing strength from its centre to solve its problems in the south, which Bock feared further endangered the prospect of resuming the advance towards Moscow. Upon discussion of this point with Halder, Bock noted in his diary on 28 July: 'Halder is in no doubt that under these circumstances a significant advance to the east by the weak forces left to the army group for the drive to the east

---

[28] Guderian, *Panzer Leader*, p. 182.   [29] Ibid., p. 183.

[30] See Guderian's letter to his wife as cited by Hürter, *Hitlers Heerführer*, p. 286, footnote 28. The use of the term *Armeegruppe* (army group) is not to be confused with Bock's Army Group Centre. This was not an independent entity, but rather a new grouping of forces under Bock's overall command.

[31] Fedor von Bock, KTB 'Osten I', Fols. 44–45, *War Diary*, p. 264 (27 July 1941); 'KTB Nr. 1 Panzergruppe 2 Bd.II vom 22.7.1941 bis 20.8.41' BA-MA RH 21–2/928, Fol. 66 (28 July 1941); Guderian, *Panzer Leader*, pp. 183–184. In Guderian's memoir he states that XX Army Corps was directed towards Yel'nya, but in fact it was IX Army Corps.

[32] Klink, 'Die Operationsführung', p. 494.   [33] Blumentritt, 'Moscow', p. 51.

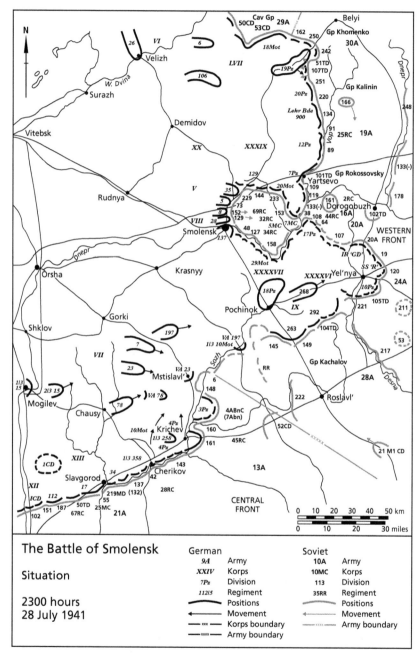

Map 12 Dispositions of Army Group Centre 28 July 1941: David M. Glantz, *Atlas of the Battle of Smolensk 7 July–10 September 1941*

will be impossible. He still hopes to change the Führer's mind.'[34] Unbeknown to the army commanders, Hitler was already beginning to accept the implausibility of Directive 33a, but was as yet uncertain how best to proceed. In the meantime, however, Bock fretted about how to carry out the clearly impracticable demands of Hitler's directive and impressed upon the OKH the offensive weakness of his army group.[35]

Although the chaotic struggle for control over the strategic direction of the campaign was dominated by the firm belief that each side knew how best to win the war, there is evidence that the Soviet Union's performance up until the end of July was having a profound impact on the German command's changing understanding of the war. Previously, the road to victory over the Soviet Union was accepted as a preordained certainty, dependent for its success entirely on German strategic manoeuvring and not to be called into question in any way by Soviet counter-measures. By late July, however, the ground was shifting and a new outlook was emerging. At Army Group Centre on 28 July the view was expressed: 'A collapse of the Russian system is for the time being not to be expected. Because the Russian is so tough his tactical methods are unpredictable.' Moreover the wide expanses of the east were acknowledged to be 'impossible to rule', while the human resources of the country were said to represent an infinite supply which 'cannot be reduced'. Accordingly more emphasis was placed on the seizure of industrial centres, such as Leningrad and Moscow, which were said to be arming the Soviet masses.[36]

Before any continuation of the offensive could be initiated, the German army had to address the fact that its motorised divisions were greatly weakened and, in the more extreme cases, barely functional. This posed extremely awkward problems for the army commanders who, owing to the woefully deficient planning before the campaign, found themselves wholly unprepared for the scale of the task, and forced actions to be undertaken on a decidedly ad hoc basis. On 28 July concern was expressed at Panzer Group 2 about the fact that just 45 replacement tank engines were being made available per month for the entire eastern front.[37] On the following day new figures were reported from all the panzer divisions showing a severe decline in the number of serviceable tanks. On 22 June 1941 Guderian's panzer group fielded 953 tanks of all

[34] Fedor von Bock, KTB 'Osten I', Fol. 45, *War Diary*, p. 265 (28 July 1941).
[35] Ibid., Fol. 46, p. 266 (29 July 1941).
[36] 'Panzerarmeeoberkommandos Anlagen zum Kriegstagebuch "Berichte, Besprechungen, Beurteilungen der Lage" Bd.IV 22.7.41 – 31.8.41' BA-MA RH 21-3/47, Fols. 13–14 and 17 (28 July 1941).
[37] 'KTB Nr.1 Panzergruppe 2 Bd.II vom 22.7.1941 bis 20.8.41' BA-MA RH 21-2/928, Fol. 68 (28 July 1941).

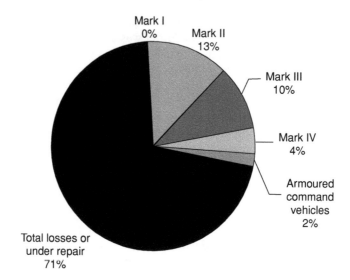

Figure 8.2 Combat readiness of Panzer Group 2 on 29 July 1941. 'KTB Nr.1 Panzergruppe 2 Bd.II vom 22.7.1941 bis 20.8.41' BA-MA RH 21–2/928. Fols. 78–79 (29 July 1941).

models,[38] but by 29 July the total had sunk to 286 tanks – only 30 per cent of the original strength. As the war diary noted, 'this figure is <u>exceedingly low</u>'.[39] More worrying still, no fewer than 132 of the remaining tanks were Mark Is (4) or Mark IIs (128), both long since outdated models. In addition, armoured command vehicles accounted for a further 19 vehicles on the list, leaving Guderian's panzer group with just 135 Mark IIIs (97) and Mark IVs (38) spread throughout four panzer divisions on divergent sectors of the front (see Figure 8.2).[40] Assessing such dramatic losses, the panzer group's war diary pointed to the disastrous combination of bad roads, dust and great distances, with the result: 'The high fallout rate is not surprising.'[41] Yet, with so many disabled tanks, the prospect of them all receiving the required repair work, and in some cases complete overhauls, was entirely unrealistic, especially given the unavailability of replacement engines and other spare parts. Recognising this fact, there was discussion in XXXXVII Panzer Corps on 30 July about merging the

---

[38] Müller-Hillebrand, *Das Heer 1933–1945*, Band III, p. 205.
[39] Underlining in the original. 'KTB Nr.1 Panzergruppe 2 Bd.II vom 22.7.1941 bis 20.8.41' BA-MA RH 21–2/928, Fol. 78 (29 July 1941).
[40] Guderian's panzer group consisted of five panzer divisions, but the 10th Panzer Division did not submit figures because the entire panzer brigade was disabled for want of fuel and spare parts.
[41] 'KTB Nr.1 Panzergruppe 2 Bd.II vom 22.7.1941 bis 20.8.41' BA-MA RH 21–2/928, Fols. 78–79 (29 July 1941).

17th and 18th Panzer Divisions to make up the personnel and material losses, but even this drastic measure could not ensure a hybrid division of anything approaching full strength in panzers.[42]

Hoth's panzer group was also suffering with Schmidt's XXXIX Panzer Corps reporting on 27 July: 'The combat strength of the panzer divisions, mainly the panzer force, especially the Mark IV, has been weakened.' In fact, Schmidt's entire corps retained just 23 Mark IVs, with an overall panzer strength at 40 per cent of their original number.[43] In a letter to Paulus, Schmidt wrote that his Panzer Corps had suffered greatly and that his material was now 'totally run down' (*total auf den Hund*).[44] Comprehensive figures for Kuntzen's LVII Panzer Corps are not available, but among the two most important tank models employed by the corps only 14 Mark IVs (from 61 at the start of the campaign) and 76 Czech Kpfw 38 (t) (from 234) remained in active service on 27 July. Based on these figures, the panzer corps could field an average of just 30 per cent of its original strength. In addition, a report from LVII Panzer Corps noted that:

It must be understood that without a rapid and plentiful supply of track rollers, track links and bolts for the Mark IV and track bolts for the Kpfw 38 (t) the number of available panzers will sink further, so that the combat strength of the panzer regiments will be greatly weakened. Still especially urgent is the delivery of fully operational motors, gearboxes, oil and specialised panzer grease.[45]

Three days later on 30 July, Hoth stated that the combat strength of his divisions had become 'especially strongly impaired' by the losses among Mark IV panzers. He then cast real doubt on the plans for the rest and refitting of the panzer divisions, claiming that, with no replacements to be expected from Germany, 'even after the forthcoming refitting period, a substantial shortfall in the number of Mark IVs will remain'.[46] Guderian too was worried by the steep decline in tank numbers and foresaw the dangers of adequate replacements not reaching the front in time to redress the critical shortages. Upon a visit by Schmundt, Hitler's chief adjutant, on 29 July, Guderian relayed an impassioned plea to Hitler (via Schmundt) imploring the dictator 'not to withhold the new tanks and our replacements'.[47] Beyond the primary subject of tanks, the maintenance of the panzer division's mobility depended on its trucks, on which Hoth

[42] Ibid., Fol. 89 (30 July 1941).
[43] 'Panzerarmeeoberkommandos Anlagen zum Kriegstagesbuch "Berichte, Besprechungen, Beurteilungen der Lage" Bd.IV 22.7.41 – 31.8.41' BA-MA RH 21–3/47, Fols. 97–98 (27 July 1941).
[44] Schmidt's letter cited by Hürter, *Hitlers Heerführer*, p. 290.
[45] Underlining in the original. 'Panzerarmeeoberkommandos Anlagen zum Kriegstagesbuch "Berichte, Besprechungen, Beurteilungen der Lage" Bd.IV 22.7.41 – 31.8.41' BA-MA RH 21–3/47, Fols. 99–100 (27 July 1941).
[46] Underlining in the original. Ibid., Fol. 116 (30 July 1941).
[47] Guderian, *Panzer Leader*, p. 185.

Figure 8.3 Army Group Centre's advance captured hundreds of thousands of Red Army POWs reinforcing the illusion that victory was only a few weeks away. Owing to German treatment, the great majority of these Soviet POWs would be dead by early 1942.

remarked on 31 July: '[A] great number of the trucks now stand at the limit of their operational capacity and any further delay in their refitting will see a greatly increased total loss in a short period of time.'[48] Clearly the panzer divisions were approaching the end of their strength, which meant any hope of resuming the blitzkrieg on a scale required for the success of Barbarossa was appearing more and more improbable.

Personnel losses in Guderian's panzer group presented a different set of problems. On 29 July casualty figures up until 25 July exceeded 20,000 men, with only 10,000 replaced, and the rest still outstanding largely because of transportation difficulties. Yet it was not simply a matter of replacing one lost man with another. The high losses included many experienced veterans and skilled specialists, while officer casualties were exceedingly high – over 1,000 in only 34 days of combat.[49] Hoth's panzer group was similarly affected, with the high casualties unable to be directly replaced and a resultant deficit of some 7,500 men and 350 officers.[50]

---

[48] 'Panzerarmeeoberkommandos Anlagen zum Kriegstagesbuch "Berichte, Besprechungen, Beurteilungen der Lage" Bd.IV 22.7.41 – 31.8.41' BA-MA RH 21–3/47, Fol. 126 (31 July 1941).

[49] 'KTB Nr.1 Panzergruppe 2 Bd.II vom 22.7.1941 bis 20.8.41' BA-MA RH 21–2/928, Fol. 79 (29 July 1941).

[50] 'Panzerarmeeoberkommandos Anlagen zum Kriegstagesbuch "Berichte, Besprechungen, Beurteilungen der Lage" Bd.IV 22.7.41 – 31.8.41' BA-MA RH 21–3/47, Fol. 18 (28 July 1941) and Fol. 96 (29 July 1941).

Furthermore, Hoth returned from a visit to the 20th Panzer Division with the impression that the high officer casualties 'were making themselves very noticeable among the troops'.[51] Bock too was worried by this development, and not only in the hard-pressed panzer groups; already on 29 July Bock commented: 'Powerful Russian attacks are in process on almost the entire front of the 9th Army. The fact is that our troops are tired and also are not exhibiting the required steadiness because of heavy officer casualties.'[52]

In the last days of July the pressure of the Soviet attacks was being absorbed more and more by the arriving divisions of the 9th and 2nd Armies. This provided a welcome relief to the motorised divisions but, given the weight of the Soviet attacks, most of Hoth's and Guderian's divisions could not yet extract themselves fully from the front to begin the technical refitting of vehicles and rest their exhausted troops.[53] On 30 July Army Group Centre reported a general increase in offensive enemy activity against the entire front (with the exception of 2nd Army's right wing). 'Above all', the report added, 'is the manifest strength of the strong artillery on every front.' Furthermore: 'The reinforced commitment of the enemy air force remains undiminished.'[54] The relentlessness of the Soviet assaults proved a harsh baptism of fire for the newly arrived infantry divisions. On the open fields, General of Infantry Hermann Geyer, commander of the IX Army Corps, noted the added difficulties infantry divisions faced over their motorised cousins in lack of mobility and communications. In addition to this, the crisis of supply was denying the infantry the use of their guns to answer the powerful Soviet bombardments. To illustrate the point, Geyer stated that during this period the 263rd Infantry Division received 1,000 shells per day which allowed each gun one shot every minute for 30 minutes a day.[55] Not surprisingly Geyer noted: 'We soon learned that in the defence not artillery duels . . . but rather digging in quick and deep proved decisive.'[56] Accordingly, Geyer also alluded to the 'changed character of the war' in which, '[w]e entered into a form of positional warfare'.[57] With the blitzkrieg stalled, Soviet strength of arms came to the fore as the predominate force on the new immobilised battlefield. Reflecting this fact,

[51] '3rd Pz. Gr. KTB 25.5.41 – 31.8.41' BA-MA Microfilm 59054, Fol. 175 (28 July 1941).

[52] Fedor von Bock, KTB 'Osten I', Fols. 46–47, *War Diary*, pp. 266–267 (29 July 1941).

[53] 'KTB Nr.1 Panzergruppe 2 Bd.II vom 22.7.1941 bis 20.8.41' BA-MA RH 21–2/928, Fol. 78 (29 July 1941); Franz Halder, KTB III, p. 132 (30 July 1941).

[54] 'Tagesmeldungen der Heeresgruppe Mitte vom 16.7.41 bis 5.8.41' BA-MA RH 19 II/129, Fol. 163 (30 July 1941).

[55] Geyer, *Das IX. Armeekorps im Ostfeldzug 1941*, pp. 97–98.

[56] Ibid., p. 99.   [57] Ibid., p. 92.

Geyer wrote that in the 137th Infantry Division 850 men were lost in the first three to four days of reaching the front, while the 263rd Infantry Division lost 750 men and the 292nd Infantry Division 300 men.[58] The attrition of Army Group Centre was proceeding rapidly.

Unable to match the Red Army in firepower, the strength of Bock's army group was dealt a further blow when orders arrived from Hitler's headquarters on 29 July removing Richthofen's VIII Air Corps from Kesselring's Air Fleet 2.[59] This was done to provide urgently needed support for Colonel-General Alfred Keller's Air Fleet 1 which was proving woefully incapable of supporting Leeb's drive towards Leningrad.[60] Hitler's decision may also have been an unspoken compromise, exchanging Hoth's panzers for Richthofen's planes. In any case, in spite of resistance from Bock and Kesselring, the transfer took immediate effect and left Army Group Centre supported only by Air General Bruno Loerzer's weaker II Air Corps. This afforded Bock little help in the face of fresh Soviet offensives striking his front. On 31 July he noted in his diary:

The pocket at Smolensk is still not done . . . very regrettable, for the enemy's attacks on the army group's eastern front are growing ever stronger . . . The Chief of Staff of the 9th Army, Weckmann, is very downcast. He is also pessimistic about the situation on the northern wing . . . Kesselring is helping me as best he can, nevertheless his remaining forces are very weak after giving up VIII Air Corps.[61]

During this period of renewed Soviet attacks, few positions were as heavily assaulted as the Yel'nya bulge (see Map 13). On 30 July no fewer than thirteen attacks were made on the salient[62] and the following day at 9.00 p.m. Vietinghoff's XXXXVI Panzer Corps reported: 'Since 3.00 a.m. uninterrupted enemy attacks which are still continuing in the south, southeast, northeast, north'. The report went on to describe a now familiar pattern of events – heavy Soviet artillery fire, attacks by enemy fighters and bombers, and at times with tanks. This resulted in heavy German material and personnel losses, with an extremely limited ability to hit back owing to munition shortages.[63]

[58] Ibid., pp. 95 and 97. Since the start of the campaign the IX Army Corps had suffered almost 5,000 casualties up until the end of July 1941 (p. 201).
[59] Fedor von Bock, KTB 'Osten I', Fol. 47, *War Diary*, p. 267 (29 July 1941).
[60] Muller, *German Air War in Russia*, p. 55.
[61] Fedor von Bock, KTB 'Osten I', Fols. 48–49, *War Diary*, pp. 268–269 (31 July 1941).
[62] Guderian, *Panzer Leader*, p. 185.
[63] 'Kriegstagesbuch Nr.2 des XXXXVI.Pz.Korps Teil II. 8.7.41 – 23.8.41' BA-MA RH 24–46/8, Fol. 148 (31 July 1941). See also: 'KTB Nr.1 Panzergruppe 2 Bd.II vom 22.7.1941 bis 20.8.41' BA-MA RH 21–2/928, Fol. 101 (31 July 1941).

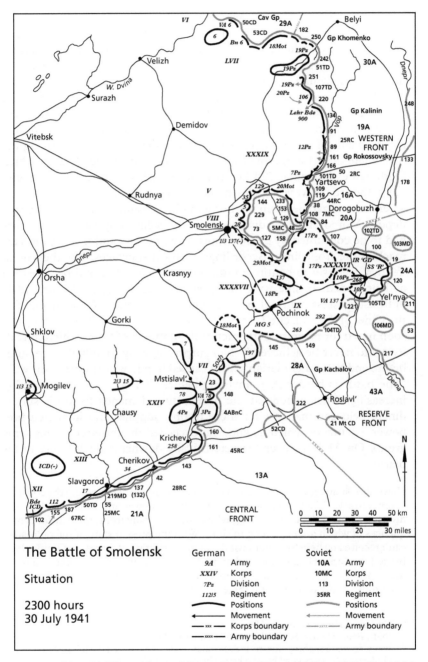

The Battle of Smolensk

Situation

2300 hours
30 July 1941

German		Soviet	
9A	Army	10A	Army
XXIV	Korps	10MC	Korps
7Pz	Division	113	Division
112/5	Regiment	35RR	Regiment
Positions		Positions	
Movement		Movement	
Korps boundary		Army boundary	
Army boundary			

Map 13 Dispositions of Army Group Centre 30 July 1941: David M.
Glantz, *Atlas of the Battle of Smolensk 7 July–10 September 1941*

The supply situation at Army Group Centre remained steadfastly dire. As Guderian wrote in his memoir: 'It is true that the railway track had already been relaid as far as Orsha to conform to the German gauge, but it was still only capable of carrying very limited traffic. The stretches of track which had not been relaid were useless since there were but few Russian locomotives available.'[64] With the railways only capable of bringing up a fraction of the supplies needed, excessive demands were being placed on the truck-based *Grosstransportraum* to meet the urgent requirements of the front. In practice, this meant the trucks driving the whole length of the German penetration into the Soviet Union, which Guderian estimated at 725 kilometres, to fetch supplies.[65] Not surprisingly, the trucks were hopelessly incapable of adequately bridging such an enormous gap between the border railheads and the front-line supply depots. Moreover, as the distance from the railheads grew, more supplies had to be consumed by the transport network itself and less net tonnage reached the front lines. Accordingly, critical shortages, like the one at Yel'nya, were set to continue until the new railroads could be extended and upgraded. In line with the German army's propensity for widely optimistic assessments of its capabilities, Lieutenant-General Gercke, the Chief of Wehrmacht Transport and responsible for the railroads, was soon noted for promising impracticable numbers of trains which in reality could never be achieved.[66] Not surprisingly, by 31 July the pressures before and behind Guderian's front caused him to write home to his wife: 'The battle is harder than anything before.'[67] Bock too was becoming increasingly melancholic at the unremitting demands from his subordinate field commanders for more troops, supplies and increased firepower – demands which he knew far exceeded the resources of his army group. On 31 July an uncharacteristically downcast Bock wrote in his diary:

I have almost no reserves left to meet the enemy massing of forces and the constant counterattacks. They took away my offensive air power and heavy artillery and diverted some of the reserves originally destined for my front, the painful consequences of which are beginning to show. With the present state of the railroads I can't receive any help from home or through the shifting of forces... Greiffenberg briefed the Army High Command and asked that any units from home – replacement formations or whatever – be moved up into the rear area, because I urgently need those of my divisions still there at the front.[68]

---

[64] Guderian, *Panzer Leader*, p. 186.
[65] Ibid.; Franz Halder, KTB III, p. 138 (1 August 1941).
[66] Van Creveld, *Supplying War*, p. 158; Schüler, 'The Eastern Campaign', p. 213.
[67] Guderian's letter as cited by Macksey, *Guderian*, p. 142.
[68] Fedor von Bock, KTB 'Osten I', Fol. 49, *War Diary*, p. 269 (31 July 1941).

Bock's troubled observations provide a striking example of the German command's looming crisis of confidence. Unlike most of his subordinates, Bock was privy to a sufficiently large view of the big picture to judge accurately the insatiable demands of the eastern front. At the same time, he was not so far removed from the battlefield that he could bask in the luxury of Halder's brazen confidence. In short, Bock's concern for the difficulties swelling in his ranks were well founded, but scantly appreciated.[69]

Although a clear and pragmatic understanding of the war in the east was still lacking at the OKH and OKW, the manifest resilience of the Red Army was swiftly deflating the bold confidence of the German command, and exposing the many myths upon which they had conceived their war against the Soviet Union. The army's difficulties also raised the stakes in the strategic dilemma of where to strike next to administer the desperately needed final blow. The evidence suggests that both Halder and Hitler were showing signs of nervous anxiety consistent with the weight of a decision on which the outcome of the campaign depended. The implications of fighting on into the winter were simply unthinkable, and therefore the war had to be largely won in the weeks remaining before the autumn rains. Halder had previously made reference to Brauchitsch's dejected and nervous state, but according to Heusinger, Halder was the more troubling of the two. Assessing the army's Chief of Staff in a letter, Heusinger concluded: 'he is near his end, on the one hand he allocates everything to me and on the other hand he constantly comes to interfere with his own ideas'.[70] Heusinger also asserted that Halder was only sleeping four hours a night and was, as a result, exhausted.[71] While Hitler was beset with doubt and indecision over what to do next,[72] Halder remained resolute in his conviction that Moscow held the key to victory, but feared

---

[69] Instructive of how polarised the debate over Barbarossa's success has become is the conclusion of Heinz Magenheimer: 'In its unparalleled drive to victory up to the end of July, the Wehrmacht had, in any event, achieved the preconditions for a successful continuation of the campaign. In detail this meant: In the north the capture of Leningrad and the union with the Finnish army; in the centre the destruction of the armies deployed for the defence of Moscow and the capture of the capital; in the south the rapid crossing of the Dnepr below Kiev with a subsequent advance in the eastern Ukraine and the Donetz basin. There was still enough time to attain these objectives' (Magenheimer, *Hitler's War*, p. 86). In similar fashion Russel Stolfi has concluded: 'The German army had the fundamental capability – the command style, the numbers of men and tanks, and the logistical system – to win World War II during this brief window of opportunity in July–August 1941 – and they would never have it again at any other time or place in the war' (Stolfi, 'Blitzkrieg Army', pp. 163–164).

[70] Interestingly this was the same complaint Halder made about Hitler.

[71] Meyer, *Heusinger*, pp. 154–155.

[72] Von Kotze (ed.), *Heeresadjutant bei Hitler 1938–1943*, p. 107 (28 July 1941); Guderian, *Panzer Leader*, p. 185.

all his cherished plans would be doomed by Hitler's nonsensical under-standing of how the war should be continued. Hence, Halder was far more afraid of the internal threat from Hitler's ruinous interference, than the external difficulties caused by the Red Army, which had become so worrisome to Bock.

Halder's perceived salvation came at midnight on 30–31 July, when Heusinger reported that a new war directive had been signed by Hitler adopting the OKH proposals.[73] It was an enormous relief for Halder, whose mood was suddenly jubilant, as if a great weight had been lifted. Writing of the new directive in his diary, Halder's frustrations with Hitler were interwoven with his unrestrained delight: 'This solution frees every thinking soldier from the horrendous nightmare of the last few days, in which the Führer's obstinacy made the complete stalling of the eastern campaign appear imminent. Finally a ray of light!'[74]

In fact, the new war directive was not the divine deliverance Heusinger had led Halder to believe. The text of the directive gives no indication that major operations were to resume towards Moscow but, importantly for Halder, the distressing implications of Directive 33 and 33a had, for the time being, been put on hold. It was also becoming clear that Hitler was no longer so certain about where the main attack was to proceed next. The official language was that all operations were simply 'postponed' until the projected ten-day rehabilitation of the panzer groups could be completed. Yet Army Group Centre appeared to retain control over both panzer groups, and Leeb was expected to invest Leningrad with his own forces (plus the addition of Richthofen's recently transferred VIII Air Corps). In addition, Bock was permitted to undertake 'limited' offen-sives to clear his flanks, especially in the direction of Gomel.[75] Above all, the directive bought Halder precious time, and with Hitler already hes-itant and Halder's preference enjoying strong backing from the military commanders, hope was renewed within the OKH that a turning point in favour of Moscow could finally be reached.

Sealing the Smolensk pocket and Army Group Centre's fate

By 1 August the pocket at Smolensk, although compressed, was still proving a major thorn in the side of Army Group Centre (see Map 14). Strauss's 9th Army didn't have enough forces to reduce the pocket as well as undertake the relief of all Hoth's motorised divisions to the east. As

---

[73] Franz Halder, KTB III, p. 134 (30 July 1941).   [74] Ibid. (30 July 1941).
[75] Trevor-Roper (ed.), *Hitler's War Directives 1939–1945*, pp. 145–146.

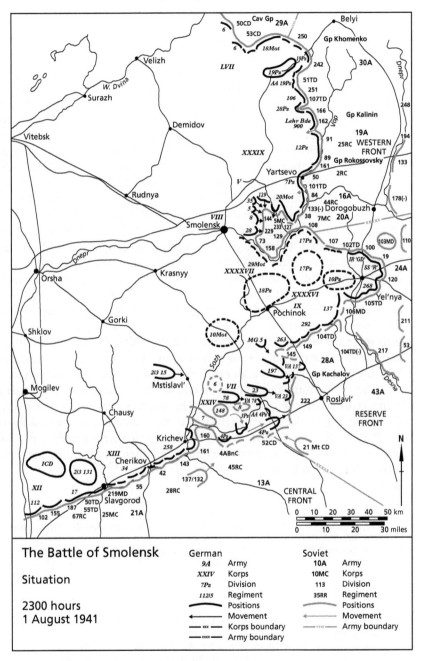

The Battle of Smolensk

Situation

2300 hours
1 August 1941

German		Soviet	
9A	Army	10A	Army
XXIV	Korps	10MC	Korps
7Pz	Division	113	Division
112/5	Regiment	35RR	Regiment
▬	Positions	⌒	Positions
◄──	Movement	◄╍╍	Movement
▬ xxx ▬	Korps boundary	╍╍ xxxx ╍╍	Army boundary
▬ xxxx ▬	Army boundary		

Map 14 Dispositions of Army Group Centre 1 August 1941: David M.
Glantz, *Atlas of the Battle of Smolensk 7 July–10 September 1941*

such Hoth's already battered front was deemed by Halder to be 'uncomfortably thin' with 'nothing behind it'.[76] The Chief of Staff of the 9th Army, Colonel Kurt Weckmann, telephoned Army Group Centre concerned that the situation was not being taken seriously enough and judged Hoth's position to be 'severely threatened'.[77] In fact, Timoshenko's residual forces did not possess adequate strength or concentration for a major breach of Hoth's front. The opposing armies had effectively battered each other to a standstill, and the enduring engagements were only further eroding their respective strengths. The battle had become attritional in nature rather than one guided by strategic manoeuvre, which only added to the urgency of removing Hoth's crucial motorised formations from the front. Hoth complained to Army Group Centre that his forces were becoming 'weaker from day to day' and pleaded for the 'urgent' replacement of his divisions by the infantry.[78] The 20th Panzer Division reported that its infantry brigades were 'severely exhausted' by the 'unceasing battles' and that officer casualties had now reached 50 per cent.[79] The 19th Panzer Division held its panzer regiment well back from the front to avoid losses, and to act as a reserve in case of an enemy breakthrough, but without relief from the infantry the war diary noted that none of the mechanical work on the tanks could begin.[80] The elimination of the Smolensk pocket was simply taking too long with Bock and Hoth becoming increasingly critical of the lack of vigour from the infantry in this sector.[81] Halder too was losing patience, but his concern was with the infantry's method of attack, which he stated was 'once again being approached the wrong way'.[82] The infantry divisions were driving the remaining Soviet forces directly into the rear of four battalions from 7th Panzer Division, who were busy defending themselves against attacks from the east. Under such circumstances, Halder expressed no surprise if the 7th Panzer Division 'eventually gets burned'.[83]

---

[76] Franz Halder, KTB III, p. 137 (1 August 1941).

[77] 'Kriegstagebuch Nr.1 (Band August 1941) des Oberkommandos der Heeresgruppe Mitte' BA-MA RH 19II/386, p. 219 (1 August 1941).

[78] 'Panzerarmeeoberkommandos Anlagen zum Kriegstagebuch "Berichte, Besprechungen, Beurteilungen der Lage" Bd.IV 22.7.41 – 31.8.41' BA-MA RH 21–3/47, Fols. 127–128 (1 August 1941). See also: '3rd Pz. Gr. KTB 25.5.41 – 31.8.41' BA-MA Microfilm 59054, Fol. 180 (1 August 1941).

[79] 'KTB 20th Pz. Div. vom 25.5.41 bis 15.8.41' BA-MA RH 27–20/2, Fol. 67 (1 August 1941).

[80] 'Kriegstagebuch 19.Panzer-Division Abt.Ib für dir Zeit vom 1.6.1941 – 31.12.1942' BA-MA RH 27–19/23, Fol. 23 (1 August 1941).

[81] Fedor von Bock, KTB 'Osten I', Fol. 50, War Diary, p. 270 (1 August 1941); 'Panzerarmeeoberkommandos Anlagen zum Kriegstagebuch "Berichte, Besprechungen, Beurteilungen der Lage" Bd.IV 22.7.41 – 31.8.41' BA-MA RH 21–3/47, Fol. 128 (1 August 1941).

[82] Franz Halder, KTB III, p. 137 (1 August 1941).   [83] Ibid. (1 August 1941).

The emerging frustration with the performance of the infantry reflects the limitations of non-motorised formations in seeking a rapid decision, and the relative inexperience of this arm of the German army. Despite having actively participated in previous campaigns, the infantry had remained in decidedly secondary roles, and were seldom called on to fight battles of the kind now being experienced on the eastern front. The war diary of the LVII Panzer Corps noted that the arrival of the 106th Infantry Division on the line was the division's first combat deployment against the Red Army. Yet, to the veteran panzer corps, it was soon evident that the infantry were 'not fully accustomed to the enemy's method of fighting and therefore suffered a disproportionately high number of losses'.[84] Similarly, a badly co-ordinated attack by the 251st Infantry Division on 2 August ended in a costly rout, which resulted in the divisional commander being relieved of his command. Within the division it was soon dubbed the 'black day' with losses so high that two regiments had to disband one battalion each.[85]

Under the intense pressure of attacks from both the east and west, on the afternoon of 1 August Schmidt's XXXIX Panzer Corps was no longer able to hold closed the eastern side of the Smolensk pocket.[86] Thus, only five days after finally closing the ring,[87] it was once again open with one German pilot reporting Soviet troops 'running off to the east'. Bock was aghast and again issued orders that the gap was to be closed jointly by Hoth's 20th Motorised Infantry Division in the north and Guderian's 17th Panzer Division to the south.[88] In spite of their joint responsibility, Bock's orders set off a new round of bickering among the panzer groups with each side insisting the other should do more to seal the gap. Guderian's panzer group asserted that the village at Ratschino, where Soviet troops had built a bridge across the river to escape eastwards, was clearly inside 9th Army's operational area and, in any case, the surrounding terrain made it 'completely impossible' for 17th Panzer Division to assault. Furthermore, Panzer Group 2's war diary complained it was

[84] 'Gen.Kdo.LVII.Pz.Korps Kriegstagesbuch Nr.1 vom 15.2. – 31.10.41' BA-MA RH 24–57/2, p. 277 (1 August 1941).
[85] Since 22 June the division had suffered 2,100 casualties. Hans Meier-Welcker, *Aufzeichnungen eines Generalstabsoffiziers 1939–1942* (Freiburg, 1982), pp. 125–126. See also Fedor von Bock, KTB 'Osten I', Fol. 51, *War Diary*, p. 271 (2 August 1941).
[86] 'Panzerarmeeoberkommandos Anlagen zum Kriegstagesbuch "Berichte, Besprechungen, Beurteilung der Lage" Bd.IV 22.7.41 – 31.8.41' BA-MA RH 21–3/47, Fol. 129 (2 August 1941).
[87] The ring may not have even held for five days as Bock wrote that the village of Ratschino, where the Soviet breakthrough was centred, had been lost 'probably three days ago'. Fedor von Bock, KTB 'Osten I', Fols. 50–51, *War Diary*, p. 271 (2 August 1941).
[88] Fedor von Bock, KTB 'Osten I', Fol. 50, *War Diary*, pp. 270–271 (2 August 1941).

'incomprehensible' why this position was 'given up' in the first place.[89] The counter-claim from Schmidt's XXXIX Panzer Corps was equally emphatic, claiming that its line was already 75 kilometres long, under attack from numerous Soviet divisions and that the original thrust to Ratschino was only undertaken because Panzer Group 2 could not fulfil its task of closing the ring from the south.[90] The dispute is an instructive example of the depths to which the army was sinking. The hole was just six kilometres wide and, although bitterly defended, the reluctance of the army's two most powerful panzer groups to undertake this task shows that they were under severe strain with greatly reduced offensive capabilities. Observing his armoured forces on 2 August, Bock commented, 'we are at the end of our tether'. He also drew attention to the great stress this was causing within his command. 'It is bad that the nerves of those burdened with great responsibility are starting to waver; today there was an argument with Strauss... Unfortunately I also became angry.'[91]

While Hoth's panzer group was stretched thin defending in the north, Guderian's forces were performing a frantic juggling act, concurrently defending at Yel'nya, attacking towards Roslavl and attempting to pull out anything not absolutely necessary for these operations to rest and refit. At Yel'nya on 1 August the attempted extraction of the 10th Panzer Division from the front had to be reversed with the withdrawn units rushed back into action to counter strong enemy pressure on Vietinghoff's right flank. Under these circumstances, the panzer group noted that no rehabilitation could take place and that more infantry was needed,[92] but Guderian's request for another infantry division was flatly rejected by Army Group Centre.[93] Meanwhile, a perpetual state of crisis hung over the German position at Yel'nya. The 60-kilometre-wide salient was caught in an unrelenting battle, typified by artillery fire which transformed the landscape into a cratered wasteland. On 1 August Vietinghoff reported to Army Group Centre that, in the average area of a company, upwards of 200 shells landed in five minutes as the troops lay helplessly in their foxholes.[94]

[89] 'KTB Nr.1 Panzergruppe 2 Bd.II vom 22.7.1941 bis 20.8.41' BA-MA RH 21–2/928, Fol. 118 (2 August 1941).
[90] 'Panzerarmeeoberkommandos Anlagen zum Kriegstagesbuch "Berichte, Besprechungen, Beurteilungen der Lage" Bd.IV 22.7.41 – 31.8.41' BA-MA RH 21–3/47, Fol. 129 (2 August 1941); '3rd Pz. Gr. KTB 25.5.41 – 31.8.41' BA-MA Microfilm 59054, Fol. 185 (2 August 1941).
[91] Fedor von Bock, KTB 'Osten I', Fol. 51, *War Diary*, p. 271 (2 August 1941).
[92] 'KTB Nr.1 Panzergruppe 2 Bd.II vom 22.7.1941 bis 20.8.41' BA-MA RH 21–2/928, Fol. 109 (1 August 1941).
[93] 'Kriegstagebuch Nr.1 (Band August 1941) des Oberkommandos der Heeresgruppe Mitte' BA-MA RH 19II/386, p. 230 (1 August 1941).
[94] Ibid. (1 August 1941).

The following day (2 August) the 268th Infantry Division reported 300–400 shells landing in one hour in the area of a battalion.[95] On 3 August during an enemy attack, Vietinghoff's corps was hit with 1,550 shells, the majority of which came from heavy-calibre 15cm guns.[96] Hearing such reports, Halder characterised Soviet artillery fire as 'insufferable'[97] – a fact borne out by the debilitating cost of holding Yel'nya. On 2 August XXXXVI Panzer Corps recorded that the SS *Das Reich* division had thus far suffered nearly 3,000 casualties with company strengths in some instances as low as 60–70 men.[98] Only two days later the same diary reported company strengths had sunk further, in some cases to just 20 men.[99] As Halder anxiously observed: 'The holding of this "bridgehead" costs us much blood.'[100] Material losses were also mounting, which led to a particularly disquieting conclusion in the XXXXVI Panzer Corps war diary: 'The losses have swelled so much that they are no longer bearable in view of later assignments.'[101] In spite of its cost, no one in the German command considered giving up the Yel'nya salient.[102] Halder was still hoping to use it as a springboard for further operations to the east and Hitler was, in general, opposed to any form of withdrawal, even if tactically advantageous.

To the south Schweppenburg's XXIV Panzer Corps began its thrust towards Roslavl on 1 August. The initial attack was supported by planes from Loerzer's II Air Corps, but these ran into very strong anti-aircraft fire over Roslavl and none of the estimated 35 aircraft returned without some form of damage.[103] On the ground Schweppenburg's 4th Panzer Division had been given considerable rest towards the end of July, substantially raising the number of combat-ready tanks[104] and allowing it to resume offensive operations. An envelopment of Roslavl, however, required a second thrust which, in the absence of additional motorised forces, fell to Geyer's IX Army Corps. In spite of the weakness of the Soviet flanks

---

[95] 'Kriegstagebuch Nr.2 der XXXXVI.Pz.Korps Teil II. 8.7.41 – 23.8.41' BA-MA RH 24–46/8, Fol. 148 (2 August 1941).

[96] Ibid., Fol. 171 (3 August 1941).

[97] Franz Halder, KTB III, p. 146 (3 August 1941).

[98] 'Kriegstagebuch Nr.2 des XXXXVI.Pz.Korps Teil II. 8.7.41 – 23.8.41' BA-MA RH 24–46/8, Fol. 158 (2 August 1941).

[99] Ibid., Fol. 178 (4 August 1941).

[100] Franz Halder, KTB III, p. 146 (3 August 1941).

[101] 'Kriegstagebuch Nr.2 des XXXXVI.Pz.Korps Teil II. 8.7.41 – 23.8.41' BA-MA RH 24–46/8, Fol. 171 (3 August 1941).

[102] Franz Halder, KTB III, p. 152 (4 August 1941).

[103] 'KTB Nr.1 Panzergruppe 2 Bd.II vom 22.7.1941 bis 20.8.41' BA-MA RH 21–2/928, Fols. 98 and 105 (31 July and 1 August 1941).

[104] On 17 July the division had only 40 serviceable tanks from an original strength of 169, but by 30 July this had been more than doubled to 90.

and the relatively small operation theatre, Geyer's offensive made clear the unsuitability of infantry as a substitute for motorised units.[105] The infantry divisions moved too slowly to exploit weaknesses or effect rapid encirclements, and their ability to concentrate firepower at the spearhead of an attack was limited. This left 4th Panzer Division to undertake the lion's share of the work, which in its rejuvenated state it succeeded in doing. Roslavl was taken from the south and by 3 August the panzers linked up with Geyer's struggling forces.[106]

The pocket was closed, but still not hermetically sealed and large numbers of Soviet troops continued to break out.[107] Days later Halder complained in his diary: 'Encircled enemy elements at Roslavl have escaped. The Russians have a remarkable ability to move on roads impassable to us and to build concealed river crossings.'[108] Although the operation was clearly another painful Soviet defeat, the fact that it was the only offensive action Army Group Centre could manage – and a small one at that – to redress the many trouble spots on its front says much about Bock's strategic paralysis. Indeed, given the degree of pressure on Bock's extensive front and the absence of any substantive reserves, Halder judged Bock's decision to attack towards Roslavl as 'downright careless'.[109] The operation was also instructive for its cost. Just two days after the start of the offensive 4th Panzer Division had lost almost a quarter of its tanks[110] and Schweppenburg's corps (including 3rd Panzer Division fighting further south) was reporting that its forces, 'irrespective of the necessary reconditioning work, must also have a 4 day rest for the physical and mental strain'.[111] This, however, was impossible to achieve as local Soviet attacks continued, one of which on 6 August succeeded in places at breaking through the 3rd Panzer Division's front.[112] Sustaining offensive operations was indeed taxing, costing material, consuming stockpiled resources of fuel and munitions and exacting a steep toll on the men. While the battle for Roslavl remains an undisputed victory at the operational level, it is instructive of the limitations of the German army

---

[105] Guderian, *Panzer Leader*, p. 188.

[106] The operations of IX Army Corps are described in detail in Geyer's memoir (Geyer, *Das IX. Armeekorps im Ostfeldzug 1941*, pp. 101–115).

[107] Ibid., pp. 112 and 114.   [108] Franz Halder, KTB III, p. 157 (6 August).

[109] Ibid., p. 146 (3 August 1941).

[110] This figure comes from the total figures given on 30 July (90 tanks) and 3 August (71 tanks); 'Kriegstagebuch 4.Panzer-Division Führungsabtl. 26.5.41 – 31.3.42' BA-MA RH 27–4/10, pp. 84 and 94 (30 July and 3 August 1941).

[111] 'KTB Nr.1 Panzergruppe 2 Bd.II vom 22.7.1941 bis 20.8.41' BA-MA RH 21–2/928, Fol. 131 (3 August 1941).

[112] 'KTB 3rd Pz. Div. vom 16.8.40 bis 18.9.41' BA-MA RH 27–3/14, p. 160 (6 August 1941).

in the east and a warning against the enduring optimism for a large-scale offensive solution to the still elusive German victory.

As all of Guderian's panzer corps concurrently parried and attacked, Lemelsen's XXXXVII Panzer Corps was juggling the demands of the front as well as attempting to begin the refitting process. The 29th Motorised Division was attacking the remnants inside the Smolensk pocket, the devastated 18th Panzer Division was licking its wounds in the rear area, and the 17th Panzer Division was split between defensive battles along the front and withdrawing some its units. The panzer divisions had lost a great deal of their combat strength and the plan was now to amalgamate certain components, 'at least to make a part fully combat ready again (especially in the 18th Panzer Division)'. Yet even this limited goal was met with difficulty as the Quartermaster-General reported, 'the spare parts have not been brought forward in the necessary quantities'. Furthermore, a shortage of oil was slowing down all movement and having an 'extremely harmful effect'. Evidently, Lemelsen's corps was caught between totally inadequate offensive strength and an extremely limited ability to bring about any form of restoration, which resulted in the worrying conclusion: 'In a further commitment, the corps intends to initially leave behind a part of the panzers until overhauling and replenishment with oil is completed.'[113]

A clear indication that German operations had fallen well short of their objectives was the contrasting discrepancy in strategic reserves available to each side. On 1 August Halder noted that the OKH reserve was entirely committed with nothing remaining beyond what the army groups now commanded.[114] By contrast, the Soviets were believed to retain some 28 divisions behind the front with 13 more in the process of formation.[115] These, in addition to the numerous Soviet armies already manning the front, would make the resumption of major eastward operations all the more difficult for the Germans, especially in their weakened state. In a letter home on 3 August, General Heinrici stated: '[When the enemy] units are all half destroyed, he stuffs new people in and attacks again. How the Russians manage this is beyond me.'[116] A report by General Walter Buhle, following a visit to Guderian's panzer group, 'cries for troop replacements for the panzer and infantry divisions'.[117] The most comprehensive study of German military losses in World War II noted that July 1941 cost the Wehrmacht more soldiers than any other month

[113] 'Kriegstagebuch der O.Qu.-Abt. Pz. A.O.K.2 von 21.6.41 bis 31.3.42' BA-MA RH 21–2/819, Fol. 265 (2 August 1941).
[114] Franz Halder, KTB III, p. 141 (1 August 1941).   [115] Ibid., p. 142 (2 August 1941).
[116] Hürter, *Ein deutscher General*, p. 72 (3 August 1941).
[117] Franz Halder, KTB III, p. 145 (2 August 1941).

on the eastern front until December 1942 and January 1943 at the battle of Stalingrad. The number of German dead in July 1941 was put at 63,099 men.[118]

Across the whole eastern front the forward movement of German reinforcements from the home replacement army was in no way keeping pace with losses. Army Group South had so far lost 63,000 men (including wounded) and gained only 10,000 replacements, Army Group Centre 74,500 men with 23,000 replacements, and Army Group North 42,000 losses to just 14,000 replacements. Bock's army group was clearly the main priority, but even here the results were disappointing. The army group had a shortfall exceeding 50,000 men and the best Halder could hope for was a further 10,000 men arriving in the next eight to ten days, although this, like everything else, depended on the tenuous German transportation system. In any case, Halder calculated that this would leave Bock's armies with the following projected shortfalls: Weichs's 2nd Army 30,500 men; Strauss's 9th Army 15,000 men; Guderian's 2nd Panzer Group 5,000 men and Hoth's 3rd Panzer Group 4,000 men.[119] Such calculations, however, could not account for losses suffered in the intervening days.

Compounding the absence of strategic reserves and the increasing gaps in the ranks was the inability to compensate with firepower owing to munition shortages. On 1 August in a telephone conversation with the Army Quartermaster-General, Bock insisted that the lack of munitions previously acknowledged as 'serious' was, after a week without improvement, 'gradually becoming a crisis'. Wagner attempted to assure Bock that the urgency of the situation was well known to him and that he was doing everything possible to alleviate the problem,[120] but these were just words and he was unable to alter substantially the realities of the German predicament. The logistical network was supposed to be sustained by a combination of Soviet and German railways bringing up the great bulk of supplies that would then be delivered to the front over relatively short distances by trucks. In practice, however, the system was so flawed that Bock was lucky to be getting enough for the bare subsistence of his army group. Gercke, the Chief of Wehrmacht Transport, explained to Halder on 2 August that the 'numerical scarcity' of captured Soviet locomotives

---

[118] Rüdiger Overmans, *Deutsche militärische Verluste im Zweiten Weltkrieg* (Munich, 2000), pp. 277–278. To add some perspective, this one-month figure is 5,000 men *higher* than the total number of American soldiers killed in all the years of the Vietnam war (58,156). Overmans gives the figure for the number of Germans killed in December 1942 as 78,759 men. January 1943 more than doubled that figure at 180,310 men.

[119] Franz Halder, KTB III, p. 145 (2 August 1941).

[120] 'Kriegstagebuch Nr.1 (Band August 1941) des Oberkommandos der Heeresgruppe Mitte' BA-MA RH 19II/386, p. 233 (1 August 1941).

and rolling stock was a major complication to the supply of the army.[121] As a result, rail supply would have to be overwhelmingly undertaken by the overstretched *Reichsbahn* and this meant that the conversion of the railways was of even more fundamental importance. This in turn gave rise to disputes over how the process should be managed. The army was clamouring for an extension of the railways as close to the front as possible, but extending the railways such a distance could only be achieved at the expense of their carrying capacity. Wagner argued for a slower extension of the railways with a higher carrying capacity, but this left a sizeable shortfall in distance which would then have to be made up by the trucks of the *Grosstransportraum*.[122] As Halder noted: 'Building a logistical system in parallel to running supplies is difficult and slow.'[123] In some cases, converted railroads replaced two-way tracks with single lines, forcing bottlenecks of one-way traffic. Moreover, liberties taken to extend the lines as fast as possible often resulted in poor quality, reducing the speed of the trains. In some instances it was not the workmanship so much as the materials which caused problems. Soviet rail beds were sometimes so weak and their rails so feeble that the only German locomotives that could be used were light models dating from World War I.[124] Gercke also complained about the inadequacy of communication infrastructure, as well as the civilian German railway workers who were, in his opinion, too inflexible and slow.[125] In the most favourable circumstance, four companies of railway engineers managed to re-lay 20 kilometres of track in a 24-hour period.[126] Overall, however, the pace was far too slow to alleviate the army's great shortages and, as Halder concluded on 3 August: 'The question of munitions is for the time being unsolvable because the trains are failing to appear.'[127] Not surprisingly, the supply situation was a major headache for the German command and Halder singled out Bock's army group as the main 'problem child'.[128]

With the railways both too limited and heavily overburdened, German commanders desperate for supplies pressed every available motor-driven vehicle into service. In the most favourable circumstances the nearest supply depots were still 150 kilometres from the front, meaning a 300-kilometre round trip, assuming there were supplies to be had. Often the trucks would have to drive a great deal further, including all the way back to the pre-war border,[129] or wait aimlessly for rail shipments while

[121] Franz Halder, KTB III, pp. 143–144 (2 August 1941).
[122] Ibid., p. 144 (2 August 1941).   [123] Ibid., p. 142 (2 August 1941).
[124] Müller, 'Das Scheitern der wirtschaftlichen "Blitzkriegstrategie"', p. 965.
[125] Franz Halder, KTB III, p. 144 (2 August 1941).
[126] Müller, 'Das Scheitern der wirtschaftlichen "Blitzkriegstrategie"', p. 962.
[127] Franz Halder, KTB III, p. 146 (3 August 1941).   [128] Ibid., p. 144 (2 August 1941).
[129] Franz Halder, KTB III, p. 138 (1 August 1941); Guderian, *Panzer Leader*, p. 186.

the men at the front pleaded for ammunition and other essentials. Thus, the stalling of Army Group Centre's offensive provided no respite for the *Grosstransportraum* which was being ground down on the dreadful Soviet roads, steadily reducing the army's future mobility. The war diary of the 19th Panzer Division noted that supplies were being brought up from a distance of 250 kilometres or more, meaning at least a 500-kilometre journey for each load.[130] The supply officer of the 10th Panzer Division informed his commanding officer, Lieutenant-General Ferdinand Schaal, that the division could only be supplied from a maximum of 200 kilometres away. Beyond that 'serious difficulties' were to be expected as only 50 per cent of the original transportation fleet remained serviceable. Particularly high was the loss of requisitioned French trucks, which Schaal acknowledged could not be replaced from Germany, meaning that the division would therefore have to 'fend for itself'.[131] Previously, about one in every ten broken-down vehicles was being replaced by new production from Germany, but, by the end of July, the OKH refused to send any more vehicles because of shortages and the planned establishment of new formations.[132]

Overall the *Grosstransportraum* of the army was in rapid decline. Halder noted on 5 August that trucks requisitioned from civilian industry had already suffered a total fallout rate of 30 per cent, while the loss of military vehicles stood at 20 per cent.[133] Army Group North was the worst off with an average total loss of 39 per cent among its transport fleet,[134] but worse still was the fact that the bulk of trucks still classed as serviceable were rapidly succumbing to the same fate. Throughout the army there were serious shortages of tyres and spare parts,[135] while the conditions in the east were noted by Guderian's Quartermaster-General to be 'very severe' in oil consumption, accounting for usage in 'frightful masses'. On the poor roads the vehicles were often forced to drive for long periods in low gears, while the hot summer temperatures and pervasive clouds of road dust combined to increase oil consumption dramatically. Not only this, but the engines were in far more frequent need of total oil changes.[136] In LVII Panzer Corps a report from 6 August noted: 'Already many vehicles are consuming 20 to 30 litres of oil per

---

[130] 'Kriegstagesbuch 19.Panzer-Division Abt.Ib für dir Zeit vom 1.6.1941 – 31.12.1942' BA-MA RH 27–19/23, Fol. 24 (2 August 1941).
[131] 'Kriegstagebuch der 10.Panzer Division Nr.5 vom: 22.5. bis: 7.10.41' BA-MA RH 27–10/26b (2 August 1941).
[132] Müller, 'Das Scheitern der wirtschaftlichen "Blitzkriegstrategie"', p. 964.
[133] Franz Halder, KTB III, p. 156 (5 August 1941).
[134] Ibid., p. 149 (3 August 1941).   [135] Ibid., p. 156 (5 August 1941).
[136] 'Kriegstagebuch der O.Qu.-Abt. Pz. A.O.K.2 von 21.6.41 bis 31.3.42' BA-MA RH 21–2/819, Fol. 267 (1 August 1941).

100 kilometres instead of the normal half litre of oil.'[137] Shortages of oil
and a general lack of careful maintenance meant that the abrasive effects
on the engines, particularly from the dust, were extremely damaging
even over short distances. A report from XXXXVII Panzer Corps on
4 August made clear that the dust in the motors of its trucks doomed
them all to an early grave. Those of the 17th Panzer Division and the 29th
Motorised Division were expected to last a further 500 to 800 kilometres
'without excessive operational demands', while the engines of the 18th
Panzer Division were forecast to last only another 200 to 400 kilometres.
The difference between the two estimates rested on the high number of
French vehicles in the 18th Panzer Division.[138] Although such lifespan
projections were only made in the XXXXVII Panzer Corps, it may be
assumed that the other panzer corps were similarly affected, spelling a
foreseeable end to the mobility of the panzer divisions even if the panzers
themselves could be brought back up to offensive strength.

As the army struggled to cope with its many burdens, the news filtering
back to the German home front was not quite the triumphant blitzkrieg
being trumpeted by Goebbels's propaganda machine. The majority of the
German population were still convinced of eventual success, but classified
SD reports (the SD *Sicherheitsdienst* were a sub-element of Himmler's SS)
undertaken to gauge the public mood detected an emerging groundswell
of anxiety about the war in the east. An SD report from 4 August read:

It is often said that the campaign has not been proceeding as might have been
assumed from reports at the start of the operation... Since then, we have had
the impression that the Soviets have plenty of materiel and that there has been
increasing resistance... From the number of reported deaths... the panzer corps
reports and front reports, one can safely assume *that casualties really are higher
than in previous campaigns.*[139]

Indeed, towards the end of July the difficulties at the front were causing
Goebbels to rein in the enthusiasm of his propaganda. He declared in his
diary: 'We must no longer promise so much.' He then signalled a new
direction for propaganda. 'It is therefore correct, when we very explicitly
inform the German people of the harshness of the battles playing out
in the east. One must tell the nation that this operation is very difficult,

---

[137] As quoted in Steiger, *Armour Tactics*, p. 124.
[138] 'Kriegstagebuch Nr.2 XXXXVII.Pz.Korps. Ia 25.5.1941 – 22.9.1941' BA-MA RH
24–47/2 (4 August 1941). See also 'KTB Nr.1 Panzergruppe 2 Bd.II vom 22.7.1941
bis 20.8.41' BA-MA RH 21–2/928, Fols. 142–143 (4 August 1941).
[139] Italics in the original. Heinz Boberach (ed.), *Meldungen aus dem Reich. Die geheimen
Lageberichte des Sicherheitsdienstes der SS 1938–1945*, Band VII (Berlin, 1984), Document 208, p. 2609 (1–4 August 1941). See also ibid., Band VIII (Berlin, 1984),
Document 208, p. 2724 (4 September 1941).

but that we can overcome it and also will overcome it.'[140] As the harsh realities of the eastern front were just dawning on many Germans, there were others to whom it came as no surprise. Anti-Hitler conspirator Helmuth James Graf von Moltke, the great-nephew of the celebrated Prussian Field Marshal Helmuth Karl Bernhard Graf von Moltke, harboured reservations from the earliest days of the war. Writing to his wife from Berlin he spoke in harsh terms about the progress of the war, which 'has already produced very heavy fighting and cost us very great losses'.[141] Two days later on 3 July Moltke concluded: 'I have come to the conclusion that we have obviously completely underestimated Russia.'[142] Another civilian and one of Moltke's compatriots, Ulrich von Hassell, judged the overall situation on 2 August in similarly bleak terms. 'The situation: heavy Russian resistance, heavy losses, heavy English air raids in the west. Very meagre results in the submarine and air war against the British merchant fleet. Consequently, low barometer readings, feeling of endlessness and doom.'[143] In Italy Goebbels ominously observed that the public mood was rife with criticism for the perceived ineptitude of Mussolini's Fascist regime and claimed that the people had placed 'their last hope in the German Wehrmacht'.[144] Even at the front, an Italian journalist travelling with the German armies, Curzio Malaparte, observed the error of German pre-war estimates and the alarming strength of the Soviet enemy.

I am thinking of the mistake made by those who hoped, at the beginning of the war against Russia, that at the first impact revolution would break out in Moscow – in other words, that the collapse of the system would precede the collapse of the army. These people showed that they failed to understand the spirit of the Soviet society. Rather than the *kolkhozi* – the great collective farms – rather than her giant factories, rather than her heavy industry, the supreme industrial creation of Soviet Russia is her Army.[145]

While the German population were only just beginning to comprehend the scale and cost of the new war in the east, any illusions held by the Soviet populace about the 'invincibility' of the Red Army were quickly dispelled in the opening days of the war. With the exception of the Soviet territories recently incorporated in to the USSR and certain regions of

[140] Elke Fröhlich (ed.), *Die Tagebücher von Joseph Goebbels*, Teil II: Diktate 1941–1945, Band 1, Juli–September 1941 (Munich, 1996), pp. 115–116 (24 July 1941).
[141] Kempowski (ed.), *Das Echolot Barbarossa '41*, p. 171 (1 July 1941).
[142] Ibid., p. 206 (3 July 1941).
[143] Von Hassell, *Vom andern Deutschland*, p. 214 (2 August 1941); von Hassell, *Diaries*, p. 185 (2 August 1941).
[144] Fröhlich (ed.), *Die Tagebücher von Joseph Goebbels*, Teil II, p. 98 (20 July 1941).
[145] Curzio Malaparte, *The Volga Rises in Europe* (Edinburgh, 2000), p. 60 (7 July 1941).

the Ukraine, the mood can generally be characterised as one of defiance and nationalistic zeal. Although Soviet post-war histories went to great lengths to demonstrate the absolute unity of the Soviet population, in truth of course there were exceptions.[146] Yet much evidence still points to widespread support for the Soviet Union's war effort, indicating that the war evoked a passion beyond a simple adherence to the Soviet state or Stalin.[147] Many people did fight for socialism, although perhaps not always Stalin's particular brand of it, while others fought, in spite of the Soviet system, for their homeland.[148] Some supported the Soviet war effort to forestall the advent of Nazi rule which they wisely feared. Of course there were also many who were simply given no choice, being drafted to the army or into the factories where draconian discipline enforced loyalty. Nevertheless, popular enthusiasm was shared by a majority of the Soviet population.[149] There was an overwhelming acceptance that the Soviet Union was the victim of Nazi aggression and the past mistakes of the political leadership were soon forgotten in the rush to defend the state. Stalin shrewdly propagated this by enacting a quiet revolution in state freedoms, previously unthinkable. Anti-religious propaganda was soon halted[150] and past national heroes,

---

[146] Research by Karel C. Berkhoff on the Ukraine has suggested that this region remained largely opposed to the Soviet cause in the initial period of war. Ukrainians drafted into the Red Army were prone to desertion, while the peasantry consistently greeted the Germans as liberators. Karel C. Berkhoff, *Harvest of Despair. Life and Death in Ukraine Under Nazi Rule* (Cambridge, 2004), p. 34. See also Merridale, *Ivan's War*, pp. 90–93 and 105–106; Braithwaite, *Moscow 1941*, pp. 70–73;. Mawdsley, *Thunder in the East*, pp. 30–31.

[147] Marius Broekmeyer, *Stalin, The Russians, and Their War 1941–1945* (London, 2004), pp. 201–203; Gennadi Bordiugov, 'The Popular Mood in the Unoccupied Soviet Union: Continuity and Change During the War' in Robert Thurston and Bernd Bonwetsch (eds.), *The People's War. Responses to World War II in the Soviet Union* (Chicago, 2000), pp. 54–70; Mikhail M. Gorinov, 'Muscovites' Moods, 22 June 1941 to May 1942' in Robert Thurston and Bernd Bonwetsch (eds.), *The People's War. Responses to World War II in the Soviet Union* (Chicago, 2000), pp. 108–134; Andrei R. Dzeniskevich, 'The Social and Political Situation in Leningrad in the First Months of the German Invasion: The Social Psychology of the Workers' in Robert Thurston and Bernd Bonwetsch (eds.), *The People's War. Responses to World War II in the Soviet Union* (Chicago, 2000), pp. 71–83.

[148] Bordiugov, 'The Popular Mood', p. 58.

[149] Alexander Werth, a British correspondent working for the BBC, was stationed in the Soviet Union throughout the war and even granted the opportunity to travel around the country (at times alone) and visit the front. After the war he wrote: 'In the fearful days of 1941-2 and in the next two and a half years of hard and costly victories, I never lost the feeling that this was a genuine People's War; first, a war waged by a people fighting for their life against terrible odds, and later a war fought by a fundamentally unaggressive people, now roused to anger and determined to demonstrate their own military superiority' (Werth, *Russia at War 1941–1945*, p. xvi).

[150] Broekmeyer, *Stalin, The Russians, and Their War 1941–1945*, p. 213; Werth, *Russia at War 1941–1945*, p. 429.

forgotten in favour of new socialist idols, were resurrected as symbols of past national glories.[151] Propaganda improved in both medium and content.[152] *Pravda*, the Soviet daily newspaper, dropped its weary peacetime slogan: 'Proletarians of all lands, unite!' Instead the new message was simple and direct: 'Death to the German invaders!'[153] The war was soon being portrayed as 'a great patriotic war' to evoke comparisons with the victorious ejection of Napoleon's invading army by Tsar Alexander I. There were also 600,000 people freed from the labour camps, 175,000 of whom where then mobilised.[154] It was a new Stalinist state with a slightly more compassionate face, designed to bleed every last drop of popular fervour from its inhabitants, while retaining an iron-fisted grip on power. The comparison with Nazi Germany at the time could hardly be more stark. The Soviets were mobilising fully on the home industrial front as well as for the Red Army, and psychologically the conflict was already being heralded as a time of great national crisis, requiring untold sacrifices. In Germany, by contrast, there was no 'total war' economy, no national state of emergency and the majority of the population still expected the war to be of short duration, ending in another triumph of German arms. It seemed only the boldest sceptic could venture to presume that in the summer of 1941 Germany was, in fact, irretrievably losing the war.

Although the motorised formations of the army were being progressively gutted on the eastern front, the German High Command was steadfastly absorbed by the strategic question of where to resume offensive operations. Hitler had resigned himself to a pause in operations while the final resistance in the Smolensk pocket was extinguished, and the necessary refitting of the panzer divisions was undertaken. This gave him time to consider his options and reflect on the weight of opinion arrayed against him. Hitler still retained his preference for Leningrad and a strike to the south over that of Moscow, but in his momentary self-doubt he wanted some form of substantiation to validate his instinctive tendency. It was also somewhat characteristic of Hitler to procrastinate over important decisions, especially when his own inner conviction was rattled. In this momentary inertia on Hitler's part, Halder saw his advantage and hoped to wrestle back the strategic initiative from Hitler's interference. Yet for all Hitler's indecision, he was not a man who could be bent to anyone else's will, something Halder consistently failed to grasp, as did many other generals later in the war. If it was ever possible to change

---

[151] Barber and Harrison, *The Soviet Home Front 1941–1945*, p. 70.
[152] Gorinov, 'Muscovites' Moods', pp. 118–119.
[153] Merridale, *Ivan's War*, p. 132.   [154] Bordiugov, 'The Popular Mood', pp. 60–61.

Hitler's mind on an issue, he would have to be tenderly cajoled and convinced in ways that sometime ignored conventional rationale, and appealed instead to Hitler's selective world-view. Confrontation was just as likely to produce the opposite effect and spark one of his thunderous tantrums.

While Hitler struggled with his flagging resolution on how to proceed, his search for conviction led him to Bock's headquarters on 4 August to hear first hand the view of his battlefield commanders – a perspective he trusted far more than the self-serving clique at OKH. Ordered to attend, Hoth and Guderian flew into Borisov to join Bock who was already hosting a visit by Heusinger – no doubt the eyes and ears of the OKH and probably with a mandate to ensure uniformity throughout the army command, which may well have been a prudent measure given that there was some evidence to suggest Guderian had favourably considered the southward strike.[155] In addition, Brauchitsch had also expressed his hope that the two panzer commanders would 'influence Hitler to release the panzer reserves'.[156]

Hitler arrived by plane with his usual entourage, which included Keitel, Jodl and Schmundt. The proceedings opened with Hitler warmly congratulating Bock on his 'unprecedented successes'.[157] Then Hitler proceeded to question each of the generals separately in another room so as to gauge their opinions individually, without each man knowing what the others had said.[158] If Hitler was looking for support within the ranks of the army he would not find it on this day, and the generals all toed Halder's line on the paramount importance of Moscow. For his part Keitel was disgusted, seeing this as an obvious sham orchestrated by the OKH. Writing before his execution at Nuremberg, Keitel recalled bitterly:

All three of them [Bock, Hoth and Guderian] were aware of the War Office's [OKH's] plan of attack and saw it as their panacea; any weakening of Army Group Centre would jeopardise this plan, a plan which had electrified them all . . . The War Office, Army Group Centre and the tank commanders had managed to put up a united front against their Führer.

It was this resistance that Keitel then blamed for ultimately having 'shipwrecked Hitler's great strategic master plan'.[159] Certainly in Bock's and Hoth's case and perhaps Guderian's too, the willingness of the generals

---

[155] 'KTB Nr.1 Panzergruppe 2 vom 22.6.1941 bis 21.7.41' BA-MA RH 21–2/927, Fol. 222 (14 July 1941).

[156] 'Kriegstagebuch Nr.1 (Band August 1941) des Oberkommandos der Heeresgruppe Mitte' BA-MA RH 19II/386, p. 240 (3 August 1941).

[157] Fedor von Bock, KTB 'Osten I', Fol. 51, *War Diary*, pp. 272 (4 August 1941).

[158] Guderian, *Panzer Leader*, p. 189.

[159] Gorlitz (ed.), *Memoirs of Field-Marshal Keitel*, pp. 150–151.

to argue for Moscow reflected not only the desires of the OKH, but also a strong degree of personal conviction. The only senior commander in Army Group Centre to have openly endorsed the diversion of panzers to the south was Kluge;[160] however, his command had been recently made redundant by the disbandment of 4th Panzer Army. As a Field Marshal, Kluge was the second-highest ranking officer in Army Group Centre and would be reinstated as an army commander. Even if the OKW had not expressly requested his attendance, Kluge had been involved in the campaign at the most senior level from the very beginning and would shortly resume his involvement, raising the question of whether there was a more devious agenda on the part of the OKH. Even if no active measures were taken to exclude him, one wonders whether there was not a passive bias against him, and whether his attendance would have been sought or even ordered had he expressed an enthusiastic devotion towards the Moscow alternative. In any case, there was no sympathetic ear for Hitler's preferred plans at Borisov.

By all accounts Hitler was still unsure how to proceed at the end of the meeting and declared that no final decision had yet been made as to future strategy. He did, however, set out the three alternatives in order of current priority. First came Leningrad, second the Donets region south of Kharkov in the eastern Ukraine, and last Moscow. Yet this was not as discouraging for the army commanders as it might first appear. Leningrad, Hitler contended, was expected to be reached by Leeb's forces without further aid by 20 August. This, he continued, left 'all the strength of the Luftwaffe currently deployed there as well as strong elements of Leeb's command to be placed at the disposal of Army Group Centre'. As for the southern operation, Hitler also made reference to the recent favourable development of Army Group South's position and that the battle strength of enemy forces there 'was no longer highly valued'.[161]

After the discussion of strategy, Hoth and Guderian were keen to seize their chance and issue a direct plea to Hitler for the urgent release of new panzers and the shipment of replacement tank engines from Germany. Guderian, in particular, couched his request in absolute terms, pointing optimistically to the prospect of renewed operations over distant reaches of the Soviet Union with a full 70 per cent of his forces fit for battle by

15 August.[162] The consequences, however, of not heeding his replacement requirements were correspondingly dire. On this point Guderian was blunt and to the point.

[T]he striking power of the decisive shock weapons [by which he had cited panzers and aircraft] would decline. The fighting would then depend more on the infantry and progress would be sluggish and bloody. Rapid, comprehensive victories would then no longer be possible and as a result of this the progress of the war would be decisively and negatively influenced.[163]

Hoth too stressed the urgency of replacement engines[164] and emphasised that newly produced tanks were also necessary to replace total losses.[165] Hoth, however, was more cautious than Guderian in giving a date for the completion of his refitting process, suggesting it would be between 18 and 20 August.[166]

Hitler listened patiently to these requests and the diarist for Guderian's second panzer group (who also appears to have been in attendance) noted that, '[t]he Führer was visibly moved'.[167] Hitler immediately authorised the release of one month's supply of engine production for the front, which equated to 400 engines,[168] and a pitiful 35 newly produced tanks.[169] Beyond this Hitler would not go. He claimed that the two remaining panzer divisions in Germany (2nd and 5th Panzer Divisions which had undergone repairs following the Balkan campaign) as well as the bulk of new production, were needed in the homeland to forestall any British landings.[170] Later it was acknowledged that, even if these

---

162 KTB OKW, Volume II, pp. 1041 and 1043, Document 88 (4 August 1941); Mendelssohn, Die Nürnberger Dokumente, pp. 396 and 398.

163 'KTB Nr.1 Panzergruppe 2 Bd.II vom 22.7.1941 bis 20.8.41' BA-MA RH 21–2/928, Fol. 138 (4 August 1941).

164 KTB OKW, Volume II, p. 1041, Document 88 (4 August 1941); Mendelssohn, Die Nürnberger Dokumente, p. 396.

165 Hoth, Panzer-Operationen, p. 117.

166 KTB OKW, Volume II, p. 1043, Document 88 (4 August 1941); Mendelssohn, Die Nürnberger Dokumente, p. 398.

167 'KTB Nr.1 Panzergruppe 2 Bd.II vom 22.7.1941 bis 20.8.41' BA-MA RH 21–2/928, Fol. 139 (4 August 1941).

168 KTB OKW, Volume II, p. 1042, Document 88 (4 August 1941); Mendelssohn, Die Nürnberger Dokumente, p. 396.

169 'KTB Nr.1 Panzergruppe 2 Bd.II vom 22.7.1941 bis 20.8.41' BA-MA RH 21–2/928, Fol. 139 (4 August 1941). The memoirs of Guderian and Hoth both claim to have received no new tanks. This does not correlate with Panzer Group 2's war diary written on 4 August 1941. Guderian's memoir, written ten years later, is littered with factual errors and oversights – he also wrote that the number of new engines was 300, which does not tally with the OKW war diary either. Hoth's memoir, which appeared later in 1956, discusses these events with a footnote to Guderian's work and therefore repeated his mistake.

170 KTB OKW, Volume II, pp. 1041–1042, Document 88 (4 August 1941); Mendelssohn, Die Nürnberger Dokumente, p. 396.

measures did not compensate for the wear and tear of the panzer divisions, 'at least it gave the troops something of the feeling that they were not forgotten.'[171] Guderian, on the other hand, protested that his panzer group alone would require 300 engines[172] and claims to have described the offer as 'totally inadequate',[173] but Hitler remained unmoved. Soviet losses, the dictator asserted, were approaching those of Imperial Russia in World War I and this after just six weeks.[174] To Hitler's mind he had already been quite generous and, in any case, the success of operations rested mainly on adopting the correct strategic approach, not haggling over a few tanks or spare parts.

At the conclusion of the conference Heusinger dutifully gave a detailed report to Halder who was gratified to note that Hitler had released the panzer engines, but added that this had already been undertaken by the OKH without Hitler's knowledge. The subject of Moscow was, however, cause for renewed frustration. Halder had hoped that the much celebrated field commanders, on the verge of another victory at Smolensk, and with all the warrior's élan that appealed so much to Hitler, would sweep aside Hitler's lingering reservations. The news that Moscow was still in third place behind Leningrad and the Ukraine was a bitter pill for Halder, who was equally frustrated at Hitler's continued procrastination in coming to a final decision. That evening, with the backing of Brauchitsch, Halder vented his frustration to Heusinger and Paulus. He insisted that the army groups needed clear-cut tasks and lamented the absence of political direction in establishing clear objectives for the campaign. Halder suggested that, if his objective was to defeat the enemy decisively, it should be left to the army with full access to resources and no interference from above. 'This', Halder assured his audience, 'would end in this year at Moscow and leave the gaining of more ground [in the Ukraine] to the development of the situation.'[175]

With the high hopes of the OKH wallowing in an atmosphere of gloom, Brauchitsch departed for the Wolf's Lair the next day (5 August) to press Hitler for more clarity on strategic questions. The meeting revealed that Hitler was also becoming concerned by the danger that the front was settling down to static warfare, like in 1914. He expressed the need to get

---

[171] 'KTB Nr.1 Panzergruppe 2 Bd.II vom 22.7.1941 bis 20.8.41' BA-MA RH 21–2/928, Fol. 139 (4 August 1941).

[172] KTB OKW, Volume II, p. 1042, Document 88 (4 August 1941); Mendelssohn, *Die Nürnberger Dokumente*, p. 396.

[173] Guderian, *Panzer Leader*, p. 190.

[174] KTB OKW, Volume II, p. 1042, Document 88 (4 August 1941); Mendelssohn, *Die Nürnberger Dokumente*, p. 397.

[175] Franz Halder, KTB III, pp. 152–153 (4 August 1941).

them moving again but, given the state of the army and the Luftwaffe, Hitler made it clear that it could not all be undertaken at the same time. He therefore proposed three areas where renewed operations were possible.[176]

Commenting in his diary after the return of Brauchitsch, Halder reviewed each of the three alternatives. The first was for a north-eastward thrust by Hoth towards the Valdai Hills, which Hitler characterised as flank support for Leeb's right wing, but Halder dismissively rejected this as superfluous. Instead Halder took heart from the fact that occupying the Valdai Hills would provide a favourable jumping-off point for Hoth's drive east to the Volga.

The second alternative raised by Hitler was for the clearing of the southern wing of Bock's army group, if possible with the capture of Korosten, followed by an advance towards Moscow. At this Halder rejoiced. 'This idea is a salvation', he proclaimed. Yet Halder was also mindful of the danger inherent in such a move. Korosten was a distant march to the south pulling forces away from the centre and endangering the prospects of a drive east. 'Let's wait and see', was his conclusive comment.

The third alternative concerned the operations within Army Group South and did not unduly impinge on Bock's forces, leaving Halder pleasantly relieved. It seemed the sum of Hitler's deliberations was largely positive and Halder hailed the 'cheering progress' these had made. According to the Army Chief of Staff, Hitler had been surreptitiously coaxed away from his obsession with tactical manoeuvre towards the OKH's operational objectives. 'That is for the moment a relief', Halder exclaimed, although he recognised that they fell well short of the clear operational objectives still being awaited.[177] Indeed, writing to his wife on 5 August, Halder's ongoing frustration was clear:

I am not the kind of person to accuse someone. However it is often extremely annoying when one must fight the authoritative people for the clear and simple lines denoting the big and deciding questions. One would not believe how big the predilection is for discussing minor questions, that every day waste hours and hours, only to evade the big decisions until the last minute.[178]

Overall, the two days of high-level meetings in early August produced little in terms of tangible results, but highlight the German command's obsession with strategic questions, while largely ignoring the diminishing

---

[176] Ibid., p. 155 (5 August 1941).   [177] Ibid. (5 August 1941).
[178] Halder's letter as cited by Schall-Riaucour, *Aufstand und Gehorsam*, p. 167 (5 August 1941).

ability of their forces to conduct such operations. Even the panzer commanders appeared singularly concerned with the serviceability of their tanks without any hint of concern for the myriad of problems which had stalled operations and forced such a long and costly struggle around Smolensk. There was no discussion of the failing logistical system, no acknowledgement of the heavy casualties in men and combined arms, and no accounting for the faltering strength of the Luftwaffe. On the other side, there was no admission that the Red Army was proving an incredibly resilient opponent, who was seemingly able to patch up the front faster than the Germans could break it down, and at the same time launch repeated offensives on multiple fronts. There could be no denying, as the German leadership was keen to point out,[179] that the Soviets had serious problems of their own, some far worse than the Germans, but the standard of success was entirely different. The Red Army had only to endure as a significant fighting force, while the Germans had to win the war and win it decisively – there was no contingency for anything else.

Victory at Smolensk? The paradox of a battle

On 5 August the great encirclement battle at Smolensk was officially declared by Army Group Centre to be over. To mark the occasion Bock issued a grandiose order of the day to his troops, which read:

With the destruction of the Russian divisions cut off at Smolensk, the three-week 'Battle at the Dnepr and Dvina and of Smolensk' has concluded in another brilliant victory for German arms and German fulfilment of duty. Taken as booty were: 309,110 prisoners, 3,205 captured or destroyed tanks, 3,000 [artillery] guns, 341 aircraft. The numbers are not yet complete. This deed of yours, too, has become part of history! It is with gratitude and pride that I look upon a force that is capable of such an accomplishment. Long Live the Führer![180]

Despite Bock's victorious proclamation being repeatedly accepted by historians as an appropriate verdict on the immense battle, the order disguises a far less favourable outcome, with the result that Bock's declaration can be more accurately understood as a simple piece of military propaganda. Bock's apparent 'brilliant victory' must of course be judged against its relative cost to Army Group Centre – which reveals a state of affairs far from brilliant. Indeed, within Bock's own command illusions

---

[179] Fröhlich (ed.), *Die Tagebücher von Joseph Goebbels*, Teil II, p. 159 (1 August 1941).
[180] Fedor von Bock, KTB 'Osten I', Fols. 53–54, *War Diary*, pp. 273–274 (5 August 1941). See also 'Tagesmeldungen der Heeresgruppe Mitte vom 16.7.41 bis 5.8.41' BA-MA RH 19 II/129, Fol. 223 (5 August 1941).

about the difficulties presented by the military situation were diminishing. Two days before declaring the end of the battle, on 3 August, the army group's war diary began:

At the beginning of the 7th week of battle the army group stands with partially worn out units, limited munitions supply and without meaningful reserves, in a difficult and costly struggle to achieve the victorious end of the encirclement at Smolensk. The enemy is in number and material greatly superior. On the outer defensive front the bridgehead at Yel'nya is a deeply endangered flashpoint.[181]

Not only was the fighting extremely hard and bloody, but the results were not as encouraging as had been hoped. In spite of acknowledging the substantial quantities of captured weapons and equipment, the army group war diary admitted 'prisoner numbers not as high as expected'.[182] This was a fundamental admission given that the purpose of the vast encirclement was to carve out a massive hole in the Soviet front and eliminate the great bulk of the enemy facing Army Group Centre. As it was, the Soviet armies were either too far east to be caught in the pocket, or those that were managed to maintain enough cohesion to offer both fierce resistance and allow large elements to flee east through the narrow opening. Thus, the overall German operation, while rich in booty, obscured their failure to strike a decisive blow. They had failed in the Belostok–Minsk pocket and failed again in the Smolensk pocket.[183] In the meantime, their motorised forces had suffered paralysing losses leaving the front stagnant and German plans in tatters. As Blumentritt later wrote of these summer battles:

The great encirclement battles had led to the capture of huge numbers of prisoners and vast quantities of booty. But the results were not quite as satisfactory as they might appear at first glance. For one thing these great encirclements made very heavy demands on our panzer forces. For another, they were seldom entirely successful and large groups of the encircled enemy frequently slipped out of the pockets eastwards.[184]

Blumentritt was not alone in rendering this verdict. Kesselring too identified the failure of Army Group Centre's large strategic movements. The operation at Smolensk aimed 'to eliminate once and for all the Russian western army' and while a victory of sorts was achieved, Kesselring admitted, it 'brought no decision'. The main problem, in his opinion, was the inability to close the gap to the east, through which he guessed over 100,000 Soviet troops escaped to form the nucleus of new Red Army

[181] 'Kriegstagebuch Nr.1 (Band August 1941) des Oberkommandos der Heeresgruppe Mitte' BA-MA RH 19II/386, p. 234 (3 August 1941).

[182] Ibid., p. 239 (3 August 1941).   [183] Hürter, Hitlers Heerführer, pp. 286–287.

[184] Blumentritt, 'Moscow', p. 52.

346   Operation Barbarossa and Germany's Defeat in the East

divisions. Yet the operation itself was an exceedingly bold one, which Kesselring acknowledged was simply too much for the German Wehrmacht. 'Our divisions, including the Luftwaffe, were simply overtaxed, at the end of their tether and far from their supply centres.'[185] Expanding further, Kesselring addressed the fundamental problem undermining the very conception of German plans in the east.

[T]he panzer groups were too weak. Our strategic mechanised forces had to be proportionate to the depth and breadth of the area to be conquered and to the strength of the enemy, and we had not anywhere near this strength. Our fully tracked vehicles, including tanks, were not adequately serviceable. There were technical limitations to constant movement. A mobile operation 1,000 kilometres in depth through strongly occupied enemy territory requires vast supplies, especially if there is no chance of falling back on large and useful enemy stores. Our lines of communication and our airfields lay mostly in enemy threatened country, and were insufficiently protected.[186]

With such deep-seated difficulties, there was a degree of hopelessness in the German operations, which Kesselring also alluded to in his description of the early summer campaign:

So the word was: march and fight, fight and march, for almost a month and a half for a depth of nearly 500 miles, for part of the time inclement weather; frontal battles with the retreating forces and with new Russian divisions brought up from the back areas, ... guerrilla bands that now made their appearance in greater strength, and with the low-flying, effectively armoured Russian ground-strafers which appeared in single formations of flight strength. Any normal hope of being brought out of the line for a rest, if only a short one, or of a regular re-equipment was just wishful thinking.[187]

In spite of such seemingly intractable problems, by the end of the battle at Smolensk Bock and his fellow officers felt entitled to claim a great victory. By conventional military precedent few campaigns could boast such an impressive advance, undertaken in just six weeks, over countless battle-fields strewn with the wreckage of huge enemy armies. Yet try as they did to cap these tumultuous weeks with a resounding stamp of victory, the rigours of this war were not to be played down or surreptitiously hidden. The British press were quick to pick up on the evident stalling of the German blitzkrieg with headlines pronouncing a Soviet victory[188] and cartoons mocking Hitler after the 'Blunting of the Blitz'.[189] Churchill

---

[185] Kesselring, *Memoirs*, pp. 92–93.   [186] Ibid., p. 99.   [187] Ibid., p. 92.

[188] An entry in Bock's diary on 29 July read: 'The English are reporting: "The battle of Smolensk has ended with a Russian victory!"' Fedor von Bock, KTB 'Osten I', Fol. 47, *War Diary*, p. 267 (29 July 1941).

[189] *Daily Express*, London, 28 July 1941; Roy Douglas, *The World War 1939–1943. The Cartoonists' Vision* (London, 1990), p. 90.

later noted that in this early period of the war, it was not particularly important where the eastern front lay, even if all the way to the Ural Mountains, so long as it continued to function as a front which continually devoured German strength. Indeed, Churchill was unequivocal in his judgement about the Soviet Union's role in the war. '[H]istory will affirm that the Russian resistance broke the power of the German armies and inflicted mortal injury upon the life-energies of the German nation.'[190]

On the Soviet side, Marshal Timoshenko's favourable summary of the battle of Smolensk to Stalin may well have been influenced by the fate of his predecessor (who was executed), but it convinced a sceptical Stalin and bears out the facts. Timoshenko told Stalin: 'I maintain that by the operations of these days we have completely upset the enemy offensive. The seven or eight tank and motorised divisions and two or three infantry divisions put into action against us have been deprived of offensive capabilities.'[191] Even the German soldiers could hardly be expected to forget what they had been through in these first weeks of the eastern campaign, nor ignore the day-to-day reality of their lives at the front. On the same day that Bock's order was being read aloud to his troops, congratulating them on the brilliance of their victory, Hans Meier-Welcker, an officer in the 9th Army, could only write home about the strength of Soviet artillery, the unremitting bombing and strafing attacks of Soviet aircraft and the strong Soviet patrols attempting to infiltrate his position each night. The war, he concluded, was now a 'positional war like that of 1914/18'.[192] Eleven days later when a letter reached Meier-Welcker from Germany talking of the 'magnificent success of arms hopefully followed by peace', he was not inclined to agree.[193] Meier-Welcker perceptively foresaw that, unlike in past wars, victory was no longer to be wrung from a battle, but only from conquest – and that was still far from being achieved. Conversely, another soldier received a letter from Germany, dated 6 August, which referred to Bock's 'special announcement' and then continued: 'One is always pleased when our troops achieve another success. At the same time, just as one can count to five, one can see that all this has cost many victims. Last year following the French campaign I never had such dark thoughts as I do now.'[194] A personal letter from General Heinrici to his wife seemed to confirm such dark thoughts.

[190] Churchill, *The Second World War*, p. 462.
[191] Albert Axell, *Stalin's War Through the Eyes of His Commanders* (London, 1997), p. 85.
[192] Meier-Welcker, *Aufzeichnungen*, p. 126 (5 August 1941).
[193] Ibid., p. 128 (16 August 1941).
[194] Anatoly Golovchansky, Valentin Osipov, Anatoly Prokopenko, Ute Daniel and Jürgen Reulecke (eds.), *'Ich will raus aus diesem Wahnsinn'. Deutsche Briefe von der Ostfront 1941–1945 Aus sowjetischen Archiven* (Hamburg, 1993), p. 25 (6 August 1941).

On 3 August Heinrici wrote: 'We wonder sometimes what the winter will bring. We will certainly have to remain here in Russia . . . So we will have to endure here a positional war along an enormous front.' Heinrici then added sarcastically: 'Wonderful prospect.'[195]

By early August 1941 Barbarossa was in deep trouble and German claims of a definitive victory at Smolensk represented a greater propaganda success than an actual military one. In fact, given German operational objectives, the battle was hardly a victory at all. Yet this does not by default make the battle a Soviet victory. Post-war Soviet historiography eulogised the battle of Smolensk as a glorious German defeat by the Red Army; this was also an embellishment of the facts. Zhukov's order on 20 July stipulated that counter-offensives by the 29th, 30th, 24th and 28th Armies were supposed to smash through German lines, relieve the nearly encircled remnants of the Soviet 19th, 20th and 16th Armies and re-take Smolensk.[196] Instead, inexperienced Soviet commanders and critical shortages in heavy weaponry transformed much of the fighting into bloody frontal assaults, which wore down the German motorised formations, but at a cost of immense Soviet casualties. By the beginning of August some of the divisions in Timoshenko's Western Front numbered only 1,000–2,000 men each.[197] Thus, while one can claim that the Germans failed in eliminating the Western Front and, in the process, sustained crucial losses to their motorised forces, it is equally true that the Soviets failed to reach their stated objectives and suffered staggering casualties in the process. Indeed, the battle of Smolensk is perhaps best represented less in terms of a rousing victory for either side but rather as a defeat for both. Yet what remains decisive in coming to any conclusive verdict as to which side benefited the most – or suffered the least as the case may be – are the strategic ramifications of their respective failures. The Soviets lost appallingly, but could go on holding the line, while replacing their losses. The Germans lost less in terms of men and equipment, but these were catastrophic to their overall war aims, especially since Bock had still not broken Soviet resistance. Additionally, the three-week battle cost Germany irreplaceable time and the repairs to their motorised divisions would cost even more. At a minimum, Bock had to win a decisive victory at Smolensk, whereas Timoshenko really only needed to survive and go on maintaining a stout resistance. The victor was simply the side with the least to lose from their failure.

Without question, the carnage wrought at Smolensk and the volume of waste the attritional battles exacted exemplified the horrors of the

---

[195] Hürter, *Ein deutscher General*, p. 73 (3 August 1941). See also his letter from 1 August, p. 72.
[196] Glantz, *Battle for Smolensk*, pp. 31–33.   [197] Ibid., p. 53.

eastern front. In this initial period the fighting was characterised by two very different approaches, which also underscored two very different opponents. If the skilful German commanders thrust and jabbed their armoured divisions with dangerous precision, the Soviet colossus swung wildly with its hammer of armies. The end result of such savage combat was telling on both sides, but ultimately more so for the Germans. One German soldier who fought in World War II from 1939 until his capture in 1945 recalled: 'The fighting around Smolensk in July and August was the heaviest and deadliest I saw during the war.'[198]

If Bock's battle at Smolensk was, as he claimed, a great victory for Army Group Centre, it certainly did not resonate far enough to relieve the growing difficulties confronting the neighbouring two army groups. By early August, Army Group North's forward progress towards Leningrad was becoming seriously complicated by the over-extension of its forces. Leeb at least had the advantage that supply ships could follow his progress up the Baltic coastline, but these still had to be delivered considerable distances overland (especially to 16th Army) and the sunken marshlands took their toll on Leeb's *Grosstransportraum* with the highest fallout rate in the whole army (39 per cent).[199] Most of Leeb's difficulties, however, stemmed from the increasingly large area in which he was operating, forcing a ceaseless dispersal of his front-line strength with every kilometre gained. As early as mid-July one of his two panzer corps was even encircled in a Soviet counter-offensive and had to commence a frantic fighting retreat, aided by air drops and a relief thrust by the SS *Totenkopf* Division.[200] Emerging from this four-day battle the 8th Panzer Division had lost 70 destroyed or damaged tanks from its remaining 150.[201] As in Army Group Centre, it was the motorised divisions of Hoepner's Panzer Group 4 that were suffering the most significant losses. Barely five weeks into the campaign, Leeb noted that 25 per cent of his panzer forces were total losses and another 25 per cent were in various states of disrepair. The SS *Totenkopf* Division and the 3rd Motorised Division were noted to have suffered particularly heavily, with the latter also recording 35 per cent casualties in officers. 'Overall losses of Panzer Group 4', Leeb concluded, were, 'very heavy. The battle strength in fact seems to me to be substantially reduced.'[202]

Along with its sharp decline in offensive strength, the geographic expansion of the front forced the army group to sustain offensives both northwards into Estonia as well as eastwards to cover Bock's left wing.

---

[198] Frisch with Jones, Jr., *Condemned to Live*, p. 74.
[199] Franz Halder, KTB III, p. 149 (3 August 1941).
[200] Von Manstein, *Lost Victories*, p. 195.
[201] David M. Glantz, *The Battle for Leningrad 1941–1944* (Lawrence, 2002), p. 45.
[202] Wilhelm Ritter von Leeb, KTB, p. 310 (27 July 1941).

The swamps and sunken roads in these regions added further difficulties even in the absence of rainfall. Whole columns became stuck fast in knee-deep mud and overtaking resulted in some vehicles disappearing almost completely into the treacherous marshes. On one day the men of the 6th Panzer Division laboured all day among swarms of insects and searing heat only to advance two kilometres per hour.[203] The army group also had to contend with a resurgent enemy, which caused the offensive to falter. In the first two weeks of Barbarossa Leeb's front had advanced some 450 kilometres, yet over the next month he struggled to manage another 120 kilometres, leaving him still 100 kilometres short of Leningrad with long, exposed flanks.[204] While Leeb concentrated his forces to reach Leningrad, he acknowledged on 31 July that defending the eastern flank was 'impossible' as it now extended 360 kilometres.[205] Two days later in a meeting with Brauchitsch, Leeb sketched out his over-extended front and told the Commander-in-Chief of the Army that he needed 35 divisions to meet his commitments, but had only 26.[206] Like Bock, Leeb desperately sought forces wherever he could find them and ordered the rear-area security divisions closer to the front.[207] He also lobbied hard for the return of four infantry divisions which had previously been transferred to Bock's 9th Army.[208] The situation remained critical and on 3 August the 32nd Infantry Division was left holding a line from Toropez to Staraia Russa – no less than 150 kilometres long.[209] Reflecting the increasingly critical situation, Hoepner, the commander of Panzer Group 4, wrote to his wife on 15 August: 'As a result of the overall supply situation and the cold the campaign *must* be *ended* by the end of September.'[210] Clearly, Army Group North was beset by many fundamental problems that were now endemic across the vast breadth of the eastern front. Leeb's forces could barely reach Leningrad, to say nothing of storming the great city, and covering their long right wing would still be cause for major concern. Obviously, if a decisive blow against the Soviet state was to be struck anywhere, it would not come from Leeb's army group.[211]

In the Ukraine Rundstedt's Army Group South faced the largest concentration of Soviet forces and with only one panzer group at his disposal,

---

[203] Lucas, *War of the Eastern Front*, pp. 108–110.
[204] Glantz, *Battle for Leningrad*, p. 45.
[205] Wilhelm Ritter von Leeb, KTB, p. 313 (31 July 1941).
[206] Ibid., pp. 316–317 (2 August 1941).   [207] Ibid., p. 316 (1 August 1941).
[208] Ibid., p. 317 (2 August 1941).   [209] Ibid., p. 318 (3 August 1941).
[210] Italics in the original. Hoepner's letter as cited by Hürter, *Hitlers Heerführer*, p. 291.
[211] In a letter to his wife on 6 August Manstein described the floundering operations of Army Group North as having developed into a 'sideshow war'. Manstein's letter cited in Hürter, *Hitlers Heerführer*, p. 288, footnote 39.

Figure 8.4 From the beginning of the war in the east the German armed forces wilfully participated in the war of annihilation. Public hangings were a common reaction to partisan activity.

the advance lagged far behind that of Bock and Leeb. On 5 July Rundstedt wrote to his wife that on account of the heavy fighting and terrible roads only slow progress could be made.[212] In addition, heavy rains had a catastrophic effect on movement with mud and dust alternating to slow progress and spoil the engines of the motorised columns. Curzio Malaparte, an Italian journalist travelling with the German armies in the south, observed:

The road, if this species of cattle-track may be so described, is covered with a thick layer of dust, which with every breath of wind rises in dense red clouds. But in places, where the clayey soil has failed to absorb the rain-water, where a stream crosses the track, the sticky, tenacious mud grips the wheels of the lorries and the tracks of the tanks, which sink slowly into the *Buna* as into quicksand.[213]

Denied rapid movement, an encirclement of the enemy forces was not initially possible as the Soviet command enacted a frustrating mixture of

[212] Rundstedt's letter cited in ibid., p. 290, footnote 47.
[213] Malaparte, *The Volga Rises in Europe*, p. 54 (7 July, 1941).

withdrawals and obstructing counter attacks. A dissipation of strength to the flanks was also inevitable, especially to the north where the 6th Army was vigorously attacked from the Pripet marshes, forcing Halder to release reserves to help cover the lines of supply.[214] The fighting in this sector was extremely bitter and within just 11 days the 98th Infantry Division alone lost 78 officers and 2,300 men.[215]

In spite of its difficulties the focal point of the attack, led by Kleist's Panzer Group 1, penetrated the defensive Stalin Line on 5 July, whereupon new objectives for Army Group South were worked out. Here Hitler and Halder were able to agree that a sharp turn of the armour to the south and a large scale encirclement of enemy forces west of the Dnepr should have priority. A secondary task was to be a deep bridgehead over the Dnepr near Kiev. Rundstedt argued for a rapid assault with elements of Kleist's panzer group to seize Kiev directly, but this was overruled owing to the apparent risk and a lack of infantry support.[216] Unlike the armoured thrusts in the two northern army groups, where a measure of freedom was achieved, Kleist's movement was continually dogged by enemy resistance and threats to his flanks. At the end of July Halder alluded to 'weeks of grinding at the Russian front in the Ukraine'.[217] One soldier, Gottlob Bidermann, wrote of the early weeks of the summer advance:

Our lines of supply became more strained with each day's advance, and as our momentum slowed to a crawl we continued to experience ever-increasing sporadic shelling... The Russian rearguard elements continued to withdraw before us, attempting to burn many of the few mud and straw huts in our path and always leaving an ever-present cadre of snipers, who slowly extracted a deadly price from our ranks at the cost of their own lives... The depth of our penetration into the Soviet Union began to take its toll, and ammunition rationing served as a first indication of the shortages that we were to encounter with disastrous results in future battles.[218]

By the first week of August Kleist's panzers manoeuvred and fought against stubborn resistance to link up with General Carl Heinrich von Stülpnagel's 17th Army and trap the Soviet 6th and 12th Armies in the Uman encirclement. Coming only days after the end of Bock's battle at Smolensk, Uman was trumpeted as another outstanding German victory.

---

[214] Klink, 'Die Operationsführung', pp. 477–478.
[215] Martin Gareis, *Kampf und Ende der Fränkisch-Sudetendeutschen 98. Infanterie-Division* (Eggolsheim, 1956), p. 103.
[216] Klink, 'Die Operationsführung', pp. 480–482.
[217] Franz Halder, KTB III, p. 131 (30 July 1941).
[218] Gottlob Herbert Bidermann, *In Deadly Combat. A German Soldier's Memoir of the Eastern Front* (Lawrence, 2000), pp. 25 and 27.

Yet, after more than six weeks of heavy fighting, the Uman pocket had netted just 103,000 Soviet prisoners,[219] one third of what Bock had taken in the Belostok–Minsk pocket a month before. Far from eliminating Soviet resistance west of the Dnepr and freeing the road to the east, the Germans found themselves with significantly reduced combat strength, little time remaining and an unbeaten enemy digging in on the Dnepr. To make matters worse, the second objective, to force a bridgehead on the eastern bank of the Dnepr, had still not been achieved. In a letter to his wife on 12 August, Rundstedt wrote: 'How much longer? I have no great hope that it will be soon. The distances in Russia devour us.'[220]

According to most accounts, by the end of the first week in August each of the three German army groups stood apparently victorious over their opposing Soviet Fronts, while plans were afoot for further advances. What is insufficiently recognised is that, operating in such vast areas, over-extension was inevitable forcing local commanders to disperse their strength and making it more and more difficult to achieve concentration for the next offensive. With the Soviet line still being doggedly held everywhere, increasing stretches of the German front passed over to defensive warfare, while strength was pulled from wherever it could be found for more limited offensives along narrower areas of the front. Only in the earliest weeks of the campaign did all three German army groups advance simultaneously and thereafter resource depletion brought combined forward operations to an abrupt halt. This heightened the importance of the strategic dispute between Hitler and Halder as Germany's shrinking offensive strength had now to be used for a final decisive blow.

In 1941 Germany's two most prominent strategic allies were Italy and Japan, who together had signed the Tripartite Pact on 27 September 1940 as a collective deterrent to hostile action, chiefly by the United States, against any member state. Despite the profession of unity, there was not much practical substance to their alliance, with each nation set on pursuing its own interests and almost no attempts being made at a genuinely co-ordinated strategy. It is, therefore, not surprising that Hitler's first official notification of his intention to wage war on the Soviet Union was given in the hours before Germany launched its invasion. Hitler's unbounded confidence in the success of Barbarossa had precluded the need to request any active participation by these allies in the war against the Soviet Union, although Hitler had been trying for months to persuade Japan to seek expansion in Southeast Asia.[221] Not only was Hitler

---

[219] KTB OKW, Volume II, p. 560 (8 July 1941).
[220] Rundstedt's letter cited in Hürter, *Hitlers Heerführer*, p. 292.
[221] KTB OKW, Volume I, pp. 328–329 (17 February 1941).

hoping to gain an ally in the war against Britain, but he hoped this would also distract American attention from Europe by threatening a war in two oceans.[222]

The Japanese government's desire for access to vital raw materials to sustain its long war in China had made further expansion a priority, and the riches of Southeast Asia were eyed keenly by the powerbrokers within the navy. Alternatively, the Japanese army had long favoured a northward strike into the Soviet Union and the launch of Barbarossa had presented a seemingly golden opportunity to realise these plans. The army wanted to annex Northern Sakhalin and the Kamchatka Peninsula, but a sphere of influence up to Lake Baikal and even a demilitarised zone from Lake Baikal to Novosibirsk were also projected.[223] The army's preference retained less political support with its only senior representative being the Japanese foreign minister, Yosuke Matsuoka. At the Imperial Conference on 2 July, chaired by Emperor Hirohito, decisive steps were taken to pursue the navy's southern offensive with an immediate occupation of southern Indochina. Matsuoka was subsequently dumped from the cabinet, but war with the Soviet Union was not yet completely ruled out, although this was now made very much conditional on the success of German operations.[224] An imminent collapse of the Soviet Union would reduce the risks of a Japanese intervention while ensuring them a lucrative share in the spoils.

In Berlin Hitler's previous ambivalence to Japanese intervention against the Soviet Union was now replaced with appeals for Japanese action. In mid-July Hitler told General Hiroshi Oshima, the Japanese ambassador in Berlin, that the 'destruction of Russia' should, in his opinion, be the 'political life's work of Germany and Japan'. Meanwhile the Japanese Kwantung Army in Manchuria was continually being reinforced, reaching a strength of 700,000 men.[225] On 16 July Oshima was given a tour of 4th Panzer Army from which he returned favourably impressed at the progress of German operations.[226] The second half of July, however, proved a major disappointment for the hawks within the Japanese army who had hoped that a decisive German victory would

---

[222] Jürgen Förster, 'Die Entscheidungen der "Dreierpaktstaaten"' in Militärgeschichtliches Forschungsamt (ed.), *Das Deutsche Reich und der Zweite Weltkrieg, Band IV: Der Angriff auf die Sowjetunion* (Stuttgart, 1983), p. 903.

[223] Gerhard Krebs, 'Japan and the German-Soviet War, 1941' in Bernd Wegner (ed.), *From Peace to War. Germany, Soviet Russia and the World, 1939–1941* (Oxford, 1997), p. 551.

[224] Förster, 'Die Entscheidungen der "Dreierpaktstaaten"', p. 904; Karl Drechsler, 'Germany and its Allies and the War Against the Soviet Union, 1940–42' in Joseph Wieczynski (ed.), *Operation Barbarossa. The German Attack on the Soviet Union June 22, 1941* (Salt Lake City, 1993), pp. 39–40.

[225] Ibid.   [226] Hillgruber, *Die Zerstörung Europas*, p. 306.

provoke a reversal in policy towards the northern alternative. Instead Bock's front was stalled east of Smolensk and the other army groups were achieving little more success. The much hoped for blitzkrieg was becoming increasingly doubtful and must have reminded the Japanese of their own bitter experiences with the Red Army in the summer of 1939 at Khalkhin-Gol.[227] As Bock observed on 25 July in his diary: 'The Japanese are taking the opportunity to establish themselves in Indochina, but in contrast they are only lukewarm about the hoped-for attack on Russia! Neither one nor the other surprises me.'[228]

Japan's occupation of southern Indochina, undertaken at the end of July, was intended as a first step towards alleviating its economic difficulties, but this was promptly rebuffed in a spectacular reversal, when the United States, Britain and the Dutch East Indies together instituted an economic embargo against Japan. The implications were dire indeed and, with major military commitments in China, the embargo represented economic strangulation. At this point Japanese strategic intentions finally became clear. There would be no easy victories in the north against the Soviet Union and the primacy of seizing economic objectives in the south now won over even hardliners in the army. On 4 August the Japanese government affirmed not to involve itself in the German–Soviet war[229] and on 6 August, the day after Bock's victorious proclamation to the troops of Army Group Centre, the Kwantung Army was ordered to avoid any border incidents with the Red Army.[230] Indeed, Japan's naval attaché in Moscow, Captain Takeda Yamaguchi, reported on 11 August that German plans for a swift victory in the east were unrealistic. 'If the war is conducted according to such plans, it will undoubtedly be lost.'[231] If there was a window of opportunity for Hitler to gain direct Japanese military assistance against the Soviet Union, it had now passed. However, the Germans were not informed of Japan's intentions and, with conditions worsening on the eastern front, the secretary of state in the foreign office, Ernst Freiherr von Weizsäcker, concluded at the end of August: 'aid from Japan more necessary than previously thought'.[232] Interestingly, thanks to Stalin's expert Japanese spy network, with such

---

[227] In this brief undeclared war the Japanese forces were badly beaten by the Red Army under Georgi Zhukov, then a corps commander and now the Chief of the General Staff who was presently overseeing operations against Army Group Centre. For the most detailed work on this war see Alvin D. Coox, *Nomanhan. Japan Against Russia 1939* (Stanford, 1990).

[228] Fedor von Bock, KTB 'Osten I', Fol. 43, *War Diary*, p. 263 (25 July 1941).

[229] Krebs, 'Japan and the German-Soviet War, 1941', p. 553.

[230] Hillgruber, *Die Zerstörung Europas*, p. 307.

[231] Nagorski, *The Greatest Battle*, p. 157.

[232] Leonidas E. Hill (ed.), *Die Weizsäcker-Papiere 1933–1950* (Frankfurt am Main, 1974), p. 265 (31 August 1941).

well placed agents as Richard Sorge and Ozaki Hotsumi, top level information regarding Japanese intentions was passed back to Moscow. These reports also confirmed Japanese concerns over the stunted success of the German armies and gave Stalin confidence enough to start moving elements of his Far Eastern Front to the European theatre. The redeployment began in June and continued throughout the summer and autumn – bringing a total of 1,700 tanks, 1,800 aircraft, 15 rifle divisions and three cavalry divisions to the west.[233]

Through a combination of the Allied economic embargo and the lacklustre progress of Hitler's war in the east, Japan's course was at last decisively set for war against the Anglo-American powers.[234] The battle of Smolensk was therefore important not only for the damage done to Germany's armies, but also for the political and strategic ramifications these involved. Hitler had lost the prospect of aid from an army larger than any of his other Axis allies deployed on the eastern front. Moreover, Japanese intervention would have forced the Soviet Union into a two-front war, further straining their resources as well as isolating them even more from outside economic assistance.

Contrary to popular assumption, Japan's ill-fated decision to seek conflict with the Anglo-American powers was not her entry into war, rather it was her first desperate move in a war she had been fighting since 1937 against China. Consequently, the summer of 1941 was the critical turning point towards eventual defeat for Japan as well as for Germany.

For all the faults inherent in Japanese strategic decision making during 1941, they can at least be said to have shown enough respect for the Red Army to await the development of Hitler's war before making a commitment themselves. Mussolini, on the other hand, was as rash as he was foolhardy and immediately committed Italy to Hitler's new war in spite of the heavy burden he was already shouldering in North Africa, the Mediterranean and the Balkans. Ultimately the CSIR (Italian Expeditionary Corps in Russia) would number just 62,000 men and were supposed to be among the best Italy had to offer so as not to make a poor impression alongside the other Axis allies.[235] When Keitel caught sight of them upon their arrival on the eastern front at the end of August, he scornfully described the army as 'a boundless disappointment' with officers who were far too old, leading what he deemed to be 'half-soldiers'

[233] Erickson, *The Soviet High Command 1918–1941*, pp. 631–632.
[234] Hillgruber, *Die Zerstörung Europas*, p. 309; Drechsler, 'Germany and its Allies', pp. 39–40; Krebs, 'Japan and the German-Soviet War, 1941', pp. 551–553; Reinhardt, *Moscow – The Turning Point*, p. 44.
[235] Förster, 'Die Entscheidungen der "Dreierpaktstaaten"', p. 899.

incapable of standing up to the Red Army.[236] Even Hitler disparagingly referred to the Italians as nothing more than 'harvest hands'.[237] In any case, the Italians were too few in number and arrived too late on the eastern front to influence the fortunes of Germany's 1941 campaign.

Thus, while Japan and Italy were Germany's two most prominent Axis allies, their overall importance to Hitler in the summer of 1941 was largely replaced by Romania and Finland.[238] At either extreme of the eastern front these two small powers contributed sizeable forces to Barbarossa and were the only two nations to be officially informed of German plans before the invasion. After Germany, Finland provided the most professional army on the eastern front, numbering 476,000 men and, because of the Winter War (1939–40), was in possession of considerable quantities of high-grade armaments supplied by Germany, Britain and the United States. In the early weeks of the war Finland recovered its recently lost territories from the Soviet Union, but the cost was very high and the country already faced critical manpower shortages with few reserves. Soviet resistance stiffened, leading the Commander-in-Chief of the Finnish Army, Field Marshal Carl Gustaf Emil Mannerheim, to suspend forward operations and to permanently go over to the defence. The escalating demands of Germany's war forced anxious requests by Hitler's OKW for renewed Finnish action, but Mannerheim informed Keitel that this went beyond the terms of their pre-war agreement and, in any case, exceeded his military capabilities. Consequently, as early as August 1941 the Finnish leadership determined that the Red Army had been badly under-estimated and the Wehrmacht over-estimated. The result they concluded was that a German victory before the onset of winter was no longer feasible and this resulted in a state of quasi non-belligerence. Thus, before the end of the summer, Germany had effectively lost its most worthy ally on the eastern front.[239]

Romania was Germany's other major ally, fielding two armies in the invasion (3rd and 4th organised as Army Group Antonescu) with some 325,685 troops between them.[240] Yet size does not equal strength. The Romanian army suffered greatly from poor training among officers and

---

[236] Görlitz (ed.), *Memoirs of Field-Marshal Keitel*, p. 160. In rendering such a severe judgement it is possible that Keitel's portrayal was somewhat influenced by later events.

[237] Förster, 'Die Entscheidungen der "Dreierpaktstaaten"', p. 899.

[238] Finland never formally became a member of the Axis and preferred instead to see its confederacy with Germany simply as 'comradeship-in-arms' against a common enemy.

[239] Manfred Menger, 'Germany and the Finnish "Separate War" against the Soviet Union' in Bernd Wegner (ed.), *From Peace to War. Germany, Soviet Russia and the World, 1939–1941* (Oxford, 1997), pp. 533–534.

[240] Mark Axworthy, Cornel Scafes and Cristian Craciunoiu, *Third Axis Fourth Ally. Romanian Armed Forces in the European War, 1941–1945* (London, 1995), p. 45.

men, obsolete equipment and a meagre standard of motorisation and domestic industrial support. Accordingly, the head of the German military mission to Romania, General Erik Hansen, described the Romanian contribution as useless for 'difficult offensive actions'.[241] Initial operations for the recovery of Bessarabia and Northern Bukovina were achieved with German aid,[242] but by late July 1941 the degree of German over-extension on the southern flank led to pleas for 'urgently desired' independent Romanian action to be taken against Odessa.[243] Unlike the Finns, the Romanian Head of State and self-appointed field commander, General Ion Antonescu, willingly heeded the call to advance further into the Soviet Union and launched successive failed assaults in an attempt to take Odessa by force. The city was eventually evacuated by the Soviets and awarded the distinctive title 'Hero City' of the Soviet Union. Antonescu tried to claim a victory, but his losses had been staggering. There were 80 per cent casualties in the 12 divisions which took part, equalling some 98,000 casualties in less than two months of fighting.[244] Even though Antonescu was willing to accept such casualties and press on with his campaign, losses of this scale naturally undercut the effectiveness of his forces and ultimately the whole army had to be reorganised and undergo further training.[245] If Hitler lost Finland to the looming danger of escalating warfare on the eastern front, he effectively lost Romania in the firing line of that danger.

Hitler's other allies on the eastern front fielded smaller contingents and proved even more vulnerable to the harsh conditions and savage fighting. The Slovak forces in Operation Barbarossa numbered some 41,000 men, divided into a motorised Rapid Group followed by the remaining bulk of the army in the Expeditionary Army Group. In the view of General Otto, head of the German Army Mission to Slovakia, the Slovak forces suffered from an 'inappropriate craving for prestige and an overestimation of strength'.[246] The tangible results of this were soon revealed at the battle of Lipovec on 22 July when the Rapid Group first encountered organised formations of the Red Army, and suffered its highest casualties of its entire war against the Soviet Union in a single day. Inadequately trained,

[241] Jürgen Förster, 'Die Gewinnung von Verbündeten in Südosteuropa', p. 345.
[242] Richard L. DiNardo, *Germany and the Axis Powers. From Coalition to Collapse* (Lawrence, 2005), pp. 112–115.
[243] Axworthy *et al.*, *Third Axis Fourth Ally*, p. 49.
[244] Mark Axworthy, 'Peasant Scapegoat to Industrial Slaughter: the Romanian Soldier at the Siege of Odessa' in Paul Addison and Angus Calder (eds.), *A Time to Kill. The Soldier's Experience of War in the West 1939–1945* (London, 1997), p. 227. See also Mihai Tone Filipescu, *Reluctant Axis: The Romanian Army in Russia 1941–1944* (Chapultepeq, 2006), Chapter Two, 'The Battle for Odessa'.
[245] Axworthy, 'Peasant Scapegoat', p. 232.
[246] Förster, 'Die Entscheidungen der "Dreierpaktstaaten"', p. 894.

poorly equipped and too large for the domestic economy to sustain, the Slovak forces had to be reorganised into a smaller army which was then relegated mostly to rear-area security tasks.[247]

At the outbreak of war with the Soviet Union the Hungarian regent, Admiral Miklós Horthy, committed the 'Carpathian Group' numbering 45,000 men to Hitler's war. This included two brigades of infantry which were left behind for security tasks and a 'Mobile Corps' of 24,000 men. This formation was the pride of the Hungarian army and gave a good account of itself even alongside the motorised divisions of Kleist's Panzer Group 1. By the beginning of August, however, heavy casualties and serious doubts about the future of Hitler's war led to much debate about Hungary's commitment. The Chief of the General Staff, Colonel-General Werth, wanted to substantially reinforce Hungary's eastern army, whereas the commander of the Carpathian Group, Lieutenant-General Szombathelyi, argued for the withdrawal of the Mobile Corps. With first-hand knowledge of the conflict Szombathelyi argued: 'The war will last for a long time, we must be prepared for that and not a lightning war.' Horthy sided with Szombathelyi and even promoted him to replace Werth. Extracting their forces, however, proved more difficult. In early September when Horthy and Szombathelyi approached Hitler, the limited progress of Army Group South, with the bulk of its forces still on the western bank of the Dnepr, caused Hitler to block the Hungarian withdrawal.[248]

Added to the overall total of Axis troops fighting in the east were volunteers from all over Europe who took up the Nazi propaganda of a 'European crusade against Bolshevism'. Of these Spain[249] contributed the most, forming their own 'Blue Division'[250] with 17,909 men. The overall total of foreign volunteers aiding the Germans in 1941 reached 43,000 men,[251] but owing to the fact that these forces still had to be trained and equipped, they did not appear on the front until autumn at the earliest – in other words, after Barbarossa had failed.

---

[247] Mark Axworthy, *Axis Slovakia: Hitler's Slavic Wedge 1938–1945* (New York, 2002), pp. 103–115.

[248] Förster, 'Die Entscheidungen der "Dreierpaktstaaten"', pp. 889–892. See also Gorlitz (ed.), *Memoirs of Field-Marshal Keitel*, p. 157; Cecil D. Eby, *Hungary at War. Civilians and Soldiers in World War II* (University Park, 1998), p. 18.

[249] Spain was an Axis ally in all but name. Franco never officially joined the alliance, just as he never formally entered World War II, but he willingly recruited volunteers for the eastern front, sent workers and raw materials to relieve the strain on German industry and aided German submarines.

[250] So named for the blue shirts worn by the Falangists.

[251] Jürgen Förster, 'Freiwillige für den "Kreuzzug Europas gegen den Bolschewismus"' in Militärgeschichtliches Forschungsamt (ed.), *Das Deutsche Reich und der Zweite Weltkrieg*, Band IV, pp. 911–913.

Clearly Germany's eastern front allies were of dubious value.[252] As the varying examples illustrate, from the earliest weeks of the campaign, each nation was decisively affected in its contribution to the overall war effort by the rapidly growing demands of the conflict. Some recoiled, seeking to minimise their involvement after astute military assessments of the horrendous warfare they found there, while those that remained, particularly those on the front line, suffered accordingly. As small powers without the resources to influence events fundamentally, they had staked everything on Hitler's victory, expecting to profit from it. Germany's failure was also their own.

Despite frequent representations of the battle of Smolensk as an unambiguous German victory, it did not achieve the main German aim of tearing open the Soviet front to allow an unhindered advance into the depths of the Soviet Union. It is important to remember that battlefield victories are not ends in themselves. Their worth is calculated from the strategic possibilities, military or political, that these stimulate. The deepening crisis within the German command underscores their failure to work out how to defeat the Soviet Union – certainly the battle of Smolensk had not provided an answer. Bock's encirclements in the centre of the front achieved impressive operational successes, but did not open up a strategic alternative through which the war could be won. Conversely his forces had been badly crippled by the effort. As a result, whatever may be said of the huge Soviet losses, these were not suffered in vain, and indeed can be seen as the price of halting the German advance. With the blitzkrieg stopped, the realisation was dawning that the war was not going to be won soon, and that it would be a long, costly struggle, decided more by economic factors than any dramatic battlefield manoeuvre. In this regard the Soviet Union, backed by its western allies, was far better placed. Even if the tangible benefits of this Allied co-operation would take many months to reach the battlefield, it still meant that time was running against Germany. The Soviet Union had to be crushed, not worn down. The prospect of spending the winter bogged down in Russia, while its frozen army continued to shed men and equipment in a violent war of attrition, was tantamount to losing World War II. The last weeks of summer were to be decisive, although the scales were already precariously tipped against Germany.

---

[252] For useful overall surveys of the Axis coalition on the eastern front see DiNardo, *Germany and the Axis Powers*; Richard L. DiNardo, 'The Dysfunctional Coalition: The Axis Powers and the Eastern Front in World War II', *The Journal of Military History* 60(4) (October, 1996) 711–730; Karl Drechsler, 'Germany and its Allies', pp. 30–47.

9   In search of resurgence

The arduous road to renewal

In his first letter to the Soviet leader after the beginning of Barbarossa, Churchill informed Stalin of his unreserved commitment to the Soviet war effort. After praising the Red Army's 'strong and spirited resistance', Churchill then promised; 'We shall do everything to help you that time, geography and our growing resources allow. The longer the war lasts the more help we can give.'[1] On 30 July Roosevelt's special representative, Harry Hopkins, met with Stalin in Moscow to discuss US assistance to the Soviet Union. Hopkins reported that Stalin was optimistic about the progress of the war and believed that a continued German offensive would be difficult in September and not possible by October when the heavy rains would begin. Thus, it was not 1941 that worried Stalin, indeed Hopkins remarked on Stalin's 'great confidence' that the Soviets would hold through the winter. Stalin was more concerned about the coming spring when mobile operations would again be possible. For this he wanted steel for more Soviet tanks and he also expressed his desire to purchase as many American tanks as possible. Additionally, he requested aluminum for aircraft construction, anti-aircraft guns, machine guns and rifles.[2] The list would be added to in September at the follow-up Three-Power conference in Moscow, attended by Lord Beaverbrook for the UK and Averell Harriman for the USA. The Three-Power conference agreed on urgent support for the USSR, even at the expense of reinforcing other theatres, and thereafter increasingly voluminous supplies began to flow, initially via Nordic convoys and the Far East (Vladivostok), but later also

---

[1] Ministry of Foreign Affairs of the U.S.S.R. (ed.), *Stalin's Correspondence with Churchill, Attlee, Roosevelt and Truman 1941–1945* (New York, 1958), p. 11 (8 July 1941).

[2] The nine-page document which Hopkins prepared for Roosevelt upon returning from his visit to the Soviet Union can be viewed online at the Franklin D. Roosevelt's Presidential Library and Museum: www.fdrlibrary.marist.edu/psf/box5/a61h08.html. See also Erickson, *Road to Stalingrad*, p. 181; George C. Herring, Jr., *Aid to Russia 1941–1946. Strategy, Diplomacy, The Origins of the Cold War* (New York, 1973), p. 12.

overland through Persia.[3] Indeed, during the period of the First Protocol, running from October 1941 to June 1942, the British and Americans undertook to ship some 400 aircraft, 500 tanks and 10,000 trucks each month, as well as a wide range of other supplies. These targets were met, but a significant proportion of these supplies were lost en route as German air and naval forces from northern Norway attempted to cut access to Murmansk and Arckangel'sk.[4]

If Stalin exuded a sublime self-assurance to Hopkins in late July, it was a premature confidence in the success of his forces. Germany's offensive strength was being weakened, but it had by no means entirely ebbed. Zhukov, the Chief of the General Staff, foresaw dangers for the Central Front, chiefly opposite Guderian's XXIV Panzer Corps and Weichs's 2nd Army. Summoned to a meeting with Stalin to give a full report of the situation on 29 July, Zhukov stated:

On the strategic axis of Moscow the Germans are unable to mount a major offensive operation in the near future owing to their heavy losses and they lack appreciable reserves to secure the right and left wings of Army Group Centre.

On the Leningrad axis it is impossible for the Germans to begin an operation to capture Leningrad and link up with the Finns without additional forces.[5]

The situation in the Ukraine was not yet so easy to determine with the Uman encirclement still in progress. According to the Soviet Chief of Staff, the real danger was that Bock would temporarily give up his thrust on Moscow and shift his attention to the south, solving the threat to his over-extended southern flank, and assisting Army Group South by cutting into the rear of Kirponos's South-Western Front. This prospect was all the more dangerous because, as Zhukov noted, the Central Front covering this area of the line 'was the weakest sector of our line' and its armies were 'badly equipped'. Zhukov recommended reinforcing it with three armies, one from the *Stavka* Reserve, one from Western Front and a last from South-Western Front. The movement of these forces, Zhukov added, could later be replaced by forces arriving from the Far East. He also advocated that Kirponos pull his front back behind the Dnepr which would mean abandoning Kiev, but Zhukov presented a solid military

---

[3] Weinberg, *A World At Arms*, p. 288; van Tuyll, *Feeding the Bear*, p. 164.

[4] Mawdsley, *Thunder in the East*, p. 191; Rolf-Dieter Müller, *Der letzte deutsche Krieg*, p. 105. Recent research from Alexander Hill suggests that British tanks played an important role in the fighting at the end of 1941. See Alexander Hill, 'British "Lend-Lease" Tanks and the Battle for Moscow, November–December 1941 – A Research Note', *Journal of Slavic Military Studies* 19(2) (June 2006), 289–294. See also Alexander Hill, 'British Lend-Lease Aid and the Soviet War Effort, June 1941 – June 1942', *Journal of Military History* 71(3) (July 2007), 773–808.

[5] Erickson, *Road to Stalingrad*, p. 178.

rationale for this course.[6] Stalin flew into a rage at the mere suggestion of deserting Kiev and accused Zhukov of 'talking nonsense'. Zhukov was one of the few Marshals who spoke his mind to Stalin and, after failing to convince him, promptly insisted: 'If you think the Chief of the General Staff talks nonsense, then I request you relieve me of my post and send me to the front.'[7] Stalin did just that. Zhukov was sent to command the new Reserve Front, and was replaced by the more amenable Marshal Boris Shaposhnikov.[8]

Stalin's rash dismissal of the threat posed to his southern flank was to bode ill for the future, yet the Soviet dictator remained convinced that Army Group Centre would push on towards Moscow after a short pause to reorganise and patch up its forces. To pre-empt this move, Stalin ordered Timoshenko to prepare new large-scale offensives all along his front with the aim of disrupting the next phase of German operations before they could begin. Additionally, Stalin directed all of his Front commanders to organise fresh counter-offensives to be undertaken from the middle of August in a co-ordinated effort from Staraia Russa in the north to the approaches of Kiev, with the biggest effort being mounted against Bock's army group.[9]

In the immediate aftermath of the battle of Smolensk the front settled down somewhat with more localised Soviet assaults replacing the larger offensives of the past two weeks. Although the intense pressure on Bock's lines had eased, certain sectors of the front were still suffering dearly, complicating the withdrawal of the motorised divisions to begin their refit. On 6 August the 12th Panzer Division, awaiting relief by the 5th Infantry Division, suffered heavily in close quarters combat with the Soviet 19th Army.[10] An officer in the division later recalled:

The 12th Panzer Division, one of the units created for fast breakthroughs and envelopments, was demoted overnight to an infantry division,... typical positional warfare developed, with minor advances on both sides... The 5th Infantry Regiment had been stretched too thinly along too long a defence line and had no reserves. If the Russians discovered that, it would be easy for them to break through here. Every single soldier was needed.[11]

[6] Ibid.
[7] Viktor Anfilov, 'Zhukov' in Harold Shukman (ed.), *Stalin's Generals* (London, 1993) p. 349.
[8] Glantz, *Barbarossa*, pp. 123–124. See also Hoffmann, 'Die Kriegführung aus der Sicht der Sowjetunion', pp. 743–744; Bullock, *Hitler and Stalin*, pp. 790–791.
[9] Glantz, *Battle for Smolensk*, pp. 56–57; Glantz, *Barbarossa*, p. 84.
[10] '3rd Pz. Gr. KTB 25.5.41 – 31.8.41' BA-MA Microfilm 59054, Fol. 194 (6 August 1941).
[11] Stahlberg, *Bounden Duty*, pp. 169–171.

Figure 9.1 From the third week of July the fighting had become a series of slogging battles, increasingly characterised by positional warfare and heavy losses on both sides.

Even without an accompanying Soviet assault, Hoth's panzer group remarked on the 'lively artillery activity', which in varying strengths was making its effects felt across the group's entire front. In addition, captured enemy prisoners revealed that the badly weakened Soviet units were being reinforced by fresh troops.[12] On Guderian's front too there was still fierce fighting, most particularly at Yel'nya where by the early afternoon of 7 August, the XXXXVI Panzer Corps reported having already fended off ten waves of enemy attacks.[13]

In contrast to the chaotic early weeks of the war when Soviet armies struggled to achieve effective command and control, the settling down of the front took a great deal of the pressure off the Soviet armies, and allowed them to improve the co-ordination of their operations. This was evident in German appraisals of Soviet combat performance. On 6 August Strauss reported that the Red Army was a 'well led, tough, powerful enemy with a great deal of artillery and a strong air

[12] '3rd Pz. Gr. KTB 25.5.41 – 31.8.41' BA-MA Microfilm 59054, Fol. 194 (6 August 1941).
[13] 'KTB Nr.1 Panzergruppe 2 Bd.II vom 22.7.1941 bis 20.8.41' BA-MA RH 21–2/928, Fol. 166 (7 August 1941).

force'.[14] Three days later a command conference at Panzer Group 3 described the enemy as a '[g]reat mass' who was 'still in a position to fight'. His armaments were described as 'good' and the artillery 'much more proficient than in the first days'. Overall, the implications of the enemy analysis were judged 'unpredictable' – a radical shift from the dismissive reports of only three weeks before. Finally the question was asked: 'How much longer should it take until the Russian's fighting strength is broken?' A dubious and uncertain answer was supplied: 'We must in this, the hardest struggle in our history, stand behind the Führer.'[15]

Given Germany's high military standards, the number of references in the various war diaries to the bravery and resilience of the average Red Army man are even more revealing. Leeb wrote in his diary on 5 August: 'Regarding the difficulty of battle and the tenacity of the Russians is a characteristic statement given in the daily report of the 18th Army on 4.8.: 40 prisoners and 500 dead Russians at Muru.'[16] Another German general commented after the war: 'The Russian civilian was tough, and the Russian soldier still tougher. He seemed to have an illimitable capacity for obedience and endurance.'[17] Although the German invaders could begrudgingly accept the fanatical concept of fighting to the last man, there were many elements of the war in the east that shocked and revolted them, underlining the totality of the Soviets' approach to war.[18] Many soldiers reacted with indignation at finding Soviet women serving as combatants in the Red Army.[19] Karl Fuchs, a soldier in the 7th Panzer Division, wrote home to his wife: 'When I get home I will tell you endless horror stories about Russia. Yesterday, for instance, we saw our

---

[14] 'Panzerarmeeoberkommandos Anlagen zum Kriegstagesbuch "Berichte, Besprechungen, Beurteilungen der Lage" Bd.IV 22.7.41 – 31.8.41' BA-MA RH 21-3/47, Fol. 131 (6 August 1941).

[15] Ibid., Fol. 142 (9 August 1941).

[16] Wilhelm Ritter von Leeb, KTB, p. 320 (5 August 1941).

[17] Liddell Hart, *History of the Second World War*, p. 169.

[18] Unlike the Germans', the Soviet 'total war' was not one in the sense defined earlier by Ludendorff.

[19] Estimates indicate that over a million Soviet women served in the Red Army or partisan detachments throughout the war and at its high point in 1943 women made up 8 per cent of the armed forces. Susanne Conze and Beate Fieseler, 'Soviet Women as Comrades-in Arms: A Blind Spot in the History of the War' in Robert Thurston and Bernd Bonwetsch (eds.), *The People's War. Responses to World War II in the Soviet Union* (Chicago, 2000), p. 212; Reina Pennington, 'Offensive Women: Women in Combat in the Red Army' in Paul Addison and Angus Calder (eds.), *A Time to Kill. The Soldier's Experience of War in the West 1939–1945* (London, 1997), p. 249. According to another source 86 women won the distinguished medal Hero of the Soviet Union (Mawdsley, *Thunder in the East*, p. 214). On 29 June 1941 Kluge issued an order that all women captured in the uniform of the Red Army were to be shot. This was contested by the OKH, but still extensively carried out (Megargee, *War of Annihilation*, p. 59).

first women soldiers – Russian women, their hair shorn, in uniform! And these pigs fired on our decent German soldiers from ambush positions.'[20] Another example of the Soviet way of war was cited by Hans von Luck, also posted to the 7th Panzer Division. He described encountering a dog in an abandoned village which ran up to meet them and then promptly disappeared under one of their armoured vehicles. This was followed by an explosion which damaged the vehicle. Incredulous, Luck explained: 'We ran to it and discovered that the dead dog had an explosive charge concealed in the furs of its back with a movable pin as detonator. When the dog crawled, the detonator tipped over and triggered off the explosion. The dog had been trained to find meat under armoured vehicles.'[21] The 'Molotov cocktail' was another feature of Soviet desperation in the face of inadequate anti-tank defences. This hand-thrown device was a gasoline- or kerosene-filled bottle that was ignited on impact by means of a burning wick. They had first been used by Franco's troops in the Spanish civil war, and were later employed to greater effect by the outgunned Finnish army during the short Winter War. It was in the Winter War that the Molotov cocktail acquired its name (an unflattering reference to the Soviet Foreign Minister Vjacheslav Molotov). In the early period of Operation Barbarossa even Molotov cocktails were in short supply, but their success soon had factories producing them at a rate of 120,000 a day.[22]

The fanaticism of Soviet resistance was not only evident in their novel use of improvised weaponry, but extended to the way the soldiers fought. Accounts speak of Soviet soldiers pretending to surrender only to open fire or stab their would-be captors at close range.[23] Numerous accounts attest to bypassed 'dead' Soviet soldiers suddenly assailing the unsuspecting Germans from behind.[24] In his memoir Manstein reported that

---

[20] Fuchs Richardson (ed.), *Sieg Heil!*, p. 119 (17 July 1941). See also Meier-Welcker, *Aufzeichnungen*, p. 127 (15 August 1941). Testimony by infantryman Walter Neustifter in Guido Knopp, *Der Verdammte Krieg. 'Unternehmen Barbarossa': Überfall auf die Sowjetunion 1939–41* (Munich, 1998), p. 135.

[21] Von Luck, *Panzer Commander*, pp. 57–58. See also: Vasily Grossman, *A Writer at War. Vasily Grossman with the Red Army 1941–1945*, ed. Antony Beevor and Luba Vinogradova (New York, 2005), p. 13; Lubbeck with Hurt, *At Leningrad's Gates*, p. 112; Erhard Raus, *Panzer Operations. The Eastern Front Memoir of General Raus, 1941–1945* ed. Steven H. Newton (Cambridge MA, 2005), p. 87. Another source claimed that the use of dogs by the Red Army was not quite so successful because the dogs could not distinguish between Soviet and German tanks and sometimes Red Army vehicles were destroyed (Lucas, *War of the Eastern Front*, p. 118).

[22] Merridale, *Ivan's War*, pp. 50–51 and 106.

[23] Kempowski (ed.), *Das Echolot Barbarossa '41*, p. 152 (29 June 1941).

[24] Erhard Rauss, 'Russian Combat Methods in World War II', pp. 21–22; Hürter, *Ein deutscher General*, p. 70 (22 July 1941); Günter K. Koschorrek, *Blood Red Snow. The Memoirs of a German Soldier on the Eastern Front* (London, 2002), pp. 69 and 152.

'there were more than enough cases where Soviet soldiers, after throwing up their hands as if to surrender, reached for their arms as soon as our infantry came near enough, or where Soviet wounded feigned death and then fired on our troops when their back were turned.'[25] The warfare on the eastern front was as ferocious as it was brutal, with combatants on both sides often unwilling to give quarter or observe the usual conventions of war. The Germans had begun a war of annihilation in the east intent on murdering millions through starvation and enslaving those that remained,[26] but in contrast to their past campaigns, this time they were being opposed by every possible means.

The sum effect of such a bitterly contested conflict manifested itself among the German troops, who were suffering to the limits of their endurance from the physical and mental strain. These led to the first doubts about the progress of the campaign, which was already Germany's longest blitzkrieg, still with no end in sight. One soldier's campaign diary, which time and again revealed the author to be a committed National Socialist, suddenly betrayed doubts. On 6 August Wilhelm Prüller recorded: 'It wouldn't be such a mistake for us to go home, for we've about 350 losses in the Battalion. August 4th alone cost us 14 dead, 47 wounded, 2 missing, 1 officer dead and 3 wounded.'[27] Another soldier from the 52nd Infantry Division, Ernst Guicking, wrote home to his wife on 10 August: 'You have no idea how we feel here after 23 days of the heaviest actions . . . This morning our battalion was called to a field mass. I can tell you it was an emotional hour. All comrades who have been lost were read out. Their number was not small.'[28] Nor were these just the bitter words of disgruntled soldiers. The matter arose in a discussion between Hoth and his subordinate commanders, with Hoth stating his belief 'that the impetus [of the men] is at times somewhat reduced'. Colonel von Bismarck tried to sound more upbeat by claiming that, if this was in fact the case, then it was only a symptom of fatigue. General Kuntzen added that one should tell the troops how successful they had been.[29] A report was subsequently issued entitled 'Morale

---

[25] Von Manstein, *Lost Victories*, pp. 180–181.
[26] On German planning for the political control and economic exploitation of the Soviet Union see Kay, *Exploitation*.
[27] Robbins Landon and Leitner (eds.), *Diary of a German Soldier*, pp. 90–91 (6 August 1941).
[28] Kleindienst (ed.), *Sei tausendmal gegrüßt*. Accompanying this book is a CD Rom with some 1,600 letters mostly unpublished in the book. The quoted letter appears only on the CD Rom and can be located by its date 10 August 1941.
[29] 'Panzerarmeeoberkommandos Anlagen zum Kriegstagesbuch "Berichte, Besprechungen, Beurteilungen der Lage" Bd.IV 22.7.41 – 31.8.41' BA-MA RH 21-3/47, Fol. 142 (9 August 1941).

Reconstitution' (*seelische Auffrischung*), intended to 'convince officers' by listing the weaknesses of the enemy and contrasting these with German successes.[30] Guderian too was feeling the strain of the campaign, as evidenced from his private letters home when he remarked on 6 August, 'how long the heart and nerves can stand this I do not know'. Days later in a second letter he asked: 'Have I not become old? These few weeks have imprinted their marks. The physical exertions and battles of the will make themselves felt.'[31]

Halder, by contrast, was still clinging to his conviction that the campaign was proceeding on track and the Red Army was nearing its end. On 8 August he compared the 'changing situation' in the Red Army to the second phase of the western campaign in France (which had allowed German forces a relatively straightforward penetration of French defences followed by a long, largely unopposed, advance through northern France). 'For further operations', Halder concluded, 'the enemy has only limited forces left.'[32] German losses, however, were hardly inconsiderable. By 6 August the German invasion armies had lost over a quarter of a million men (266,352 casualties) in just six weeks of fighting,[33] with Army Group Centre accounting for 88,400 of these.[34]

With the end of the encirclement at Smolensk and the relative decline in the scale of Soviet attacks, aside from what Bock dubbed 'small-scale attacks at the hot-spots', the withdrawal of the motorised divisions from the front could proceed.[35] Nevertheless, once all the infantry divisions had fully closed up on the front (including those previously employed at the Smolensk encirclement) their distribution along the eastern front was inadequate to cover the full line of the army group. Even for a defensive posture against lacklustre enemy attacks, Army Group Centre could not manage without the aid of the motorised divisions, and the more they released the more precarious the front became. Not only were the infantry divisions stretched too thinly to allow any depth to their defensives but, unlike the motorised divisions, when a crisis did occur they lacked the mobility to react quickly. As a consequence their casualties were higher and, by the time local reserves arrived, they were sometimes unable to restore the situation, escalating the crisis. On 7 August, after detailing

[30] Ibid., Fol. 160 (no date given on document).
[31] Guderian's letters as cited by Macksey, *Guderian*, p. 142.
[32] Franz Halder, KTB III, p. 164 (8 August 1941).
[33] Ibid., p. 169 (10 August 1941).
[34] 'Kriegstagebuch Nr.1 (Band August 1941) des Oberkommandos der Heeresgruppe Mitte' BA-MA RH 19II/386, p. 277 (9 August 1941).
[35] Fedor von Bock, KTB 'Osten I', Fol. 56, *War Diary*, p. 275 (7 August 1941).

the ongoing withdrawal of the motorised divisions from the front, Bock noted:

The situation is nevertheless extremely tense. If I want to create a reserve and try to pull out a division to do so, it is declared 'impossible,' if a division deployed in the rear army area arrives at the front it is snatched from my hands! I therefore wrote to the commanders of the armies and armoured groups, made them aware of the results of such a blinkered policy, and asked them to be reasonable on this point. – I don't exactly know how a new operation is to take place out of this situation and with the slowly sinking fighting strength of our constantly attacking forces – but things are undoubtedly even worse for the Russians![36]

By 7 August the majority of Schmidt's XXXIX Panzer Corps had been relieved with only parts of the 12th Panzer Division still awaiting replacement.[37] To the south Lemelsen's XXXXVII Panzer Corps included the shattered 18th Panzer Division, which had been pulled out of the line in late July, but was only now being joined by the 29th Motorised Division, and shortly thereafter by the 17th Panzer Division. In Vietinghoff's XXXXVI Panzer Corps, the attempted extraction of the 10th Panzer Division had only been partially successful, and it had to be kept close to the front for sporadic commitment because of the perpetual state of crisis in the Yel'nya salient. The SS division *Das Reich* and infantry regiment *Grossdeutschland* were released on 7 August. On the army group's flanks, however, the situation was more complex. To the south Schweppenburg's XXIV Panzer Corps had managed to rest and refit for a number of days at the end of July, but had been ordered back onto the offensive at Roslavl and by 8 August had only just finished eliminating the last pockets of resistance inside its encirclement (see Map 15). Schweppenburg, however, was to be the victim of his own success with the new strategic possibilities created by his victory allowing no rest for his weary corps. On the northern flank Kuntzen's LVII Panzer Corps was simply too far away and could not be fully relieved until 11 August.[38]

By 7 August the refitting phase of the motorised divisions had begun in earnest, yet Guderian had promised to have it completed by 15 August – in just eight days. Hoth had been more cautious in his estimate and had originally proposed to be finished between 18 and 20 August.[39] On 9 August Halder asked if a panzer division or even a whole panzer corps

---

[36] Ibid., Fol. 56, p. 276 (7 August 1941).
[37] '3rd Pz. Gr. KTB 25.5.41 – 31.8.41' BA-MA Microfilm 59054, Fol. 196 (7 August 1941).
[38] Ibid. (7 August 1941).
[39] KTB OKW, Volume II, p. 1043, Document 88 (4 August 1941); Mendelssohn, *Die Nürnberger Dokumente*, p. 398.

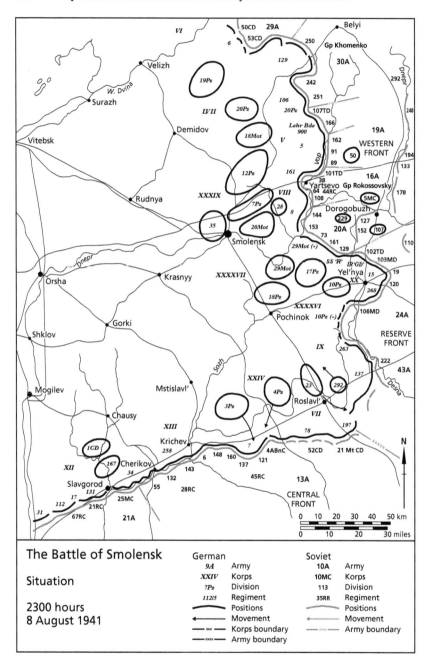

The Battle of Smolensk

Situation

**2300 hours
8 August 1941**

German		Soviet	
9A	Army	10A	Army
XXIV	Korps	10MC	Korps
7Pz	Division	113	Division
112/5	Regiment	35RR	Regiment
——	Positions	～～	Positions
◄———	Movement	◄———	Movement
—— xxx ——	Korps boundary	～～ xxxx ～～	Army boundary
—— xxxx ——	Army boundary		

Map 15 Dispositions of Army Group Centre 8 August 1941: David M. Glantz, *Atlas of the Battle of Smolensk 7 July–10 September 1941*

could be ready by 17 August on the condition that the necessary motors
were given preferential delivery status. Strauss, the commander of the
9th Army, to whom Panzer Group 3 was subordinated, answered that
the delivery of motors was only part of the problem and rejected the
earlier date in favour of 20 August.[40]

With time becoming an increasingly important factor for the Germans,
there was no minimum standard for what determined a reconstituted
division; it was a matter of doing whatever could be done in the limited
time available. As Strauss indicated, the success of the refitting process
was dependent on a number of factors. The essential spare parts, including motors, were an obvious requirement, but these had to be transported
to the front via a supply system that was grossly inadequate and, in any
case, overwhelmed by meeting the existing urgent demands for ammunition. Transport was also a problem within the motorised divisions. The
initial advance had placed great strain on their mobility, and the past
three weeks of frantic defensive battles had kept virtually every vehicle in
action to offset critical shortages of supplies and shift reserves. The high
fallout rates in trucks, especially those of civilian or non-German design,
reduced the net transport capacity and placed an even greater burden
on the vehicles that remained. Now, as the motorised divisions pulled
back from the line, a further obstacle intervened. Just as in early July,
on 7 August thunderstorms deluged the front with heavy rainfalls, converting the primitive roads into seas of mud. The strong rain continued
throughout 8 August,[41] compounding the difficulties of movement 'in
parts heavily'.[42] Hans Meier-Welcker wrote home on 9 August: 'It has
been raining for days. The rain counts against the goal . . . The roads have
become terrible, so that the dispatch riders can hardly get through. With
normal vehicles one does not get any further. The east *begins* to show its
true face.'[43] For horses, men and machines forging a path through the
mud required inordinate effort causing Army Group Centre to issue an
'urgent appeal' that 'all troop movement behind the front, not absolutely
necessary, be avoided'. Otherwise it warned, the 'motorised troops and
the infantry would be "marched to death"'.[44]

---

[40] '3rd Pz. Gr. KTB 25.5.41 – 31.8.41' BA-MA Microfilm 59054, Fol. 199 (9 August
1941). See also Fedor von Bock, KTB 'Osten I', Fol. 58, *War Diary*, p. 278 (9 August
1941).
[41] Weather reports are provided in the Panzer Group 3's war diary for each day.
[42] '3rd Pz. Gr. KTB 25.5.41 – 31.8.41' BA-MA Microfilm 59054, Fol. 198 (8 August
1941).
[43] Italics in the original. Meier-Welcker, *Aufzeichnungen*, p. 127 (9 August 1941).
[44] 'Kriegstagebuch Nr.1 (Band August 1941) des Oberkommandos der Heeresgruppe
Mitte' BA-MA RH 19II/386, p. 261 (8 August 1941).

Although Hoth's panzer group had opted not to accept a staggered return of its motorised units to action, and preferred instead to rest the entire group for as long as possible, Guderian was more impatient. His success at Roslavl made him particularly eager to exploit the hole in the Soviet line and push the advance rapidly forward.[45] To do so, however, he faced an even greater complication to his already dire logistical problems. From the beginning of August Schweppenburg's XXIV Panzer Corps had been involved in the encirclement and elimination of the Roslavl pocket claiming 38,000 prisoners on 8 August.[46] Yet the corps was only receiving 50 per cent of what it needed to undertake further offensive action. The unreliable railroads were ruled out as an option to supply enough provisions for the attack, leaving the suggestion to requisition 2,000 tons of supplies from the XXXXVI and XXXXVII Panzer Corps. The difficulty was finding enough transportation capacity to transfer all these supplies to Schweppenburg's panzer corps as most of the trucks were fully supporting the refitting of the panzer group and bringing up more ammunition. In addition, the war diary of the panzer group's Quartermaster-General noted that 'the heavy strain on the wheeled transportation has risen greatly recently'. The conclusion was that the operation remained possible, but only at a considerable cost to XXXXVI and XXXXVII Panzer Corps.[47] Even at this late stage Guderian refused to acknowledge the constraints of his over-extension, preferring instead to press on with another offensive.

Without a doubt, the delusionary assessments upon which Barbarossa's pre-war logistical plans were built now revealed themselves. Not only was the army struggling to meet the most rudimentary needs of the front, while also supporting the refitting process, but, in theory, the whole army would soon need to continue advancing a great deal further to the east. The Achilles heel of the whole process was the rail network. The trucks were never supposed to be bridging so many supplies over such great distances, but the absence of trains forced desperate measures. On 8 August the 3rd Panzer Division noted that sending its trucks to the eastern railheads often resulted in them sitting idle for days on end while waiting for a train to arrive.[48] As if mocking the armies with an empty promise, the focus was geared towards extending the

[45] 'KTB Nr.1 Panzergruppe 2 Bd.II vom 22.7.1941 bis 20.8.41' BA-MA RH 21–2/928, Fol. 170 (7 August 1941).
[46] 'Tagesmeldungen der Heeresgruppe Mitte vom 6.8.41 bis 26.8.41' BA-MA RH 19 II/130, Fol. 18 (8 August 1941).
[47] 'Kriegstagebuch der O.Qu.-Abt. Pz. A.O.K.2 von 21.6.41 bis 31.3.42' BA-MA RH 21–2/819, Fols. 254–255 (7 August 1941).
[48] 'KTB 3rd Pz. Div. I.b 19.5.41 – 6.2.42' BA-MA RH 27–3/218 (8 August 1941).

railways closer to the front, but there was insufficient carrying capacity to provide the volume of trains required. Accordingly, the trucks of the *Grosstransportraum* were left to pick up the slack and it soon became common practice for units to bypass the Quartermaster-General altogether and independently dispatch trucks back to Germany to obtain what was needed.[49] The limitations sometimes caused the corps command to override divisional jurisdiction and snatch trucks for other operations, causing much friction, especially when this required long detours and the trucks returned in an even worse state.[50] Not surprisingly the fallout rate within the *Grosstransportraum* continued to rise dramatically and by 10 August Panzer Group 2's Quartermaster-General indicated that a further 1,500 tons of transport capacity was 'urgently necessary' and that one-third of all the *Grosstransportraum* was in need of repair.[51]

The implications of the failing transportation system for the all-important refitting process were clear. Without the necessary preconditions, the panzer divisions could not be restored. Guderian noted on 10 August: 'So long as the agreed motors and spare parts remain undelivered the panzer situation cannot be decidedly improved. It would be false to remain inactive waiting for further refitting. In the absence of spare parts and motors, the rest period will produce no noticeable improvement.' Guderian therefore determined to continue his attack in the south. Ultimately he concluded: 'The time ticks for the enemy, not for us.'[52]

While the refitting process was seriously hindered by the internal weaknesses of Bock's army, the Red Army played its part too. Even the comparatively quiet rumblings of the front were on a scale too great for the overstretched infantry to cope with. Not surprisingly, the first crisis came at Yel'nya from which the SS division *Das Reich* and infantry regiment *Grossdeutschland* had been released on 7 August. Only the following day the XXXXVI Panzer Corps, to which they belonged, declared 'that a rest and refitting of the troops is no longer to be considered'.[53] A 30-kilometre section of the front was threatening to buckle under enemy pressure for which *Das Reich*, along with what was referred to as 'the badly worn out

---

[49] Müller, 'Das Scheitern der wirtschaftlichen "Blitzkriegstrategie"', p. 976.

[50] 'Kriegstagesbuch 19.Panzer-Division Abt.Ib für die Zeit vom 1.6.1941 – 31.12.1942' BA-MA RH 27–19/23, Fol. 25 (6 August 1941).

[51] 'Kriegstagebuch der O.Qu.-Abt. Pz. A.O.K.2 von 21.6.41 bis 31.3.42' BA-MA RH 21–2/819, Fols. 237 (10 August 1941).

[52] Underlining in the original. 'Panzerarmeeoberkommandos Anlagen zum Kriegstagesbuch "Berichte, Besprechungen, Beurteilungen der Lage" Bd.IV 22.7.41 – 31.8.41' BA-MA RH 21–3/47, Fol. 176 (10 August 1941).

[53] Underlining in the original.

infantry regiment' *Grossdeutschland*, were urgently needed.[54] Two days after their recall to active duty (10 August), the situation at Yel'nya was still worsening, with the 15th Infantry Division suffering a deep breakthrough and losing control of a commanding height. The division's last reserves (2 engineer companies) were committed, but a further expansion of the breakthrough to the south was still expected.[55] Bock observed: 'The enemy at Yel'nya is still not worn down – on the contrary! Powerful reserves have been identified behind his front.'[56] Far from increasing their combat strength, the elite units were again locked into the vicious attritional warfare at Yel'nya, which was now threatening to drag in even more German strength.

Nor was Yel'nya the only area where the Germans were attempting to stave off crisis. The IX Infantry Corps holding the line to the south of Yel'nya was likewise caught in a desperate struggle to contain a Soviet offensive against its front, but Vietinghoff's panzer corps observed that 'there can be no practical question of offering support'.[57] To the north of Yel'nya the 17th Panzer Division was similarly under pressure on a wide 30-kilometre front, with enemy breakthroughs requiring the commitment of the panzer regiment to throw them back. Under such conditions any hope of rest or refitting was simply impossible and casualties continued to mount, as the war diary of XXXXVII Panzer Corps noted on 9 August: 'The battle is especially hard . . . our losses are high. Alone on 8.8. the [17th Panzer] division lost over 300 men.'[58]

Soviet attacks were also causing trouble in the north for 9th Army which was incapable of holding its positions without the support of Hoth's panzer group. Unlike Guderian, however, after the disbandment of Kluge's 4th Panzer Army, Hoth was re-subordinated to 9th Army and not allowed an independent command. This was now to become a renewed source of friction as Strauss ordered elements of Hoth's group to break off their rest and rejoin the fighting. Hoth, on the other hand, insisted that his forces be allowed an uninterrupted respite and wrote to Bock requesting that his panzer group be withdrawn from 9th Army's

---

[54] 'Kriegstagesbuch Nr.2 des XXXXVI.Pz.Korps Teil II. 8.7.41 – 23.8.41' BA-MA RH 24–46/8, Fol. 204 (8 August 1941).

[55] 'KTB Nr.1 Panzergruppe 2 Bd.II vom 22.7.1941 bis 20.8.41' BA-MA RH 21–2/928, Fol. 203 (10 August 1941).

[56] Fedor von Bock, KTB 'Osten I', Fol. 59, *War Diary*, p. 278 (10 August 1941).

[57] 'Kriegstagesbuch Nr.2 des XXXXVI.Pz.Korps Teil II. 8.7.41 – 23.8.41' BA-MA RH 24–46/8, Fol. 204 (8 August 1941).

[58] 'Kriegstagebuch Nr.2 XXXXVII.Pz.Korps. Ia 25.5.1941 – 22.9.1941' BA-MA RH 24–47/2 (9 August 1941).

jurisdiction.[59] Strauss was also petitioning Bock for more reserves, as well as the allocation of Hoth's 14th Motorised Division which had only just been pulled out of the line. Bock ultimately sided with Strauss and even authorised a limited withdrawal to shorten the overall defensive line.[60] From Halder's diary it seems that Brauchitsch was in favour of a more offensive solution to the menacing Soviet assaults, advocating 'attacks in all directions', which Halder held to be quite wrong. Instead Halder favoured Hoth's preference to refit in peace, but did not intervene in Bock's command.[61] In spite of getting his way, Strauss was still unable to counter every crisis and, only days later, the 5th Infantry Division suffered a Soviet breakthrough right up to its artillery positions.[62]

While the motorised divisions endeavoured to refit in the face of the unrelenting demands of the front, the Luftwaffe was in an even more desperate position. Kesselring's Air Fleet 2 was reduced to just Loerzer's II Air Corps, having lost Richthofen's VIII Air Corps to Army Group North. Loerzer's corps was kept in constant action, but could not hope to adequately screen Bock's enormous area of operations and therefore concentrated on aiding Guderian's operations in the south. Even then the demands of constant action resulted in the corps being 'in substantial need of replenishment', which was naively intended to be undertaken 'as soon as the combat situation allows'. Richthofen's VIII Air Corps was due to be returned to Kesselring's command between 15 and 20 August, but was expected to be 'completely worn out' and not available for operational use.[63] Thus Soviet planes operated with a degree of freedom over the German front, strafing and bombing in small groups and disappearing before German fighters arrived.[64]

Brauchitsch's visit to Hitler's headquarters on 5 August had produced a calming effect at OKH, bringing renewed hope that Hitler was moving closer to accepting the Moscow alternative. In truth, however, Hitler had still not made up his mind[65] and his moderate tone was probably just calculated to pacify the nervous sensitivities of the OKH, especially in the absence of any final decision. Nevertheless, Halder was still hopeful he would prevail and, after discussions with Bock, the commander

[59] '3rd Pz. Gr. KTB 25.5.41 – 31.8.41' BA-MA Microfilm 59054, Fol. 200 (9 August 1941).
[60] Fedor von Bock, KTB 'Osten I', Fols. 56–57, War Diary, pp. 276–277 (8 August 1941).
[61] Franz Halder, KTB III, p. 164 (8 August 1941).
[62] Fedor von Bock, KTB 'Osten I', Fol. 61, War Diary, p. 280 (12 August 1941).
[63] 'Kriegstagebuch Nr.1 (Band August 1941) des Oberkommandos der Heeresgruppe Mitte' BA-MA RH 19II/386, p. 273 (9 August 1941).
[64] Boog, 'Die Luftwaffe', p. 661.
[65] Von Kotze (ed.), Heeresadjutant bei Hitler 1938–1943, p. 108 (6 August 1941).

of Army Group Centre wrote in his diary: 'apparently the ideas of the Supreme Command are now developing in the direction we wish'.[66] Halder saw his next opportunity to sway Hitler when the Führer and his staff visited Army Group South on 6 August. Just as he had done at the 4 August meeting at Bock's headquarters, Halder dispatched a representative (this time Paulus) to report on the proceedings and provide a reminder of OKH's interests. Halder also spoke with Rundstedt before Hitler's arrival and gained the Field Marshal's assurance that he would attempt to influence Hitler on the matter of Moscow, in spite of the fact that this would mean a secondary role for Army Group South's operations in the Ukraine. Hitler was probably expecting a much more receptive response than he had received at Army Group Centre to his suggestion of turning Guderian's panzers to the south and aiding Rundstedt's forward drive. Nevertheless, Hitler's eagerness to find some support for his own ideas within the army, and thereby pacify his self-doubts, was to be disappointed yet again when Rundstedt advocated the Moscow alternative. In frustration Hitler stubbornly restated the same priorities he had outlined at Army Group Centre – first Leningrad, second the eastern Ukraine and third Moscow.[67]

Halder was perplexed by Hitler's ardent determination to seize the Ukraine over Moscow and he felt that securing economic gains was a deflection from the immediate goal of crushing the Soviet Union in the time remaining. Halder was also coming to the realisation that an indirect approach was needed to gain Hitler's approval and therefore pitched a new position to Jodl with the hope that it would finally move Hitler to accept OKH strategy. On 7 August Halder met with Jodl and posed the question: 'Do we want to defeat the enemy or pursue economic objectives (Ukraine, Caucasus)?' Jodl replied that Hitler probably considered both goals to be simultaneously attainable. The answer confirmed to Halder the wisdom of his new scheme, which sought to offer Hitler everything he wanted by presenting him with subtly controlled information that supported his desires, and allowed the OKH and OKW to pursue theirs. In short, Hitler would be persuaded that Leeb and Rundstedt were capable of reaching their objectives on their own, leaving Bock free to march on Moscow with his armoured groups intact. The plan was not pure deception on Halder's part as he naively believed that a continued general offensive would work, but he wanted to assuage Hitler's doubts, practically in the south, by minimising the importance of enemy strengths. In the north Leningrad could be reached, Halder assured Jodl, with

[66] Fedor von Bock, KTB 'Osten I', Fol. 58, *War Diary*, p. 278 (9 August 1941).
[67] Franz Halder, KTB III, pp. 157–158 (6 August 1941).

Leeb's available forces. 'We need not, nor may we, expend any forces
for this objective that we need for Moscow.' Shifting his attention to the
main operation Halder declared: 'The question Moscow *or* Ukraine or
Ukraine *and* Moscow must be answered with emphasis on the *and*.'[68]
Thus, Halder's grand solution to the strategic impasse was to advocate
everything, a stance which took astonishingly little account of the dreadful state of his eastern armies. Nevertheless, Halder convinced Jodl who
agreed to 'pull together with us in this direction'. Halder concluded:
'For us agreement on two ideas is necessary: All of Bock's strength for
Moscow . . . and minimise the importance of the Korosten group.'[69]

   While Halder was alarmingly ignorant of the strength of his own forces,
his intelligence concerning Soviet strengths was even more misleading.
On 8 August Halder asserted with assurance that, applying the empiri-
cal yardstick that two divisions could be raised from every million people within a population, the Soviet Union had reached the end of its
mobilisation and could raise no further major formations. According to
his calculations, this left Army Group North's 26 divisions (including
6 motorised) facing 23 Soviets divisions (including 2 motorised), Army
Group Centre's 60 divisions (including 17 motorised) against 70 Soviet
divisions (including $8\frac{1}{2}$ motorised), and Army Group South's $50\frac{1}{2}$ divisions (including $9\frac{1}{2}$ motorised) confronting an equal number of Soviet
divisions (including $6\frac{1}{2}$ motorised divisions). To this Halder confidently
asserted:

This confirms my old judgement that [Army Group] North is strong enough to
carry out its own task. [Army Group] Centre must concentrate all its strength
to destroy the mass of the enemy. [Army Group] South is sufficiently strong to
complete its task and maybe even help [Army Group] Centre.[70]

The much lauded victories of Bock's battle at Smolensk and Rundstedt's
at Uman fortified Halder's sanguine faith in the success of his new plan
to both turn Hitler's will to his own and finally break the Soviet Union.
Halder hoped to emulate the success of the French campaign and achieve
a final breakthrough to destroy the remaining Soviet armies. His plans
reveal that he was as much deluded by his successes, as he was emboldened to surpass them. The fallacy of such assumptions, reminiscent of
the deplorable pre-war planning for Barbarossa, proved that the harsh
realities of the eastern campaign were still grossly unappreciated by the
Chief of the German General Staff.

---

[68] Ibid., p. 159 (7 August 1941). Italics in the original.
[69] Ibid., pp. 159–160 (7 August 1941).   [70] Ibid., pp. 164–165 (8 August 1941).

If Halder was captivated by the allure of impending success, Hitler was less certain. The dictator felt the weight of strategic decision being forced upon him and vacillated as he tried to identify the shortest possible road to victory. From intelligence and past Soviet deployments it seemed clear that the greatest enemy strength was to be found on the road to Moscow, but Hitler was sceptical of treading this path, and not just for the historical parallels with Napoleon's ill-fated campaign. Bock's powerful forces had twice lunged in this direction, destroying large Soviet armies, but bringing no result and entangling themselves in long, fierce battles. Hitler had already identified the problem of such large strategic manoeuvres and had proposed smaller encirclements, but he was soon forced to accept that, while these held better prospects for operational success, because of their size they had far less strategic importance. The fact remained that the Red Army had not, as intended, been destroyed in the initial battles and a renewed thrust on Moscow, as the OKH advocated, seemed too much like reinforcing failure having already failed twice to acieve the desired result. Hitler also saw no war-winning potential in seizing Moscow. To the south, however, he saw the prospect of an immediate success over the Soviet South-Western Front and the opening of the resource-rich eastern Ukraine to his forces. Yet this was hardly an annihilation strategy and would mean the bulk of the Red Army remained active in the field with even less time to deal with it before the onset of winter. As a result, there was hardly a general to be found who supported such a move. For the first time, Hitler may have begun to feel that control of events was slipping from his grasp, as there was no obvious solution to his dilemma without risking major drawbacks. Gripped with indecision, he reacted by steadfastly refusing to make any decision at all. Hitler's army adjutant, Major Gerhard Engel, noted after the OKW military conference on 8 August: 'One notices immediately how irresolute the Führer is concerning the further direction of the operation. Constantly vacillating between the ideas and objectives. From the situation conferences one comes out knowing nothing more than when one went in.'[71]

Despite the weight of indecision, or perhaps even because of it, once away from the situation room Hitler's mind warmly indulged delusional fantasies of his future empire and conjured visions of his wars as historical comparatives to Cannae, Sedan and Tannenberg.[72] These wild protestations are unhelpful in determining Hitler's true perception of

[71] Von Kotze (ed.), *Heeresadjutant bei Hitler 1938–1943*, p. 108 (8 August 1941).
[72] Trevor-Roper (ed.), *Hitler's Table Talk*, p. 25 (nights of 8–11 August).

events, since his illusions, particularly of the '*Endsieg*' (ultimate victory), persisted until the final days of April 1945. In the situation room Hitler's conceited bravado had to confront another reality, frightening in its implications for the Nazi state. If Hitler had any sense of that danger it might have added to, or even precipitated, the dictator's sudden paralysis. In May 1940 Hitler had nervously halted the crucial drive to the English Channel because of an unwarranted fear of a military disaster. If his fears were again aroused in early August 1941, he showed better strategic judgement. There was no immediate danger to German forces, but there was a very real question about how Germany could end the war, and Hitler knew better than many of his generals that Germany was unfit to bear the economic burden of a long war. Thus, it remains open to speculation whether Hitler's desire to secure economic objectives in the south, which were made abundantly clear during the planning stages of Operation Barbarossa, now assumed a heightened sense of urgency, betraying perhaps a lack of faith in an outright German victory and revealing Hitler's growing concern over control of the Soviet Union's economic heartland.

As the days passed without clear direction, Brauchitsch's impatience spilled over into anger and disgust. According to Engel, Brauchitsch bemoaned the constant agitation from the OKW in insignificant matters and the 'ridiculous nervous reaction' to every movement of the enemy. Moreover, by 9 August Brauchitsch shared none of Halder's optimism in swaying Hitler to the OKH's wishes and in fact despaired that 'Moscow will obviously be abandoned'.[73]

On the following day (10 August) Jodl followed through on his commitment to Halder and delivered a new proposal to Hitler, prepared by the OKW's Section L in accordance with the Operations Section of OKH.[74] The plan argued for an attack on Moscow at the end of August, with Hoth and Guderian's panzer groups operating on the wings and the infantry in the centre. Jodl ended his presentation with a proposal that was clearly calculated to impress Hitler. He suggested that a later operation by Guderian's panzer group could be launched towards the south-east to seize control of the Don River, effectively giving Germany the Ukraine.[75] Hitler's immediate response is not recorded but, from the emphatic support it offered to Hitler's least favoured alternative, one can surmise that it only added to his uncertainty.

---

[73] Von Kotze (ed.), *Heeresadjutant bei Hitler 1938–1943*, p. 109 (9 August 1941).
[74] Warlimont, *Im Hauptquartier*, Band I, p. 201.
[75] KTB OKW, Volume II, pp. 1043–1044 (10 August 1941).

'Today is the beginning of positional warfare!'
(Fedor von Bock)

Although a number of valuable studies have recently taken issue with the long-standing Soviet assessment of early partisan warfare, the debate is focused on how widespread the movement was, and its actual effect on military operations. Justifiable doubt has been cast on the spontaneous national uprising mythologised in Soviet-era publications, but none disputes that a form of clandestine warfare was being conducted parallel to the main fighting at the front. Evidence from the army's files in August 1941 indicates that the partisan war was not simply a problem for the rear echelon units; it was affecting the main formations at the front. Indeed there was genuine concern at the impact of these camouflaged forces. On 10 August the Chief of Staff of the 9th Army, Colonel Weckmann, complained to Army Group Centre about the treacherous conditions in the rear area which he stated 'constantly increased'. Elaborating further, Weckmann added: 'Confrontations with partisans increase daily... Army has the impression that the Russian rebels come together in bands and use every opportunity to attack.'[76] A week later on 17 August Weckmann complained to Greiffenburg about the drain on motorised forces which were being drawn away to 'fight the still very disruptive and damaging partisan activities'.[77]

A similar problem was being experienced in the rear area of 2nd Army. In early August Weichs asked that additional forces of the SD be committed in order to allow the smooth flow of supplies. He was informed, however, that these forces were fully occupied and could spare no resources, resulting in the 252nd Infantry Division being detained for this purpose throughout August and September.[78] The army's own security divisions (of which just three were available to Army Group Centre[79]) were utterly overwhelmed by the sheer size of the rear area they were charged to control. Already by the end of July, the 221st Security Division, with at most 9,000 men, was charged with securing an area 35,000 square kilometres in size. It is estimated that, of the three million German soldiers involved in Operation Barbarossa, only about 100,000 were allocated to rear-area security. By the autumn of 1941 Bock's rear area extended to

---

[76] 'Kriegstagebuch Nr.1 (Band August 1941) des Oberkommandos der Heeresgruppe Mitte' BA-MA RH 19II/386, p. 283 (10 August 1941).

[77] Ibid., p. 340 (17 August 1941).

[78] Munoz and Romanko, *Hitler's White Russians*, pp. 157–158.

[79] These were the 221st, 403rd and the 286th Security Divisions. Army Groups North and South were also allocated three security divisions each.

some 145,000 square kilometres, an area roughly equal to the size of England and Wales.[80]

Frequently the partisan attacks targeted the vital supply trucks operating in the vast spaces of the rear area, which helps to explain why the relatively weak early partisan movement had such a disproportionately worrying effect on the German armies. Organised civilian groups were still few in number and at an embryonic stage of development, meaning that the real backbone of the partisan movement came from the many cut-off and isolated Soviet soldiers still operating behind German lines. Their motives were not always governed by a devotion to the Soviet cause and were often dominated by a simple desire to find food and other imperatives. Nevertheless, with or without intention, their actions were striking at the weakest link in the German army, placing further demands on the stretched and exhausted German forces. Motorised units were especially important for responding quickly to partisan assaults and hunting down the attackers; it was yet another diversion the panzer groups could scarcely afford. On 16 August the 14th Motorised Infantry Division was asked to provide a battalion for operations in the Tury area against an estimated 500 enemy partisans.[81] The 29th Motorised Infantry Division was soon heavily engaged in similar work.[82] Lemelsen's XXXXVII Panzer Corps noted on 19 August that in the large forested areas different partisan groups were operating in groups of 30–40 men. Equipped with good weapons, these groups were said to be striking at any trucks driving alone through the region.[83] Three days later on 22 August the same war diary stated: 'New is the increased partisan activity.'[84] The 4th Panzer Division received orders to conduct 'security actions' against partisans on 24 August, but its operation failed to find the enemy.[85] The same problem was noted by Hoth's panzer group which reported on 23 August: 'The partisans are obviously always informed as soon as German soldiers arrive in a village. The large forests and swamp areas

---

[80] In the United States this equals about the size of Iowa or in Germany the combined states of Bavaria, Baden-Württemberg, Rhineland-Palatinate and Hesse. See Hürter, *Hitlers Heerführer*, p. 410.

[81] 'Kriegstagesbuch Ia. 14.Inf.Div. (mot) vom 25.5.41 – 1.10.41' BA-MA RH 26–14/10, Fol. 120 (16 August 1941).

[82] 'Kriegstagebuch Nr.2 der 29.I.D. (mot) vom: 30.7.1941 bis 25.8.1941' BA-MA RH 26–29/16, pp. 50 and 52 (20 and 22 August 1941).

[83] 'Kriegstagebuch Nr.2 XXXXVII.Pz.Korps. Ia 25.5.1941 – 22.9.1941' BA-MA RH 24–47/2 (19 August 1941).

[84] Ibid. (22 August 1941).

[85] 'Kriegstagebuch 4.Panzer-Division Führungsabtl. 26.5.41 – 31.3.42' BA-MA RH 27–4/10, p. 118 (23 August 1941).

always offer enough cover, so that finding them is extremely difficult.'[86] The 10th Panzer Division took stringent pre-emptive measures and on 10 August the division started sending all men of military age to POW camps and seizing hostages from villages to be shot if hostile action was taken against its forces.[87]

As the front-line units struggled with the partisan menace, the seeds of rebellion against German rule were steadily being sown in the occupied territories. A report on 5 August from Himmler's notorious *Einsatzgruppe B* (Action Group B) operating in Army Group Centre's rear area noted: 'Among the population of the erstwhile Soviet Republic of Belorussia a worsening mood has recently become apparent. This is due, above all, to the constant plunder and requisitioning, in both town and country, by the German troops.'[88] By the start of September the new civilian-administered Reich Commissariat Ostland took over from Army Group Centre,[89] supporting mass repression and the retention of the hated Soviet collective farms. This quickly dispelled the myth of benevolent German rule and fuelled sympathies for underground communist propaganda. Nevertheless, in the summer of 1941 the majority of the civilian population in the occupied territories were preoccupied with their own survival, and most felt it wiser to await a clearer outcome of the conflict before becoming actively involved in the struggle on either side. For the German troops, the perceived danger, whether from Red Army fugitives or armed civilians, was widespread enough to have a manifest psychological affect which, at this early stage, was more potent than the actual military threat posed by the partisans.[90]

Even before Guderian had completed his encirclement at Roslavl, Bock was keen to seize the opportunity and launch an offensive with 2nd Army to solve the problems on his southern flank. Bock, however, determined Weichs's forces to be too weak and therefore ordered Guderian to give up one panzer division to support the attack. Though not opposed to the idea of an offensive, Guderian was loath to relinquish any of his forces and protested to the point of refusing the order, which in the end had to

---

[86] '3rd Pz. Gr. KTB 25.5.41 – 31.8.41' BA-MA Microfilm 59054, Fol. 232 (23 August 1941).

[87] 'Kriegstagebuch der 10.Panzer Division Nr.5 vom: 22.5. bis: 7.10.41' BA-MA RH 27–10/26b (10 August 1941).

[88] Shepherd, *War in the Wild East*, p. 95.

[89] Lithuania was handed over starting in late July and ending on 1 August. Latvia and Belorussia were added on 1 September and Estonia was incorporated on 5 December 1941.

[90] Hill, *The War Behind the Eastern Front*, p. 12; Shepherd, *War in the Wild East*, pp. 77–78.

come directly from OKH.[91] Guderian vented his fury and despair in a letter to his wife. '[S]omebody [he chose not to name Bock or Halder] interferes as before and endeavours to deploy the tanks in dribs and drabs, ruining them by useless journeys. One despairs! How I can overcome this stupidity I do not know. Nobody helps me.'[92] On the following day Guderian was saved from having to begin the transfer by a general Soviet withdrawal from the Roslavl area, which he immediately seized upon to propose a new offensive to the south-west, thereby relieving himself of the need to give up a division by directly assisting 2nd Army's advance. Bock approved the operation[93] and, early on 9 August, Schweppenburg's XXIV Panzer Corps was again in action attempting to cut off Soviet forces at Krasnopolye.[94]

In spite of Guderian's desire to maintain his offensive operations, the panzers of Schweppenburg's corps had not been adequately rested or refurbished and lacked sufficient supplies, especially of oil. Hastily conducted field repairs to the 4th Panzer Division resulted in about 50 per cent of its panzer strength being available for the attack, but the desperate shortage of oil supplies was to prove a greater obstacle than enemy resistance.[95] Moreover, the heavy rains slowed the attack and hindered movement even for the tanks, with the added consequence that oil consumption rose by 75 per cent above normal levels.[96] Bock wrote on 9 August: 'The tanks are making slow progress over bottomless roads.'[97]

Before the attack began, Bock chose Krasnopolye as Guderian's first objective (about 120 kilometres south-west of Roslavl), to be followed by a further advance to Checkersk (a further 60 kilometres to the south-west). At the time, Guderian was dismissive of Checkersk and proposed marching immediately to the vital Soviet concentration point at Gomel[98] (a distance of about 90 kilometres from Krasnopolye). In the light of the difficulties, on only the second day of the attack, Bock enquired as to whether the more limited advance on Checkersk was still possible, to

[91] Fedor von Bock, KTB 'Osten I', Fol. 54, *War Diary*, p. 274 (6 August 1941); Franz Halder, KTB III, p. 158 (6 August 1941); Guderian, *Panzer Leader*, p. 193.
[92] Guderian's letter as cited by Macksey, *Guderian*, p. 144.
[93] Fedor von Bock, KTB 'Osten I', Fol. 55, *War Diary*, p. 275 (7 August 1941).
[94] 'KTB Nr.1 Panzergruppe 2 Bd.II vom 22.7.1941 bis 20.8.41' BA-MA RH 21–2/928, Fol. 186 (8 August 1941).
[95] 'Kriegstagebuch 4.Panzer-Division Führungsabtl. 26.5.41 – 31.3.42' BA-MA RH 27–4/10, pp. 96 and 101 (6, 7 and 9 August 1941).
[96] 'Tagesmeldungen der Heeresgruppe Mitte vom 6.8.41 bis 26.8.41' BA-MA RH 19 II/130, Fol. 27 (9 August 1941).
[97] Fedor von Bock, KTB 'Osten I', Fol. 57, *War Diary*, p. 277 (9 August 1941).
[98] Ibid., Fol. 57, p. 277 (8 August 1941).

which Guderian replied: 'No, that would mean the end of the corps.'[99]
It is indeed instructive to note the continual over-estimation of strength
on behalf of the German command, as well as the profound decline of
the German offensive capacity. The operation to Krasnopolye was being
undertaken by an entire panzer corps (3rd and 4th Panzer Divisions,
followed by the 10th Motorised Infantry Division) against fleeing Soviet
resistance, over a distance hardly comparable with the vast stretches of
land to be conquered if Soviet resistance was indeed to be crushed. Yet
instead of the panzers' difficulties causing Guderian to exercise caution,
the very fact that they were moving spurred him to precisely the opposite course of action. He came up with a bold new offensive plan to
roll up the Soviet flanks to the north of Roslavl, just as he was now
doing in the south. This would mean that, after its small encirclement
around Krasnopolye, Schweppenburg's panzer corps would have to perform a complete about-face and retrace its steps back to the area around
Roslavl, before launching an even more ambitious offensive against much
stronger Soviet formations. Guderian believed that if he added the available strength from his other two panzer corps he could relieve the Yel'nya
salient, while also destroying the Soviet reserve armies in the rear.[100] After
the war Guderian alleged that this plan would have opened the road to
Moscow, and claimed that its rejection by Bock and Halder was evidence
of their hesitant commitment to the thrust on Moscow.[101] As usual Guderian only saw one way of going about things and that was his way.

In fact, Bock's rejection of Guderian's proposal was based on a far
more sound military assessment. Bock believed that such an operation
might yield a brief tactical success, before resulting in another costly
battle, with Guderian's exposed right flank providing a vulnerable target
for the Soviet reserves to attack. Clearly Bock was better informed as
to the depth and strength of the Soviet reserves. On the whole, Bock
concluded:

Army Group Guderian is too weak to also defeat these forces on its own. 4th
and 9th Armies are busy, Panzer Group Hoth will not be ready to attack until
the 20th [of August]. The whole thing becomes a partial blow which places the
armoured groups at risk without promising a strategic success.[102]

[99] Ibid., Fol. 59, p. 279 (10 August 1941); 'KTB Nr.1 Panzergruppe 2 Bd.II vom
22.7.1941 bis 20.8.41' BA-MA RH 21–2/928, Fol. 202 (10 August 1941).
[100] 'KTB Nr.1 Panzergruppe 2 Bd.II vom 22.7.1941 bis 20.8.41' BA-MA RH 21–2/928,
Fols. 211–215 (11 August 1941); Fedor von Bock, KTB 'Osten I', Fols. 58–59, War
Diary, p. 278 (10 August 1941).
[101] Guderian, Panzer Leader, pp. 194–195.
[102] Fedor von Bock, KTB 'Osten I', Fol. 59, War Diary, pp. 278–279 (10 August 1941).
Bock's assessment was supported by the OKH: see 'KTB Nr.1 Panzergruppe 2 Bd.II
vom 22.7.1941 bis 20.8.41' BA-MA RH 21–2/928, Fol. 217 (11 August 1941).

By 11 August Schweppenburg's corps was shattering the weak Soviet 13th Army, but its own forces were likewise being ground down. The 4th Panzer Division had only 64 tanks left and only 33 of these were Mark IIIs (25) and IVs (8).[103] On the same day the panzer group's war diary noted: 'The technical requirements of this attack are not favourable. In spite of the rest period, it was not possible to bring up the necessary spare parts. The number of panzers in the army group [Army Group Guderian] has not increased significantly. It is also not known whether or when the spare parts (motors etc.) will be delivered.'[104] At this point Brauchitsch abruptly declared that Checkersk and Gomel would also have to be taken, which probably reflected his recognition that Hitler would never allow the march on Moscow before being convinced that the problems on Bock's southern flank were solved. Bock was very doubtful that Schweppenburg's corps had the strength to undertake such an order and suggested that more panzer forces would have to be transferred to the south, but even then he concluded: 'With the poor equipment state of the panzer divisions, I have doubts whether they can force this order to be carried out.'[105]

As the Soviet position opposite 2nd Army became untenable, Weichs's infantry divisions launched their own offensive on 12 August. The infantry attacks were generally able to move forward, but at certain points the attacks were thrown back with heavy casualties. In the attack on Kostjaschowo, an entire German battalion advanced to within 10 metres of a large, but well concealed, Soviet force defending the town. The Soviets waited till this point to open fire, routing the Germans and wiping out half the battalion. In one company only 35 men survived.[106] Nevertheless, by 13 August Schweppenburg's corps had eliminated a pocket at Krichev, capturing 16,000 prisoners, 76 guns and 15 tanks.[107] Bock, however, was still unconvinced that the seizure of Gomel was possible, writing: 'material and human strengths will probably no longer be sufficient.'[108] This was certainly reflective of the strain Schweppenburg's corps was under and, as the heavy fighting continued, the 4th Panzer Division's war diary noted on the evening of 14 August: 'Battles on 13 and 14 [August] very costly, also in material. There was little benefit [in the fighting] because the enemy mass had already evacuated. Trucks in bad condition. Men

---

[103] 'Kriegstagebuch 4.Panzer-Division Führungsabtl. 26.5.41 – 31.3.42' BA-MA RH 27–4/10, p. 103 (11 August 1941).
[104] 'KTB Nr.1 Panzergruppe 2 Bd.II vom 22.7.1941 bis 20.8.41' BA-MA RH 21–2/928, Fol. 215 (11 August 1941).
[105] Fedor von Bock, KTB 'Osten I', Fol. 60, *War Diary*, p. 280 (11 August 1941).
[106] Lammers (ed.), *'Fahrtberichte'*, p. 235 (12 August 1941).
[107] 'KTB Nr.1 Panzergruppe 2 Bd.II vom 22.7.1941 bis 20.8.41' BA-MA RH 21–2/928, Fol. 237 (13 August 1941).
[108] Fedor von Bock, KTB 'Osten I', Fol. 61, *War Diary*, p. 281 (13 August 1941).

tired. Division increasingly more worn out... Russian tanks, especially the <u>heavy</u> ones, are good.'[109]

On 8 August, as Guderian was about to commence his attack in the south, Bock asked 9th Army if there was any prospect of conducting a renewed attack towards Velikie Luki in the north. The difficulties facing Strauss convinced Bock that, as in the south, the infantry would be unable to advance without support from Hoth's panzers. On 9 August, when Halder expressed an interest in Bock's plans, the Chief of the General Staff proposed a new large-scale operation in the north. Bock, however, was careful to point out to Halder Strauss's reservations concerning his ability to attack because, Bock remarked: 'I have the feeling that the Army High Command has overestimated the army's forces.' With Hoth's refit not projected to be finished until 20 August, Bock was prepared to put off the northern offensive until approximately 23 August.[110]

As Bock's offensive strength floundered, the importance of refitting the panzer divisions assumed critical importance, but this required uninterrupted rest, spare parts and sufficient time. The corps with the greatest success in meeting these requirements was Lemelsen's XXXXVII Panzer Corps, which on 11 August recorded an improvement in its combat strength. Despite the rigours of continually running supplies, by remaining stationary the corps had been able to arrest the decline in its transportation fleet and even raise vehicle numbers through a combination of repairs and the seizure of 300 captured vehicles (mostly trucks) from the Soviet material around Smolensk. In addition, the 18th Panzer Division, which had been kept out of the line for the past two weeks and allowed complete rest, had raised its combat strength to 129 serviceable tanks. The 17th Panzer Division was still fighting, but managed to field 80 tanks.[111]

Lemelsen's corps, however, was the exception, not the rule. There were not enough spare parts to service all the divisions, and the endless demands of the front denied many of the motorised and panzer divisions the time and rest they needed to conduct repairs. Indeed, it was only on 11 August that the remaining elements of the 20th and 19th Panzer Divisions were finally relieved by the infantry and able to begin their refitting, while the 18th Motorised Division would not be fully released from the front until 15 August.[112]

---

[109] Underlining in the original. 'Kriegstagebuch 4.Panzer-Division Führungsabtl. 26.5.41–31.3.42' BA-MA RH 27–4/10, p. 109 (14 August 1941).

[110] Fedor von Bock, KTB 'Osten I', Fol. 58, *War Diary*, pp. 277–278 (9 August 1941).

[111] 'Kriegstagebuch Nr.2 XXXXVII.Pz.Korps. Ia 25.5.1941 – 22.9.1941' BA-MA RH 24–47/2 (11 August 1941).

[112] '3rd Pz. Gr. KTB 25.5.41 – 31.8.41' BA-MA Microfilm 59054, Fol. 200 (11 August 1941).

By 13 August the problem of significantly raising tank numbers within the panzer divisions reached a critical apex. Time was exceedingly short and the promised delivery of tank motors had still not materialised. It was at this point that Army Group Centre revealed there were now only 150 tank engines to be expected – although still not delivered – for both Hoth's and Guderian's panzer groups.[113] At the 4 August conference Hitler had promised 400 engines, a figure Guderian had described as 'totally inadequate'.[114] With the scaled down number of new engines to be expected, Hoth's panzer group determined that only a 15 per cent increase in panzer strength could now be anticipated.[115] Yet even achieving this slight rise was provisional to when the delivery would take place, especially given the inadequate field installations and working conditions of the army technicians.[116]

In spite of such unpromising conditions for improvement within in the panzer groups, estimates circulating around the OKH stubbornly insisted upon upwards of 70 per cent of the 'full authorized establishment' being restored during the refitting period. Colonel Burmeister, who had reported this figure to Paulus on 12 August, however, also made the ominous admission that once operations began again the army would have to expect swift losses of up to 25 per cent.[117] Clearly, the extent of the repairs and the serviceability of many tanks was highly provisional and not to be counted on for the wide-ranging operations to come.

In spite of the dark clouds swelling over the army, Halder remained defiantly optimistic about the prospects of a decisive blow being dealt to the Soviet Union when operations resumed towards the end of August. In part this was based on a serious over-estimation of the army's offensive strength, but there was also a corresponding under-estimation of the Red Army, fed by the inept submissions of the intelligence department Foreign Armies East. Halder's dismissive estimation of the Red Army had recently prompted him to compare it with France's desperate position in early June 1940, and he continued to insist that Soviet reserves had reached their end. This delusional perception of Soviet strength was one of the central pillars sustaining Halder's faith in the coming victory, but his bubble was burst with dramatic effect when new information from Foreign Armies East finally revealed the fearsome potential of the Soviet

[113] Ibid., Fol. 207 (13 August 1941).   [114] Guderian, *Panzer Leader*, p. 190.
[115] '3rd Pz. Gr. KTB 25.5.41 – 31.8.41' BA-MA Microfilm 59054, Fol. 207 (13 August 1941).
[116] Müller, 'Das Scheitern der wirtschaftlichen "Blitzkriegstrategie"', p. 976.
[117] Letter from Burmeister to Paulus dated 12 August 1941 as cited in Görlitz, *Paulus and Stalingrad*, p. 138.

colossus. Halder's diary entry for 11 August conveys his shock, disbelief and sudden misgivings.

Regarding the general situation, it stands out more and more clearly that we underestimated the Russian colossus, which prepared itself consciously for war with the complete unscrupulousness that is typical of totalitarian states [*sic*]. This statement refers just as much to organizational as to economic strengths, to traffic management, above all to pure military potential. At the start of the war we reckoned with 200 enemy divisions. Now we already count 360. These divisions are not armed and equipped in our sense, and tactically they are inadequately led in many ways. But they are there and when we destroy a dozen of them, then the Russians put another dozen in their place. The time factor favours them, as they are near to their own centres of power, while we are always moving further away from ours.

And so our troops, sprawled over an immense front line, without any depth, are subject to the incessant attacks of the enemy. These are sometimes successful, because in these enormous spaces far too many gaps must be left open.[118]

It was this dispersal of units that sapped the army's strength and revealed a critical shortage of resources, which undercut every attempt at concentration. This realisation made a sobering impression on Halder, as he bluntly outlined the difficulty of the German predicament.

[W]hat we are now doing is the last desperate attempt to avoid positional warfare. The High Command is very limited in its means. The army groups are separated by natural boundaries (marshes). Our last reserves have been committed. Any new grouping now is a movement on the baseline within the army groups. This takes time and consumes the power of men and machines.[119]

Without question this was Halder's most accurate assessment to date on the harsh reality of war against the Soviet Union.

Given the general severity of Germany's position in the east, it would be incorrect to highlight any individual problem and attribute to it a decisive importance. A few hundred tank engines more or less would not have radically altered the German predicament, any more than a particular command decision in one direction over another. Such hypothetical matters may have affected the war in individual areas, or at best across a broad section of the front, but the general lack of military resources, in almost every significant category, locked Germany into a long war. Although barely understood by the German command at the time, this created an alarming strategic dilemma. The dilapidated state of the motorised and panzer divisions rendered them unable to eliminate

---

[118] Franz Halder, KTB III, p. 170 (11 August 1941). See also Hürter, *Ein deutscher General an der Ostfront*, p. 71 (1 August 1941).
[119] Halder, KTB III, p. 170 (11 August 1941).

Figure 9.2 As Hitler intended to disperse Army Group Centre's panzers to the north and south, Halder (left) and Brauchitsch desperately schemed to maintain the attack on Moscow.

Soviet power in 1941, yet by the same token, the longer the war dragged on, the more the Soviets would benefit from Allied economic assistance and direct military aid.

Not only was the restoration of Bock's motorised divisions proving an uphill battle against an intractable mechanical deficit, but the race to offset the widening gaps in the ranks of the panzer groups was also being lost. Personnel losses from 22 June to 10 August revealed the scale of internal erosion that the replacement system was proving too slow to counter. Guderian's panzer group had suffered the heaviest casualties with 26,230 men lost, including 1,275 officers.[120] For the same seven-week period, Hoth's panzer group recorded 17,201 casualties, including 763 officers.[121] Throughout the whole army the loss of officers had reached a worrying proportion, with some 10,000 having been killed or wounded in the first 50 days of the campaign, a staggering average of 200 a day. On 15 August Halder noted that some 16,000 officers would be required for the rest of the year, but that only 5,000 replacements would be available.[122]

Army Group Guderian's continuing juggling act to simultaneously attack in the south, refit in the rear and defend at Yel'nya was symptomatic of Army Group Centre's excessive commitments. All three placed inordinate demands on resources which simply could not be met, and Guderian's penchant for the offensive left the Yel'nya salient, already in crisis, under threat of total collapse. Soviet attacks were proving indefatigable and growing in strength, against which the recommitment of the weakened SS division *Das Reich* and infantry regiment *Grossdeutschland* had provided only a short-term solution. On 11 August XXXXVI Panzer Corps reported that the latest enemy breakthrough had been achieved on a 2½-kilometre front to a depth of three kilometres. *Das Reich* was reported to be at the end of its strength and not in a position to hold its line against sustained enemy pressure.[123] The desperate position of Vietinghoff's panzer corps and the XX Army Corps now forced plans to be prepared for a major reinforcement of the salient in the event of a complete military collapse. In this instance, the entire 18th Panzer Division and parts of the 10th Panzer Division would be mobilised, as well as the 17th Panzer Division if still available.[124] It was indeed a troubling commentary on both the offensive strength of the Red Army and the corresponding weakness of the German front, that they deemed it would now require the great majority of two panzer corps to simply hold one section of the front.

Bock was now paying the price for the gross over-extension of his army group, and the frantic demands of the front required that he raise more

---

[120] 'Verlustmeldungen 5.7.1941 – 25.3.1942' BA-MA RH 21-2/757, Fol. 1 (Casualty lists until 10 August 1941, report dated 14 August 1941). Exact figures: Officers fallen 359, wounded 881, missing 35. Non-commissioned officers and lower ranks, fallen 5,848, wounded 17,839, missing 1,268.

[121] 'Panzerarmeeoberkommandos Anlagen zum Kriegstagebuch "Berichte, Besprechungen, Beurteilungen der Lage" Bd.IV 22.7.41 – 31.8.41' BA-MA RH 21-3/47, Fol. 49 (10 August 1941).

[122] Franz Halder, KTB III, p. 179 (15 August 1941).

[123] 'KTB Nr.1 Panzergruppe 2 Bd.II vom 22.7.1941 bis 20.8.41' BA-MA RH 21-2/928, Fol. 209 (11 August 1941).

[124] Ibid., Fol. 220 (11 August 1941).

reserves. He sought to do this by stripping the rear areas. 'I need every man up front', he wrote in his diary on 12 August. Yet the absence of reserves was a crisis that pervaded the whole of the eastern front. Bock observed with growing concern that Army Group North's advance to Leningrad was sluggish, and Army Group South was stuck at the Dnepr River. For his own army group, Bock recognised that resuming forward operations depended on refitting the panzer groups; he foresaw, however, the motorised and panzer divisions being restored to no more than half of their initial strength. Even then, he noted, they would have to engage the main body of the Red Army on a 700-kilometre-wide front. Overall, Bock concluded: 'If the Russians don't soon collapse somewhere, the objective of defeating them so badly that they are eliminated will be difficult to achieve before the winter.'[125]

As Soviet pressure mounted at Yel'nya, the lack of German reserves was only part of the problem. On 13 August Vietinghoff's panzer corps complained that the ongoing shortage of ammunition supplies further contributed to its difficulties and that so long as these continued the Stuka dive-bomber constituted its artillery.[126] Even this was thrown into doubt when Hermann Göring, as the Commander-in-Chief of the Luftwaffe, abruptly directed Kesselring's concentration of strength away from Yel'nya to support Guderian's drive in the south. This was done without Bock's consultation or consent, which, as the Field Marshal protested, made rational command 'impossible'.[127] Vietinghoff's panzer corps had no doubts about the consequences of this decision and noted in its war diary 'it is questionable whether the front, especially the Yel'nya salient, will hold. The losses remain continually high.'[128]

With the profound threat of collapse hanging over the German position at Yel'nya, Guderian ordered Vietinghoff and Materna (the respective commanders of XXXXVI Panzer Corps and XX Army Corps) to a meeting on 14 August. Already on 13 August the idea had been mooted to withdraw from the salient, thereby shortening the German defensive line, but Guderian was extremely reluctant. In his opinion, withdrawal was akin to permitting a significant Soviet victory, and Guderian was very sensitive about allowing the first major retreat of the entire war to take place on his front, which he felt the Soviets would use to good effect

[125] Fedor von Bock, KTB 'Osten I', Fol. 61, *War Diary*, pp. 280–281 (12 August 1941).
[126] 'KTB Nr.1 Panzergruppe 2 Bd.II vom 22.7.1941 bis 20.8.41' BA-MA RH 21–2/928, Fols. 235–236 (13 August 1941).
[127] Fedor von Bock, KTB 'Osten I', Fol. 62, *War Diary*, p. 282 (14 August 1941). See also Franz Halder, KTB III, p. 176 (14 August 1941).
[128] 'Kriegstagebuch Nr.2 des XXXXVI.Pz.Korps Teil II. 8.7.41 – 23.8.41' BA-MA RH 24–46/8, Fol. 237 (13 August 1941).

as propaganda.[129] The emergency meeting on 14 August was intended to decide the fate of the Yel'nya salient and sharply divergent opinions were exchanged. General Materna was adamant that the German position must be evacuated. The evening before he had complained bitterly to Vietinghoff that his 15th Infantry Division was particularly threatened, having lost 35 officers over the preceding two days alone, and insisting that holding the current position was 'pure insanity'.[130] On 14 August, Materna stated that a serious enemy attack could no longer be held by either of his two infantry divisions and pleaded for a withdrawal.[131] Vietinghoff took the opposing view and argued that a retreat would allow the Soviets to concentrate their forces in the same way that Materna was proposing to benefit. Guderian was inclined to back Vietinghoff's standpoint but, in the absence of any clear idea of future operational priorities, he found it difficult to make a decision.[132] As Bock observed, if major operations were to be continued towards the east, then it was important to hold the salient as an offensive springboard. On the other hand, if the front was to remain on the defensive against costly Soviet attacks, then withdrawal was the correct course of action.[133] Clearly, the enduring strategic uncertainty was making reasoned command decisions hopelessly impracticable. Bock referred the matter to Brauchitsch, but ultimate responsibility for a decision was returned to him.[134] At this point Guderian gave a strong hint of his lack of faith in the Moscow alternative by advocating the salient be evacuated.[135] Halder, on the other hand, spoke with Greiffenberg, Bock's Chief of Staff, and warned him against a withdrawal, claiming that however bad the situation was, it had to be a lot worse for the enemy.[136] Eventually Bock too decided to hold at Yel'nya and consulted Guderian to find out what was needed to make this possible. Most notably, Guderian stipulated a sizeable increase in the flow of munitions and the recommitment of the Luftwaffe to Yel'nya.[137]

The army's uncertainty about Yel'nya was only one symptom of Hitler's continuing indecision over the further prosecution of the war. His customary decisiveness had temporarily deserted him, and he stood

[129] 'KTB Nr.1 Panzergruppe 2 Bd.II vom 22.7.1941 bis 20.8.41' BA-MA RH 21–2/928, Fol. 240 (13 August 1941).
[130] 'Kriegstagesbuch Nr.2 des XXXXVI.Pz.Korps Teil II. 8.7.41 – 23.8.41' BA-MA RH 24–46/8, Fol. 238 (13 August 1941).
[131] Ibid., Fol. 244 (14 August 1941).
[132] 'KTB Nr.1 Panzergruppe 2 Bd.II vom 22.7.1941 bis 20.8.41' BA-MA RH 21–2/928, Fols. 248–249 (14 August 1941).
[133] Fedor von Bock, KTB 'Osten I', Fol. 63, *War Diary*, p. 283 (15 August 1941).
[134] Ibid., Fols. 62–63, p. 282 (14 August 1941).
[135] Franz Halder, KTB III, p. 176 (14 August 1941); Guderian, *Panzer Leader*, p. 195.
[136] Franz Halder, KTB III, p. 177 (14 August 1941).
[137] Fedor von Bock, KTB 'Osten I', Fol. 62, *War Diary*, pp. 281–282 (14 August 1941).

day after day at his military conferences struggling to find a way of closing the Pandora's Box he had opened in the east. Caught between his own instinctive strategic judgement and the resounding opposition of his commanders, Hitler anxiously sought a solution that would allow him to cover all options. Jodl's submission to Hitler on 10 August had advocated much of what Halder had earlier proposed (from their meeting on 7 August) and was, therefore, endowed with a hefty dose of Halder's previously insatiable optimism. The continued drive on Moscow by Bock's armoured forces was, of course, central to what Jodl had argued, with the two flanking army groups deliberately presented as being strong enough to carry out the tasks Hitler desired of them. Not surprisingly, Hitler found in this a degree of solace, as it purported to offer a joint solution to the seemingly intractable impasse over the strategic direction of the campaign. Although not accepted in its purest form, Jodl's submission was convincing enough for Hitler to initiate it in an amendment to Directive 34, to be known as Directive 34a. This new dictate took a major step towards the Moscow alternative, albeit with Hitler's own stringently attached conditions. Dated 12 August, Directive 34a made clear that Rundstedt's army group was expected to achieve its objectives in the Ukraine without assistance from Bock. Leeb's army group was likewise expected to encircle Leningrad and achieve a junction with Finnish forces. In this case, however, Bock was expected to extend his front further to the north to allow Leeb's offensive a greater concentration of forces. The directive also repeated Hitler's long-standing insistence that Bock deal decisively with the Soviet forces on his southern flank before renewing his advance eastward.[138] Regarding Moscow, the directive stated:

Only after these threats to our ranks have been entirely overcome and armoured formations have been rehabilitated will it be possible to continue the offensive, on a wide front and with echeloning of both flanks, against the strong enemy forces which have been concentrated for the defence of Moscow. The object of operations must then be to deprive the enemy, before the coming of winter, of his government, armament, and traffic centre around Moscow, and thus prevent the rebuilding of his defeated forces and the orderly working of government control.[139]

When Halder received news of the new directive on 13 August he reacted with cautious optimism. While acknowledging that it freed the path to Moscow, he was wary of the many conditions Hitler attached, particularly the success of Leeb's operations towards Leningrad. These, he determined, 'severely handicapped' the operational freedom of the

---

[138] Trevor-Roper (ed.), *Hitler's War Directives 1939–1945*, pp. 148–150.
[139] Ibid., p. 150.

army.[140] Essentially Halder was annoyed that Bock's decisive drive on Moscow was being made secondary to the lesser concerns of Leeb's front. This concern was greatly exacerbated on the following day (14 August) when a powerful Soviet offensive south of Staraia Russa proved too strong for Leeb's over-extended X Army Corps. To Halder's mind this was an inconsequential development, but when word reached Hitler's headquarters it evoked, in Halder's view, a wholly unwarranted response. Jodl was first told by Hitler that an entire panzer corps would need to be sent, but later changed his mind to a single panzer division. Halder complained bitterly in his diary about disproportionate 'reactions to pinpricks' which frustrated planning and the concentration of forces.[141] On 15 August Hitler changed his mind again, and insisted to Brauchitsch that one panzer division and two motorised infantry divisions would need to be sent to Army Group North as fast as possible. Halder was incensed: 'Once again the old mistake, with the result that a brash thrust by a single Russian division ties down 3 to 4 German divisions. In view of our limited resources and the immensity of space, we will never come to a success.'[142] Yet Halder's assessment failed to appreciate the seriousness of the Soviet offensive, which only became clear to him over the course of the day. Instead of one Soviet division, by the evening of 15 August Halder was made aware that X Army Corps had been attacked by 'motorised divisions and a cavalry division' as well as '6 new divisions and 2 cavalry divisions of the Soviet 34th Army'.[143] The situation was hardly inconsequential and Army Group North, which had already ordered elements of Manstein's LVI Panzer Corps north to aid the drive on Leningrad, now reversed the decision, sending them back to the south. Having taken eight hours to travel a distance of 200 kilometres on 15 August, Manstein noted that on the following day the corps was ordered down to Dno – 257 kilometres to the south, 'along the same dreadful route we had covered the day before... what the troops thought of it all I do not care to imagine'.[144] The situation so concerned Leeb that he made what Halder referred to as '[w]ild requests' for engineers, artillery, anti-aircraft guns and anti-tank guns, all of which Halder rejected.[145]

When the order reached Bock's headquarters that he would have to give up a panzer division and two motorised infantry divisions, despite

---

[140] Franz Halder, KTB III, p. 175 (13 August 1941).
[141] Ibid., pp. 176–177 (14 August 1941).
[142] Ibid., p. 178 (15 August 1941).   [143] Ibid., p. 180 (15 August 1941).
[144] Von Manstein, *Lost Victories*, p. 199. See also Wilhelm Ritter von Leeb, KTB, p. 333 (15 August 1941).
[145] Franz Halder, KTB III, p. 180 (15 August 1941).

the already excessive demands of his front, Bock was stirred to a frantic outburst of dismay. In a telephone call with Halder, Bock sharply criticised the removal of the three motorised divisions, claiming this would leave his own front unbearably weakened and without the strength for further offensive operations. Army Group Centre's war diary then quotes the following exchange:

BOCK: In this case I don't know any more how I can move the army group forward. Today is the beginning of positional warfare!
  The units to be given up can only be moved in a partly finished condition [owing to their incomplete refitting]. I must make you aware, that after the loss of this corps an attack by Strauss's army, except for the special action towards Velikie Luki, is no longer possible. The offensive intention of 9th Army is dead.
HALDER: In my opinion this goes for 2nd Army too.
BOCK: Please inform the Commander-in-Chief of the Army [Brauchitsch], that with this order any thought of an offensive posture by the 9th Army, and as a result probably by the whole army group, ceases to exist. It is also to be borne in mind, that going over to a defensive position is not possible given the current position. The existing line is not adequate for a lengthy defence. I have the intention to inform the Führer's chief adjutant [Schmundt] of the same thing.
HALDER: I don't know myself what I should do. I am utterly desperate and will try to save what there is to save.[146]

Such depressing assessments of the situation speak for themselves about the stark decline in Germany's fortunes. There was now real doubt in the minds of senior commanders about the direction the war was taking. Beyond this, Bock was even expressing deep-seated doubts about the ability of his weakened forces to remain on the defensive in the open expanses of the Soviet Union. As Bock repeated in his diary, 'I told Halder that after being so weakened, a major offensive by the 9th Army and thus probably the army group as well, would no longer be possible. At the same time I pointed out that going over to the defensive was no simple matter considering the large frontages held by my weak divisions.'[147] Halder's diary also alluded to the problem in the most dire terms. He too reiterated the conclusion that 9th Army, and by extension the whole army group, was probably now unalterably stalled. Halder wrote:

Moreover it should be taken into consideration that changing over to the defensive in the present position is not possible. The front of the army group, with its 40 divisions over 730 kilometres is so strained that moving to a determined

---

[146] 'Kriegstagebuch Nr.1 (Band August 1941) des Oberkommandos der Heeresgruppe Mitte' BA-MA RH 19II/386, pp. 328–329 (15 August 1941).
[147] Fedor von Bock, KTB 'Osten I', Fol. 64, *War Diary*, p. 283 (15 August 1941).

defence entails far-reaching considerations, which have not been thought through in detail. The present deposition and line organisation is in no way suited for a sustained defence.[148]

The implications of Bock and Halder's conclusions spelled unmitigated disaster for German operations in the east. By mid-August 1941, it had already become exceedingly difficult to move the front forward and yet it was also impossible to maintain a sustainable, long-term defence. German resources were simply overtaxed and grossly inadequate for their assigned tasks, especially with more Soviet offensives being planned (see Map 16). The rigours of long marches and heavy fighting had exhausted the army, leaving too many units badly worn out, insufficiently supplied and sprawled out over the vast expanse of the Soviet hinterland. Added to this was the wayward strategic direction of the campaign which had become so haphazard that it was now being improvised on a day-to-day basis, without any semblance of inter-command agreement or joint long-term objectives. Indeed Halder had become so disillusioned with the turn of events that the re-assignment of Bock's motorised forces caused him to conclude in despair: 'everything that has so far been achieved is for nothing.'[149]

If there was an exception to the dejection and melancholy at OKH it came, oddly enough, from Brauchitsch. This is somewhat curious given his own deeply pessimistic remarks to Hitler's army adjutant, Major Engel, as recently as 9 August. On that occasion Brauchitsch appeared to have given up all hope of implementing the Moscow alternative, but his optimism was probably reignited with the issuing of Directive 34a on 12 August. Bolstered with renewed hope, Brauchitsch called Bock on 15 August (shortly after the call between Halder and Bock) and attempted to allay his fears, claiming that the three motorised divisions would be returned to him and it was therefore only a temporary loss. Bock, however, was not to be so easily distracted from the magnitude of the problem and pertinently pointed out that, due to the great distances involved and the current condition of the units, a return of the divisions was out of the question. Bock then stubbornly restated his belief that the whole army group suffered from 'a hardly bearable weakness in offensive strength'. Brauchitsch was equally blunt in his response and told Bock: 'I don't see the situation in such catastrophic terms as the army group.'[150]

---

[148] Franz Halder, KTB III, p. 180 (15 August 1941).   [149] Ibid. (15 August 1941).
[150] 'Kriegstagebuch Nr.1 (Band August 1941) des Oberkommandos der Heeresgruppe Mitte' BA-MA RH 19II/386, pp. 329–330 (15 August 1941). See also Fedor von Bock, KTB 'Osten I', Fol. 64, *War Diary*, pp. 283–284 (15 August 1941).

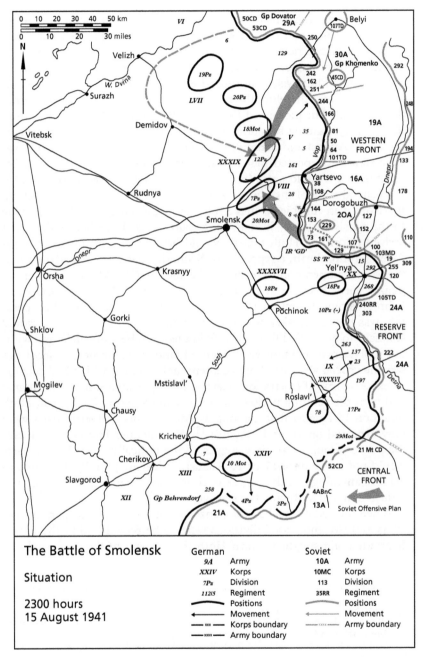

Map 16 Dispositions of Army Group Centre 15 August 1941: David
M. Glantz, *Atlas of the Battle of Smolensk 7 July–10 September 1941*

Even before the Soviet offensive against Leeb's weakened forces south of Staraia Russa had caused such a commotion in the German command and placed new demands on Hoth's forces, Panzer Group 3 was already confronting grave difficulties. It was proving impossible to make a complete withdrawal of all motorised forces from the heavy demands of the front, and therefore the refitting process was still staggered rather than general. The motorised *Lehrbrigade 900*, a special unit formed from the infantry training school at Döberitz, was still tied up in the fighting on 15 August and Schmidt's XXXIX Panzer Corps, to which it was subordinated, reported that it would need eight days of refitting after relief before it could again be committed.[151] Of far greater concern for the general state of the panzer group was that the units already behind the front were unable to make full use of the time for refitting owing to the persistent delay in delivering spare parts. Even before the order arrived informing Hoth that he would have to give up forces to assist Army Group North, a report from Schmidt's panzer corps advised that the foreseen operation to recapture Velikie Luki would require an entire panzer corps because of the reduced strength of the panzer divisions. Schmidt's report, sent on 14 August, also stated that, even if this operation was not undertaken for another six days, until 20 August, it would still have to be carried through with limited numbers of trucks and without replacement manpower.[152] Central among the numerous shortages was the crucial absence of replacement tank engines, which had become a vexing source of frustration. Having already waited since early August and with the refitting period due to be completed by 20 August, Hoth noted on 15 August that the long overdue motors and spare parts were only expected on 16 or 17 August.[153] Shortly after Hoth's assessment, the panzer group's war diary suggested the critically needed spare parts would not arrive until 17 or 18 August,[154] leaving pitifully little time to achieve anything like the degree of restoration originally hoped for, and indeed demanded, by the tasks ahead.

When the orders reached the panzer group that one of its panzer divisions and two motorised divisions were to be redeployed in the north, Schmidt again sought to warn Hoth that instead of the requested one

---

[151] '3rd Pz. Gr. KTB 25.5.41 – 31.8.41' BA-MA Microfilm 59054, Fol. 211 (15 August 1941).

[152] Ibid., Fol. 210 (14 August 1941).

[153] 'Kriegstagebuch Nr.1 (Band August 1941) des Oberkommandos der Heeresgruppe Mitte' BA-MA RH 19II/386, p. 330 (15 August 1941).

[154] '3rd Pz. Gr. KTB 25.5.41 – 31.8.41' BA-MA Microfilm 59054, Fol. 212 (15 August 1941).

Figure 9.3 Having failed to convince Hitler of Moscow's importance, Halder sent Guderian in a last-ditch attempt to change the Führer's mind. Yet the popular panzer commander did not want to fall out of favour and soon backed Hitler's plan.

panzer division, two should be sent because one would simply not have sufficient strength. This, however, was immediately rejected by Bock. Schmidt also made Hoth aware that in the course of the 500-kilometre march 'a large number of the trucks will reach the end of their serviceability'.[155]

As Army Group Centre sought to attack in the south, hold hundreds of kilometres of front and now shed some of its mobile forces in the north, Bock's fears for his offensive capabilities were well justified. On top of this, the enduring supply difficulties and the disappointing results of the refitting process made for an even bleaker outlook. This undermined any prospect of eradicating major Soviet resistance in the little time remaining before the onset of adverse seasonal conditions.

[155] Ibid. (15 August 1941).

Embracing world war and apocalypse – Hitler reaches resolution

Although Directive 34a raised the prospect of a direct thrust on Moscow by Army Group Centre, it fell well short of ordering it and Hitler was careful to attach his own conditions before pledging any authorisation. Jodl, Brauchitsch and Halder were gambling on convincing Hitler that the conquest of Leningrad and the Ukraine could be achieved by the respective northern and southern army groups in the hope of freeing Bock to undertake operations against Moscow. Three days after issuing War Directive 34a, at a conference with Brauchitsch and Jodl on 15 August, Hitler again insisted that attacking Moscow could not be considered until after the success of Army Group North's operations. In the meantime Bock was forbidden to make any attacks in the direction of the Soviet capital.[156] Evidently Hitler was not so easily taken in by the assurances of his commanders, which is probably as much a commentary on his distrust of the generals as his own reading of the difficulties confronting the campaign. For the army commanders, Hitler's steadfast refusal to budge on Moscow, while at the same time giving no firm indication of where Bock's embattled motorised divisions would next be employed, was an unending source of frustration and anxiety. The inordinate amount of time which had now elapsed while awaiting a decision and the corresponding daily depletion of resources had the inevitable effect of radicalising the strategic crisis to the point where all hopes of ultimately winning the war increasingly seemed to rest on Hitler's final decision. Yet while Hitler fussed about the success of Leeb's drive on Leningrad and the army commanders impatiently eyed Moscow, none was able to see how irrelevant their whole debate was becoming and that defeating the Soviet Union in 1941 was simply beyond the Wehrmacht's available strength.

The chain of events that ended the strategic impasse in the German High Command was well beyond the comprehension of Hitler's generals, but it struck at the very root of Hitler's obsessive world-view. The result would sweep away Hitler's indecision about strategy in the east and at the same time proceed rapidly towards the unfolding Jewish Holocaust. Understanding the symbiosis between the future progress of the war and Hitler's Jewish policy, it is important to recognise that in Hitler's view there existed two forms of war, the conventional kind fought between nation states, and the second, a racial war in which

---

[156] KTB OKW, Volume II, p. 1045, Document 91 (15 August 1941); Mendelssohn, *Die Nürnberger Dokumente*, p. 403.

the two principal groups, Arians and Jews, were now competing for supremacy.[157]

Since his earliest days of public life Hitler had consistently cast history and his contemporary world in terms of an inter-racial struggle for survival. Indeed the Nazi regime's search for a solution to its 'Jewish problem' in the early part of World War II was not seen as a distraction from the war; on the contrary, it was an integral element of the war itself. While it was deemed that the Jews under German control had to be increasingly repressed, the still outstanding problem was the Jews outside of German control, whom Hitler referred to as 'international Jewry' and blamed for undermining Germany's position with increasingly belligerent anti-German policies, particularly from the United States. To Hitler's mind, this global Jewish conspiracy sought the destruction of Germany by arraying against it the powers of the world in a new world war. It was this eventuality that provoked Hitler to the most extreme form of racial warfare. Addressing the Reichstag on 30 January 1939, Hitler publicly prophesied: 'Should the international Jewry of finance succeed, both within and beyond Europe, in plunging mankind into yet another world war, then the result will not be a Bolshevisation of the earth and the victory of Jewry, but the annihilation of the Jewish race in Europe.'[158]

After the defeat of France, Hitler had resolved to crush the Soviet Union in the hope of forcing Britain to make terms and at the same time eliminating what Hitler saw as the antithesis of Nazi ideology – Jewish Bolshevism. Not only was this intended to be a decisive move to win the war, but the conquest of Soviet lands would yield immeasurable wealth for contemplating global warfare and, above all, forestall the prospect of foreign encirclement by hostile powers.

Assessing the situation in mid-August 1941 it was clear that the Soviet Union had not yet crumbled under the weight of German arms and that the war in the east was still far from over. By implication, instead of discouraging the British will to fight, Germany's failure to achieve a rapid and convincing conquest would spur British resolve to fight on. Added to this was the news, which had just reached Hitler, of the first

[157] Tobias Jersak, 'A Matter of Foreign Policy: "Final Solution" and "Final Victory" in Nazi Germany', *German History* 21(3) (2003), 379. See also Tobias Jersak, 'Die Interaktion von Kriegsverlauf und Judenvernichtung. Ein Blick auf Hitlers Strategie im Spätsommer 1941', *Historische Zeitschrift*, Band 268 (1999), 311–374; Tobias Jersak 'Holocaust im Krieg' in Militärgeschichtliches Forschungsamt (ed.), *Das Deutsche Reich und der Zweite Weltkrieg*, Band IX, Erster Halbband: *Die Deutsche Kriegsgesellschaft 1939 bis 1945. Politisierung, Vernichtung, Überleben* (2004), pp. 275–318; Tobias Jersak, 'Blitzkrieg Revisited: A New Look at Nazi War and Extermination Planning', *Historical Journal* 43(2) (2000), 565–582; Müller, *Der letzte deutsche Krieg 1939–1945*, p. 108.
[158] Domarus, *Hitler*, Volume III, p. 1449. See also Domarus, *Hitler*, Volume IV, p. 2367.

face-to-face meeting between Churchill and Roosevelt, at which the two leaders agreed on eight points that came to be known as the Atlantic Charter. Ulrich von Hassell's diary alluded to the importance of the Atlantic Charter and its significance for Hitler.

The chief political event is the publication of the joint declaration of Churchill and Roosevelt... The points, whose effects Hitler evidently fears, cannot be mentioned, but they are nevertheless disputed and crudely picked to pieces [in the press].[159]

Below, Hitler's Luftwaffe adjutant, was more specific. He said that upon hearing of the Charter's content, especially point six, Hitler 'flew into a passionate rage'.[160] Point six of the Charter began with the opening phrase, 'after the final destruction of the Nazi tyranny', confirming for Hitler that a new world war to include the United States was becoming inevitable and that his prophecy surrounding the conspiracy of international Jewry had indeed come true. In this same period Hitler was overcome with what was referred to as a severe case of dysentery, but the momentous nature of events has led to speculation by at least one historian that Hitler, in fact, suffered a nervous breakdown.[161] When Goebbels flew to Hitler's headquarters on 18 August, he was informed that Hitler's health was not good and, upon seeing the Führer in person, noted that Hitler 'looked somewhat assailed and sickly'.[162] Goebbels then joined Hitler for a lengthy meeting in which the dictator astonishingly portrayed serious doubts about the war in the east and even suggested that a peace initiative from Stalin would be accepted. Bolshevism without the Red Army, Hitler told Goebbels, would be no danger to Germany.[163] In the frightful reality of his strategic position, Hitler was clutching at straws. At another point he told Goebbels of his certainty that Japan would soon invade the Soviet Union.[164] Phantom peace deals and imaginary allies were no doubt soothing remedies to Hitler's troubled state of mind, but in concrete terms Hitler knew he was facing the sum of all his strategic fears – a global anti-German coalition. This was a decisive point for Hitler, which would help determine future strategy in both his conventional and his racial war.

Contemplating racial warfare Goebbels wrote after his meeting with Hitler:

---

[159] Von Hassell, *Vom andern Deutschland*, pp. 217–218 (18 August 1941); von Hassell, *Diaries*, pp. 188–189 (18 August 1941).
[160] Von Below, *Als Hitlers Adjutant 1937–45*, p. 287.
[161] Jersak, 'Die Interaktion', p. 350.
[162] Fröhlich (ed.), *Die Tagebücher von Joseph Goebbels*, Teil II, p. 259 (19 August 1941).
[163] Ibid., p. 262 (19 August 1941).   [164] Ibid., p. 263 (19 August 1941).

We talked about the Jewish problem. The Führer is convinced that his earlier prophecy in the Reichstag is proving correct, that if the Jews succeed again in provoking another world war it would end with the annihilation of the Jews. This is being proved in these weeks and months with an apparently eerie certainty. In the east the Jews must pay for this . . .[165]

August and September saw a dramatic increase in the killing of Jews, but Hitler's path to unrestrained genocide in the Soviet Union cannot be pinpointed so precisely. The Holocaust proceeded, for the most part, with verbal instructions and meetings without written records. The absence of a paper trail makes it difficult for historians to agree on the exact timing of decisions, while the available testimonies, together with surviving evidence, are sometimes contradictory or open to several interpretations.[166] Nevertheless, there can be little doubt that, by mid-August, the progress of the war had further radicalised Hitler's conception of a racial war, and drove him to authorise more extreme measures in the mass extermination of the Soviet Union's Jewish population. To implement this Himmler's mobile death squads, known as the *Einsatzgruppen*, which had been operating since the first days of the war under a more limited mandate, now undertook the systematic mass murder of whole Jewish communities. Mass shootings throughout the occupied territories were soon killing thousands of Jews every day. If there were any doubts about the nature of German occupation in the east, the mass graves of Jewish men, women and children proved there was no limit to the excesses of Nazi rule. Nor was the genocide restricted to the activities of the SS. The army assisted the *Einsatzgruppen* by marking and registering Jews, providing the killing units with supplies and transport, and sometimes assembling, guarding and even shooting the victims.[167] Even the scattered reports that were reaching the outside world were enough to hint at the horrific scale of

---

[165] Ibid., p. 269 (19 August 1941).

[166] Geoffrey Megargee has observed: 'Some historians believe that Hitler made the decision to eradicate the Jews completely before the campaign even started, and that only tactical considerations, such as a shortage of shooters, limited the killing in the first weeks. Others maintain that he decided on extermination while the campaign was going on and communicated it to the units in the field through Himmler. Still others emphasize the role of field commanders themselves in instigating actions that Himmler and Hitler then approved and encouraged. There is no way to settle the debate with any degree of certainty – we have no written order' (Megargee, *War of Annihilation*, p. 93). For a more in-depth investigation into the origins of the Holocaust see Christopher R. Browning and Jürgen Matthäus, *The Origins of the Final Solution: The Evolution of Nazi Jewish Policy, September 1939–March 1942* (London, 2005); Peter Longerich, *Der ungeschriebene Befehl: Hitler und der Weg zur 'Endlösung'* (Munich, 2001); Hilberg, *Destruction of the European Jews*.

[167] Megargee, *War of Annihilation*, p. 95. For an excellent new study assessing the role of the German army in the mass killings now taking place in the east see Hürter, *Hitlers Heerführer*, Section II, Chapter 5, 'Judenmord'.

the killing in the Soviet Union, which in fact was only just beginning. As Churchill broadcast on 24 August, 'whole districts are being extermi- nated. Scores of thousands – literally scores of thousands – of executions in cold blood are being perpetrated by the German police-troops . . . We are in the presence of a crime without a name.'[168]

Just as the anticipation of a world war brought Hitler's racial policy to its horrifying conclusion, so too did it finally bring resolution in his direc- tion of the war in the east. The clear signal from the western allies that they would not accept limited war aims, and the phenomenal demands of the fighting in the east, led Hitler to urgently reassess the course of the military campaign in the east. Even before the war, Hitler had eyed the Soviet Union's economic wealth with special interest, but this was in context of an ongoing war against Britain and possibly later the United States. There was no thought given to a continuing, high-intensity war in the east. Yet now that this prospect was an emerging reality, Hitler's interest in economic objectives assumed greatly increased importance, both as a method of weakening the Soviet state and sustaining Germany through a long conflict. Accordingly, Hitler was no longer concerned with the submissions of his generals; Moscow had never been more than a secondary objective and Hitler was now acutely aware that Germany's lack of resources could be ruinous in a world war. Thus, the mineral-rich Donets Basin in the eastern Ukraine and the oil fields of southern Russia were now unambiguously the focus of Hitler's strategic thinking. On the night of 19–20 August, Hitler was steadfastly preoccupied with visions of his economic autarky to be won in the next phase of the campaign:

It is not tolerable that the life of the peoples of the continent should depend upon England. The Ukraine, and then the Volga basin, will one day be the granaries of Europe. We shall reap much more than what actually grows from the soil . . . If one day Sweden declines to supply any more iron, that's alright. We'll get it from Russia.[169]

Although the declaration of the Atlantic Charter may well have instigated the changes in Hitler's war policy, these were not immediately apparent to Hitler's military commanders in either the OKW or OKH. Accordingly, although the Moscow operation was now a forlorn hope, Halder was still under the impression that the recently issued War Directive 34a represented grounds for encouragement that Hitler was finally being won over. Believing his approach was working, Halder sought to capitalise on his erroneous assurance that the three army groups could simultaneously

---

[168] As cited in Martin Gilbert, *The Holocaust. The Jewish Tragedy* (London, 1986), p. 186.
[169] Trevor-Roper (ed.), *Hitler's Table Talk*, p. 28 (night of 19–20 August).

achieve everything Hitler and the army wanted. Halder now sought to present his plan in written form and to give it maximum weight by again enlisting Jodl's support to produce a similar proposal from the OKW. Thus Heusinger set to work on one plan for the OKH, while Warlimont prepared another for the OKW, with both essentially arguing for the same strategic solution.

Warlimont's 'Assessment of the Eastern Situation' concluded that: 'The eastern army is strong enough for Army Groups North and South to accomplish their tasks with their own strengths, and Army Group Centre to undertake the decisive thrust on Moscow.' It was believed that a line from the Donets Basin, through Kharkov and Moscow to Leningrad could be reached by the end of the next phase of operations.[170]

Heusinger's plan began by reasserting that the enemy's main strength was concentrated opposite Bock's army group and that it was here that a decisive blow could be struck against the Red Army. Moscow's industrial potential was also highlighted, while the attainment of economic objectives in the north and south were suggested to be within the strengths of the two flanking army groups. Interestingly, the OKH plan sounded a note of urgency over the time remaining for operations and, at the same time, warned that the motorised divisions, even after their refitting, could be employed 'only over limited distances and with reduced combat strength. As a result,' the OKH plan made clear, 'their employment must be on the *one deciding operation* so that the offensive remains limited to absolutely necessary actions.'[171] Clearly, the OKH was envisioning the coming offensive as the last chance to end the war in 1941 and for this everything depended on Bock driving towards Moscow.

Warlimont's and Heusinger's plans were both presented to Hitler on 18 August, the same day on which Goebbels arrived at the Wolf's Lair. By this stage Hitler was already absorbing the implications of the unfavourable international developments, which, in addition to the escalating demands of the war, allowed him to recover his inner resolve over future strategy. Accordingly, if the latest submissions by the generals generated any doubts at all in the dictator's mind, they were short-lived. More likely, Hitler was not at all surprised, or pleased, by yet more submissions in favour of Moscow. This he may have rejected as simply the wrong strategy under the circumstances, or he may have even seen through Halder's ploy and suspected that the army was attempting to

---

[170] KTB OKW, Volume II, pp. 1054–1055, Document 94 (18 August 1941); Mendelssohn, *Die Nürnberger Dokumente*, pp. 404–405.

[171] Italics in the original. KTB OKW, Volume II, pp. 1055–1056, Document 95 (18 August 1941); Mendelssohn, *Die Nürnberger Dokumente*, pp. 406–408.

manipulate him by deliberately over-estimating German strength to gain approval for the army's plans. In any case, Hitler's mind was now made up and with the lines drawn for one last showdown, the army commanders would finally be forced to accept who really controlled events on the eastern front.

It is instructive of the muddled procedures within the German command that strategic possibilities were debated with such vigour in spite of a near total disregard for operational realities. A major operation towards Moscow was questionable not just for the demands it would place on the worn-out motorised divisions; even the most superficial assessment reveals that a further push to the east would first require large stockpiles of supplies to service the army over the long distances to come. As it was, in mid-August the 9th and 2nd Armies were living hand to mouth, unable to spare any ammunition for future operations, while the supply of fuel, oil and lubricants was likewise insufficient and did not take account of the worn state of the engines which greatly increased consumption.[172] Maintaining even these inadequate levels of supply, the trucks of the *Grosstransportraum* were being ruined on long journeys that should have been bridged by the railroads. Any hope of a renewed offensive would have to depend on an improvement in the railways for which Wagner's promises never matched reality. In August Army Group Centre needed at least 24 trains a day just to cover day-to-day consumption; in the first half of the month barely half that number arrived.[173] Thereafter Wagner promised an increase to first 30 and then 35 trains a day to establish adequate magazines for the next stage of the advance, but in practice only about 18 trains a day came through.[174]

Transporting sufficient supplies to the eastern front was the main problem, but distributing them to the forward units was also a major challenge, especially in the case of Schweppenburg's XXIV Panzer Corps which was attacking away towards the south. Although the distances covered in the advance were not large, the over-extended supply system still had great difficulty keeping up over the terrible roads. On 18 August, the diary of the 3rd Panzer Division's Quartermaster-General stated: 'The forward advance of the division is so fast that the columns are not able to

---

[172] Van Creveld, *Supplying War*, pp. 168–169.

[173] Wagner reported to Halder on 15 August that over a period of ten days in the first half of August 22, seven trains a day were reaching Army Group Centre, but this has been challenged in recent research. See Schüler, 'The Eastern Campaign', p. 213, footnote 7; Klaus Schüler, *Logistik im Russlandfeldzug. Die Rolle der Eisenbahn bei Planung, Vorbereitung und Durchführung des deutschen Angriffs auf die Sowjetunion bis zur Krise vor Moskau im Winter 1941/42* (Frankfurt am Main, 1987).

[174] Franz Halder, KTB III, pp. 178 and 183 (15 and 17 August 1941); Schüler, 'The Eastern Campaign', p. 213, footnote 7. See also van Creveld, *Supplying War*, p. 170.

keep pace.'[175] On the following day (19 August) a Soviet counter-attack caused mayhem in the rear areas by cutting across German supply lines. Schweppenburg's corps then informed Guderian's headquarters that fuel shortages and flagging offensive strengths did not allow for the capture of Novozybkov, an important town to the east of Gomel.[176] When pressed to continue the attack on 20 August, Schweppenburg's corps replied that 3rd Panzer Division was almost without fuel, the 10th Motorised Infantry Division had lost, and had to leave behind, many trucks on the bad roads, and the 4th Panzer Division was still too far to the north.[177] The war diary of 4th Panzer Division also states that on the same day (20 August) oil supplies were 'very tight' and that the division did not expect any substantial supplies for the coming two to three days. Furthermore, the number of serviceable tanks was reported to have sunk to just 44 machines, only 26 of which were Mark IIIs (20) and Mark IVs (6).[178] Accordingly, in spite of the support of the 17th Panzer Division, which was covering the eastern flank of Schweppenburg's corps against heavy enemy opposition at Pochep,[179] the corps restated that a further advance towards Novozybkov was simply not possible.[180] Bock recorded in his diary on 20 August: 'Guderian informed me that he was no longer able to take Novozybkov because XXIV Panzer Corps was at the end of its tether.'[181] Clearly, supply difficulties and declining combat strengths were inadequate for sustained offensives like those undertaken in the early weeks of the campaign. It is also apparent that, in contemplating an offensive towards Moscow, the army high command repeated its pre-invasion mistake of ignoring the immense logistical constraints under which its armies would labour. Indeed, the enforced halt of Army Group Centre throughout September still only allowed for a partial stockpiling of resources for the later advance on Moscow (Operation Typhoon), and this did not include any of the winter equipment that would shortly be required in vast quantities.[182]

As the offensive in the south was desperately struggling for modest territorial gains, further north Bock's front was staggering under the

---

[175] 'KTB 3rd Pz. Div. I.b 19.5.41 – 6.2.42' BA-MA RH 27–3/218 (18 August 1941).
[176] 'KTB Nr.1 Panzergruppe 2 Bd.II vom 22.7.1941 bis 20.8.41' BA-MA RH 21–2/928, Fol. 296 (19 August 1941).
[177] Ibid., Fol. 302 (20 August 1941).
[178] 'Kriegstagebuch 4.Panzer-Division Führungsabtl. 26.5.41 – 31.3.42' BA-MA RH 27–4/10, p. 115 (20 August 1941).
[179] Guderian, Panzer Leader, p. 196.
[180] 'KTB Nr.1 Panzergruppe 2 Bd.II vom 22.7.1941 bis 20.8.41' BA-MA RH 21–2/928, Fol. 302 (20 August 1941).
[181] Fedor von Bock, KTB 'Osten I', Fol. 68, War Diary, p. 287 (20 August 1941).
[182] Müller, 'Das Scheitern der wirtschaftlichen "Blitzkriegstrategie"', p. 979.

weight of wide dispersal and repeated enemy attacks. Hoth was concerned that his panzer group, already reduced by the dispatch of forces to the north, was too widely spread and subordinated to four separate command posts supporting 9th Army. Hoth wanted a unification of command and, owing to the losses in men and tanks, a concentration of all available forces; otherwise, he warned, a breakthrough of the Soviet front could not be achieved anywhere.[183] He was soon in a position to have his way. Strauss's ailing health allowed Hoth to replace him temporarily as commander of 9th Army.[184] In spite of his new found freedom of action, Hoth could not ignore the perpetual state of crisis which gripped his long front. On 17 August Timoshenko's heavily reinforced 19th Army, under General Ivan Konev,[185] struck the German V and VIII Army Corps, forcing them back and, over the coming days, exerted major pressure on the German front around Dukhovshchina.[186] By 20 August, the raging defensive battles had left the 161st Infantry Division so exhausted that Hoth reported to Bock he would have to commit the 7th Panzer Division to stabilise the front. Bock was wary of Soviet strength and urged Hoth to also commit the 14th Motorised Infantry Division – Hoth's last reserve. Hoth, however, did not want to wait for it to arrive and ordered the 7th Panzer Division to attack alone.[187] The result was a debacle. The 7th Panzer Division's attack ran into two fortified Soviet lines and was promptly beaten off with a loss of 30 tanks.[188]

In spite of the immense pressure being exerted against 9th Army and the disappointing results of the refitting period, Hoth was determined

[183] 'Panzerarmeeoberkommandos Anlagen zum Kriegstagesbuch "Berichte, Besprechun-gen, Beurteilungen der Lage" Bd.IV 22.7.41 – 31.8.41' BA-MA RH 21-3/47, Fol. 53 (16 August 1941).
[184] '3rd Pz. Gr. KTB 25.5.41 – 31.8.41' BA-MA Microfilm 59054, Fol. 216 (17 August 1941). Strauss returned to command the 9th Army on 5 September 1941. In January 1942 he again had to request a leave of absence on the basis of poor health, but this time his condition was much more serious. A doctor's report in April 1942 made it clear that Strauss had suffered severe heart problems and that over the past four years he had been addicted to sleeping pills. See 'Personalakten für Strauss, Adolf' BA-MA Pers 6/56, Fol. 34 (14 April 1942).
[185] Glantz, *Battle for Smolensk*, p. 62.
[186] Fedor von Bock, KTB 'Osten I', Fols. 66–67, *War Diary*, pp. 285–287 (17, 18 and 19 August 1941).
[187] 'Kriegstagebuch Nr.1 (Band August 1941) des Oberkommandos der Heeresgruppe Mitte' BA-MA RH 19II/386, pp. 355–356 (20 August 1941); Fedor von Bock, KTB 'Osten I', Fols. 67–68, *War Diary*, p. 287 (20 August 1941).
[188] '3rd Pz. Gr. KTB 25.5.41 – 31.8.41' BA-MA Microfilm 59054, Fol. 227 (21 August 1941); 'Kriegstagebuch Nr.3 der 7.Panzer-Division Führungsabteilung 1.6.1941 – 9.5.1942' BA-MA RH 27-7/46, Fol. 104 (21 August 1941). See also Bock's comments: Fedor von Bock, KTB 'Osten I', Fol. 68, *War Diary*, p. 288 (21 August 1941); Werner Haupt, *Army Group Center. The Wehrmacht in Russia 1941–1945* (Atglen, 1997), p. 67.

not to give up the planned offensive against Velikie Luki, preferring an offensive solution to try and regain the initiative and force the Soviets onto the back foot. The offensive had been set for 21 August, but this was delayed a day owing to bad weather. The offensive was undertaken by Kuntzen's LVII Panzer Corps with the attack spearheaded by the 19th and 20th Panzer Divisions, supported by the XXXX Army Corps. The attack enjoyed immediate success and by 26 August the Germans had captured Velikie Luki with 34,000 prisoners and more than 300 guns,[189] but Bock was all too aware that limited offensives like this were not going to achieve the destruction of the Red Army, nor was it adequately alleviating the pressure on his front. He wrote in his diary on 24 August:

This is the seventh or eight time in this campaign that the army group has succeeded in encircling the enemy. But I'm not really happy about it, because the objective to which I have devoted all my thought, the destruction of the enemy armies, has been dropped. [By this point Bock had learned that the offensive towards Moscow would not take place.][190]

Continuing on 25 August Bock added:

[P]erhaps we will overrun the Russians in front of my northern wing and thus get things going to the point that at least the pressure on my eastern front is relieved. It can't hold much longer the way things look now. I am being forced to spread the reserves which I so laboriously scraped together for the hoped for attack behind my front just to have some degree of security that it will not be breached. If, after all the successes, the campaign in the east now trickles away in dismal defensive fighting for my army group, it is not my fault.[191]

While Hoth was able to provoke a new crisis in the north for Soviet forces, it did not prevent more heavy assaults against the 9th Army which by 28 August worried Bock enough to consider ordering Hoth's panzers to strike south and come to the aid of the beleaguered 9th Army's left wing. Bock also contemplated a major withdrawal of 9th and 4th Army resulting in the loss of Smolensk.[192] This did not come to pass, but it demonstrates the dire state of affairs in Army Group Centre, and the effect of the seldom discussed defensive battles which hammered the German front and exacted numerous casualties from the already weakened infantry divisions. It may well be added that these Soviet attacks were only achieved at a correspondingly high cost to the Red Army,

[189] Fedor von Bock, KTB 'Osten I', Fol. 74, *War Diary*, p. 294 (26 August 1941).
[190] Ibid., Fol. 72, pp. 292–293 (24 August 1941).
[191] Ibid., Fol. 73, pp. 292–293 (24 August 1941). The English translation of this quotation incorrectly dates it to 24 August.
[192] Ibid., Fols. 75–76, p. 295 (28 August 1941); Franz Halder, KTB III, p. 202 (28 August 1941).

but while they were often extraordinarily bloody affairs their cumulative effect, since the third week of July, in bludgeoning the German blitzkrieg to a halt and plunging German forces into a sustained state of crisis should not be under-estimated.[193]

On 22 August Kluge's 4th Army was again reinstated between 2nd and 9th Armies,[194] but unlike the old 4th Panzer Army, Kluge's new army was made up of infantry divisions with extremely limited armoured support. As the static warfare took hold, Blumentritt (Kluge's Chief of Staff) commented on the ebb and flow of activity from the middle of August to the end of September.

> Without any considerable armoured support, we were reduced to trench warfare along the Desna, which made very heavy demands on the troops. The Russians attacked violently and over and over again succeeded in breaking through our thinly held lines. Tank units had to be called in to make good the damage. This taught us that in modern warfare infantry requires armoured support not only in the attack but also in the defence.
>
> When I say our lines were thin, this is not an understatement. Divisions were assigned sectors almost twenty miles wide. Furthermore, in view of the heavy casualties already suffered in the course of the campaign, these divisions were usually under strength and tactical reserves were non-existent.[195]

The problem, which was all too apparent to the infantry, if not sufficiently so to their higher commanders, was that there were nowhere near enough mobile units to back up the strung-out infantry. The result was a greatly increased level of attrition, constantly grinding down the infantry divisions in thousands of small nameless battles along the front. Describing one such encounter in late August, Heinrich Haape wrote:

> Under cover of early morning mist two regiments of Russians burst through the thinly-held lines of our neighbouring Regiment 37 and penetrated as far as their regimental battle-post... the 37th regimental commander had fallen as well as ten other officers; eight more officers were severely wounded and more than two hundred N.C.O.s and men had been killed.[196]

---

[193] It is an instructive background to the megalomaniac practices of the Nazi state that throughout 1941, in spite of the demands of the front, Hitler refused to scale back any of the enormous building projects he had commissioned for Berlin and Nuremberg. Albert Speer, Hitler's architect and later minister for armaments, explained that on 20 August he told an astonished Admiral Lorey, the commander of the Berlin armoury, that on Hitler's orders he needed 230 captured pieces of heavy enemy artillery to line Berlin's central boulevard. Any extra large tanks were to be reserved for positioning in front of important buildings. In addition, contracts to the value of 30 million Reichsmarks were awarded to companies in Sweden, Norway and Finland for granite. Speer, *Inside the Third Reich*, p. 259.

[194] Franz Halder, KTB III, p. 187 (18 August 1941).

[195] Blumentritt, 'Moscow', pp. 51–52.

[196] Haape with Henshaw, *Moscow Tram Stop*, p. 112.

Another soldier from 9th Army serving in the 35th Infantry Division wrote home on 19 August of the worrying toll the fighting was having.

At the moment we are part of the Army reserve – and high time – we have already lost 50 men in the company. It should not be allowed to continue much longer otherwise the burden will be really too heavy. We normally have four men on the [anti-tank] gun, but for two days at a particularly dangerous point, we only had two. The others were wounded.[197]

On 20 August a report from the 2nd Army's 267th Infantry Division stated that in the preceding six days the division had lost around 1,000 men and that, since the start of the war in the east, the division had suffered some 2,700 casualties. In the LIII Army Corps (to which the 267th Infantry Division belonged) losses by 22 August totalled 192 officers and 5,500 men.[198] At the beginning of the war the average German infantry division consisted of about 17,000 men.[199] By the end of August 1941 casualties affected the divisions as follows: in 14 divisions losses exceeded 4,000 men; in 40 divisions over 3,000; in 30 divisions over 2,000 and in 58 under 2,000.[200]

On 21 August the fighting around the Yel'nya salient began to ease off as the Soviet 24th Army regrouped and received reinforcements in preparation for a major offensive at the end of the month.[201] Even in this period of relative quiet, the German IX Army Corps defending the northern flank of the salient was so badly under strength that the engineers, desperately needed behind the front building roads, spent weeks fighting as infantry. The description of this period as 'quiet' is all the more remarkable for the rate of losses still being sustained. The 137th Infantry Division was losing over 50 men a day in local actions between 20 and 30 August, while the neighbouring 263rd Infantry Division lost 1,200 men between 20 and 27 August, equalling about 150 men every day.[202] After a tour of inspection at Yel'nya, Halder was informed: 'Troops very strained. Enemy artillery activity very unpleasant. Our munition use limited. Mines and wire absent.'[203] At the end of August, the looming Soviet offensive finally struck with eight Soviet rifle divisions, two tank divisions and one motorised infantry division, backed by 800 guns, mortars and

[197] As quoted in Kershaw, *War Without Garlands*, p. 117.
[198] Lammers (ed.), *Fahrtberichte*, pp. 255–257 (20 and 22 August 1941).
[199] Overmans, *Deutsche militärische Verluste*, p. 277.
[200] Müller-Hillebrand, *Das Heer 1933–1945*, Band III, p. 19.
[201] Glantz, *Battle for Smolensk*, p. 74.
[202] Geyer, *Das IX. Armeekorps im Ostfeldzug 1941*, p. 122. See also 'Kriegstagebuch Nr.1 (Band August 1941) des Oberkommandos der Heeresgruppe Mitte' BA-MA RH 19II/386, p. 381 (25 August 1941).
[203] Franz Halder, KTB III, p. 182 (16 August 1941).

multiple rocket launchers. The Soviet forces of Zhukov's Reserve Front were organised into two shock groups to the north and south of the salient, and for the first time the whole offensive was co-ordinated with simultaneous offensives by Western Front in the north at Dukhovshchina and Briansk Front in the south at Roslavl and Novozybkov.[204] On the first day of the offensive (30 August) the Soviets penetrated ten kilometres into Kluge's southern flank and Bock was forced to send two divisions (including the 10th Panzer Division) to restore the situation.[205] Heavy fighting ensued, until finally on 2 September Bock decided to abandon the Yel'nya salient, claiming that it served no purpose and that divisions deployed there were simply 'bled white' over time.[206] Thus, after six weeks of the heaviest fighting and untold losses, the Yel'nya salient ulti-mately proved worthless – an appalling example of Army Group Centre's aimless strategic direction. As Franz Frisch, who fought in those battles, later wrote:

Officially it was called a 'planned withdrawal', and a 'correction of the front lines.' . . . But to me it was so much bullshit. The Russians were kicking us badly and we had to regroup . . . The next day – or maybe a few days later – we heard on the radio, in the 'news from the front' (*Wehrmachtsbericht*) about the 'successful front correction' in our Yel'nya defensive line, which was east of Smolensk, and the enormous losses we had inflicted on the enemy. But no single word was heard about a retreat, about the hopelessness of the situation, about the mental and emotional stagnation and numbness of the German soldiers. In short, it was again a 'victory'. But we on the front line were running back like rabbits in front of the fox. This metamorphosis of the truth from 'all shit' to 'it was a victory' baffled me, and those of my comrades who dared to think.[207]

Frisch was not the only German soldier to be shocked by the huge discrepancy between wartime propaganda and the reality of life at the front. Georg Grossjohann, an officer who had been stationed in France during the first weeks of Barbarossa, wrote after the war:

When I was moved to the east [in the late summer of 1941] I was actually convinced that I would be too late to see action. *Reichspressechef* [German press chief] Dr Dietrich declared on the radio that all that was needed in Russia from that point in the late summer would be 'police actions'. Well, I was taught differently when I arrived there . . . There was tremendous bitterness amongst the

---

[204] Glantz, *Battle for Smolensk*, pp. 74–76.
[205] Fedor von Bock, KTB 'Osten I', Fol. 78, *War Diary*, p. 298 (30 August 1941).
[206] Ibid., Fol. 82, p. 302 (2 September 1941).
[207] Frisch with Jones, Jr., *Condemned to Live*, pp. 74–77.

infantry soldiers at the front over the misinterpretation and misunderstanding of the realities of their situation.[208]

In the late summer of 1941 images of long victorious advances into the open spaces of enemy territory belonged to propaganda reels of past wars. For the average German *Landser* the day-to-day reality of life on the eastern front had assumed a more frightening similarity to the torments of trench warfare. Corporal W.F. wrote on 22 August: 'We have suffered greatly under the Russian artillery fire and we must live day and night in our foxholes in order to gain protection from shrapnel. The holes are full of water. Lice and other types of vermin have already snuck in.'[209] Erich Mende noted how it was impossible to dig down deep because after just 50 centimetres ground water was already appearing.[210] Another soldier, Harald Henry, wrote home in a letter on 18 August: 'It would be no overstatement to declare "a dog wouldn't want to go on living like this", as no animal could live lower or more primitively than us. All day long we squat under the ground, twisted in narrow holes, taking sun and rain with no respite and try to sleep.'[211] If the living conditions were harsh, they were made worse by the terrors of combat which dominated life on the front. In another letter written only days later (22 August) Henry despaired at the mental anguish he was enduring.

Yesterday was a day so immersed in blood, so full of dead and wounded, so blasted by crackling salvoes, shrapnel from shells and groans and shrieks of the wounded, that I can not yet write about it . . . As if by a wonder I was drawn from the heaviest fighting in the afternoon and remain until now unhurt . . . At any rate my old non-commissioned officer Grabke and many other comrades are dead.[212]

Far from the triumphant announcements of unprecedented victories, the war in the east was only just settling down to a steady rhythm of murderous routine. As Theodor Mogge, a non-commissioned artillery officer in 2nd Army, poignantly observed, 'every day brought new victims'.[213] By the end of August, after only nine weeks of war against the Soviet Union, German losses had reached 14,457 officers and almost 400,000 men. Statistically, slightly more than one man in every ten was now a casualty.[214] Reserves from the Replacement Army were already marching

[208] Georg Grossjohann, *Five Years, Four Fronts. The War Years of Georg Grossjohann, Major, German Army (Retired)* (Bedford, 1999), pp. 40–41.
[209] As quoted in Fritz, *Frontsoldaten*, p. 62.
[210] As quoted in Knopp, *Der verdammte Krieg*, p. 91.
[211] Bähr and Bähr (eds.), *Kriegsbriefe gefallener Studenten*, p. 74 (18 August 1941).
[212] Ibid., p. 75 (22 August 1941).
[213] Theodor Mogge's unpublished account was recorded in 1978.
[214] Franz Halder, KTB III, p. 213 (3 September 1941).

east to cover some of these losses,[215] but manpower replacements were rapidly being exhausted and the war was only just beginning. The long bloody battles and soaring losses had a profound effect on the men who were reminded time and again of how cheap life was on the eastern front. Having already seen so much death on the march to Smolensk Siegfried Knappe chose to accept his own death would result from the war.

> I had to become fatalistic about it and assume that eventually it would happen to me and there was nothing I could do to prevent it . . . I knew that I was going to be killed or badly wounded sooner or later. The odds against my escaping unscathed were impossibly high, and I accepted my eventual death or maiming as part of my fate. Once I forced myself to accept that, I could put it out of my mind and go on about my duties.[216]

Just as the infantry were enduring at first hand the trials of attritional warfare, so too was the Luftwaffe having to adapt to ever more extreme operational conditions. In past campaigns a hallmark of the Luftwaffe's success was its versatile ability to move forward with the army, and provide constant air support even as the axis of operations shifted from one front to another and the army penetrated ever deeper into enemy territory. This was initially true of the Luftwaffe's operations in the east too, but here the method quickly revealed a conspicuous fragility, which the unceasing fighting and depth of operations badly exacerbated. The forward airfields were poorly serviced, exposed to attack and severely under-supplied. The result was predictably calamitous, as one German officer observed: 'The constant movement of flying formations, usually without adequate ground personnel, resulted in such bad servicing that a *Luftflotte* [Air Fleet] had often on a sector of about 400 km only 10–12 serviceable fighter aircraft.'[217] As sectors of the German front rapidly became devoid of protective air cover, the Soviet air force was left an increasingly free hand. Heinrici wrote on 9 August that one Soviet bomber attack had alone killed 90 horses and 'a great many men'.[218] The 7th Panzer Division's war diary for 22 August reported: 'Throughout the whole day the enemy had complete air superiority. The division has until now heavy losses through bombing attacks.'[219] On the same day the diary of the 3rd Panzer Division noted: 'In the course of the afternoon there were constant, and at times costly, attacks on the division by

---

[215] Ibid., p. 199 (26 August 1941).   [216] Knappe with Brusaw, *Soldat*, p. 219.
[217] As quoted in Muller, *The German Air War in Russia*, p. 57.
[218] Hürter, *Ein deutscher General*, p. 74 (9 August 1941).
[219] 'Kriegstagebuch Nr.3 der 7.Panzer-Division Führungsabteilung 1.6.1941 – 9.5.1942' BA-MA RH 27-7/46, Fol. 104 (22 August 1941).

high flying bombers.'[220] Lemelsen's XXXXVII Panzer Corps reported
on 30 August: 'Absolute enemy air supremacy. Up to midday a total of
69 bomber attacks.' Days later the same panzer corps complained that
the 'Red air force is master of the skies. No fighter cover. Human and
material losses due to bombing.'[221] A tour of the front on 21 August
by Field Marshal Erhard Milch, the Inspector-General of the Luftwaffe,
revealed that the airfields in the east were littered with scores, sometimes
hundreds, of damaged aircraft.[222] From an assessment of Richthofen's
VIII Air Corps it is not hard to see why. The VIII Air Corps had been
transferred to Leeb's army group to aid the drive on Leningrad, but in
just 12 days from 10 to 21 August the corps lost an astonishing 10.3
per cent of its aircraft to enemy action and had another 54.5 per cent of
its aircraft classed as damaged but repairable. At the same time, 3.9 per
cent of its flying personnel were killed, 5.7 per cent were wounded and
2.9 per cent were listed as missing, equalling a combined attrition rate of
12.5 per cent in less than two weeks.[223] General Karl Koller, the Luftwaffe's last Chief of the General Staff, described Richthofen's high losses
as 'heartless' and felt that 'owing to his privileged position' with Göring
and Jeschonnek, Richthofen was untroubled by high casualties, always
certain that he could count on an adequate flow of replacements.[224] Yet
owing to the Luftwaffe's incompetent management and wayward strategic direction, not to mention Germany's industrial bottlenecks, there was
no appreciable increase in aircraft production to cover the heavy losses
now being sustained.[225] As a result, the Luftwaffe was seriously over-
committed and beginning its long decline, as it attempted to maintain
operations simultaneously in the east, the Mediterranean and against
Britain.

Just as Bock's army group was suffering from a critical lack of resources
to deal with the excessive demands of its long front, so too were the
two neighbouring army groups feeling the stress of over-extension. In
the south, following Rundstedt's victory at Uman, General Georg von
Sodenstern, the Chief of the General Staff of Army Group South, warned
Halder on 10 August of the mounting difficulties confronting operations
in the south. As Sodenstern explained, 'the sudden change in the estimate of the situation' was based less on an evaluation of the enemy

---

[220] 'KTB 3rd Pz. Div. vom 16.8.40 bis 18.9.41' BA-MA RH 27–3/14, p. 187 (22 August
1941).
[221] As quoted in Steiger, *Armour Tactics*, p. 69.
[222] David Irving, *The Rise and Fall of the Luftwaffe: The Life of Erhard Milch* (London,
1973), p. 131.
[223] Murray, *The Luftwaffe*, p. 84.   [224] Muller, *German Air War in Russia*, p. 57.
[225] Boog, 'Die Luftwaffe', pp. 300–301.

situation than 'a revised assessment of the capabilities of our own troops. They are simply exhausted and have heavy losses.'[226] The following day (11 August) Halder recorded in his diary that the 6th Army was suffering a daily loss of 1,600 casualties, of which some 380 were deaths.[227] In the 98th Infantry Division (belonging to the 6th Army) one regiment alone reported losing 1,200 men and 37 officers between 31 July and 10 August.[228] Towards the end of August the motorised divisions of Kleist's panzer group were estimated to be at 50 per cent strength.[229] Nor was it possible to provide the army group with the promised 12 supply trains a day; indeed on some days only half this number arrived.[230]

In Army Group North, over-extension increasingly slowed operations throughout August, but Leeb's offensive was buttressed by Hitler's Leningrad bias and this ensured him the support of first Richthofen's VIII Air Corps and then Schmidt's XXXIX Panzer Corps. Even with such external aid, the drive to cut off Leningrad was not achieved until 8 September and the following assault to break through to the city proved a costly failure. Supply trains were also well short of the required number in August, and while the ratio improved in September it was still less than the minimum needed.[231] Further north, on the distant Finnish Front, the German XXXVI Army Corps had been heavily engaged in a failed operation to cut the vital Murmansk railway at Kandalaksha. By 13 September the Corps' two divisions had together sustained 9,463 casualties and the 169th Infantry Division was judged no longer capable of holding even a defensive position.[232]

To have any confidence about breaking the Red Army's resistance and ending the war in 1941, a great deal of hope was placed in the refitting of the two panzer groups in Army Group Centre that had been underway since early August. Guderian had originally said he would have finished his refitting by 15 August, but delays in the arrival of spare parts and replacement engines, as well as the constant action of his forces especially in the south, meant that his panzer group was scarcely in better shape than before the refitting began. On 19 August Panzer Group 2 notified Army Group Centre of the results of its refitting and the subsequent combat readiness of its panzer corps. Schweppenburg's XXIV Panzer Corps and Lemelsen's XXXXVII Panzer Corps were still in action south

---

[226] Franz Halder, KTB III, p. 167 (10 August 1941).
[227] Ibid., p. 172 (11 August 1941).   [228] Gareis, *Kampf*, p. 125.
[229] Franz Halder, KTB III, p. 202 (28 August 1941).
[230] Klaus Schüler, 'The Eastern Campaign', p. 213, footnote 6.
[231] Ibid., p. 213, footnotes 6 and 8.
[232] Earl F. Ziemke, *The German Northern Theater of Operations 1940–1945* (Washington DC, 1959), p. 176.

of Roslavl and their respective time spent refitting was reported as: 'XXIV Panzer Corps at no time since the beginning of the war. XXXXVII Panzer Corps only with the 18th Panzer Division fully allowed rest.' The recommendation of the panzer group was that both panzer corps needed ten days of technical refitting to make good material losses and four days of rest for the personnel. Vietinghoff's XXXXVI Panzer Corps was only relieved from its latest commitment to the volatile Yel'nya salient on the same day the report was prepared (19 August), and even then one brigade remained at the front. The corps was reported to be in need of rest and repairs, which for personnel and equipment would require until 23 August. Yet undermining any prospective extension to the refitting process were the same two problems which until now had proved so detrimental. The first was the constant commitment of panzer forces to action, and the second was the persistent lack of spare parts. Even on 19 August, four days after the refitting was due to be completed, Panzer Group 2 informed Bock's command: 'The technical refitting of all corps depends on the arrival of the spare parts.' Furthermore, with a view to the worn and dust-spoilt engines of the panzer group, the report advised that future operations would need to take into account the increased oil consumption.[233] As an example of how extreme the situation was becoming, the 10th Panzer Division reported on 17 August:

The condition of the trucks is in large part bad... For major repairs, which are necessary for many trucks, there are no spare parts. It must therefore be understood that with the beginning of a new operation, trucks will have to be towed in order to take them with us.[234]

Hoth's panzer group also prepared a report to Army Group Centre on its combat readiness with a similarly pessimistic conclusion regarding its success in refitting the panzer divisions. Hoth had originally stated that his refitting would be finished on 20 August, but the report produced on 21 August revealed that the number of available panzers had not substantially increased at all. Figures for the combat readiness of the individual panzer divisions were listed as follows: 7th Panzer Division 45 per cent (it had been at 60 per cent until the aforementioned total loss of 30 panzers), 19th Panzer Division 60 per cent, 20th Panzer Division 49 per cent and 12th Panzer Division 45 per cent

[233] 'KTB Nr.1 Panzergruppe 2 Bd.II vom 22.7.1941 bis 20.8.41' BA-MA RH 21–2/928, Fol. 294 (19 August 1941).
[234] 'Kriegstagebuch der 10.Panzer Division Nr.5 vom: 22.5. bis: 7.10.41' BA-MA RH 27–10/26b (17 August 1941).

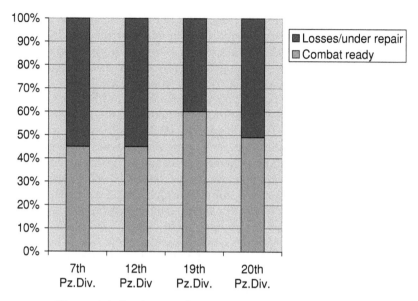

Figure 9.4 Combat readiness of Panzer Group 3 on 21 August 1941. 'Panzerarmeeoberkommandos Anlagen zum Kriegstagesbuch "Berichte, Besprechungen, Beurteilungen der Lage" Bd.IV 22.7.41–31.8.41' BA-MA RH 21-3/47, Fols. 78–79 (21 August 1941).

(see Figure 9.4).[235] The overall average panzer strength was therefore about 50 per cent, which is the same figure Halder reported almost a month before at the end of the long advance towards Smolensk.[236] Figures demonstrating personnel shortages also highlight the manpower deficiency within the panzer group. The 19th and 20th Panzer Divisions were at 75–80 per cent of full strength. The 7th Panzer Division was at 70 per cent strength and the 14th Motorised Infantry Division was at 50–60 per cent strength. Both of these divisions, however, were expected to be raised to 80 per cent strength with the arrival of reinforcements, although it is not clear from the document when this was expected to take place.[237] The serviceability of trucks for the panzer group was one area where the refitting period appeared to have made some significant improvements, although these were, in practice, short-term remedies. At

[235] 'Panzerarmeeoberkommandos Anlagen zum Kriegstagesbuch "Berichte, Besprechungen, Beurteilungen der Lage" Bd.IV 22.7.41 – 31.8.41' BA-MA RH 21-3/47, Fols. 78–79 (21 August 1941).
[236] Franz Halder, KTB III, p. 104 (23 July 1941).
[237] Figures for Schmidt's XXXIX Panzer Corps (12th Panzer Division, 18th and 20th Motorised Infantry Divisions) were not listed.

first glance the figures appear rather encouraging. Among the motorised infantry divisions the 20th was at 92 per cent of full strength, the 14th at 90 per cent and the 18th at 75 per cent strength. For the panzer divisions the results were somewhat less successful. The 12th was at 82 per cent of its full complement, the 19th at 80 per cent, the 7th at 75 per cent and the 20th at 70 per cent. As if to dissuade Bock's army group from drawing an overly optimistic conclusion, it was made clear that the high number of French vehicles in the panzer group were almost at the end of their serviceability. For example, it was warned that the trucks in the 14th Motorised Infantry Division, which was now outfitted with 90 per cent of its original fleet, had 'only a limited life expectancy'. Similarly the 20th Panzer Division, with 70 per cent of its full strength, was noted to have 'French trucks, which will not survive much longer'.[238] Yet, even for those divisions with German trucks, the outlook was not fundamentally different and the prospect of a long advance over terrible roads would quickly see a sharp spike in the fallout rate.

On 22 August Army Group Centre's war diary concluded: 'The armoured units are so battle-weary and worn-out that there can be no question of a mass operative mission until they have been completely replenished and repaired.'[239] Two days later General Buhle reported to Halder that the combat strength of the infantry divisions across the eastern front had been reduced on average by 40 per cent and the panzer divisions by 50 per cent.[240] By the end of August panzer losses across the whole of the eastern front had reached 1,488, with Hitler still determined to withhold most of the new domestic production of panzers for later campaigns. As a result, only 96 replacements were released out of 815 new models produced between June and August 1941. Based on starting totals given on 22 June 1941, on 4 September the number of available panzers were as follows: total losses constituted about 30 per cent, those classified as under repair came to 23 per cent, leaving just 47 per cent ready for action. Within Army Group Centre, however, only 34 per cent of tanks were classed as ready for action.[241] Hoth's panzer group, reduced to three panzer divisions

[238] 'Panzerarmeeoberkommandos Anlagen zum Kriegstagesbuch "Berichte, Besprechungen, Beurteilungen der Lage"' Bd.IV 22.7.41 – 31.8.41' BA-MA RH 21-3/47, Fols. 78–79 (21 August 1941). See also '3rd Pz. Gr. KTB 25.5.41 – 31.8.41' BA-MA Microfilm 59054, Fol. 231 (23 August 1941).
[239] 'Kriegstagebuch Nr.1 (Band August 1941) des Oberkommandos der Heeresgruppe Mitte' BA-MA RH 19II/386, p. 364 (22 August 1941).
[240] Franz Halder, KTB III, p. 195 (23 August 1941).
[241] Müller, 'Das Scheitern der wirtschaftlichen "Blitzkriegstrategie"', p. 976.

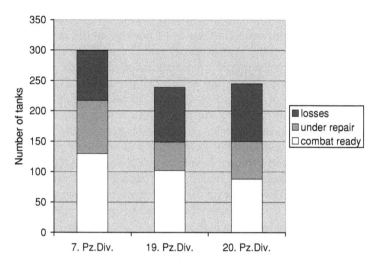

Figure 9.5 Combat readiness of Panzer Group 3 on 4 September 1941.
Burkhart Müller-Hillebrand, *Das Heer 1933–1945*, Band III, p. 205.

after the 12th Panzer Division was subordinated to the 16th Army, retained only 41 per cent of its initial strength (see Figure 9.5). Guderian's panzer group, reduced to four panzer divisions after the 10th Panzer Division was subordinated to 4th Army, fielded just 25 per cent of its original strength (see Figure 9.6).[242] The fact that Bock's advance had already been stalled for a month clearly shows that the stiff Soviet resistance had had a ruinous impact on German plans. Even after the long pause, on 22 August large-scale operations were judged to be out of the question. At the same time, a long-term defence of the eastern front was determined to be 'unbearable'.[243] The principal commanders at Army Group Centre and at the OKH correctly determined that Hitler's preference for a southward swing would not lead to a comprehensive victory over the Soviet Union in 1941, yet their own plans for shattering the Red Army and seizing Moscow were reflective of the same wildly unrealistic optimism that had undermined Barbarossa from the very beginning. By the end of August it was clear that Operation Barbarossa would fail in its essential goal to conquer the Soviet Union, which by extension destined Germany to almost certain defeat in a world war. The short window of opportunity to strike down the Soviet colossus had passed and the so-called 'Russian front' would continue to devour strength at

---

[242] Müller-Hillebrand, *Das Heer 1933–1945*, Band III, pp. 20 and 205.
[243] Franz Halder, KTB III, p. 195 (22 August 1941).

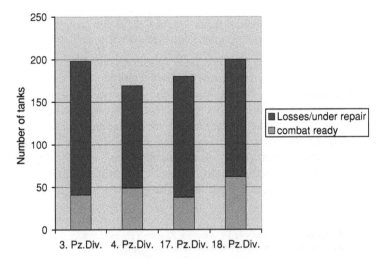

Figure 9.6 Combat readiness of Panzer Group 2 on 4 September 1941.
Burkhart Müller-Hillebrand, *Das Heer 1933–1945*, Band III, p. 205.

an insufferable rate for German manpower reserves and military production. The arrival of winter would hit the struggling German armies with devastating effect and complete the 'hollowing out' of German divisions, leaving many undermanned and inadequately equipped for much of the rest of the war. The implications of Barbarossa's failure were already disturbingly apparent to some commanders. Hans von Luck records the commander of the 7th Panzer Division telling his men: 'This war is going to last longer than we would like . . . The days of the Blitzkrieg are over.'[244] Another German officer, Colonel Bernd von Kleist, described the situation metaphorically: 'The German Army in fighting Russia is like an elephant attacking a host of ants. The elephant will kill thousands, perhaps even millions, of ants, but in the end their numbers will overcome him, and he will be eaten to the bone.'[245] On the Soviet side, Stalin's most successful commander of the war, Marshal Zhukov, summed up the German summer campaign.

Gross miscalculations and mistakes were made in political and strategic estimates. The forces at Germany's disposal, even including satellite reserves, were clearly inadequate for waging simultaneous operations in the three major sectors of the Soviet–German front. Because of this the enemy was compelled to halt his drive

[244] Von Luck, *Panzer Commander*, p. 60.
[245] As quoted in Clark, *Barbarossa*, p. 55. Clark provides no date for this quote, but includes it in his discussion of the early summer campaign.

towards Moscow and to assume defensive positions on that front in order to divert part of the forces of Army Group Centre to the support of Army Group South, facing our troops on the Central and Southwest fronts.[246]

While the German generals later found it convenient to blame Hitler's interference, the harshness of the Soviet climate, and the sheer numerical superiority of the Soviet Union, the fact remains that their plans for the conquest of the Soviet Union were simply attempting too much. Germany's successes in the early weeks of the war were enough to severely batter the Red Army, yet these came at an unexpectedly high cost to the motorised divisions upon which the blitzkrieg's success depended. While Germany still needed to do more – in fact much more – to topple the Soviet Union in late August 1941, the offensive strength simply no longer existed.

[246] Harrison E. Salisbury (ed.), *Marshal Zhukov's Greatest Battles* (London, 1971), p. 155. See also Besymenski, *Sonderakte Barbarossa*, pp. 299–300.

10 Showdown

Hitler's triumph in defeat

Hitler's long period of procrastination before finally reaching a decision over strategy in the east was not without consequences for commanders on the front. The absence of a clear strategic directive caused hesitancy and confusion about where particular forces were to be deployed along the front, and what timetable they could expect for the commencement of operations. There were also major strategic questions such as the holding of the Yel'nya salient which was being stubbornly defended on nothing more than an assumption of what the next phase of the campaign would be. The uncertainty was especially troubling for Guderian as he was constantly unsure how much strength he should devote to his offensive in the south. On 18 August he wrote in a letter to his wife:

This situation has a bad effect upon on the troops, for everyone is aware of the absence of harmony. That is the product of unclear orders and counter-orders, absence of instructions sometimes for weeks . . . we are missing so many opportunities. But it is annoying when no one knows the reasons. These most probably cannot be put right in this war which we will win despite it all. That is human nature in great moments and with great men.[1]

Guderian's Chief of Staff, Colonel Kurt Freiherr von Liebenstein, also noted the absence of clarity and even the outright contradictions in the issuing of orders, leading to his conclusion: 'The troops must think we are crazy.'[2] While Guderian's forces were constantly being pushed south by Hitler's desire to clean up the southern flank and exploit successes, at the army group headquarters, under Bock's wilful tutelage, there was an attempt to resolve the ambiguity by favouring Moscow as the clear priority. When Greiffenburg met with Weckmann on 17 August to clarify the coming offensive operations, the Chief of Staff of Army Group Centre told his counterpart at 9th Army: 'The enemy in front of the army group is to be destroyed. The armies will break through

---

[1] Guderian's letter as cited by Macksey, *Guderian*, p. 144.   [2] Ibid., p. 146.

in the general direction of Moscow.'[3] Similarly, on 19 August Bock set his sights firmly on Moscow and urged Weichs to make all haste in concluding the operations in the south. This, together with a successful drive towards Velikie Luki, would mean in Bock's estimation, 'the entire army group can attack towards the east'.[4]

The joint proposals prepared and submitted by Warlimont and Heusinger on 18 August had received no direct response from Hitler by 20 August and so Heusinger was sent to meet with Jodl in order to gauge the mood at the Wolf's Lair. Jodl had certainly been predisposed towards Halder's plans, but his interview with Heusinger now betrayed real doubts. Jodl certainly possessed an intimate knowledge of Hitler's moods and frame of mind, and the events of the past days must have impressed upon Jodl the dictator's rejuvenated determination and stubborn unwillingness for any further deliberation on his chosen strategic solution. Jodl was also extremely wary of challenging Hitler when he knew his mind was made up, which stemmed partly from raw pragmatism, but also owed a debt to the enduring Führer myth of which Jodl was a compliant disciple. Thus, according to Heusinger's account, Jodl was now quite reluctant to have anything more to do with the OKH's plans. Undeterred, Heusinger again pressed the importance of Moscow and defeating the 'life strength' of the Red Army. After this, he concluded, 'everything else will fall into our lap'. Jodl is said to have retorted: 'That's what *you* say. Now let me tell you what the Führer's answer will be: There is at the moment a much better possibility of beating the Russian forces. Their main grouping is now east of Kiev.' Heusinger, however, stood his ground and raised the issue of the coming winter which, he reminded Jodl, would arrive earlier in the northern and central sectors than in the south. Ultimately Jodl agreed to continue doing what he could to support the OKH's plans, but his resolve was clearly weakening and he warned Heusinger: 'You must admit that the Führer's reasons are well thought out though and cannot be pushed aside just like that . . . One must not try to compel him to do something which goes against his inner convictions. His intuition has generally been right. You can't deny that!'[5]

The fact that Halder's support at the OKW was drying up came as a direct result of Hitler's new found sense of purpose and the emphatic tone with which he now dictated the strategic goals of the campaign. On the same day that Heusinger was appealing for continued support from Jodl (20 August), Hitler was unequivocal in his rejection of the

---

[3] 'Kriegstagebuch Nr.1 (Band August 1941) des Oberkommandos der Heeresgruppe Mitte' BA-MA RH 19II/386, p. 341 (17 August 1941).
[4] Fedor von Bock, KTB 'Osten I', Fol. 67, *War Diary*, p. 287 (19 August 1941).
[5] Italics in original. Heusinger, *Befehl im Widerstreit*, pp. 132–135.

OKH's memorandum.[6] With clear instructions for the future course of the war, the subservient OKW soon abandoned any independent ideas, and indeed sought to rein in the wayward OKH. On 21 August the head of the OKW, Field Marshal Keitel, appeared at Halder's headquarters with the task, according to Warlimont, of winning Halder over to Hitler's point of view, or at least weakening his opposition to the diversion of Bock's panzers.[7] Keitel must have known that Hitler's mind was already firmly made up; he was careful, however, not to disappoint all of Halder's hopes and left the army's Chief of Staff with the impression that Hitler's final decision was still pending. Instead, Keitel told Halder that Hitler was insisting on carrying through the northern operation towards Leningrad, and in the south sought to eliminate the Soviet 5th Army.[8] If Keitel tried to convince Halder of Hitler's strategic wisdom it was probably nothing more than Halder expected from a man with such blind obedience to the Führer. In any case, Halder had never hoped for, nor counted on, support from Keitel. Whatever passed between them that day, it seems from Halder's record of the meeting that he still had no idea just how far events had progressed against him. On that same day (21 August), Hitler instructed Jodl to draft new orders for the OKH detailing the direction of future operations.[9] These would reach Halder's office late in the evening and strike, according to Heusinger, 'like a bomb'.[10] Hitler's army adjutant, Major Engel, simply dubbed it: 'A black day for the army'.[11]

As soon as Halder had read the new dictate from Hitler he knew all his plans and hopes had come to nothing. Hitler's order was a devastating blow and left Halder uncertain of how exactly the war was to be won. Writing in his diary Halder ominously pronounced: 'It is decisive for the outcome of the campaign.'[12] Hitler's directive began:

The proposal by the army for the continuation of the operations in the east, dated 18.8, do not meet with my approval. I order the following:
    The principal objective that must be achieved before the onset of winter is not the capture of Moscow, but rather in the south the occupation of the Crimea and the industrial and coal region of the Donets, together with the isolation of the Russian oil regions in the Caucasus. In the north, the encirclement of Leningrad and the union with the Finns.[13]

---

[6] KTB OKW, Volume II, p. 1061, Document 97 (20 August 1941); Mendelssohn, *Die Nürnberger Dokumente*, p. 411.
[7] Warlimont, *Im Hauptquartier*, Band I, p. 203. Warlimont's memoir states that Jodl accompanied Keitel, but Halder's diary makes no mention of Jodl.
[8] Franz Halder, KTB III, p. 191 (21 August 1941).
[9] Warlimont, *Im Hauptquartier*, Band I, p. 204.
[10] As cited in Meyer, *Heusinger*, p. 156.
[11] Von Kotze (ed.), *Heeresadjutant bei Hitler 1938–1943*, p. 110 (21 August 1941).
[12] Franz Halder, KTB III, p. 192 (22 August 1941).
[13] KTB OKW, Volume II, p. 1062, Document 99 (21 August 1941).

Army Group Centre was now to co-operate with Army Group South in order to enact an encirclement of the Soviet 5th Army in the region east of Kiev. With the Dneper crossed and the Soviet southern front in ruins, Army Group South would then be free to advance eastwards and seize the industrial centres of Rostov and Kharkhov. Hitler also placed great importance on the capture of the Crimea insisting it was 'of paramount importance for safeguarding our oil supply from Romania'.[14]

As the OKH reeled from the totality of its rebuff, there was still worse to come when on the following day (22 August) a second memorandum arrived personally dictated by Hitler. It was a so-called 'study' of the general situation and purported to lecture the generals at OKH on the importance of strategic goals and operational methods. It also included a scathing attack on the leadership of the army, citing poor management and a failure to provide adequate direction which, by contrast, was being superbly exhibited by Göring in command of the Luftwaffe. The study began with Hitler's long-espoused argument that eliminating the Soviet Union would deny Britain its last remaining continental ally, and thereby eradicate all hope of altering the course of events in Europe. To do this Hitler stated that two objectives had to be achieved. First, the resistance of the Red Army had to be broken and, second, the industrial base of the Soviet Union had to be either occupied or destroyed to prevent any reorganisation of Soviet forces. Having emphasised the strategic goals of the campaign, Hitler turned his attention to operational aspects and returned in veiled fashion to his earlier preoccupation with smaller encirclements. Hitler wanted the infantry to participate more directly in the battles of encirclement in order to prevent the escape of Soviet forces from the pockets. Following the OKH's plan and continuing operations into the distant east, in Hitler's opinion, failed to acknowledge what had been learned from past battles and also ignored the favourable strategic opportunity to hit the Soviet flanks in the north and especially in the south. Hitler also criticised the OKH for failing to grasp the concept of concentration and splitting up the valuable motorised divisions and Luftwaffe units among the various armies and army corps along the front. Failure to recognise that successful mobile warfare depended on unifying these forces under a single high command was only fully understood by Göring and, accordingly, he came in for much praise at the expense of the army.

In spite of his determination to divert Bock's remaining strength to the flanks, Hitler was not opposed to the idea of an operation towards Moscow, but this would have to wait until after Leningrad and the

[14] Ibid., p. 1063 (21 August 1941).

Ukraine were within Germany's reach. The argument that a delay in the drive on Moscow would not leave enough time or find the motorised and panzer divisions primed for such a plan, was also countered by Hitler. The elimination of the threat to Bock's southern flank would compensate for any other loss of strength and in fact make the later offensive, in Hitler's words, 'not more difficult, but considerably easier'.[15]

At the OKH Halder was beside himself with fury. After the crushing setback of Hitler's first directive, the arrival of Hitler's 'study' effectively blaming the OKH for all the army's woes, was simply too much. Writing in the privacy of his diary Halder openly criticised Hitler. 'I regard the situation created by the Führer's interference unendurable for the OKH. No other but the Führer himself is to blame for the zigzag course caused by his successive orders.' Furthermore, Halder protested that the 'study' was 'filled with contradictory statements' and inexcusably placed Göring well above Brauchitsch. Halder also recorded that Brauchitsch was accused of being swayed by the special interests of the individual army groups.[16] Although Halder singles out Brauchitsch as the subject of Hitler's criticism, the document is not so specific and should rather be taken to include the whole OKH, especially Halder given his central position in the organisation. Still, Halder preferred to single out Brauchitsch.

The afternoon and evening Halder spent in consultation with Brauchitsch and Heusinger. There was some discussion about how Hitler's new orders could to be put into effect, but the mood was dominated by abject despair and loss of hope. Halder was insistent that after four victorious campaigns the OKH had had its 'good name tarnished'. He also considered the way Brauchitsch (and thereby the OKH) was treated to be 'outrageous'. The embittered discussion finally reached a point where Halder proposed to Brauchitsch that they both resign their posts in protest over Hitler's new orders and his treatment of the army. Brauchitsch, however, refused on the grounds that such a move 'would not result in them quitting their posts [because he felt Hitler would not accept such a move] and so nothing would be changed'.[17] Halder then also opted not to resign, but he was still not quite prepared to admit defeat over the question of Moscow.

Halder and Heusinger attempted to persuade Brauchitsch to confront Hitler over the matter and to push again for the Moscow alternative, but Brauchitsch took Hitler's rebuke as a stern warning and refused any further opposition to his plans. A split now developed within the OKH

[15] KTB OKW, Volume II, pp. 1063–1068, Document 100 (22 August 1941).
[16] Franz Halder, KTB III, p. 193 (22 August 1941).   [17] Ibid. (22 August 1941).

with Brauchitsch resisting all attempts to prompt him into action. Under pressure from Halder and Heusinger, the Field Marshal declared, 'what is the purpose of presenting everything to the Führer again?' Whereupon a frustrated Heusinger retorted: 'God, should we lead our whole life as if everything we do has to have a purpose?'[18] Halder was also bitterly disappointed with what seemed to be Brauchitsch's betrayal. Writing to his wife Halder confided: 'Alone I can not stand against a world of cowardice that shares my opinion, but will not fight for it.'[19] Desperate for more support, Halder decided to visit Bock on the following day to discuss the situation further.

At Bock's headquarters news of Hitler's memorandum arrived on 22 August, just as orders were about to be sent out to the entire army group detailing plans for a major offensive to the east. Bock was stupefied by the news. 'I want to smash the enemy army', he wrote in his diary, 'and the bulk of this army is opposite my front!' He termed the turn south a 'secondary operation' and claimed it would jeopardise the main goal which he defined as: 'the destruction of the Russian armed forces before winter'. When Bock had the chance to confer with Guderian he asked him which units could be released for the turn south. According to Bock, Guderian 'flatly rejected the operation' citing the utter fatigue of XXIV Panzer Corps, the inability to spare forces for a secondary operation, and the impassability of the Maglin–Unecha–Starodub road.[20] Guderian himself claims to have protested the move as 'criminal folly'.[21] It was not only Guderian's offensive strength that was placed in doubt for the new operation; the defence of the army group's long front was also determined to be 'over time unbearable' and therefore 'the attack eastwards must proceed'. With this, although the army group reluctantly began planning to implement Hitler's new directive, there was also no abandonment of planning for an attack to the east.[22] Halder had already told Bock he wanted to visit him on the following day (23 August), and Bock hoped something could still be done to bring about a change of plans. Bock also spoke on the telephone with Brauchitsch and, after outlining which forces could be dispatched south in accordance with Hitler's orders, he ominously added that no other major offensive could

---

[18] As cited in Meyer, *Heusinger*, p. 156.
[19] Halder's letter as cited by Schall-Riaucour, *Aufstand und Gehorsam*, p. 168 (23 August 1941). See also Hartmann, *Halder Generalstabschef Hitlers 1938–1942*, p. 283.
[20] Fedor von Bock, KTB 'Osten I', Fols. 69–70, *War Diary*, pp. 288–289 (22 August 1941). Fol. 70 of Bock's KTB 'Osten I' has been bound in the wrong order and can be found between fols. 52 and 53.
[21] Guderian, *Panzer Leader*, p. 198.
[22] 'Kriegstagebuch Nr.1 (Band August 1941) des Oberkommandos der Heeresgruppe Mitte' BA-MA RH 19II/386, pp. 364–365 (22 August 1941).

be considered 'for this year'.[23] Brauchitsch then asked: 'If the designated strength is deployed to the south, then you will not have any motorised units behind your front. Can the front then hold another 8 days?' To which Bock answered:

8 days yes, if the motorised divisions that must be refitted, can be made ready behind the front. This concerns the SS *Das Reich*, the 14th Motorised Infantry Division and the 7th Panzer Division. To this must be added the badly battle-worn 161st Infantry Division. The whole thing is naturally only an emergency solution. 8–10 days can be somehow managed, but not longer, especially if the enemy continues with strong attacks.[24]

Brauchitsch was clearly shaken by this and replied that either the attack eastward had to proceed or Army Group Centre would have to be withdrawn to a more defensible line.[25]

On 23 August Halder flew to Bock's headquarters at Borisov, ostensibly to see what could be done to hasten the attack set out by Hitler's memorandum.[26] This did indeed take up a good deal of discussion, but they also hatched a final plot for one last desperate effort to bring Hitler around to the views of the army. When Halder arrived in the afternoon a meeting was convened to discuss possibilities. In attendance were Bock, Heusinger, Halder, Lieutenant-Colonel Chrift, two junior officers and, summoned specially for the meeting, Guderian. Halder began with an overview of Hitler's orders, whereupon discussion followed of their implementation. Bock and Guderian were steadfastly critical, Guderian almost to the point of dismissing Hitler's orders as impossible. The panzer general stated that his divisions, after nine weeks of uninterrupted fighting, required a respite before undertaking any big operation. Guderian then stated that, in the best case scenario, only four divisions could be made available for the operation and that, because of the long lengths of atrocious roads, the ability of the divisions to reach Starodub (Guderian's southernmost position) in good time and with sufficient strength was 'completely impossible'. Guderian even went so far as to add 'that under the best conditions 30 per cent of the fighting strength would reach Starodub'.[27] A second suggestion to conduct a sweeping movement through Briansk and then strike deep into the Ukraine was also condemned as requiring too much strength. Finally, it was decided

[23] Underlining in the original. 'Kriegstagebuch Nr.1 (Band August 1941) des Oberkommandos der Heeresgruppe Mitte' BA-MA RH 19II/386, p. 365 (22 August 1941).
[24] Underlining in the original. Ibid., p. 366 (22 August 1941).
[25] Ibid. (22 August 1941).   [26] Franz Halder, KTB III, p. 194 (23 August 1941).
[27] Underlining in the original. 'Kriegstagebuch Nr.1 (Band August 1941) des Oberkommandos der Heeresgruppe Mitte' BA-MA RH 19II/386, pp. 371–372 (23 August 1941).

to move the mobile divisions behind the front all the way to Gomel, a distance of 200 kilometres.[28]

Although the new southern operation was being taken seriously by the army and planning was in full swing, there were still deep reservations about where this was leading the whole campaign. Time remained for just one more major offensive, and none were optimistic that Hitler's drive to seize the Ukraine and isolate Leningrad would be sufficient to force an end to the war. Bock also expressed concern that the morale of the troops should not be forgotten; according to him, they asked only one question: 'When will we march to Moscow? We don't want to get stuck here in winter.'[29] As things now stood, there could be only one answer to this question. The whole war in the east was being improvised on an almost daily basis, which was the consequence of a fragmented command and competing strategic conceptions. The generals themselves did not know if or when Moscow would be attacked, just as they did not know whether Hitler's thrust south could be carried out with the available strength, and what risk this would entail for the security of Bock's weakened army group. One thing, however, was certain, although scarcely understood at the time; the fears the men held of spending the winter deep in the Soviet Union were now assured. The army simply did not have the resources to avoid it and the grinding daily attrition slowly but steadily made this eventuality ever clearer. For the time being, the mass of German troops still believed in the ultimate victory of their Wehrmacht, although none were of any doubt that the Red Army demonstrated an incredible resilience, and that the war still had much hard fighting left in it. Yet the men of Army Group Centre recognised that Moscow was their objective and its capture, it was widely assumed, would bring about an end to the fighting. Many soldiers reasoned that, with two-thirds of the distance covered from the German border to the Soviet capital, only one-third of the war remained. As Heinrich Haape wrote:

Our marching column... wanted to get to Moscow. It was their only objective. They had been told it would be taken soon and to each man it meant the end of the march, rest, an organised life again, excitement, civilisation, women, relaxation of discipline perhaps... We measured it out on the map – one hundred and eighty

---

[28] This figure comes from Bock's diary, although Army Group Centre's war diary discusses the same problem and cites the distance as 300 kilometres. The discrepancy may be explained by the difference in distance that individual divisions would have to travel. Fedor von Bock, KTB 'Osten I', Fol. 71, *War Diary*, p. 291 (23 August 1941). 'Kriegstagebuch Nr.1 (Band August 1941) des Oberkommandos der Heeresgruppe Mitte' BA-MA RH 19II/386, p. 374 (23 August 1941).

[29] 'Kriegstagebuch Nr.1 (Band August 1941) des Oberkommandos der Heeresgruppe Mitte' BA-MA RH 19II/386, p. 374 (23 August 1941).

miles [290 kilometres] across country to Moscow! We had marched six hundred miles [965 kilometres] from East Prussia... we could do it in a fortnight at the most, even with resistance stiffening as we approached the capital.[30]

Signs were commonly hung by the men reading 'TO MOSCOW'[31] and hope was sustained by the idea that heavy losses were local rather than general. Thus, when orders finally arrived directing forces to the north and south, there was a sudden feeling of bewilderment and confusion, with some men even sensing that the campaign was now in trouble. An artilleryman, Werner Adamczyk, wrote:

I had a chance to look at a map of Russia. It showed the distance between Smolensk and Leningrad to be about 600km. On the other hand, the distance from where we were to Moscow was less than 400km... Definitely the Russians confronting us on our way to Moscow had been beaten. And now, it seemed we were to turn away from our greatest chance to get to Moscow and bring the war to an end. My instinct told me that something was very wrong.[32]

Erich Mende noted how his troops were 'agitated' and couldn't understand why there was not an immediate offensive towards Moscow.

Moscow was only 280 kilometres away. The troops hoped that we would be in the Soviet capital in August or latest September and then the resistance of the Red Army would probably be broken. We were very angry that the panzer divisions were pulled out and sent to the Ukraine to fight at Kiev. We saw this as a completely wrong strategy.[33]

Alexander Stahlberg recalled his 'shock' when the order was given to discontinue the advance to Moscow and assume defensive positions. 'What strategy was intended?' he asked himself. 'The word had gone around at once that it had come from the highest level, from Hitler himself. After a few days the riddle was solved... Moscow was no longer the objective, Leningrad was to be taken first.'[34] As confusion over strategy pervaded the ranks of the German army, for many at the front thoughts were quickly overtaken by day-to-day hardships and the suffering caused by harsh fighting. One man summed it up in a letter to his mother on 28 August: 'I passionately wanted to be part of the attack on Moscow, but now would be more pleased if I could get out of this hellish situation.'[35]

With preliminary planning for Hitler's directive underway at Army Group Centre, discussion switched to what was most likely Halder's real

[30] Haape with Henshaw, *Moscow Tram Stop*, p. 88.
[31] Guderian, *Panzer Leader*, p. 195; Frisch with Jones, Jr., *Condemned to Live*, p. 74.
[32] As quoted in Kershaw, *War Without Garlands*, p. 121.
[33] As quoted in Knopp, *Der verdammte Krieg*, p. 91.
[34] Stahlberg, *Bounden Duty*, p. 172.
[35] As quoted in Kershaw, *War Without Garlands*, p. 122.

interest in visiting Bock's command – securing a way to subvert Hitler's order. Guderian noted that Halder seemed 'deeply upset' and in the lengthy discussion that followed a new scheme emerged to challenge Hitler's 'unalterable will'.[36] Almost a month before, Halder had spoken to the Chiefs of Staff of the three army groups and emphasised the importance Hitler attached to the views of battlefield commanders. At this time Halder was already considering the value of pressing the OKH's point of view using such 'courier generals', which as Halder accurately assessed, were 'more trusted than us!'[37] Halder had just witnessed first-hand Guderian's rigid forcefulness for which he was well known throughout the army. Halder was undoubtedly also impressed by the dire terms in which Guderian set out his current predicament and the manifest difficulties of fulfilling Hitler's orders. Furthermore, Guderian's status as an 'heroic' panzer general was firmly established, and he was one of the most celebrated military idols in Goebbels's propaganda machine which constantly lauded his victories and heaped praise on his leadership. It also happened that Guderian's panzer army was at the centre of the strategic dispute over where the bulk of Bock's armour should strike. Thus, it did not take long for a new plan to form – a last-ditch throw of the dice to gain what until now had eluded the army. Bock telephoned Hitler's headquarters and asked Schmundt to secure a meeting with Hitler that same evening for Guderian. Bock carefully explained the reason as giving Hitler an opportunity, 'to form a picture of the situation for himself'.[38] According to one eyewitness, Colonel Rudolf-Christoph Freiherr von Gersdorff, when Guderian took his leave of Bock he did so with the words: 'Only over my dead body will it come to another solution [other than Moscow]'.[39] Guderian then accompanied Halder for the flight back to Lötzen airfield in East Prussia, near to Hitler's Wolf's Lair headquarters.

When Guderian arrived he reported first to Brauchitsch, who categorically forbade him from raising the question of Moscow in Hitler's presence. 'The operation to the south has been ordered,' Brauchitsch insisted. 'The problem now is how it is to be carried out. Discussion is pointless.'[40] Brauchitsch had never been a particularly strong character in his time as Commander-in-Chief of the Army and his resolve to push so vigorously for Moscow resulted partly from his own inner convictions, but mainly from two external factors. One was the dominance of Halder and his followers in the OKH which bolstered Brauchitsch's nerve and instilled

[36] Guderian, *Panzer Leader*, p. 198.   [37] Franz Halder, KTB III, p. 111 (25 July 1941).
[38] Fedor von Bock, KTB 'Osten I', Fol. 71, *War Diary*, p. 291 (23 August 1941).
[39] Von Gersdorff, *Soldat im Untergang*, p. 95.   [40] Guderian, *Panzer Leader*, p. 199.

in him an artificial robustness. The other, however, was the absence of staunch opposition. Since the end of July when the strategic issue became a crisis of two opposing and equally inflexible factions within the German command, Hitler did not end the dispute there and then with his customary intolerance for dissent. Rather, he himself was seized by indecision, which enabled Brauchitsch to go on actively supporting the Moscow alternative, although even in this period the Commander-in-Chief of the Army at times experienced grave doubts and even spells of utter despair. Once Hitler had recovered his nerve and sought to impose his will with ardent determination, Brauchitsch predictably buckled, exposing the frail man that hid behind a facade of high rank and position. Now, as Guderian threatened to pursue the matter of Moscow further, Brauchitsch, who had already accepted defeat on the matter and was in damage control over the army's confrontation with Hitler, sought to prevent upsetting the Führer any further. Upon receiving such a stern command, Guderian claims that he threatened to turn around and fly straight back to his panzer army, as his meeting with Hitler would now be a waste of time. Yet that too was unacceptable to Brauchitsch and he ordered Guderian to make his report as expected, 'but without mentioning Moscow!'[41]

Guderian was shown in to see Hitler who was surrounded by the usual cast of OKW officers including Keitel, Jodl and Schmundt. Guderian began to outline the state of his forces and claims to have initially adhered to Brauchitsch's instructions by not raising the issue of Moscow. Finally, Hitler asked: 'In view of their past performance, do you consider that your troops are capable of making another great effort?' To which Guderian responded: 'If the troops are given a major objective, the importance of which is apparent to every soldier, yes.' Hitler was under no illusions about what was meant by this and raised the topic himself. 'You mean, of course, Moscow', he rejoined. Guderian then seized his chance and began: 'Yes. Since you have broached the subject, let me give you the reasons for my opinions.'[42] Guderian then entered into a long exposition of all the evidence that counted in favour of an attack towards Moscow, recounting the many familiar arguments Hitler had no doubt heard in varying forms before. Probably in deference to his high standing, Guderian was not interrupted once and allowed to speak his mind freely to the end. Only then did Hitler begin to speak and it was soon apparent that he remained wholly unconvinced. Keeping his composure, Hitler set about expounding the opposing arguments for a strike into the Ukraine. His focus was unmistakably fixed on economic objectives, claiming they were vitally necessary for the future prosecution of the war. This was

[41] Ibid.   [42] Ibid.

backed by Hitler's insistence that: 'My generals know nothing about the economic aspects of war.'

Guderian's account leaves no doubt about Hitler's resolve and it was clear that the 'strict orders' for the attack to the south would proceed and that 'all actions were to be carried out with that in mind'.[43] Guderian also observed how all those present nodded in agreement with everything that Hitler said, revealing the presiding dominance of the Führer myth, which quickly captivated Guderian as well. His memoir explains his sudden compliance by the hopelessness of his position in changing a decision that had clearly already been taken.[44] As he explained: 'I did not think it right to make an angry scene with the head of the German state when he was surrounded by his advisers.' Yet Guderian also sought to blame Halder and Brauchitsch, stating he was 'extremely sorry' that neither of them accompanied him to the meeting, 'on the outcome of which, according to them, so very much depended, perhaps even the result of the war as a whole'.[45] If this was true, and the fate of the whole war potentially rested on his success, it seems a distinctly half-hearted effort on his part to convince Hitler, especially when he had previously felt no aversion to bitterly contesting the orders of superiors over decidedly lesser matters. According to his leading biographer, he was also being unofficially discussed as an eventual replacement for Brauchitsch and it was clear, from his private correspondence, that Guderian was well aware he was under consideration for the post.[46] Thus, his placid behaviour and accommodating attitude towards Hitler appear suddenly less mysterious for a man who was usually extremely reluctant to compromise, and exceedingly ambitious. Additionally, Guderian's explanation that he could not challenge Hitler in front of his entourage is difficult to accept when, in his later career as Chief of the Army General Staff, there were numerous occasions where he clashed openly with Hitler in fiery displays of temper. Guderian was not the dutiful soldier compelled to humbly follow orders as he suggests. There is enough evidence to show that he was, in fact, far closer to the regime, its policies and its leader than the

---

[43] Ibid., p. 200.

[44] According to Gersdorff, an unidentified officer of the OKH who was also said to have attended Guderian's meeting with Hitler later gave another version of events. Hitler apparently dominated the conference, refusing to allow Guderian to get a word in, and only after an unending monologue spanning economic and political considerations did Hitler say: 'Now then my dear Colonel-General, you will do what I order.' To which Guderian is said to have simply replied: 'Yes, my Führer.' Von Gersdorff, *Soldat im Untergang*, pp. 95–96.

[45] Guderian, *Panzer Leader*, p. 200.

[46] Macksey, *Guderian*, pp. 145–147; Macksey, 'Generaloberst Heinz Guderian', p. 83; Macksey, 'Guderian', pp. 452–453.

general himself was prepared to admit.[47] Furthermore, in criticising the absence of Halder and Brauchitsch, what Guderian did not acknowledge (or mistakenly undervalued) in his post-war account was the degree of antipathy that now existed between Hitler and the OKH. Halder was all too aware that his presence would not have advanced his cause, or stayed Hitler's temper on the issue. The difference now in this eleventh-hour attempt to change Hitler's mind was not so much the nature of the message, as the status of the man who was arguing for it. While Guderian counted greatly in that regard, Halder and Brauchitsch were clearly liabilities. Nevertheless, the fact remains that Guderian's mission was doomed from the very beginning, both because Hitler's mind was not to be changed on the issue and because he was far too malleable to deal with Hitler.

In adopting the southern operation, Guderian was not so much reluctantly abiding by Hitler's orders, as actively converted to carrying out Hitler's will.[48] He was simply overawed in Hitler's company and the result finally spelled defeat for Halder's cherished plans. On the following day (24 August), when Guderian told Halder of his failure to convince Hitler and that the southern operation would have to be adopted, Halder, according to Guderian, 'suffered a complete nervous collapse'. Halder unloaded all his pent-up frustrations onto Guderian in a tirade of resentful accusations. Guderian explained Halder's outburst as an unreasonable over-reaction, resulting from over-strained nerves, to news which he should have known to expect.[49] Halder, on the other hand, could not understand how Guderian could have presented such a blatantly critical critique of Hitler's plan and now freely propose to carry it out with the same forces that only yesterday were regarded as incapable of doing so. Guderian defended his behaviour by saying that his previous comments were given to provide the OKH with arguments against Hitler's proposal, but he also alluded to the difficulties the coming operation would entail by claiming that he was now duty bound to 'make the impossible

[47] In spite of his claims to the contrary, in his time as an active field commander in the east Guderian's units have been shown to have repeatedly implemented Hitler's criminal orders. Later Guderian avoided giving any aid to the plotters planning to assassinate Hitler and he even sat briefly on the notorious Court of Honour set up to condemn and execute many of the plot's participants. During his time as Chief of the General Staff he presided over some of the most draconian orders ever issued in the German army. These accounted for the deaths of thousands of German soldiers who were hanged or shot as deserters. For two contrasting depictions of Guderian's role in the war see Macksey, 'Guderian', pp. 441–460 and Hans-Heinrich Wilhelm, 'Heinz Guderian – "Panzerpapst" und Generalstabschef' in Ronald Smelser and Enrico Syring (eds.), *Die Militärelite des Dritten Reiches. 27 biographische Skizzen* (Berlin, 1995), pp. 187–208.

[48] Von Below, *Als Hitlers Adjutant 1937–45*, p. 288.

[49] Guderian, *Panzer Leader*, p. 202.

possible'. Halder was disgusted by such a flagrant twisting of the facts to suit Guderian's own standpoint. Brauchitsch insisted that he would issue strict new orders on the drafting of reports. Halder, however, was dismissive of such an action, declaring: 'You can not change character through orders.'[50] The confrontation between Halder and Guderian ended on hostile terms and without any form of agreement; indeed Guderian later claimed that Halder actively sought to hinder his operations by denying him adequate strength.[51] The recriminations were also felt at Army Group Centre, whom Halder contacted immediately to report news of Guderian's duplicity and betrayal.[52] When Bock heard the news, his bitter disappointment at the loss of the Moscow operation was mixed with resentment and confusion for Guderian's apparently inexplicable role in the final act of the long-drawn-out command crisis.[53]

Operations now shifted to the south and north, and with them a degree of strategic clarity emerged which had been absent for many weeks. Still, the gruelling effects of the long period of indecision and internal wrangling left their mark on the higher command with frayed nerves and bitter personal animosity reflective of an army that had suffered a major reversal. The daily business of directing the war went on, of course, but it was no longer a blitzkrieg campaign; now it was a war of endurance – and in such a war the Soviet Union, backed by its allies in the west, was already in the favoured position. No one could yet predict the collapse of the Third Reich, nor a Soviet occupation of Berlin, but by forfeiting its only possibility of eliminating the Soviet Union, Germany was destined for a long war, against an emerging superpower, which it could not hope to overcome. Operation Barbarossa's failure was more than just a lost campaign; the scale and importance of the eastern theatre ensured that the summer of 1941 was the turning point of World War II.

Throughout late August and September operations on the flanks of Army Group Centre became the focus of German operations and led to more hard won battlefield victories, but at an ever increasing cost to their dwindling offensive strength.[54] Even the great encirclement battle at

---

[50] Franz Halder, KTB III, p. 195 (24 August 1941).

[51] Guderian, *Panzer Leader*, p. 202.

[52] 'Kriegstagebuch Nr.1 (Band August 1941) des Oberkommandos der Heeresgruppe Mitte' BA-MA RH 19II/386, p. 375 (24 August 1941).

[53] Fedor von Bock, KTB 'Osten I', Fols. 71–72, *War Diary*, pp. 291–292 (24 August 1941).

[54] Michael Geyer accurately summed up the German strategic dilemma at the end of the 1941 summer: 'What more could be done than to defeat major parts of the Russian army? How could one break the will of a nation that would not surrender, but recuperated again and again, while German forces became weaker and weaker? More battles could be won, perhaps at Leningrad, at Moscow, or in the Ukraine, but obviously one could win battles and lose the war. This was the main operational problem after August

Kiev, which has in the past attracted attention for its supposed significance as the quintessential example of German operational perfection-
ism, is in need of careful revision. The same problems, so devastat-
ingly prevalent in the summer campaign, worsened in the autumn, while
the German command remained incurably divided and fatally blind to
its growing weaknesses. The attritional drain that had begun from the
first day of Operation Barbarossa had progressed so far by the end of
two months that Germany no longer possessed the ability to defeat the
Soviet Union in 1941. Future battles, whether centred on Moscow or
the Ukraine, were simply not able to crush the Red Army and conquer the Soviet Union, undermining the persistent arguments favouring
one strategic alternative over another. Failure to end the war in another
blitzkrieg campaign entailed destructive consequences for Germany and
this was a foreseeable reality by the late summer of 1941. On 23 August
Ribbentrop conceded to the Japanese ambassador in Berlin, General
Oshima, that the war against the Soviet Union might last into 1942.[55]
Furthermore, an OKW memorandum dated 27 August stated: 'The
mandatory collapse of Russia is the next, decisive objective, which must
be reached by employing all the troops that can be spared on other fronts.
If this aim is not achieved in 1941, the continuation of the eastern campaign will have first priority in 1942.'[56] Three days later on 30 August
von Hassell wrote in his diary: 'Hitler is pressing hard for swift advances,
but the Army High Command has certain misgivings... In any event,
it is generally believed that there will be a Russian front through the
winter.'[57] Even Halder now recognised the futility of seeking a knockout
blow against the USSR and on 23 August, presumably after hearing the
result of Guderian's fateful meeting with Hitler, he wrote to his wife: 'The
goal which I had set myself to achieve, namely to finish off the Russians in
this year, will not be attained and we will have a strength-draining eastern
front over the winter.'[58] Yet Halder was still incapable of understanding the full implications of this for Germany's chances in the ongoing
world war. It was only in late November 1941, long after the intended
blitzkrieg had failed, that Halder belatedly observed: 'It is possible that

---

1941. It was the insoluble operational problem for an army and a political leadership
that had come to believe that the mere accumulation of success would ensure victory.
This is a prime example of strategic decadence, but by no means the last of its kind'
(Geyer, 'German Strategy', p. 591).

[55] Chapman, 'The Imperial Japanese Navy', p. 178.
[56] Document as cited by Reinhardt, *Moscow – The Turning Point*, p. 39; Reinhardt, 'Moscow
1941. The Turning Point', p. 210.
[57] Von Hassell, *Vom andern Deutschland*, p. 220 (30 August 1941); von Hassell, *Diaries*,
p. 191 (30 August 1941).
[58] Halder's letter as cited by Schall-Riaucour, *Aufstand und Gehorsam*, p. 168 (23 August
1941).

the war is shifting from the level of military success to the level of moral and economic endurance.'[59] To others in the German command, the decisive importance of the summer of 1941 became clear after the war. Although erroneously claiming that Hitler ruined the army's grand plan for assured victory by not striking towards Moscow, Heusinger and Hoth both identified the summer campaign as the turning point of the war. As Heusinger wrote:

The Army High Command's opposition to this decision [to send Guderian and Weichs south into the Ukraine] had been in vain. Hitler had brushed all their arguments aside. He left the ground of purely operational command following basic military principles in favour of other aspects. This was the decisive turning point of the Eastern campaign.[60]

Likewise, Hoth described Hitler's plan to strike towards the north and south as 'the decision of the war'.[61]

In the strategic crisis that dominated the German command for a month in July and August 1941, Hitler emerged the undisputed victor. He not only asserted his authority over the army and prevailed against almost unanimous opposition, but his strategic choice was certainly the wiser alternative given both German logistical constraints and the dreadful Soviet strategic deployment in the south. Yet his triumph in taking control of the campaign from the OKH was never really in doubt once he had made up his mind to do so, and even if he did offer a better alternative for the next phase of the campaign, by the late summer of 1941, he could not change the fundamentally flawed undertaking that Barbarossa represented. If Hitler's victory over the army was any kind of victory at all, it was only a hollow success in a war that was doomed to be lost. Perhaps, therefore, the historical reference to a 'July/August crisis' should be thought of, not in reference to a somewhat trivial strategic debate fought out between the military commanders and Hitler, but rather as a reflection of the catastrophic predicament Germany now confronted in the east.

[59] Franz Halder, KTB III, p. 306 (23 November 1941).
[60] As cited by Dieter Ose, 'Smolensk: Reflections on a Battle' in David M. Glantz (ed.), The Initial Period of War, p. 351.
[61] Italics in the original. Hoth, Panzer-Operationen, p. 124.

Conclusion

Having focused in this study primarily on the problems of the German summer offensive, there might be those who would wish to point out that things were much worse on the Soviet side of the line. That the summer of 1941 represented a Soviet debacle of grand proportions, typified by mass confusion and an enormous wastage of men and material, is not in question here. The fact remains, however, that these losses, while dreadfully costly to the Soviet war effort, were bearable. Indeed, far from crumbling, the Red Army was in fact growing in size, fed by the huge pool of non-active reserves. Moreover, unlike the German army, the Red Army did not have to win the war in 1941, it only had to survive long enough for Germany's offensive strength to exhaust itself. The winter granted the Soviet Union a reprieve, which was sweetened by the entry of the United States into the war. Thus, whatever may be said of the Red Army's weaknesses in the summer of 1941, it was entirely successful in one fundamental respect – it confounded the German leadership's plan to conquer the Soviet Union in a Blitz-style campaign in the early weeks of the war.[1] As Jacob Kipp concluded in his study on the battle of Smolensk:

At a horrible cost in losses, Russia gave up her sons and her land to bleed the Wehrmacht white, even if the losses were 10 to 1 in favour of the German invader. Nazi ideology and occupation policies in the end made such sacrifices seem justified and legitimized Soviet totalitarianism . . . After Smolensk it was clear that this would be a long war, not a Blitzkrieg. The Soviet state and society, which Lenin and Stalin had cast as a vast mechanism for mobilization and militarization, had begun that process in earnest.[2]

A further challenge to the conclusions of this study may arise from those seeking to showcase the results of the German battles at Kiev, Briansk and Viaz'ma in September and October 1941. These battles collectively yielded well over a million additional Soviet prisoners of war and, on the

---

[1] Chor'kov, 'The Red Army', p. 429.
[2] Kipp, 'Barbarossa and the Crisis', pp. 117 and 150.

surface, seem to suggest that German operational mobility was still capable of crushing Soviet resistance. Unfortunately, space does not permit a more detailed analysis of these battles, but one of the key aspects to understanding the extent of the German successes in the autumn is the complicity of Stalin himself. In the same way that Hitler's obstinate insistence on holding the line at all costs dogged German defensive operations from 1943 to 1945, by September 1941 Stalin grossly over-estimated the success of his counter-attacks on the German armies and refused to permit the abandonment of Kiev. In any case, the Soviet dictator was confident Bock would only strike towards Moscow and took no account of Zhukov's warning that Kirponos's South-Western Front was in grave danger.[3] Accordingly, Bock's path to the south was left dangerously open, inviting another Soviet calamity. The extent of Stalin's blunder was compounded by the fact that, once German intentions became clear, Stalin still refused to allow Kirponos to retreat with whatever he could save until it was much too late.[4] Guderian's and Kleist's weary panzer groups were thus handed a victory far in excess of what their reduced forces could have achieved had Zhukov not been dismissed and his counter-measures ignored. Even with Stalin's spectacular mismanagement, it still took the Germans another month to exploit their good fortune and eliminate the huge Kiev pocket. By the time German armies were able to reassemble for their renewed drive on Moscow in Operation Typhoon, it was already 30 September. The available combat strength and logistical support had fallen far below what would be required to seize the Soviet capital. Following the pattern of early offensives, the attack began well and again took advantage of the dreadful Soviet strategic direction to bag another huge haul of Soviet prisoners in two enormous pockets. As Halder recorded on 4 October: 'Operation Typhoon is following an altogether classic course . . . The enemy is standing fast on all parts of the front not under attack, which gives hope for the creation of pockets.'[5] As in the past German offensives, however, the pace could not be sustained. Over vast distances, the spearheads weakened as their flanks grew and their supply lines became impossibly long. Soviet counter-attacks became unrelenting. The road conditions worsened along with the weather, and soon German troops everywhere were finding themselves in freezing temperatures with little more than their worn-out summer uniforms. Deprived of the chance to win the war, or even to extract itself from the slogging

---

[3] Erickson, *Road to Stalingrad*, p. 178; Bullock, *Hitler and Stalin*, pp. 790–791.
[4] Bernd Bonwetsch, 'Stalin, the Red Army, and the "Great Patriotic War" ' in Ian Kershaw and Moshe Lewin (eds.), *Stalinism and Nazism. Dictatorships in Comparison* (Cambridge, 2003), pp. 197–199.
[5] Franz Halder, KTB III, p. 267 (4 October 1941).

battles of attrition, Germany's stalled eastern front underwent a rapid de-modernisation. This accentuated the bitter deprivations of life at the front, especially as the winter took hold. As one German soldier wrote in December 1941: 'Technology no longer plays a role... The elemental power of nature broke the operations of our engines. What do we do?'[6] As historians have been keen to show, the launch of the Soviet winter offensive before Moscow in December 1941 spelled the end of Operation Barbarossa, but it was really only the final nail in the coffin; a coffin which had already been built by the end of the summer. The German victories at Kiev, Briansk and Viaz'ma in September and October 1941 did not change this fact, nor did they achieve what the battles at Minsk, Smolensk and Uman had not. Nazi Germany's last chance for a successful military outcome in World War II ended in the summer of 1941.

Summing up the first two years of the war Michael Geyer observed: 'However successful the first two years of the war, the Third Reich never came close to escaping the dilemma posed by the fact that the political and military-strategic costs of the expansion continuously outran the benefits of a newly gained hegemonic position.'[7] When the hoped-for lightning victory against the Soviet Union proved beyond the Wehrmacht's strength, a longer-term war-winning solution was all that remained open to Germany, but the prospects of success for this option can be immediately dismissed. As Omer Bartov has written:

Once blitzkrieg failed, production, industrial capacity, material and manpower resources, organisation and technical skill, all became more important than tactics, training, and courage. Of course blitzkrieg itself depended on technology, indeed, it made a fetish of modern fighting machines. But now technological innovation had to be paralleled by quantities produced, while the initial psychological impact of mass (but spatially and temporally limited) use of modern weaponry lost much of its force. In this area Germany had no chance of competing successfully with its enemies.[8]

Raw statistics make this clear. In 1941 German industry managed to produce a total of 5,200 tanks, 11,776 aircraft and 7,000 artillery pieces (over 37mm).[9] In the first half of 1941 the Soviet Union produced 1,800 modern tanks, 3,950 aircraft and 15,600 artillery pieces and mortars. What is extraordinary is that these figures rise considerably in the second

[6] As quoted in Fritz, *Frontsoldaten*, p. 126.   [7] Geyer, 'German Strategy', p. 578.

[8] Omer Bartov, 'From Blitzkrieg to Total War: Controversial Links between Image and Reality' in Ian Kershaw and Moshe Lewin (eds.), *Stalinism and Nazism*, pp. 165–166.

[9] Figures from Richard Overy, 'Statistics' in Dear and Foot (eds.), *The Oxford Companion to the Second World War* (Oxford, 1995), Table 2: Military Production, p. 1060.

half of 1941 in spite of the loss of important production centres, and the massive industrial relocation to the east. In the midst of the war on its doorstep, Soviet factories turned out another 4,740 tanks, 8,000 aircraft and 55,500 artillery pieces and mortars.[10] Thus the Soviet Union out-performed Germany in all the major armaments even in the first year of the war and thereafter production almost always exceeded losses in the main categories.[11] The disparity becomes even clearer when one adds production figures from Britain and the United States (who were shipping considerable quantities of military aid to Europe even before their direct entry into the war). In 1942 Germany significantly raised its armament output, but this was still hopelessly out-performed by Allied production. Even allowing for the fact that a sizeable portion of British and American production would be sent to the Pacific theatre, the disparity between Allied and German industrial production was still staggering. In 1942 Germany produced 15,409 aircraft, while the combined Allied total reached 96,944 (25,436 USSR, 23,672 UK, 47,836 USA). In the same year, German tank production numbered 9,200 units, while the Allies turned out 58,054 units (24,446 USSR, 8,611 UK, 24,997 USA).[12] In November 1941 Stalin confidently exclaimed: 'Modern war is a war of motors. The war will be won by the one who produces the most motors. The combined motor production of the USA, Britain, and the USSR is at least three times that of Germany.'[13] In fact the combined motor production of the three Allied powers was far in excess of Stalin's three-fold estimate. The remaining years of the war continued to see a commanding Allied lead in armament production, dooming Germany to eventual defeat by sheer weight of arms. The ebb and flow of battlefield successes affected only the length of the war, not its eventual outcome.[14]

In 1942 the Germans could only resume the offensive on the southern part of the front. This new offensive pushed all the way to the Volga, but

---

[10] Hoffmann, 'Die Kriegführung aus der Sicht der Sowjetunion', p. 734.

[11] Walter S. Dunn, Jr., *Stalin's Keys to Victory. The Rebirth of the Red Army in WWII* (Mechanicsburg, 2006), p. 41.

[12] Overy, 'Statistics', Table 2: Military Production, p. 1060.

[13] As quoted in Mawdsley, *Thunder in the East*, p. 193.

[14] This assertion is strongly contested by Richard Overy, who argues: 'Economic size as such does not explain the outcome of wars ... The line between material resources and victory on the battlefield is anything but a straight one. The history of war is littered with examples of smaller, materially disadvantaged states defeating a larger, richer enemy' (Overy, *Why the Allies Won*, pp. 316–317). Generally speaking Overy is quite correct, but not in the case of World War II. In this author's opinion, Overy considerably over-estimates both Germany's outright military strength and Hitler's woeful strategic direction, both of which would have to compensate massively for her inferior economic resources.

here again, the Germans fatally over-extended themselves and met with disaster at the battle of Stalingrad. In 1943 they lost the strategic initiative altogether when their third summer offensive was stopped cold after only a few days. From this point on until the end of the war, Germany's eastern front became an entirely defensive war.

This study presents a revealing picture of the German generals at war. It is not a picture that will be familiar to many readers, especially those in the English-speaking world, where military histories abound and the German generals of World War II are often portrayed (and even unfortunately admired) as consummate military professionals. In Germany that picture is very different. The focus on the criminal legacy of the Nazi state has, in the last 25 years, shifted more and more attention towards the role of the army and its extensive activity in the war of annihilation, particularly on the eastern front.[15] As a result, unlike military histories in the Anglo-American world, the campaigns and battles fought by the German generals do not form the principal subject of interest for academics. The question more commonly asked in contemporary German debates is to what extent the German army and its commanders were complicit in issuing, or at least condoning, criminal orders. The weight of research supports the conclusion that this was very extensive indeed. Yet the all too common tendency among Anglo-American historians to separate the strictly military performance of the German generals from their wider political and ideological actions has, in this author's opinion, allowed too many favourable judgements to be passed. In doing so many English language publications have inadvertently set a worrying precedent. One would never conclude that Joseph Goebbels was an excellent propaganda minister without rendering a fuller and morally deserving judgement on the consequence of his actions. In the same vein the German generals should not escape a fuller accounting of their actions in World War II. The men in control of Hitler's armies were not honourable men, carrying out their orders as dutiful servants of the state. With resolute support for the regime, the generals unquestioningly waged one war of aggression after the other, and, once Barbarossa began, willingly

---

[15] There is a long list of historians (both German and international) who have produced first-rate studies on the many diverse aspects of this topic. On the treatment of Soviet prisoners of war see Streit, *Keine Kameraden*. For the relationship between the German army and NS State see Bartov, *Hitler's Army*. For the army's role in the occupation of the Soviet Union see Theo Schulte, *The German Army and the Nazi Policies in Occupied Russia* and Gerlach, *Kalkulierte Morde*. On the war against the partisans see Shepherd, *War in the Wild East*. For an overview of the German army's criminal activity in 1941 see Jürgen Förster's contribution to the fourth volume of *Das Deutsche Reich und der Zweite Weltkrieg* and Megargee, *War of Annihilation*.

partook in the genocide of the Nazi regime.[16] For historians to comment exclusively on military matters, and render judgements about these
men on those facts alone, allows a distorted and potentially dangerous
perception of the generals to arise.[17]

While the German generals cannot avoid a degree of guilt for the
crimes committed during the war, from a strictly professional standpoint
one must also question their role in the military failure of the war against
the Soviet Union. Far from the picture presented in many publications,
which in the early years of World War II laud the German field marshals
as grand operators and the panzer commanders as dashing innovators
of a revolutionary military concept, this study presents a contrasting
image. In addition to the complicity of the field commanders in the many
planning and conceptual blunders inherent in Barbarossa, these same
men compounded these initial oversights with an enduring blindness
towards the difficulties encountered during the summer campaign. Even
in August 1941, when the supply system was greatly over-extended, the
army group's offensive strength widely dispersed, and the refitting process
incomplete, the generals argued for an offensive towards Moscow, which
was in practical terms impossible to realise. The fatal inability to recognise
the limitations of the forces under their command was inherent to the
campaign itself, but what is more surprising is the slow learning curve
among the generals at the front who were confronted with the day-to-
day problems of the advance. Surely these men could see the problem
posed by the vast extent of the Soviet Union and could calculate for
themselves the logistical and military costs of continued operations? Even
if future planning was too much of a distraction from the day-to-day
operations, one wonders what they had learned from weeks of warfare
over the Soviet Union's roads and against the Red Army's relentless

---

[16] One recent study by Klaus J. Arnold seeks a radical reinterpretation of the army's
role in the east. Arnold attempts to argue that the Wehrmacht's crimes were merely
a reaction to circumstances either beyond their control or 'forced' on them by enemy
elements such as the partisans. Such an argument has no factual credibility and should
remain sidelined. Klaus J. Arnold, *Die Wehrmacht und die Besatzungspolitik in den besetzten
Gebieten der Sowjetunion. Kriegführung und Radikalisierung im 'Unternehmen Barbarossa'*
(Berlin, 2005).

[17] For one of the best studies of the Wehrmacht, which addresses its ideological bias and
criminal activity as well as the many enduring post-war myths, see: Wolfram Wette,
Die Wehrmacht. Feindbilder, Vernichtungskrieg, Legenden (English translation: Wolfram
Wette, *The Wehrmacht. History, Myth, Reality*). Equally indispensable is Hannes Heer
and Klaus Naumann, *War of Extermination. The German Military in World War II 1941–
1944* (Oxford, 2006). For more recent research see the outstanding study by Hürter,
Hitlers Heerführer. In addition, Johannes Hürter, 'Konservative Akteure oder totale
Krieger? Zum Transformationsprozess einer militärischen Elite' in Christian Hartmann,
Johannes Hürter and Ulrike Jureit (eds.), *Verbrechen der Wehrmacht. Bilanz einer Debatte*
(Munich, 2005), pp. 50–59.

counter-attacks. Had these not weakened the all-important motorised formations to a critical point? How were the chronic supply problems going to be solved adequately to sustain the next big push before too much time elapsed? Where were the reserve units to help plug the gaps in the line and later fill the vacuum of space in the still-to-be-conquered territories? Positive answers simply didn't exist, and each of the field commanders prominently featured in this study retained a sufficiently large overview of the strategic situation to be able to identify this dire state of affairs.[18] The fact that none of these men were pointing to Barbarossa's impending failure, to say nothing of urging some form of negotiated settlement before it was too late, is itself an indication that the German generals were unaware of how much trouble the campaign was in.

To explain this extraordinary weakness one must take a step back and see the German generals in a wider context than the immediate events of Operation Barbarossa. All of the generals had served in World War I and some had direct experiences fighting on the eastern front (Halder, Rundstedt, Manstein, Kesselring, Kleist). Memories of Russia's poor performance in that war, exemplified most dramatically by the battle of Tannenberg in 1914, undoubtedly coloured the perceptions of junior officers of the period. The ultimate defeat of Russia in 1917, despite the division of German forces between multiple fronts, gave weight to the view of Russia as a backward land, fielding a peasant army that was technically ill-equipped and badly led. By contrast events in the same war on Germany's western front had encouraged the misleading conclusion that this was where the one real threat to German military ambitions stood. By 1941 with France defeated, England isolated and the Soviet Union facing Germany essentially alone, the temptation to under-estimate the Red Army, especially in the absence of an objective appraisal of Soviet power, was always going to be great. Once Barbarossa was underway and the mounting difficulties of the campaign began to surface, memories of World War I again played a defining role. In September 1914, as the attacking German armies were compelled to assume defensive positions on the western front, which quickly transformed into the stalemate of trench warfare, the so-called 'Miracle of the Marne' was proclaimed by the Allies and German victory plans for 1914 were doomed. In the eyes of many later German commanders (including Guderian who fought in the battle of the Marne), the German failure was not a reflection of an overly ambitious campaign objective or the prevailing battlefield conditions; it was the result of excessive caution and a failure to press the attack on Paris with every possible means in the hope of clinching the decisive

[18] Hürter, *Hitlers Heerführer*, p. 276.

success. The lesson seemed justified by the first campaigns of World War II and formed a new cult of the offensive which subsequently pushed the German armies well beyond their limits in Operation Barbarossa. While historical context may help explain why Halder and his generals acted as they did, it does not excuse the oversights these included.

If the German generals are to be seen as efficient operators of the blitzkrieg war method,[19] one can say that even at the height of their wartime experience in offensive operations, they still failed to grasp the fundamental underpinnings of blitzkrieg in strategic matters. This is no small oversight and it raises the question of how well they really understood the formula of their success and its related limitations.[20] Certainly there was a great over-confidence going into Barbarossa, supported by an overarching ideological and racial bias, but these factors alone don't fully explain the phenomenon. At its root the generals demonstrated a clear professional failing. They could lead their men well towards a limited operational objective so long as they could maintain their dynamic movement, which in Poland, France and the Balkans also sufficed to achieve the strategic objective. In the Soviet Union, however, this same concept produced an initial success, but not anywhere near enough to achieve the overall strategic objective. Even after the battle of Smolensk and the changing relationship between German offensive and Soviet defensive strength, the generals could do no more than propose yet another grand offensive towards Moscow, entirely oblivious to the essential underpinning of such an operation. Operational thinking predominated within the Wehrmacht at the expense of a vigilant strategic overview.[21] This

---

[19] Especially positive assessments of Guderian, Hoth, Strauss and Weichs can be found in their personal files. The appraisals were written at different times during the war by Bock, Leeb, Rundstedt, Manstein and Kluge. See: 'Personalakten für Strauss, Adolf' BA-MA Pers 6/56, Fol. 20 (13 February 1941); 'Personalakten für Guderian, Heinz' BA-MA Pers 6/27, Fol. 44 (29 September 1939); 'Personalakten für Hoth, Hermann' BA-MA Pers 6/38, Fol. 21 (20 February 1941); Fol. 25 (6 April 1942); Fol. 28 (23 March 1943); Fol. 29 (18 December 1943); 'Personalakten für Weichs, Max. Frhr. von' BA-MA Pers 6/62, Fol. 33 (20 February 1941); Fol. 36 (No date given).

[20] One can also see examples of this in the preliminary planning and conceptualisation of the Western campaign in 1940. See Frieser, *Blitzkrieg-Legende*, Zweiter Teil (English translation: *The Blitzkrieg Legend*, Chapter 2).

[21] The over-emphasis on operational matters was already evident under the tenure of Colonel-General Ludwig Beck, the Army Chief of Staff before Halder. Beck complained that younger officers were fixated on maximising the use of weapons without learning to evaluate operations in the context of wider strategic factors. As Michel Geyer concluded: 'To be sure, military technocrats with their functional outlook and National Socialists with their goal of ideological war remained apart and often were at cross purposes, but they complemented each other and, in crucial moments, when the Third Reich turned from preparing to fighting war, achieved a symbiosis' (Geyer, 'German Strategy', p. 572). See also Hartmann, *Halder Generalstabschef Hitlers 1938–1942*, p. 239.

forestalled an informed understanding of what was possible and not possible, and allowed the war to degenerate into strategically senseless battles
without any clear appreciation of how it could eventually be won. The
generals merely concentrated on the tasks at hand; the next city to conquer, the next Soviet army to defeat. This blinkered view endured not
only throughout 1941, but into the summer of 1943. It was only after the
disaster at Stalingrad, when the war was increasingly recognised as being
lost, that the plots to kill Hitler, emanating from within the army, gathered pace. Even then the decision to join the conspiracy was largely based
on the deteriorating military situation, and not the well-known criminal
activity of the regime. In the summer of 1941 there was hardly a mur-
mur of recognition that the strategic outlook was dooming Germany's
war effort. For this the generals were far too short-sighted; indeed, most
believed in some form of victory until the Soviet winter offensive finally
dispelled all remaining illusions. Professionally, therefore, it may be said
that the men who led the German armies in Operation Barbarossa were
functionally competent, but strategically inept. Accordingly, Hitler's generals, with very few exceptions, were both morally compromised in the
war of annihilation behind the front and professionally incapable in
the war against the Red Army.

   For Anglo-American readers there should be no military idols in the
German High Command. In 1941 the top echelon of command were at
one with their Führer over his erroneous military and ideological objectives. Not even when these reached their frightening conclusion in a
strategic quagmire and mass murder did even a single general resign in
disgust. From Brauchitsch down this was indeed Hitler's army.

   A central problem for military historians in assessing Germany's 'victories' on the eastern front in 1941 has been the occupational hazard
of evaluating these battles in context of countless other historical conflicts. In almost any other war, a battle on the scale of Belystok–Minsk,
Smolensk or even Uman would constitute a crushing blow and, most
likely, prove decisive. Barbarossa produced multiple battles of this magnitude, and in quick succession, which, together with the deep advance of
the German armies, seem to provide sufficient evidence that the Soviet
Union must have been on the brink of defeat. Yet, the extraordinary
robustness of the Soviet state is rarely taken into account; likewise the
difficulties of completely eliminating such an enormous power in a short
campaign, especially given the structural weaknesses of the German invasion force, are often overlooked. The resilience of the Soviet state, therefore, defies straightforward comparisons with previous empires and past
wars. As Stalin himself remarked in November 1941, 'any other government which had suffered such losses of territory as we did would not

have stood the test and would have collapsed'.[22] With this in mind, the benchmark for what constitutes a decisive battle is accordingly a good deal higher. The Soviet Union was nothing less than a militarised juggernaut and, while deeply wounded in Germany's 1941 campaign, there is no evidence to suggest it was about to collapse either politically or militarily. This is not to say that historical comparisons are inappropriate in evaluating the German–Soviet war, rather that a suitable appreciation of scale needs to be borne in mind. Reconciling the early German 'victories' with the ultimate task at hand – the defeat of the Soviet Union – should in future forestall the ingratiating descriptions which have previously defined German operations in the summer of 1941.

Historical comparisons reveal that many fundamental points that denote Hitler's failure in 1941 were actually foreshadowed in past campaigns. The most obvious example is Napoleon's ill-fated invasion of Russia in 1812. The German High Command's inability to grasp some of the essential hallmarks of this military calamity highlights another angle of their flawed conceptualisation and planning in anticipation of Operation Barbarossa. Like Hitler, Napoleon was the conqueror of Europe and foresaw his war on Russia as the key to forcing England to make terms. Napoleon invaded with the intention of ending the war in a short campaign centred on a decisive battle in western Russia. As the Russians withdrew, Napoleon's supply lines grew and his strength was in decline from week to week. The poor roads and harsh environment took a deadly toll on both horses and men, while politically Russia's oppressed serfs remained, for the most part, loyal to the aristocracy. Worse still, while Napoleon defeated the Russian army at Smolensk and Borodino, it did not produce a decisive result for the French and each time left Napoleon with the dilemma of either retreating or pushing deeper into Russia. Neither was really an acceptable option, the retreat politically and the advance militarily, but in each instance Napoleon opted for the latter. In doing so the French emperor outdid even Hitler and successfully took the Russian capital in September 1812, but it counted for little when the Russians simply refused to acknowledge defeat and prepared to fight on through the winter. By the time Napoleon left Moscow to begin his infamous retreat, the Russian campaign was doomed.[23] As Clausewitz observed:

---

[22] As quoted in Mawdsley, *Thunder in the East*, p. 44. See also Braithwaite, *Moscow 1941*, p. 254.

[23] For a first-rate account of the Napoleon's 1812 campaign see: Adam Zamoyski, *1812. Napoleon's Fatal March on Moscow* (London, 2004). See also Michael Howard's Foreword to Carl von Clausewitz, *The Campaign of 1812 in Russia* (New York, 1995).

The Russia campaign of 1812 demonstrated in the first place that a country of such size could not be conquered (which might well have been foreseen), and in the second that the prospect of eventual success does not always decrease in proportion to lost battles, captured capitals, and occupied provinces, which is something that diplomats used to regard as dogma, and made them always ready to conclude a peace however bad. On the contrary, the Russians showed us that one often attains one's greatest strength in the heart of one's own country, when the enemy's offensive power is exhausted, and the defensive can then switch with enormous energy to the offensive.[24]

Despite the intervening 129 years, the parallels with Hitler's advance into the Soviet Union are unmistakable. A point almost entirely lost on the German generals, who, in spite of reading accounts of the 1812 campaign and other Russian wars,[25] preferred to trust in their technological advancement and 'natural' German superiority.

The war of 1812 was certainly not the only invasion from which German generals could have learned instructive lessons. The German army's own failure to successfully implement the famous Schlieffen plan in 1914 also merits strong comparisons with Barbarossa. Just as the defeat of France in 1940 had swelled the superiority myth to dangerous proportions within the German army, so too had the memory of 1870[26] seriously influenced planning and expectations on the eve of World War I. As the powerful right wing of the German western front wheeled through Belgium in the opening act of World War I, serious problems soon undermined the success of Schlieffen's planned strategic envelopment. The German railways proved magnificent at mobilising and concentrating the great mass of the German army, but from here the German field armies had to march to war, leaving supply railheads further behind with every day.[27] Efforts to extend the railways suffered from poor planning and inadequate resources.[28] Trucks were too few in number and too slow over the congested roads to bridge the gap. The constant demands also

---

[24] Howard and Paret (eds.), Carl von Clausewitz, *On War*, p. 258.
[25] Guderian makes reference to having studied the campaigns of Charles XII of Sweden and Napoleon I (Guderian, *Panzer Leader*, p. 142). Kluge's desk at his headquarters in Warsaw was said to be laden with books and maps on Russia and, according to Blumentritt, he read General de Caulaincourt's account of the 1812 campaign with 'the greatest attention'. Blumentritt himself studied the Soviet-Polish war (1919–1920) and delivered a series of lectures on the subject (Blumentritt, 'Moscow', pp. 34–35). In a separate publication, Blumentritt wrote about Napoleon's 1812 campaign and then commented: 'In 1941 the German commanders all remembered these French misadventures' (Blumentritt, *Von Rundstedt*, p. 102).
[26] In this year the Prussian army decisively defeated the French at the battle of Sedan, the high point of the Franco-Prussian war (1870–1871).
[27] When the pivotal battle of the Marne began the railheads of the 1st, 2nd and 3rd Armies were between 136 and 168 kilometres behind the front.
[28] Hew Strachan, *The First World War*, Volume I: *To Arms* (Oxford, 2003), pp. 239–240.

led to a high vehicle fallout rate, which by early September 1914, at the critical battle of the Marne, left only 40 per cent of the fleet serviceable. Horses were of course the main motor of the army's transportation system, but they were inadequately cared for and almost no provision had been made to provide fodder for the horses on the march.[29] The result was masses of sick and weakened horses, which soon succumbed in high numbers. Allied resistance also took its toll on German offensive strength, with casualties throughout the German field armies reaching some 265,000 men by 6 September 1914. The expansion of the front further exacerbated this weakness, while French losses were being made good by not having committed so many of their reserves from the outset and falling back on the country's interior.[30] These were not the only factors that contributed to the German failure in 1914, but they all reflect essential problems later encountered, to a lesser or greater extent, in Operation Barbarossa. Summing up the failure of the Schlieffen plan, historian Hew Strachan's judgement could apply as much to 1941 as it did to 1914. Strachan wrote:

Moltke's [the Chief of the German General Staff] lines of communication were lengthening by the day; his front broadened as the movement through France developed . . . The combination of the detached corps, the heavy losses . . . and exhaustion through the march and its attendant supply problems meant that a stage would be reached when the Germans had too few men. Thus, in almost every key index of military strength – in command, in communications, in manpower . . . – the balance was swinging from Germany to France. Much of the swing was inherent in the advance itself and the plan which had given rise to it.[31]

Later in his summary of the battle of the Marne, which may be contrasted with the battle of Smolensk, Strachan concluded: 'Germany had failed to secure the quick victory on which its war plan rested. From now on it was committed to a war on two fronts. With hindsight, some would say that Germany had already lost the war.'[32]

Operation Barbarossa's much lauded success began as just another episode of Nazi propaganda, yet this has been given amazing longevity, and even a guise of historical truth, by continual acceptance in stoutly uncritical military histories. In spite of some severe early blows to the Red Army, the German army never really came close to their definitive goal

---

[29] This is because of the sheer scale of the undertaking. Kluck's 1st Army alone had 84,000 horses, which required some two million pounds of fodder a day. Living off the land was, therefore, the only option available in spite of its inadequacy (van Creveld, *Supplying War*, pp. 124–126).

[30] Strachan, *The First World War*, pp. 230–231 and 241.   [31] Ibid., p. 242.

[32] Ibid., p. 261. Evan Mawdsley's discussion is also enlightening: Mawdsley, *Thunder in the East*, pp. 44 and 53.

of conquering the Soviet Union. Indeed, it was these early 'successes' which led to the Wehrmacht's own rapid exhaustion and insurmountable difficulties. By mid-August 1941, it was already abundantly clear that Barbarossa would fall well short of achieving its operational objectives, while the ongoing scale of attrition would paradoxically transform its legacy from the annihilation of the Red Army to the ceaseless destruction of the German Wehrmacht. While the precise path to an Allied victory was by no means clear in late August 1941, Germany's inability to win the war was at least assured. Accordingly, if on 22 June 1941 Hitler was right and the world did indeed collectively hold its breath – the course of operations ensured that, by the middle of August, the world could breathe again.

Bibliography

ARCHIVAL REFERENCES

BA-MA RH 2/247. 'Oberkommando des Heeres/Generalstab des Heeres'
BA-MA RW 19/164. 'OKW/Wehrwirtschafts- und Rüstungsamt'

FIELD MARSHAL FEDOR VON BOCK

BA-MA N-22/7. 'Tagebuchnotizen Osten – Vorbereitungszeit, 20.9.1940 bis 21.6.1941'
BA-MA N-22/9. 'Tagebuchnotizen Osten I, 22.6.1941 bis 5.1.1942'

PERSONAL FILES

BA-MA Pers 6/27. 'Personalakten für Guderian, Heinz'
BA-MA Pers 6/38. 'Personalakten für Hoth, Hermann'
BA-MA Pers 6/56. 'Personalakten für Strauss, Adolf'
BA-MA Pers 6/62. 'Personalakten für Weichs, Max. Frhr. von'

ARMY GROUP CENTRE

BA-MA RH 19 II/386. 'Kriegstagebuch Nr.1 (Band August 1941) des Oberkommandos der Heeresgruppe Mitte'
BA-MA RH 19 II/128. 'Tagesmeldungen der Heeresgruppe Mitte vom 22.6.41 bis 15.7.41'
BA-MA RH 19 II/129. 'Tagesmeldungen der Heeresgruppe Mitte vom 16.7.41 bis 5.8.41'
BA-MA RH 19 II/130. 'Tagesmeldungen der Heeresgruppe Mitte vom 6.8.41 bis 26.8.41'

4TH PANZER ARMY

BA-MA RH 20–4/162. 'A.O.K.4 Ia Anlage zum K.T.B. Nr.8 Tagesmeldungen des Korps von 21.6.41 – 9.7.41'

PANZER GROUP 2

BA-MA RH 21–2/927. 'KTB Nr.1 Panzergruppe 2 vom 22.6.1941 bis 21.7.41'

BA-MA RH 21–2/928. 'KTB Nr.1 Panzergruppe 2 Bd.II vom 22.7.1941 bis 20.8.41'

BA-MA RH 21–2/819. 'Kriegstagebuch der O.Qu.-Abt. Pz. A.O.K.2 von 21.6.41 bis 31.3.42'

BA-MA RH 21–2/757. 'Verlustmeldungen 5.7.1941 – 25.3.1942'

BA-MA RH 24–47/2. 'Kriegstagebuch Nr.2 XXXXVII.Pz.Korps. Ia 25.5.1941 – 22.9.1941'

BA-MA RH 26–29/6. 'Kriegstagebuch der 29.I.D. (mot) vom: 25.5.1941 bis 29.7.1941'

BA-MA RH 26–29/16. 'Kriegstagebuch Nr.2 der 29.I.D. (mot) vom: 30.7.1941 bis 25.8.1941'

BA-MA RH 27–18/20. '18. Panzer Division, Abt. Ia. Kriegstagebuch Teil I vom: 22.6 – 20.8.41'

BA-MA RH 24–46/8. 'Kriegstagesbuch Nr.2 des XXXXVI.Pz.Korps Teil II. 8.7.41 – 23.8.41'

BA-MA RH 27–10/26a. 'Kriegstagebuch der 10.Panzer Division Nr.5 vom: 22.5. bis: 7.10.41'

BA-MA RH 27–3/14. 'KTB 3rd Pz. Div. vom 16.8.40 bis 18.9.41'

BA-MA RH 27–3/218. 'KTB 3rd Pz. Div. I.b 19.5.41 – 6.2.42'

BA-MA RH 27–4/27. 'Kriegstagebuch 4.Panzer-Division Führungs Abtl. 26.5.41 – 31.3.42'

BA-MA RH 29–1/5. '1.Kav.Div. Ia: KTB Anl. Von 1.4.1941 – 23.7.1941'

PANZER GROUP 3

BA-MA Microfilm 59054. '3rd Pz. Gr. KTB 25.5.41 – 31.8.41'

BA-MA RH 21–3/46. 'Panzerarmeeoberkommandos Anlagen zum Kriegstagesbuch "Berichte, Besprechungen, Beurteilungen der Lage" Bd.III 25.5.41 – 22.7.41'

BA-MA RH 21–3/47. 'Panzerarmeeoberkommandos Anlagen zum Kriegstagesbuch "Berichte, Besprechungen, Beurteilungen der Lage" Bd.IV 22.7.41 – 31.8.41'.

BA-MA RH 21–3/43. 'Panzerarmeeoberkommandos Tagesmeldungen 21.6 – 31.8.41'

BA-MA RH 24–57/2. 'Gen.Kdo.LVII.Pz.Korps Kriegstagesbuch Nr.1 vom 15.2. – 31.10.41'

BA-MA RH 26–14/10. 'Kriegstagesbuch Ia. 14.Inf.Div. (mot) vom 25.5.41 – 1.10.41'

BA-MA RH 27–12/2. 'Kriegstagebuch Nr.1 der 12.Pz.Div. vom 25.5.41 – 30.9.41'

BA-MA RH 27–19/23. 'Kriegstagesbuch 19.Panzer-Division Abt.Ib für die Zeit vom 1.6.1941 – 31.12.1942'

BA-MA RH 27–20/2. 'KTB 20th Pz. Div. vom 25.5.41 bis 15.8.41'

BA-MA RH 27–7/46. 'Kriegstagebuch Nr.3 der 7.Panzer-Division Führungsabteilung 1.6.1941 – 9.5.1942'

PRIMARY AND SECONDARY SOURCES

Anfilov, Viktor, 'Timoshenko' in Harold Shukman (ed.), *Stalin's Generals* (London, 1993), pp. 239–253.

'Zhukov' in Harold Shukman (ed.), *Stalin's Generals* (London, 1993), pp. 343–360.

Arnold, Klaus J., *Die Wehrmacht und die Besatzungspolitik in den besetzten Gebieten der Sowjetunion. Kriegführung und Radikalisierung im 'Unternehmen Barbarossa'* (Berlin, 2005).

Axell, Albert, *Stalin's War Through the Eyes of His Commanders* (London, 1997).

Russia's Heroes, 1941–45: An Epic Account of Struggle and Survival on the Eastern Front (London, 2001).

Axworthy, Mark, 'Peasant Scapegoat to Industrial Slaughter: the Romanian Soldier at the Siege of Odessa' in Paul Addison and Angus Calder (eds.), *A Time to Kill. The Soldier's Experience of War in the West 1939–1945* (London, 1997), pp. 221–232.

Axis Slovakia: Hitler's Slavic Wedge 1938–1945 (New York, 2002).

Axworthy, Mark, Cornel Scafes and Cristian Craciunoiu, *Third Axis Fourth Ally. Romanian Armed Forces in the European War, 1941–1945* (London, 1995).

Bähr, Walter and Hans Bähr (eds), *Kriegsbriefe gefallener Studenten, 1939–1945* (Tübingen and Stuttgart, 1952).

Barber, John and Mark Harrison, *The Soviet Home Front 1941–1945: A Social and Economic History of the USSR in World War II* (London, 1991).

Bartov, Omer, *The Eastern Front, 1941–45, German Troops and the Barbarisation of Warfare* (London, 1985).

'Soldiers, Nazis, and War in the Third Reich', *Journal of Modern History* 63 (1991), 44–60.

Hitler's Army. Soldiers, Nazis, and War in the Third Reich (Oxford, 1992).

'From *Blitzkrieg* to Total War: Controversial Links between Image and Reality' in Ian Kershaw and Moshe Lewin (eds.), *Stalinism and Nazism. Dictatorships in Comparison* (Cambridge, 2003), pp. 158–184.

Beevor, Antony, *Stalingrad* (London, 1998).

Bellamy, Chris, *Absolute War. Soviet Russia in the Second World War* (New York, 2007).

Below, Nicolaus von, *Als Hitlers Adjutant 1937–45* (Mainz, 1999).

Berkhoff, Karel C., *Harvest of Despair. Life and Death in Ukraine Under Nazi Rule* (Cambridge, 2004).

Besymenski, Lew, *Sonderakte Barbarossa. Dokumentarbericht zur Vorgeschichte des deutschen Überfalls auf die Sowjetunion – aus sowjetischer Sicht* (Reinbek, 1973).

Bidermann, Gottlob Herbert, *In Deadly Combat. A German Soldier's Memoir of the Eastern Front* (Lawrence, 2000).

Blau, George, *The Campaign Against Russia (1940–1942)* (Washington, 1955).

Blumentritt, Günther, *Von Rundstedt. The Soldier and the Man* (London, 1952).

'Moscow' in William Richardson and Seymour Freidin (eds.), *The Fatal Decisions* (London, 1956), pp. 29–74.

Boberach, Heinz (ed.), *Meldungen aus dem Reich. Die geheimen Lageberichte des Sicherheitsdienstes der SS 1938–1945*, Band 7 (Berlin, 1984).

(ed.), *Meldungen aus dem Reich. Die geheimen Lageberichte des Sicherheitsdienstes der SS 1938–1945*, Band 8 (Berlin, 1984).

Bock, Fedor von, *Generalfeldmarschall Fedor von Bock. The War Diary 1939–1945*, ed. Klaus Gerbet (Atglen, 1996).

Bond, Brian, 'Brauchitsch' in Correlli Barnett (ed.), *Hitler's Generals* (London, 1989), pp. 75–99.

The Pursuit of Victory. From Napoleon to Saddam Hussein (Oxford, 1998).

Bonwetsch, Bernd, 'Stalin, the Red Army, and the "Great Patriotic War"' in Ian Kershaw and Moshe Lewin (eds.), *Stalinism and Nazism. Dictatorships in Comparison* (Cambridge, 2003), pp. 185–207.

Boog, Horst, 'Die Luftwaffe' in Militärgeschichtliches Forschungsamt (ed.), *Das Deutsche Reich und der Zweite Weltkrieg. Band 4. Der Angriff auf die Sowjetunion* (Stuttgart, 1983), pp. 277–318 and 652–712.

Bordiugov, Gennadi, 'The Popular Mood in the Unoccupied Soviet Union: Continuity and Change During the War' in Robert Thurston and Bernd Bonwetsch (eds.), *The People's War. Responses to World War II in the Soviet Union* (Chicago, 2000), pp. 54–70.

Braithwaite, Rodric, *Moscow 1941. A City and Its People at War* (New York, 2006).

Brett-Smith, Richard, *Hitler's Generals* (London, 1976).

Broekmeyer, Marius, *Stalin, The Russians, and Their War 1941–1945* (London, 2004).

Browning, Christopher R. and Jürgen Matthäus, *The Origins of the Final Solution: The Evolution of Nazi Jewish Policy, September 1939–March 1942* (London, 2005).

Bullock, Alan, *Hitler. A Study in Tyranny* (London, 1962).

Hitler and Stalin. Parallel Lives (London, 1993).

Burleigh, Michael, *Germany Turns Eastwards. A Study of 'Ostforschung' in the Third Reich* (Cambridge, 1988).

The Third Reich. A New History (London, 2001).

Busse, Hans, 'Das Scheitern des Operationsplanes "Barbarossa" im Sommer 1941 und die militaristische Legende von der "Führungskrise"', *Zeitschrift für Militärgeschichte* 1 (1962), 62–83.

Butler, Rupert, *Hitler's Jackals* (Barnsley, 1998).

Carell, Paul, *Hitler's War on Russia. The Story of the German Defeat in the East* (London, 1964).

Cecil, Robert, *Hitler's Decision to Invade Russia 1941* (London, 1975).

Chapman, John, 'The Imperial Japanese Navy and the North–South Dilemma' in John Erickson and David Dilks (eds.), *Barbarossa. The Axis and the Allies* (Edinburgh, 1998), pp. 150–206.

Chor'kov, Anatoli G., 'The Red Army During the Initial Phase of the Great Patriotic War' in Bernd Wegner (ed.), *From Peace to War. Germany, Soviet Russia and the World, 1939–1941* (Oxford, 1997), pp. 415–429.

Churchill, Winston S., *The Second World War. Abridged Edition* (London, 1959).

Never Give In: The Best of Winston Churchill's Speeches (New York, 2003).

Citino, Robert M., *Death of the Wehrmacht. The German Campaigns of 1942* (Lawrence, 2007).

Clark, Alan, *Barbarossa. The Russian–German Conflict 1941–1945* (London, 1996).

Clausewitz, Carl von, *The Campaign of 1812 in Russia* (New York, 1995).

Conze, Susanne and Beate Fieseler, 'Soviet Women as Comrades-in Arms: A Blind Spot in the History of the War' in Robert Thurston and Bernd Bonwetsch (eds.), *The People's War. Responses to World War II in the Soviet Union* (Chicago, 2000), pp. 211–234.

Cooper, Matthew, *The Phantom War. The German Struggle Against Soviet Partisans 1941–1944* (London, 1979).

The German Army 1933–1945. Its Political and Military Failure (New York, 1984).

Coox, Alvin D., *Nomanhan. Japan Against Russia 1939* (Stanford, 1990).

Creveld, Martin van, *Supplying War. Logistics from Wallenstein to Patton* (Cambridge, 1984).

Dallin, Alexander, *German Rule in Russia 1941–1945. A Study of Occupation Policies* (London, 1957).

Davies, Norman, *No Simple Victory. World War II in Europe, 1939–1945* (London, 2007).

Dawidowicz, Lucy, *The War Against the Jews 1933–45* (London, 1987).

Deighton, Len, *Blitzkrieg. From the Rise of Hitler to the Fall of Dunkirk* (London, 1980).

Deist, Wilhelm, 'Die militärische Planung des "Unternehmens Barbarossa"' in Roland G. Foerster (ed.), *'Unternehmen Barbarossa'* (Munich, 1993), pp. 109–122.

Department of the U.S. Army (ed.), *Military Improvisations During the Russian Campaign* (Washington, 1951).

(ed.), *German Armored Traffic Control During the Russian Campaign* (Washington, 1952).

(ed.), *Small Unit Actions During the German Campaign in Russia* (Washington, 1953).

DiNardo, Richard L., *Mechanized Juggernaut or Military Anachronism: Horses and the German Army in World War II* (London, 1991).

'The Dysfunctional Coalition: The Axis Powers and the Eastern Front in World War II', *The Journal of Military History* 60(4) (October, 1996), 711–730.

Germany and the Axis Powers. From Coalition to Collapse (Lawrence, 2005).

Domarus, Max, *Hitler. Speeches and Proclamations 1932–1945. The Chronicle of a Dictatorship*, Volume III: *The Years 1939 to 1940* (Würzburg, 1997).

Hitler. Speeches and Proclamations 1932–1945. The Chronicle of a Dictatorship, Volume IV: *The Years 1941 to 1945* (Wauconda, 2004).

Douglas, Roy, *The World War 1939–1943. The Cartoonists' Vision* (London, 1990).

Drabkin, Artem (ed.), *The Red Air Force At War. Barbarossa & the Retreat to Moscow. Recollections of Fighter Pilots on the Eastern Front* (Barnsley, 2007).

Drechsler, Karl, 'Germany and its Allies and the War Against the Soviet Union, 1940–42' in Joseph Wieczynski (ed.), *Operation Barbarossa. The German Attack on the Soviet Union June 22, 1941* (Salt Lake City, 1993), pp. 30–47.

Dunn, Walter S., Jr., *Stalin's Keys to Victory. The Rebirth of the Red Army in WWII* (Mechanicsburg, 2006).
Durrwanger, Alfred, '28th Infantry Division Operations' in David M. Glantz (ed.), *The Initial Period of War on the Eastern Front 22 June–August 1941* (London, 1997), pp. 232–237 and 438–439.
Dzeniskevich, Andrei R., 'The Social and Political Situation in Leningrad in the First Months of the German Ivasion: The Social Psychology of the Workers' in Robert Thurston and Bernd Bonwetsch (eds.), *The People's War. Responses to World War II in the Soviet Union* (Chicago, 2000), pp. 71–83.
Eberle, Henrik and Matthias Uhl (eds.), *The Hitler Book. The Secret Dossier Prepared for Stalin from the Interrogations of Hitler's Personal Aides* (New York, 2005).
Eby, Cecil D., *Hungary at War. Civilians and Soldiers in World War II* (University Park, 1998).
Emelianenko, Vasily B., *Red Star Against the Swastika. The Story of a Soviet Pilot over the Eastern Front* (London, 2005).
Erickson, John, *The Soviet High Command 1918–1941. A Military–Political History 1918–1941* (London, 1962).
The Road to Stalingrad. Stalin's War with Germany, Volume I (London, 1975).
'Soviet War Losses. Calculations and Controversies' in John Erickson and David Dilks (eds.), *Barbarossa. The Axis and the Allies* (Edinburgh, 1998), pp. 255–277.
Fest, Joachim, *Hitler* (Orlando, 1974).
Filipescu, Mihai Tone, *Reluctant Axis: The Romanian Army in Russia 1941–1944* (Chapultepeq, 2006).
Foot, M. R. D., 'USSR' in I. C. B. Dear and M. R. D. Foot (eds.), *The Oxford Companion to the Second World War* (Oxford, 1995), pp. 1207–1243.
Förster, Jürgen, 'Das Unternehmen "Barbarossa" als Eroberungs- und Vernichtungskrieg' in Militärgeschichtliches Forschungsamt (ed.), *Das Deutsche Reich und der Zweite Weltkrieg*, Band 4: *Der Angriff auf die Sowjetunion* (Stuttgart, 1983), pp. 413–447.
'Die Entscheidungen der "Dreierpaktstaaten"' in Militärgeschichtliches Forschungsamt (ed.), *Das Deutsche Reich und der Zweite Weltkrieg*, 1983, pp. 883–907.
'Die Gewinnung von Verbündeten in Südosteuropa' in Militärgeschichtlichen Forschungsamt (ed.), *Das Deutsche Reich und der Zweite Weltkrieg*, 1983, pp. 327–364.
'Die Sicherung des "Lebensraumes" Sowjetunion' in Militärgeschichtlichen Forschungsamt (ed.), *Das Deutsche Reich und der Zweite Weltkrieg*, 1983, pp. 1030–1078.
'Freiwillige für den "Kreuzzug Europas gegen den Bolschewismus"' in Militärgeschichtliches Forschungsamt (ed.), *Das Deutsche Reich und der Zweite Weltkrieg*, 1983, pp. 908–926.
'Hitlers Entscheidung für den Krieg gegen die Sowjetunion' in Militärgeschichtliches Forschungsamt (ed.), *Das Deutsche Reich und der Zweite Weltkrieg*, 1983, pp. 3–37.

'New Wine in Old Skins? The Wehrmacht and the War of "Weltanschauungen", 1941' in Wilhelm Deist (ed.), *The German Military in the Age of Total War* (Warwickshire, 1985), pp. 304–322.

'The German Army and the Ideological War against the Soviet Union' in Gerhard Hischfeld (ed.), *The Politics of Genocide: Jews and Soviet Prisoners of War in Nazi Germany* (London, 1986), pp. 15–29.

'The Dynamics of Volksgemeinschaft: The Effectiveness of the German Military Establishment in the Second World War' in Allan Millett and Williamson Murray (eds.), *Military Effectiveness*, Volume III: *The Second World War* (Winchester, 1988), pp. 180–220.

'Zum Russlandbild der Militärs 1941–1945' in Hans-Erich Volkmann (ed.), *Das Russlandbild im Dritten Reich* (Köln, 1994), pp. 141–163.

'Hitler Turns East – German War Policy in 1940 and 1941' in Bernd Wegner (ed.), *From Peace to War. Germany, Soviet Russia and the World, 1939–1941* (Oxford, 1997), pp. 115–133.

'Motivation and Indoctrination in the Wehrmacht, 1933–45' in Paul Addison and Angus Calder (eds.), *A Time to Kill. The Soldier's Experience of War in the West 1939–1945* (London, 1997), pp. 263–273.

Forty, George, *German Tanks of World War II* (London, 1999).

Frieser, Karl-Heinz, *Blitzkrieg-Legende. Der Westfeldzug 1940* (Munich, 1996). English translation: Frieser, Karl-Heinz, *The Blitzkrieg Legend. The 1940 Campaign in the West* (Annapolis, 2005).

Frisch, Franz A. P. in association with Wilbur D. Jones, Jr., *Condemned to Live. A Panzer Artilleryman's Five-Front War* (Shippensburg, 2000).

Fritz, Stephen G., *Frontsoldaten. The German Soldier in World War II* (Lexington, 1995).

Fröhlich, Elke (ed.), *Die Tagebücher von Joseph Goebbels*, Teil II: Diktate 1941–1945, Band 1, Juli–September 1941 (Munich, 1996).

(ed.), *Die Tagebücher von Joseph Goebbels*, Teil I: Aufzeichnungen 1923–1941, Band 9, Dezember 1940–Juli 1941 (Munich, 1998).

Fuchs Richardson, Horst (ed.), *Sieg Heil! War Letters of Tank Gunner Karl Fuchs 1937–1941* (Hamden, 1987).

Fugate, Bryan, *Operation Barbarossa. Strategy and Tactics on the Eastern Front, 1941* (Novato, 1984).

Fugate, Bryan and Lev Dvoretsky, *Thunder on the Dnepr. Zhukov–Stalin and the Defeat of Hitler's Blitzkrieg* (Novato, 1997).

Gareis, Martin, *Kampf und Ende der Fränkisch-Sudetendeutschen 98. Infanterie-Division* (Eggolsheim, 1956).

Geddes, Giorgio, *Nichivó. Life, Love and Death on the Russian Front* (London, 2001).

Gerlach, Christian, *Kalkulierte Morde. Die deutsche Wirtschafts- und Vernichtungspolitik in Weißrussland 1941 bis 1944* (Hamburg, 2000).

Gersdorff, Rudolf-Christoph Frhr. von, *Soldat im Untergang* (Frankfurt am Main, 1977).

Geyer, Hermann, *Das IX. Armeekorps im Ostfeldzug 1941* (Neckargemünd, 1969).

Geyer, Michael, 'German Strategy in the Age of Machine Warfare,1914–1945' in Peter Paret (ed.), *Makers of Modern Strategy. From Machiavelli to the Nuclear Age* (Oxford, 1999), pp. 527–597.

Gibbons, Robert, 'Opposition gegen "Barbarossa" im Herbst 1940 – Eine Denkschrift aus der deutschen Botschaft in Moskau', *Vierteljahrshefte für Zeitgeschichte* 23 (1975), 332–340.

Gilbert, Martin, *The Holocaust. The Jewish Tragedy* (London, 1986).

Glantz, David M., 'Introduction: Prelude to Barbarossa. The Red Army in 1941' in David M. Glantz (ed.), *The Initial Period of War on the Eastern Front 22 June–August 1941* (London, 1993), pp. 1–39.

'The Border Battles on the Bialystok–Minsk Axis: 22–28 June 1941' in David M. Glantz (ed.), *The Initial Period of War on the Eastern Front 22 June–August 1941* (London, 1997), pp. 184–225.

Stumbling Colossus. The Red Army on the Eve of World War (Lawrence, 1998).

'The Red Army at War, 1941–1945: Sources and Interpretations', *The Journal of Military History* 62(3) (July, 1998), 595–617.

Forgotten Battles of the German-Soviet War (1941–1945), Volume I: *The Summer–Fall Campaign (22 June–4 December 1941)* (Privately published study by David M. Glantz, 1999).

Atlas of the Battle of Smolensk 7 July–10 September 1941 (Privately published by David M. Glantz, 2001).

Barbarossa. Hitler's Invasion of Russia 1941 (Stroud, 2001).

The Battle for Smolensk: 7 July–10 September 1941 (Privately published study by David M. Glantz, 2001), pp. 14–15.

'Forgotten Battles' in The Military Book Club (ed.), *Slaughterhouse. The Encyclopedia of the Eastern Front* (New York, 2002), pp. 471–496.

'Introduction' in The Military Book Club (ed.), *Slaughterhouse. The Encyclopedia of the Eastern Front* (New York, 2002), pp. 1–14.

The Battle for Leningrad 1941–1944 (Lawrence, 2002).

Atlas and Operational Summary The Border Battles 22 June–1 July 1941 (Privately published by David M. Glantz, 2003).

Colossus Reborn. The Red Army at War, 1941–1943 (Lawrence, 2005).

The Soviet–German War 1941–1945: Myths and Realities: A Survey Essay (Privately published study by David M. Glantz).

Glantz, David M. and Jonathan House, *When Titans Clashed. How the Red Army Stopped Hitler* (Lawrence, 1995).

Golovchansky, Anatoly, Valentin Osipov, Anatoly Prokopenko, Ute Daniel and Jürgen Reulecke (eds.), *'Ich will raus aus diesem Wahnsinn': Deutsche Briefe von der Ostfront 1941–1945 aus sowjetischen Archiven* (Hamburg, 1993).

Göpfert, Helmut, 'Zur Anfangsperiode des faschistischen Überfalls auf die Sowjetunion', *Zeitschrift für Militärgeschichte* 4(2) (1965), 161–173.

'Das Scheitern des Blitzkrieges der faschistischen Wehrmacht an der deutsch-sowjetischen Front' in Erhard Moritz (ed.), *Das Fiasko der antisowjetischen Aggression. Studien zur Kriegführung des deutschen Imperialismus gegen die UdSSR (1941–1945)* (East Berlin, 1978), pp. 45–73.

Gorinov, Mikhail M., 'Muscovites' Moods, 22 June 1941 to May 1942' in Robert Thurston and Bernd Bonwetsch (eds.), *The People's War. Responses to World War II in the Soviet Union* (Chicago, 2000), pp. 108–134.

Görlitz, Walter, *Paulus and Stalingrad* (London, 1963).

(ed.), *The Memoirs of Field-Marshal Keitel. Chief of the German High Command, 1938–1945* (New York, 1966).

Gorodetsky, Gabriel, 'Stalin and Hitler's Attack on the Soviet Union' in Bernd Wegner (ed.), *From Peace to War. Germany, Soviet Russia and the World, 1939–1941* (Oxford, 1997), pp. 343–359.

Grand Delusion. Stalin and the German Invasion of Russia (New Haven, 1999).

Graichen, Patrick, 'Deutsche Vergangenheitspolitik und deutscher "National-stolz"' in Stiftung für die Rechte zukünftiger Generationen (ed.), *Was bleibt von der Vergangenheit? Die junge Generation im Dialog über den Holocaust* (Berlin, 1999), pp. 222–229.

Greiner, Helmuth, *Die Oberste Wehrmachtführung 1939–1943* (Wiesbaden, 1951).

Grenkevich, Leonid, *The Soviet Partisan Movement 1941–1944* (London, 1999).

Gretschko, A. A. (ed.), *Geschichte des Zweiten Weltkrieges 1939–1945*, Volume II: *Am Vorabend des Krieges* (East Berlin, 1975).

Groehler, Olaf, 'Goals and Reason: Hitler and the German Military' in Joseph Wieczynski (ed.), *Operation Barbarossa. The German Attack on the Soviet Union June 22, 1941* (Salt Lake City, 1993), pp. 48–61.

Grossjohann, Georg, *Five Years, Four Fronts. The War Years of Georg Grossjohann, Major, German Army (Retired)* (Bedford, 1999).

Grossman, Vasily, *A Writer at War. Vasily Grossman with the Red Army 1941–1945*, ed. Antony Beevor and Luba Vinogradova (New York, 2005).

Guderian, Heinz, *Panzer Leader* (New York, 1952).

Achtung-Panzer! The Development of Tank Warfare (London, 2002).

Günther, Helmut, *Hot Motors, Cold Feet. A Memoir of Service with the Motorcycle Battalion of SS-Division 'Reich' 1940–1941* (Winnipeg, 2004).

Haape, Heinrich in association with Dennis Henshaw, *Moscow Tram Stop. A Doctor's Experiences with the German Spearhead in Russia* (London, 1957).

Habeck, Mary, *Storm of Steel. The Development of Armor Doctrine in Germany and the Soviet Union, 1919–1939* (London, 2003).

Hagen, Mark von, 'Soviet Soldiers and Officers on the Eve of the German Invasion: Towards a Description of Social Psychology and Political Attitudes' in Robert Thurston and Bernd Bonwetsch (eds.), *The People's War. Responses to World War II in the Soviet Union* (Chicago, 2000), pp. 187–210.

Halder, Franz, *Hitler als Feldherr* (Munich, 1949).

Hitler as Warlord (London, 1950).

Kriegstagebuch: Tägliche Aufzeichnungen des Chefs des Generalstabes des Heeres 1939–1942, Band I: *Vom Polenfeldzug bis zum Ende der Westoffensive (14.8.1939 – 30.6.1940)*; Band II: *Von der geplanten Landung in England bis zum Beginn des Ostfeldzuges (1.7.1940 – 21.6.1941)*, ed. Hans-Adolf Jacobsen and Alfred Philippi (Arbeitskreis für Wehrforschung, Stuttgart, 1962); Band III: *Der Russlandfeldzug bis zum Marsch auf Stalingrad (22.6.1941 – 24.9.1942)*, ed. Hans-Adolf Jacobsen and Alfred Philippi (Arbeitskreis für Wehrforschung, Stuttgart, 1964). Abridged English translation: Halder, Franz, *The Halder*

War Diary 1939–1942, ed. Charles Burdick and Hans-Adolf Jacobsen (London, 1988).

Hancock, Eleanor, *The National Socialist Leadership and Total War 1941–45* (New York, 1991).

Hansmann, Claus, *Vorüber – Nicht Vorbei. Russische Impressionen 1941–1943* (Frankfurt, 1989).

Hardesty, Von, *Red Phoenix. The Rise of Soviet Air Power 1941–1945* (Washington DC, 1982).

Hartmann, Christian, *Halder Generalstabschef Hitlers 1938–1942* (Munich, 1991).

'Franz Halder – Der verhinderte Generalstabschef' in Ronald Smelser and Enrico Syring (eds.), *Die Militärelite des Dritten Reiches. 27 biographische Skizzen* (Berlin, 1995), pp. 209–222.

Hassell, Ulrich von, *Vom andern Deutschland* (Freiburg, 1946). English translation: Hassell, Ulrich von, *The Von Hassell Diaries 1938–1944* (London, 1948).

Haupt, Werner, *Die Schlachten der Heeresgruppe Mitte. Aus der Sicht der Divisionen* (Friedberg, 1983).

Army Group Center. The Wehrmacht in Russia 1941–1945 (Atglen, 1997).

Hayward, Joel, *Stopped at Stalingrad. The Luftwaffe and Hitler's Defeat in the East, 1942–1943* (Lawrence, 1998).

Healy, Mark, *Kursk 1943: Tide Turns in the East* (Oxford, 2000).

Heer, Hannes and Klaus Naumann, *War of Extermination. The German Military in World War II 1941–1944* (Oxford, 2006).

Herbst, Ludolf, *Das nationalsozialistische Deutschland 1933–1945. Die Entfesselung der Gewalt Rassismus und Krieg* (Frankfurt am Main, 1996).

Herring, George C., Jr., *Aid to Russia 1941–1946. Strategy, Diplomacy, The Origins of the Cold War* (New York, 1973).

Heuser, Beatrice, *The Bomb. Nuclear Weapons in their Historical Strategic and Ethical Context* (Harlow, 2000).

Heusinger, Adolf, *Befehl im Widerstreit. Schicksalsstunden der deutschen Armee 1923–1945* (Tübingen, 1957).

Hilberg, Raul, *The Destruction of the European Jews* (Chicago, 1973).

Hildebrand, Klaus, 'Hitlers "Programm" und seine Realisierung 1939–1942' in Manfred Funke (ed.), *Hitler, Deutschland und die Mächte. Materialien zur Außenpolitik des Dritten Reiches* (Düsseldorf, 1976), pp. 63–93.

Deutsche Außenpolitik, 1933–1945. Kalkül oder Dogma? 4th edn (Stuttgart, 1980).

Hill, Alexander, *The War Behind the Eastern Front. The Soviet Partisan Movement in North-West Russia 1941–1944* (New York, 2005).

'British "Lend-Lease" Tanks and the Battle for Moscow, November–December 1941 – A Research Note', *Journal of Slavic Military Studies* 19(2) (June 2006), 289–294.

'British Lend-Lease Aid and the Soviet War Effort, June 1941–June 1942', *Journal of Military History* 71(3) (July 2007), 773–808.

Hill, Leonidas E. (ed.), *Die Weizsäcker-Papiere 1933–1950* (Frankfurt am Main, 1974).

Hillgruber, Andreas, *Der Zenit des Zweiten Weltkrieges Juli 1941* (Wiesbaden, 1977).

'Die Bedeutung der Schlacht von Smolensk in der zweiten Juli-Hälfte 1941 für den Ausgang des Ostkrieges' in Inge Auerbach, Andreas Hillgruber and Gottfried Schramm (eds.), *Felder und Vorfelder russischer Geschichte. Studien zu Ehren von Peter Scheibert* (Freiburg, 1985), pp. 266–279.

Die Zerstörung Europas. Beiträge zur Weltkriegsepoche 1914 bis 1945 (Frankfurt am Main, 1988), pp. 296–312.

Hitlers Strategie. Politik und Kriegführung 1940–1941 (Bonn, 1993).

'The German Military Leaders' View of Russia Prior to the Attack on the Soviet Union' in Bernd Wegner (ed.), *From Peace to War. Germany, Soviet Russia and the World, 1939–1941* (Oxford, 1997), pp. 169–185.

Hinsley, H. F., 'British Intelligence and Barbarossa' in John Erickson and David Dilks (eds.), *Barbarossa. The Axis and the Allies* (Edinburgh, 1998), pp. 43–75.

Hitler, Adolf, *Mein Kampf* (New York, 1999).

Hofer, Walter, *War Premeditated* (London, 1954).

Hoffmann, Joachim, 'Die Kriegführung aus der Sicht der Sowjetunion' in Militärgeschichtlichen Forschungsamt (ed.), *Das Deutsche Reich und der Zweite Weltkrieg*, Band 4: *Der Angriff auf die Sowjetunion.* (Stuttgart, 1983), pp. 713–809.

'The Soviet Union's Offensive Preparations in 1941' in Bernd Wegner (ed.), *From Peace to War. Germany, Soviet Russia and the World, 1939–1941* (Oxford, 1997), pp. 361–380.

Höhn, Hans (ed.), *Auf antisowjetischem Kriegskurs. Studien zur militärischen Vorbereitung des deutschen Imperialismus auf die Aggression gegen die UdSSR (1933–1941)* (Berlin, 1970).

Holz, Rick, *Too Young to be a Hero* (Sydney, 2000).

Hoth, Hermann, *Panzer-Operationen. Die Panzergruppe 3 und der operative Gedanke der deutschen Führung Sommer 1941* (Heidelberg, 1956).

Howard, Michael and Peter Paret (eds.), Carl von Clausewitz, *On War* (New York, 1993).

Howell, Edgar M., *The Soviet Partisan Movement 1941–1944* (Washington, 1956).

Hürter, Johannes, *Ein deutscher General an der Ostfront. Die Briefe und Tagebücher des Gotthard Heinrici 1941/42* (Erfurt, 2001).

'Konservative Akteure oder totale Krieger? Zum Transformationsprozess einer militärischen Elite' in Christian Hartmann, Johannes Hürter and Ulrike Jureit (eds.), *Verbrechen der Wehrmacht. Bilanz einer Debatte* (Munich, 2005), pp. 50–59.

Hitlers Heerführer. Die deutschen Oberbefehlshaber im Krieg gegen die Sowjetunion 1941/24 (Munich, 2006).

Irving, David, *The Rise and Fall of the Luftwaffe: The Life of Erhard Milch* (London, 1973).

Hitler's War, Volume I (New York, 1977).

Jächel, Eberhard, *Hitlers Weltanschauung. Entwurf einer Herrschaft* (Stuttgart, 1991).

Jacobsen, Hans-Adolf (ed.), *Kriegstagebuch des Oberkommandos der Wehrmacht (Wehrmachtführungsstab)*, Band I/1: *1. August 1940–31. Dezember 1941*; Band I/2: *1. August 1940–31. Dezember 1941* (Munich, 1982).

Jacobsen, Otto, *Erich Marcks: Soldat und Gelehrter* (Göttingen, 1971).

Jersak, Tobias, 'Die Interaktion von Kriegsverlauf und Judenvernichtung. Ein Blick auf Hitlers Strategie im Spätsommer 1941', *Historische Zeitschrift*, Band 268 (1999), 311–374.

'Blitzkrieg Revisited: A New Look at Nazi War and Extermination Planning', *Historical Journal* 43(2) (2000), 565–582.

'A Matter of Foreign Policy: "Final Solution" and "Final Victory" in Nazi Germany', *German History* 21(3) (2003), 369–391.

'Holocaust im Krieg' in Militärgeschichtlichen Forschungsamt (ed.), *Das Deutsche Reich und der Zweite Weltkrieg*, Band 9, Erster Halbband: *Die Deutsche Kriegsgesellschaft 1939 bis 1945. Politisierung, Vernichtung, Überleben* (2004), pp. 275–318.

Kay, Alex J., '"Neuordnung" and "Hungerpolitik": The Development and Compatibility of Political and Economic Planning within the Nazi Hierarchy for the Occupation of the Soviet Union, July 1940–July 1941' (PhD dissertation from the Humboldt University, 2005).

Exploitation, Resettlement, Mass Murder: Political and Economic Planning for German Occupation Policy in the Soviet Union, 1940–1941 (Oxford, 2006).

Keegan, John, *The Second World War* (New York, 1989).

Kempowski, Walter (ed.), *Das Echolot Barbarossa '41. Ein kollektives Tagebuch* (Munich, 2004).

Kern, Ernst, *War Diary 1941–45. A Report* (New York, 1993).

Kershaw, Ian, *Hitler 1936–1945. Nemesis* (London, 2001).

Kershaw, Robert, *War Without Garlands. Operation Barbarossa 1941/42* (New York, 2000).

Kesselring, Albrecht, *The Memoirs of Field-Marshal Kesselring* (London, 1953).

Kipp, Jacob W., 'Barbarossa and the Crisis of Successive Operations: The Smolensk Engagements, July 10–August 7, 1941' in Joseph Wieczynski (ed.), *Operation Barbarossa. The German Attack on the Soviet Union June, 1941* (Salt Lake City, 1993), pp. 113–150.

'Overview Phase 1: to 20 July 1941' in David M. Glantz (ed.), *The Initial Period of War on the Eastern Front 22 June–August 1941* (London, 1997), pp. 354–379.

Klein, Friedhelm and Ingo Lachnit, 'Der "Operationsentwurf Ost" des Generalmajors Marcks vom 5. August 1940', *Wehrforschung* 4 (1972), 114–123.

Kleindienst, Jürgen (ed.), *Sei tausendmal gegrüßt. Briefwechsel Irene und Ernst Guicking 1937–1945* (Berlin, 2001).

Klink, Ernst, 'Die militärische Konzeption des Krieges gegen die Sowjetunion' in Militärgeschichtlichen Forschungsamt (ed.), *Das Deutsche Reich und der Zweite Weltkrieg*, Band 4: *Der Angriff auf die Sowjetunion* (Stuttgart, 1983).

'Die Operationsführung' in Militärgeschichtliches Forschungsamt (ed.), *Das Deutsche Reich und der Zweite Weltkrieg*, Band 4: *Der Angriff auf die Sowjetunion* (Stuttgart, 1983), pp. 451–652.

Knappe, Siegfried with Ted Brusaw, *Soldat. Reflections of a German Soldier, 1936–1949* (New York, 1992).

Knopp, Guido, *Der verdammte Krieg. 'Unternehmen Barbarossa': Überfall auf die Sowjetunion 1939–41* (Munich, 1998).

Koch-Erpach, R., '4th Panzer Division's Crossing of the Dnepr River and the Advance to Roslavl' in David M. Glantz (ed.), *The Initial Period of War on the Eastern Front 22 June–August 1941* (London, 1997), pp. 403–404.

Koschorrek, Günter K., *Blood Red Snow. The Memoirs of a German Soldier on the Eastern Front* (London, 2002).

Köstring, Ernst, *Der militärische Mittler zwischen dem Deutschen Reich und der Sowjetunion 1921–1941*, ed. Hermann Teske (Frankfurt am Main, 1965).

Kotze, Hildegard von (ed.), *Heeresadjutant bei Hitler 1938–1943. Aufzeichnungen des Majors Engel* (Stuttgart, 1974).

Krausnick, Helmut and Hans-Heinrich Wilhelm, *Die Truppe des Weltanschauungskrieges: Die Einsatzgruppen der Sicherheitspolizei und des SD 1938–1942* (Stuttgart, 1981).

Krebs, Gerhard, 'Japan and the German-Soviet War, 1941' in Bernd Wegner (ed.), *From Peace to War. Germany, Soviet Russia and the World, 1939–1941* (Oxford, 1997), pp. 541–560.

Kroener, Bernhard R., 'Squaring the Circle. Blitzkrieg Strategy and the Manpower Shortage, 1939–1942' in Wilhelm Deist (ed.), *The German Military in the Age of Total War* (Warwickshire, 1985), pp. 282–303.

'Die Winter 1941/42. Die Verteilung des Mangels oder Schritte zu einer rationelleren Personalbewirtschaftung' in Militärgeschichtlichen Forschungsamt (ed.), *Das Deutsche Reich und der Zweite Weltkrieg*, Band V/1: *Organisation und Mobilisierung des deutschen Machtbereichs. Erster Halbband: Kriegsverwaltung, Wirtschaft und Personelle Ressourcen 1939–1941* (Stuttgart, 1988), pp. 871–989.

'The "Frozen *Blitzkrieg*". German Strategic Planning against the Soviet Union and the Causes of its Failure' in Bernd Wegner (ed.), *From Peace to War. Germany, Soviet Russia and the World, 1939–1941* (Oxford, 1997), pp. 135–149.

Krumpelt, Ihno, *Das Material und die Kriegführung* (Frankfurt am Main, 1968).

Kumanev, G. A., 'The Soviet Economy and the 1941 Evacuation' in Joseph Wieczynski (ed.), *Operation Barbarossa. The German Attack on the Soviet Union June 22, 1941* (Salt Lake City, 1993), pp. 163–193.

Lakowski, Richard, 'Between Professionalism and Nazism. The Wehrmacht on the Eve of its Invasion of the USSR' in Bernd Wegner (ed.), *From Peace to War. Germany, Soviet Russia and the World, 1939–1941* (Oxford, 1997), pp. 151–167.

Lamb, Richard, 'Kluge' in Correlli Barnett (ed.), *Hitler's Generals* (London, 1989), pp. 395–409.

Lammers, Walther (ed.), *'Fahrtberichte' aus der Zeit des deutsch-sowjetischen Krieges 1941. Protokolle des Begleitoffiziers des Kommandierenden Generals LIII. Armeekorps* (Boppard am Rhein, 1988).

Landon, H. C. Robbins and Sebastian Leitner (eds.), *Diary of a German Soldier* (London, 1963).

Leach, Barry, *German Strategy Against Russia 1939–1941* (Oxford, 1973).
'Halder' in Correlli Barnett (ed.), *Hitler's Generals* (London, 1989), pp. 101–126.
Lemelsen, Joachim, *29.Division* (Bad Nauheim, 1960).
Lemm, 'Discussion' in David M. Glantz (ed.), *The Initial Period of War on the Eastern Front 22 June–August 1941* (London, 1997), pp. 440–453.
Liddell Hart, Basil, *History of the Second World War* (London, 1970).
The Other Side of the Hill. Germany's Generals: Their Rise and Fall, With Their Own Account of Military Events, 1939–1945 (London, 1999).
Lingenthal, 'Discussion' in David M. Glantz (ed.), *The Initial Period of War on the Eastern Front 22 June–August 1941* (London, 1997), pp. 440–453.
Longerich, Peter, *Der ungeschriebene Befehl: Hitler und der Weg zur 'Endlösung'* (Munich, 2001).
Lubbeck, William with David Hurt, *At Leningrad's Gates. The Story of a Soldier with Army Group North* (Philadelphia, 2006).
Lucas, James, *War of the Eastern Front 1941–1945. The German Soldier in Russia* (London, 1980).
Das Reich. The Military Role of the 2nd SS Division (London, 1991).
Luck, Hans von, *Panzer Commander. The Memoirs of Colonel Hans von Luck* (New York, 1989).
Ludendorff, Erich, *Der Totale Krieg* (Munich, 1935).
Lukas, Richard C., *The Forgotten Holocaust. The Poles Under German Occupation 1939–1944* (New York, 1997).
Macksey, Kenneth, *Guderian. Panzer General* (London, 1975).
'Guderian' in Correlli Barnett (ed.), *Hitler's Generals* (London, 1989), pp. 441–460.
'Generaloberst Heinz Guderian' in Gerd R. Ueberschär (ed.), *Hitlers militärische Elite* (Darmstadt, 1998), pp. 80–87.
Magenheimer, Heinz, *Hitler's War. Germany's Key Strategic Decisions 1940–1945* (London, 1999).
Malaparte, Curzio, *The Volga Rises in Europe* (Edinburgh, 2000).
Manstein, Erich von, *Lost Victories* (Novato, 1958).
Mawdsley, Evan, *Thunder in the East. The Nazi-Soviet War 1941–1945* (London, 2005).
Mazower, Mark, *Inside Hitler's Greece. The Experience of Occupation, 1941–1944* (London, 1993).
Megargee, Geoffrey P., *Inside Hitler's High Command* (Lawrence, 2000).
War of Annihilation. Combat and Genocide on the Eastern Front 1941 (Lanham, 2006).
Meier-Welcker, Hans, *Aufzeichnungen eines Generalstabsoffiziers 1939–1942* (Freiburg, 1982).
Mendelssohn, Peter de, *Die Nürnberger Dokumente. Studien zur deutschen Kriegspolitik 1937–45* (Hamburg, 1947).
Menger, Manfred, 'Germany and the Finnish "Separate War" against the Soviet Union' in Bernd Wegner (ed.), *From Peace to War. Germany, Soviet Russia and the World, 1939–1941* (Oxford, 1997), pp. 525–539.

Merridale, Catherine, *Ivan's War. Life and Death in the Red Army, 1933–1945* (New York, 2006).

Messerschmidt, Manfred, 'June 1941 Seen Through German Memoirs and Diaries' in Joseph Wieczynski (ed.), *Operation Barbarossa. The German Attack on the Soviet Union June 22, 1941* (Utah, 1993), pp. 214–227.

Meyer, Georg (ed.), *Generalfeldmarschall Wilhelm Ritter von Leeb. Tagebuchaufzeichnungen und Lagebeurteilungen aus zwei Weltkriegen* (Stuttgart, 1976).

Adolf Heusinger. Dienst eines deutschen Soldaten 1915 bis 1964 (Berlin, 2001).

Middlebrook, Martin, 'Paulus' in Correlli Barnett (ed.), *Hitler's Generals* (London, 1989), pp. 361–372.

Militärgeschichtliches Forschungsamt (ed.), *Germany and the Second World War,* Volume IV: *The Attack on the Soviet Union* (Oxford, 1998).

Ministry of Foreign Affairs of the U.S.S.R. (ed.), *Stalin's Correspondence with Churchill, Attlee, Roosevelt and Truman 1941–1945* (New York, 1958).

Mitcham, Samuel, *Hitler's Field Marshals and Their Battles* (Chatham, 1988).

Mitcham, Samuel and Gene Mueller, *Hitler's Commanders. Officers of the Wehrmacht, the Luftwaffe, the Kriegsmarine, and the Waffen-SS* (Lanham, 2000).

Mogge, Theodor, unpublished personal recollections recorded in 1978.

Moritz, Erhard (ed.), *Fall Barbarossa. Dokumente zur Vorbereitung der faschistischen Wehrmacht auf die Aggression gegen die Sowjetunion (1940/41)* (Berlin, 1970).

Muggeridge, Malcolm (ed.), *Ciano's Diary 1939–1943* (Kingswood, 1947).

Mühleisen, Horst, 'Fedor von Bock – Soldat ohne Fortune' in Ronald Smelser and Enrico Syring (eds.), *Die Militärelite des Dritten Reiches. 27 biographische Skizzen* (Berlin, 1995), pp. 66–82.

Muller, Richard, *The German Air War in Russia* (Baltimore, 1992).

'Close Air Support. The German, British and American Experiences, 1918–1941' in Williamson Murray and Allan R. Millett (eds.), *Military Innovation in the Interwar Period* (Cambridge, 1998), pp. 144–190.

Müller, Rolf-Dieter, 'Das Scheitern der wirtschaftlichen "Blitzkriegstrategie"' in Militärgeschichtliches Forschungsamt (ed.), *Das Deutsche Reich und der Zweite Weltkrieg. Band 4. Der Angriff auf die Sowjetunion* (Stuttgart, 1983), pp. 936–1029.

'Von der Wirtschaftsallianz zum kolonialen Ausbeutungskrieg' in Militärgeschichtliches Forschungsamt (ed.), *Das Deutsche Reich und der Zweite Weltkrieg. Band 4. Der Angriff auf die Sowjetunion* (Stuttgart, 1983), pp. 98–189.

'Das "Unternehmen Barbarossa" als wirtschaftlicher Raubkrieg' in Gerd R. Ueberschär and Wolfram Wette (eds.), *'Unternehmen Barbarossa'. Der deutsche Überfall auf die Sowjetunion 1941* (Paderborn, 1984), pp. 173–196.

Der letzte deutsche Krieg 1939–1945 (Stuttgart, 2005).

Müller, Rolf-Dieter and Gerd R. Ueberschär, *Hitler's War in the East 1941–1945. A Critical Assessment* (Oxford, 1997).

Müller-Hillebrand, Burkhart, *Das Heer 1933–1945. Band III. Der Zweifrontenkrieg. Das Heer vom Beginn des Feldzuges gegen die Sowjetunion bis zum Kriegsende* (Frankfurt am Main, 1969).

Munoz, Antonio and Oleg V. Romanko, *Hitler's White Russians: Collaboration, Extermination and Anti-Partisan Warfare in Byelorussia 1941–1944. A Study of White Russian Collaboration and German Occupation Policies* (New York, 2003).

Murray, Williamson, *The Luftwaffe 1933–45. Strategy for Defeat* (Washington, 1996).

'Strategic Bombing. The British, American and German Experiences' in Williamson Murray and Allan R. Millett (eds.), *Military Innovation in the Interwar Period* (Cambridge, 1998), pp. 96–143.

Musial, Bodan, *'Konterrevolutionäre Elemente sind zu erschiessen'. Die Brutalisierung des deutsch-sowjetischen Krieges im Sommer 1941* (Berlin, 2000).

Nagorski, Andrew, 'Stalin's Tipping Point', *Newsweek* (US edition, 10 September 2007), 44.

The Greatest Battle. Stalin, Hitler, and the Desperate Struggle for Moscow That Changed the Course of World War II (New York, 2007).

Newton, Steven H., *Hitler's Commander. Field Marshal Walther Model – Hitler's Favorite General* (Cambridge MA, 2006).

Niepold, Gerd, 'Plan Barbarossa' in David M. Glantz (ed.), *The Initial Period of War on the Eastern Front 22 June–August 1941* (London, 1997), pp. 66–77.

Nolte, Ernst, 'Zwischen Geschichtslegende und Revisionismus? Das Dritte Reich im Blickwinkel des Jahres 1980' in *Historikerstreit. Die Dokumentation der Kontroverse um die Einzigartigkeit der nationalsozialistischen Judenvernichtung*, 6th edn (Munich, 1987).

Obryn'ba, Nikolai I., *Red Partisan. The Memoir of a Soviet Resistance Fighter on the Eastern Front* (Washington DC, 2007).

Ohrloff, Horst, 'XXXIX Motorized Corps Operations' in David M. Glantz (ed.), *The Initial Period of War on the Eastern Front 22 June–August 1941* (London, 1997), pp. 167–183.

Ose, Dieter, 'Smolensk: Reflections on a Battle' in David M. Glantz (ed.), *The Initial Period of War on the Eastern Front 22 June–August 1941* (London, 1997).

Overmans, Rüdiger, *Deutsche militärische Verluste im Zweiten Weltkrieg* (Munich, 2000).

Overy, Richard, *The Air War 1939–1945* (London, 1980).

'Statistics' in I. C. B. Dear and M. R. D. Foot (eds.), *The Oxford Companion to the Second World War* (Oxford, 1995), pp. 1059–1062.

Why the Allies Won (New York, 1996).

Russia's War (London, 1997).

Interrogations. The Nazi Elite in Allied Hands, 1945 (London, 2001).

The Dictators. Hitler's Germany and Stalin's Russia (London, 2004).

Pabst, Helmut, *The Outermost Frontier. A German Soldier in the Russian Campaign* (London, 1957).

Parker, R. A. C., *Struggle for Survival. The History of the Second World War* (Oxford, 1989).

Paulus, Wilhelm-Ernst, *Die Entwicklung der Planung des Russland Feldzuges 1940/41* (Bonn, 1957).

Pennington, Reina, 'Offensive Women: Women in Combat in the Red Army' in Paul Addison and Angus Calder (eds.), *A Time to Kill. The Soldier's Experience of War in the West 1939–1945* (London, 1997), pp. 249–262.

Perel, Solomon, *Europa Europa* (New York, 1997).

Perello, Chris, 'German Infantry on the Eastern Front in 1941' in Command Magazine (ed.), *Hitler's Army. The Evolution and Structure of German Forces, 1933–1945* (Boston, 2003), pp. 17–23.

Philippi, Alfred, 'Das Pripjetproblem: Eine Studie über die operative Bedeutung des Pripjetgebietes für den Feldzug des Jahres 1941' in *Wehrwissenschaftliche Rundschau*, suppl. 2 (Darmstadt, 1956).

Pleshakov, Constantine, *Stalin's Folly. The Tragic First Ten Days of WWII on the Eastern Front* (New York, 2005).

Plocher, Hermann, *The German Air Force Versus Russia, 1941* (New York, 1965).

Raus, Erhard, *Panzer Operations. The Eastern Front Memoir of General Raus, 1941–1945*, ed. Steven H. Newton (Cambridge MA, 2005).

'Russian Combat Methods in World War II' in Peter G. Tsouras (ed.), *Fighting in Hell. The German Ordeal on the Eastern Front* (New York, 1998), pp. 13–153.

Reese, Roger R., *Stalin's Reluctant Soldiers. A Social History of the Red Army 1925–1941* (Lawrence, 1996).

Reese, Willy Peter, *A Stranger to Myself. The Inhumanity of War: Russia, 1941–1944* (New York, 2005).

Reinhardt, Klaus, *Moscow – The Turning Point. The Failure of Hitler's Strategy in the Winter of 1941–42* (Oxford, 1992).

'Moscow 1941. The Turning Point' in John Erickson and David Dilks (eds.), *Barbarossa. The Axis and the Allies* (Edinburgh, 1998), pp. 207–224.

Reitlinger, Gerald, *The House Built on Sand. The Conflicts of German Policy in Russia 1939–45* (London, 1960).

Rich, Norman, *Hitler's War Aims. Ideology, the Nazi State, and the Course of Expansion* (New York, 1972).

Ritgen, Helmut, '6th Panzer Division Operations' in David M. Glantz (ed.), *The Initial Period of War on the Eastern Front 22 June–August 1941* (London, 1993), pp. 108–120.

Roberts, Geoffrey, *The Soviet Union and the Origins of the Second World War. Russo-German Relations and the Road to War, 1933–1941* (London, 1995).

Victory at Stalingrad. The Battle that Changed History (London, 2002).

Robertson, E. M., *Hitler's Pre-War Policy and Military Plans: 1933–1939* (London, 1963).

Röhricht, Edgar, *Probleme der Kesselschlacht. Dargestellt an Einkreisungs-Operationen im zweiten Weltkrieg* (Karlsruhe, 1958).

Rothe, Hermann and H. Ohrloff, '7th Panzer Division Operations' in David M. Glantz (ed.), *The Initial Period of War on the Eastern Front 22 June–August 1941* (London, 1997), pp. 380–392.

Rutherford, Jeffrey, 'Soldiers into Nazis? The German Infantry's War in Northwest Russia, 1941–1944' (unpublished PhD dissertation from the University of Texas at Austin, 2007).

Salisbury, Harrison E. (ed.), *Marshal Zhukov's Greatest Battles* (London, 1971).

The Unknown War (London, 1978).

Schall-Riaucour, Gräfin Heidemarie, *Aufstand und Gehorsam. Offizierstum und Generalstab im Umbruch. Leben und Wirken von Generaloberst Franz Halder Generalstabchef 1938–1942* (Wiesbaden, 1972).

Schreiber, Gerhard, 'Mussolinis Überfall auf Griechenland oder der Anfang vom Ende der italienischen Großmachtstellung' in Militärgeschichtliches Forschungsamt (ed.), *Das Deutsche Reich und der Zweite Weltkrieg. Band III. Der Mittelmeerraum und Südosteuropa. Von der 'non belligeranza' Italiens bis zum Kriegseintritt der Vereinigten Staaten* (Stuttgart, 1984), pp. 368–414.

'Deutsche Politik und Kriegführung 1939 bis 1945' in Karl Dietrich Bracher, Manfred Funke and Hans-Adolf Jacobsen (eds.), *In Deutschland 1933–1945. Neue Studien zur nationalsozialistischen Herrschaft* (Bonn, 1992), pp. 333–356.

Schröder, Hans Joachim, 'German Soldiers' Experiences During the Initial Phase of the Russian Campaign' in Bernd Wegner (ed.), *From Peace to War. Germany, Soviet Russia and the World, 1939–1941* (Oxford, 1997), pp. 309–324.

Schüler, Klaus, *Logistik im Russlandfeldzug. Die Rolle der Eisenbahn bei Planung, Vorbereitung und Durchführung des deutschen Angriffs auf die Sowjetunion bis zur Krise vor Moskau im Winter 1941/42* (Frankfurt am Main, 1987).

'The Eastern Campaign as a Transportation and Supply Problem' in Bernd Wegner (ed.), *From Peace to War. Germany, Soviet Russia and the World, 1939–1941* (Oxford, 1997), pp. 205–222.

Schulte, Theo, *The German Army and the Nazi Policies in Occupied Russia* (Oxford, 1989).

Schwabedissen, Walter, *The Russian Air Force in the Eyes of the German Commanders* (New York, 1960).

Seaton, Albert, *The Russo-German War 1941–45* (Novato, 1971).

The German Army 1933–45 (London, 1982).

Senger und Etterlin, Ferdinand Maria von, *German Tanks of World War II. The Complete Illustrated History of German Armoured Fighting Vehicles 1926–1945* (Harrisberg, 1969).

Shepherd, Ben, *War in the Wild East. The German Army and Soviet Partisans* (Cambridge, 2004).

Shilin, P. A., *Der Grosse Vaterländische Krieg der Sowjetunion*, Vol. I (Berlin, 1975).

Shirer, William, *The Rise and Fall of the Third Reich* (New York, 1960).

Shtemenko, Sergei M., *The Soviet General Staff at War 1941–1945* (Moscow, 1975).

Slepyan, Kenneth, *Stalin's Guerrillas. Soviet Partisans in World War II* (Lawrence, 2006).

Smelser, Ronald and Edward J. Davies II, *The Myth of the Eastern Front. The Nazi–Soviet War in American Popular Culture* (Cambridge, 2008).

Sontag, Raymond James and James Stuart Beddie (eds.), *Nazi–Soviet Relations, 1939–1941. Documents from the Archives of the German Foreign Office* (Washington DC, 1948).

Soviet Information Bureau, *The Falsifiers of History* (Moscow and London, 1948).

Speer, Albert, *Inside the Third Reich* (London, 1971).

Stahlberg, Alexander, *Bounden Duty. The Memoirs of a German Officer 1932–45* (London, 1990).

Steiger, Rudolf, *Armour Tactics in the Second World War. Panzer Army Campaigns of 1939–41 in German War Diaries* (Oxford, 1991).

Stern, Wolf and Ernst Stenzel, 'Die Blitzkriegsstrategie des deutschen Militaris-
    mus und ihr Scheitern beim Überfall auf die Sowjetunion' in *Jahrbuch für
    die Geschichte der UdSSR und der volksdemokratischen Länder Europas*, Vol. 5
    (1961), pp. 23–42.
Stolfi, R. H. S., *Hitler's Panzers East. World War II Reinterpreted* (Norman,
    1993).
'Blitzkrieg Army, Siege Führer. A Reinterpretation of World War II in Europe'
    in Command Magazine (ed.), *Hitler's Army. The Evolution and Structure of
    German Forces, 1933–1945* (Boston, 2003), pp. 153–164.
Strachan, Hew, *The First World War*, Volume I: *To Arms* (Oxford, 2003).
Streit, Christian, *Keine Kameraden: Die Wehrmacht und die sowjetischen Kriegsge-
    fangenen 1941–1945* (Stuttgart, 1978).
'The German Army and the Policies of Genocide' in Gerhard Hirschfeld (ed.),
    The Policies of Genocide: Jews and Soviet Prisoners of War in Nazi Germany
    (London, 1986).
'Partisans – Resistance – Prisoners of War' in Joseph Wieczynski (ed.), *Opera-
    tion Barbarossa. The German Attack on the Soviet Union June 22, 1941* (Salt
    Lake City, 1993), pp. 260–275.
Suvorov, Victor, *Icebreaker: Who Started the Second World War* (London, 1990).
Tashjean, John E., 'Smolensk 1941. Zum Kulminationspunkt in Theorie und
    Praxis' in Militärgeschichtliches Forschungsamt (ed.), *Die operative Idee und
    ihre Grundlagen. Ausgewählte Operationen des Zweiten Weltkrieges. Vorträge zur
    Militärgeschichte*, Volume X (Herford, 1989), pp. 39–51.
Taylor, A. J. P., *The Origins of The Second World War* (London, 1961).
Taylor, Brian, *Barbarossa To Berlin. A Chronology of the Campaigns on the Eastern
    Front 1941 to 1945*, Volume I: *The Long Drive East 22 June 1941 to 18
    November 1942* (Staplehurst, 2003).
Thilo, Karl Wilhelm, 'A Perspective from the Army High Command (OKH)'
    in David M. Glantz (ed.), *The Initial Period of War on the Eastern Front 22
    June–August 1941* (London, 1997), pp. 290–307.
Thomas, David, 'Foreign Armies East and German Military Intelligence in Rus-
    sia 1941–45', *Journal of Contemporary History* 22 (1987), 261–301.
Thomas, Georg, *Geschichte der deutschen Wehr- und Rüstungswirtschaft (1918–
    1943/45)*, ed. Wolfgang Birkenfeld (Boppard am Rhein, 1966).
Thurston, Robert, 'Cauldrons of Loyalty and Betrayal: Soviet Soldiers' Behav-
    ior, 1941 and 1945' in Robert Thurston and Bernd Bonwetsch (eds.), *The
    People's War. Responses to World War II in the Soviet Union* (Chicago, 2000),
    pp. 235–257.
Tilemann, Walter, *Ich, das Soldatenkind* (Munich, 2005).
Tooze, Adam, *The Wages of Destruction. The Making and Breaking of the Nazi
    Economy* (London, 2007).
Topitsch, Ernst, *Stalin's War: A Radical New Theory of the Origins of the Second
    World War* (New York, 1987).
Trevor-Roper, Hugh R. 'A.J.P Taylor, Hitler and the War' in *Outbreak of the
    Second World War: Design or Blunder?* (Boston, 1962).
(ed.), *Hitler's War Directives 1939–1945* (London, 1964).
(ed.), *Hitler's Table Talk, 1941–1944. His Private Conversations* (London, 2000).

True To Type. A Selection From Letters and Diaries of German Soldiers and Civilians Collected on the Soviet-German Front (London). This book makes no reference to its editor or date of publication.

Tsouras, Peter (ed.), *Panzers on the Eastern Front. General Erhard Raus and his Panzer Divisions in Russia 1941–1945* (London, 2002).

Turney, Alfred W., *Disaster At Moscow: Von Bock's Campaigns 1941–1942* (Albuquerque, 1970).

Tuyll, Hubert P. van, *Feeding the Bear. American Aid to the Soviet Union, 1941–1945* (Westport, 1989).

Ueberschär, Gerd R., 'Das Scheitern des Unternehmens "Barbarossa". Der deutsch-sowjetische Krieg vom Überfall bis zur Wende vor Moskau im Winter 1941/42' in Gerd Ueberschär and Wolfram Wette (eds.), *'Unternehmen Barbarossa': Der deutsche Überfall auf die Sowjetunion 1941* (Paderborn, 1984), pp. 140–172.

'Hitlers Entschluß zum "Lebensraum" – Krieg im Osten. Programmatisches Ziel oder militärstrategisches Kalkül?' in Gerd Ueberschär and Wolfram Wette (eds.), *'Unternehmen Barbarossa': Der deutsche Überfall auf die Sowjetunion 1941* (Paderborn, 1984), pp. 83–110.

Generaloberst Franz Halder (Zürich, 1991).

'Hitler's Decision to Attack the Soviet Union in Recent German Historiography' in Joseph Wieczynski (ed.), *Operation Barbarossa. The German Attack on the Soviet Union June, 1941* (Salt Lake City, 1993), pp. 293–309.

Vogel, Detlef, 'Der deutsche Überfall auf Jugoslawien und Griechenland' in Militärgeschichtliches Forschungsamt (ed.), *Das Deutsche Reich und der Zweite Weltkrieg*, Band III: *Der Mittelmeerraum und Südosteuropa. Von der 'non belligeranza' Italiens bis zum Kriegseintritt der Vereinigten Staaten* (Stuttgart, 1984).

'Die deutsche Balkanpolitik im Herbst 1940 und Frühjahr 1941' in Militärgeschichtliches Forschungsamt (ed.), *Das Deutsche Reich und der Zweite Weltkrieg*, Band III: *Der Mittelmeerraum und Südosteuropa. Von der 'non belligeranza' Italiens bis zum Kriegseintritt der Vereinigten Staaten* (Stuttgart, 1984).

Waddington, Geoffrey, 'Rippentrop and the Soviet Union, 1937–1941' in John Erickson and David Dilks (eds.), *Barbarossa. The Axis and the Allies* (Edinburgh, 1998), pp. 7–33.

Wagner, Elisabeth (ed.), *Der Generalquartiermeister. Briefe und Tagebuchaufzeichnungen des Generalquartiermeisters des Heeres General der Artillerie Eduard Wagner* (Munich, 1963).

Warlimont, Walter, *Im Hauptquartier der deutschen Wehrmacht 1939 bis 1945*, Band I: *September 1939–November 1942* (Koblenz, 1990). English translation: Warlimont, Walter, *Inside Hitler's Headquarters, 1939–1945* (New York, 1964).

Wegner, Bernd, "'My Honour is Loyalty". The SS as a Military Factor in Hitler's Germany' in Wilhelm Deist (ed.), *The German Military in the Age of Total War* (Warwickshire, 1985), pp. 220–239.

Weinberg, Gerhard, 'The Yelnya–Dorogobuzh Area of Smolensk Oblast' in John A. Armstrong (ed.), *Soviet Partisans in World War II* (Madison, 1964), pp. 389–457.

'Some Thoughts on World War II', *The Journal of Military History* 56(4) (October, 1992), 659–668.

A World At Arms. A Global History of World War II (Cambridge, 1994).

Germany, Hitler, and World War II – Essays in Modern German and World History (New York, 1995).

'22 June 1941: The German View', *War in History* 3(2) (1996), 225–233.

(ed.), *Hitler's Second Book* (New York, 2003).

Weizsäcker, Ernst von, *Erinnerungen. Mein Leben*, ed. Richard von Weizsäcker (Munich, 1950).

Werth, Alexander, *Russia at War 1941–1945* (New York, 1964).

Wette, Wolfram, *Die Wehrmacht. Feindbilder, Vernichtungskrieg, Legenden* (Frankfurt am Main, 2002). English translation: *The Wehrmacht. History, Myth, Reality* (Cambridge, 2006).

Whaley, Barton, *Codeword Barbarossa* (Cambridge, 1973).

Wheeler-Bennett, John, *The Nemesis of Power. The German Army in Politics 1918–1945* (New York, 1969).

Wilhelm, Hans-Heinrich, 'Heinz Guderian – "Panzerpapst" und Generalstabschef' in Ronald Smelser and Enrico Syring (eds.), *Die Militärelite des Dritten Reiches. 27 biographische Skizzen* (Berlin, 1995), pp. 187–208.

Wilt, Alan F., 'Hitler's Late Summer Pause in 1941', *Military Affairs* 45(4) (1981), 187–191.

Young, Peter (ed.), *The World Almanac of World War II. The Complete and Comprehensive Documentary of World War II* (London, 1981).

Zamoyski, Adam, *1812. Napoleon's Fatal March on Moscow* (London, 2004).

Zeidler, Manfred, 'Das Bild der Wehrmacht von Russland und der Roten Armee zwischen 1933 und 1939' in Hans-Erich Volkmann (ed.), *Das Russlandbild im Dritten Reich* (Köln, 1994), pp. 105–123.

Ziemke, Earl F., *The German Northern Theater of Operations 1940–1945* (Washington DC, 1959).

'Book Review – *Thunder on the Dnepr*', *The Journal of Military History* 62(2) (April 1998), 432–433.

The Red Army 1918–1941: From Vanguard of World Revolution to US Ally (London, 2004).

Ziemke, Earl F. and Magna E. Bauer, *Moscow to Stalingrad: Decision in the East* (New York, 1988).

Zobel, Horst, '3rd Panzer Division Operations' in David M. Glantz (ed.), *The Initial Period of War on the Eastern Front 22 June–August 1941* (London, 1997), pp. 238–247.

'3rd Panzer Division's Advance to Mogilev' in David M. Glantz (ed.), *The Initial Period of War on the Eastern Front 22 June–August 1941* (London, 1997), pp. 393–397.

INTERNET SITES

www.jewishvirtuallibrary.org/jsource/ww2/churchill062241.html
www.fdrlibrary.marist.edu/psf/box5/a61h08.html

Kipp, Jacob W., 'Barbarossa, Soviet Covering Forces and the Initial Period of War: Military History and Airland Battle' published online by the Foreign Military Studies Office (Fort Leavenworth, 1989). http://fmso.leavenworth.army.mil/fmsopubs/issues/barbaros.htm

Miller, John J., 'Sounding Taps. Why Military History is being Retired', *National Review Online* (October 2006). http://nrd.nationalreview.com/article/?q=YTdiMDkzZDJjYTYwOWM4YmIyMmE4N2IwODFlNWU0MjE=

Index

Brauchitsch, Walter von (*cont.*)
  planning for Barbarossa 63, 92–95, 116, 142–143
  problems at Army Group Centre 161–163, 211, 428–429
  strategic thinking (June/July) 156–157, 197, 252–253
  (August) 375, 379, 385
Brest Litovsk 143, 155, 164, 211–212, 223
Briansk 292, 429
  battle of 439–441
Britain 1–2
  bombing of 124–125
  German planning for Barbarossa 43, 71–72, 75, 95, 104
  Japanese relations 355
  perception of Barbarossa 148
  war against Germany 105, 139–140
Britain, Battle of 123
Bucharest 305
Bug River 143, 155, 158
Buhle, Walter 243, 331, 419
Busch, Ernst 170

Canaris, Wilhelm 147, 253
Cannae, battle of 378
Carpathian Group 359
Checkersk 383, 385
Cherikov 282
China 1, 354, 356
Churchill, Winston 1, 24, 274, 347, 361, 402, 404
Ciano, Galeazzo 140, 231, 253, 274
Clausewitz, Carl von 3, 19, 54, 247, 261, 448–449
Cohrs, Alexander 202–203, 213
Commissar Order 100, 146
Crete 124, 126, 141
CSIR (Italian Expeditionary Corps in Russia) 356
Czechoslovakia 91, 108

Disna 199, 205, 219
Dittri, Helmuth 308–309
divisions (German)
  1st (Cavalry) 156, 176
  3rd (Motorised) 349
  5th (Infantry) 363, 375
  6th (Infantry) 206
  7th (Parachute) 141
  10th (Motorised) 156, 264, 384, 407
  14th (Motorised) 173, 260–261, 303, 375, 381, 408, 418–419
  15th (Infantry) 374, 392
  18th (Motorised) 173, 286, 386, 419
  20th (Motorised) 173, 286, 327, 419

28th (Infantry) 164
29th (Motorised) 155, 163, 174–176, 180, 257, 331, 335, 369, 381
32nd (Infantry) 350
34th (Infantry) 411
45th (Infantry) 164, 211
52nd (Infantry) 266, 367
60th (Motorised) 141
87th (Infantry) 198
98th (Infantry) 352, 416
106th (Infantry) 327
137th (Infantry) 320, 411
161st (Infantry) 408, 429
167th (Infantry) 155
169th (Infantry) 416
221st (Security) 380
251st (Infantry) 327
252nd (Infantry) 380
255th (Infantry) 156, 195, 290
263rd (Infantry) 319–320, 411
267th (Infantry) 411
268th (Infantry) 329
292nd (Infantry) 320
293rd (Infantry) 182
Das Reich (SS) 176, 286–288, 307, 309–311, 329, 369, 373, 390
  equipment and training 117–121
Grossdeutschland (SS infantry regiment) 286, 288–289, 369, 373, 390
Totenkopf (SS) 349
Dnepr River
  drive to 158, 161, 178–179, 180, 187–188, 196
  operations on the eastern bank 252, 257, 344
  in planning Barbarossa 40, 42, 77, 89, 93
  planning to cross 210, 212, 219, 221–223
Dniester River 89
Dno 394
Döberitz 398
Don River 50, 379
Dorogobuzh 268–269, 286, 289
Dubyssa River 167
Dukhovshchina 408, 412
Dutch East Indies 355
Dvina River
  drive to 158, 161, 170–171, 178, 186–188, 196
  operations on the eastern bank 205, 257, 344
  in planning Barbarossa 41, 77, 81, 93–94
  planning to cross 212, 219, 220
Dvinsk 170